Study Guide
to Accompany
McConnell and Brue
Economics

Study Guide
to Accompany
McConnell and Brue

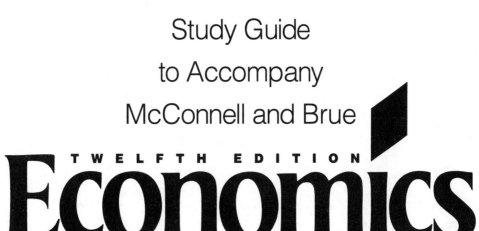

TWELFTH EDITION
Economics

William B. Walstad
Professor of Economics
University of Nebraska—Lincoln

Robert C. Bingham
Late Professor of Economics
Kent State University

McGraw-Hill, Inc.

New York   St. Louis   San Francisco   Auckland   Bogotá
Caracas   Lisbon   London   Madrid   Mexico   Milan   Montreal   New Delhi
Paris   San Juan   Singapore   Sydney   Tokyo   Toronto

Study Guide to Accompany McConnell and Brue: Economics

2 3 4 5 6 7 8 9 0   **SEM SEM**   9 0 9 8 7 6 5 4 3 2

ISBN 0-07-045590-2

This book was set in Helvetica by Waldman Graphics, Inc.
The editors were Scott D. Stratford, Michael R. Elia, and Edwin Hanson;
the production supervisor was Annette Mayeski.
The cover was designed by Joseph A. Piliero.
Semline Inc., was printer and binder.

About the Authors

William B. Walstad is a professor of economics at the University of Nebraska—Lincoln where he directs the Center for Economic Education and the National Center for Research in Economic Education. He received his Ph.D. degree from the University of Minnesota and taught at the University of Missouri—St. Louis before moving to Nebraska. Professor Walstad has been honored by the College of Business Administration at Nebraska with a Distinguished Teaching Award. He also received the Henry H. Villard Research Award for his published research in economic education. He co-edited *The Principles of Economics Course: A Handbook for Instructors* (McGraw-Hill) and developed three national tests on economics for the Joint Council on Economic Education. He enjoys being with his family and likes to travel.

Robert C. Bingham was an undergraduate student at DePauw University and obtained M.A. and Ph.D. degrees from Northwestern University. He taught at the University of Nebraska—Lincoln where he was a colleague of Professor McConnell before coming to Kent State University from which he retired in 1985. He was the author of several other study guides and supplements for the principles of economics courses.

To
Karen, Laura, and Kristin

Contents

How to Use the Study Guide to Learn Economics

This **Study Guide** is designed to help you read and understand Campbell R. McConnell and Stanley L. Brue's textbook, **Economics**, Twelfth Edition. If used properly, a guide can be a great aid to you in what is probably your first course in economics.

No one pretends that the study of economics is easy, but it can be made easier. Of course a study guide will not do your work for you, and its use is no substitute for reading the text. You must be willing to read the text, spend time on the subject, and work at learning if you wish to understand economics.

Many students do read their text and work hard on their economics course and still fail to learn the subject. This is because principles of economics is a new subject for them, and they have had no previous experience in learning economics. They want to learn but do not know just how to go about it. Here is where the **Study Guide** can help. Let us first see what the **Study Guide** contains and then how to use it.

■ WHAT THE STUDY GUIDE IS

The **Study Guide** contains forty chapters—one for each chapter in the text and a **glossary**. Each **Study Guide** chapter has ten parts.

1. An **introduction** explains what is in the chapter of the text and how it is related to material in earlier and later chapters. It points out topics to which you should give special attention, and reemphasizes difficult or important principles and facts.

2. A **checklist** tells you the things you should be able to do when you have finished the chapter.

3. A **chapter outline** shows how the chapter is organized and summarizes briefly the essential points made in the chapter.

4. A list of the **important terms** found in the chapter points out what you must be able to define in order to understand the material in the chapter. A definition of each of these terms will be found in the glossary at the end of the **Study Guide**.

5. **Fill-in questions** (short-answer and list questions) help you to learn and remember the important generalizations and facts in the chapter.

6. **Problems and projects** assist you in learning and understanding economic relationships and get you to think about certain economic problems.

7. **True-false questions** can be used to test your understanding of the material in the chapter.

8. **Multiple-choice questions** also give you a chance to check your knowledge of the chapter content and to prepare for this type of course examination.

9. **Discussion questions** can be used to test yourself, to identify important questions in the chapter, and to prepare for examinations.

10. **Answers** to fill-in questions, to the problems and projects, to true-false questions, and to the multiple-choice questions are found at the end of each chapter. You are also given the references to the specific pages in the textbook for each true-false, multiple choice, and discussion question.

■ HOW TO STUDY AND LEARN WITH THE HELP OF THE STUDY GUIDE

1. **Read and outline.** For best results, quickly read the introduction, outline, list of terms, and checklist in the **Study Guide** before you read the chapter in the text. Then read the chapter in the text slowly and keep one eye on the **Study Guide** outline and the list of terms. The outline contains only the major points in the chapter. Highlight the chapter as you read it by identifying the major **and the minor** points and by placing outline numbers or letters (such as I or A or 1 or a) in the margins. Circle the important terms. When you have completed the chapter, you will have the chapter outlined and it will give you a set of notes on the chapter. Be careful to highlight or underline only the really important or summary statements.

2. **Review and reread.** After you have read the chapter in the text once, return to the introduction, outline, and list of terms in the **Study Guide**. Reread the introduction and outline. Does everything there make sense? If not, go to the text and reread the topics that you do not remember well or that still confuse you. Look at the outline. Try to recall each of the minor topics or points that were contained in the text under each of the major points in the outline. When you come to the list of terms go over them

one by one. Define or explain each to yourself and then look for the definition of the term either in the text chapter or in the glossary. Compare your own definition or explanation with that in the text or glossary. The quick way to find the definition of a term in the text is to look in the index of the text for the page or pages on which that term or concept is mentioned. Make any correction or change in your own definition or explanation that is necessary.

3. *Test and check answers.* When you have done all this, you will have a pretty fair general idea of what is in the text chapter. Now take a look at the fill-in questions, the problems and projects, and the self-test questions. Tackle each of these three sections one at a time, using the following procedure. (1) Answer as many questions as you can without looking in the text or in the answer section. (2) Check the text for whatever help you need. It is a good idea to do more than merely look for answers in the text. Reread any section for which you were not able to answer questions. (3) Then consult the answer section at the end of the chapter for the correct answers and reread any section of the text for which you missed questions. (See the text page references that are given with the answer to each true-false or multiple choice question.)

The questions in these three sections are not all of equal difficulty. Do not expect to get them all right the first time. Some are designed to pinpoint things of importance which you will probably miss the first time you read the text and to get you to read about them again. None of the questions is unimportant. Even those that have no definite answers will bring you to grips with many important economic questions and increase your understanding of economic principles and problems.

For the discussion questions, it is not necessary to write out answers. All you need to do is mentally outline your answer. For the more difficult questions you may want to write out a brief outline of the answer or a full answer. Do not avoid the difficult questions just because they are more work. Answering these questions is often the most valuable work a student can do toward acquiring an understanding of economic relationships and principles. Although no answers are given in the *Study Guide* to the discussion questions, the answer section does list page references in the text for each question. You are *strongly* encouraged to read those text pages for an explanation to the question or for better insight into the question content.

4. *Double check.* Before you turn to the next chapter in the text and *Study Guide*, return to the checklist. If you cannot honestly check off each of the items in the list, you have not learned what the author of the text and of this *Study Guide* hoped you would learn.

■ **SOME FINAL WORDS**

Perhaps the method of using the *Study Guide* outlined above seems like a lot of work. It is! Study and learning necessarily entail work on your part. This is a fact you must accept if you are to learn economics.

After you have used the *Study Guide* to study three or four chapters, you will find that some sections are of more value to you than others. Let your own experience determine how you will use it. But do not discontinue use of the *Study Guide* after three or four chapters merely because you are not sure whether it is helping you. *Stick with it.*

In addition to the material in the *Study Guide*, there are questions at the end of each chapter in the text. Some of these questions are similar to questions in the *Study Guide*, but none is identical. It will be worthwhile for you to examine all the questions at the end of each chapter and to work out or outline answers for them. Students who have trouble with the problems in the *Study Guide* will find the end-of-chapter problems useful in determining whether they have actually mastered their difficulties.

For those of you who either have trouble with or wish to learn more rapidly the sections of the text containing explanations of economic theory (or principles), let me recommend *Economic Concepts: A Programmed Approach*, by Professor Robert Bingham as revised by Professor Henry Pope. A programmed book is a learning device which speeds and increases comprehension. Its use will greatly expand your understanding of economics.

■ **ACKNOWLEDGMENTS**

The late Professor Robert Bingham prepared the first ten editions of the *Study Guide*. He worked with great care and wanted the *Study Guide* to be a valuable aid for students. Many past users of the *Study Guide* will attest to his success. Although Professor Bingham did not participate directly in this revision, his work remains a major contribution to this edition.

I also wish to acknowledge other help I received. Campbell McConnell and Stanley Brue offered many helpful comments for the revision. Professor Thomas Phelps of Pierce College and Professor Janet West of the University of Nebraska–Omaha provided many good suggestions in their reviews of the *Study Guide*. Bart Nemmers, a graduate student at the University of Nebraska–Lincoln, helped me check the self-test questions and identify the textbook pages given with the answers. Students in my principles of economics classes also helped me with their comments and questions about material. Finally, the team at McGraw-Hill, especially Scott Stratford, Michael Elia, and Edwin Hanson, gave me great assistance with the editorial and production work. Despite the many contributions from others, all responsibility for errors and omissions is mine.

William B. Walstad

Study Guide
to Accompany
McConnell and Brue
Economics

CHAPTER 1

The Nature and Method of Economics

Chapter 1 introduces you to economics—the study of how people decide how to use scarce productive resources to satisfy material wants. Knowledge of economics is important because it is essential for well-informed citizenship and it has many practical applications to personal decisions. The purpose of this chapter is to explain the nature of the subject and to describe the methods that economists use to study economic questions.

Economists use three different approaches to examine economic topics. The gathering of relevant facts about an economic problem is called **descriptive economics**. **Economic theory** or economic analysis involves the derivation of principles using inductive or deductive methods. **Policy economics** entails the formulation of policies or recommended solutions to economic problems.

The heart of the chapter is the discussion of economic principles in the economic theory section. Economic principles are generalizations. Because the economist cannot employ laboratory experiments to test the generalizations, these principles are always imprecise and subject to exceptions. Economics is a science but it is not an exact science. Economic principles are also simplifications—approximations of a complex world—and both the formulation and application of these principles present many opportunities for making serious mistakes. Economic principles are not the answers to economic questions but are tools—intellectual tools—for analyzing economic problems and for finding policies to solve these problems.

The selection of economic policies to follow depends not only on economic principles but also on the value judgments and the weight given to particular economic goals. Here we move from economic theory and positive economics, which investigates **what is**, to normative economics, which incorporates subjective or value-laden views of **what ought to be**. Many of the apparent disagreements among economists are over normative policy issues and involve deciding which economic goals for our economy are most important in making the case for a policy solution.

Clear thinking about economic questions requires that the beginning student avoid many pitfalls. Errors of commission and omission can occur from bias, loaded terminology, imprecise definitions, fallacies of composition, and confusing correlation with causation. If you can guard against these potential hazards, you can use the economic perspective to improve your understanding of actions and events at the macroeconomic or the microeconomic level.

■ CHECKLIST

When you have studied this chapter you should be able to:

☐ Write a formal definition of economics.
☐ Give two good reasons for studying economics.
☐ Define descriptive economics, economic theory, and policy economics.
☐ Distinguish between induction and deduction in economic reasoning.
☐ Explain what an economic principle is and how economic principles are obtained.
☐ Discuss how economic principles are generalizations and abstractions.
☐ Explain what the "other things equal" (**ceteris paribus**) assumption is and why this assumption is employed in economics.
☐ Discuss the distinction between macroeconomics and microeconomics.
☐ Give examples of positive and normative economics.
☐ Identify the eight economic goals.
☐ State four significant points about economic goals.
☐ Recognize the "pitfalls to straight thinking" when confronted with examples of them.
☐ Describe the economic perspective and give an example of its application.

■ CHAPTER OUTLINE

1. Economics is concerned with the efficient use of limited productive resources to achieve the maximum satisfaction of human material wants.

2. Citizens in a democracy must understand elementary economics to comprehend the present-day problems of their society and to make intelligent decisions when they vote. Economics is an academic rather than a vocational subject, but a knowledge of it is valuable to business executives, consumers, and workers.

3. Economists gather relevant facts to obtain economic principles that may be used to formulate policies which will solve economic problems.

    a. Descriptive economics is the gathering of relevant facts about the production, exchange, and consumption of goods and services.

    b. Economic theory is the analysis of the facts and the derivation of economic principles.

    (1) To obtain and test their principles economists use both the inductive and the deductive methods.

    (2) Economic principles are also called laws, theories, and models.

    (3) Each of these principles is a generalization.

    (4) Economists employ the *ceteris paribus* (or "other things equal") assumption to obtain these generalizations.

    (5) These principles are also abstractions from reality.

    (6) Economists can derive principles about economic behavior at the macroeconomic or the microeconomic level of analysis.

    c. Policy economics is the combination of economic principles and economic values (or goals) to control economic events.

    (1) Values are the judgments people make about what is desirable (good, just) and what is undesirable (bad, unjust).

    (2) Positive economics concerns **what is**, or the scientific analysis of economic behavior; normative economics suggests **what ought to be** in offering answers to policy questions.

    (3) There are eight major economic goals that are often important to consider—economic growth, full employment, economic efficiency, price level stability, economic freedom, equitable distribution of income, economic security, and a balance of trade.

    (4) Economic goals can be complementary or conflicting; issues related to goal interpretation or setting priorities can cause problems.

    (5) The three steps in creating an economic policy designed to achieve an economic goal involve defining the goal, identifying the effects of alternative policies, and evaluating the results.

4. Straight thinking in the study and use of economic principles requires strict application of the rules of logic in which personal emotions are irrelevant, if not detrimental. The pitfalls encountered by beginning students in studying and applying economic principles include:

    a. bias or preconceived beliefs not warranted by facts;

    b. loaded terminology or the use of terms in a way which appeals to emotion and leads to a nonobjective analysis of the issues;

    c. the definition by economists of terms in ways which may not be the same as the ways in which these terms are more commonly used;

    d. the fallacy of composition or the assumption that what is true of the part is necessarily true of the whole;

    e. and the ***post hoc fallacy*** or the mistaken belief that when one event precedes another the first event is the cause of the second.

5. The economic perspective is a cost-benefit perspective. People, either as individuals or in groups, make economic choices by evaluating the costs and benefits of decisions.

■ **IMPORTANT TERMS**

Economics	Microeconomics
Descriptive economics	Positive and normative statements
Economic theory (analysis)	Economic goals
Policy economics	Value judgment
Economic principles (law)	Conflicting or complementary goals
Induction	Loaded terminology
Deduction	Fallacy of composition
Generalization	*Post hoc, erto propter hoc fallacy*
Economic model	
Abstraction	Correlation
"Other things equal" (*ceteris paribus*) assumption	Causation
	Economic perspective
Macroeconomics	

■ **FILL-IN QUESTIONS**

  1. Economics as a subject:
  a. Is, first of all, the study of the

_____,

_____,

and _____
of the material goods and services that satisfy human wants.

  b. But, more formally, it is concerned with the efficient

use of _____ productive resources to

achieve the _____ satisfaction of these wants.

  2. An understanding of economics is essential if we are

to be well-informed _____ and it has many
personal applications even though it is an academic and

not a _____ subject.

  3. Economics, like other sciences, begins with the facts found in the world around us.

a. The gathering of relevant facts is the part of the economics called _____ economics.

b. Economic _____ involves deriving general principles about the economic behavior of people and institutions. When economists develop economic principles from studying facts, they are using the

_____ method; whereas

the _____ method uses facts to test the validity of hypotheses or economic theories.

c. The formulation of recommended solutions or remedies for economic problems is referred to as

_____ economics.

4. Economic principles are also called _____.

These principles are _____
about people's economic behavior and as such necessar-

ily involve _____ from reality.

5. Economists know that the amount consumers spend for goods and services in any year depends upon their after-tax income in that year and several factors other than their income. To look at the relationship between the spending and income of consumers, economists often assume that these other factors are constant and do not change; and when economists do this they make the

_____ assumption.

6. Macroeconomics is concerned with the _____

output of the economy and the _____ level of prices, while microeconomics is concerned with output

in a(n) _____

_____

and the price of a(n) _____

_____

7. There are two different types of statements that can be made about economic topics. A (positive, normative)

_____ statement explains **what is** by offering a scientific proposition about economic behavior that is

based on economic theory and facts. A _____ statement includes a value judgment about an economic policy or the economy that suggests **what ought to be**. Many of the reported disagreements among economists

usually involve _____ statements.

8. Eight widely accepted economic goals in the United States are the following:

a. _____

b. _____

c. _____

d. _____

e. _____

f. _____

g. _____

h. _____

9. Increases in economic growth that promote full employment would be an example of a set of (conflicting,

complementary) _____ economic goals. Efforts to achieve an equitable distribution of income that reduce economic efficiency and growth would be an ex-

ample of a set of _____ economic goals.

10. The three steps involved in the formulation of economic policy are:

a. _____

b. _____

c. _____

11. There are many pitfalls to straight thinking in economics. For example, the statement that "what is good for the individual is also good for the group" may not be correct

because of the fallacy of _____. The person who believes that "washing a car will cause it to rain to-

morrow" is expressing a _____ fallacy.

12. The economic perspective is a _____ perspective. People and institutions are assumed to make

(rational, irrational) _____ decisions by weigh-

ing the _____ and _____ of economic actions.

■ **PROBLEMS AND PROJECTS**

1. **News report:** "The Russian demand for wheat in the United States increased and caused the price of wheat in the United States to rise." This is a **specific** instance of a more **general** economic principle. Of which economic

generalization is this a particular example? _____

_____

_____

2. Below are four statements. Each of them is an example of one of the pitfalls frequently encountered in the study of economics. Indicate in the space following each statement the type of pitfall involved.

a. "Investment in stocks and bonds is the only way to build real capital assets." _____

b. "An unemployed worker can find a job if he looks diligently and conscientiously for employment; therefore, all unemployed workers can find employment if they are diligent and conscientious in looking for a job."

_____

c. *Walstad:* "Regulation of public utilities in the United States is an immoral and unconscionable interference with the God-given right of private property and, as you know, old chum, there is no private property in the communist nations." *McConnell:* "It is far from that, my boy. You know perfectly well that it is an attempt to limit the unmitigated avarice of mammoth corporations in order, as the Constitution commands, to promote the general welfare of a democratic America." _____

_____

d. "The stock market crash of 1929 was followed by and resulted in 10 years of Depression." _____

_____

3. Below is a list of economic statements. Indicate in the space to the right of each whether they are positive (P) or normative (N). Then in the last four lines below, write two of your own examples of positive statements and two examples of normative economic statements.

a. New York City should control the rental price of apartments. _____

b. Consumer prices rose at an annual rate of 5% last year. _____

c. Most people who are unemployed are just too lazy to work. _____

d. Generally speaking, if you lower the price of a product, people will buy more of that product. _____

e. The profits of drug companies are too large and ought to be used to conduct research on new medicines. _____

f. Government should do more to help the poor.

_____

g. _____ P

h. _____ P

i. _____ N

j. _____ N

Circle the T if the statement is true; the F if it is false.

1. Economics deals with the activities by which humans can earn a living and improve their standard of living. **T** **F**

2. Economics is academic and of little value because it does not teach the student how to earn a living. **T** **(F)**

3. Gathering the relevant economic facts from which economic principles are derived is called economic analysis. **T** **(F)**

4. In economics the terms "law," "principle," "theory," and "model" mean essentially the same thing. **(T)** **F**

5. The "other things equal" or *ceteris paribus* assumption is made in order to simplify the reasoning process. **(T)** **F**

6. The deductive method is the scientific method and the method used to derive economic principles from economic facts. **T** **(F)**

7. Economic principles enable us to predict the economic consequences of many human actions. **(T)** **F**

8. One of the widely (though not universally) accepted economic goals of Americans is an equal distribution of income. **T** **(F)**

9. The first step in the formulation of an economic policy, the statement of goals, may be an occasion for disagreement because different people may have different and conflicting goals to be achieved. **(T)** **F**

10. Once a single goal or end has been determined as the sole objective of economic policy, there is seldom any question of which policy to adopt to achieve that goal. **T** **(F)**

11. If you speak of "capital" to most people, they understand you to be referring to money. The economist, therefore, is obligated to use the term "capital" to mean money. **T** **(F)**

12. When value judgments are made about the economy or economic policy, this is referred to as positive economics. **T** **(F)**

13. Microeconomic analysis is concerned with the performance of the economy as a whole or its major aggregates. **T** **(F)**

14. The economic perspective views individuals or institutions as making rational choices based on the analysis of the costs and benefits of decisions. **(T)** **F**

15. The statement that "the legal minimum wage should be raised to give working people a decent income" is an example of a normative statement. **(T)** **F**

From facts to theory — induction.

Circle the letter that corresponds to the best answer.

1. Which statement would be the best one to use to complete a short definition of economics? "Economics is the study of:
(a) how business produces goods and services."
(b) the efficient use of scarce productive resources."
(c) the equitable distribution of society's income and wealth."
(d) the printing and circulation of money in the economy."

2. Which of the following terms is **not** found in a sophisticated definition of economics?
(a) efficient use
(b) unlimited productive resources
(c) maximum satisfaction
(d) human and material wants

3. Economics is a practical field of study in several ways. Which one of the following is **not** an element of its practicality?
(a) every person affects and is affected by the operation of the economy
(b) every person has to earn a living in some manner, and economics develops skills and trains the student in the art of making a living
(c) every person in a democracy is confronted with its political problems, many of which are economic in nature
(d) every person who understands the overall operation of the economy is in a better position to solve personal economic problems

4. One economic principle states that the lower the price of a commodity, the greater will be the quantity of the commodity which consumers will wish to purchase. On the basis of this principle **alone**, it can be concluded that:
(a) if the price of mink coats falls, more mink coats will be purchased by consumers
(b) if the price of mink coats falls, Mrs. James will purchase two instead of one
(c) if the price of mink coats falls and there are no important changes in the other factors affecting their demand, the public will probably purchase a greater quantity of mink coats than it did at the higher price
(d) if more mink coats are purchased this month than last month, it is because the price of mink coats has fallen

5. An economic model is **not**:
(a) an ideal type of economy or an economic policy for which we ought to strive to achieve
(b) a tool which the economist employs in order to predict
(c) one or a collection of economic principles
(d) an explanation of how the economy or a part of the economy functions in its essential details

6. When economic principles or theories are developed from factual evidence, this method of economic reasoning is called:
(a) descriptive economics
(b) hypothesis testing
(c) deduction
(d) induction

7. Knowing that as the price of a commodity rises the quantity of the commodity sold decreases and that the imposition of a higher tax on a commodity increases its price, the economist concludes that if a government increases the tax on gasoline, less gasoline will be sold. This is an example of:
(a) prediction
(b) control
(c) policy
(d) the fallacy of composition

8. Which of the following economic goals is subject to reasonably accurate measurement?
(a) economic security
(b) full employment
(c) economic freedom
(d) an equitable distribution of income

9. To say that two economic goals are conflicting or mutually exclusive means that:
(a) it is not possible to achieve both goals
(b) these goals are not accepted as goals
(c) the achievement of one of the goals results in the achievement of the other
(d) it is possible to quantify both goals

10. Which of the following would be studied in **microeconomics**?
(a) the output of the entire economy
(b) the total number of workers employed in the United States
(c) the general level of prices in the American economy
(d) the output and price of wheat in the United States

11. Sandra states that "there is a high correlation between consumption and income." Arthur replies that it occurs because "people consume too much of their income and don't save enough."
(a) both Sandra's and Arthur's statements are positive
(b) both Sandra's and Arthur's statements are normative
(c) Sandra's statement is positive and Arthur's statement is normative
(d) Sandra's statement is normative and Arthur's statement is positive

12. During World War II the United States employed price control to prevent inflation; this was referred to as "a fascist and arbitrary restriction of economic freedom" by some and as "a necessary and democratic means of pre-

venting ruinous inflation" by others. Both labels are examples of:
- **(a)** economic bias
- **(b)** the fallacy of composition
- **(c)** the misuse of commonsense definitions
- **(d)** loaded terminology

13. If an individual determines to save a larger percentage of his/her income he/she will no doubt be able to save more. To reason, therefore, that if all individuals determine to save a larger percentage of their incomes they will be able to save more is an example of:
- **(a)** the **post hoc, ergo propter hoc** fallacy
- **(b)** the fallacy of composition
- **(c)** economic bias
- **(d)** using loaded terminology

14. The government increases its expenditures for road-construction equipment and later the average price of this equipment falls. The reason that the lower price was due to the increase in government expenditures may be an example of:
- **(a)** the **post hoc, ergo propter hoc** fallacy
- **(b)** the fallacy of composition
- **(c)** imprecise definition
- **(d)** using loaded terminology

15. Which one of the following is a normative economic statement?
- **(a)** the consumer price index rose 5.6% last month
- **(b)** the unemployment rate of 6.8% is too high
- **(c)** the average rate of interest on loan is 8.6%
- **(d)** the economy grew at an annual rate of 2.6%

16. The economist sometimes assumes that "other things are held constant" when studying an economic problem. This statement would best be an example of:
- **(a)** the **post hoc, ergo propter hoc** fallacy
- **(b)** the fallacy of composition
- **(c)** deductive reasoning
- **(d)** **ceteris paribus**

From Theory → fact to fill

17. The development of an economic theory and the testing of this theory by an appeal to facts is:
- **(a)** induction   *deduction*
- **(b)** deduction
- **(c)** policy economics
- **(d)** normative economics

18. Which economic goal is associated with the idea that we want to get the maximum benefits at the minimum cost from the limited productive resources which are available?
- **(a)** full employment
- **(b)** economic growth
- **(c)** economic security
- **(d)** economic efficiency

19. If economic growth tends to produce a more equitable distribution of income among people in a nation, then this relationship between the two economic goals appears to be:
- **(a)** deductive
- **(b)** conflicting
- **(c)** complementary
- **(d)** mutually exclusive

20. When we look at the whole economy or its major aggregates, our analysis would be at the level of:
- **(a)** microeconomics
- **(b)** macroeconomics
- **(c)** positive economics
- **(d)** normative economics

■ **DISCUSSION QUESTIONS**

1. Define economics in both a less and a more sophisticated way. In your latter definition, explain the meaning of "resources" and "wants."

2. What are the principal reasons for studying economics?

3. What is the relationship between facts and theory?

4. Define and explain the relationships between descriptive economics, economic theory, and applied economics.

5. What is a "laboratory experiment under controlled conditions"? Does the science of economics have any kind of laboratory? Why do economists employ the "other things equal" assumption?

6. Why are economic principles and models necessarily generalizations and abstract?

7. Why do economists disagree?

8. What does it mean to say that economic principles can be used for prediction?

9. Of the eight economic goals listed in the text, which one would you **rank** first, second, third, etc.? Would you add any other goals to this list? If economic goals 2 and 4 were conflicting, which goal would you prefer? Why? If goals 1 and 5 were conflicting, which would you prefer? Why?

10. What procedure should be followed in formulating sound economic policies?

11. Explain each of the following:
- **(a)** fallacy of composition;
- **(b)** loaded terminology;
- **(c)** the **post hoc, ergo propter hoc** fallacy.

12. Explain briefly the difference between
- **(a)** macroeconomics and microeconomics;
- **(b)** deduction and induction; and
- **(c)** correlation and causation.

13. What are some current examples of positive economic statements and normative economic statements?

14. Describe the economic perspective and give an example of its application.

■ **ANSWERS**

Chapter 1 The Nature and Method of Economics

FILL-IN QUESTIONS

1. *a.* production, distribution, consumption; *b.* limited (scarce), maximum

2. citizens, vocational

3. *a.* descriptive; *b.* theory, inductive, deductive; *c.* policy

4. laws (or theories or models), generalizations, abstractions

5. "other things equal" (*ceteris paribus*)

6. total, general, individual industry, particular product

7. positive, normative, normative

8. *a.* economic growth; *b.* full employment; *c.* economic efficiency; *d.* price stability; *e.* economic freedom; *f.* equitable distribution of income; *g.* economic security; *h.* balance of trade

9. complementary, conflicting

10. *a.* a clear statement of the objectives and goals; *b.* an analysis of all possible solutions; *c.* an evaluation of the results

11. composition; *post hoc, ergo propter hoc*

12. cost-benefit, rational, costs, benefits (either order for last two)

PROBLEMS AND PROJECTS

1. An increase in the demand for an economic good will cause the price of that good to rise.

2. *a.* definitions; *b.* the fallacy of composition; *c.* loaded terminology; *d.* the *post hoc, ergo propter hoc* fallacy.

3. *a.* N; *b.* P; *c.* N; *d.* P; *e.* N; *f.* N

SELF-TEST*

1. T, p. 1	**5.** T, p. 5	**9.** T, pp. 7–8	**13.** F, p. 5
2. F, pp. 2–3	**6.** F, pp. 3–4	**10.** F, pp. 7–8	**14.** T, pp. 9–10
3. F, p. 3	**7.** T, pp. 3–4	**11.** F, p. 8	**15.** T, p. 6
4. T, p. 4	**8.** F, p. 7	**12.** F, p. 6	

1. *b*, pp. 1–2	**6.** *d*, pp. 3–4	**11.** *c*, p. 6	**16.** *d*, p. 5
2. *b*, p. 1	**7.** *a*, p. 5	**12.** *d*, p. 8	**17.** *b*, pp. 3–4
3. *b*, pp. 2–3	**8.** *b*, p. 7	**13.** *b*, pp. 8–9	**18.** *d*, pp. 6–7
4. *c*, pp. 4–5	**9.** *a*, p. 7	**14.** *a*, pp. 8–9	**19.** *c*, p. 7
5. *a*, p. 4	**10.** *d*, p. 5	**15.** *b*, p. 6	**20.** *b*, p. 5

Page references are for the textbook.

DISCUSSION QUESTIONS

1. p. 1	**5.** pp. 4–5	**9.** pp. 6–8	**12.** pp. 3–4; 5; 9
2. pp. 2–3	**6.** pp. 4–5	**10.** pp. 7–8	**13.** p. 6
3. pp. 3–4	**7.** p. 6	**11.** pp. 8–9	**14.** pp. 9–11
4. p. 4	**8.** p. 6		

Appendix to Chapter 1 Graphs and Their Meaning

This appendix provides an introduction to graphing in economics. Graphs help illustrate and simplify the economic theories and models that will be presented throughout this book. The old saying that "a picture is worth a thousand words" applies to economics; graphs are the way that economists "picture" relationships between economic variables.

You will need to master the basics of graphing if these "pictures" are to be of any help to you. The appendix explains how to achieve that mastery. It begins by showing you how to construct a graph from a table of data on two variables, such as income and consumption. Economists usually, but not always, place the independent variable (income) on the horizontal axis and the dependent variable (consumption) on the vertical axis of the graph. Once the data points are plotted and a line drawn to connect the plotted points, you can determine whether there is a direct or an inverse relationship between the variables. Identifying a direct and an inverse relationship between variables is an essential skill that will be used repeatedly in this book.

Information from data in graphs and tables can be written in an equation. This work involves determining the slope and intercept from a straight line in a graph or data in a table. Using values for the slope and intercept, you can write a linear equation that will enable you to calculate what the dependent variable would be for a given level of the independent variable.

Some graphs used in the book are nonlinear. With nonlinear curves, the slope of the line is no longer constant throughout but varies as one moves along the curve. This slope can be estimated at a point by determining the slope of a straight line that is drawn tangent to the curve at that point. Similar calculations can be made for other points to see how the slope changes along the curve.

■ **APPENDIX CHECKLIST**

When you have studied this appendix you should be able to:

☐ Explain why economists use graphs.
☐ Construct a graph of two variables using the numerical data from a table.
☐ Make a table with two variables from data on a graph.
☐ Distinguish between a direct and an inverse relationship when given data on two variables.

☐ Identify dependent and independent variables in economic examples and graphs.

☐ Calculate the slope of a straight line between two points and determine the vertical intercept for the line.

☐ Write a linear equation using the slope of a line and the vertical intercept; when given values for the independent variable, determine values for the independent variable.

☐ Estimate the slope of a nonlinear curve at a point using a line that is tangent to the curve at that point.

■ **APPENDIX OUTLINE**

1. Graphs illustrate the relationship between variables to give economists and students another means, in addition to verbal explanation, of understanding economic phenomena. Graphs serve as an aid in describing economic theories and models.

2. The construction of a simple graph involves the plotting of numerical data about two variables from a table.

   a. Each graph has a horizontal and a vertical axis that can be labeled for each variable and then scaled for the range of the data point that will be measured on the axis.

   b. Data points are plotted on the graph by drawing perpendiculars from the scaled points on the two axes to the place on the graph where the perpendiculars intersect.

   c. A line or curve can then be drawn to connect the points plotted on the graph.

3. A graph provides information about relationships between variables.

   a. A line that is upward sloping to the right on a graph indicates that there is a positive or *direct* relationship between two variables: an increase in one is associated with an increase in the other; a decrease in one is associated with a decrease in the other.

   b. A line that is downward sloping to the right means that there is a negative or *inverse* relationship between the two variables because the variables are changing in opposite directions: an increase in one is associated with a decrease in the other; a decrease in one is associated with an increase in the other.

4. Economists are often concerned with determining cause and effect in economic events.

   a. A dependent variable changes (increases or decreases) because of a change in another variable.

   b. An independent variable produces or "causes" the change in the dependent variable.

   c. In a graph, mathematicians place an independent variable on the horizontal axis and a dependent variable on the vertical axis; economists are more arbitrary about which variable is placed on an axis.

5. Economic graphs are simplifications of economic relationships. When graphs are plotted, there is usually an implicit assumption made that all other factors are being held constant. This "other things equal" or ***ceteris paribus*** assumption is used to simplify the analysis so the study can focus on the two variables of interest.

6. A slope and intercept can be calculated for a straight line and written in the form of a linear equation.

   a. The slope of a straight line is the ratio of the vertical change to the horizontal change between two points. A positive slope indicates that the relationship between two variables is direct; a negative slope means there is an inverse relationship between the variables.

   b. Where the line intersects the vertical axis of the graph is the vertical intercept.

   c. A linear equation is written as $y = a + bx$. Once the values for the intercept (a) and the slope (b) are calculated, then given any value of the independent variable (x), the value of the dependent variable (y) can be determined.

7. The slope of a straight line is constant, but the slope of a nonlinear curve changes throughout. To estimate the slope of a nonlinear curve at a point, the slope of a line tangent to the curve at that point is calculated.

■ **IMPORTANT TERMS**

Vertical and horizontal axes	Slope of a line
	Vertical intercept
Direct (positive) and inverse (negative) relationships	Linear equation
	Nonlinear curve
Dependent and independent variables	Tangent

■ **FILL-IN QUESTIONS**

1. The relationship between two economic variables can be visualized with the aid of a two-dimensional graph.

   a. Customarily, the (dependent, independent) _____ _____ variable is placed on the horizontal axis and the _____ variable is placed on the vertical axis. The _____ variable is said to change because of a change in the _____ variable.

   b. The vertical and horizontal (scales, ranges) _____ on the graph are calibrated to reflect the _____ of values in a table of data points on which the graph is based.

   c. Other variables, beyond the two in the graph, that might affect the economic relationship are assumed to be (changing, held constant) _____.

Ceteris paribus also means that other variables are

_____

2. The graph of a straight line that slopes downward to the right indicates that there is (a direct, an inverse)

_____ relationship between the two variables. A graph of a straight line that slopes upward to the right tells us that the relationship is (direct, inverse)

_____. When the value of one variable increases and the value of the other variable increases, then

the relationship is _____; when the value of one increases, while the other decreases, the relationship is

_____

3. The slope of a straight line between two points is defined as the ratio of the (vertical, horizontal)

_____ change to the _____ change. When two variables move in the same direction,

the slope will be (negative, positive) _____; when the variables move in opposite directions the slope

will be _____. The point at which the line

meets the vertical axis is called the _____

4. We can express the graph of a straight line with a linear equation that can be written as $y = a + bx$.

    a. *a* is the (slope, intercept) _____ and *b* is

    the _____

    b. *y* is the (dependent, independent) _____

    variable and *x* is the _____
    variable.
    c. If *a* was 2, *b* was 4, and *x* was 5, then *y* would be

    _____ . If the value of *x* changed to 7, then

    y would be _____. If the value of *x* changed

    to 3, then *y* would be _____

5. The slope of a (straight line, nonlinear curve)

_____ is constant throughout; the slope of a

_____ varies from point to point. An estimate of the slope of a nonlinear curve at a point can be made by calculating the slope of a straight line that is

_____ to the point on the curve.

■ **PROBLEMS AND PROJECTS**

1. Next are three exercises in making graphs. On the graphs plot the economic relationships contained in each exercise. Be sure to label each axis of the graph and to

indicate the unit of measurement and scale used on each axis.

    a. Graph national income on the horizontal axis and consumption expenditures on the veritcal axis; connect the seven points and label the curve "Consumption Schedule." The relationship between national income and consumption expenditures is a(n) (direct, inverse)

_____ one and the Consumption Schedule

a(n) (up-, down-) _____ sloping curve.

National income, billions of dollars	Consumption expenditures, billions of dollars
$ 600	$ 600
700	640
800	780
900	870
1000	960
1100	1050
1200	1140

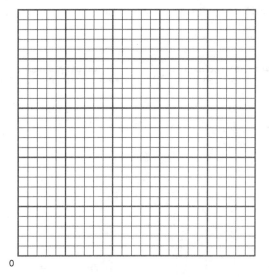

    b. Graph investment expenditures on the horizontal axis and the rate of interest on the vertical axis; connect the seven points and label the curve "Investment Schedule." The relationship between the rate of interest and investment expenditures is a(n) (direct, inverse)

_____ one and the Investment Schedule a(n)

(up-, down-) _____ sloping curve.

Rate of interest, %	Investment expenditures, billions of dollars
8	$220
7	280
6	330
5	370
4	400
3	420
2	430

0

c. Graph average salary on the horizontal axis and wine consumption on the vertical axis; connect the seven points.

Average salary, American college professors	Annual per capita wine consumption in liters
$52,000	11.5
53,000	11.6
54,000	11.7
55,000	11.8
56,000	11.9
57,000	22.0
58,000	22.1

0

(1) The average salary of a college professor and wine consumption (are, are not) _____ **correlated**. The higher average salary (is, is not)

_____ the **cause** of the greater consumption of wine.
(2) The relationship between the two variables may be purely _____ ; or, as is more likely, both the higher salaries and the greater consumption of wine may be the result of the higher _____ in the American economy.

2. This question is based on the graph below.

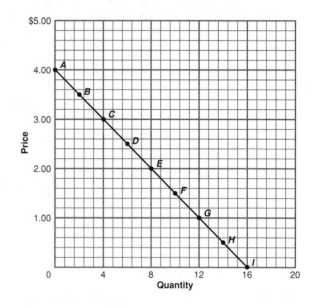

a. Construct a table for points **A–I** from the data shown in the graph.
b. According to economists, price is the (independent, dependent) _____ variable and quantity is the _____ variable.
c. Write a linear equation that summarizes the data.

3. The following three sets of data each show the relationship between an independent variable and a dependent variable. For each set, the independent variable is in the left column and the dependent variable is in the right column.

(1)		(2)		(3)	
A	B	C	D	E	F
0	10	0	100	0	20
10	30	10	75	50	40
20	50	20	50	100	60
30	70	30	25	150	80
40	90	40	0	200	100

a. Write an equation that summarizes the data for each set: (1), (2), and (3).
b. State whether each data set shows a positive or inverse relationship between the two variables.

$y = 0.5x + 5$

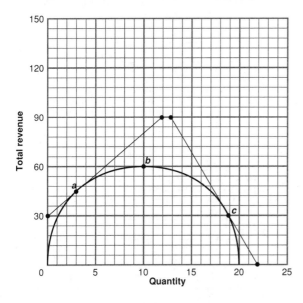

$\frac{\text{con}}{\text{in}} = 0.9$

c. Graph data sets 1 and 2 on the graph above. Use the same horizontal scale for both sets of independent variables and the same vertical scale for both sets of dependent variables.

4. This problem is based on the following graph.

a. The slope of the straight line through point **a** is?
b. The slope of the straight line through point **b** is?
c. The slope of the straight line through point **c** is?

■ SELF-TEST

Circle the T if the statement is true; the F if it is false.

1. Graphs are designed by economists to confuse students and the public.   T F

2. If the straight line on a two-variable graph is downward sloping to the right, then there is a positive relationship between the two variables.   T **F**

3. A variable that changes as a consequence of a change in another variable is considered to be a dependent variable.   **T** F

4. Economists always put the independent variable on the horizontal axis and the dependent variable on the vertical axis of a two-variable graph.   T **F**

5. *Ceteris paribus* means that other variables are changing at the same time.   T **F**

6. In the ratio for the calculation of the slope of a straight line, the vertical change is in the numerator and the horizontal change is in the denominator.   **T** F

7. If the slope of the linear relationship between consumption and income was .90, then it tells us that for every $1 increase in income there will be a $.90 increase in consumption.   **T** F

8. If a linear equation was $y = 10 + 5x$, the vertical intercept is 5.   T **F**

9. When a line is tangent to a nonlinear curve, then it intersects the curve at a particular point.   T **F**

10. If the slope of a straight line on a two-variable (x, y) graph was .5 and the vertical intercept was 5, then a value of 10 for x means y is also 10.   **T** F

11. A slope of -4 for a straight line in a two-variable graph indicates that there is an inverse relationship between the two variables.   **T** F

12. If x is an independent variable and y is a dependent variable, then a change in y results in a change in x.   T **F**

13. An upward slope for a straight line that is tangent to a nonlinear curve would indicate that the slope of the line is positive. $\frac{-10}{5}$ (-2) **T** F

14. If one pair of x, y points was (13, 10) and the other was (8, 20), then the slope of the straight line between the two sets of points in the two-variable graph, with x on the horizontal axis and y on the vertical axis, would be 2.   T **F**

15. When the value of x is 2, a value of 10 for y would be calculated from a linear equation of $y = -2 + 6x$. **T** F

Circle the letter that corresponds to the best answer.

1. If an increase in one variable is associated with a decrease in another variable, then we can conclude that the variables are:
  (a) nonlinear
  (b) directly related
  (c) inversely related
  (d) positively related

$y = mx + b.$
B   A

2. The ratio of the absolute vertical change to the absolute horizontal change between two points of a straight line is the:
(a) slope
(b) vertical intercept
(c) horizontal intercept
(d) point of tangency

$x = 0 \quad y = 5$
$slope = \dfrac{15}{5} = 3$

3. There are two sets of **x, y** points on a straight line in a two-variable graph with **y** on the vertical axis and **x** on the horizontal axis. If one set of points was (0, 5) and the other set (5, 20), the linear equation for the line would be:
(a) $y = 5x$
(b) $y = 5 + 3x$
(c) $y = 5 + 15x$
(d) $y = 5 + .33x$

$y = 3x + 5$

4. In a two-variable graph of data on the price and quantity of a product, economists place:
(a) price on the horizontal axis because it is the independent variable and quantity on the vertical axis because it is the dependent variable
(b) price on the vertical axis because it is the dependent variable and quantity on the horizontal because it is the independent variable
(c) price on the vertical axis even though it is the independent variable and quantity on the horizontal axis even though it is the dependent variable
(d) price on the horizontal axis even though it is the dependent variable and quantity on the vertical axis even though it is the independent variable

5. In a two-dimensional graph of the relationship between two economic variables, an assumption is usually made that:
(a) both variables are linear
(b) both variables are nonlinear
(c) other variables are held constant
(d) other variables are permitted to change

6. When the slope of a straight line to a point tangent to a nonlinear curve is zero, then the straight line is:
(a) vertical
(b) horizontal
(c) upward sloping
(d) downward sloping

*The next four questions (**7, 8, 9,** and **10**) are based on the following four data sets. In each set, the independent variable is in the left column and the dependent variable is in the right column.*

(1)		(2)		(3)		(4)	
A	B	C	D	E	F	G	H
0	1	0	12	4	5	0	4
3	2	5	8	6	10	1	3
6	3	10	4	8	15	2	2
9	4	15	0	10	20	3	1

7. There is an inverse relationship between the independent and dependent variable in data sets:
(a) 1 and 4
(b) 2 and 3
(c) 1 and 3
(d) 2 and 4

8. The vertical intercept is 4 in data set:
(a) 1
(b) 2
(c) 3
(d) 4

9. The linear equation for data set 1 is:
(a) $B = 3A$
(b) $B = 1 + 3A$
(c) $B = 1 + .33A$
(d) $A = 1 + .33B$

10. The linear equation for data set 2 is:
(a) $C = 12 - 1.25D$
(b) $D = 12 + 1.25C$
(c) $D = 12 - .80C$
(d) $C = 12 - .80D$

*Answer the next four questions (**11, 12, 13,** and **14**) on the basis of the following diagram.*

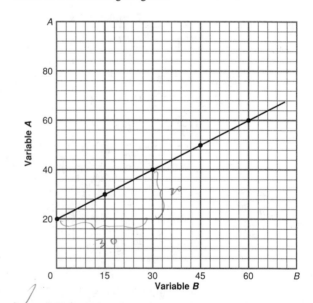

11. The variables **A** and **B** are:
(a) positively related
(b) negatively related
(c) indirectly related
(d) nonlinear

12. The slope of the line is:
(a) .33
(b) .67

(c) 1.50
(d) 3.00

13. The vertical intercept is:
(a) 80
(b) 60
(c) 40
(d) 20

14. The linear equation for the slope of the line is:
(a) $A = 20 + .33B$
(b) $B = 20 + .33A$
(c) $A = 20 + .67B$
(d) $B = 20 + .67A$

Answer the next two questions (15 and 16) on the basis of the following diagram.

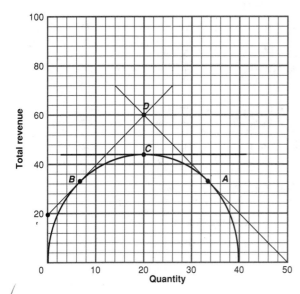

15. The slope of the line tangent to the curve at point **A** is:
(a)   2
(b) −2
(c) −1.5
(d) −0.5

16. The slope of the line tangent to the curve at point **B** is:
(a) −2
(b)   2
(c)   3
(d)   0.5

17. The slope of the line tangent to the curve at point **C** is:
(a) −1
(b)   1
(c)   0
(d)   undefined

18. Assume that the relationship between concert ticket prices and attendance is expressed in the equation $P = 25 - 1.25Q$, where P equals ticket price and Q equals concert attendance in thousands of people. On the basis of this equation, it can be said that:
(a) more people will attend the concert when the price is high compared to when the price is low
(b) if 12,000 people attended the concert, then the ticket price was $10
(c) if 18,000 people attend the concert, then entry into the concert was free
(d) an increase in ticket price by $5 reduces concert attendance by 1,000 people

19. If you know that the equation relating consumption (C) to income (Y) is $C = \$7,500 + .2Y$, then:
(a) consumption is inversely related to income
(b) consumption is the independent variable and income is the dependent variable
(c) if income is $15,000, then consumption is $10,500
(d) if consumption is $30,000, then income is $10,000

20. If the dependent variable changes by 22 units when the independent variable changes by 12 units, then the slope of the line is:
(a) 0.56
(b) 1.83
(c) 2.00
(d) 3.27

■ **DISCUSSION QUESTIONS**

1. Why do economists use graphs in their work? Give two examples of a graph that illustrates the relationship between two economic variables.

2. What does the slope tell you about a straight line? How would you interpret a slope of 4? A slope of −2? A slope of .5? A slope of −.25?

3. If the vertical intercept increases in value but the slope of a straight line stays the same, what happens to the graph of the line? If the vertical intercept decreases in value, what will happen to the line?

4. How do you interpret a vertical line on a two-variable graph? How do you interpret a horizontal line?

5. When you know that the price and quantity of a product are inversely related, what does this tell you about the slope of a line? What do you know about the slope when the two variables are positively related?

6. Which variable is the dependent and which is the independent in the following economic statement: "A decrease in business taxes had a positive effect on investment spending." How do you tell the difference between a dependent and independent variable when examining economic relationships?

7. Why is an assumption made that all other variables are held constant when we construct a two-variable graph of the price and quantity of a product?

8. How do mathematicians and economists differ at times in the way that they construct two-dimensional graphs? Give an example.

9. If you know that the equation relating consumption (C) to income (Y) is $C = 10,000 + 5Y$, then what would consumption be when income is $5,000? Construct an income-consumption table for five different levels of income.

10. How do the slopes of a straight line and a nonlinear curve differ? How do you estimate the slope of a nonlinear curve?

Point	Price	Quantity
A	$4.00	0
B	3.50	2
C	3.00	4
D	2.50	6
E	2.00	8
F	1.50	10
G	1.00	12
H	.50	14
I	.00	16

b. independent, dependent; *c.* $P = 4.00 - .25Q$

3. *a.* (1) $B = 10 + 2A$; (2) $D = 100 - 2.5C$; (3) $F = 20 + .4E$; *b.* (1) positive; (2) inverse; (3) positive

4. *a.* 5; *b.* 0; *c.* -10

■ **ANSWERS**

Appendix to Chapter 1 Graphs and Their Meaning

FILL-IN QUESTIONS

1. *a.* independent, dependent, dependent, independent; *b.* scales, ranges; *c.* held constant, held constant

2. inverse, direct, direct, inverse

3. vertical, horizontal, positive, negative, vertical intercept

4. *a.* intercept, slope; *b.* dependent, independent; *c.* 22, 30, 14

5. straight line, nonlinear curve, tangent

PROBLEMS AND PROJECTS

1. *a.* direct, up-; *b.* inverse, down-; *c.* (1) are, is not; (2) coincidental, incomes (standard of living, or some other such answer)

2. *a.*

SELF-TEST

1. F, p. 13
2. F, p. 14
3. T, pp. 14–15
4. F, p. 15
5. F, p. 15
6. T, p. 15
7. T, pp. 15–16
8. F, p. 16
9. F, pp. 16–17
10. T, p. 16
11. T, p. 15
12. F, pp. 14–15
13. T, pp. 16–17
14. F, pp. 15–16
15. T, pp. 15–16

1. *c*, p. 14
2. *a*, p. 15
3. *b*, pp. 15–16
4. *c*, pp. 14–15
5. *c*, p. 15
6. *b*, pp. 16–17
7. *d*, p. 14
8. *d*, pp. 15–16
9. *c*, pp. 16–17
10. *c*, pp. 15–16
11. *a*, p. 14
12. *b*, p. 15
13. *d*, p. 16
14. *c*, p. 16
15. *b*, pp. 16–17
16. *b*, pp. 16–17
17. *c*, pp. 16–17
18. *b*, p. 16
19. *c*, p. 15
20. *b*, p. 15

DISCUSSION QUESTIONS

1. p. 13
2. pp. 15–16
3. pp. 15–16
4. pp. 13–14
5. p. 14
6. pp. 14–15
7. p. 15
8. p. 15
9. p. 16
10. pp. 16–17

CHAPTER 2

The Economizing Problem

The aim of Chapter 2 is to explain the central problem of economics. The problem is that resources—the ultimate means of satisfying material wants—are scarce *relative* to the insatiable wants of society. Economics as a science is the study of the various aspects of the behavior of society in its effort to allocate the scarce resources—land, labor, capital, and entrepreneurial ability—in order to satisfy as best it can its unlimited desire for consumption.

The production possibilities table and curve are used in this chapter to illustrate the meaning of the scarcity of resources and increasing opportunity costs. It is both an illustrative device that will help you to understand several economic concepts and problems and a tool that has many applications in the real world.

Every economy is faced with the problem of scarce resources and has to find ways to respond to the economic problem. No economy answers the problem in the same way that another economy does. Between the extremes of pure (or laissez faire) capitalism and the command economy (communism) are various economic systems; all these systems are different devices—different methods of organization—for finding an answer to the economic problem of relative scarcity. Chapters 3 through 6 will explain in greater detail how the United States economy is organized and operates to address the economizing problem.

In Chapter 2 of the textbook are a number of economic definitions and classifications. It would be worthwhile for you to learn these definitions *now.* They will be used later on and it will be necessary for you to know them if you are to understand what follows.

■ CHECKLIST

When you have studied this chapter you should be able to:

☐ Write a definition of economics that incorporates the relationship between resources and wants.
☐ Identify the four economic resources and the type of income associated with each.
☐ Explain why full employment and full production are necessary for the efficient use of resources.

☐ Distinguish between allocative efficiency and productive efficiency.
☐ State the four assumptions made when a production possibilities table or curve is constructed.
☐ Construct a production possibilities curve when you are given the appropriate data.
☐ Define opportunity cost and utilize a production possibilities curve to explain the concept.
☐ State the law of increasing opportunity costs and, in as few words as possible, present the economic rationale for this law.
☐ Use a production possibilities curve to illustrate economic growth, underemployment of resources, and increasing opportunity costs.
☐ Give real-world applications of the production possibilities curve.
☐ List the two major characteristics of pure capitalism and the command economy.

■ CHAPTER OUTLINE

1. The bases upon which the study of economics rests are two facts.
    a. Society's material wants are unlimited.
    b. The economic resources which are the ultimate means of satisfying these wants are scarce in relation to the wants.
    (1) Economic resources are classified as land, capital, labor, and entrepreneurial ability.
    (2) The payments received by those who provide the economy with these four resources are rental income, interest income, wages, and profits, respectively.
    (3) Because these resources are scarce (or limited) the output that the economy is able to produce is also limited.

2. Economics, then, is the study of how society's scarce resources are used (administered) to obtain the greatest satisfaction of its material wants.
    a. To be efficient in the use of its resources an economy must achieve both full employment and full production. Full production implies that there are

(1) allocative efficiency, which means that resources are devoted to those goods most wanted by society; and

(2) productive efficiency, which means that goods and services are being produced in the least-cost way.

b. The production possibilities table indicates the alternative combinations of goods and services an economy is capable of producing when it has achieved full employment and full production.

(1) The four assumptions that are usually made when a production possibilities table is constructed is that there are economic efficiency, fixed resources, fixed technology, and two products being considered.

(2) The table illustrates the fundamental choice every society must make: what quantity of each product it wants produced.

c. The data contained in the production possibilities table can be plotted on a graph to obtain a production possibilities curve.

d. Which of these alternative combinations society chooses—which product-mix it selects—depends upon the preferences of that society; and preferences are subjective and nonscientific.

e. The opportunity cost of producing an additional unit of one product is the amounts of other products that are sacrificed; and the law of increasing opportunity costs is that the opportunity cost of producing additional units of a product increases as more of that product is produced.

(1) The law of increasing opportunity cost results in a production possibilities curve that is concave (from the origin).

(2) The opportunity cost of producing additional units of a product increases as more of the product is produced because resources are not completely adaptable to alternative uses.

(3) The production possibilities curve illustrates the concepts of scarcity, choice, opportunity cost, and increasing opportunity costs.

3. The following modifications make the production possibilities concept more realistic.

a. The failure to achieve full employment or full production reduces the output of the economy.

b. Improvements in technology and increased amounts of resources expand the output the economy is capable of producing.

c. The combination of goods and services an economy chooses to produce today helps to determine its production possibilities in the future.

d. There are many real-world applications of the production possibilities curve and table.

4. Different economic systems differ in the way they respond to the economizing problem.

a. At one extreme is pure capitalism, which relies upon the private ownership of its economic resources and the market system.

b. At the other extreme, the command economy uses the public ownership of its resources and central planning.

c. Economies in the real world lie between these two extremes and are hybrid systems.

d. Some underdeveloped nations have traditional (or customary) economies which are shaped by the customs and traditions of the society.

■ **IMPORTANT TERMS**

The economizing problem

Unlimited wants

Scarce resources

Land, capital, labor, and entrepreneurial ability

Factors of production

Investment

Consumer goods

Capital goods

Real capital

Money (financial) capital

Rental income, interest income, wages, and profit

Utility

Economics

Economic efficiency

Full employment

Full production

Allocative efficiency

Productive efficiency

Production possibilities table

Production possibilities curve

Optimal product mix

Opportunity cost

Law of increasing opportunity costs

Unemployment

Underemployment

Economic growth

Pure (laissez-faire) capitalism

Command economy (communism)

Authoritarian capitalism

Market socialism

Traditional (customary) economies

■ **FILL-IN QUESTIONS**

1. The two fundamental facts that provide the foundation of economics are:

a. _____

b. _____

2. Complete the following classification of resources:

a. _____

(1) _____

_____

(2) _____

b. _____

(1) _____

(2) _____

3. Both consumer goods and capital goods satisfy human wants. The consumer goods satisfy these wants (directly, indirectly) _____ and the capital goods satisfy them _____

4. The incomes of individuals are received from supplying resources. Four types of incomes are _____, _____, _____, and _____

5. Economics can be defined as _____ _____ _____ _____

6. Economic efficiency requires that there be both full (employment, production) _____ of resources, and full _____ so as to make the most valued contributions to national output. Full _____ implies that there is both (allocative, productive) _____ efficiency, which means that resources are devoted to those goods most wanted by society, and that there is _____ efficiency, which means that goods and services are being produced in the least-cost way.

7. When a production possibilities table or curve is constructed, four assumptions are made. These assumptions are:

a. _____

b. _____

c. _____

d. _____

8. In the next column is a production possibilities curve for tractors and suits of clothing.

a. If the economy moves from point **A** to point **B** it will produce (more, fewer) _____ tractors and (more, fewer) _____ suits of clothing.

b. If the economy is producing at point **X,** some of the resources of the economy are either _____ or _____

c. If the economy moves from point **X** to point **B** (more, fewer) _____ tractors and (more, fewer) _____ suits will be produced.

d. If the economy is to produce at point **Y,** it must either _____ or _____

9. All the combinations of products shown in the production possibilities table (or on the curve) can be achieved only if there are full employment and full production in the economy; the best combination of products depends upon the (values, resources, technology) _____ of that society and is a (scientific, nonscientific) _____ matter.

10. The quantity of other goods and services an economy must go without in order to produce more low-cost housing is the _____ of producing the additional low-cost housing.

11. The cost of producing a commodity tends to increase as more of the commodity is produced because _____ _____ _____

12. The more an economy consumes of its current production, the (more, less) _____ it will be capable of producing in future years if other things are equal.

13. In:

a. pure capitalism property resources are (publicly, privately) _____ owned and the means employed to direct and coordinate economic activity is the _____ system.

b. a command economy the property resources are (publicly, privately) _____ owned and the coordinating device is central _____

■ PROBLEMS AND PROJECTS

1. Below is a list of resources. Indicate in the space to the right of each whether the resource is land, capital (C), labor, entrepreneurial ability (EA), or some combinations of these.

a. Fishing grounds in the North Atlantic _____

b. A cash register in a retail store _____

c. Uranium deposits in Canada _____

d. An irrigation ditch in Nebraska _____

e. The work performed by the late Henry Ford _____

f. The oxygen breathed by human beings _____

g. An IBM plant in Rochester, Minnesota _____

h. The food on the shelf of a grocery store _____

i. The work done by a robot at an auto plant _____

j. The tasks accomplished in perfecting a new computer for commercial sales _____

k. A carpenter building a house _____

2. A production possibilities table for two commodities, wheat and automobiles, is found below. The table is constructed employing the usual assumptions. Wheat is measured in units of 100,000 bushels and automobiles in units of 100,000.

Combination	Wheat	Automobiles
A	0	7
B	7	6
C	13	5
D	18	4
E	22	3
F	25	2
G	27	1
H	28	0

a. Follow the general rules for making graphs (see Chapter 1); plot the data from the table on the graph below to obtain a production possibilities curve. Place wheat on the vertical axis and automobiles on the horizontal axis.

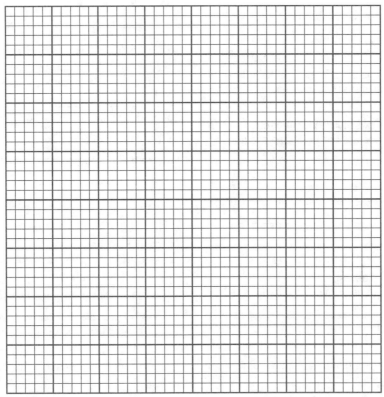

0

b. Fill in the table below showing the opportunity cost per unit of producing the 1st through the 7th automobile.

Automobiles	Cost of production
1st	_____
2d	_____
3d	_____
4th	_____
5th	_____
6th	_____
7th	_____

3. Below is a production possibilities curve.

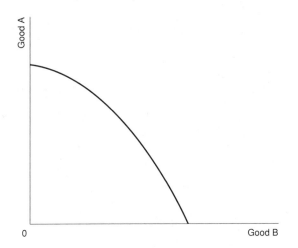

Draw on this graph:
   a. A production possibilities curve which indicates greater efficiency in the production of good A.
   b. A production possibilities curve which indicates greater efficiency in the production of good B.
   c. A production possibilities curve which indicates an increase in the resources available to the economy.

4. Below is a list of economic goods. Indicate in the space to the right of each whether the good is a consumer good (CON), a capital good (CAP), or that it depends (DEP) upon who is using it and for what purpose.

   a. An automobile _____

   b. A tractor _____

   c. A taxicab _____

   d. A house _____

   e. A factory building _____

   f. An office building _____

   g. An ironing board _____

   h. A refrigerator _____

   i. A telephone _____

   j. A quart of a soft drink _____

   k. A cash register _____

   l. A screwdriver _____

■ **SELF-TEST**

Circle the T if the statement is true; the F if it is false.

1. The wants with which economics is concerned include only those wants which can be satisfied by goods and services.　　T (F)

2. Money is a resource and is classified as "capital."　　T (F)

3. Profit is the reward paid to those who provide the economy with capital.　　T (F)

4. Resources are scarce because society's material wants are unlimited and productive resources are limited.　　(T) F

5. Economic efficiency requires that there be both full employment of resources and full production.　　(T) F

6. Allocative efficiency means that goods and services are being produced by society in the least-cost way.　　T (F)

7. Only allocative efficiency is necessary for there to be full production.　　T (F)

8. The opportunity cost of producing antipollution devices is the other goods and services the economy is unable to produce because it has decided to produce these devices.　　(T) F

9. The opportunity cost of producing a good tends to increase as more of it is produced because resources less suitable to its production must be employed.　　(T) F

10. Drawing a production possibilities curve concave to the origin is the geometric way of stating the law of increasing opportunity costs.　　(T) F

11. Given full employment and full production, it is not possible for an economy capable of producing just two goods to increase its production of both.　　(T) F

12. Economic growth means an increase in the ability of an economy to produce goods and services; and it is shown by a movement of the production possibilities to the right.　　(T) F

13. The more capital goods an economy produces today, the greater will be the total output of all goods it can produce in the future, other things being equal.　　(T) F

14. It is economically desirable for a nation to have unemployed resources at the outset of a war because it can increase its production of military goods without having to decrease its production of civilian goods.   T F

15. In the economic system called authoritarian capitalism most property is publicly owned but the market system is used to coordinate economic activity.   T F

Circle the letter that corresponds to the best answer.

1. An "innovator" is defined as an entrepreneur who:
(a) makes basic policy decisions in a business firm
(b) combines factors of production to produce a good or service
(c) invents a new product or process for producing a product
(d) introduces new products on the market or employs a new method to produce a product

2. An economy is efficient when it has achieved:
(a) full employment
(b) full production
(c) either full employment or full production
(d) both full employment and full production

3. When a production possibilities schedule is written (or a production possibilities curve is drawn) four assumptions are made. Which of the following is *not* one of those assumptions?
(a) only two products are produced
(b) the nation is not at war
(c) the economy has both full employment and full production
(d) the quantities of all resources available to the economy are fixed

4. At point *A* on the production possibilities curve in the following illustration:

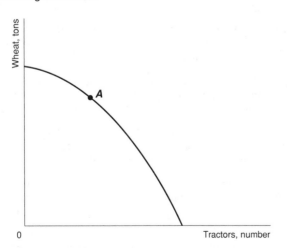

(a) more wheat than tractors is being produced

(b) more tractors than wheat are being produced
(c) the economy is employing all its resources
(d) the economy is not employing all its resources

5. The combinations of products in a society's production possibilities table which is its optimal product-mix depends upon that society's:
(a) resources
(b) technology
(c) level of employment
(d) values

6. The production possibilities curve is:
(a) concave
(b) convex
(c) linear
(d) positive

7. What is the economic rationale for the law of increasing opportunity cost?
(a) full production and full employment of resources has not been achieved
(b) economic resources are not completely adaptable to alternative uses
(c) economic growth is being limited by the pace of technological advancement
(d) an economy's present choice of output is determined by fixed technology and fixed resources

8. A farmer who produces his crops by inefficient methods is:
(a) an unemployed worker
(b) an underemployed worker
(c) a fully employed worker
(d) an apparently unemployed worker

9. If there is an increase in the resources available within the economy:
(a) more goods and services will be produced in the economy
(b) the economy will be capable of producing more goods and services
(c) the standard of living in the economy will rise
(d) the technological efficiency of the economy will improve

10. If the production possibilities curve on the next page moves from position *A* to position *B,* then:
(a) the economy has increased the efficiency with which it produces wheat
(b) the economy has increased the efficiency with which it produces tractors
(c) the economy has put previously idle resources to work
(d) the economy has gone from full employment to less-than-full employment

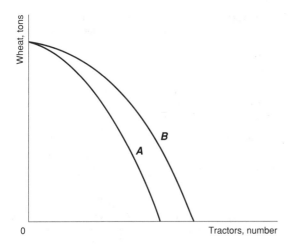

11. Which would be the best example of allocative efficiency? When society devoted resources to the production of:
(a) slide rules instead of hand-held calculators
(b) horse-drawn carriages instead of automobiles
(c) word processors instead of manual typewriters
(d) long-play records instead of compact discs or cassettes

12. Which situation would most likely shift the production possibilities curve for a nation in an outward direction?
(a) deterioration in product quality
(b) reductions in the supply of resources
(c) increases in technological advances
(d) rising levels of discrimination

13. The opportunity cost of a new public stadium is the:
(a) money cost of hiring guards and staff for the new stadium
(b) cost of constructing the new stadium in a future year
(c) change in the real estate tax rate to pay off the new stadium
(d) other goods and services that must be sacrificed to construct the new stadium

14. The public ownership of property resources and the use of a market system to direct and coordinate economic activity is characteristic of:
(a) pure capitalism
(b) the command economy
(c) market socialism
(d) authoritarian capitalism

Answer the next three questions (15, 16, and 17) on the basis of the data given in the following production possibilities table.

	Production possibilities (alternatives)					
	A	B	C	D	E	F
Capital goods	100	95	85	70	50	0
Consumer goods	0	100	180	240	280	300

15. The choice of alternative B compared with alternative D would tend to promote:
(a) a slower rate of economic growth
(b) a faster rate of economic growth
(c) increased consumption in the present
(d) central economic planning

16. If the economy is producing at production alternative D, the opportunity cost of 40 more units of consumer goods is about:
(a) 5 units of capital goods
(b) 10 units of capital goods
(c) 15 units of capital goods
(d) 20 units of capital goods

17. In the table, the law of increasing opportunity costs is suggested by the fact that:
(a) greater and greater quantities of consumer goods must be given up to get more capital goods
(b) smaller and smaller quantities of consumer goods must be given up to get more capital goods
(c) capital goods are relatively more scarce than consumer goods
(d) the production possibilities curve will eventually shift outward as the economy expands

18. Productive efficiency means that:
(a) the law of increasing opportunity cost has reached a maximum
(b) the least-costly methods are being used to produce a product
(c) resources are being devoted to the production of products most desired by society
(d) the amount of other products which must be sacrificed to obtain production of a given product is at a minimum

19. Which situation would most likely cause a nation's production possibilities curve to shift inward?
(a) investing more resources in new plants and equipment
(b) eliminating discrimination based on race and ethnic background
(c) increasing international trade or incurring a trade deficit
(d) going to war with another nation and suffering a major defeat

20. The private ownership of property resources and use of the market system to direct and coordinate economic activity is characteristic of:
- **(a)** pure capitalism
- **(b)** the command economy
- **(c)** market socialism
- **(d)** the traditional economy

■ **DISCUSSION QUESTIONS**

1. Explain what is meant by the "economizing problem." Why are resources scarce?

2. In what sense are wants satiable and in what sense are they insatiable?

3. What are the four economic resources? How is each of these resources defined? What is the income earned by each of them called?

4. When is a society economically efficient? What is meant by "full production" and how does it differ from "full employment"? Explain why full production implies both allocative and productive efficiency.

5. What four assumptions are made in drawing a production possibilities curve or schedule? How do technological advance and an increased supply of resources in the economy affect the curve or schedule?

6. Why cannot an economist determine which of the combinations in the production possibilities table is "best"? What determines the optimal product-mix?

7. What is opportunity cost? What is the law of increasing opportunity cost? Why do costs increase?

8. What is the important relationship between the **composition** of the economy's current output and the **location** of future production possibilities curves?

9. Describe some real-world applications of the production possibilities curve.

10. Pure capitalism and the command economy differ in two important ways. Compare these two economic systems with each other and with authoritarian capitalism and market socialism.

■ **ANSWERS**

Chapter 2 The Economizing Problem

FILL-IN QUESTIONS

1. *a.* society's material wants are unlimited; *b.* economic resources, which are the ultimate means of satisfying these wants, are scarce in relation to these wants

2. *a.* property resources; (1) land or raw materials, (2) capital; *b.* human resources; (1) labor, (2) entrepreneurial ability

3. directly, indirectly

4. rental income, interest income, wages profits

5. the social science concerned with the problem of using or administering scarce resources to attain maximum fulfillment of unlimited wants

6. employment, production, production, allocative, productive

7. *a.* the economy is operating at full employment and full production; *b.* the available supplies of the factors of production are fixed; *c.* technology does not change during the course of the analysis; *d.* the economy produces only two products

8. *a.* fewer, more; *b.* unemployed, underemployed; *c.* more, more; *d.* increase resource supplies, improve its technology

9. values, nonscientific

10. opportunity cost

11. economic resources are not completely adaptable among alternate uses

12. less

13. *a.* privately, market; *b.* publicly, planning

PROBLEMS AND PROJECTS

1. *a.* land; *b.* C; *c.* land; *d.* C; *e.* EA; *f.* land; *g.* C; *h.* C; *i.* C; *j.* EA; *k.* labor

2. *b.* 1, 2, 3, 4, 5, 6, 7 units of wheat

4. *a.* DEP; *b.* CAP; *c.* CAP; *d.* CAP; *e.* CAP; *f.* CAP; *g.* DEP; *h.* DEP; *i.* DEP; *j.* DEP; *k.* CAP; *l.* DEP

SELF-TEST

1. T, pp. 19–20	**6.** F, p. 22	**11.** T, pp. 23–24
2. F, pp. 20–21	**7.** F, p. 22	**12.** T, p 26
3. F, p. 21	**8.** T, p. 23	**13.** T, pp. 27–28
4. T, pp. 20–21	**9.** T, pp. 23–24	**14.** F, p. 29
5. T, p. 22	**10.** T, p. 25	**15.** F, p. 31

1. *d,* p. 21	**8.** *b,* p. 22	**15.** *b,* pp. 27–28
2. *d,* p. 22	**9.** *b,* p. 26	**16.** *d,* pp. 27–28
3. *b,* p. 23	**10.** *b,* p. 27	**17.** *a,* p. 25
4. *c,* p. 24	**11.** *c,* p. 22	**18.** *b,* p. 22
5. *d,* pp. 24–25	**12.** *c,* pp. 26–27	**19.** *d,* pp. 28–29
6. *a,* p. 25	**13.** *d,* p. 25	**20.** *a,* p. 30
7. *b,* p. 25	**14.** *c,* p. 30	

DISCUSSION QUESTIONS

1. pp. 19–20	**5.** pp. 23–25	**8.** p. 25
2. pp. 20–21	**6.** p. 24	**9.** pp. 27–28
3. pp. 20–21	**7.** p. 24	**10.** pp. 30–31
4. p. 22		

CHAPTER 3

Pure Capitalism and the Circular Flow

Chapter 3 has three principal aims: to outline six ideological and institutional characteristics of pure capitalism, to explain three practices found in all modern economies, and to sketch in extremely simple terms the fundamental operation of a capitalistic economy. A more detailed explanation of the institutions, practices, and behavior of the United States economy—which is not *purely* capitalistic—is found in the chapters that follow. If the aims of this chapter are accomplished, you can begin to understand the system and methods employed by our economy to solve the economizing problem presented in Chapter 2 and to find answers to the Five Fundamental Questions that will be discussed later in Chapter 5.

The resources of the American economy are owned by its citizens, who are free to use them as they wish in their own self-interest; prices and markets serve to express the self-interests of resource owners, consumers, and business firms; and competition serves to regulate self-interest—to prevent the self-interest of any person or any group from working to the disadvantage of the economy as a whole and to make self-interest work for the benefit of the entire economy.

The three practices of all modern economies are the employment of large amounts of capital, extensive specialization, and the use of money. Economies use capital and engage in specialization because it is a more efficient use of their resources; it results in larger total output and the greater satisfaction of wants. But when workers, business firms, and regions within an economy specialize they become dependent on each other for the goods and services they do not produce for themselves. To obtain these goods and services they must engage in trade. Trade is made more convenient by using money as a medium of exchange.

The principle of comparative advantage is the basis for all trade between individuals, firms, regions, and nations. You ought to be sure that you understand what is meant by comparative advantage, and how specialization is determined by comparative advantage. You should also know why specialization and trade tend to increase the production possibilities in an economy and the interdependence among the members of an economy.

The circular-flow-of-income model (or diagram) is a device which illustrates for a capitalistic economy the relation between households and businesses, the flow of money and economic goods and services between households and businesses, their dual role as buyers and sellers, and the two basic types of markets essential to the capitalistic process.

Understand these essentials of the economic skeleton first; then a little flesh—a little more reality, a little more detail—can be added to the bones. Understanding the skeleton makes it much easier to understand the whole body and its functioning.

■ CHECKLIST

When you have studied this chapter you should be able to:

☐ Identify and explain the six important institutional characteristics of capitalism.

☐ Name and explain the three characteristics of all modern economies.

☐ Compute the comparative costs of production from production possibilities data.

☐ Determine which of two economic units has a comparative advantage and show the gains from trade when you are given cost data for the two units.

☐ Indicate the range in which the terms of trade will be found.

☐ Draw the circular flow diagram; and correctly label the real and money flows and the two major types of markets.

■ CHAPTER OUTLINE

1. The United States economy is not pure capitalism, but it is a close approximation of pure capitalism. Pure capitalism has the following six peculiarities that distinguish it from other economic systems.

   a. Private individuals and organizations own and control its property resources by means of the institution of private property.

b. These individuals and organizations possess both the freedom of enterprise and the freedom of choice.

c. Each of them is motivated largely by self-interest.

d. Competition prevents them as buyers and sellers from exploiting others.

e. Markets and prices (the market system) are used to communicate and coordinate the decisions of buyers and sellers.

f. And the role of government is limited in a competitive and capitalistic economy.

2. In common with other advanced economies of the world, the American economy has three major characteristics.

a. It employs complicated and advanced methods of production and large amounts of capital equipment to produce goods and services efficiently.

b. It is a highly specialized economy; and this specialization increases the productive efficiency of the economy.

c. It also uses money extensively to facilitate trade and specialization.

3. Specialization and trade among economic units (individuals, firms, states, regions, or nations) are based on the principle of comparative advantage. This concept can be illustrated with a hypothetical example of trade between two states that produce two products.

a. Suppose the production possibilities curve for each state is a straight line (there is a constant cost ratio), and the slope of each line is different for each state.

b. Each state will find it profitable to trade because there will be a comparative (cost) advantage in the production of one of the two products; each state can produce one of the products at a lower opportunity cost than the other state.

c. The terms of trade—the ratio at which one product is traded for another—lies between the cost ratios for the two states.

d. Each state gains from this trade because specialization allows more total production from the same resources and permits a better allocation of resources; specialization and trade have the effect of easing the fixed constraints of the production possibilities curve for each state.

e. Specialization can have three potential drawbacks: more monotonous work; more dependence on the production of others; and more conflict over the exchange of the increased output.

4. The circular flow model is a device used to clarify the relationships between households and business firms in a purely capitalistic economy.

a. In resource markets households supply and firms demand resources and in product markets the firms supply and households demand products. Households use the incomes they obtain from supplying resources to purchase the goods and services produced by the firms; and in the economy there is a real flow of resources and products and a money flow of incomes and expenditures.

b. The circular flow model has several limitations.

■ **IMPORTANT TERMS**

Private property	Terms of trade
Self-interest	Money
Competition	Medium of exchange
Market	Barter
Freedom of choice	Coincidence of wants
Freedom of enterprise	Circular flow model
Roundabout production	Households
Specialization	Resource market
Division of labor	Product market
Comparative advantage	

■ **FILL-IN QUESTIONS**

1. The ownership of property resources by private individuals and organizations is the institution of _____

_____

2. Two basic freedoms encountered in a capitalistic economy are the freedoms of _____

and _____

3. Self-interest means that each economic unit attempts

to _____;

this self-interest might work to the disadvantage of the economy as a whole if it were not regulated and constrained by _____

4. According to the economist, competition is present if two conditions prevail; these two conditions are:

a. _____

b. _____

5. If the number of buyers and sellers in a market is

large, no single buyer or seller is able to _____

the price of the commodity bought and sold in that market.

6. In a capitalistic economy individual buyers communicate their demands and individual sellers communicate

their supplies in the _____ of the economy;

and their decisions are coordinated by the _____

determined there by demand and supply.

7. In the ideology of pure capitalism government is assigned (no, a limited, an extensive) _____ role.

8. The three practices or institutions common to all modern economies are _____

_____,

_____,

and _____

9. Modern economies make extensive use of capital goods and engage in roundabout production because it is more _____ than direct production.

10. If an economy engages in extensive specialization the individuals living in the economy are extremely _____; and if these individuals are to enjoy the benefits of specialization there must be _____ among them.

11. Modern economies practice specialization and the division of labor because the self-sufficient producer or worker tends to be a(n) _____ one.

12. When one state or nation has a lower opportunity cost of producing a product relative to another state or nation it has a _____; the amount of one product that must be given up to obtain one unit of another product is the _____

13. In modern economies money functions chiefly as a(n) _____

14. Barter between two individuals will take place only if there is a(n) _____

15. For an item to be "money," it must be _____ _____

16. In the circular flow model:
  a. Households are demanders and businesses are suppliers in the _____ markets; and businesses are demanders and households are suppliers of the _____ markets of the economy.

  b. The two flows are called the _____ flow and the _____ flow.

  c. The expenditures made by businesses are a _____ to them and become the _____ of households.

■ **PROBLEMS AND PROJECTS**

1. The countries of Lilliput and Brobdingnag have the production possibilities tables for apples and bananas shown below.
  Note that the costs of producing apples and bananas are constant in both countries.

LILLIPUT PRODUCTION POSSIBILITIES TABLE

Product	Production alternatives					
(lbs.)	A	B	C	D	E	F
Apples	40	32	24	16	8	0
Bananas	0	4	8	12	16	20

BROBDINGNAG PRODUCTION POSSIBILITIES TABLE

Product	Production alternatives					
(lbs.)	A	B	C	D	E	F
Apples	75	60	45	30	15	0
Bananas	0	5	10	15	20	25

  a. In Lilliput the cost of producing:
  (1) 8 apples is _____ bananas
  (2) 1 apple is _____ bananas
  b. In Brobdingnag the cost of producing:
  (1) 15 apples is _____ bananas
  (2) 1 apple is _____ bananas
  c. In Lilliput the cost of producing:
  (1) 4 bananas is _____ apples
  (2) 1 banana is _____ apples
  d. In Brobdingnag the cost of producing:
  (1) 5 bananas is _____ apples
  (2) 1 banana is _____ apples
  e. The cost of producing 1 apple is lower in the country of _____ and the cost of producing 1 banana is lower in the country of _____
  f. Lilliput has a comparative advantage in the production of _____ and Brobdingnag has a comparative advantage in the production of _____
  g. The information in this problem is not sufficient to determine the exact terms of trade; but the terms of trade will be *greater* than _____ apples for 1 banana and *less* than _____ apples for 1 banana. Put another way, the terms of trade will be between _____ bananas for 1 apple and _____ bananas for 1 apple.

h. If neither nation could specialize, each would produce production alternative C. The combined production of apples in the two countries would be _____ apples and the combined production of bananas would be _____ bananas.

(1) If each nation specializes in producing the fruit for which it has a comparative advantage, their combined production will be _____ apples and _____ bananas.

(2) Their gain from specialization will be _____ apples and _____ bananas.

2. Here is another problem to help you understand the principle of comparative advantage and the benefits of specialization. A tailor named Hart has the production possibilities table for trousers and jackets given below. He chooses production alternative D.

HART'S PRODUCTION POSSIBILITIES TABLE

Product	Production alternatives					
	A	**B**	**C**	**D**	**E**	**F**
Trousers	75	60	45	30	15	0
Jackets	0	10	20	30	40	50

Another tailor, Schaffner, has the production possibilities table below and produces production alternative E.

SCHAFFNER'S PRODUCTION POSSIBILITIES TABLE

Product	Production alternatives						
	A	**B**	**C**	**D**	**E**	**F**	**G**
Trousers	60	50	40	30	20	10	0
Jackets	0	5	10	15	20	25	30

a. To Hart

(1) the cost of one pair of trousers is _____ jackets

(2) the cost of one jacket is _____ pairs of trousers

b. To Schaffner

(1) the cost of one pair of trousers is _____ jackets

(2) the cost of one jacket is _____ pairs of trousers

c. If Hart and Schaffner were to form a partnership to make suits

(1) _____ should specialize in the making of trousers because he can make a pair of trousers at the cost of _____ of a jacket while it costs his partner _____ of a jacket to make a pair of trousers.

(2) _____ should specialize in the making of jackets because he can make a jacket at the cost of _____ pairs of trousers while it costs his partner _____ pairs of trousers to make a jacket.

d. Without specialization and between them Hart and Schaffner were able to make 50 pairs of trousers and 50 jackets. If each specializes completely in the item in the production of which he has a comparative advantage, their combined production will be _____ pairs of trousers and _____ jackets. Thus the gain from specialization is _____

e. When Hart and Schaffner come to divide the income of the partnership between them, the manufacture of a pair of trousers should be treated as the equivalent of from _____ to _____ jackets (or a jacket should be treated as the equivalent of from _____ to _____ pairs of trousers).

3. In the circular flow diagram below, the upper pair of flows (**a** and **b**) represent the resource market and the lower pair (**c** and **d**) the product market.

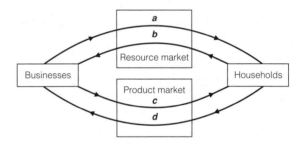

Supply labels or explanations for each of the four flows:

a. _____

b. _____

c. _____

d. _____

■ **SELF-TEST**

Circle the T if the statement is true; the F if it is false.

1. The United States economy can correctly be called "pure capitalism."   T **F**

2. There are in the United States legal limits to the right of private property.   **T** F

3. The freedom of business firms to produce a particular consumer good is always limited by the desires of consumers for that good.   **T** F

4. When a market is competitive the individual sellers of the commodity are unable to reduce the supply of the commodity enough to drive its price upward.   **T** F

5. In a purely capitalistic economy it is consumers who ultimately decide what goods and services the economy will produce. Ⓣ F

6. The market system is not employed in communistic and socialistic economies. T Ⓕ

7. The employment of capital to produce goods and services requires that there be "roundabout production" but it is more efficient than "direct" production. Ⓣ F

8. Increasing the amount of specialization in an economy generally leads to the more efficient use of its resources. Ⓣ F

9. Money is a device for facilitating the exchange of goods and services. Ⓣ F

10. "Coincidence of wants" means that two persons desire to acquire the same good or service. T Ⓕ

11. Cigarettes may serve as money if sellers are generally willing to accept them as money. Ⓣ F

12. In the circular flow model, the household functions on the demand side of the resource and product markets. T Ⓕ

13. The pursuit of economic self-interest is the same thing as selfishness. T Ⓕ

14. A gas station is an example of a market. Ⓣ F

15. Human and geographic specialization are both essential in achieving efficiency in the use of resources. Ⓣ F

16. If a person, firm, or region has a comparative advantage in the production of a particular commodity, it should specialize in the production of that commodity. Ⓣ F

17. One way that human specialization can be achieved is through a division of labor in productive activity. Ⓣ F

18. If one nation has a better comparative advantage in the production of a commodity than another nation, then it has a higher opportunity cost of production than the other nation. T Ⓕ

19. The economic effects of specialization and trade between nations are similar to increasing the quantity of resources or to achieving technological progress. Ⓣ F

20. One of the limitations of the simple model of the circular flow is that flows of output and income are constant. T Ⓕ

Circle the letter that corresponds to the best answer.

1. Which of the following is **not** one of the six characteristics of capitalism?
(a) competition
Ⓑ central economic planning

(c) private property
(d) freedom of enterprise and choice

2. Maximization of profits appears to be in the self-interest of:
Ⓐ business firms
(b) landowners
(c) workers
(d) consumers

3. To decide how to use its scarce resources to satisfy human wants pure capitalism relies on:
(a) central planning
(b) roundabout production
Ⓒ a price system
(d) the coincidence of wants

4. In pure capitalism the role of government is best described as:
Ⓐ nonexistent
(b) limited
(c) significant
(d) extensive

5. Which of the following is **not** a necessary consequence of specialization?
Ⓐ people will use money
(b) people will engage in trade
(c) people will be dependent upon each other
(d) people will produce more of some things than they would produce in the absence of specialization

6. In an economy in which there are full employment and full production, constant amounts of resources, and unchanging technology:
(a) to increase the production of capital goods requires an increase in the production of consumer goods
(b) to decrease the production of capital goods necessitates a decrease in the production of consumer goods
(c) to increase the production of capital goods is impossible
Ⓓ to increase the production of capital goods requires a decrease in the production of consumer goods

7. Which of the following is **not** a characteristic of competition as the economist sees it?
(a) the widespread diffusion of economic power
(b) a large number of buyers in product markets
Ⓒ several sellers of all products
(d) the relatively easy entry into and exit of producers from industries

Answer the next four questions (8, 9, 10, and 11) on the basis of the data given for two regions, Slobovia and Utopia, which have the production possibilities tables below.

3 cams : 1 Widget

SLOBOVIA PRODUCTION POSSIBILITIES TABLE

Product	Production alternatives					
	A	B	C	D	E	F
Cams	1,500	1,200	900	600	300	0
Widgets	0	100	200	300	400	500

UTOPIA PRODUCTION POSSIBILITIES TABLE

Product	Production alternatives				
	A	B	C	D	E
Cams	4,000	3,000	2,000	1,000	0
Widgets	0	200	400	600	800

5 Cams : 1 widgets

8. In Slobovia, the comparative cost of:
(a) 1 cam is 3 widgets
(b) 1 widget is ⅓ cam   3 cam   1 widgets
(c) 1 cam is ⅓ widget
(d) 3 widgets is 1 cam

9. Which of the following statements is **not** true?
(a) Slobovia should specialize in the production of widgets
(b) Slobovia has a comparative advantage in the production of widgets
(c) Utopia should specialize in the production of widgets
(d) Utopia has a comparative advantage in the production of cams

10. The terms of trade will be:
(a) greater than 7 cams for 1 widget
(b) between 7 cams for 1 widget and 5 cams for 1 widget
(c) between 5 cams for 1 widget and 3 cams for 1 widget
(d) less than 3 cams for 1 widget

11. Assume that if Slobovia did not specialize it would produce alternative C and that if Utopia did not specialize it would select alternative B. The gains from specialization are:
(a) 100 cams and 100 widgets
(b) 200 cams and 200 widgets
(c) 400 cams and 500 widgets
(d) 500 cams and 400 widgets

12. When workers specialize in various tasks to produce a commodity, the situation is referred to as:
(a) double coincidence of wants
(b) roundabout production
(c) division of labor
(d) terms of trade

13. The two kinds of market found in the circular flow model are:
(a) the real and the money markets
(b) the real and the product markets
(c) the money and the resource markets
(d) the product and the resource markets

14. In the circular flow model businesses:
(a) demand both products and resources
(b) supply both products and resources
(c) demand products and supply resources
(d) supply products and demand resources

15. One of the limitations of the circular flow model found in this chapter is that:
(a) no mention is made of the role of government
(b) it is assumed households save some of their income
(c) too much attention is paid to how resource and produce prices are determined
(d) it "ensnares the viewer in a maze of detail"

■ DISCUSSION QUESTIONS

1. Explain the several elements—institutions and assumptions—embodied in pure capitalism.

2. What do each of the following seek if they pursue their own self-interest? Consumers, resource owners, and business firms.

3. Explain what economists mean by competition. Why is it important to have competition in an economy whose members are motivated by self-interest?

4. What are the advantages of "indirect" or "roundabout" production?

5. How does an economy benefit from specialization and the division of labor?

6. What disadvantages are there to specialization and the division of labor?

7. Explain what is meant by comparative cost and comparative advantage. What determines the terms of trade? What is the gain that results from specialization in the products in the production of which there is a comparative advantage?

8. What are the principal disadvantages of barter?

9. What is money? What important function does it perform? Explain how money performs this function and how it overcomes the disadvantages associated with barter. Why are people willing to accept paper money in exchange for the goods and services which they sell?

10. In the circular-flow-of-income model:
(a) What two markets are involved?
(b) What roles do households play in each of these markets?
(c) What roles do businesses play in each of these markets?
(d) What two income flows are pictured in money terms? In real terms?
(e) What two expenditure flows are pictured in money terms? In real terms?

11. What are the shortcomings of the circular-flow-of-income model?

12. Give several international examples of specialization and efficiency.

■ **ANSWERS**

Chapter 3 Pure Capitalism and the Circular Flow

FILL-IN QUESTIONS

1. private property

2. enterprise, choice

3. do what is best for itself, competition

4. *a.* large numbers of independently acting buyers and sellers operating in the markets; *b.* freedom of buyers and sellers to enter or leave these markets

5. control (rig, affect)

6. markets, prices

7. a limited

8. the extensive use of capital, specialization, the use of money

9. efficient

10. interdependent, exchange (trade)

11. inefficient

12. comparative advantage; terms of trade

13. medium of exchange

14. coincidence of wants

15. generally acceptable by sellers in exchange

16. *a.* product, resource; *b.* real, money (either order); *c.* cost, income

PROBLEMS AND PROJECTS

1. *a.* (1) 4, (2) ½; *b.* (1) 5, (2) ⅓; *c.* (1) 8, (2) 2; *d.* (1) 15, (2) 3; *e.* Brobdingnag, Lilliput; *f.* bananas, apples; *g.* 2, 3, ⅓, ½; *h.* 69, 18, (1) 75, 20, (2) 6, 2

2. *a.* (1) ⅔, (2) 1½; *b.* (1) ½, (2) 2; *c.* (1) Schaffner, ½, ⅔; (2) Hart, 1½, 2; *d.* 60, 50, 10 pairs of trousers; *e.* ½, ⅔, 1½, 2

3. *a.* money income payments (wages, rent, interest, and profit); *b.* services or resources (land, labor, capital, and entrepreneurial ability); *c.* goods and services; *d.* expenditures for goods and services

SELF-TEST

1. F, p. 35	11. T, p. 42
2. T, p. 36	12. F, p. 44
3. T, p. 36	13. F, p. 36
4. T, pp. 36–37	14. T, p. 37
5. T, p. 36	15. T, p. 39
6. F, p. 38	16. T, pp. 39–40
7. T, p. 38	17. T, p. 39
8. T, p. 39	18. F, pp. 39–40
9. T, p. 42	19. T, pp. 40–41
10. F, pp. 41–42	20. F, p. 45

1. *b,* pp. 36–37	9. *c,* pp. 39–40
2. *a,* p. 36	10. *c,* p. 40
3. *c,* p. 36	11. *a,* pp. 39–40
4. *b,* p. 38	12. *c,* p. 39
5. *a,* pp. 40–41	13. *d,* pp. 43–44
6. *d,* p. 39	14. *d,* pp. 44–45
7. *c,* pp. 36–37	15. *a,* p. 45
8. *c,* pp. 39–40	

DISCUSSION QUESTIONS

1. pp. 35–36	7. pp. 39–41
2. p. 36	8. pp. 41–42
3. pp. 36–37	9. pp. 41–42
4. pp. 38–39	10. pp. 43–45
5. p. 39	11. p. 45
6. p. 41	12. p. 39

Understanding Individual Markets: Demand and Supply

Chapter 4 is an introduction to the most fundamental tools of economic analysis: demand and supply. If you are to progress successfully into the later chapters it is essential that you understand what is meant by demand and supply and how to use these powerful tools.

Demand and supply are simply "boxes" or categories into which all the forces and factors that affect the price and the quantity of a good bought and sold in a competitive market can conveniently be placed. Demand and supply determine price and quantity exchange and it is necessary to see **why** and **how** they do this.

Many students never do understand demand and supply because they never learn to **define** demand and supply **exactly** and because they never learn (1) what is meant by an increase or decrease in demand or supply, (2) the important distinctions between "demand" and "quantity demanded" and between "supply" and "quantity supplied," (3) the equally important distinctions between an increase (or decrease) in demand and an increase (or decrease) in quantity demanded and between an increase (or decrease) in supply and an increase (or decrease) in quantity supplied.

Having learned these, however, it is no great trick to comprehend the so-called "law of supply and demand." The equilibrium price—that is, the price which will tend to prevail in the market as long as demand and supply do not change—is simply the price at which **quantity demanded** and **quantity supplied** are equal. The quantity bought and sold in the market (the equilibrium quantity) is the quantity demanded and supplied at the equilibrium price. If you can determine the equilibrium price and quantity under one set of demand and supply conditions, you can determine them under any other set and so will be able to analyze for yourself the effects of changes in demand and supply upon equilibrium price and quantity.

The chapter includes a brief examination of the factors that determine demand and supply and of the ways in which changes in these determinants will affect and cause changes in demand and supply. A graphic method is employed in this analysis in order to facilitate an understanding of demand and supply, equilibrium price and quantity, changes in demand and supply, and the resulting changes in equilibrium price and quantity. In addition to understanding the **specific** definitions of demand and supply, it is necessary to understand the two counterparts of demand and supply: the demand **curve** and the supply **curve**. These are simply graphic (or geometric) representations of the same data contained in the schedules of demand and supply.

If you wonder why an entire chapter has been devoted to demand and supply you will find the answer in the last major section of the chapter. Demand and supply have so many applications that they are the most important single tool in economics. The example given in the last section is the application of supply and demand to the foreign exchange market.

You will use supply and demand over and over again. It will turn out to be as important to you in economics as jet propulsion is to the pilot of a Boeing 767. You can't get off the ground without it.

■ **CHECKLIST**

When you have studied this chapter you should be able to:

☐ Define a market.
☐ Define demand and state the law of demand.
☐ Graph the demand curve when you are given a demand schedule.
☐ Explain the difference between individual and market demand.
☐ List the major nonprice determinants of demand and explain how each one shifts the demand curve.
☐ Distinguish between a change in demand and a change in the quantity demanded.
☐ Define supply and state the law of supply.
☐ Graph the supply curve when you are given a supply schedule.
☐ List the major nonprice determinants of supply and explain how each shifts the supply curve.
☐ Distinguish between a change in supply and a change in the quantity supplied.

☐ Determine when you are given the demand for and the supply of a good what the equilibrium price and the equilibrium quantity will be.
☐ Explain why the price of a good and the amount of the good bought and sold in a competitive market will be the equilibrium price and the equilibrium quantity, respectively.
☐ Predict the effects of changes in demand and supply on equilibrium price and equilibrium quantity; and on the prices of substitute and complementary goods.
☐ Explain the meaning of the rationing function of prices.
☐ Explain why violations of the "other things equal" assumption may cause confusion about the validity of the laws of demand and supply.
☐ Define the characteristics of the foreign exchange market.
☐ Demonstrate how supply and demand analysis applies to the foreign exchange market.

■ CHAPTER OUTLINE

1. A market is any institution or mechanism that brings together the buyers and the sellers of a particular good or service; and in this chapter it is assumed that markets are purely competitive.

2. Demand is a schedule of prices and the quantities which buyers would purchase at each of these prices during some period of time.
   a. As price rises, other things being equal, buyers will purchase smaller quantities, and as price falls they will purchase larger quantities; this is the law of demand.
   b. The demand curve is a graphic representation of demand and the law of demand.
   c. Market (or total) demand for a good is a summation of the demands of all individuals in the market for that good.
   d. The demand for a good depends upon the tastes, income, and expectations of buyers; the number of buyers in the market; and the prices of related goods.
   e. A change (either an increase or a decrease) in demand is caused by a change in any of the factors (in d) which determine demand, and means that the demand schedule and demand curve have changed.
   f. A change in demand and a change in the quantity demanded are *not* the same thing.

3. Supply is a schedule of prices and the quantities which sellers will offer to sell at each of these prices during some period of time.
   a. The law of supply means, other things being equal, that as the price of the good rises larger quantities will be offered for sale, and that as the price of the good falls smaller quantities will be offered for sale.
   b. The supply curve is a graphic representation of supply and the law of supply; the market supply of a good is the sum of the supplies of all sellers of the good.

   c. The supply of a good depends upon the techniques used to produce it, the prices of the resources employed in its production, the extent to which it is taxed or subsidized, the prices of other goods which might be produced, the price expectations of sellers, and the number of sellers of the product.
   d. Supply will change when any of these determinants of supply changes; a change in supply is a change in the entire supply schedule or curve.
   e. A change in supply must be distinguished from a change in quantity supplied.

4. The market or equilibrium price of a commodity is that price at which quantity demanded and quantity supplied are equal; and the quantity exchanged in the market (the equilibrium quantity) is equal to the quantity demanded and supplied at the equilibrium price.
   a. The rationing function of price is the elimination of shortages and surpluses of the commodity.
   b. A change in demand, supply, or both changes both the equilibrium price and the equilibrium quantity in specific ways.
   c. In resource markets suppliers are households and demanders are business firms, and in product markets suppliers are business firms and demanders are householders; and supply and demand are useful in the analysis of prices and quantities exchanged in both types of markets.
   d. When demand and supply schedules (or curves) are drawn up it is assumed that all the nonprice determinants of demand and supply remain unchanged.

5. Understanding how demand and supply determine price and quantity in a competitive market is a powerful tool which has a large number of applications; for example, supply and demand can be used to explain the market for foreign exchange.
   a. National currencies are traded in the *foreign exchange market* where exchange rates are established; the *exchange rate* is the price paid in one nation's currency to buy 1 unit of another nation's currency ($0.01 U.S. = 1 Japanese yen).
   b. The exchange rate for a nation's currency is determined by the supply of that currency and the demand for that currency; when the supply or demand for this currency changes, then the exchange rate of this currency will change (move from $0.01 = 1 yen to $0.02 = 1 yen).
   c. Increases in exchange rate or price of a unit of foreign currency (the dollar price of a yen increases) means that there has been a *depreciation* in the value of one currency (the dollar) relative to the foreign currency (the yen); conversely, decreases in the exchange rate for a foreign currency (a decrease in the dollar price of the yen) means that there has been an *appreciation* in the value of one currency (the dollar) relative to the foreign currency (the yen).

■ IMPORTANT TERMS

Market

Demand schedule

Law of demand

Diminishing marginal utility

Quantity demanded

Income effect

Substitution effect

Demand curve

Individual demand

Total or market demand

Nonprice determinant of demand

Increase (or decrease) in demand

Normal (superior) good

Inferior good

Substitute (competing) goods

Complementary goods

Independent goods

Supply schedule

Quantity supplied

Law of supply

Supply curve

Nonprice determinant of supply

Increase (or decrease) in supply

Equilibrium price

Equilibrium quantity

Rationing function of prices

Price-increasing (-decreasing) effect

Quantity-increasing (-decreasing) effect

Foreign exchange market

Depreciation and appreciation of the dollar

■ FILL-IN QUESTIONS

1. A market is the institution or mechanism that brings together the _____ and the _____ of a particular good or service.

   a. In resource markets prices are determined by the demand decisions of (business firms, households) _____ and the supply decisions of _____.

   b. In product markets prices are determined by demand decisions of _____ and the supply decisions of _____

2. The relationship between price and quantity in the demand schedule is a(n) (direct, inverse) _____ _____ relationship; in the supply schedule the relationship is a(n) _____ one.

3. The added satisfaction or pleasure obtained by a consumer from additional units of a product decreases as her or his consumption of the product increases. This phenomenon is called _____

4. A consumer tends to buy more of a product as its price falls because:

   a. The purchasing power of the consumer is increased and the consumer tends to buy more of this product (and of other products); this is called the (income, substitution) _____ effect;

   b. The product becomes less expensive relative to similar products and the consumer tends to buy more of this and less of the similar products; and this is called the _____ effect.

5. When demand or supply is graphed, price is placed on the (horizontal, vertical) _____ axis and quantity on the _____ axis.

6. When a consumer demand schedule or curve is drawn up, it is assumed that five factors that determine demand are fixed and constant. These five determinants of consumer demand are:

   a. _____

   b. _____

   c. _____

   d. _____

   e. _____

7. A decrease in demand means that consumers will buy (larger, smaller) _____ quantities at every price or will pay (more, less) _____ for the same quantities.

8. A change in income or in the price of another product will result in a change in the (demand for, quantity demanded of) _____ the given product, while a change in the price of the given product will result in _____

9. The fundamental factors which determine the supply of any commodity in the product market are:

   a. _____

   b. _____

   c. _____

   d. _____

   e. _____

   f. _____

10. The equilibrium price of a commodity is the price at which _____

11. If quantity demanded exceeds quantity supplied, price is (above, below) _____ the equilibrium price; and the (shortage, surplus) _____ will cause the price to (rise, fall) _____.

12. In the spaces below each of the following, indicate the effect [*increase* (+), *decrease* (−), or *indeterminate* (?)] upon equilibrium price (*P*) and equilibrium quantity (*Q*) of each of these changes in demand and/or supply.

	P	Q
a. Increase in demand, supply constant	___	___
b. Increase in supply, demand constant	___	___
c. Decrease in demand, supply constant	___	___
d. Decrease in supply, demand constant	___	___
e. Increase in demand, increase in supply	___	___
f. Increase in demand, decrease in supply	___	___
g. Decrease in demand, decrease in supply	___	___
h. Decrease in demand, increase in supply	___	___

13. If supply and demand establish a price for a good such that there is no shortage or surplus of the good, then price is successfully performing its _____.

14. To assume that all the nonprice determinants of demand and supply do not change is to employ the _____ assumption.

15. When the dollar price of foreign currency increases, there has been a(n) (appreciation, depreciation) _____ in value of the dollar. When the dollar price of foreign currency decreases, there has been a(n) _____ in the value of the dollar; for example, if the dollar price of a German mark (DM) decreases from $0.60 = 1 DM to $0.50 = 1 DM, then it means that there has been a(n) _____ in the value of the dollar; but if the dollar price of a German mark increases from $0.40 = 1 DM to $0.55 = 1 DM, then it means that there has been a(n) _____ in the value of the dollar.

16. In the market for Japanese yen, an increase in the (demand for, supply of) _____ yen will decrease the dollar price of yen, while an increase in the _____ yen will increase the dollar price of yen.

If the dollar price of the yen increases, then Japanese goods imported into the United States will be (more, less) _____ expensive to American consumers, while American goods exported to Japan will be _____ expensive for Japanese consumers.

■ **PROBLEMS AND PROJECTS**

1. Using the demand schedule below, plot the demand curve on the graph on the next page. Label the axes and indicate for each axis the units being used to measure price and quantity.

Price	Quantity demanded, 1,000 bushels of soybeans
$7.20	10
7.00	15
6.80	20
6.60	25
6.40	30
6.20	35

a. Plot the supply schedule which follows on the same graph.

Price	Quantity supplied, 1,000 bushels of soybeans
$7.20	40
7.00	35
6.80	30
6.60	25
6.40	20
6.20	15

b. The equilibrium price of soybeans will be $_____

c. How many thousand bushels of soybeans will be exchanged at this price? _____

d. Indicate clearly on the graph the equilibrium price and quantity by drawing lines from the intersection of the supply and demand curves to the price and quantity axes.

e. If the Federal government supported a price of $7.00 per bushel there would be a (shortage, surplus) _____ of _____ bushels of soybeans.

2. The demand schedules of three individuals (Robert, Charles, and Lynn) for loaves of bread are shown on the next page. Assuming there are only three buyers of bread, draw up the total or market demand schedule for bread.

0

	Quantity demanded, loaves of bread			
Price	Robert	Charles	Lynn	Total
$.40	1	4	0	_____
.36	3	5	1	_____
.32	6	6	5	_____
.28	10	7	10	_____
.24	15	8	16	_____

3. Below is a demand schedule for bushels of apples. In columns 3 and 4 insert *any* new figures for quantity which represent in column 3 an increase in demand and in column 4 a decrease in demand.

(1) Price	(2) Quantity demanded	(3) Demand increases	(4) Demand decreases
$6.00	400	_____	_____
5.90	500	_____	_____
5.80	600	_____	_____
5.70	700	_____	_____
5.60	800	_____	_____
5.50	900	_____	_____

4. Assume that O'Rourke has, when his income is $100 per week, the demand schedule for good A shown in columns 1 and 2 of the table below and the demand schedule for good B shown in columns 4 and 5. Assume that the prices of A and B are $.80 and $5, respectively.

Demand for A (per week)			Demand for B (per week)		
(1) Price	(2) Quantity demanded	(3) Quantity demanded	(4) Price	(5) Quantity demanded	(6) Quantity demanded
$.90	10	0	$5.00	4	7
.85	20	10	4.50	5	8
.80	30	20	4.00	6	9
.75	40	30	3.50	7	10
.70	50	40	3.00	8	11
.65	60	50	2.50	9	12
.60	70	60	2.00	10	13

a. How much A will O'Rourke buy? _____

How much B? _____

b. Suppose that, as a consequence of a $10 increase in O'Rourke's weekly income, the quantities demanded of A become those shown in column 3 and the quantities demanded of B become those shown in column 6.

(1) How much A will he now buy? _____

How much B? _____

(2) Good A is (normal, inferior) _____

(3) Good B is _____

5. The market demand for good X is shown in columns 1 and 2 of the table below. Assume the price of X to be $2 and constant.

(1) Price	(2) Quantity demanded	(3) Quantity demanded	(4) Quantity demanded
$2.40	1,600	1,500	1,700
2.30	1,650	1,550	1,750
2.20	1,750	1,650	1,850
2.10	1,900	1,800	2,000
2.00	2,100	2,000	2,200
1.90	2,350	2,250	2,450
1.80	2,650	2,550	2,750

a. If as the price of good Y rises from $1.25 to $1.35 the quantities demanded of good X become those shown in column 3, it can be concluded that X and Y are (substitute, complementary) _____ goods.

b. If as the price of good Y rises from $1.25 to $1.35 the quantities of good X become those shown in column 4, it can be concluded that X and Y are _____ goods.

6. In a local market for hamburger on a given date, each of 300 identical sellers of hamburger has the following supply schedule.

(1) Price	(2) Quantity supplied— one seller, lb.	(3) Quantity supplied— all sellers, lb.
$2.05	150	_____
2.00	110	_____
1.95	75	_____
1.90	45	_____
1.85	20	_____
1.80	0	_____

a. In column 3 construct the market supply schedule for hamburger.

b. At the top of the next column is the market demand schedule for hamburger on the same date and in the same local market as that given above.

Price	Quantity demanded, lb.
$2.05	28,000
2.00	31,000
1.95	36,000
1.90	42,000
1.85	49,000
1.80	57,000

If the Federal government sets a price on hamburger at $1.90 a pound the result would be a (shortage, surplus)

_____

of _____ pounds of hamburger in this market.

7. Each of the following events would tend to increase or decrease either the demand for or the supply of computer games and, as a result, increase or decrease the price of these games. In the first blank indicate the effect upon demand or supply (increase, decrease); and in the second indicate the effect on price (increase, decrease).

a. It becomes known that a local department store is going to have a sale on these games three months from now. _____;

_____

b. The workers who produce the games go on strike for over two months. _____;

_____

c. The workers in the industry receive a 90-cent-an-hour wage increase. _____;

_____

d. The average price of movie tickets increases. _____; _____

e. The firms producing the games undertake to produce a large volume of missile components for the Defense Department. _____;

_____

f. It is announced by a private research institute that children who have taken to playing computer games also improve their grades in school. _____;

_____

g. Because of the use of mass-production techniques, the amount of labor necessary to produce a game decreases. _____;

_____

h. The price of computers increases _____;

_____

i. The average consumer believes that a shortage of games is developing in the economy. _____;

_____

j. The Federal government imposes a $5 per game tax upon the manufacturers of computer games. _____

_____ ; _____

■ SELF-TEST

Circle the T if the statement is true; the F if it is false.

1. A market is any arrangement that brings the buyers and sellers of a particular good or service together. **T** F

2. Demand is the amount of a commodity or service which a buyer will purchase at a particular price. **T** (**F**)

3. The law of demand states that as price increases, other things being equal, the quantity of the product demanded increases. **T** (**F**)

4. In graphing supply and demand schedules, supply is put on the horizontal axis and demand on the vertical axis. **T** (**F**)

5. If price falls, there will be an increase in demand. **T** (**F**)

6. If the demand curve moves from D_1 to D_2 in the graph shown below, demand has increased. (**T**) F

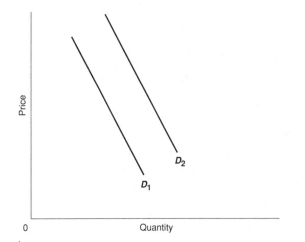

7. A fall in the price of a good will cause the demand for goods which are substitutes for it to increase. **T** (**F**)

8. If two goods are complementary, an increase in the price of one will cause the demand for the other to increase. **T** (**F**)

9. If the market price of a commodity is for a time below its equilibrium price, the market price will tend to rise because demand will decrease and supply will increase. **T** (**F**)

10. The equilibrium price of a good is the price at which the demand and the supply of the good are equal. **T** (**F**)

11. The rationing function of prices is the elimination of shortages and surpluses. (**T**) **F**

12. The interaction of the demand for, and supply of, Japanese yen will establish the dollar price of Japanese yen. (**T**) **F**

13. An increase in incomes in the United States would tend to cause the dollar price of the Japanese yen to fall. **T** (**F**)

14. When the dollar price of another nation's currency increases, there has been an appreciation in the value of the dollar. **T** (**F**)

15. When the dollar depreciates relative to the value of the currencies of the trading partners of the United States, then goods imported into the United States will tend to become more expensive. (**T**) **F**

Circle the letter that corresponds to the best answer.

1. The markets examined in this chapter are:
(a) purely competitive markets
(b) markets for goods and services
(c) markets for products and resources
(d) all of the above

2. Which of the following could cause a decrease in consumer demand for product X?
(a) a decrease in consumer income
(b) an increase in the prices of goods which are good substitutes for product X
(c) an increase in the price which consumers expect will prevail for product X in the future
(d) a decrease in the supply of product X

3. If two goods are substitutes for each other, an increase in the price of one will necessarily:
(a) decrease the demand for the other
(b) increase the demand for the other
(c) decrease the quantity demanded of the other
(d) increase the quantity demanded of the other

4. The income of a consumer decreases and his/her demand for a particular good increases. It can be concluded that the good is:
(a) normal
(b) inferior
(c) a substitute
(d) a complement

5. If the supply curve moves from S_1 to S_2 on the graph below, there has been:
(a) an increase in supply
(b) a decrease in supply
(c) an increase in quantity supplied
(d) a decrease in quantity supplied

6. An increase in demand and a decrease in supply will:
(a) increase price and increase the quantity exchanged
(b) decrease price and decrease the quantity exchanged
(c) increase price and the effect upon quantity exchanged will be indeterminate
(d) decrease price and the effect upon quantity exchanged will be indeterminate

7. An increase in supply and an increase in demand will:
(a) increase price and increase the quantity exchanged
(b) decrease price and increase the quantity exchanged
(c) affect price in an indeterminate way and decrease the quantity exchanged
(d) affect price in an indeterminate way and increase the quantity exchanged

8. Which of the following could *not* cause an increase in the supply of cotton?
(a) an increase in the price of cotton
(b) improvements in the art of producing cotton
(c) a decrease in the price of the machinery and tools employed in cotton production
(d) a decrease in the price of corn

9. The law of supply states that, other things being constant, as price increases:
(a) supply increases
(b) supply decreases
(c) quantity supplied increases
(d) quantity supplied decreases

10. Demand and supply may be employed to explain how price is determined in:
(a) product markets
(b) resource markets
(c) markets for foreign currency
(d) all of the above markets

11. When government sets the price of a good and that price is below the equilibrium price the result will be:
(a) a surplus of the good
(b) a shortage of the good
(c) an increase in the demand for the good
(d) a decrease in the supply of the good

12. A decrease in supply and a decrease in demand will:
(a) increase price and decrease the quantity exchanged
(b) decrease price and increase the quantity exchanged
(c) increase price and affect the quantity exchanged in an indeterminate way
(d) affect price in an indeterminate way and decrease the quantity exchanged

13. A decrease in the price of a product would most likely be caused by:
(a) an increase in business taxes
(b) an increase in consumer incomes
(c) a decrease in resource costs for production
(d) a decrease in the price of a complementary good

The next three questions (14, 15, and 16) refer to the following table. Consider the following supply and demand schedules for corn.

Price	Quantity demanded	Quantity supplied
$20	395	200
22	375	250
24	350	290
26	320	320
28	280	345
30	235	365

14. The equilibrium price in this market is:
(a) $22
(b) $24
(c) $26
(d) $28

15. An increase in the cost of labor lowers the quantity supplied by 65 units at each price. The new equilibrium price would be:
(a) $22
(b) $24
(c) $26
(d) $28

16. If the quantity demanded increases by 130 units, then the new equilibrium quantity will be:
(a) 290
(b) 320
(c) 345
(d) 365

Complementary

17. Assume that in a competitive market video tape players (VCRs) double in price. What will most likely happen in that market to the equilibrium price and quantity of video tapes?

(a) price will increase; quantity will decrease
(b) price will decrease; quantity will increase
(c) price will decrease; quantity will decrease
(d) price will increase; quantity will increase

18. If the equilibrium exchange rate changes so that the dollar price of Japanese yen increases:

(a) the dollar has appreciated in value
(b) the dollar has depreciated in value
(c) Americans will be able to buy more Japanese goods
(d) Japanese will be able to buy fewer U.S. goods

19. A decrease in the United States demand for Japanese goods will:

(a) increase the demand for Japanese yen and increase the dollar price of yen
(b) increase the demand for Japanese yen but decrease the dollar price of yen
(c) decrease the demand for Japanese yen and decrease the dollar price of yen
(d) decrease the demand for Japanese yen but increase the dollar price of yen

20. If the exchange rate for one United States dollar changes from 1.4 German marks to 1.7 German marks, then there has been:

(a) an appreciation in the value of the mark
(b) a depreciation in the value of the dollar
(c) a depreciation in the value of the mark
(d) an increase in the price of the mark

■ **DISCUSSION QUESTIONS**

1. How is a market defined?

2. Carefully define demand and state the law of demand. Now define supply and state the law of supply.

3. Two decades ago the price of coffee in the United States rose as a result of bad weather in coffee-producing regions. Employ the income-effect and the substitution effect concepts to explain why the quantity of coffee demanded in the U.S. declined dramatically. A few years later when the weather became normal the price of coffee fell. Use the diminishing-marginal-utility notion to explain why the quantity of coffee demanded rose.

4. Explain the difference between an increase in demand and an increase in quantity demanded, and between a decrease in supply and a decrease in quantity supplied.

5. Neither demand nor supply remains constant for long because the factors which determine demand and supply

do not long remain constant. What are these factors? How do changes in them affect demand and supply?

6. How are normal, inferior, substitute, complementary, and independent goods defined, and how can these concepts be used to predict the way in which a change in income or in the price of another good will affect the demand for a given good?

7. Given the demand for and the supply of a commodity, what price will be the equilibrium price of this commodity? Explain why this price will tend to prevail in the market and why higher (lower) prices, if they do exist temporarily, will tend to fall (rise).

8. Analyze the following quotation and explain the fallacies contained in it: "An increase in demand will cause price to rise; with a rise in price, supply will increase and the increase in supply will push price down. Therefore, an increase in demand results in little change in price because supply will increase also."

9. What is meant by the "rationing function of prices"?

10. What is the difference between individual and market demand; and what is the relationship between these two types of demand? Does this distinction and relationship also apply to individual and market supply?

11. Why might an appreciation of the value of the United States dollar relative to the Japanese yen depress the American economy and stimulate the Japanese economy? Why might a government intervene in the foreign exchange market and try to increase or decrease the value of its currency?

■ **ANSWERS**

Chapter 4 Understanding Individual Markets: Demand and Supply

FILL-IN QUESTIONS

1. buyers (demanders), sellers (suppliers) (either order); *a.* business firms, households; *b.* households, business firms

2. inverse, direct

3. diminishing marginal utility

4. *a.* income; *b.* substitution

5. vertical, horizontal

6. *a.* the tastes or preferences of consumers; *b.* the number of consumers in the market; *c.* the money income of consumers; *d.* the prices of related goods; *e.* consumer expectations with respect to future prices and incomes

7. smaller, less

8. demand for, a change in the quantity demanded of the product

9. *a.* the technique of production; *b.* resource prices; *c.* taxes and subsidies; *d.* prices of other goods; *e.* price expectations; *f.* the number of sellers in the market

10. quantity demanded and quantity supplied are equal

11. below, shortage, rise

12. *a.* +, +; *b.* −, +; *c.* −, −; *d.* +, −; *e.* ?, +; *f.* +, ?; *g.* ?, −; *h.* −, ?

13. rationing function

14. other things being equal

15. depreciation, appreciation, appreciation, depreciation

16. supply of, demand for, more, less

PROBLEMS AND PROJECTS

1. *b.* 6.60; *c.* 25,000; *e.* surplus, 20,000

2. Total: 5, 9, 17, 27, 39

3. Each quantity in column 3 is greater than in column 2, and each quantity in column 4 is less than in column 2.

4. *a.* 30, 4; *b.* (1) 20, 7; (2) inferior; (3) normal (superior)

5. *a.* complementary; *b.* substitute

6. *a.* 45,000; 33,000; 22,500; 13,500; 6,000; 0 *b.* shortage, 28,500

7. *a.* decrease demand, decrease price; *b.* decrease supply, increase price; *c.* decrease supply, increase price; *d.* increase demand, increase price; *e.* decrease supply, increase price; *f.* increase demand, increase price; *g.* increase supply, decrease price; *h.* decrease demand, decrease price, *i.* increase demand, increase price; *j.* decrease supply, increase price

SELF-TEST

1. T, p. 47
2. F, p. 48
3. F, p. 48
4. F, pp. 49−50
5. F, pp. 49−50
6. T, pp. 51−52
7. F, p. 52
8. F, p. 52
9. F, p. 57
10. F, p. 57
11. T, p. 58
12. T, pp. 62−63
13. F, pp. 63−64
14. F, pp. 63−64
15. T, p. 64

1. *d,* p. 47
2. *a,* pp. 50−51
3. *b,* p. 49
4. *b,* p. 52
5. *a,* pp. 55−56
6. *c,* pp. 60−61
7. *d,* p. 61
8. *a,* pp. 55−56
9. *c,* p. 54
10. *d,* p. 61
11. *b,* pp. 57−58
12. *d,* pp. 60−61
13. *c,* pp. 59−60
14. *c,* pp. 57−58
15. *d,* pp. 55−57
16. *d,* pp. 51, 59
17. *c,* p. 52
18. *b,* pp. 63−64
19. *c,* p. 64
20. *c,* pp. 63−64

DISCUSSION QUESTIONS

1. p. 47
2. pp. 48−49, 54
3. pp. 48−49
4. pp. 51−53; 55−56
5. pp. 50−53; 55−56
6. p. 52
7. pp. 57−58
8. pp. 58−61
9. p. 58
10. pp. 50, 54
11. pp. 63−64

CHAPTER 5

The Private Sectors and the Market System

In the American economy, there are private sectors and a public sector. Chapter 5 discusses the private sectors: the 94 million households, the roughly 18 million business firms in the country, and our trade with other nations in the foreign sector. Chapter 6 deals with the public sector of the economy: the Federal, state, and local governments found in the United States. These two chapters will acquaint you with a few of the facts relevant to an understanding of our economy.

Also, in Chapters 2, 3, and 4 you examined the institutions and characteristics of pure capitalism and saw how supply and demand determine equilibrium prices and equilibrium quantities in resource and product markets. The second part of Chapter 5 draws these elements together into an explanation of the ways in which the market system finds answers to basic economic questions.

Chapter 5 begins with an examination of the households of the economy, the distribution of income in the United States, and the uses to which the households put their incomes. Two different distributions of income are examined. American households earn five kinds of income and receive transfer payments. The way in which the total personal income received by all American households is divided among the five types of earned income and transfer payments is called the **functional distribution.** The way in which the total personal income received by all households is distributed among the various income classes is called the **personal** distribution of income. Attention should be concentrated on the **general** facts of income distribution (not the exact figures), the conclusions which are drawn from these general facts, and the definitions of the new terms employed. In the examination of the different uses households make of their incomes, several new terms and concepts are introduced; and figures are employed in the discussion. Again, attention should be paid to the generalizations and to the new terms.

Business firms of the United States are the next focus of the chapter. It is apparent that what most characterizes American business is the differences among firms insofar as their size and legal form are concerned, as well as in the products they produce. You should note the distinctions between a proprietorship, a partnership, and a corporation and the advantages and disadvantages of each.

You will also find that the American economy can be divided into ten sectors or industry classes. The privately owned business firms are found in eight of these industry classes. These eight sectors are not equal in terms of the number of firms in the class, the contribution to the national income made by the industry class, and the number of full-time workers employed by the sector. These facts serve as an introduction to two major observations. In the economy as a whole and in the manufacturing sector a relatively few firms produce a relatively large part of the output of that sector.

These two observations indicate that big business is an important characteristic of the American economy. The corollary of these observations is that the American economy also has a large number of small business firms. But the problems created by big business and the ways in which government deals with these problems are topics examined later in the text.

The discussion of the private sectors concludes with a look at the foreign sector of the economy of the United States. The volume, patterns, and linkages of our trade with the rest of the world are described. In addition, our growing international trade has economic implications for our: (1) living standards; (2) ability to compete in a world economy; (3) banking and finance; and (4) macroeconomic instability and policy.

The latter part of Chapter 5 describes the operation of the competitive market system. There are Five Fundamental Questions that any economic system must answer in attempting to use its scarce resources to satisfy its material wants. The five questions or problems are: (1) How much output is to be produced? (2) What is to be produced? (3) How is the output to be produced? (4) Who is to receive the output? (5) Can the economic system adapt to change? Only the last four questions will be discussed in this chapter. Answers to the first question will await the presentation of material on macroeconomics.

The explanation of how the market system finds answers to the last four of the Five Fundamental Questions is only an approximation—a simplified version or a model—of the methods actually employed by the American economy. Yet this simple model, like all good models, contains enough realism to be truthful and is general enough to be understandable.

The "Operation of the Market System" is both the most important part of this chapter and the part you will find most difficult. If you will try to understand how the American system of prices and markets finds answers for each of the four basic questions by examining them *individually* and in the order in which they are presented, you will more easily understand how the market system as a whole operates. Actually the market system finds answers for all these questions simultaneously, but it is much simpler to consider them as if they were separate questions.

A few final words of advice to you. Be sure to understand the *importance* and *role* of each of the following in the operation of the market system: (1) the rationing and directing functions of prices, (2) the profit motive of business firms, (3) the entry into and exodus of firms from industries, (4) competition, and (5) consumer sovereignty.

■ **CHECKLIST**

When you have studied this chapter you should be able to:

☐ Define and distinguish between a functional and a personal distribution of income.
☐ State the relative size of the five sources of personal income in the functional distribution.
☐ List the three uses to which households put their personal incomes and state the relative size of each.
☐ Distinguish among durable goods, nondurable goods, and services.
☐ Explain the difference among a plant, a firm, and an industry; and between limited and unlimited liability.
☐ State the advantages and disadvantages of the three legal forms of business enterprise.
☐ Report the relative importance of each of the legal forms of business enterprise in the American economy.
☐ State which two industry classes contain the largest and the smallest number of privately owned business firms, produce the largest and the smallest percentages of the national income, and employ the greatest and the smallest number of full-time workers.
☐ Cite evidence to indicate that large corporations dominate the economy and some major American industries; and indicate in which industry classes big business is and is not a dominant force.
☐ Describe the main characteristics of our volume and pattern of trade with other nations.
☐ Explain four economic implications of our growing international trade.
☐ Identify the Five Fundamental Questions.

☐ Explain how a competitive market system determines what will be produced.
☐ Distinguish between normal profit and economic profit.
☐ Predict what will happen to the price charged by and the output of a prosperous and an unprosperous industry; and explain why these events will occur.
☐ Explain how production is organized in a competitive market system.
☐ Find the least-cost combination of resources when you are given the technological data and the prices of the resources.
☐ Explain how a competitive market system determines the distribution of total output.
☐ Describe the guiding function of prices to accommodate change in the competitive market system.
☐ Explain how the competitive market system initiates change by fostering technological advances and capital accumulation.
☐ State how the "invisible hand" in the competitive market system tends to promote public or social interests.
☐ Present the case for the competitive market system.

■ **CHAPTER OUTLINE**

1. Households play a dual role in the economy. They supply the economy with resources, and they purchase the greatest share of the goods and services produced by the economy. They obtain their personal incomes in exchange for the resources they furnish the economy and from the transfer payments they receive from government.
   a. The functional distribution of income indicates the way in which total personal income is divided among the five sources of earned income (wages and salaries, proprietors' income, corporate profits, interest, and rents) and transfer payments.
   b. The personal distribution of income indicates the way in which total personal income is divided among households in different income classes.

2. Households use their incomes to purchase consumer goods, to pay taxes, and to accumulate savings.
   a. Personal taxes constitute a deduction from a household's personal income; what remains after taxes can be either saved or spent.
   b. Saving is what a household does not spend of its after-tax income.
   c. Households spend for durable goods, nondurable goods, and services.

3. The business population of the American economy consists of many imperfectly defined and overlapping industries; business firms which operate one or more plants and produce one or more products are the components of these industries.

4. The three principal legal forms of organization of firms are the proprietorship, the partnership, and the corporation; each form has special characteristics, advantages, and disadvantages. The form of organization which any business firm should adopt depends primarily upon the amount of money capital it will require to carry on its business. Although the proprietorship is numerically dominant in the United States, the corporation accounts for the major portion of the economy's output.

5. An examination of the ten industry classes found in the American economy reveals at least four important facts and leads to the conclusion that large firms are a characteristic of the American economy and that many of its industries are dominated by big businesses.

6. The merchandise trade of the United States with other nations has increased in absolute terms and as a percentage of our national output. Our major trading partner is Canada, not Japan. In recent years, the United States has had trade deficits because our economy has imported more goods and services than it has exported to other nations. These large trade deficits are financed by borrowing from other nations.

7. International trade produces sizable economic benefits because there is more efficient use of world resources and it strengthens competition. The dramatic improvements in communications also mean that the banking industry and financial markets operate on a global basis. The one potential drawback of the increased trade is that the domestic economy is more vulnerable to influence from changes in the world economy. The involvement in a world economy becomes a potential source of macroeconomic instability in the domestic economy and can present new problems for economic policymakers.

8. There are Five Fundamental Questions which must be answered by every economic system:
(1) How much output is to be produced?
(2) What is to be produced?
(3) How is output to be produced?
(4) Who is to receive the output?
(5) Can the economic system adapt to change?

9. The system of prices and markets and the choices of households and business firms furnish the economy with answers to the last four Fundamental Questions.
a. The demands of consumers for products and the desires of business firms to maximize their profits determine what and how much of each product is produced (and its price).
b. The desires of business firms to maximize profits by keeping their costs of production as low as possible guide them to employ the most efficient techniques of production and determine their demands for and prices of the various resources; competition forces them to use the most efficient techniques and ensures that only the most efficient will be able to stay in business.

c. With resource prices determined, the money income of each household is determined; and with product prices determined, the quantity of goods and services which these money incomes will buy is determined.
d. The market system is able to accommodate itself to changes in consumer tastes, technology, and resource supplies.
(1) The desires of business firms for maximum profits and competition lead the economy to make the appropriate adjustments in the way it uses its resources.
(2) Competition and the desire to increase profits promote both better techniques of production and capital accumulation.
e. Competition in the economy compels firms seeking to promote their own interests to promote (as though led by an "invisible hand") the best interest of society as a whole: an allocation of resources appropriate to consumer wants, production by the most efficient means, and the lowest possible prices.

10. The market system has been praised for its merits. The two major merits of the system are that it efficiently allocates scarce resources and allows individuals large amounts of personal freedom.

■ **IMPORTANT TERMS**

Private sectors	Limited liability
Functional distribution of income	Double taxation
Personal distribution of income	Separation of ownership and control
Personal consumption expenditures	Five Fundamental Questions
Durable good	Normal profit
Nondurable good	Economic cost
Services	Economic profit
Personal taxes	Expanding (prosperous) industry
Personal saving	Declining (unprosperous) industry
Plant	
Firm	Dollar votes
Industry	Consumer sovereignty
Horizontal combination	Derived demand
Vertical combination	Guiding function of prices
Conglomerate combination	Self-limiting adjustment
Sole proprietorship	Technological advance
Partnership	Capital accumulation
Corporation	Invisible hand
Unlimited liability	Allocative efficiency

■ FILL-IN QUESTIONS

1. The approximately _____ million households in the United States play a dual role in the economy because they _____ and _____ _____

2. The largest single source of income in the United States is _____ and is equal to about _____% of total income.

3. In the United States the poorest 20% of all American families receive about _____% of total personal income and the richest 20% of these families receive about _____% of total personal income.

4. The total income of households is disposed of in three ways: _____, _____, and _____

5. Households use about _____% of their total income to pay personal taxes; and the greatest part of their personal taxes are the personal _____ taxes which they pay to the (Federal, state, local) _____ government.

6. Households save primarily in order to obtain _____ and for purposes of _____

7. Based on their durability, consumer spending is classified as spending for _____, _____, and _____

8. There are today about _____ business firms in the United States. The legal form of the great majority of these firms is the _____; but the legal form that produces over one-half the output of the American economy is the _____

9. The liabilities of a sole proprietor and of partners are _____ but the liabilities of stockholders in a corporation are _____

10. Indicate in the spaces to the right of each of the following whether these business characteristics are associated with the proprietorship (PRO), partnership (PART), corporation (CORP), two of these, or all three of these legal forms.
   a. Much red tape and legal expense in beginning the firm _____
   b. Unlimited liability _____
   c. No specialized management _____
   d. Has a life independent of its owner(s) _____
   e. Double taxation of income _____
   f. Greatest ability to acquire funds for the expansion of the firm _____
   g. Permits some but not a great degree of specialized management _____
   h. Possibility of an unresolved disagreement among owners over courses of action _____
   i. The potential for the separation of ownership and control of the business _____

11. Of the eight industry classes in which privately owned business firms are found:
   a. The two which contain the greatest number of firms are _____ and _____
   b. The two which employ the most full-time workers are _____ and _____

12. The public sector produces roughly one-_____-th of all the goods and services produced in the American economy.

13. The United States is often called a big business economy because a relatively _____ firms produce a relatively _____ part of the output of the economy and of some industries.

14. The imports and exports of the United States are about _____% of the domestic output.

15. Our major trading partner is _____

16. The United States incurred a $_____ billion trade (surplus, deficit) _____ in 1990.

17. List four economic implications of growing international trade and finance:
   a. _____
   b. _____
   c. _____
   d. _____

18. List the Five Fundamental Questions which every economy must answer.

a. _____

b. _____

c. _____

d. _____

e. _____

19. The competitive market system is a mechanism for both _____ the decisions of producers and households and _____ these decisions.

20. A *normal* profit (is, is not) _____ an economic cost because it is a payment that (must, need not) _____ be paid to (workers, landowners, suppliers of capital goods, entrepreneurs) _____ but a *pure* (or *economic*) profit (is, is not) _____ an economic cost because it (must, need not) _____ be paid to them to obtain and retain the services they provide to the firm.

21. Pure or economic profits are equal to the total _____ of a firm less its total _____

22. Business firms tend to produce those products from which they can obtain:

a. at least a (pure, normal) _____ profit; and

b. the maximum _____ profit.

23. If firms in an industry are obtaining economic profits, firms will (enter, leave) _____ the industry, the price of the industry's product will (rise, fall) _____, the industry will employ (more, fewer) _____ resources, produce a (larger, smaller) _____ output, and the industry's economic profits will (increase, decrease) _____ until they are equal to _____

24. Consumers:

a. vote with their _____ for the production of a good or service when they buy that good or service;

b. are said, because firms are motivated by their desire for profits to produce the goods and services consumers vote for in this way, to be (dependent, sovereign) _____

c. (restrict, expand) _____ the freedom of firms and resource suppliers.

25. Because firms are interested in obtaining the largest economic profits possible the technique they select to produce a product is the one that enables them to produce that product in the least _____ly way.

26. In determining how the total output of the economy will be divided among its households the market system is involved in two ways:

a. it determines the money _____ each of the households receives; and

b. it determines the _____ they have to pay for each of the goods and services produced.

27. In industrial economies:

a. the changes which occur almost continuously are changes in consumer _____, in _____, and in the supplies of _____;

b. to make the adjustments in the way it uses its resources that are appropriate to these changes a market economy allows price to perform its _____ function.

28. The competitive market system tends to foster technological change.

a. The incentive for a firm to be the first to employ a new and improved technique of production or to produce a new and better product is a greater economic _____;

b. and the incentive for other firms to follow its lead is the avoidance of _____

29. The entrepreneur uses money which is obtained either from _____ or from _____ to acquire capital goods.

30. If the market system is competitive, there is an identity of _____ interests and the _____ interest: firms seem to be guided by an _____ to allocate the economy's resources efficiently.

31. The chief economic advantage of the market system is that _____ and its chief noneconomic advantage is that _____ _____

■ **PROBLEMS AND PROJECTS**

1. The table below shows the functional distribution of total income in the United States for a year.

	Billions of dollars
Wages and salaries	$2,905
Proprietors' income	325
Corporate profits	324
Interest	392
Rents	19
Total earnings	3,964

Of the total earnings about _____% were wages and salaries, and about _____% were corporate profits.

2. Below are six numbers and each of them is a percentage. Match these six numbers with the six phrases that follow:

82	12
35	11
56	9

A. Percentage of U.S. merchandise exports going to developing countries. _____

B. Percentage of the domestic output which is contributed by the government sector of the economy. _____

C. Percentage of the privately owned business firms in the United States which are in the agriculture, forestry, and fishing sector of the economy. _____

D. Percentage of business firms in the United States which are partnerships. _____

E. Percentage of personal consumption expenditures which are for services. _____

F. Percentage of the income of consumers which is used for personal consumption expenditures. _____

3. Indicate to the best of your ability in which industry *class* you would put each of these firms.
  a. Sears, Roebuck and Company
  b. The General Electric Company
  c. A used-car dealer in your town
  d. Macy department stores
  e. Your local electric company
  f. A new-car dealer
  g. The Mars Candy Company
  h. The Aluminum Company of America
  i. The Revere Copper and Brass Company
  j. General Mills

4. Assume that a firm can produce *either* product A, product B, or product C with the resources it currently employs.

These resources cost the firm a total of $50 per week. Assume, for the purposes of the problem, that the firm's employment of resources cannot be changed. The market prices of and the quantities of A, B, and C these resources will produce per week are given below. Compute the firm's profit when it produces A, B, or C; and enter these profits in the table below.

Product	Market price	Output	Economic profit
A	$7.00	8	$_____
B	4.50	10	_____
C	.25	240	_____

a. Which product will the firm produce? _____

b. If the price of A rose to $8, the firm would _____

(Hint: You will have to recompute the firm's profit from the production of A.)

c. If the firm were producing A and selling it at a price of $8, what would tend to happen to the number of firms producing A?

5. Suppose that a firm can produce 100 units of product X by combining labor, land, capital, and entrepreneurial ability in three different ways. If it can hire labor at $2 per unit, land at $3 per unit, capital at $5 per unit, and entrepreneurship at $10 per unit; and if the amounts of the resources required by the three methods of producing 100 units of product X are indicated in the table, answer the questions below it.

Resource	Method		
	1	2	3
Labor	8	13	10
Land	4	3	3
Capital	4	2	4
Entrepreneurship	1	1	1

a. Which method is the least expensive way of producing 100 units of X? _____

b. If X sells for 70 cents per unit, what is the economic profit of the firm? $_____

c. If the price of labor should rise from $2 to $3 per unit and if the price of X is 70 cents,
(1) the firm's use of:

Labor would change from _____ to _____

Land would change from _____ to _____

Capital would change from _____ to _____

Entrepreneurship would not change.

(2) The firm's economic profit would change from

$_____ to $_____

■ **SELF-TEST**

Circle the T if the statement is true; the F if it is false.

1. The personal distribution of income describes the manner in which society's total personal income is divided among wages and salaries, corporate profits, proprietors' income, interest, and rents.   T **F**

2. Limited liability refers to the fact that all members of a partnership are liable for the debts incurred by one another.   *page 73*   T (F)

3. In both relative and absolute terms, personal taxes have exceeded personal saving in recent years.   (T) F

4. Most of the personal saving in the American economy is done by those households in the top 10% of its income receivers.   (T) F

5. *Dissaving* means that personal consumption expenditures exceed after-tax income.   (T) F

6. A "durable good" is defined as a good which has an expected life of one year or more.   (T) F

7. A plant is defined as a group of firms under a single management.   T (F)

8. An industry is a group of firms that produce the same or nearly the same products.   (T) F

9. The corporate form of organization is the least used by firms in the United States.   *72*   (T) F

10. The corporation in the United States today always has a tax advantage over other legal forms of business organization.   T (F)

11. Whether a business firm should incorporate or not depends chiefly upon the amount of money capital it must have to finance the enterprise.   (T) F

12. The wholesale and retail trade and the service industries contain a relatively large number of firms but are not important sources of income and employment in the American economy.   T (F)

13. Corporations produce over one-half the total output produced by privately owned business firms in the United States.   T (F)

14. Increased international trade creates more macroeconomic stability for the United States.   T (F)

15. Foreign competition gives consumers a greater variety of goods and services and forces domestic producers to be more efficient.   T (F)

16. Business firms try to maximize their normal profits.   T (F)

17. Industries in which economic profits are earned by the firms in the industry will attract the entry of new firms into the industry.   T F

18. If firms have sufficient time to enter industries, the economic profits of an industry will tend to disappear.   T F

19. Business firms are really only free to produce whatever they want in any way they wish if they do not want to maximize profits or to minimize losses.   T F

20. To say that the demand for a resource is a derived demand means that it depends upon the demands for the products the resource is used to produce.   T (F)

21. Resources will tend to be used in those industries capable of earning normal or economic profits.   (T) F

22. Economic efficiency requires that a given output of a good or service be produced in the least costly way.   (T) F

23. If the market price of resource A decreases, firms will tend to employ smaller quantities of resource A.   T (F)

24. Changes in the tastes of consumers are reflected in changes in consumer demand for products.   (T) F

25. The incentive which the market system provides to induce technological improvement is the opportunity for economic profits.   T (F)

26. In a capitalistic economy it is from the entrepreneur that the demand for capital goods arises.   T (F)

27. The tendency for individuals pursuing their own self-interests to bring about results which are in the best interest of society as a whole is often called the "invisible hand."   (T) F

28. The basic economic argument for the market system is that it promotes an efficient allocation of resources.   (T) F

29. One of the Five Fundamental Questions is who will control the output.   T (F)

Circle the letter that corresponds to the best answer.

1. The functional distribution for the United States shows that the largest part of the personal income is:
   (a) wages and salaries
   (b) proprietors' income
   (c) corporate profits
   (d) interest and rents

2. The part of after-tax income which is not consumed is defined as:
(a) saving
(b) capital investment
(c) wages and salaries
(d) nondurable goods expenditure

3. If in an economy personal consumption expenditures were 80% of income and personal taxes were 8% of income, then personal savings would be:
(a) 8% of income
(b) 10% of income
(c) 12% of income
(d) 88% of income

4. Expenditures for _nondurable_ goods in recent years have amounted to approximately what percentage of personal consumption expenditures?
(a) 32%
(b) 42%
(c) 50%
(d) 65%

5. Which of the following is a true statement?
(a) the durable goods and service parts of personal consumption expenditures vary more over time than do the expenditures for nondurables
(b) expenditures for nondurables vary more than do the expenditures for durable goods and services
(c) expenditures for nondurables vary more than the expenditures for services and less than the expenditures for durables
(d) expenditures for nondurables vary more than the expenditures for durables and less than the expenditures for services

6. In recent years personal taxes have been approximately what percentage of total income?
(a) 13%
(b) 22%
(c) 24%
(d) 80%

7. Approximately how many million business firms are there in the United States?
(a) 5
(b) 8
(c) 18
(d) 28

8. A group of three plants which is owned and operated by a single firm and which consists of a farm growing wheat, a flour milling plant, and a plant which bakes and sells bakery products is an example of:
(a) a horizontal combination
(b) a vertical combination
(c) a conglomerate combination
(d) a corporation

9. Limited liability is associated with:
(a) only proprietorships
(b) only partnerships
(c) both proprietorships and partnerships
(d) only corporations

10. Which of the following forms of business organization can most effectively raise money capital?
(a) corporation
(b) partnership
(c) proprietorship
(d) vertical combination

11. Which of the following industry classes has the largest number of firms?
(a) agriculture, forestry, and fishing
(b) manufacturing
(c) wholesale and retail trade
(d) mining

12. About what percentage of the domestic output of the United States is produced by government?
(a) 3%
(b) 5%
(c) 10%
(d) 12%

13. A deficit in merchandise trade with other nations is produced when a nation's:
(a) exports are greater than imports
(b) imports are greater than exports
(c) imports are greater than currency appreciation
(d) exports are greater than currency appreciation

14. One of the major benefits of international trade and finance for the United States is:
(a) lower living standards
(b) less efficient use of world resources
(c) greater competition among businesses
(d) greater economic security for domestic banks and financial markets

15. If incomes increased significantly in the major industrial countries that trade with the United States, this development would most likely:
(a) increase United States exports
(b) decrease United States exports
(c) decrease United States imports of oil
(d) have no significant effect on the imports or exports of the United States

16. The competitive market system is a method of:
(a) communicating and synchronizing the decisions of consumers, producers, and resource suppliers
(b) centrally planning economic decisions
(c) promoting productive efficiency, but not allocative efficiency
(d) promoting allocative efficiency, but not productive efficiency

17. Which of the following best defines economic costs?
(a) total payments made to workers, landowners, suppliers of capital, and entrepreneurs
(b) only total payments made to workers, landowners, suppliers of capital, and entrepreneurs which must be paid to obtain the services of their resources
(c) total payments made to workers, landowners, suppliers of capital, and entrepreneurs less normal profits
(d) total payments made to workers, landowners, suppliers of capital, and entrepreneurs plus normal profits

18. If less-than-normal profits are being earned by the firms in an industry, the consequences will be that:
(a) lower-priced resources will be drawn into the industry
(b) firms will leave the industry, causing the price of the industry's product to fall
(c) firms will leave the industry, causing the price of the industry's product to rise
(d) the price of the industry's product will fall and thereby cause the demand for the product to increase

19. Which of the following would *not* necessarily result, sooner or later, from a decrease in consumer demand for a product?
(a) a decrease in the profits of the industry producing the product
(b) a decrease in the output of the industry
(c) a decrease in the supply of the product
(d) an increase in the prices of resources employed by the firms in the industry

20. If firm A does not employ the most "efficient" or least costly method of production, which of the following will *not* be a consequence?
(a) firm A will fail to earn the greatest profit possible
(b) other firms in the industry will be able to sell the product at lower prices
(c) new firms will enter the industry and sell the product at a lower price than that at which firm A now sells it
(d) firm A will be spending less on resources and hiring fewer resources than it otherwise would

21. Which of the following is *not* a factor in determining the share of the total output of the economy received by any household?
(a) the price at which the household sells its resources
(b) the quantities of resources which the household sells
(c) the tastes of the household
(d) the prices which the household must pay to buy products

22. If an increase in the demand for a product and the resulting rise in the price of the product cause the supply of the product, the size of the industry producing the prod-

uct, and the amounts of resources devoted to its production to expand, price is successfully performing its:
(a) guiding function
(b) rationing function
(c) medium-of-exchange function
(d) standard-of-value function

23. In a capitalistic economy characterized by competition, if one firm introduces a new and better method of production, other firms will be forced to adopt the improved technique:
(a) to avoid less-than-normal profits
(b) to obtain economic profits
(c) to prevent the price of the product from falling
(d) to prevent the price of the product from rising

24. Which of the following would be an indication that competition does not exist in an industry?
(a) less-than-normal profits in the industry
(b) inability of the firms in the industry to expand
(c) inability of firms to enter the industry
(d) wages lower than the average wage in the economy paid to workers in the industry

25. The chief economic virtue of the competitive market system remains that of:
(a) allowing extensive personal freedom
(b) efficiently allocating resources
(c) providing an equitable distribution of income
(d) eliminating the need for decision making

Answer the next two questions (26 and 27) on the basis of the following information.

Suppose 50 units of product X can be produced by employing just labor and capital in the four ways shown below. Assume the prices of labor and capital are $5 and $4, respectively.

	A	B	C	D
Labor	1	2	3	4
Capital	5	3	2	1

26. Which technique is economically most efficient in producing product X?
(a) A
(b) B
(c) C
(d) D

27. If the price of product X is $1.00, then the firm will realize:
(a) an economic profit of $28
(b) an economic profit of $27
(c) an economic profit of $26
(d) an economic profit of $25

■ **DISCUSSION QUESTIONS**

1. Explain the difference between a functional and a personal distribution of income. Rank the five types of earned income in the order of their size.

2. Which would result in greater total saving and less consumption spending out of a national income of a given size: a more or less nearly equal distribution of income?

3. The purchase of what type of consumer goods is largely postponable? Why is this? How is it possible for a family's personal consumption expenditures to exceed its after-tax income?

4. What is the difference between a plant and a firm? Between a firm and an industry? Which of these three concepts is the most difficult to apply in practice? Why? Distinguish between a horizontal, a vertical, and a conglomerate combination.

5. What are the principal advantages and disadvantages of each type of the three legal forms of business organization? Which of the disadvantages of the proprietorship and partnership accounts for the employment of the corporate form among the big businesses of the American economy?

6. Explain what "separation of ownership and control" of the modern corporation means. What problems does this separation create for stockholders and the economy?

7. What figures can you cite to show that the typical firm engaged in agriculture is relatively small and that the average firm engaged in manufacturing is relatively large? Are firms engaged in wholesaling and retailing; mining; finance, insurance, and real estate; and services relatively large or relatively small?

8. Is the American economy and manufacturing in the United States dominated by big business? What evidence do you use to reach this conclusion?

9. Describe the merchandise trade import and export patterns for the United States. What percentage of our exports and imports are with
   (a) industrial countries;
   (b) OPEC countries; and
   (c) developing countries other than OPEC

10. Explain how increasing international trade for the United States affects
   (a) living standards;
   (b) competition;
   (c) banking and finance; and
   (d) macroeconomic stability and policy.

11. What are the Five Fundamental Questions?

12. In what way do the desires of entrepreneurs to obtain economic profits and to avoid losses make consumer sovereignty effective?

13. Why is the ability of firms to enter industries which are prosperous important to the effective functioning of competition?

14. Explain *in detail* how an increase in the consumer demand for a product will result in more of the product being produced and in more resources being allocated to its production.

15. To what extent are firms "free" to produce what they wish by methods which they choose? Do resource owners have freedom to use their resources as they wish?

16. What is meant when it is said that competition is the mechanism which "controls" the market system? How does competition do this? What do critics of the price system argue tends to happen to this controlling mechanism as time passes, and why do they so argue?

17. What are the two important functions of prices? Explain the difference between these two functions.

18. "An invisible hand operates to identify private and public interests." What are private interests and what is the public interest? What is it that leads the economy to operate as if it were directed by an invisible hand?

19. If the basic economic decisions are not made in a capitalistic economy by a central authority, how are they made?

20. Households use the dollars obtained by selling resource services to "vote" for the production of consumer goods and services. Who "votes" for the production of capital goods, why do they "vote" for capital-goods production, and where do they obtain the dollars needed to cast these "votes"?

■ **ANSWERS**

Chapter 5 The Private Sectors and the Market System

FILL-IN QUESTIONS

1. 94, furnish resources, buy the bulk of the total output of the economy

2. wages and salaries, 75

3. 5, 44

4. personal consumption, personal saving, personal taxes

5. 13, income, federal

6. security, speculation

7. services, nondurable goods, durable goods (any order)

8. 18 million, sole proprietorship, corporation

9. unlimited, limited

10. *a.* CORP; *b.* PRO and PART; *c.* PRO; *d.* CORP; *e.* CORP; *f.* CORP; *g.* PART; *h.* PART; *i.* CORP

11. *a.* wholesale and retail trade; services; *b.* services, wholesale and retail

12. eight

13. few, large

14. 7–9

15. Canada

16. 108, deficit

17. *a.* increased productive efficiency and living standards; *b.* increased worldwide competition; *c.* financial markets and banking industries operate globally; and *d.* more macroeconomic instability and possibly less effective domestic policy

18. *a.* at what level to utilize resources in the productive process; *b.* what collection of goods and services best satisfies its wants; *c.* how to produce this total output; *d.* how to divide this output among the various economic units of the economy; *e.* how to make the responses required to remain efficient over time

19. communicating, synchronizing (coordinating)

20. is, must, entrepreneurs, is not, need not

21. revenues, costs

22. *a.* normal; *b.* pure (economic)

23. enter, fall, more, larger, decrease, zero

24. *a.* dollars; *b.* sovereign; *c.* restrict

25. cost

26. *a.* income; *b.* prices

27. *a.* preferences (tastes), technology, resources; *b.* guiding

28. *a.* profit; *b.* losses (bankruptcy)

29. profits, borrowed funds

30. private, public (social), invisible hand

31. it efficiently allocates resources, it emphasizes personal freedom

PROBLEMS AND PROJECTS

1. 13, 8

2. A. 35; B. 12; C. 11; D. 9; E. 56; F. 82

3. Firms **a, c, d,** and **f** are in wholesale and retail trade; firms **b, g, h, i,** and **j** are in manufacturing; firms **h** and **i** are also in mining; firm **e** is in transportation, communications, and public utilities

4. $6, −$5, $10; *a.* C; *b.* produce A and have an economic profit of $14; *c.* it would increase

5. *a.* method 2; *b.* 15; *c.* (1) 13, 8; 3, 4; 2, 4; (2) 15, 4

SELF-TEST

1. F, p. 68	**17.** T, p. 79
2. T, p. 73	**18.** T, p. 79
3. T, pp. 68–69	**19.** T, p. 80
4. T, p. 69	**20.** T, p. 80
5. T, p. 69	**21.** T, pp. 80–81
6. T, p. 70	**22.** T, p. 81
7. F, p. 71	**23.** F, p. 81
8. T, p. 71	**24.** T, p. 82
9. F, p. 72	**25.** T, p. 83
10. F, pp. 73–74	**26.** T, p. 83
11. T, p. 74	**27.** T, p. 83
12. F, p. 75	**28.** T, p. 85
13. T, pp. 75–76	**29.** F, pp. 78, 85
14. F, p. 77	
15. T, p. 77	
16. F, p. 79	

1. *a,* p. 67	**15.** *a,* p. 77
2. *a,* p. 69	**16.** *a,* p. 78
3. *c,* pp. 68–69	**17.** *b,* p. 79
4. *a,* p. 70	**18.** *c,* p. 79
5. *a,* p. 70	**19.** *d,* pp. 79–80
6. *a,* p. 69	**20.** *d,* p. 81
7. *c,* p. 72	**21.** *c,* pp. 81–82
8. *b,* p. 71	**22.** *a,* p. 82
9. *d,* p. 73	**23.** *a,* p. 83
10. *a,* p. 73	**24.** *c,* pp. 83–84
11. *c,* p. 75	**25.** *b,* p. 85
12. *d,* p. 75	**26.** *b,* p. 81
13. *b,* p. 77	**27.** *a,* pp. 79, 81
14. *c,* p. 77	

DISCUSSION QUESTIONS

1. pp. 67–68	**11.** p. 78
2. pp. 68–69	**12.** p. 80
3. pp. 69–70	**13.** p. 79
4. p. 71	**14.** p. 80
5. pp. 72–74	**15.** p. 80
6. p. 74	**16.** pp. 83–85
7. p. 75	**17.** pp. 82–83
8. pp. 75–76	**18.** pp. 83–84
9. pp. 76–77	**19.** p. 85
10. p. 77	**20.** p. 83

CHAPTER 6

The Public Sector

Chapter 6 introduces you to the five basic functions performed by the Federal, state, and local governments in America's mixed capitalistic economy. This is an examination of the role of government (the public sector) in an economy which is neither a purely planned nor a purely market-type economy. The discussion points out the degree and the ways in which government causes the American economy to differ from pure capitalism. The chapter does not attempt to list all the *specific* ways in which government affects the behavior of the economy. Instead it provides a *general* classification of the tasks performed by government.

The chapter begins by discussing the two major functions of government. First, the legal and social framework for the operation of the market system is provided by government. Second, government actions can be taken to maintain competition in the economy. In addition, the chapter explains how government influences the market system in three other ways: by redistributing wealth and income; altering domestic output; and stabilizing the economy.

The chapter also returns to the circular flow model that was first presented in Chapter 3. The model has now been modified to include government along with businesses and households. The addition of government changes the real and monetary flows in the model. The twelve linkages among the household, business, and government sectors in the model are described in detail.

The facts of public-sector or government finance in the United States presented in the second half of Chapter 6 center on two questions: Where do governments get their incomes? On what do they spend these incomes?

The organization of the government finance discussion is relatively simple. First, the trends which taxes collected and expenditures made by all levels of government—Federal, state, and local—have taken since 1929 and the causes of the increases in expenditures and taxes are examined briefly. Second, a closer look is taken at the major items upon which the Federal government spends its income, the principal taxes it levies to obtain its income, and the relative importance of these taxes. Third, the chapter looks at the major expenditures of and the major taxes of

the state and the local governments, and at fiscal federalism.

What should you get out of this discussion of government finance? There are at least two important sets of facts: (1) the trends which taxes and government expenditures have taken in recent years and why; and (2) the relative importance of the principal taxes and the relative importance of the various expenditure items in the budgets of the three levels of government. Also, remember to avoid memorizing statistics. You should look instead for the trends and generalizations which these statistics illuminate.

■ CHECKLIST

When you have studied this chapter you should be able to:

☐ Explain in one or two sentences why the American economy is *mixed* rather than *pure* capitalism.
☐ Enumerate the five economic functions of government in the United States and explain the difference between the purpose of the first two and the purpose of the last three functions.
☐ Define monopoly and explain why government wishes to prevent monopoly and to preserve competition in the economy.
☐ Explain why government feels it should redistribute income and list the three principal policies it employs for this purpose.
☐ Define a spillover cost and a spillover benefit; explain why a competitive market fails to allocate resources efficiently when there are spillovers; and list the things government may do to reduce spillovers and improve the allocation of resources.
☐ Define a public good and a private good and explain how government goes about reallocating resources from the production of private to the production of public goods.
☐ Draw a circular flow diagram that includes businesses, households, and government; label all the flows in the diagram; and use the diagram to explain how government

Quasi-public good

Free-rider problem

Government purchase

Government transfer payment

Personal income tax

Marginal tax rate

Average tax rate

Progressive tax

Payroll tax

Corporate income tax

Sales tax

Excise tax

Property tax

Fiscal federalism

■ **FILL-IN QUESTIONS**

1. All actual economies are "mixed" because they combine elements of a _____ economy and a role for _____.

2. List the five economic functions of government.

   a. _____

   b. _____

   c. _____

   d. _____

   e. _____

3. To control monopoly in the United States government has:

   a. created commissions to _____ the prices and the services of the _____ monopolies; and taken over at the local level the _____ of electric and water companies;

   b. enacted _____ laws to maintain competition.

4. The market system, because it is an impersonal mechanism, results in an (equal, unequal) _____ distribution of income. To redistribute income from the upper- to the lower-income groups the Federal government has:

   a. provided _____ payments;

   b. engaged in _____ intervention;

   c. used the _____ tax to raise much of its revenues.

5. Government frequently reallocates resources when it finds instances of _____ failure; and the two major cases of such failure occur when the competitive market system either

   a. _____

   b. or _____

6. Competitive markets bring about an optimum allocation of resources only if there are no _____ costs or benefits in the consumption and production of the good or service.

7. There is a spillover whenever some of the costs of producing a product or some of the benefits from consuming it accrue to _____

8. Whenever in a competitive market there are:

   a. spillover costs the result is an (over-, under-) _____ allocation of resources to the production of the good or service;

   b. spillover benefits the result is an _____ _____ allocation of resources to the production of the good or service.

9. What two things can government do to:

   a. Make the market reflect spillover costs?

   (1) _____

   (2) _____

   b. Make the market reflect spillover benefits?

   (1) _____

   (2) _____

10. Public (social) goods tend to be goods which are not subject to the _____ principle and which are (divisible, indivisible) _____. Quasi-public goods are goods which could be subjected to the exclusion principle but which are provided by government because they have large spillover _____

11. To reallocate resources from the production of private to the production of public goods government reduces the demand for private goods by _____ consumers and firms and then _____ _____ public goods.

12. To stabilize the economy, government:

   a. when there is less than full employment (increases, decreases) _____ aggregate demand by (increasing, decreasing) _____ its expenditures for public goods and services and by (increasing, decreasing) _____ taxes.

   b. where there are inflationary pressures _____ _____ aggregate demand by _____ its expenditures for public goods and services and by _____ taxes.

13. Throughout most of its history government in the United States has performed in some degree each of the five functions except that of _____

_____

14. The functions of government are most directly felt by the economy through the _____ it makes and the _____ it collects.

15. An examination of the public sector of the American economy reveals that:

  a. between 1929 and 1991 government **purchases** of goods and services as a percentage of domestic output have tended to (increase, decrease, remain constant) _____ and since the early 1950s have been about (10, 20, 33) _____% of the domestic output;

  b. but government **transfer payments** as a percentage of domestic output during the past 20 or so years have (increased, decreased, remained constant) _____;

  c. and the tax revenues required to finance both government expenditures and transfer payments are today about (10, 20, 30) _____% of domestic output.

16. Government transfer payments are defined as _____ _____ and are (exhaustive, nonexhaustive) _____

17. When government raises $20 billion by taxation and uses it to purchase goods it shifts resources from the production of (private, public) _____ goods to the production of _____ goods; but these expenditures are (exhaustive, nonexhaustive) _____ because they absorb resources and are part of current production.

18. The most important source of revenue for the Federal government is the _____ tax; next in importance are the _____ taxes. The three largest categories of Federal expenditures are for _____, for _____, and for interest on the _____

19. The Federal government uses the personal income tax to obtain most of the _____ it requires to finance its expenditures. In fact, the personal income tax accounts for _____% of Federal tax revenues. The Federal government also receives _____% from payroll taxes and _____% from corporate income taxes.

20. The state governments rely primarily upon _____ and _____ taxes for their incomes which they spend mostly on _____ and _____

21. At local levels of government the single most important source of revenue is the _____ tax and the single most important expenditure is for _____

22. The amount by which the expenditures of state and local governments exceed their tax revenues is largely filled by grants from the _____ government; these grants account for _____% to _____% of all revenue received by state and local governments.

■ **PROBLEMS AND PROJECTS**

1. Below is a list of various government activities. Indicate in the space to the right of each into which of the five classes of government functions the activity falls. If it falls under more than one of the functions, indicate this.

  a. Maintaining an army _____
  b. Providing for a system of unemployment compensation _____

  c. Establishment of the Federal Reserve Banks _____

_____

  d. Insuring employees of business firms against industrial accidents _____
  e. Establishment of an Antitrust Division in the Department of Justice _____
  f. Making it a crime to sell stocks and bonds under false pretenses _____
  g. Providing low-cost lunches to school children _____

_____

  h. Taxation of whisky and other spirits _____

_____

  i. Regulation of organized stock, bond, and commodity markets _____
  j. Setting tax **rates** higher for larger incomes than for smaller ones _____

2. The circular flow diagram below includes business firms, households, and government (the public sector). Also shown are the product and resource markets.

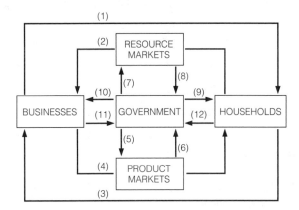

a. Supply a label or an explanation for each of the twelve flows in the model:

(1) _____

(2) _____

(3) _____

(4) _____

(5) _____

(6) _____

(7) _____

(8) _____

(9) _____

(10) _____

(11) _____

(12) _____

b. If government wished to
(1) expand output and employment in the economy it

would increase expenditure flows _____ or

_____, decrease net tax flows

_____ or _____, or do both;
(2) increase the production of public (social) goods and decrease the production of private goods in the

economy it would increase flows _____

and _____ or _____;
(3) redistribute income from high-income to low-income households it would (increase, decrease)

_____ the net taxes (taxes minus transfers)

paid by the former and _____ the net taxes

paid by the latter in flow _____

3. On the following graph are the demand and supply curves for a product bought and sold in a competitive market. Assume that there are no spillover benefits or costs.

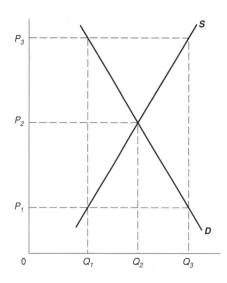

a. Were this market to produce an output of Q_1 there

would be an (optimal, under-, over-) _____
allocation of resources to the production of this product.
b. Were this market to produce Q_3 there would be an

_____ allocation of resources to this
product.
c. The equilibrium output is _____

and at this output there is an _____
allocation of resources.

4. On two graphs that follow are product demand and supply curves that do **not** reflect either the spillover costs of producing the product or the spillover benefits obtained from its consumption.
a. On the first graph draw in another curve that reflects the inclusion of spillover costs.

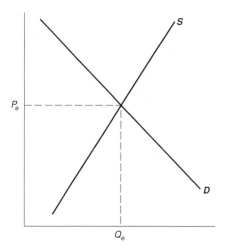

(1) Government might force the (demand for, supply of) _____ the product to reflect the spillover costs of producing it by (taxing, subsidizing) _____ the producers.
(2) The inclusion of spillover costs in the total cost of producing the product (increases, decreases) _____ the output of the product and _____ its price.
b. On the next graph draw in a supply curve that reflects the inclusion of spillover **benefits.**

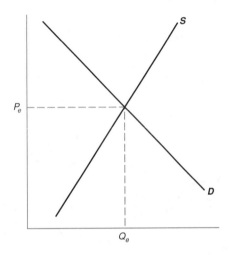

(1) Indicate on the graph the output that is optimal when spillover benefits are included.
(2) To bring about the production of this optimal output government might (tax, subsidize) _____ the producers of this product, and this would (increase, decrease) _____ the supply of the product.
(3) This optimal output is (greater than, less than, equal to) _____ Q_e; and the price of the product is (above, below, equal to) _____ P_e.

5. In the table below are several levels of taxable income and hypothetical marginal tax rates for each $1000 increase in income.

Taxable income	Marginal tax rate, %	Tax	Average tax rate, %
$1500		$300	20
2500	22	520	20.8
3500	25	___	___
4500	29	___	___
5500	34	___	___
6500	40	___	___

a. At the four income levels compute the tax and the average tax rate.
b. As the marginal tax rate:
(1) increases the average tax rate (increases, decreases, remains constant) _____
_____
(2) decreases the average tax rate _____
c. This tax is _____ because the average tax rate increases as income _____

■ SELF-TEST

Circle the T if the statement is true; the F if it is false.

1. The American economy cannot be called "capitalistic" because its operation involves some "planning by government."   **T F**

2. When the Federal government provides for a monetary system, it is functioning to provide the economy with public goods and services.   **T F**

3. An economy in which strong and effective competition is maintained will find no need for programs designed to redistribute income.   **T F**

4. Competitive product markets ensure an optimal allocation of an economy's resources.   **T F**

5. In a competitive product market and in the absence of spillover costs, the supply curve or schedule reflects the costs of producing the product.   **T F**

6. If demand and supply reflected all the benefits and costs of a product, the equilibrium output of a competitive market would be identical with its optimal output.   **T F**

The following graph should be used to answer true-false question 7 and multiple-choice question 3.

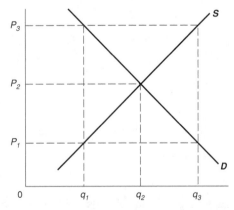

7. Assuming there are no spillover costs or benefits, the production of q_1 units of this product would result in an overallocation of resources to the production of the product. T F

8. The inclusion of the spillover benefits would increase the demand for a product. T F

9. When there are spillover costs involved in the production of a product, more resources are allocated to the production of that product and more of the product is produced than is optimal or most efficient. T F

10. Subsidizing the firms producing goods which provide spillover benefits will usually result in a better allocation of resources. T F

11. Governments have undertaken to provide lighthouse services because these services have social benefits and private producers of such services encounter the free-rider problem. T F

12. In performing its stabilization function when there is widespread unemployment and no inflation in the economy, government should decrease its spending for public goods and services and increase taxes. T F

13. Net taxes for businesses are taxes paid by business less a depreciation allowance. T F

14. Flood control projects are usually undertaken by government because of the free-rider problem. T F

15. When the Federal government takes actions to control unemployment or inflation it is performing the allocative function of government. T F

16. Government purchases of goods and services are called **nonexhaustive** and government transfer payments are called **exhaustive** expenditures. T F

17. When a government levies taxes and uses the tax revenue to make transfer payments it shifts resources from the production of private goods to the production of public goods. T F

18. The level of Federal expenditures in 1990 was about $1,031 billion. T F

19. The chief source of revenue for the Federal government is the corporate income tax. T F

20. The Federal government levies sales taxes on tobacco and gasoline. T F

21. Total taxes collected by the Federal government are approximately equal to the amount of taxes collected by all state and local governments. T F

22. If the marginal tax rate is higher than the average tax rate, the average tax rate will fall. T F

23. Property taxes are the largest percentage of the total budget of local governments. T F

24. The largest expenditure by state governments is for highways. T F

25. Fiscal federalism involves the sharing of sales tax receipts among local, state, and Federal governments. T F

Circle the letter that corresponds to the best answer.

1. Which of the following is **not** one of the methods utilized by government to control monopoly?
(a) the imposition of special taxes on monopolists
(b) government ownership of monopolies
(c) government regulation of monopolies
(d) antitrust laws

2. One of the following is **not** employed by government to redistribute income. Which one?
(a) the negative income tax
(b) direct market intervention
(c) income taxes which take a larger part of the incomes of the rich than the poor
(d) public assistance programs

Use the graph on page 58 to answer the following question.

3. If there are neither spillover costs nor spillover benefits, the output which results in the optimal allocation of resources to the production of this product is:
(a) q_1
(b) q_2
(c) q_3
(d) none of these outputs

4. When the production and consumption of a product entail spillover costs, a competitive product market results in an:
(a) underallocation of resources to the product
(b) overallocation of resources to the product
(c) optimal allocation of resources to the product
(d) a higher price for the product

5. Which of the following is the best example of a good or service providing the economy with spillover benefits?
(a) an automobile
(b) a drill press
(c) a high school education
(d) an operation for appendicitis

6. In the American economy the reallocation of resources needed to provide for the production of public goods is:
(a) government subsidies to the producers of social goods
(b) government purchases of social goods from producers
(c) direct control of producers of both private and social goods
(d) direct control of producers of social goods only

7. Which of the following is characteristic of public goods?
(a) they are indivisible
(b) they are sold in competitive markets
(c) they are subject to the exclusion principle
(d) they can be produced only if large spillover costs are incurred

8. Quasi-public goods are goods and services:
(a) to which the exclusion principle could not be applied
(b) which have large spillover benefits
(c) which would not be produced by private producers through the market system
(d) which are indivisible

9. To redistribute income from high-income to low-income households government might:
(a) increase transfer payments to high-income and decrease transfer payments to low-income households
(b) increase the taxes paid by high-income and increase the transfer payments to low-income households
(c) increase the taxes paid by low-income and decrease the taxes paid by high-income households
(d) decrease the taxes paid by high-income and decrease the transfer payments to low-income households

10. To reallocate resources from the private to the public sector of the economy government should:
(a) increase its expenditures for the goods it purchases from business firms
(b) increase the transfer payments it makes to households
(c) increase its expenditures for the labor services it purchases from households
(d) do either or both *a* and *c*

11. To prevent or slow inflation in the economy government would most likely:
(a) increase its expenditures for the goods and services it purchases from business firms and households
(b) increase the transfer payments it makes to business firms and the public
(c) increase the taxes it collects from business firms and the public
(d) do either or both *a* and *c*

12. Which of the following is the best example of a good or service providing the economy with a spillover cost?
(a) a textbook
(b) an automobile
(c) a business suit
(d) an audit of a business firm's books

13. There is a "free-rider" problem when people:
(a) are willing to pay for what they want

(b) are not willing to pay for what they want
(c) benefit from a good without paying for its cost
(d) want to buy more than is available for purchase in the market

14. In the circular flow model, net taxes are:
(a) taxes minus depreciation
(b) taxes minus transfer payments
(c) subsidies minus transfer payments
(d) business receipts minus household expenditures

15. In the circular flow model, government provides goods and services and receives net taxes from:
(a) colleges and universities
(b) businesses and households
(c) resource and product markets
(d) foreign nations and corporations

16. Today all government expenditures (purchases plus transfer payments) equal approximately what percentage of the American economy's total output?
(a) 10%
(b) 18%
(c) 23%
(d) 33%

17. Which of the following is *not* one of the causes of the present size of government expenditures in the United States?
(a) national defense
(b) property taxes
(c) population growth
(d) egalitarianism

18. Which of the following would *not* be a government transfer expenditure?
(a) salaries and benefits for military personnel
(b) social security payments to the aged
(c) unemployment compensation benefits
(d) payments to the widows of war veterans

19. Which of the following accounts for the largest percentage of all Federal expenditures?
(a) income security
(b) national defense
(c) interest on the public debt
(d) veterans' services

20. Which of the following is the largest source of the tax revenues of the Federal government?
(a) sales and excise taxes
(b) property taxes
(c) payroll taxes
(d) personal income taxes

21. A tax that would most likely alter consumer expenditures on a product would be:
(a) an excise tax
(b) a general sales tax
(c) a personal income tax
(d) a corporate income tax

22. Which of the following pairs represents the chief source of income and the most important type of expenditure of state governments?
(a) personal income tax and expenditures for education
(b) personal income tax and expenditures for highways
(c) sales and excise taxes and expenditures for highways
(d) sales and excise taxes and expenditures for public welfare

23. Which of the following pairs represents the chief source of income and the most important type of expenditure of *local* governments?
(a) property tax and expenditures for highways
(b) property tax and expenditures for education
(c) sales and excise taxes and expenditures for public welfare
(d) sales and excise taxes and expenditures for police, fire, and general government

The next two questions (24 and 25) are based on the portion of the tax table given below.

Taxable income	Total tax
$ 0	$ 0
30,000	5,000
70,000	15,000
150,000	42,000

24. The marginal tax rate at the $70,000 level of taxable income is:
(a) 16.6
(b) 21.4
(c) 25.0
(d) 28.0

25. The average tax rate at the $150,000 level of taxable income is:
(a) 21.4
(b) 28.0
(c) 31.5
(d) 33.8

■ **DISCUSSION QUESTIONS**

1. Why is it proper to refer to the United States economy as "mixed capitalism"?

2. What are the five economic functions of government in America's mixed capitalistic economy? Explain what the performance of each of these functions requires government to do.

3. Would you like to live in an economy in which government undertook only the first two functions listed in the text? What would be the advantages and disadvantages of living in such an economy?

4. Why does the market system provide some people with lower income than it provides others?

5. What is "market failure" and what are the two major kinds of such failures?

6. What is meant by a spillover in general and by spillover cost and spillover benefit in particular? How does the existence of such costs and benefits affect the allocation of resources and the prices of products? If a market could be required to take these costs and benefits into account, how would the allocation of resources and the price of the product bought and sold in that market be changed?

7. What methods do government employ to:
(a) redistribute income;
(b) reallocate resources to take account of spillover costs;
(c) reallocate resources to take account of spillover benefits?

8. Distinguish between a private and a public good. Include in your answer an explanation of the "exclusion principle" and the distinction between divisible and indivisible goods.

9. What basic method does government employ in the United States to reallocate resources away from the production of private goods and toward the production of social goods?

10. In a circular flow diagram that includes not only business firms and households but also government (or the public sector), what are the four flows of money into or out of the government sector of the economy? Using this diagram, explain how government redistributes income, reallocates resources from the private to the public sector, and stabilizes the economy.

11. What are the causes of the historical growth and the present size of government spending and taxes in the American economy?

12. Government expenditures fall into two broad classes: expenditures for goods and services, and transfer payments. Explain the difference between these and give examples of expenditures which fall into each of the two classes.

13. Explain the difference between exhaustive and nonexhaustive government spending.

14. When government collects taxes and spends the tax revenues it affects the composition of the total output of the economy. What is the effect on total output if government uses the tax revenues to purchase goods and services? What is the effect if it uses them to make transfer payments?

15. Explain precisely the difference between the marginal tax rate and the average tax rate.

16. Explain how the Federal personal income tax enables the Federal government to perform three (of the five) economic functions.

17. Explain in detail the differences that exist among Federal, state, and local governments in the taxes upon which they primarily rely for their revenues and the major purposes for which they use these revenues.

18. Why does the Federal government share its tax revenues with state and local governments? How has this fiscal federalism changed in recent years?

■ ANSWERS

Chapter 6 The Public Sector

FILL-IN QUESTIONS

1. market, government

2. *a.* provide legal foundation and social environment; *b.* maintain competition; *c.* redistribute income and wealth; *d.* reallocate resources; *e.* stabilize the economy

3. *a.* regulate, natural, ownership; *b.* antitrust (antimonopoly)

4. unequal; *a.* transfer; *b.* market; *c.* income

5. market; *a.* produces the "wrong" amounts of certain goods and services; *b.* fails to allocate any resources to the production of certain goods and services whose production is economically justified

6. spillover

7. people other than the buyers and sellers (third parties)

8. *a.* over; *b.* under

9. *a.* (1) enact legislation, (2) pass special taxes; *b.* (1) subsidize production, (2) finance or take over the production of the product

10. exclusion, indivisible, benefits

11. taxing, spends the revenue to buy

12. *a.* increases, increasing, decreasing; *b.* decreases, decreasing, increasing

13. stabilizing the economy

14. expenditures, taxes

15. *a.* increase, 20; *b.* increased; *c.* 33

16. expenditures for which government currently receives no good or service in return, nonexhaustive

17. exhaustive

18. personal income, payroll, income security, national defense, public debt

19. revenue, 45, 37, 9

20. sales and excise, personal income, public welfare, education

21. property, education

22. federal, 15, 20

PROBLEMS AND PROJECTS

1. *a.* reallocates resources; *b.* redistributes income; *c.* provides a legal foundation and social environment *and* stabilizes the economy; *d.* reallocates resources; *e.* maintains competition; *f.* provides a legal foundation and social environment *and* maintains competition; *g.* redistributes income; *h.* reallocates resources; *i.* provides a legal foundation and social environment; *j.* redistributes income

2. *a.* (1) business pay costs for resources that becomes money income for households; (2) households provide resources to businesses; (3) household expenditures become receipts for businesses; (4) business provide goods and services to households; (5) government spends money in product market; (6) government receives goods and services from product market; (7) government spends money in resource market; (8) government receives resources from resource market; (9) government provides goods and services to households; (10) government provides goods and services to businesses; (11) business pays net taxes to government; (12) households pay net taxes to government; *b.* (1) 5, 7 (either order), 11, 12 (either order); (2) 9, 10, 11 (either order); (3) increase, decrease, 12

3. *a.* under; *b.* over; *c.* Q_2, optimal

4. *a.* (1) supply of, taxing, (2) decreases, increases; *b.* (2) subsidize, increase, (3) greater than, below

5. *a.* tax: $770, 1,060, 1,400, 1,800; average tax rate: 22%, 23.6%, 25.5%, 27.7%; *b.* (1) increases, (2) decreases; *c.* progressive, increases

SELF-TEST

1. F, p. 88	8. T, p. 92	14. T, pp. 93–94	20. F, p. 99
2. F, p. 89	9. T, p. 91	15. F, p. 94	21. F, pp. 98, 100
3. F, p. 90	10. T, pp. 92–93	16. F, p. 96	22. F, p. 99
4. F, pp. 90–91	11. T, p. 93	17. F, pp. 96–97	23. T, p. 100
5. T, p. 91	12. F, p. 94	18. T, p. 98	24. F, p. 100
6. T, p. 90	13. F, p. 96	19. F, p. 98	25. F, p. 102
7. F, p. 91			

1. *a*, p. 90	8. *b*, pp. 93–94	14. *b*, p. 96	20. *d*, p. 98
2. *a*, p. 90	9. *b*, p. 90	15. *b*, p. 96	21. *a*, p. 99
3. *b*, p. 92	10. *d*, p. 94	16. *d*, p. 97	22. *d*, p. 100
4. *d*, p. 91	11. *c*, p. 94	17. *b*, pp. 97–98	23. *b*, p. 100
5. *c*, p. 92	12. *b*, pp. 90–91	18. *a*, pp. 97–98	24. *c*, p. 99
6. *b*, p. 94	13. *c*, p. 93	19. *a*, p. 98	25. *b*, p. 99
7. *a*, pp. 93–94			

DISCUSSION QUESTIONS

1. p. 88	6. pp. 90–93	11. pp. 97–98	15. p. 99
2. pp. 88–89	7. pp. 90–93	12. pp. 96–97	16. pp. 98–99
3. pp. 88–94	8. p. 93	13. pp. 96–97	17. pp. 98–101
4. p. 90	9. p. 94	14. p. 96	18. p. 102
5. p. 90	10. pp. 94–96		

Measuring Domestic Output, National Income, and the Price Level

The subject of Chapter 7 is national income accounting. The first measure that you will learn about in the chapter is the gross domestic product (GDP). The GDP is an important economic statistic because it provides the best estimate of the total market value of all final goods and services produced by our economy in one year. (In 1992, GDP replaced a similar measure—the gross national product [GNP]—as the chief economic measure of the economy's output to make it comparable to the ones reported by other nations.) The chapter also explains the relationship of GDP to four other measures in our national accounts: net domestic product (NDP), national income (NI), personal income (PI), and disposable income (DI).

National income accounting involves estimating output or income for the nation society as a whole, rather than for an individual business firm or family. Note that the terms "output" and "income" are interchangeable because the nation's domestic output and its income are identical. The value of the nation's output equals the total expenditures for this output, and these expenditures become the income of those who have produced this output. Consequently, there are two equally acceptable methods, both discussed in the chapter, for obtaining each of the five income-output measures listed above. These two methods are the expenditures method and the income method.

Accounting is essentially an adding-up process. This chapter explains in detail and lists the items which must be added to obtain by both methods each of the five income-output measures. It is up to you to learn precisely **what** to add, i.e., how to compute GDP, NDP, NI, PI, and DI by both methods. This is a fairly difficult chapter, and the only way to learn the material is simply to sit down and learn it—memorize it if necessary! A careful reading of the chapter, however, will enable you to avoid the necessity of memorizing. You should first try to understand what each of the five income-output measures measures and the two alternative approaches to these measurements. Remembering the items to be added will then be much simpler.

In addition to explaining the two methods of computing the five income-output measures and each of the items used in the computation process, the chapter discusses the measurement of the price level in the economy. By measuring the price level, economists are able to determine how much inflation (an increase in the price level) or deflation (a decrease in the price level) has occurred in the economy. This information is important because income-output measures are expressed in monetary units, so if accurate comparisons are to be made between years, these monetary measures must be adjusted to take account of changes in the price level. A simple example is presented to show how a GDP price index or deflator is constructed and then the index is used to adjust nominal GDP to determine real GDP for comparison purposes. But, as the last section of the chapter points out, it is especially dangerous to assume that GDP is a good measure of the welfare of the society.

Chapter 7 is the essential background for Parts 2 and 3, which explain the history of and the factors that determine the level of domestic output and income in the economy. This chapter is important because it explains the several methods used to measure the performance of the economy in a given year and make the adjustments necessary to ensure accurate measurements of performance over time.

■ **CHECKLIST**

When you have studied this chapter you should be able to:

☐ Give a definition of the gross domestic product (GDP) and the gross national product (GNP).
☐ Identify the major difference between the GDP and GNP.
☐ Explain why GDP is a monetary measure.
☐ Discuss how GDP avoids double counting.
☐ Give examples of nonproductive transactions that are excluded from GDP.
☐ Describe the four basic expenditure components of GDP.
☐ Explain: (1) the difference between gross and net investment; (2) why changes in inventories are investment; and (3) the relationship between net investment and economic growth.

☐ Compute GDP using the expenditures approach when you are given national income accounting data.
☐ Identify the major income and nonincome allocations of GDP in the income approach to GDP.
☐ Describe the effect of net American income earned abroad on national income accounts.
☐ Compute GDP using the income approach when you are given national income accounting data.
☐ Define net domestic product (NDP), national income (NI), personal income (PI), and disposable income (DI).
☐ Compute NDP, NI, PI, and DI by two different methods when you are given the necessary data.
☐ Use Figure 7-2 in the text to describe the circular flow model as it relates to GDP.
☐ Explain how a price index or the GDP deflator is constructed.
☐ Calculate the GDP deflator or a price index when you are given the necessary price and quantity data.
☐ Find real GDP when you are given related data on nominal GDP and the price index.
☐ Present seven reasons why GDP may overstate or understate real output, and why it may not be a good measure of social welfare.

■ **CHAPTER OUTLINE**

1. National income accounting consists of concepts which enable those who use them to measure the economy's output, to compare it with past outputs, to explain its size and the reasons for changes in its size, and to formulate policies designed to increase it.

2. The market value of all final goods and services produced in the economy during the year is measured by the gross domestic product (GDP).
   a. A very similar measure to GDP is the gross national product (GNP).
   (1) The basic accounting difference between the two is that GDP *excludes* the market value of final output produced abroad by Americans and *includes* the market value of output produced domestically by foreign companies, whereas GNP accounting does the opposite; however, the GDP and GNP estimates of the size of the United States economy are virtually the same.
   (2) GDP replaced GNP as the chief measure of the output of the economy in 1992 because it is more comparable with the way most other nations measure the output of their economy.
   (3) Given its importance as the primary economic measure of the economy, GDP is the focus of discussion throughout the remainder of Chapter 7.
   b. GDP is measured in dollar terms rather than in terms of physical units of output.
   c. To avoid double counting, GDP includes only *final* goods and services (goods and services that will not be processed further during the *current* year).

   d. Nonproductive transactions are not included in GDP; purely financial transactions and second-hand sales are, therefore, excluded.
   e. Measurement of GDP can be accomplished by either the expenditures or the income method but the same result is obtained by the two methods.

3. Computation of the GDP by the expenditures method requires the addition of the total amounts of the four types of spending for final goods and services.
   a. Personal consumption expenditures (*C*) are the expenditures of households for durable and nondurable goods and for services.
   b. Gross private domestic investment (*I_g*) is the sum of the spending by business firms for machinery, equipment, and tools; spending by firms and households for new buildings; and the changes in the inventories of business firms.
   (1) A change in inventories is included in investment because it is the part of output of the economy which was not sold during the year.
   (2) Investment does not include expenditures for stocks or bonds or for second-hand capital goods.
   (3) Gross investment exceeds net investment by the value of the capital goods worn out during the year.
   (4) An economy in which net investment is positive (zero, negative) is an expanding (a static, a declining) economy.
   c. Government purchases (*G*) are the expenditures made by all governments in the economy for products produced by business firms and for resource services from households.
   d. Net exports (*X_n*) in an economy equal the expenditures made by foreigners for goods and services produced in the economy less the expenditures made by the consumers, governments, and investors of the economy for goods and services produced in foreign nations
   e. In symbols, $C + I_g + G + X_n = $ GDP

4. Computation of GDP by the income method requires the addition of the nine uses to which the income derived from the production and sales of final goods and services are put. These nine items are:
   a. Depreciation (consumption of fixed capital).
   b. Indirect business taxes.
   c. Compensation of employees (the sum of wages and salaries *and* wage and salary supplements).
   d. Rents.
   e. Interest (only the interest payments made by business firms are included and the interest payments made by government are excluded).
   f. Proprietors' income (the profits or net income of unincorporated firms).
   g. Corporate profits which are subdivided into:
   (1) Corporate income taxes
   (2) Dividends
   (3) Undistributed corporate profits

h. Adding these nine items together gives you GNP, not GDP. To obtain GDP, you must subtract net American income earned abroad from GNP.

5. In addition to GDP, four other national income measures are important in evaluating the performance of the economy. Each has a distinct definition and can be computed by making additions to or deductions from another measure.

　a. NDP is the annual output of final goods and services over and above the capital goods worn out during the year; and is equal to the GDP minus depreciation (consumption of fixed capital).

　b. NI is the total income ***earned*** by owners of land and capital and by the suppliers of labor and entrepreneurial ability during the year; and equals NDP *plus* net American income earned abroad, but *minus* indirect business taxes.

　c. PI is the total income ***received***—whether it is earned or unearned—by the households of the economy before the payment of personal taxes; and is found by ***adding*** transfer payments to and ***subtracting*** social security contributions, corporate income taxes, and undistributed corporate profits from the NI.

　d. DI is the total income available to households after the payment of personal taxes; and is equal to PI less personal taxes and also equal to personal consumption expenditures plus personal saving.

　e. The relations among the five income-output measures are summarized for you in Table 7-5.

　f. Figure 7-2 is a more realistic and complex circular flow diagram that shows the flows of expenditures and incomes among the households, business firms, and governments in the economy.

6. Because price levels change from year to year it is necessary to adjust the nominal GDP (or money GDP) computed for any year to obtain the real GDP before year-to-year comparisons between the outputs of final goods and services can be made.

　a. The price level is stated as an index number that measures the price ratio of a market basket of goods in a given year to a market basket of goods in a base year, and that ratio is multiplied by 100.

　b. Although there are many price indexes, the GDP price index or deflator is used to adjust GDP measures for changes in the price level.

　c. To adjust the GDP figures, divide the nominal GDP in any year by the price index for that year; the result is the adjusted or real GNP.

　d. When the price index in a year is below (above) the 100 it was in the base year the nominal GDP figure for that year is inflated (deflated) by this adjustment.

7. The GDP is not, for the following reasons, a measure of social welfare in the economy.

　a. It excludes the value of final goods and services not bought and sold in the markets of the economy.

　b. It excludes the amount of leisure the citizens of the economy are able to have.

　c. It does not record the improvements in the quality of products which occur over the years.

　d. It does not measure changes in the composition and the distribution of the domestic output.

　e. It is not a measure of per capita output because it does not take into account changes in the size of the economy's population.

　f. It does not record the pollution costs to the environment of producing final goods and services.

　g. It does not measure the market value of the final goods and services produced in the underground sector of the economy.

■ **IMPORTANT TERMS**

National income accounting	Net exports
Gross national product	Nonincome charges
Gross domestic product	Consumption of fixed capital (depreciation)
Final goods	Indirect business taxes
Intermediate goods	Compensation of employees
Double counting	
Value added	Wage and salary supplements
Nonproductive transaction	Net domestic product
Nonmarket transaction	National income
Expenditures approach	Personal income
Income approach	Disposable income
Personal consumption expenditures	Personal saving
Government purchases	Nominal GDP
Gross private domestic investment	Real GDP
Noninvestment transaction	Price index
	Base year
Net private domestic investment	Given year
	Inflating
Expanding economy	Deflating
Static economy	GDP deflator
Declining economy	

■ **FILL-IN QUESTIONS**

　1. National income accounting is valuable because it provides a means of keeping track of the level of

_____ in the economy and the course it has followed over the long run; and the information required to

devise and put into effect the public _____ that will improve the performance of the economy.

2. Gross domestic product and gross national product are monetary measures of all final goods and services produced during a year; to measure the value of these goods and services, the goods and services are valued at their

_____. The basic difference between the gross domestic product (GDP) and the gross national product (GNP) is that GDP (includes, excludes)

_____ the market value of final goods and services produced by foreign producers in the United States, whereas GNP accounting _____ it, and GDP

_____ the market value of final goods and services produced by Americans abroad, whereas GNP

_____ it.

3. In measuring GDP only final goods and services are included; if intermediate goods and services were included, the accountant would be _____

4. A firm buys materials for $2,000 from other firms in the economy and produces from them a product which sells for $3,015. The $1,115 is the _____ by the firm.

5. The total value added to a product at all stages of production equals the _____ value of the _____ product; and the total value added to all products produced in the economy during a year is the _____ product.

6. Personal consumption expenditures are the expenditures of households for _____ and _____ goods and for _____

7. Gross private domestic investment basically includes

_____,

_____,

and _____.
Net private domestic investment is less than gross private domestic investment by an amount equal to _____

_____

8. If gross private domestic investment is less than depreciation, net private domestic investment is (positive, zero, negative) _____ and the economy is (static, declining, expanding) _____

9. An economy's *net* exports equal its _____ _____ less its _____

10. In symbols, the GDP by the expenditures approach

= _____ + _____ + _____ + _____

11. The consumption of fixed capital and indirect business taxes, by the income approach, are referred to as

_____ charges or allocations.

12. The compensation of employees in the system of social accounting consists of actual wages and salaries *and*

wage and salary _____
The latter are the payments employers make to social

_____ programs and to _____ pension, health, and welfare funds.

13. Corporate profits are disposed of in three ways: ___

_____, _____,

and _____

14. Gross domestic product overstates the economy's net production because it fails to make allowance for that part of the output which replaces the _____ worn out or used up in producing the output. To compute the net domestic product it is, therefore, necessary to subtract the _____

_____

15. National income equals net domestic product plus

_____

and minus _____

16. Personal income:

a. equals national income plus _____ and minus the sum of _____,

_____,

and _____;

b. also equals _____

plus _____

plus _____

17. Disposable income:

a. equals personal income minus _____

_____;

b. also equals _____

_____

18. In order to compare the real gross domestic product in two different years, it is necessary to adjust the nominal GDP because _____

_____

a. A price index is the ratio of the price of a market basket of goods and services in a given year to

_____ in the base year, with the ratio being multiplied by 100.

b. The price index used to adjust nominal GDP for changes in the price level is called _____

c. Real GDP is calculated by dividing _____ GDP by the _____ (in hundredths).

19. For several reasons the GDP is not a measure of social welfare in an economy.

a. It does not include the _____ transactions that result in the production of goods and services or the amount of _____ enjoyed by the citizens of the economy.

b. It fails to record improvements in the _____ of the products produced, changes in the composition and distribution of the economy's total _____, the undesirable effects of producing the GDP upon the _____ of the economy, and the goods and services produced in the _____ economy.

c. And because it is a measure of the *total* output of the economy it does not measure the _____ output of the economy.

20. When the population of an economy grows at a more rapid rate than its real GDP grows, the standard of living in that economy (rises, falls, remains constant) _____

■ **PROBLEMS AND PROJECTS**

1. Below are national income accounting figures for the United States.

	Billions of dollars
Exports	$ 367
Dividends	60
Consumption of fixed capital	307
Wages and salaries	1442
Government purchases	577
Rents	33
Indirect business taxes	255
Wage and salary supplements	280
Gross private domestic investment	437
Corporate income taxes	88
Transfer payments	320
Interest	201
Proprietors' income	132
Personal consumption expenditures	1810
Imports	338
Social security contributions	148
Undistributed corporate profits	55
Personal taxes	372
Net American income earned abroad	0

a. Compute each of the following.

(1) Compensation of employees: $_____

(2) Net exports: $_____

(3) Net private domestic investment: $_____

b. Use any of these figures and any of your computations in (**a**) above to prepare in the table below an Income Statement for the Economy similar to the one found in Table 7-4 (on page 113 of the text).

Receipts: Expenditures approach		Allocations: Income approach
$_____		$_____
$_____		$_____
$_____		$_____
$_____		$_____
		$_____
		$_____
		$_____
		$_____
		$_____
		$_____
		$_____
Gross domestic product $_____		Gross domestic product $_____

c. In this economy:

(1) Net domestic product is $_____

(2) National income is $_____

(3) Personal income is $_____

(4) Disposable income is $_____

2. A farmer who owns a plot of ground sells the right to pump crude oil from his land to a crude-oil producer. The crude-oil producer agrees to pay the farmer $20 a barrel for every barrel pumped from the farmer's land.

a. During one year 10,000 barrels are pumped.

(1) The farmer receives a payment of $_____ from the crude-oil producer.

(2) The value added by the farmer is $_____

b. The crude-oil producer sells the 10,000 barrels pumped to a petroleum refiner at a price of $25 a barrel.

(1) The crude-oil producer receives a payment of $_____ from the refiner.

(2) The value added by the crude-oil producer is $_____

c. The refiner employs a pipeline company to transport the crude oil from the farmer's land to the refinery and pays the pipeline company a fee of $1 a barrel for the oil transported.

(1) The pipeline company receives a payment of $_____ from the refiner.

(2) The value added by the pipeline company is $_____

d. From the 10,000 barrels of crude oil the refiner produces 315,000 gallons of gasoline and various by-products which are sold to distributors and gasoline service stations at an average price of $1 per gallon.

(1) The total payment received by the refiner from its customers is $_____

(2) The value added by the refiner is $_____

e. The distributors and service stations sell the 315,000 gallons of gasoline and by-products to consumers at an average price of $1.30 a gallon.

(1) The total payment received by distributors and service stations is $_____

(2) The value added by them is $_____

f. The total value added by the farmer, crude-oil producer, pipeline company, refiner, and distributors and service stations is $_____ and the market value of the gasoline and by-products (the final good) is $_____

3. Below is a list of items which may or may not be included in the five income-output measures. Indicate in the space to the right of each which of the income-output measures includes this item; it is possible for the item to be included in none, one, two, three, four, or all of the measures. If the item is included in none of the measures, indicate why it is not included.

a. Interest on the national debt _____

b. The sale of a used computer _____

c. The production of shoes which are not sold by the manufacturer _____

d. The income of a bootlegger in a "dry" state _____

e. The purchase of a share of common stock on the New York Stock Exchange _____

f. The interest paid on the bonds of the General Motors Corporation _____

g. The labor performed by a homemaker _____

h. The labor performed by a paid baby-sitter _____

i. The monthly check received by an idler from his rich aunt _____

j. The purchase of a new tractor by a farmer _____

k. The labor performed by an assembly-line worker in repapering his own kitchen _____

l. The services of a lawyer _____

m. The purchase of shoes from the manufacturer by a shoe retailer _____

n. The monthly check received from the Social Security Administration by a college student whose parents have died _____

o. The rent a homeowner would receive if she did not live in her own home _____

4. Below is hypothetical data for a market basket of goods in year 1 and year 2 for an economy.

a. Compute the expenditures for year 1.

Market Basket for Year 1 (base year)

Products	Quantity	Price	Expenditures
Toys	3	$10	$____
Pencils	5	2	$____
Books	7	5	$____
Total			$____

b. Compute the expenditures for year 2.

Market Basket for Year 2

Products	Quantity	Price	Expenditures
Toys	3	$11	$____
Pencils	5	3	$____
Books	7	6	$____
Total			$____

c. In the space below, show how you computed the GDP price index for year 2.

_____.

5. In the table below are nominal GDP figures for three years and the price indices for each of the three years. (The GDP figures are in billions.)

Year	Nominal GDP	Price index	Real GDP
1929	$104	121	$____
1933	56	91	$____
1939	91	100	$____

a. Which of the three years appears to be the base year? _____

b. Between:

(1) 1929 and 1933 the economy experienced (inflation, deflation) _____

Handwritten notes at top:

GDP − CFC = NDP.

NI = NDP + NAIEA − IBT − UCP + TP

PI = NI − SS − CIT

DI = PI − PT.

(2) 1933 and 1939 it experienced _____

c. Use the price indices to compute the real GDP in each year. (You may round your answers to the nearest billion dollars.)

d. The nominal GDP figure:

(1) for 1929 was (deflated, inflated, neither) _____

_____

(2) for 1933 was _____

(3) for 1939 was _____

e. The price level:

(1) fell by _____% from 1929 to 1933.

(2) rose by _____% from 1933 to 1939.

■ **SELF-TEST**

Circle the T if the statement is true; the F if it is false.

1. Gross domestic product measures at their market values the total output of all goods and services produced in the economy during a year. **T** (**F**)

2. The gross domestic product (GDP) is equal to the gross national product (GNP) when net American income earned abroad is subtracted from GNP. (**T**) **F**

3. The total market value of the wine produced in the United States during a year is equal to the number of bottles of wine produced in that year multiplied by the (average) price at which a bottle sold during that year. (**T**) **F**

4. The total value added to a product and the value of the final product are equal. (**T**) **F**

5. The two approaches to the measurement of the gross domestic product yield identical results because one approach measures the total amount spent on the products produced by business firms during a year while the second approach measures the total income of business firms during the year. **T** (**F**)

6. In computing gross domestic product, net domestic product, and national income by the expenditures approach, transfer payments are excluded because they do not represent payments for currently produced goods and services. (**T**) **F**

7. The expenditure made by a household to have a new home built for it is a personal consumption expenditure. **T** (**F**)

8. In national income accounting any increase in the inventories of business firms is included in gross private domestic investment. (**T**) **F**

9. If gross private domestic investment is greater than depreciation during a given year, the economy has declined during that year. **T** (**F**)

10. The net exports of an economy equal its exports of goods and services less its imports of goods and services. (**T**) **F**

The data in the following table should be used to answer true-false questions 11 through 14.

Handwritten: GDP = 305   NDP = 298

	Billions of dollars
Net private domestic investment *(hw: G. = 32+7 = 39)*	$ 32
Personal taxes	39
Transfer payments	19
Indirect business taxes	8
Corporate income taxes	11
Personal consumption expenditures	217
Consumption of fixed capital	7
United States exports	15
Dividends	15
Government purchases	51
Net American income earned abroad	0
Undistributed corporate profits	10
Social security contributions	4
United States imports	17

Handwritten: NI = NDP − IBT = 290

11. The stock of capital goods in the economy has expanded. (**T**) **F**

12. Gross private domestic investment is equal to $25 billion. **T** (**F**)

13. National income equals the net domestic product minus $8 billion. (**T**) **F**

14. Disposable income is equal to $245 billion. (**T**) **F**

15. Comparison of a gross domestic product with the gross domestic product of an earlier year when the price level has risen between the two years necessitates the "inflation" of the GDP figure in the later year. **T** (**F**)

16. To adjust nominal gross domestic product for a given year, it is necessary to divide nominal GDP by the price index—expressed in hundredths—for that year. (**T**) **F**

17. The consumer price index (CPI) is the price index used to adjust nominal GDP to measure real GDP. **T** (**F**)

18. The GDP is a good measure of the social welfare of society. **T** (**F**)

19. The productive services of a homemaker are included in GDP. **T** (**F**)

20. The spillover costs from pollution and other activities associated with the production of the GDP are deducted from total output. **T** (**F**)

Circle the letter that corresponds to the best answer.

1. Which of the following is *not* an important use for national income accounting?

(a) it provides a basis for formulation and application

of policies designed to improve the economy's performance

(b) it permits measurement of the economic efficiency of the economy

(c) it makes possible an estimate of the output of final goods and services in the economy

(d) it enables the economist to chart the growth or decline of the economy over a period of time

2. To include the value of the parts used in producing the automobiles turned out during a year in gross domestic product for that year would be an example of:

(a) including a nonmarket transaction

(b) including a nonproductive transaction

(c) including a noninvestment transaction

(d) double counting

3. Which of the following is *not* a purely financial transaction?

(a) the sale of a used (second-hand) ironing board at a garage sale

(b) the sale of shares of stock in the United States Steel Corporation

(c) the payment of social-security benefits to a retired worker

(d) the birthday gift of a check for $5 sent by a grandmother to her grandchild

4. The sale in 1993 of an automobile produced in 1992 would not be included in the gross domestic product for 1993; doing so would involve:

(a) including a nonmarket transaction

(b) including a nonproductive transaction

(c) including a noninvestment transaction

(d) double counting

5. The service a baby-sitter performs when she stays at home with her baby brother while her parents are out and for which she receives no payment is not included in the gross domestic product because:

(a) this is a nonmarket transaction

(b) this is a nonproductive transction

(c) this is a noninvestment transaction

(d) double counting would be involved

6. Which of the following does *not* represent investment?

(a) an increase in the quantity of shoes on the shelves of a shoe store

(b) the construction of a house which will be occupied by its owner

(c) the purchase of newly issued shares of stock in the General Motors Corporation

(d) the construction of a factory building using money borrowed from a bank

7. A refrigerator is produced by its manufacturer in 1992, sold during 1992 to a retailer, and sold by the retailer to a final consumer in 1993. The refrigerator was:

(a) counted as consumption in 1992

(b) counted as investment in 1993

(c) counted as investment in 1992

(d) not included in the gross domestic product of 1992

8. GDP in an economy is $3,452 billion. Consumer expenditures are $2,343 billion, government purchases are $865, and gross investment is $379 billion. Net exports are:

(a) + $93 billion $GDP = C + G + I + Z$

(b) + $123 billion

(c) − $45 billion

(d) − $135 billion

9. The annual charge which estimates the amount of capital equipment used up in each year's production is called:

(a) indirect business taxes

(b) inventory reduction

(c) depreciation

(d) investment

10. The income approach to GDP sums the total income earned by resource suppliers, subtracts the net American income earned abroad, and then adds two nonincome charges:

(a) net investment and the consumption of fixed capital

(b) the consumption of fixed capital and indirect business taxes

(c) indirect business taxes and undistributed corporate profits

(d) undistributed corporate profits and financial transactions

Questions 11 through 17 use the national income accounting data given in the table in the true-false section.

11. The nonincome charges are equal to:

(a) $11 billion

(b) $15 billion

(c) $17 billion

(d) $19 billion

$7 + 5$
$IBT + CFC$
Indirect Business Tax
+ Consumption of Fixed Capital

12. Corporate profits are equal to:

(a) $15 billion

(b) $25 billion

(c) $26 billion

(d) $36 billion

$CT + D + NDCP$

13. Net exports are equal to:

(a) − $2 billion

(b) $2 billion

(c) − $32 billion

(d) $32 billion

14. The gross domestic product is equal to:

(a) $298 billion

(b) $302 billion

(c) $317 billion

(d) $305 billion

15. The net domestic product is equal to:
(a) $298 billion
(b) $302 billion
(c) $317 billion
(d) $321 billion

16. National income exceeds personal income by:
(a) $6 billion
(b) $15 billion
(c) $21 billion
(d) $44 billion

17. Personal saving is equal to:
(a) − $28 billion
(b) − $8 billion
(c) $8 billion
(d) $28 billion

18. If both nominal gross domestic product and the level of prices are rising, it is evident that:
(a) real GDP is constant
(b) real GDP is rising but not so rapidly as prices
(c) real GDP is declining
(d) no conclusion can be drawn concerning the real GDP of the economy on the basis of this information

19. Suppose nominal GDP rose from $500 billion to $600 billion while the GDP deflator increased from 125 to 150. The real GDP
(a) remained constant
(b) increased
(c) decreased
(d) cannot be calculated from these figures

20. In an economy, the total expenditures for a market basket of goods in year 1 (the base year) was $4,000 billion. In year 2, the total expenditure for the same market basket of goods was $4,500 billion. What was the GDP price index for the economy in year 2?
(a) .88
(b) 1.13
(c) 188
(d) 113

21. Nominal GDP is less than real GDP in an economy in year 1. In year 2, nominal GDP is equal to real GDP. In year 3, nominal GDP is slightly greater than real GDP. In year 4, nominal GDP is significantly greater than real GDP. Which year is most likely to be the base year that is being used to calculate the price index for this economy?
(a) 1
(b) 2
(c) 3
(d) 4

22. Nominal GDP was $3,774 billion in year 1 and the GDP deflator was 108 and nominal GNP was $3,989 in year 2 and the GDP deflator that year was 112. What was real GDP in years 1 and 2, respectively?

(a) $3,494 billion and $3,562 billion
(b) $3,339 billion and $3,695 billion
(c) $3,595 billion and $3,725 billion
(d) $3,643 billion and $3,854 billion

23. A price index one year was 145, and the next year it was 167. What is the approximate percentage change in the price level from one year to the next as measured by that index?
(a) 12%
(b) 13%
(c) 14%
(d) 15%

24. The GDP includes:
(a) the goods and services produced in the underground economy
(b) expenditures for equipment to reduce the pollution of the environment
(c) the value of the leisure enjoyed by citizens
(d) the goods and services produced but not bought and sold in the markets of the economy

25. Changes in the real GDP from one year to the next do **not** reflect:
(a) changes in the quality of the goods and services produced
(b) changes in the size of the population of the economy
(c) changes in the average length of the workweek
(d) any of the above changes

■ **DISCUSSION QUESTIONS**

1. Of what use is national income accounting to the economist and to the policymakers in the economy?

2. Why is GDP a monetary measure, and why is it necessary that it be a monetary measure? How does GDP differ from GNP? Explain.

3. Why does GDP exclude nonproductive transactions? What are the two principal types of nonproductive transactions? List some examples of each.

4. Why are there two ways, both of which yield the same answers, of computing GDP, NDP, etc.?

5. Why are transfer payments excluded from GNP, NNP, and NI?

6. Is residential construction counted as investment or consumption? Why? Why is a change in inventories an investment?

7. How do you define a static, an expanding, and a declining economy? What is the relationship between gross private domestic investment and the capital consumption allowance in these three economies?

8. What is meant by a nonincome charge or allocation? What are the two principal nonincome charges included in GDP? Why are they excluded from NI?

9. What are the basic differences between the GDP deflator and the consumer price index (CPI)? Why do economists use the GDP deflator to adjust GDP figures?

10. Why do economists find it necessary to inflate and deflate GDP when comparing GDP in different years? How do they do this?

11. Why is GDP not a measure of the social welfare of society?

■ **ANSWERS**

Chapter 7 Measuring Domestic Output, National Income, and the Price Level

FILL-IN QUESTIONS

1. production, policies

2. market prices, includes, excludes, excludes, includes

3. double counting

4. value added

5. market, final, gross domestic

6. durable, nondurable (either order), services

7. all final purchases of machinery, tools, and equipment by business firms; all construction; changes in inventories; the consumption of fixed capital

8. negative, declining

9. exports, imports

10. C, I_g, G, X_n

11. nonincome

12. supplements, insurance, private

13. corporate income taxes, dividends, undistributed corporate profits

14. capital goods, consumption of fixed capital

15. net American income earned abroad, indirect business taxes

16. *a.* transfer payments, social security contributions, corporate income taxes, undistributed corporate profits; *b.* personal consumption expenditures, personal taxes, personal saving

17. *a.* personal taxes; *b.* personal consumption expenditures plus personal saving

18. the price level changes *a.* the price of the same market basket; *b.* GDP deflator; *c.* nominal, price index

19. *a.* nonmarket, leisure; *b.* quality, output, environment, underground; *c.* per capita

20. falls

PROBLEMS AND PROJECTS

1. *a.* (1) 1722, (2) 29, (3) 130; *b.* see table in the next column; *c.* (1) 2546, (2) 2291, (3) 2320, (4) 1948

2. *a.* (1) 200,000, (2) 200,000; *b.* (1) 250,000, (2) 50,000; *c.* (1)

Receipts: Expenditures approach		Allocations: Income approach	
Personal consumption expenditures	$1810	Consumption of fixed capital	$ 307
Gross private domestic investment	437	Indirect business taxes	255
Government purchases	577	Compensation of employees	1722
Net exports	29	Rents	33
		Interest	201
		Proprietors' income	132
		Corporate income taxes	88
		Dividends	60
		Undistributed corporate profit	55
		Net American income earned abroad	0
Gross domestic product	2853	Gross domestic product	2853

10,000, (2) 10,000; *d.* (1) 315,000, (2) 55,000; *e.* (1) 409,500, (2) 94,500; *f.* 409,500, 409,500

3. *a.* personal income and disposable income, a public transfer payment; *b.* none; a second-hand sale; *c.* all, represents investment (additions to inventories); *d.* all, illegal production and incomes are included when known; *e.* none, a purely financial transaction; *f.* all; *g.* none, a nonmarket transaction; *h.* all; *i.* none, a private transfer payment; *j.* all; *k.* none, a nonmarket transaction; *l.* all; *m.* all, represents additions to the inventory of the retailer; *n.* personal income and disposable income, a public transfer payment; *o.* all; estimate of rental value of owner-occupied homes is included in rents as if it were income and in personal consumption expenditures as if it were payment for a service

4. *a.* 30, 10, 35, 75; *b.* 33, 15, 42, 90; *c.* ($90/$75) 100 = 120

5. *a.* 1939; *b.* (1) deflation, (2) inflation; *c.* 86, 62, 91; *d.* (1) deflated, (2) inflated, (3) neither; *e.* (1) 24.8 (2) 9.9

SELF-TEST

1. F, p. 106	8. T, p. 110	15. F, p. 119
2. T, pp. 115, 106	9. F, pp. 111–112	16. T, p. 121
3. T, pp. 107–108	10. T, pp. 112–113	17. F, p. 121
4. T, pp. 107–108	11. T, pp. 110–111	18. F, pp. 122–123
5. F, pp. 108–109	12. F, pp. 110–111	19. F, p. 123
6. T, pp. 110–111	13. T, p. 116	20. F, p. 124
7. F, p. 110	14. T, p. 117	

1. *b*, p. 106	10. *b*, p. 113	18. *d*, pp. 120–121
2. *d*, pp. 107–108	11. *b*, pp. 113–114	19. *a*, p. 121
3. *a*, p. 108	12. *d*, pp. 114–115	20. *d*, p. 120
4. *b*, p. 110	13. *a*, pp. 112–113	21. *b*, p. 122
5. *a*, pp. 108, 123	14. *d*, p. 115	22. *a*, p. 122
6. *c*, pp. 108, 110	15. *a*, p. 116	23. *d*, pp. 120–121
7. *c*, p. 110	16. *a*, pp. 116–117	24. *b*, pp. 122–125
8. *d*, p. 113	17. *d*, p. 117	25. *d*, pp. 123–125
9. *c*, pp. 113–114		

DISCUSSION QUESTIONS

1. p. 106	5. p. 108	9. p. 119
2. pp. 106–107	6. p. 110	10. pp. 121–122
3. p. 108	7. p. 111	11. pp. 122–125
4. pp. 108–109	8. pp. 113–114	

CHAPTER 8

Macroeconomic Instability: Unemployment and Inflation

In the last chapter you learned how to define and how to compute the gross and net domestic product and domestic, personal, and disposable income in any year. This chapter begins the explanation of what determines how large each of these five income-output measures will tend to be. In the chapters that follow you will learn what causes the income and output of the economy to be what they are, what causes them to change, and how they might be controlled for the welfare of society.

Chapter 8 is concerned with the instability of the American economy or with what is commonly called the business cycle: the ups and downs in the employment of labor and the real output of the economy that occur over the years. That there have been expansions and contractions in economic (or business) activity since the end of the American Civil War is evident from even a casual look at American economic history. What is not immediately evident, however, is that these alternating and relatively short periods of prosperity and "hard times" have taken place over a longer period in which the trends in output, employment, and the standard of living have been upward. During this long history booms and busts have occurred quite irregularly; and their duration and intensity have been so varied that it is better to think of economic instability than of business cycles.

There are two principal problems that result from the instability of the economy—from the business cycle. After a brief look in the first major section of the chapter at the business cycle, its phases, and its impact on the production of different kinds of goods, Professors McConnell and Brue turn to the first of these two problems in the second major section. Here you will find an examination of the unemployment that accompanies a downturn in the level of economic activity in the economy. You will discover that there are three different kinds of unemployment, that full employment means about 5% to 6% of the labor force is unemployed, and that there are at least three problems encountered in measuring the percentage of the labor force actually unemployed at any time. That unemployment has an economic cost and that this cost is unequally distributed among different sectors of our society you will also learn; and you probably won't be too surprised to dis-

cover that widespread unemployment can be the cause of other social problems.

The second of the two problems that result from economic instability is inflation and it is examined in the remainder of the chapter. Inflation is an increase in the general (or average) level of prices in an economy. It does not have a unique cause: it may result from increases in demand; from increases in costs; or from both. But regardless of its cause, it works a real hardship on certain sectors within the economy. If it occurs at too rapid a rate it may bring about a severe breakdown in the economy.

One last word. The thing to keep your eye on when you consider economic fluctuations and unemployment and inflation in the American economy is the changes in aggregate expenditures which can occur because consumers, business firms, or the public sector decide to spend more or less for goods and services.

■ CHECKLIST

When you have finished this chapter you should be able to:

☐ Explain what is meant by the business cycle.
☐ Describe the four phases of an idealized business cycle.
☐ Identify the two types of noncyclical fluctuations.
☐ Identify the "immediate determinant" or cause of the levels of output and employment.
☐ Distinguish between the impact of cyclical fluctuations on industries producing capital and consumer durable goods and on those producing consumer nondurable goods; and on high- and low-concentration industries.
☐ Distinguish between frictional, structural, and cyclical unemployment, and explain the causes of these three kinds of unemployment.
☐ Define full employment and the full-employment unemployment rate (the natural rate of unemployment).
☐ Describe the process employed (by the Bureau of Labor Statistics) to measure the rate of unemployment; and list the three criticisms of the BLS data.

☐ Identify the economic cost of unemployment and three groups that bear the unequal burdens of unemployment.
☐ Define the GDP gap and state Okun's law.
☐ Define inflation and the rate of inflation.
☐ Make international comparisons of inflation rate and unemployment rate data.
☐ Define demand-pull inflation and explain its effects in ranges 1, 2, and 3 of a price level and real domestic output graph.
☐ Define cost-push inflation and its relation to per unit production costs.
☐ Identify two types of cost-push or supply-side inflation.
☐ Distinguish between real and nominal income and calculate real income when given data on nominal income and the price level.
☐ List three groups that are hurt by and two groups that benefit from unanticipated inflation.
☐ Describe how the redistributive effects of inflation are changed when it is anticipated.
☐ Present three scenarios that describe the possible effects of inflation on real output and employment.

■ CHAPTER OUTLINE

1. The history of the American economy is a record of exceptional economic growth.
   a. But this growth has been accompanied by periods of inflation, of depression, and of both.
   b. The business cycle means alternating periods of prosperity and depression. These recurrent periods of ups and downs in employment, output, and prices are irregular in their duration and intensity; but the typical pattern is peak, recession, trough, and recovery to another peak.
   c. Changes in the levels of output and employment are largely the result of changes in the level of aggregate spending or demand in the economy.
   d. Not all changes in employment and output which occur in the economy are cyclical; some are due to seasonal and secular influences.
   e. The business cycle affects almost the entire economy, but it does not affect all parts in the same way and to the same degree: the production of capital and durable consumer goods fluctuates more than the production of consumer nondurable goods during the cycle because
   (1) the purchase of capital and durable consumer goods can be postponed, and
   (2) the industries producing these goods are largely dominated by a few large firms that hold prices constant and let output decline when demand falls.

2. Full employment does not mean that all workers in the labor force are employed and that there is no unemployment; some unemployment is normal.

   a. There are at least three kinds of unemployment.
   (1) There is always some frictional unemployment; and this kind of unemployment is generally desirable.
   (2) And in addition there is the structural unemployment that is the result of changes in technology and in the types of goods and services consumers wish to buy.
   (3) Cyclical unemployment is the result of insufficient aggregate demand in the economy.
   b. Because some frictional and structural unemployment is unavoidable, the full-employment unemployment rate (the natural rate of unemployment) is the sum of frictional and structural unemployment; is achieved when cyclical unemployment is zero (the real output of the economy is equal to its potential output); and is about 5% to 6% of the labor force.
   c. Surveying 60,000 households each month, the Bureau of Labor Statistics finds the unemployment rate by dividing the number of persons in the labor force who are unemployed by the number of persons in the labor force; but the figures collected in the survey have been criticized for at least three reasons.
   d. Unemployment has an economic cost.
   (1) The economic cost is the unproduced output (or the GDP gap), and Okun's law is that for every 1% the actual unemployment rate exceeds the natural rate of unemployment there is 2.5% GDP gap.
   (2) This cost is unequally distributed among different groups of workers in the labor force.
   e. Unemployment also leads to serious social problems.

3. Over its history the American economy has experienced not only periods of unemployment but periods of inflation.
   a. Inflation is an increase in the general level of prices in the economy; and a decline in the level of prices is deflation.
   b. The rate of inflation in any year is equal to the percentage change in the price index between that year and the preceding year; and the rule of 70 can be used to calculate the number of years it will take for the price level to double at any given rate of inflation.
   c. There are at least two causes of inflation; and these two causes may operate separately or simultaneously to raise the price level.
   (1) Demand-pull inflation is the result of excess aggregate demand in the economy; and while increases in aggregate demand do not increase the price level when the unemployment rate is high (in a depression) they do bring about inflation as the economy nears and reaches full employment.
   (2) Cost-push or supply-side inflation is the result of factors that raise per unit production costs. This average cost is found by dividing the total cost of the resource inputs by the amount produced. There are two

variants that explain this rise in costs: (a) excessive wage increases that push up unit costs; and (b) a supply shock from an increase in the prices of resource inputs. With cost-push inflation, output and employment are declining as the price level rises.

4. Even if the total output of the economy did not change, inflation would arbitrarily redistribute real income and wealth; and would benefit some groups and hurt other groups in the economy.

   a. Whether someone benefits or is hurt by inflation is measured by what happens to real income. Inflation injures those whose real income falls and benefits those whose real income rises.

(1) Real income is determined by dividing nominal income by the price level expressed in hundredths; and

(2) the percentage change in real income can be approximated by subtracting the percentage change in the price level from the percentage change in nominal income.

   b. It also injures savers because it decreases the real value of any savings the money value of which is fixed.

   c. And it benefits debtors and hurts creditors because it lowers the real value of debts.

   d. But when the inflation is anticipated and people can adjust their nominal incomes to reflect the expected rise in the price level the redistribution of income and wealth is lessened.

   e. Since World War II inflation in the United States has redistributed wealth from the household to the public sector of the economy.

   f. In short, inflation acts to tax some groups and to subsidize other groups.

5. Inflation may also affect the total output of the economy but economists disagree over whether it is likely to expand or contract total output.

   a. Mild demand-pull inflation seems likely to expand output and employment in the economy.

   b. Cost-push inflation is apt to contract output and employment.

   c. And hyperinflation may well lead to the breakdown of the economy.

■ **IMPORTANT TERMS**

Business cycle
Peak
Recession
Trough
Recovery
Seasonal variation
Secular trend
Frictional unemployment
Structural unemployment
Cyclical unemployment
Full employment
Full-employment unemployment rate
Natural rate of unemployment
Potential output
Unemployment rate
Labor force
Discouraged workers
GDP gap
Okun's law
Inflation
Deflation
Rule of 70
Demand-pull inflation
Cost-push inflation
Per unit production cost
Nominal income
Real income
Cost-of-living adjustment (COLA)
Anticipated inflation
Unanticipated inflation
Nominal interest rate
Real interest rate
Hyperinflation

■ **FILL-IN QUESTIONS**

1. The history of the American economy is one of (steady, unsteady) _____ economic growth; and at times its growth has been accompanied by _____ and at other times its expansion has been interrupted by low levels of _____ and _____

2. The business cycle is a term which means the recurrent _____ and _____ in the level of business activity in the economy; and the four phases of a typical business cycle are peak, _____ _____, _____, and _____

3. The basic determinant of the levels of employment and output in an economy is the level of total _____ or aggregate _____ in the economy.

4. In addition to the changes brought about by the operation of the business cycle, noncyclical fluctuations in output and employment may be due to _____ variations and to a _____ trend.

5. Production and employment in the (durable, nondurable) _____ and (capital, consumer) _____ goods industries are affected to a greater extent by the expansion and contraction of the economy than they are in the _____ goods industries; and prices vary to a greater extent in the (low-, high-) _____ concentration industries.

6. The three types of unemployment are:

   a. _____

   b. _____

   c. _____

7. The full-employment unemployment rate is:

   a. sometimes called the _____ rate of unemployment;

   b. equal to the total of the _____ and the _____ unemployment in the economy;

   c. realized when the _____ unemployment in the economy is equal to zero and when the _____ output of the economy is equal to its _____ output; and

   d. assumed in this chapter to be about _____%.

8. When the economy achieves its natural rate of unemployment the number of job seekers is (greater than, less than, equal to) _____ the number of job vacancies; and the price level is (rising, falling, constant) _____

9. The unemployment **rate** is found by dividing _____
_____
by the _____

10. The GDP gap is equal to _____ GDP **minus** _____ GDP; and for every percentage point the unemployment rate rises above the natural rate the GDP gap will, according to Okun's law, (increase, decrease) _____ by ____%.

11. The burdens of unemployment are borne more heavily by (black, white) _____, (adult, teenage) _____, and (white-collar, blue-collar) _____ workers; and the percentage of the labor force unemployed for 15 or more weeks is (greater, less) ____ than the unemployment rate.

12. Inflation means a _____ in the general level of _____ in the economy; and the rate of inflation in year 1993 is equal to the price index for year _____ less the price index for year

_____ all divided by the price index for year _____

13. To find the approximate number of years it takes the price level to double you divide the percentage _____ into _____. This approximation is called the _____

14. Since the 1920s, the experience of the United States with inflation has varied.

   a. The price level decreased during the early years of the Great Depression, which means there was _____ occurring in the economy.

   b. The post–World War II period (1945–1948) was characterized by (high, low) ____ rates of inflation, the 1961–1965 period was a period of ____ inflation, and the mid-to-late 1970s was a period of ____ inflation for the United States.

   c. Compared with other industrialized countries, the rate of inflation in the United States during the 1980s has neither been usually _____.

15. The basic cause of:

   a. demand-pull inflation is (an increase, a decrease) _____ in aggregate demand;

   b. cost-push inflation is explained in terms of factors that raise _____. Two sources of cost-push inflation are increases in _____ and increases in _____

   c. In practice, it is (easy, difficult) _____ to distinguish the two types of inflation.

16. The amount of goods and services one's nominal income can buy is called _____

   a. If one's nominal income rises by 10% and the price level rose by 7%, the percentage increase in _____ _____ would be _____

   b. If nominal income was $30,000 and the price index, expressed in hundredths, was 1.06, then _____ _____ would be _____

17. Inflation:

   a. hurts those whose nominal incomes are relatively (fixed, flexible) _____

   b. penalizes savers when the inflation is (expected, unexpected) _____

   c. hurts (creditors, debtors) _____ and benefits _____

d. has since World War II shifted wealth from (the public sector, households) _____

to _____

18. The redistributive effects of inflation are less severe when it is (anticipated, unanticipated) _____

a. Clauses in labor contracts that call for automatic adjustments of workers' income from the effects of inflation are called _____

b. The percentage increase in purchasing power that the lender receives from the borrower is the (real rate of interest, nominal rate of interest) _____; the percentage increase in money that the lender receives is the _____

19. Despite considerable disagreement and uncertainty among economists it seems that:

a. demand-pull inflation, unless there is full employment in the economy, will (increase, decrease) _____ _____ total output and employment;

b. cost-push inflation will _____ output and employment in the economy;

c. hyperinflation may bring about an economic _____ _____

■ **PROBLEMS AND PROJECTS**

1. In the table below are statistics showing the labor force and total employment during year 1 and year 5. Make the computations necessary to complete the table. (Numbers of persons are in thousands.)

	Year 1	Year 5
Labor force	84,889	95,453
Employed	80,796	87,524
Unemployed	_____	_____
Unemployment rate	_____	_____

a. How is it possible that *both* employment and unemployment increased? _____

b. In relative terms, if unemployment increases employment will decrease? Why? _____

c. Would you say that year 5 was a year of full employment? _____

d. Why is the task of maintaining full employment over the years more than just a problem of finding jobs for those who happen to be employed at any given time?

_____

2. Suppose that in 1993 an economy is at full employment, has a potential and actual real GDP of $3,000 billion, and has an unemployment rate of 6%.

a. Compute the GDP gap in 1993 and enter it in the table below.

Year	Potential GDP	Actual GDP	GDP gap
1993	$3000	$3000	$_____
1994	3800	3705	_____
1995	4125	3712.5	_____

b. The potential and actual real GDPs in 1994 and 1995 are also shown in the table. Compute and enter into the table the GDP gaps in these two years.

c. In 1994 the actual real GDP is _____% of the potential real GDP. (*Hint:* divide the actual real GDP by the potential real GDP.)

(1) The actual real GDP is _____% *less* than the potential real GDP.
(2) Using Okun's law, the unemployment rate will rise from 6% in 1993 and be _____% in 1994.

d. In 1995 the actual real GDP is _____% of the potential real GDP.

(1) The actual real GDP is _____% *less* than the potential real GDP.
(2) The unemployment rate, according to Okun's law, will be _____%.

3. The table below shows the price index in the economy at the end of four different years.

Year	Price index	Rate of inflation
1	100.00	
2	112.00	_____%
3	123.20	_____
4	129.36	_____

a. Compute and enter in the table the rates of inflation in years 2, 3, and 4.
b. Employing the "rule of 70," how many years would it take for the price level to double at each of these three inflation rates? _____

_____

c. If nominal income increased by 15% from year 1 to year 2, what was the approximate percentage change in real income? _____

d. If nominal income increased by 7% from year 2 to year 3, what was the approximate percentage change in real income? _____

e. If nominal income was $25,000 in year 2, what was real income that year? _____

f. If nominal income was $25,000 in year 3, what was real income that year? _____

g. If the nominal interest rate was 14% to borrow money from year 1 to year 2, what was the approximate real rate of interest over that period? _____

h. If the nominal interest rate was 8% to borrow money from year 3 to year 4, what was the approximate real rate of interest over that period? _____

4. Indicate in the space to the right of each of the following the most likely effect—beneficial (B), detrimental (D), or indeterminate (I)—of unanticipated inflation on these persons:

a. A retired business executive who now lives each month by spending a part of the amount that was saved and deposited in a savings and loan association.

_____

b. A retired private-school teacher who lives on the dividends received from the shares of stock owned.

_____

c. A farmer who (by mortgaging a farm) borrowed at the local bank $500,000 that must be repaid during the next ten years. _____

d. A retired couple whose sole source of income is the pension they receive from a former employer.

_____

e. A widow whose income consists entirely of interest received from the corporate bonds she owns.

_____

f. A public school teacher. _____

g. A member of union who works for a firm that produces computers. _____

5. In the space below, indicate for each of the following situations the effects of an increase in total spending on *real GDP*, *nominal GDP*, the *unemployment rate*, and the *price level*, respectively, using the following symbols: A, little or no effect; B, increase; C, decrease; and D, sharp increase.

a. Depression and widespread unemployment

_____ _____ _____ _____

b. Prosperity, but moderate unemployment

_____ _____ _____ _____

c. Prosperity and full employment

_____ _____ _____ _____

6. On the graph below and the graph on the next page the price *level* is measured along the vertical axis and real *national* output is measured along the horizontal axis. The demand for and the supply of domestic output are shown by the curves labeled **D** and **S**.

a. Applying the principles of demand and supply which you learned in Chapter 4, the equilibrium price level is the price level at which the domestic output demanded

and the domestic output supplied are _____

and the equilibrium domestic output is _____

_____

b. Draw on the first graph a new demand curve which represents an *increase* in the demand for domestic output.

Real domestic output

(1) The effect of this increase in demand is a rise in the equilibrium price level and a(n) _____ in the equilibrium domestic output.

(2) This rise in the price level is an example of _____

_____ inflation.

c. On the graph on the next page draw a new supply curve which represents a *decrease* in the supply of domestic output.

(1) The effect of this decrease in supply is a _____ in the equilibrium price level and a _____ in the equilibrium domestic output.

(2) These effects are an example of _____

_____

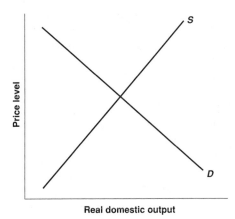

Real domestic output

■ **SELF-TEST**

Circle the T if the statement is true; the F if it is false.

1. The American economy has experienced a long period of substantial economic growth and shorter periods of inflation and of high employment. Ⓣ F

2. The business cycle is best defined as alternating periods of increases and decreases in the rate of inflation in the economy. T Ⓕ

3. Individual business cycles tend to be of roughly equal duration and intensity. T Ⓕ

4. Not all changes which occur in output and employment in the economy are due to the business cycle. Ⓣ F

5. Industries which are highly concentrated show small relative decreases in output and large relative decreases in prices during a downswing of the business cycle. T Ⓕ

6. Frictional unemployment is not only inevitable but largely desirable. Ⓣ F

7. The essential difference between frictionally and structurally unemployed workers is that the former **do not have** and the latter **do have** salable skills. T Ⓕ

8. When the number of people seeking employment is less than the number of job vacancies in the economy the actual rate of unemployment is less than the natural rate of unemployment and the price level will tend to rise. Ⓣ F

9. If unemployment in the economy is at its natural rate, the actual and potential outputs of the economy are equal. Ⓣ F

10. The natural rate of unemployment in the American economy is a constant 6% of the labor force. T Ⓕ

11. An economy cannot produce an actual real GDP that exceeds its potential real GDP. T Ⓕ

12. The unemployment rate is equal to the number of persons in the labor force divided by the number of people who are unemployed. T Ⓕ

13. The percentage of the labor force unemployed for fifteen or more weeks is always less than the unemployment rate and tends to rise during a recession. Ⓣ F

14. The economy's GDP gap is measured by deducting its actual GDP from its potential GDP. Ⓣ F

15. The economic cost of cyclical unemployment is the goods and services that are not produced. Ⓣ F

16. Inflation is defined as an increase in the total output of an economy. T Ⓕ

17. From one year to the next the consumer price index rose from 311.1 to 322.2. The rate of inflation was, therefore, 5.6%. T Ⓕ

18. If the price level increases by 10% each year the price level will double every ten years. T Ⓕ

19. With a moderate amount of unemployment in the economy, an increase in aggregate spending will generally increase both the price level and the output of the economy. Ⓣ F

20. The theory of cost-push inflation explains rising prices in terms of factors which increase per unit production cost. Ⓣ F

21. A person's real income is the amount of goods and services which the person's nominal (or money) income will enable him or her to purchase. Ⓣ F

22. Whether inflation is anticipated or unanticipated, the effects of inflation on the distribution of income are much the same. T Ⓕ

23. Suppose a household has $10,000 on deposit in a savings and loan association upon which it earns 7% interest during a year and the rate of inflation is 9% in that year. By the end of the year the purchasing power of the $10,000 and the interest it has earned will have decreased to about $9,817. Ⓣ F

24. Unemployment and inflation rates vary greatly among major industrialized nations. Ⓣ F

25. Inflation in the United States has transferred wealth from the public sector to the households of the economy. T Ⓕ

Circle the letter that corresponds to the best answer.

1. Which one of the following is **not** one of the four phases of an idealized business cycle?
(a) inflation
(b) recession *peak.*
(c) recovery
(d) trough

2. Most economists believe that the immediate determinant of the levels of domestic output and employment is:
(a) the price level
(b) the size of the civilian labor force
(c) the nation's stock of capital goods
(d) the level of aggregate spending

3. Total employment in December of this year was greater than total employment in December of 1928. This is no doubt due to the effect of:
(a) seasonal variations
(b) secular trend
(c) the business cycle
(d) business fluctuations

4. If employment in the agricultural sector of the American economy during last August and September was 112% of what it normally is in those months, this is probably a consequence of:
(a) seasonal variations
(b) secular trend
(c) the business cycle
(d) both seasonal variations and the business cycle

5. Production and employment in which of the following industries would be least affected by a depression?
(a) nondurable consumer goods
(b) durable consumer goods
(c) capital goods
(d) iron and steel

6. A worker who loses a job at a petroleum refinery because consumers and business firms switch from the use of oil to the burning of coal is an example of:
(a) frictional unemployment
(b) structural unemployment
(c) cyclical unemployment
(d) disguised unemployment

7. A worker who has quit one job and is taking two weeks off before reporting to a new job is an example of:
(a) frictional unemployment
(b) structural unemployment
(c) cyclical unemployment
(d) disguised unemployment

8. Insufficient aggregate demand results in:
(a) frictional unemployment
(b) structural unemployment
(c) cyclical unemployment
(d) disguised unemployment

9. The full-employment unemployment rate in the economy has been achieved when:
(a) frictional unemployment is zero
(b) structural unemployment is zero
(c) cyclical unemployment is zero
(d) the natural rate of unemployment is zero

10. Which of the following has increased the natural rate of unemployment in the United States since the 1960s?
(a) the increased size of unemployment benefits
(b) more workers covered by unemployment programs
(c) having more young workers in the labor force
(d) all of the above

11. The labor force includes those who are:
(a) under sixteen years of age
(b) in mental institutions
(c) not seeking work
(d) employed

12. The unemployment rate in an economy is 8%. The total population of the economy is 250 million and the size of the civilian labor force is 150 million. The number of employed workers in this economy is:
(a) 12 million
(b) 20 million
(c) 138 million
(d) 140 million

13. The price level has doubled in about fourteen years. The approximate annual percentage rate of increase in the price level over this period has been:
(a) 2%
(b) 3%
(c) 4%
(d) 5%

14. The unemployment data collected by the Bureau of Labor Statistics have been criticized because:
(a) part-time workers are not counted in the number of workers employed
(b) discouraged workers are treated as a part of the labor force
(c) some workers who are not working may claim they are looking for work and are included in the labor force
(d) the underground economy may understate unemployment

15. Okun's law predicts that when the actual unemployment rate exceeds the natural rate of unemployment by two percentage points the GDP gap will equal:
(a) 2% of the potential GDP
(b) 3% of the potential GDP
(c) 4% of the potential GDP
(d) 5% of the potential GDP

16. If the GDP gap were equal to 7.5% of the potential GDP the actual unemployment rate would exceed the natural rate of unemployment by:
(a) two percentage points
(b) three percentage points
(c) four percentage points
(d) five percentage points

17. The burden of unemployment is *least* felt by:
(a) white-collar workers
(b) teenagers

(c) blacks
(d) males

18. If the consumer price index was 110 in one year and 117 in the next year, then the rate of inflation from one year to the next was:
(a) 3.5%
(b) 4.7%
(c) 6.4%
(d) 7.1%

$$\frac{117-110}{110} \times 100 \, 100.$$

19. Only two resources, capital and labor, are used in an economy to produce an output of 300 million units. If the total cost of capital resources is $150 million and the total cost of labor resources is $50 million, then the per unit production costs in this economy are:
(a) $0.67 million
(b) $1.50 million
(c) $2.00 million
(d) $3.00 million

$$\frac{150+50}{300} = 0.67 \, mil$$

20. If the resources of the economy are fully employed, an increase in aggregate spending will cause:
(a) output and employment to increase
(b) output and prices to increase
(c) nominal income and prices to increase
(d) employment and nominal income to increase

21. If the economy is experiencing a depression with substantial unemployment, an increase in total spending will cause:
(a) a decrease in the *real* income of the economy
(b) little or no increase in the level of prices
(c) an increase in the *real* income and a decrease in the *nominal* income of the economy
(d) proportionate increases in the price level, output, and income in the economy

22. If a person's nominal income increases by 8% while the price level increases by 10% the person's real income will have:
(a) increased by 2%
(b) increased by 18%
(c) decreased by 18%
(d) decreased by 2%

23. The average level of nominal income is $21,000 and the price level index is 154. The average real income would be about:
(a) $12,546
(b) $13,636
(c) $15,299
(d) $17,823

$$\frac{21,000}{154}.$$

24. With no inflation a bank would be willing to lend a business firm $10 million at an annual interest rate of 8%. But, if the rate of inflation was anticipated to be 6% the bank would charge the firm an annual interest rate of:
(a) 2%
(b) 6%

$$6+8$$

(c) 8%
(d) 14%

25. Which of the following would *not* be hurt by unanticipated inflation?
(a) those living on fixed nominal incomes
(b) those who find prices rising more rapidly than their nominal incomes
(c) those who have money savings
(d) those who became debtors when prices were lower

26. Many economists argue that mild demand-pull inflation at less than full employment results in:
(a) rising output
(b) rising real income
(c) falling unemployment
(d) all of the above

27. Which of the following is *not* related to the cost-push theory of inflation?
(a) an increase in employment and output
(b) an increase in per unit production costs
(c) excessive wage gains
(d) supply-shocks

28. Which of the following is *not* associated with hyper-inflation?
(a) war or its aftermath
(b) rising output in the economy
(c) the hoarding of goods and speculation
(d) a halt to the use of money as both a medium of exchange and a standard of value

29. In recent years, Peru has experienced an inflation rate of over 3000% per year. This economic condition would best be described as:
(a) a wage-price inflationary spiral
(b) a cost-of-living adjustment
(c) cost-push inflation
(d) hyperinflation

■ **DISCUSSION QUESTIONS**

1. What is the historical record of American economy with respect to economic growth, full employment, and price-level stability?

2. Define the business cycle. Why do some economists prefer the term "business fluctuations" to "business cycle"? Describe the four phases of an idealized cycle.

3. What, in the opinion of most economists, is the immediate determinant or cause of the levels of output and employment in the economy?

4. The business cycle is only one of three general causes of changes in output and employment in the economy. What are the other influences which affect these variables?

5. Compare the manner in which the business cycle affects output and employment in the industries producing capital and durable goods with industries producing nondurable goods and services. What causes these differences?

6. Distinguish among frictional, structural, and cyclical unemployment.

7. When is there full employment in the American economy? (Answer in terms of the unemployment rate, the actual and potential output of the economy, and the markets for labor.)

8. How is the unemployment rate measured in the United States? What criticisms have been made of the method used by the Bureau of Labor Statistics to determine the unemployment rate?

9. What is the economic cost of unemployment and how is this cost measured? What is the quantitative relationship (called Okun's law) between the unemployment rate and the cost of unemployment?

10. What groups in the economy tend to bear the burdens of unemployment? How are women affected by unemployment and how is the percentage of the labor force unemployed fifteen or more weeks related to the unemployment rate in the economy?

11. What is inflation and how is the rate of inflation measured?

12. Compare and contrast demand-pull and cost-push inflation.

13. What groups benefit from and what groups are hurt by inflation and how has the public sector of the economy been affected by it?

14. What is the difference between the effects of unanticipated and the effects of anticipated inflation on the redistribution of real incomes in the economy?

15. Explain what will tend to happen to employment, output, nominal and real income, and the price level if total spending increases and the resources of the economy are: (*a*) widely unemployed, (*b*) moderately unemployed, (*c*) fully employed. If total spending ***decreased*** would the effects on employment, output, income, and the price level be just the opposite?

16. Write three scenarios that describe the effects of inflation on the domestic output.

17. How do the unemployment rate and inflation rate in the United States compare with those for other industrialized nations in recent years?

■ **ANSWERS**

Chapter 8 Macroeconomic Instability: Unemployment and Inflation

FILL-IN QUESTIONS

1. unsteady, inflation, output, employment

2. ups (increases), downs (decreases), recession, trough, recovery

3. spending, demand

4. seasonal, secular

5. durable, capital, nondurable, low-

6. *a.* frictional unemployment; *b.* structural unemployment; *c.* cyclical unemployment (any order)

7. *a.* natural; *b.* frictional, structural (either order); *c.* cyclical, actual, potential (either order); *d.* 5 to 6

8. equal to, constant

9. the number of unemployed persons, labor force

10. the potential, the actual, increase, 2.5

11. black, teenage, blue-collar, less

12. rise (increase), prices, 1993, 1992, 1992

13. annual increase in the rate of inflation, rule of 70

14. *a.* deflation; *b.* high, low, high; *c.* high nor low

15. *a.* increase; *b.* per unit production costs, wages, nonwage inputs; *c.* difficult

16. real income; *a.* real income, 3; *b.* real income, $28,301.88

17. *a.* fixed; *b.* unexpected; *c.* creditors, debtors; *d.* households, the public sector

18. anticipated; *a.* cost-of-living adjustments (COLA); *b.* real rate of interest, nominal rate of interest

19. *a.* increase; *b.* decrease; *c.* breakdown (collapse)

PROBLEMS AND PROJECTS

1. year 1: 4,093, 4.8; year 5: 7,929, 8.3; *a.* the labor force increased more than employment increased; *b.* because unemployment and employment in relative terms are percentages of the labor force and ***always*** add to 100%, and if one increases the other must decrease; *c.* no economist would argue that the full-employment unemployment rate is as high as 8.3% and year 5 was not a year of full employment; *d.* the number of people looking for work expands

2. *a.* 0; *b.* 95, 412.5; *c.* 97.5, (1) 2.5, (2) 7; *d.* 90, (1) 10, (2) 10

3. *a.* 12, 10, 5; *b.* 5.83, 7, 14; *c.* 3; *d.* −3; *e.* $22,321; *f.* $20,292; *g.* 2; *h.* 3

4. *a.* D; *b.* I; *c.* B; *d.* D; *e.* D; *f.* I; *g.* B

5. *a.* B, B, C, A; *b.* B, B, C, B; *c.* A, D, A,

6. *a.* equal, the domestic output demanded and supplied at the equilibrium price level; *b.* (1) increase, (2) demand-pull; *c.* (1) rise, fall, (2) cost-push inflation

SELF-TEST

1. T, p. 129
2. F, pp. 129–130
3. F, p. 130
4. T, p. 132
5. F, p. 132
6. T, pp. 133–134
7. F, p. 134
8. T, p. 134
9. T, p. 134
10. F, p. 135
11. F, p. 138
12. F, p. 136
13. T, p. 138

14. T, p. 136
15. T, p. 134
16. F, p. 139
17. F, p. 140
18. F, p. 140
19. T, p. 142
20. T, p. 142
21. T, p. 144
22. F, p. 144
23. T, p. 145
24. T, p. 140
25. F, p. 146

1. *a*, pp. 130–131
2. *d*, p. 131
3. *b*, p. 132
4. *c*, pp. 131–132
5. *a*, p. 132
6. *b*, p. 134
7. *a*, p. 133
8. *c*, p. 134
9. *c*, p. 134
10. *d*, p. 135
11. *d*, p. 136
12. *c*, p. 136
13. *d*, p. 140
14. *c*, p. 136
15. *d*, p. 137

16. *b*, p. 137
17. *a*, p. 138
18. *c*, p. 140
19. *a*, p. 142
20. *c*, p. 142
21. *b*, pp. 141–142
22. *d*, p. 144
23. *b*, p. 144
24. *d*, pp. 145–146
25. *d*, p. 145
26. *d*, p. 146
27. *a*, pp. 142–143
28. *b*, p. 147
29. *d*, p. 147

DISCUSSION QUESTIONS

1. pp. 129–130
2. pp. 130–131
3. p. 131
4. pp. 131–132
5. p. 132
6. pp. 133–134
7. pp. 134–137
8. pp. 135–136
9. pp. 136–138

10. p. 138
11. pp. 139–140
12. pp. 141–143
13. pp. 143–145
14. pp. 145–146
15. pp. 141–142
16. pp. 140–143
17. pp. 139, 141

Aggregate Demand and Aggregate Supply

You learned in Chapter 7 how the GDP and the NDP are measured and how to adjust them when the price level changes to find the real GDP and the real NDP. Then in Chapter 8 you found that over the years the American economy has at times suffered from unemployment, has at other times experienced inflation, and has at still other times had both unemployment and inflation.

In Chapter 9 you will begin learning what determines how large the real domestic output (the real GDP or NDP) and the price level at any time will be; what causes them to change; and what policies the Federal government can use to prevent unemployment and inflation.

The tools employed to explain what determines the economy's real output and price level are demand and supply. You first encountered these tools in Chapter 4 where they were used to explain what determines the output and the price of a particular product. These same tools are now employed in a slightly different way. To use these tools of aggregate demand and aggregate supply you will have to think not of the price of a particular good or service but of the price level in the economy. And instead of thinking about the quantity of a particular good or service demanded or supplied it is necessary to think about the total (the aggregate) quantity of all final goods and services demanded (purchased) and supplied (produced) in the economy. You will have no difficulty with the way demand and supply are used in this chapter once you adjust the way you think about them from a particular good or service and its price to all final goods and services and their average price.

Having made this adjustment in your way of thinking about demand and supply, the rest is not too difficult. The aggregate-demand curve is downsloping because of the interest-rate, real-balances, and foreign-purchases effects of changes in the price level. With the downsloping aggregate demand, changes in the price level cause changes in the level of spending by domestic consumers, businesses, government, and foreign buyers that affect the amount of real domestic output, assuming **other things equal**. This change would be equivalent to a movement along an existing aggregate-demand curve: a lower price level increases the quantity of real domestic output and a

higher price level decreases the quantity of real domestic output. But other things may not be equal and so the entire aggregate-demand curve can also shift due to a change in one of the nonprice level determinants of aggregate demand. You should pay attention to these "aggregate-demand shifters" that are outlined in Table 9–1.

The aggregate-supply curve differs from the shape of the aggregate-demand curve because it reflects what happens to per unit production costs as real domestic output increases or decreases. For the purposes of this analysis, it has three ranges: (1) at low level of real domestic output, the price level is relatively constant, so the aggregate-supply curve in this range is horizontal; (2) at high level of real domestic output, the aggregate-supply curve is vertical; and (3) in the intermediate range, the level of real domestic output rises along with the price level, so the curve is upsloping.

You should remember that an assumption has also been made that other things are equal, when one moves along an aggregate-supply curve. When other things change, then the aggregate-supply curve can shift. The determinants of aggregate supply include changes in input prices, changes in productivity, and changes in the legal and institutional environment for production.

Like the ordinary demand and supply curves of Chapter 4, the intersection of the aggregate-demand and the aggregate-supply curves determines equilibrium quantity and price: the equilibrium quantity is the equilibrium real domestic output and the equilibrium price is the equilibrium price level. With the knowledge of how aggregate demand and supply determine the real domestic output and the price level you have acquired the ability to explain the basic causes of inflation (an increase in demand or a decrease in supply), of a decrease in domestic output and employment (a decrease in demand or in supply).

Aggregate demand and aggregate supply are the skeleton upon which macroeconomic theory and policies are based. The next ten chapters "flesh-out" this skeleton. As you study these chapters you may forget the aggregate-demand–aggregate-supply framework. Don't!

■ CHECKLIST

When you have studied this chapter you should be able to:

☐ Define aggregate demand.
☐ Explain why the aggregate-demand curve slopes downward.
☐ Identify the major determinants of aggregate demand and explain how they shift the aggregate-demand curve.
☐ Define aggregate supply.
☐ Describe the shape of the aggregate-supply curve and name the three ranges on it.
☐ List the major nonprice level determinants of aggregate supply and describe how they shift the aggregate-supply curve.
☐ Explain what the real domestic output and price level will be in equilibrium and why the economy will tend to produce this output and price level (rather than another combination).
☐ State the effects on the real domestic output and on the price level of an increase in aggregate demand when the economy is in the Keynesian, classical, and intermediate ranges.
☐ Explain why a decrease in aggregate demand will not reduce the price level so much as an equal increase in aggregate demand would have raised it.

■ CHAPTER OUTLINE

1. Aggregate demand and aggregate supply determine the real domestic output and the price level of the economy; and they are used in this chapter to explain why output and the price level fluctuate.

2. Aggregate demand is a curve which shows the total quantity of goods and services that will be purchased (demanded) at different price levels; and the curve slopes downward for three reasons.

   a. An increase in the price level also decreases the purchasing power of financial assets with a fixed money value, and because those who own such assets are now poorer they spend less for goods and services; and a decrease in the price level has the opposite effects.

   b. With the supply of money fixed, an increase in the price level increases the demand for money, increases interest rates, and as a result reduces those expenditures (by consumers and business firms) which are sensitive to increased interest rates; and a decrease in the price level has the opposite effects.

   c. In addition, an increase in the price level (relative to foreign price levels) will reduce American exports, expand American imports, and decrease the quantity of goods and services demanded in the American econ-

omy; and a decrease in the price level (relative to foreign price levels) will have opposite effects.

3. Spending by domestic consumers, businesses, government, and foreign buyers that is independent of changes in the price level shifts aggregate demand, as outlined in Table 9–1.

   a. For domestic consumers, increases in wealth, improved expectations, reductions in indebtedness, or lower taxes can increase consumer spending and aggregate demand; decreases in consumer wealth, less positive expectations, increases in indebtedness, and higher taxes decrease consumer spending and aggregate demand.

   b. For businesses, lower interest rates, improved profit expectations, lower taxes, improved technology, and less excess capacity may increase investment spending and aggregate demand; whereas higher interest rates, worse profit expectations, higher taxes, and more excess capacity may retard investment spending and aggregate demand.

   c. More government spending tends to increase aggregate demand and less government spending will decrease it, assuming that tax collections and interest rates do not change as a result.

   d. Net export spending and aggregate demand are increased by increases in the national incomes of other nations and by a dollar depreciation; declines in the incomes of foreign buyers and a dollar appreciation tend to reduce net exports and aggregate demand.

4. Aggregate supply is a curve that shows the total quantity of goods and services that will be produced (supplied) at different price levels; and the curve has three ranges.

   a. In the Keynesian range (when the economy is in a severe recession or depression) the aggregate-supply curve is horizontal; the price level need not rise to induce producers to supply larger quantities of goods and services.

   b. In the classical range (when the economy is at full employment) the aggregate-supply curve is vertical: a rise in the price level cannot result in an increase in the quantity of goods and services supplied.

   c. Between these two ranges is the intermediate range in which the supply curve slopes upward: the price level must rise to induce producers to supply larger quantities of goods and services.

5. Factors that shift the aggregate-supply curve include changes in the prices of inputs for production, changes in productivity, and changes in the legal and institutional environment in the economy, as outlined in Table 9–2.

   a. Lower prices for productive domestic resources (land, labor, capital, and entrepreneurial ability) and imported resources tend to reduce unit costs of production and increase aggregate supply, whereas higher input prices, which may be brought about by more market power on the part of resource suppliers, will tend to decrease aggregate supply.

b. As productivity improves, per unit production costs fall and aggregate supply increases; the converse occurs when productivity falls.

c. A decrease in the level of business taxation or reduced regulation of business may improve the business environment and increase aggregate supply; the opposite actions may reduce aggregate supply.

6. The equilibrium real domestic output and the equilibrium price level are at the intersection of the aggregate-demand and the aggregate-supply curves. Were the actual output greater (less) than the equilibrium output producers would find that their inventories were increasing (decreasing) and they would contract (expand) their output to the equilibrium output.

7. The aggregate-demand and aggregate-supply curves shift to change equilibrium.

a. An increase in aggregate demand in:

(1) the Keynesian range would result in an increase in real output but the price level would remain unchanged;

(2) the classical range would result in an increase in the price level but the real domestic output would remain unchanged;

(3) the intermediate range would result in an increase in both real domestic output and the price level.

b. But a decrease in aggregate demand may not have the opposite effect on the price level because prices (for several reasons) tend to be inflexible (sticky) downward.

c. A decrease in aggregate supply means there will be a decrease in real domestic output (economic growth) and employment, and at the same time a rise in the price level, or cost-push inflation.

d. An increase in aggregate supply, however, has the beneficial effects of improving real domestic output and employment, while simultaneously reducing the price level.

■ **IMPORTANT TERMS**

Aggregation	Classical range
Aggregates	Intermediate range
Aggregate-demand curve	Determinants of aggregate supply
Wealth or real balances effect	Productivity
Interest-rate effect	Equilibrium price level
Foreign-purchases effect	Equilibrium real domestic output
Determinants of aggregate demand	Demand-pull inflation
Aggregate-supply curve	Ratchet effect
Keynesian range	Cost-push inflation

■ **FILL-IN QUESTIONS**

1. Aggregate demand and aggregate supply together determine the equilibrium real domestic _____ and the equilibrium price _____

2. The aggregate-demand curve shows the quantity of goods and services that will be _____ at various price _____

a. It slopes (upward, downward) _____

b. because of the _____,

the _____,

and the _____ effects.

3. For the aggregate-demand curve:

a. An increase in the price level leads to a(n) (increase, decrease) _____ in the quantity of real domestic output;

b. whereas a decrease in the price level leads to a(n) _____ in the quantity of real domestic output,

c. assuming _____

4. When the price level changes:

a. there is a (movement along, change in) _____ _____ the aggregate-demand curve;

b. when the entire aggregate-demand curve shifts, there is a (change in the quantity of real output demanded, change in aggregate demand) _____,

c. and that change is caused by one or more of the _____ of aggregate demand.

5. List the determinants of aggregate demand by type:

a. From changes in consumer spending due to changes in:

(1) _____

(2) _____

(3) _____

(4) _____

b. From changes in investment spending due to changes in:

(1) _____

(2) _____

(3) _____

(4) _____

(5) _____

c. From government due to changes in:

(1) _____

d. From net export spending due to changes in:

(1) _____

(2) _____

6. The aggregate-supply curve shows the quantity of goods and services that will be _____ at various price _____; and in the:

a. Keynesian range is (vertical, horizontal, upsloping)

_____

b. the intermediate range is _____

c. the classical range is _____

7. The basic cause of a decrease in aggregate supply is a(n) (increase, decrease) _____ in the per unit costs of producing goods and services; and the basic cause of an increase in aggregate supply is ____

_____,

all other things equal.

8. List the determinants of aggregate supply:

a. From a change in input prices due to a change in:

(1) _____

(2) _____

(3) _____

b. From a change in _____

c. From a change in the legal and institutional environment due to a change in:

(1) _____

(2) _____

9. The equilibrium real domestic output and price level are found at the _____ of the aggregate-demand and the aggregate-supply curves.

a. At this price level the aggregate quantity of goods and services _____ is equal to the aggregate quantity of goods and services _____

b. And at this real domestic output the prices producers are willing to (pay, accept) _____ are equal to the prices buyers are willing to ____

10. Were the actual real domestic output:

a. greater than the equilibrium domestic output producers would find that their inventories are (increasing, decreasing) _____ and they would (expand, reduce) _____ their production;

b. less than the equilibrium domestic output producers would find that their inventories are _____ and they would _____ their production.

11. When the economy is producing in:

a. the Keynesian range an increase in aggregate demand will (increase, decrease, have no effect on) _____ real domestic output and will _____ the price level;

b. the intermediate range an increase in aggregate demand will _____ real domestic output and will _____ the price level;

c. the classical range an increase in aggregate demand will _____ real domestic output and will _____ the price level.

12. Were the economy operating in the intermediate or classical ranges and aggregate demand were to decrease, the price level would decline by (a larger, a smaller, the same) _____ amount as an equal increase in aggregate demand would have raised the price level; this is called the (interest-rate, real-balances, ratchet) _____ effect.

13. An increase in aggregate supply will not only (raise, lower) _____ real domestic output and (lead to, prevent) _____ inflation but will also (increase, decrease) _____ the full-employment level of domestic output; a decrease in aggregate supply will _____ real output and _____ the price level.

14. Demand-pull inflation is the result of a(n) (increase, decrease) _____ in aggregate demand and is accompanied by a (rise, fall) _____ in real output; but cost-push inflation is the result of a(n) _____ in aggregate supply and is accompanied by a _____

■ **PROBLEMS AND PROJECTS**

1. In the table below is an aggregate-supply schedule.

Price level	Real domestic output supplied
250	2000
225	2000
200	1900
175	1700
150	1400
125	1000
125	500
125	0

a. The economy is in the:
(1) Keynesian range when the real domestic output is

between _____ and _____
(2) classical range when the real domestic output is

_____ and the price level is _____
or more
(3) intermediate range when the real domestic output

is between _____ and _____

b. Plot this aggregate-supply schedule on the graph below.

c. In the table below are three aggregate-demand schedules.

Price level (1)	Real domestic output demanded		
	(2)	(3)	(4)
250	1400	1900	400
225	1500	2000	500
200	1600	2100	600
175	1700	2200	700
150	1800	2300	800
125	1900	2400	900
100	2000	2500	1000

(1) Plot the aggregate-demand curve shown in columns (1) and (2) on the graph below; and label this curve **AD₁**. At this level of aggregate demand the equi-

librium real domestic is _____

and the equilibrium price level is _____
(2) On the same graph plot the aggregate-demand curve shown in columns (1) and (3); and label this curve

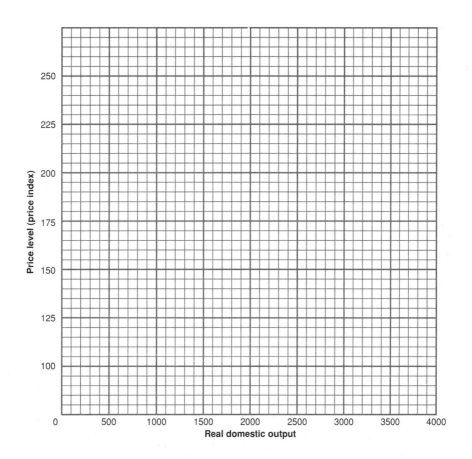

AD₂. The equilibrium real domestic output is _____

and the equilibrium price level is _____
(3) Now plot the aggregate-demand curve in columns
(1) and (4) and label it **AD₃**. The equilibrium real do-

mestic output is _____ and the equilib-

rium price level is _____

2. In the first diagram in the next column are an aggregate-supply curve and six aggregate-demand curves.
    a. The movements of the aggregate-demand curves
from **AD₁** to **AD₂**, from **AD₃** to **AD₄**, and from **AD₅** to

AD₆ all portray (increases, decreases) _____
in aggregate demand.
(1) The movement from **AD₁** to **AD₂** increases the (real

domestic output, price level) _____

but does not change the _____
(2) The movement from **AD₃** to **AD₄** will (raise, lower)

_____ the price level and will (expand,

contract) _____ the real domestic output.

(3) The movement from **AD₅** to **AD₆** will _____

_____
    b. The movements of the aggregate-demand curves

to the left all portray (increases, decreases) _____
in aggregate demand.
(1) If prices are flexible in a downward direction, what
effects will these changes in aggregate demand have

upon the real domestic output and the price level? ___

_____
(2) If prices are **not** flexible in a downward direction,
what effects will these changes in aggregate demand

have? _____

_____

3. In the second diagram in the next column there are two
aggregate-supply curves and three aggregate-demand
curves.
    a. The movement of the aggregate-supply curve
from **AS₁** to **AS₂** represents a(n) (increase, decrease)

_____ in aggregate supply.
(1) If the price level is flexible downward and upward,
this change in aggregate supply in each of the three
ranges along the aggregate supply curve will (raise,

lower) _____

the price level and (expand, contract) _____
the real domestic output.
(2) But if prices are inflexible in a downward direction,
this change in aggregate supply will (increase, de-

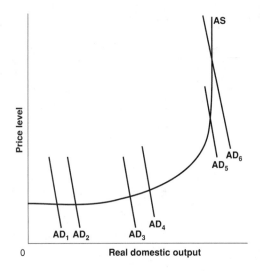

crease) _____ real domestic output

but (will, will not) _____ affect the
price level.
    b. The movement of aggregate supply from **AS₂** to

AS₁ portrays a(n) _____ in aggre-

gate supply and in each of the three ranges will _____

the price level and _____ the real domestic output.

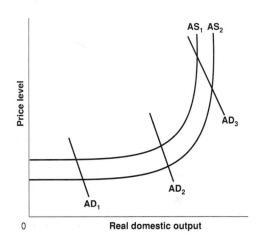

4. Below are hypothetical data showing the relationship
between the real domestic output and the quantity of input
resources needed to produce each level of output.

Output	Input	Productivity		Per unit cost		
		(1)	(2)	(3)	(4)	(5)
2500	500	_____	_____	_____	_____	_____
2000	400	_____	_____	_____	_____	_____
1500	300	_____	_____	_____	_____	_____

a. In column (1) compute the level of productivity at each level of real domestic output.

b. In column (2) compute the level of productivity if there is a doubling in the quantity of inputs required to produce each level of output.

c. In column (3) compute the per unit production cost at each level of output, if each unit of input costs $15, given the level of productivity in column (1).

d. In column (4) compute the new per unit production cost at each level of output given that input price is $15 per unit, given that there has been a doubling in the required quantity of inputs to produce each level of output as shown in column (2). What will happen to the aggregate-supply curve if this situation occurs?

_____

e. In column (5), compute the new per unit production cost at each level of output, given that input price is now $10 instead of $15, but the level of productivity stays as it was originally, as shown in column (1). What will happen to the aggregate-supply curve if this situation occurs? _____

5. In the list below, what will most likely happen as a result of each event to: (1) aggregate demand (AD), (2) aggregate supply (AS); (3) the equilibrium price level; and (4) equilibrium real domestic output (**Q**). Assume that all other things remain constant when the event occurs and that the economy is operating in the intermediate range of the aggregate-supply curve. Use the following symbols to indicate the expected effects: **I** = increase; **D** = decrease; **S** = remains the same; and **U** = uncertain.

a. A decrease in labor productivity.

AD _____   AS _____   **P** _____   **Q** _____

b. A fall in the interest rate for business loans.

AD _____   AS _____   **P** _____   **Q** _____

c. Consumer incomes decline as the economy moves into a recession.

AD _____   AS _____   **P** _____   **Q** _____

d. The price of oil on the world market falls to a low level.

AD _____   AS _____   **P** _____   **Q** _____

e. There is an appreciation in the value of the United States dollar.

AD _____   AS _____   **P** _____   **Q** _____

■ **SELF-TEST**

Circle the T if the statement is true; the F if it is false.

1. The aggregate-demand curve slopes downward. **T F**

2. A fall in the price level increases the real value of financial assets with fixed money values and, as a result, increases spending by the holders of these assets. **T F**

3. A fall in the price level reduces the demand for money in the economy and drives interest rates upward. **T F**

4. A rise in the price level of an economy (relative to foreign price levels) tends to increase that economy's exports and to reduce its imports of goods and services. **T F**

5. The aggregate-supply curve is horizontal in the classical range. **T F**

6. At the equilibrium price level the real domestic output purchased is equal to the real domestic output produced. **T F**

7. In the intermediate range on the aggregate-supply curve an increase in aggregate demand will increase both the price level and the real domestic output. **T F**

8. A decrease in aggregate demand will lower the price level by the same amount as an equal increase in aggregate demand would have raised it because of the ratchet effect. **T F**

9. An increase in aggregate supply increases both the equilibrium real domestic output and the full-employment output of the economy. **T F**

10. A decrease in aggregate supply is "doubly good" because it increases the real domestic output and prevents inflation. **T F**

11. Aggregation in macroeconomics is the process of combining all the prices of individual products and services into a price level and merging all the equilibrium quantities into real domestic output. **T F**

12. Per unit production cost is determined by dividing total input cost by units of output. **T F**

13. A change in aggregate demand is caused by a change in the price level, *other things equal*. **T F**

14. A fall in excess capacity, or unused existing capital goods, will retard the demand for new capital goods and therefore reduce aggregate demand. **T F**

15. The wealth or real-balances effect is one of the non-price-level determinants of aggregate demand. **T F**

16. A high level of consumer indebtedness will tend to increase consumption spending and aggregate demand. **T F**

17. Appreciation of the dollar relative to foreign currencies will tend to increase net exports and aggregate demand. **T F**

18. When the determinants of aggregate supply change they alter the per unit production cost and thereby aggregate supply. **T F**

19. Productivity is a measure of real output per unit of input.   T F

20. A change in the degree of market power or monopoly power held by sellers of resources can affect input prices and aggregate supply.   T F

Circle the letter that corresponds to the best answer.

1. The slope of the aggregate-demand curve is the result of:
(a) the wealth effect
(b) the interest-rate effect
(c) the foreign-purchases effect
(d) all of the above effects

2. The aggregate-demand curve is the relationship between the:
(a) price level and the real domestic output purchased
(b) price level and the real domestic output produced
(c) price level which producers are willing to pay
(d) real domestic output purchased and the real domestic output produced

3. The aggregate-supply curve is the relationship between the:
(a) price level and the real domestic output purchased
(b) price level and the real domestic output produced
(c) price level which producers are willing to accept and the price level purchasers are willing to pay
(d) real domestic output purchased and the real domestic output produced

4. In the Keynesian range the aggregate-supply curve is:
(a) upsloping
(b) downsloping
(c) vertical
(d) horizontal

5. In the intermediate range the aggregate-supply curve is:
(a) upsloping
(b) downsloping
(c) vertical
(d) horizontal

6. An increase in aggregate supply will:
(a) reduce the price level and real domestic output
(b) reduce the price level and increase the real domestic output
(c) increase the price level and real domestic output
(d) reduce the price level and decrease the real domestic output

7. When the price level rises:
(a) holders of financial assets with fixed money values increase their spending
(b) the demand for money and interest rates rise
(c) spending which is sensitive to interest-rate changes increases
(d) holders of financial assets with fixed money values have more purchasing power

8. If the real domestic output is less than the equilibrium real domestic output producers find:
(a) their inventories decreasing and expand their production
(b) their inventories increasing and expand their production
(c) their inventories decreasing and contract their production
(d) their inventories increasing and contract their production

9. When the economy is in the Keynesian range an increase in aggregate demand will:
(a) increase the price level and have no effect on real domestic output
(b) increase the real domestic output and have no effect on the price level
(c) increase both real output and the price level
(d) increase the price level and decrease the real domestic output

10. The ratchet effect is the result of:
(a) a price level that is inflexible upward
(b) a price level that is inflexible downward
(c) a domestic output that cannot be increased
(d) a domestic output that cannot be decreased

11. If there were stagflation in the economy that decreased aggregate supply:
(a) both the real domestic output and the price level would decrease
(b) the real domestic output would increase and rises in the price level would become smaller
(c) the real domestic output would decrease and the price level would rise
(d) both the real domestic output and rises in the price level would become greater

12. The aggregate-demand curve will tend to be increased by:
(a) a decrease in the price level
(b) an increase in the price level
(c) an increase in the excess capacity of factories
(d) a depreciation in the value of the United States dollar

13. A sharp decline in the real value of stock prices, which is independent of a change in the price level, would best be an example of:
(a) the wealth effect
(b) the real balance effect
(c) a change in real wealth
(d) a change in consumer indebtedness

Suppose that real domestic output in an economy is 50 units, the quantity of inputs is 10, and the price of each input is $2. Answer the next four questions (14, 15, 16, and 17) on the basis of this information.

14. The level of productivity in this economy is:
  (a) 5
  (b) 4
  (c) 3
  (d) 2

15. The per unit cost of production is:
  (a) $0.40
  (b) $0.50
  (c) $2.50
  (d) $3.50

16. If real domestic output in the economy rose to 60 units, then per unit production costs would:
  (a) remain unchanged and aggregate supply would remain unchanged
  (b) increase and aggregate supply would decrease
  (c) decrease and aggregate supply would increase
  (d) decrease and aggregate supply would decrease

17. All else equal, if the price of each input increases from $2 to $4, productivity would:
  (a) decrease from $4 to $2 and aggregate supply would decrease
  (b) decrease from $5 to $3 and aggregate supply would decrease
  (c) increase from $4 to $2 and aggregate supply would increase
  (d) remain unchanged and aggregate supply would decrease

18. If the prices of imported resources increase, then this event would most likely:
  (a) decrease aggregate supply
  (b) increase aggregate supply
  (c) increase aggregate demand
  (d) decrease aggregate demand

19. If Congress passed much stricter laws to control the air pollution from business, then this action would tend to:
  (a) increase per unit production costs and shift the aggregate-supply curve to the right
  (b) increase per unit production costs and shift the aggregate-supply curve to the left
  (c) increase per unit production costs and shift the aggregate-demand curve to the left
  (d) decrease per unit production costs and shift the aggregate-supply curve to the left

20. An increase in business taxes will tend to:
  (a) decrease aggregate demand but not change aggregate supply
  (b) decrease aggregate supply but not change aggregate demand

  (c) decrease aggregate demand and decrease aggregate supply
  (d) decrease aggregate supply and increase aggregate demand

Answer the next four questions (21, 22, 23, and 24) on the basis of the following aggregate demand and supply schedule for a hypothetical economy.

Real domestic output demanded (in billions)	Price level	Real domestic output supplied (in billions)
$1500	170	$4000
$2000	150	$4000
$2500	125	$3500
$3000	100	$3000
$3500	75	$2500
$4000	75	$2000

21. The equilibrium price level and quantity of real domestic output will be:
  (a) 100 and $2500
  (b) 100 and $3000
  (c) 125 and $3500
  (d) 150 and $4000

22. The Keynesian range of the aggregate-supply curve is associated with the quantity supplied of:
  (a) $4000
  (b) $4000 and $3500
  (c) $3500 and $3000
  (d) $2500 and $2000

23. If the quantity of real domestic output demanded increased by $2000 at each price level, the new equilibrium price level and quantity of real domestic output would be:
  (a) 175 and $4000
  (b) 150 and $4000
  (c) 125 and $3500
  (d) 100 and $3000

24. Using the original data from the table, if the quantity of real domestic output demanded *increased* by $500 and quantity of real domestic output supplied *decreased* by $500 at each price level, the new equilibrium price level and quantity of real domestic output would be:
  (a) 175 and $4000
  (b) 150 and $4000
  (c) 125 and $3000
  (d) 100 and $3500

25. If aggregate demand decreases but the price level does not fall as much as would be expected if price were flexible, then this situation could be the result of:
  (a) an increase in aggregate supply
  (b) the foreign-purchases effect
  (c) lower interest rates
  (d) a ratchet effect

■ DISCUSSION QUESTIONS

1. What are an aggregate-demand curve and an aggregate-supply curve?

2. Explain:
(a) the interest-rate effect,
(b) the wealth effect, and
(c) the foreign-purchases effect of change in the price level on the quantity of goods and services demanded in an economy.

3. The aggregate-supply curve is divided into three distinct ranges. Describe the slope of this curve in each of the three ranges. What conditions prevail in the economy in each of the ranges? Why is one range called the Keynesian and another called the classical range?

4. Why does the aggregate-supply curve slope upward in the intermediate range?

5. What real domestic output is the equilibrium real domestic output? Why will business firms that produce the domestic output reduce or expand their production when they find themselves producing more or less than the equilibrium output?

6. What are the effects on the real domestic output and the price level when aggregate demand increases in each of the three ranges along the aggregate-supply curve?

7. If prices were as flexible downward as they are upward, what would be the effects on real domestic output and the price level of a decrease in aggregate demand in each of the three ranges along the aggregate-supply curve?

8. Prices in the economy tend to be "sticky" or inflexible in a downward direction. Why? How does this downward inflexibility alter your answers to question **7** (above)?

9. What are the effects on the real domestic output and the price level of a decrease in aggregate supply? What are the effects of an increase in aggregate supply on the real domestic output, the price level, and the maximum real output the economy is able to produce?

10. Why is a decrease in aggregate supply "doubly bad" and an increase in aggregate supply "doubly good"?

11. Using the aggregate-demand and aggregate-supply concepts, explain the difference between demand-pull and cost-push inflation.

12. What roles do the expectations of consumers and businesses play in influencing aggregate demand?

13. Explain the difference between the wealth effect and "a change in the real value of consumer wealth" for the interpretation of aggregate demand.

14. Describe how changes in the international economy influence aggregate demand or aggregate supply.

15. How does an increase or decrease in per unit production costs change aggregate supply? Give examples.

16. Explain how a change in business taxes affects aggregate demand and aggregate supply.

17. How does the legal and institutional environment affect the price level and real domestic output? Give examples.

18. What is the relationship between the production possibilities curve and aggregate supply?

■ ANSWERS

Chapter 9 Aggregate Demand and Aggregate Supply

FILL-IN QUESTIONS

1. output, level

2. demanded (purchased), levels *a.* downward; *b.* wealth (real-balances), interest-rate, foreign-purchases (any order)

3. *a.* decrease; *b.* increase; *c.* other things equal

4. *a.* movement along; *b.* change in aggregate demand; *c.* determinants

5. *a.* (1) consumer wealth, (2) consumer expectations; (3) consumer indebtedness, (4) personal taxes (any order); *b.* (1) interest rates, (2) profit expectations, (3) business taxes, (4) technology, (5) degree of excess capacity (any order); *c.* (1) government purchases; *d.* (1) national income of other nations; (2) exchange rates (any order)

6. supplied (produced), levels; *a.* horizontal; *b.* upsloping; *c.* vertical

7. increase, a decrease in the per unit costs of production

8. *a.* (1) domestic resource availability, (2) prices of imported resources, (3) market power (any order); *b.* productivity; *c.* (1) business taxes and subsidies, (2) government regulation (either order)

9. intersection; *a.* purchased (demanded), produced (supplied) (either order); *b.* accept, pay

10. *a.* increasing, reduce; *b.* decreasing, expand

11. *a.* increase, have no effect on; *b.* increase, increase; *c.* have no effect on, increase

12. smaller, ratchet

13. raise, prevent, increase; lower, raise

14. increase, rise, decrease, fall in real output

PROBLEMS AND PROJECTS

1. *a.* (1) 0, 1000, (2) 2000, 225, (3) 1000, 2000; *c.* (1) 1700, 175, (2) 2000, 225, (3) 900, 125

2. *a.* increases, (1) real domestic output, price level, (2) raise, expand, (3) increase the price level but will not affect domestic output; *b.* decreases, (1) Decrease the price level in the classical and intermediate ranges and decrease domestic output in the intermediate and Keynesian ranges, (2) Decrease only output in the intermediate and Keynesian ranges

3. *a.* increase, (1) lower, expand, (2) increase, will not; *b.* decrease, increase, decrease

4. *a.* 5, 5, 5; *b.* 2.5, 2.5, 2.5; *c.* $3, $3, $3; *d.* $6, $6, $6, it will decrease; *e.* $2, $2, $2, it will increase

5. *a. S, D, I, D; b. I, S, I, I; c. D, S, D, D; d. I, I, U, I; e. D, I, D, U*

SELF-TEST

1. T, p. 152	**11.** T, p. 152
2. T, p. 153	**12.** T, p. 161
3. F, p. 153	**13.** F, p. 154
4. F, p. 153	**14.** F, p. 156
5. F, pp. 157–158	**15.** F, p. 153
6. T, p. 162	**16.** F, p. 155
7. T, pp. 163–164	**17.** F, p. 156
8. F, p. 164	**18.** T, p. 159
9. T, p. 166	**19.** T, p. 161
10. F, p. 166	**20.** T, p. 161

1. *d,* pp. 152–153	**14.** *a,* p. 161
2. *a,* p. 152	**15.** *a,* p. 161
3. *b,* p. 157	**16.** *c,* p. 161
4. *d,* p. 157	**17.** *d,* p. 161
5. *a,* p. 158	**18.** *a,* pp. 160–161
6. *b,* p. 159	**19.** *b,* p. 162
7. *b,* p. 153	**20.** *c,* pp. 155–156, 161–162
8. *a,* p. 162	**21.** *b,* p. 162
9. *b,* p. 163	**22.** *b,* pp. 163–164
10. *b,* p. 164	**23.** *b,* p. 162
11. *c,* p. 167	**24.** *c,* p. 162
12. *d,* p. 156	**25.** *d,* p. 164
13. *c,* p. 155	

DISCUSSION QUESTIONS

1. pp. 152–153, 157	**10.** p. 166
2. pp. 153–154	**11.** pp. 163–164, 166
3. pp. 157–158	**12.** p. 155
4. pp. 162–163	**13.** pp. 153, 155
5. pp. 163–164	**14.** p. 156
6. pp. 163–164	**15.** p. 161
7. p. 164	**16.** pp. 155–156, 161–162
8. pp. 164–165	**17.** pp. 164–165
9. pp. 165–166	**18.** p. 166

Classical and Keynesian Theories of Employment

Chapters 10 and 11 are really one chapter which has been divided into two parts. They continue the explanation begun in the last chapter of how aggregate demand and aggregate supply determine the real domestic output and price level of the economy. In these two chapters you will learn what determines the total quantity of goods and services that will be purchased (or demanded) at various price levels: the focus in these chapters is on aggregate demand.

Most of the material contained in these two chapters deals with the Keynesian theory or explanation of what determines the demand for the real domestic output (the real GDP) and how the equilibrium level of output (and of employment) is determined. The Keynesian explanation is not the only possible explanation, however. It is with the alternative classical theory that the first part of Chapter 10 deals. The classical theory is described there for several reasons: to impress upon you the fact that an alternative theory does exist; to examine its assumptions and its "cures" for depression; and to prepare you for discussion of macroeconomic theory in later chapters.

The outstanding thing about the classical theory is its conclusion that the economy will *automatically* function to produce the maximum output it is capable of producing and to provide employment for all those who are willing and able to work. Compare this with the conclusion drawn by the exponents of the Keynesian theory that the economy functions in no such way, that both depression and inflation can prevail with no automatic tendency to be corrected, and that full employment and maximum output, when achieved, are accidental. Compare also the political philosophies of the proponents of the two theories. Those accepting the classical theory have advocated as little government interference with the economy as possible in the belief that such interference prevents the achievement of full employment and maximum output. Adherents of the Keynesian theory argue that government action is necessary to eliminate the periods of depression that occur. The basic proposition contained in the Keynesian theory is that the level of total or aggregate expenditures in the economy determines the location of the economy's aggregate-demand curve and, as a result, determines real output and employment and, as you learned in the last chapter, therefore determines the price level. The latter part of

the chapter analyzes the economic factors which determine two principal components of aggregate expenditures—consumption expenditures and investment expenditures. You should pay particular attention to the relationships called the consumption schedule, the saving schedule, and their characteristics; to the four propensity concepts; and to the "nonincome" determinants of consumption and saving.

Investment expenditures—that is, the purchase of capital goods—depend upon the rate of net profits which business firms **expect** to earn from an investment and upon the real rate of interest they have to pay for the use of money. Because firms are anxious to make profitable investments and to avoid unprofitable ones, they undertake all investments which have an expected rate of net profit greater than (or equal to) the real rate of interest and do not undertake an investment when the expected rate of net profit is less than the real interest rate. You should see that because business firms behave this way the lower the real rate of interest the larger will be the dollar amount invested; and that this relationship between the real interest rate and the level of investment spending, called the investment-demand schedule, is an inverse one. But you should not confuse the investment-demand schedule (or curve) with the investment schedule (or curve) which relates investment spending to the GDP and which may show investment is either unrelated to or directly related to the GDP. Five noninterest determinants of investment spending influence the profit expectations of business firms; and these are analyzed. You should learn how changes in these determinants affect investment and why investment spending is unstable.

In the next chapter the tools and ideas developed and explained in Chapter 10 are put together to form a complete and coherent picture of how aggregate expenditures determine the level of GDP in the Keynesian theory.

■ CHECKLIST

When you have studied this chapter you should be able to:

☐ Contrast the views of classical and Keynesian economists on unemployment in a market (or capitalistic) economy and the type of policy government should pursue.

☐ List the three simplifying assumptions made in this and the next chapter and the two implications of these assumptions.

☐ State Say's law and explain how classical economists were able to reason that all saving would be borrowed and spent for capital goods.

☐ Explain how classical economists were able to reason that price-wage flexibility would eliminate a recession and unemployment.

☐ Present two reasons why the rate of interest may not guarantee the quantity of saving and investment, and two reasons why price-wage flexibility may not guarantee full employment; and state the classical response to the latter Keynesian contention.

☐ Compare and contrast the classical and Keynesian views of the aggregate-demand curve and the aggregate-supply curve.

☐ State what determines the amount of goods and services produced and the level of employment in the Keynesian theory.

☐ Explain how consumption and saving are related to disposable income.

☐ Compute, when you are given the necessary data, the four propensities.

☐ Explain what happens to the size of the two average propensities as income increases.

☐ Demonstrate that the MPC is the numerical value of the slope of the consumption schedule and that the MPS is the numerical value of the slope of the saving schedule.

☐ List five nonincome determinants of consumption and saving; and explain how a change in each of these determinants will affect the consumption and saving schedules.

☐ Explain the difference between a change in the amount consumed (or saved) and a change in the consumption (or saving) schedule.

☐ List the two basic determinants of investment; and explain when a firm will and will not invest.

☐ Compute, when given the appropriate data, the investment-demand schedule; and explain why the relationship between investment spending and the real rate of interest is inverse.

☐ List the five noninterest determinants of investment; and explain how a change in each of these determinants will affect the investment-demand curve.

☐ Explain the two variables found in an investment schedule; and the two kinds of relationships that might be found to exist between these two variables.

☐ List the four factors which explain why investment spending tends to be unstable.

■ CHAPTER OUTLINE

1. Classical economists contend that full employment is the norm in a market (or capitalistic) economy and laissez-faire is the best policy for government to pursue; but

Keynesian economists argue that unemployment is typical of such economies and activist policies are required to eliminate it.

2. To simplify the explanation of Keynesian employment theory in this and the next chapter four assumptions are made: the economy is "closed"; government neither spends nor collects taxes; all saving is personal saving; and depreciation and net American income earned abroad are zero. These assumptions have two important implications.

3. The classical theory of employment reached the conclusion that the economy would automatically tend to employ its resources fully and produce a full-employment level of output; this conclusion is based on Say's law and the assumption that prices and wages are flexible.

   a. Say's law stated that the production of goods produced an equal demand for these goods because changes in the rate of interest would ensure that all income not spent (that is, income saved) by consumers would be lent to investors who would spend these borrowed funds for capital goods.

   b. If there were an excess supply of goods or an excess supply of labor (unemployment), prices and wages would fall until the excesses were eliminated and full employment and maximum output again prevailed in the economy.

   c. Believing that capitalism would automatically ensure a full-employment level of output, the classical economists saw no need for government interference with the operation of the economy.

4. J. M. Keynes, in *The General Theory of Employment, Interest and Money,* denied that flexible interest rates, prices, and wages would automatically promote full employment; he set forth the theory that there was nothing automatic about full employment and that both depression and inflation might prevail without any tendency existing for them to be self-correcting.

   a. According to Keynes, flexible interest rates do not guarantee that all income saved by consumers will be spent by investors for capital goods because savers and investors are differently motivated and because saving is neither the only source of the funds to finance investment nor the only use to which consumers can put these funds.

   b. Keynes also argued that prices and wages
   (1) are not, in fact, flexible downward; and
   (2) that even if they were a reduction in prices and wages would not reduce unemployment in the economy; but
   (3) the defenders of classical theory responded that they would be flexible downward if it were not for government policies that prevented them from falling.

5. Classical and Keynesian economics can be compared by examining their aggregate-demand–aggregate-supply models of the economy.

a. In the classical model the aggregate-supply curve is vertical at the economy's full-employment output; and a decrease in aggregate demand will lower the equilibrium price level and have no effect on the real output of (or employment in) the economy because of Say's law, flexible interest rates, and responsive prices and wages.

b. In the Keynesian model the aggregate-supply curve is horizontal at the current price level; and a decrease in aggregate demand will lower the real output of (and employment in) the economy and have no effect on the equilibrium price level because of the downward inflexibility of prices and wages.

c. In both the classical and Keynesian models the aggregate-demand curve slopes downward.

(1) In the classical model it slopes downward because (with a fixed money supply in the economy) a fall in the price level increases the purchasing power of money and enables consumers and business firms to purchase a larger real output; aggregate demand will be reasonably stable if the nation's monetary authorities maintain a constant supply of money.

(2) Keynesians view aggregate demand as being unstable over time, even if the supply of money is held constant, in part because of fluctuations in investment spending; and a decline in aggregate demand decreases real domestic output, but has no effect on the price level, thereby causing output to stay permanently below the full-employment level.

6. Aggregate output and employment in the Keynesian theory are directly related to the level of total or aggregate expenditures in the economy; and to understand what determines the level of total expenditures at any time it is necessary to explain the factors that determine the levels of consumption and investment expenditures.

7. Consumption is the largest component of aggregate expenditures; and saving is disposable income not spent for consumer goods.

a. Disposable income is the most important determinant of both consumption and saving; the relationships between income and consumption and between income and saving are both direct (positive) ones.

b. The consumption schedule shows the amounts that households plan to spend for consumer goods at various levels of income, given a price level.

c. The saving schedule indicates the amounts households plan to save at different income levels, given a price level.

d. The average propensities to consume and to save and the marginal propensities to consume and to save can be computed from the consumption and saving schedules.

(1) The APC and the APS are, respectively, the percentages of income spent for consumption and saved; and their sum is equal to 1.

(2) The MPC and the MPS are, respectively, the percentages of **additional** income spent for consumption and saved; and their sum is equal to 1.

(3) The MPC is the slope of the consumption schedule and the MPS is the slope of the saving schedule when the two schedules are graphed.

e. In addition to income, there are several other important determinants of consumption and saving; and changes in these nonincome determinants will cause the consumption and saving **schedules** to change.

f. A change in the amount consumed (or saved) is not the same thing as a change in the consumption (or saving) schedule. If these schedules change they change in opposite directions; but the schedules are very stable.

8. The two important determinants of the level of gross investment spending in the economy are the expected rate of net profits from the purchase of additional capital goods and the real rate of interest.

a. The expected rate of net profits is directly related to the net profits (revenues less operating costs) that are expected to result from an investment and inversely related to the cost of making the investment (purchasing capital goods).

b. The rate of interest is the price paid for the use of money. When the expected real rate of net profits is greater (less) than the real rate of interest a business will (will not) invest because the investment will be profitable (unprofitable).

c. For this reason, the lower (higher) the real rate of interest, the greater (smaller) will be the level of investment spending in the economy; and the investment-demand curve (schedule) indicates this inverse relationship between the real rate of interest and the level of spending for capital goods.

d. There are at least five noninterest determinants of investment demand; and a change in any of these determinants will shift the investment-demand curve (schedule).

e. Investment spending in the economy may also be either independent or directly related to the real GDP; and the investment schedule may show that investment either remains constant or increases as real GDP increases.

f. Because the five noninterest determinants of investment are subject to sudden changes, investment spending tends to be unstable.

■ **IMPORTANT TERMS**

Classical theory of employment	Money market
Say's law	Savings
Rate of interest	Investment
	Price-wage flexibility

Keynesian economics

Aggregate total expenditures

Dissaving

Consumption schedule

Saving schedule

Break-even income

Average propensity to consume

Average propensity to save

Marginal propensity to consume

Marginal propensity to save

Nonincome determinants of consumption and saving

Change in amount consumed (saved)

Change in the consumption (saving) schedule

Expected rate of net profits

Real rate of interest

Investment-demand schedule (curve)

Noninterest determinants of investment

Investment schedule (curve)

■ FILL-IN QUESTIONS

1. Classical economists believe a market (or capitalistic) economy will tend to produce an output at which its labor force is (fully, less than fully) _____ employed but Keynesian economists argue it will tend to produce an output at which its labor force is _____ employed; and for this reason the classical economists favor a(n) (activist, laissez faire) _____ government policy and the Keynesian economists favor a(n) _____ policy.

2. Four "simplifying assumptions" used throughout most of the chapter are that the economy is a(n) (open, closed) _____ economy; that all saving is (personal, business) _____ saving; that government does not collect _____, make _____ payments, or _____ for goods and services; and that depreciation and net American income earned abroad are _____ The implications of these assumptions are:

  a. GDP = _____ =

  _____ = _____

  b. total spending = _____ +

  _____

3. Full employment, in the classical theory, was ensured by the operation of _____ law and price-wage _____.

4. According to Say's law, the production of goods and services creates an equal _____

_____

5. Changes in _____, according to the classical economists, ensure that what is not spent on consumer goods is spent on capital goods.

6. In the classical theory, if saving is greater than investment the rate of interest will (rise, fall) _____; and if investment is greater than saving it will _____; and the rate of interest will move to the level at which _____ and _____ are equal.

7. According to the classical way of thinking, if the interest rate did not equate saving and investment, and if total output exceeded the level of spending, prices in the output markets would tend to (rise, fall) _____ because of competition among business firms; this would make some production unprofitable and temporarily cause _____ in labor markets; but competition among workers would tend to drive wage rates (upward, downward) _____ and (increase, decrease) _____ their employment. This process would continue until _____

_____

8. According to the Keynesian theory of employment:
  a. saving and investment are done for different _____

  b. the funds to finance investment come not only from current saving but from the _____ of households and from _____
  c. current saving may not be lent to investors in the money market but added to the money _____ of consumers or used to retire outstanding bank _____

9. Keynes, in attacking the classical theory of employment, contended that in the modern economy prices and wages (do, do not) _____ fall when there is unemployment; and that wage reductions would lead to (smaller, larger) _____ money incomes, a (fall, rise) _____ in total spending, a(n) (increase, decrease) _____ in prices, and little or no change in total _____ in the economy.

10. Reasoning that if a price and wage-rate reduction would increase the output and employment of an individual firm, then a general reduction in prices and wages will increase output and employment in the economy as a whole is an example of the (**post hoc, ergo propter hoc** fallacy, fallacy of composition) _____

_____

11. The aggregate-supply curve of the classical economists is (horizontal, vertical) _____ and the aggregate-supply curve of the Keynesian economists is _____ up to the full-employment level of output. Therefore, a decrease in aggregate demand will have no effect on the price level and will decrease output and employment in the (classical, Keynesian) _____ model; but a decrease in aggregate demand will decrease the price level and have no effect on output and employment in the _____ model.

12. The views of classical and Keynesian economists also differ on the nature of the aggregate-demand curve.
   a. In the classical way of thinking, the money supply sets the basis for aggregate demand: if the price level falls and the money supply is constant, the purchasing power of money will (rise, fall) _____ and consumers and business firms will (expand, contract) _____ their expenditures for goods and services; aggregate demand will be reasonably stable if the nation's monetary authorities maintain a _____

_____
   b. From the Keynesian perspective, aggregate demand is (stable, unstable) _____, even if there are no changes in the supply of money, in part because business investment tends to be _____

13. Keynes argued that:
   a. the domestic output and employment depend (directly, inversely) _____ on the level of aggregate _____ in the economy;
   b. the most important determinant of consumption and of saving in the economy is the economy's _____;
   c. and both consumption and saving are (directly, inversely) _____ related to this determinant.

14. As disposable income falls, the average propensity to consume will (rise, fall) _____ and the average propensity to save will _____

15. The MPC is the change in (consumption, saving, income) _____ divided by the change in _____; it is the numerical value of the slope of the

_____ schedule. The MPS is the change in _____ divided by the change in _____; it is the numerical value of the slope of the _____ schedule.

16. The most important determinants of consumption spending, other than the level of income, are:
   a. the wealth or the sum of the _____ and the _____ assets households have accumulated
   b. _____
   c. _____
   d. _____
   e. _____

17. A change in the consumption (or saving) schedule means that _____

_____ but a change in the amount consumed (or saved) means that _____

18. Investment is defined as spending for additional _____; and the total amount of investment spending in the economy depends upon:
   a. the _____ rate of net _____
   b. the real rate of _____

_____

19. A business firm will invest in more capital if the expected rate of net profits on this investment is (greater, less) _____ than the real rate of interest it must pay for the use of money.

20. The relation between the rate of interest and the total amount of investment in the economy is (direct, inverse)

_____ This means that if the real rate of interest:
   a. rises, investment will _____
   b. falls, investment will _____

21. Five noninterest determinants of investment demand are:
   a. _____
   b. _____
   c. _____
   d. _____
   e. _____

22. The consumption schedule and the saving schedule tend to be (stable or unstable) _____ while investment demand tends to be _____ _____

23. The demand for new capital goods tends to be unstable because of the _____ of capital goods, the _____ of innovation, and the _____ of actual and expected profits.

GDP	C	S	APC, %	APS, %
$1500	$1540	$_____	1.027	−.027
1600	1620	_____	1.025	−.025
1700	1700	_____	_____	_____
1800	1780	_____	.989	.011
1900	1860	_____	.979	.021
2000	1940	_____	_____	_____
2100	2020	_____	.962	.038
2200	2100	_____	_____	_____

■ **PROBLEMS AND PROJECTS**

1. At the top of the next column is a consumption schedule. Assume taxes and transfer payments are zero and that all saving is personal saving.
  a. Compute saving at each of the eight levels of GDP and the missing average propensities to consume and to save.
  b. The break-even level of income (GDP) is $_____
  c. As GDP rises the marginal propensity to consume remains constant. Between each two GDPs the MPC can be found by dividing $_____ by $_____; and is equal to _____%

  d. The marginal propensity to save also remains constant when the GDP rises. Between each two GDPs the MPS is equal to $_____ divided by $_____; or to _____%
  e. Plot the consumption schedule, the saving schedule, and the 45° line on the graph below.
  (1) The numerical value of the slope of the consumption schedule is _____ and the term that is used to describe it is the _____
  (2) If the relevant saving schedule were constructed the numerical value of the slope of the saving schedule would be _____ and the term that is used to describe it is the _____

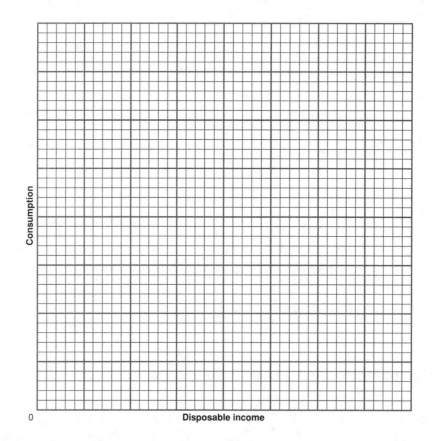

0   **Disposable income**

2. Indicate in the space to the right of each of the following events whether the event will tend to increase ($+$) or decrease ($-$) the **saving** schedule.

a. Development of consumer expectations that prices will be higher in the future _____

b. Gradual shrinkage in the quantity of real assets owned by consumers _____

c. Increase in the volume of consumer indebtedness

_____

d. Growing belief that disposable income will be lower in the future _____

e. Rumors that a current shortage of consumer goods will soon disappear _____

f. Rise in the actual level of disposable income

_____

g. A build-up in the dollar size of the financial assets owned by consumers _____

h. Development of a belief by consumers that the Federal government can and will prevent depressions in the future _____

3. The schedule below has eight different rates of net profit and the dollar amounts of the investment projects expected to have each of these net profit rates.

Expected rate of net profit	Investment projects (billions)
18%	$ 0
16	10
14	20
12	30
10	40
8	50
6	60
4	70

a. If the real rate of interest in the economy were 18%, business firms would plan to spend $_____ billion for investment; but if the real interest rate were 16% they would plan to spend $_____ for investment.

b. Should the real interest rate be 14% they would still wish to make the investments they were willing to make at real interest rates of 18% and 16%; they would also plan to spend an additional $_____ billion for investment; and their total investment would be $_____ billion.

c. Were the real rate of interest 12% they would make all the investments they had planned to make at higher real interest rates plus an additional $_____

billion; and their total investment spending would be $_____ billion.

d. Complete the table below by computing the amount of planned investment at the four remaining real interest rates.

Real rate of interest	Amount of investment (billions)
18%	$ 0
16	10
14	30
12	60
10	_____
8	_____
6	_____
4	_____

e. Graph the schedule you completed on the graph below. Plot the real rate of interest on the vertical axis and the amount of investment planned at each real rate of interest on the horizontal axis.

f. Both the graph and the table show that the relation between the real rate of interest and the amount of investment spending in the economy is _____. This means that when the real rate of interest:

(1) increases, investment will (increase, decrease)

_____

(2) decreases, investment will _____

g. It also means that should we wish to;

(1) increase investment, we would need to _____ the real rate of interest

(2) decrease investment, we would have to _____ the real rate of interest

0

h. This graph (or table) is the _____

_____ curve (or schedule).

4. Indicate in the space to the right of the following events whether the event would tend to increase (+) or decrease (−) investment expenditures.

a. Rising stock market prices _____

b. Development of expectations by businessmen that

business taxes will be higher in the future _____

c. Step-up in the rates at which new products and new

production processes are being introduced _____

d. Business belief that wage rates may be lower in the

future _____

e. A mild recession _____

f. A belief that business is "too good" and the economy is due for a period of "slow" consumer demand

_____

g. Rising costs in the construction industry _____

h. A rapid increase in the size of the economy's

population _____

i. A period of a high level of investment spending which has resulted in productive capacity in excess of

the current demand for goods and services _____

5. Below are two schedules showing several GDPs and the level of investment spending (*I*) at each GDP. (All figures are in billions of dollars.)

Schedule number 1		Schedule number 2	
GDP	*I*	**GDP**	*I*
$1850	$90	$1850	$ 75
1900	90	1900	80
1950	90	1950	85
2000	90	2000	90
2050	90	2050	95
2100	90	2100	100
2150	95	2150	105

a. Each of these schedules is an _____ schedule.

b. When such a schedule is drawn up it is assumed

that the real rate of interest is _____

c. In schedule:

(1) number 1, GDP and *I* are (unrelated, directly

related) _____

(2) number 2, GDP and *I* are _____

d. Should the real rate of interest rise, investment spending at each GDP would (increase, decrease)

_____ and the curve relating GDP and investment spending would shift (upward, downward)

_____

■ **SELF-TEST**

Circle the T if the statement is true; the F if it is false.

1. According to the classical economists, full employment is normal in market economies. **T** F

2. The classical economists believed that government assistance was **not** required to bring about full employment and full production in the economy. **T** F

3. Say's law states that demand for goods and services creates an equal supply of goods and services. **T** F

4. In both the classical and Keynesian theories of employment saving is income not expended for consumer goods and services. **T** F

5. In the classical theory, if saving exceeds investment the rate of interest will rise until saving and investment are equal. T **F**

6. Keynesians contend that most saving is done by business firms and most investment is done by households in the economy. T **F**

7. Classical economists contend that prices and wages would be sufficiently flexible to assure full employment in the economy if it were not for the government policies that reduce their downward flexibility. **T** F

8. The classical economists' view of aggregate demand is that if the money supply is constant a decrease in the price level will decrease the purchasing power of money and increase the quantities of goods and services demanded by consumers and business firms. T **F**

9. The level of saving in the economy, according to the Keynesians, depends primarily upon the level of its disposable income. **T** F

10. The consumption schedule which is employed as an analytical tool is also a historical record of the relationship of consumption to disposable income. T **F**

11. Empirical data suggest that households will tend to spend a smaller proportion of a small disposable income than of a larger disposable income. T **F**

12. An increase in the price level will increase the consumption schedule (shift the consumption curve upward). T **F**

13. An increase in the taxes paid by consumers will decrease both the amount they spend for consumption and the amount they save. **T** F

14. Both the consumption schedule and the saving schedule tend to be relatively stable over time. **T** F

15. The **real** interest rate is the nominal interest rate minus the rate of inflation. **T** F

16. A business firm will purchase additional capital goods if the real rate of interest it must pay exceeds the expected rate of net profits from the investment. T (F)

17. An increase in an economy's income may induce an increase in investment spending. (T) F

18. The relationship between the rate of interest and the level of investment spending is called the investment schedule. T (F)

19. The investment-demand schedule (or curve) tends to be relatively stable over time. T (F)

20. The irregularity of innovations and the variability of business profits contribute to the instability of investment expenditures. (T) F

Circle the letter that corresponds to the best answer.

1. Keynesian economists believe:
(a) unemployment is characteristic of capitalistic economies, and the government should engage in activist policies
(b) unemployment is characteristic of capitalistic economies, and in a government policy of laissez-faire
(c) full employment is characteristic of capitalistic economies, and the government should engage in activist policies
(d) full employment is characteristic of capitalistic economies, and in a government policy of laissez-faire

2. If the economy is closed, government neither taxes nor spends; all saving done in the economy is personal saving; and depreciation and net American income earned abroad are zero:
(a) gross domestic product equals personal consumption expenditures
(b) gross domestic product equals personal saving
(c) gross domestic product equals disposable income
(d) disposable income equals personal consumption expenditures

3. In the classical theory of employment, a decline in the rate of interest will:
(a) decrease saving and investment
(b) decrease saving and increase investment
(c) increase saving and decrease investment
(d) increase saving and investment

4. The classical theory predicts that an increase in the supply of savings will:
(a) lower interest rates and reduce investment
(b) raise interest rates and reduce investment
(c) lower interest rates and expand investment
(d) raise interest rates and expand investment

5. If the rate of interest did not equate saving and investment and total output was greater than total spending, the classical economists argued, competition would tend to force:
(a) product and resource prices down

(b) produce prices up and resource prices down
(c) product prices up and resource prices up
(d) product prices down and resource prices up

6. Which of the following is *not* involved in Keynes's criticism of the classical theory of employment?
(a) a reduction in wage rates will lead only to a reduction in total spending, not to an increase in employment
(b) investment spending is not influenced by the rate of interest
(c) prices and wages are simply not flexible downward in modern capitalistic economies
(d) saving in modern economies depends largely upon the level of disposable income and is little influenced by the rate of interest

7. Keynesian economists argue the source of the funds which finance investment are:
(a) current saving
(b) the accumulated money balances of households
(c) commercial banks
(d) all of the above

8. The Keynesian economists also argue that saving is:
(a) used to finance investment expenditures
(b) added to the money balances of savers
(c) used to retire the loans made previously by banks
(d) utilized for all of the above

9. The Keynesian aggregate-supply curve:
(a) is horizontal (to full-employment output)
(b) slopes upward
(c) is vertical
(d) slopes downward

10. The aggregate-supply curve of classical economists:
(a) is horizontal (to full-employment output)
(b) slopes upward
(c) is vertical
(d) slopes downward

11. In the classical theory of employment a decrease in aggregate demand results in:
(a) a decrease in both the price level and domestic output
(b) a decrease in the price level and no change in domestic output
(c) no change in the price level and a decrease in domestic output
(d) no change in either the price level or domestic output

12. A decrease in aggregate demand, in the Keynesian theory of employment, results in:
(a) a decrease in both the price level and domestic output
(b) a decrease in the price level and no change in domestic output
(c) no change in the price level and a decrease in domestic output

(d) no change in either the price level or domestic output

13. In the Keynesian theory, output and employment in the economy depend:
(a) directly on the level of total expenditures
(b) inversely on the quantity of resources available to it
(c) directly on the level of disposable income
(d) directly on the rate of interest

14. As disposable income decreases, *ceteris paribus:*
(a) both consumption and saving increases
(b) consumption increases and saving decreases
(c) consumption decreases and saving increases
(d) both consumption and saving decrease

15. If consumption spending increases from $358 to $367 billion when disposable income increases from $412 to $427 billion, it can be concluded that the marginal propensity to consume is:
(a) 0.4
(b) 0.6
(c) 0.8
(d) 0.9

16. If when disposable income is $375 billion the average propensity to consume is 0.8, it can be concluded that:
(a) the marginal propensity to consume is also 0.8
(b) consumption is $325 billion
(c) saving is $75 billion
(d) the marginal propensity to save is 0.2

17. As the disposable income of the economy increases:
(a) both the APC and the APS rise
(b) the APC rises and the APS falls
(c) the APC falls and the APS rises
(d) both the APC and the APS fall

18. Which of the following would *not* cause the consumption schedule to increase (that is, cause the consumption curve to rise)?
(a) a decrease in the expected price level
(b) an increase in consumers' ownership of financial assets
(c) a decrease in the amount of consumers' indebtedness
(d) an increase in the income received by consumers

19. A decrease in the price level tends to:
(a) increase the amount consumed
(b) decrease the amount consumed
(c) shift the consumption schedule upward
(d) shift the consumption schedule downward

20. A decrease in the level of investment spending would be a consequence of:
(a) a decline in the rate of interest
(b) a decline in the level of wages paid
(c) a decline in business taxes
(d) a decline in stock market prices

21. Which of the following relationships is an inverse one?
(a) the relationship between consumption spending and disposable income
(b) the relationship between investment spending and the rate of interest
(c) the relationship between saving and the rate of interest
(d) the relationship between investment spending and net national product

22. The slope of the consumption schedule or line for a given economy is the:
(a) marginal propensity to consume
(b) average propensity to consume
(c) marginal propensity to save
(d) average propensity to save

23. According to the classical economists, aggregate demand will be reasonably stable if:
(a) aggregate supply is reasonably stable
(b) business investment does not fluctuate
(c) there is a constant supply of money
(d) interest rates are flexible

*Answer the next two questions (**24** and **25**) on the basis of the following diagram.*

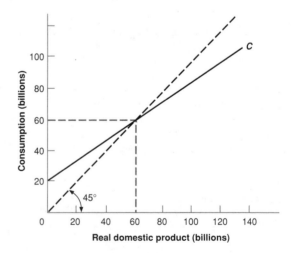

24. This diagram indicates that:
(a) consumption decreases after the $60 billion level of GDP
(b) the marginal propensity to consume decreases after the $60 billion level of GDP
(c) consumption decreases as a percentage of GDP as GDP increases
(d) consumption increases as GDP decreases

25. If the relevant saving schedule were constructed, one would find that:
(a) the marginal propensity to save is negative up to the $60 billion level of GDP

(b) the marginal propensity to save increases after the $60 billion level of GDP
(c) saving is zero at the $60 billion level of GDP
(d) saving is $20 billion at the $0 level of GDP

*Answer the next three questions (**26, 27,** and **28**) on the basis of the following disposable income (**DI**) and consumption (**C**) schedules for a private, closed economy. All figures are in billions of dollars.*

DI	C
$ 0	$ 4
40	40
80	76
120	112
160	148
200	184

26. If plotted on a graph, the slope of the consumption schedule would be:
(a) .6
(b) .7
(c) .8
(d) .9

27. At the $160 billion level of disposable income, the average propensity to save is:
(a) .015
(b) .075
(c) .335
(d) .925

28. If consumption increases by $5 billion at each level of disposable income, then the marginal propensity to consume will:
(a) change, but the average propensity to consume will *not* change
(b) change, and the average propensity to consume will change
(c) *not* change, but the average propensity to consume will change
(d) *not* change, and the average propensity to consume will *not* change

29. If the slope of a linear saving schedule decreases in a private, closed economy, then it can be concluded that the:
(a) MPS has decreased
(b) MPC has decreased
(c) income has decreased
(d) income has increased

30. Which one of the following best explains the variability of investment?
(a) the predictable useful life of capital goods
(b) constancy or regularities in business innovations
(c) instabilities in the level of profits
(d) business pessimism about the future

■ **DISCUSSION QUESTIONS**

1. How do the classical and Keynesian economists differ on:
(a) the normal amount of unemployment that will prevail in a capitalistic (or market) economy; and
(b) the role they would assign to government in such an economy?

2. What are the three simplifying assumptions used in this chapter and what are the two implications of these assumptions?

3. According to the classical economists, what level of employment would tend to prevail in the economy? On what two basic assumptions did their analysis of the level of employment rest?

4. What is Say's law? How were the classical economists able to reason that whatever is saved is spent?

5. In the classical analysis Say's law made it certain that whatever was produced would be sold. How did flexible prices, flexible wages, and competition drive the economy to full employment and maximum output?

6. On what grounds did J. M. Keynes argue that flexible interest rates would not assure the operation of Say's law? What were his reasons for asserting that flexible prices and wages would not assure full employment; and what was the classical response to his assertion?

7. What is:
(a) the difference between the classical and the Keynesian aggregate-supply curve; and
(b) the difference between the effects a decrease in aggregate demand would have on the price level and on the real national output in the two models? Why does the classical aggregate-demand curve have a negative (downward) slope?

8. "Savers and investors are largely motivated by different factors." Explain in detail what motivates savers and investors. Does the rate of interest play any role in determining saving and investment?

9. Describe the relation between consumption and disposable income called the consumption schedule and the one between saving and disposable income known as the saving schedule; and then define the two average propensities and the two marginal propensities.

10. Explain briefly how the average propensity to consume and the average propensity to save vary as disposable income varies. Why do APC and APS behave this way? What happens to consumption and saving as disposable income varies?

11. Why do the sum of the APC and the APS and the sum of the MPC and the MPS always equal exactly one?

12. Explain briefly and explicitly *how* changes in the five nonincome determinants will affect the consumption schedule and the saving schedule and *why* such changes will affect consumption and saving in the way you have indicated.

13. Explain:
(a) when a business firm will or will not purchase additional capital goods;
(b) how changes in the five noninterest determinants of investment spending will affect the investment-demand curve;
(c) why investment spending tends to rise when the rate of interest falls; and
(d) how changes in GDP might affect investment spending.

14. Why does the level of investment spending tend to be highly unstable?

15. Explain why the amount consumers spend and the amount investors spend matter all that much to the performance of the economy.

■ **ANSWERS**

Chapter 10 Classical and Keynesian Theories of Employment

FILL-IN QUESTIONS

1. fully, less than fully, laissez-faire, activist

2. closed, personal, taxes, transfer, spend, zero; *a.* national income, personal income, disposable income; *b.* consumption, investment

3. Say's, flexibility

4. demand for these goods and services

5. the rate of interest

6. fall, rise, saving, investment

7. fall, unemployment, downward, increase, all who are willing to work at the going wage rate are employed and total output equals total spending

8. *a.* reasons (motives); *b.* accumulated money balances, commercial banks; *c.* balances, loans (debts)

9. do not, smaller, fall, decrease, employment (output)

10. fallacy of composition

11. vertical, horizontal, Keynesian, classical

12. *a.* rise, expand, constant supply of money; *b.* unstable, unstable

13. *a.* directly, expenditures; *b.* disposable income; *c.* directly

14. rise, fall

15. consumption, income, consumption, saving, income, saving

16. *a.* real, financial (either order); *b.* the price level; *c.* expectations; *d.* consumer indebtedness; *e.* taxation of consumer income

17. the amount consumers plan to consume (save) will be different at every level of income, the level of income has changed and that consumers will change their planned consumption (saving) as a result

18. capital goods; *a.* expected, profits; *b.* interest

19. greater

20. inverse; *a.* decrease; *b.* increase

21. *a.* the cost of acquiring, maintaining, and operating the capital goods; *b.* business taxes; *c.* technological change; *d.* the stock of capital goods on hand; *e.* expectations

22. stable, unstable

23. durability, irregularity, variability

PROBLEMS AND PROJECTS

1. *a.* S: −40, −20, 0, 20, 40, 60, 80, 100; APC: 1.000, 0.970, 0.955; APS: 0.000, 0.030, 0.045; *b.* 1,700; *c.* 80, 100, 80; *d.* 20, 100, 20; *e.* (1) .8, MPC; (2) .2, MPS

2. *a.* −; *b.* −; *c.* +; *d.* +; *e.* +; *f.* none; *g.* −; *h.* −

3. *a.* 0, 10; *b.* 20, 30; *c.* 30, 60; *d.* 100, 150, 210, 280; *f.* inverse, (1) decrease, (2) increase; *g.* (1) lower, (2) raise; *h.* investment-demand

4. *a.* +; *b.* −; *c.* +; *d.* +; *e.* −; *f.* −; *g.* −; *h.* +; *i.* −

5. *a.* investment; *b.* constant (given); *c.* (1) unrelated, (2) directly related; *d.* decrease, downward

SELF-TEST

1. T, p. 171	8. F, p. 179	15. T, p. 187
2. T, p. 171	9. T, p. 180	16. F, pp. 187–188
3. F, p. 172	10. F, pp. 181–182	17. T, pp. 190–191
4. T, pp. 173, 176	11. F, p. 182	18. F, p. 190
5. F, p. 173	12. F, p. 185	19. F, p. 191
6. F, pp. 175–176	13. T, p. 185	20. T, pp. 191–192
7. T, pp. 174–175	14. T, p. 186	

1. *a*, p. 171	11. *b*, pp. 178–179	21. *b*, p. 188
2. *c*, p. 172	12. *c*, pp. 178–179	22. *a*, p. 184
3. *b*, pp. 173–174	13. *a*, p. 180	23. *c*, p. 179
4. *c*, pp. 173–174	14. *d*, p. 182	24. *c*, p. 183
5. *a*, p. 174	15. *b*, p. 184	25. *c*, p. 183
6. *b*, p. 176	16. *c*, pp. 182–184	26. *d*, p. 184
7. *d*, p. 176	17. *c*, p. 183	27. *b*, p. 183
8. *d*, pp. 176–177	18. *d*, p. 185	28. *c*, pp. 182–184
9. *a*, p. 179	19. *c*, p. 185	29. *a*, p. 184
10. *c*, p. 178	20. *d*, pp. 189–190	30. *c*, pp. 191–193

DISCUSSION QUESTIONS

1. p. 171	6. pp. 175–177	11. pp. 183–184
2. p. 172	7. pp. 177–179	12. p. 185
3. p. 172	8. p. 176	13. pp. 187–190
4. pp. 172–173	9. pp. 180–184	14. pp. 191–193
5. pp. 174–175	10. pp. 182–183	15. pp. 186, 191–193

CHAPTER 11

Equilibrium Domestic Output in the Keynesian Model

Chapter 11, building on the tools developed in the last chapter, continues the Keynesian explanation of what determines the equilibrium level of real GDP—the real GDP an economy will tend to produce. You **must** understand this chapter if you are to acquire an understanding of what causes the real GDP to rise and fall; of what causes unemployment, depression, inflation, and prosperity; and of what can be done to foster price stability, full employment, and economic growth.

In the Keynesian model of the economy the equilibrium level of real GDP is determined **only** by the level of **aggregate expenditures** because it is assumed in this model that the economy is operating in the Keynesian (or horizontal) range of the aggregate-supply curve (and that the price level does not rise or fall). The two components of aggregate expenditures in an economy which is closed (neither exports nor imports goods and services) and in which governments do not spend or tax are consumption expenditures and gross investment expenditures; and they were analyzed in the last chapter. In this chapter the equilibrium level of real GDP is explained with both tables and graphs, first by using the expenditures-output approach and then by employing the leakages-injections approach. These two approaches are complementary and are two different ways of analyzing the same process and of reaching the same conclusions. For each approach it is important for you to know, given the consumption (or saving) schedule and the level of gross investment expenditures, **what** real GDP will tend to be produced and **why** this will be the real GDP which will be produced.

It is also important that you understand the significant distinction between **planned** investment and **actual** investment. Saving and actual gross investment are always equal because they are defined in exactly the same way: the output of the economy minus its consumption. But saving and planned gross investment are not, however, equal by definition. They are equal only when real GDP is at its equilibrium level. When real GDP is **not** at its equilibrium level, saving and planned gross investment are **not** equal even though saving and actual investment are, as always, equal because the actual investment includes **un**planned investment or disinvestment. Remember: Equilibrium real GDP is achieved when saving and **planned** gross invest-

ment—**not** saving and **actual** gross investment—are equal.

The consumption (and the saving) schedule and the investment schedule—especially the latter—are subject to change, and when they change equilibrium real GDP will also change. The relationship between an initial change in the investment or consumption schedules and a change in equilibrium real GDP is called the multiplier. Three things to note here are: **how** the multiplier is defined, **why** there is a multiplier effect, and upon **what** the size of the multiplier depends. Because of the multiplier, the paradoxical consequence of an attempt by the economy to save more is either no increase or a decrease in the level of saving in the economy. The explanation of this paradox will be evident to you when you understand the equilibrium real GDP and the multiplier effect.

It is important to be aware that the equilibrium real GDP is not necessarily the real GDP at which full employment with inflationary pressures is achieved. Aggregate expenditures may be greater or less than the full-employment noninflationary real GDP; if they are greater there is an inflationary gap, and if they are less there exists a recessionary gap. Be sure that you know how to measure the size of each of these gaps: the amount by which the aggregate-expenditures schedule (or curve) must change to bring the economy to its full-employment real GDP without there being inflation in the economy.

The Keynesian model of the economy can be extended by adding the **net** exports of an economy to the aggregate-expenditures schedule. Net exports are nothing more than the economy's exports less its imports of goods and services. Like investment, the exports of a nation are an injection into its circular flow of income; and they increase the flow. But imports are, like saving, a leakage from the circular flow, and decrease the flow.

The generalization used to find the equilibrium real GDP in an open economy (one that exports and imports) is the same one as for a closed economy: the economy will tend to produce a real GDP which is equal to aggregate expenditures. The only difference is that the aggregate expenditures include not only consumption and planned gross investment expenditures but the expenditures for net exports. So the equilibrium real GDP will equal $C + I_g + X_n$ (when X_n is the symbol used for net exports).

An increase in X_n, like an increase in I_g, will increase the equilibrium real GDP; and a decrease in X_n will decrease the equilibrium real GDP. And like a change in I_g, a change in X_n has a multiplier effect on real GDP.

The price level in the Keynesian model, as noted above, is assumed to be constant; but in the aggregate demand-aggregate supply model (examined in Chapter 9) the price level can rise or fall. These two models do not, however, contradict each other; and the last section of the chapter reconciles them. The important thing to understand is that prices can be constant at different levels. The price index in the economy, for example, might be constant at 100, at 75, or at 120. The AD curve is derived from the Keynesian model by letting prices be **constant at different levels.** Once you realize that it is no great problem to see that the lower (the higher) the level at which prices are constant in the Keynesian model the larger (the smaller) will be the equilibrium real GDP in that model of the economy; and that the AD curve slopes downward.

The AD curve derived in this way from the Keynesian model and the AS curve together determine the price level and the equilibrium real GDP in the aggregate-demand–aggregate-supply model. But aggregate demand can increase (or decrease); and when it does both the price level and the equilibrium real GDP may be changed. How the price level and real GDP are affected depends upon the range on the aggregate-supply curve in which the economy is initially operating. Here the important thing to see is that because the change in AD may also affect the price level in the economy, the change in AD may not have its *full* multiplier effect on the real GDP of the economy.

The next chapter deals with the fiscal policies that can be employed by government to eliminate recessionary and inflationary gaps in the economy. Chapter 11 has purposely ignored government and assumed an economy in which government neither taxes nor spends. But Chapter 12 does not ignore the role of government in the economy and discusses fiscal policies and their effects upon the equilibrium real GDP and the price level.

■ **CHECKLIST**

When you have studied this chapter you should be able to:

☐ State the range along the aggregate supply in which the economy is assumed to operate and the assumption made about the price level in the Keynesian model.
☐ Find the equilibrium real GDP, when you are given the necessary tabular or graphical data, by employing either the aggregate-expenditures–national-output or the leakages-injections approach.
☐ Explain why the economy will tend to produce its equi-

librium real GDP rather than some smaller or larger real GDP.
☐ State the difference between planned investment and actual investment.
☐ Explain how it is possible for saving and actual investment to be equal when saving and planned investment are not equal.
☐ Determine the economy's new equilibrium real GDP when there is a change in the consumption (or saving) schedule or in the investment schedule.
☐ Find the value of the multiplier when you are given the needed information.
☐ Cite the two facts upon which the multiplier effect (a multiplier greater than one) is based.
☐ Draw a graph to explain the paradox of thrift.
☐ Distinguish between the equilibrium real GDP and the full-employment noninflationary level of real GDP.
☐ Find the recessionary and the inflationary gaps when you are provided the relevant data.
☐ Use the concept of net exports to define aggregate expenditures in an open economy.
☐ Explain what the equilibrium real GDP in an open economy will be when net exports are positive and when net exports are negative.
☐ Find the equilibrium real GDP in an open economy when you are given the appropriate data.
☐ Give examples of how circumstances or policies abroad can affect domestic GDP.
☐ Contrast the Keynesian expenditures-output and the aggregate-demand–aggregate-supply models by comparing the variability of the price level and real GDP in the two models in the three ranges along the aggregate-supply curve.
☐ Derive the aggregate-demand curve (or schedule) from the Keynesian model.
☐ Explain the effect of a change in aggregate expenditures (in the Keynesian model) on the aggregate-demand curve (or schedule).
☐ Predict the effects of a change in aggregate demand on the price level and the equilibrium real GDP in the three ranges along the aggregate-supply curve.
☐ Explain what determines how large the multiplier effect on the equilibrium real GDP will be in the aggregate-demand–aggregate-supply model.

■ **CHAPTER OUTLINE**

1. In this chapter it is assumed (unless otherwise explicitly specified) that the economy is operating within the Keynesian range of the aggregate-supply curve and the price level is, therefore, constant; two approaches are used to explain what *real* domestic output (or GDP) the economy will tend to produce; but both approaches yield the same conclusion.

2. Employing the aggregate-expenditures–national-output approach, the equilibrium real GDP is the real GDP at which:

a. aggregate expenditures (consumption plus planned gross investment) equal the real GDP; or

b. in graphical terms, the aggregate-expenditures curve crosses the 45-degree line and its slope is equal to the marginal propensity to consume.

3. Using the leakages-injections approach, the equilibrium real GDP is the real GDP at which:

a. saving and planned gross investment are equal; or

b. in graphical terms, the saving curve crosses the planned gross investment curve.

4. The gross investment schedule indicates what investors **plan** to do; and when saving is greater (less) than planned gross investment,

a. **un**planned gross investment (disinvestment) in inventories will occur; and

b. producers will reduce (expand) their production and the real GDP will fall (rise) until there is no unplanned gross investment (disinvestment); but the **actual** gross investment and saving are always equal because the former includes unplanned investment or disinvestment.

5. Changes in planned gross investment (or in the consumption and saving schedules) will cause the equilibrium real GDP to change in the same direction by an amount greater than the initial change in investment (or consumption).

a. This is called the multiplier effect; and the multiplier is equal to the ratio of the change in the real GDP to the initial change in spending.

(1) The multiplier effect occurs because a change in the dollars spent by one person alters the income of another person in the same direction and because any change in the income of one person will change the person's consumption and saving in the same direction by a fraction of the change in income.

(2) The value of the simple multiplier is equal to the reciprocal of the marginal propensity to save.

(3) The significance of the multiplier is that relatively small changes in the spending plans of business firms or households bring about large changes in the equilibrium real GDP.

(4) The simple multiplier has this value only in an economy in which the only leakage is saving; and the complex multiplier takes into account such other leakages as taxes and imports.

b. The paradox of thrift is that an increase in the saving schedule results in no increase, and may result in a decrease, in saving: the increase in the saving schedule causes a multiple contraction in real GDP and at the lower real GDP the same amount or even less saving takes place; but saving is not socially undesirable

if it limits demand-pull inflation or if it leads to more investment and growth in the economy.

6. The equilibrium level of real GDP may turn out to be an equilibrium at less than full employment, at full employment, or at full employment with inflation.

a. If the equilibrium real GDP is **less** than the real GDP consistent with full employment, there exists a recessionary gap; the size of the recessionary gap equals the amount by which the aggregate-expenditures schedule must increase (shift upward) to increase the real GDP to its full-employment noninflationary level.

b. If equilibrium real GDP is **greater** than the real GDP consistent with stable prices there is an inflationary gap. The size of the inflationary gap equals the amount by which the aggregate-expenditures schedule must decrease (shift downward) if the economy is to achieve full employment without inflation.

c. It is, however, likely that a full-employment noninflationary real GDP is unattainable in the real world; and this likelihood complicates the elimination of an inflationary gap.

7. In an open economy the exports (X) of a nation increase and its imports (M) decrease aggregate expenditures in that economy; and aggregate expenditures are equal to the sum of consumption spending, planned gross investment spending, and net exports (X_n) when X_n is defined as X minus M.

a. The equilibrium real GDP is an open economy is the real GDP equal to consumption plus planned gross investment plus net exports; and

b. any increase (decrease) in its X_n will increase (decrease) its equilibrium real GDP with a multiplier effect.

c. In an open economy model, circumstances and policies abroad, such as a change in the level of national incomes of trading partners, changes in tariffs or quotas, or changes in exchange rates can affect domestic GDP.

8. The Keynesian expenditures-output model and the aggregate-demand–aggregate-supply model are reconciled by recalling that the price level is assumed to be constant in the former and is a variable (can rise or fall) in the latter model.

a. The AD curve is derived from the intersections of the aggregate-expenditures curves and the 45-degree curve: as the price level falls (rises) the aggregate-expenditures curve shifts upward (downward) and the equilibrium real GDP increases (decreases); and this inverse relationship between the price level and the equilibrium real GDP is the AD schedule (or curve).

As the price level falls (rises):

(1) the consumption curve shifts upward (downward) because of the **real balances** or **wealth** effect;

(2) the investment curve shifts upward (downward) because of the **interest-rate** effect; and

(3) the net export curve shifts upward (downward) because of the **foreign purchases** effect.

b. If the price level is constant, any change in the non-price level determinants of consumption and planned investment that shifts the aggregate-expenditures curve upward (downward) will increase (decrease) the equilibrium real GDP and shift the AD curve to the right (left) by an amount equal to the increase (decrease) in aggregate expenditures times the multiplier.

c. If the economy is operating along the:

(1) Keynesian range of the AS curve an increase in AD will have no effect on the price level and the increase in the equilibrium real GDP will equal the full multiplier effect of the increase in aggregate expenditures;

(2) intermediate range the increase in AD will increase the price level and the increase in the equilibrium real GDP will be less than the full multiplier effect of the increase in aggregate expenditures;

(3) classical range the increase in AD will increase the price level and have no effect on the equilibrium real GDP.

d. The Keynesian expenditures-output model is expanded in the next chapter (by including the effects of government expenditures and tax collections on real GDP).

■ **IMPORTANT TERMS**

Real domestic output (real GDP)	Injection
	Actual investment
Nominal domestic output (nominal GDP)	Unplanned investment
	Multiplier effect
Aggregate-expenditures–national-output approach	Multiplier
	Simple multiplier
Leakages-injections approach	Complex multiplier
	Paradox of thrift
Aggregate expenditures	Recessionary gap
Aggregate-expenditures schedule (curve)	Inflationary gap
	Open economy
Planned investment	Closed economy
Equilibrium (real) GDP	Net exports
45-degree line	
Leakage	

■ **FILL-IN QUESTIONS**

1. In this chapter (unless explicitly indicated to the contrary),

a. it is assumed that the economy is operating within the (Keynesian, classical) _____ range of the aggregate supply and the price level is (variable, constant) _____;

b. the explanation is in terms of the (real, nominal) _____ domestic output or real GDP.

2. Two complementary approaches which are employed to explain the equilibrium level of real domestic output are the _____ approach and the _____ approach.

3. Assuming a private and closed economy, the equilibrium level of real GDP is the real GDP at which:

a. aggregate _____ equal real domestic _____

b. real GDP equals _____ plus _____

c. the aggregate-expenditures schedule or curve intersects the _____ line.

4. When the leakages-injections approach is used:

a. In this chapter the only leakage considered is _____ and the only injection considered is _____

b. Later the two additional:

(1) leakages considered are _____ and _____

(2) injections considered are _____ and _____

5. If:

a. Aggregate expenditures are greater than the real domestic output, saving is (greater, less) _____ than planned gross investment, there is unplanned (investment, disinvestment) _____ in inventories, and the real GDP will (rise, fall) _____

b. Aggregate expenditures are less than the real domestic output, saving is _____ than planned gross investment, there is unplanned _____ in inventories, and the real GDP will _____

c. Aggregate expenditures are equal to the real domestic output, saving is _____ planned gross investment, unplanned investment in inventories is _____, and the real GDP will _____

6. At every level of real GDP saving is equal to (planned, actual) _____ gross investment.

a. But if planned gross investment is greater than saving by $10:

(1) there is $10 of unplanned (investment, disinvestment) _____

(2) the real GDP will (rise, fall) _____

b. And if planned gross investment is less than saving by $5:

(1) there is $5 of unplanned _____

(2) the real GDP will _____

7. The multiplier:

a. is the ratio of the change in _____ to an initial change in spending in the economy;

b. has a value equal to the one divided by the

_____

which is the same thing as one divided by the quantity

of one minus _____

8. The multiplier effect is based on two facts:

a. an initial increase in spending by business firms or

consumers will increase the _____ of the households in the economy; and

b. the latter increase will expand the (consumption, investment) _____ spending of the households by an amount equal to the increase in income

times the _____

9. When planned gross investment spending increases

the equilibrium real GDP (increases, decreases) _____

_____ and when planned gross investment spend-

ing decreases the equilibrium real GDP _____

a. The changes in the equilibrium real GDP are

(greater, less) _____ than the changes in planned gross investment spending.

b. The size of the multiplier varies (directly, inversely)

_____ with the size of the marginal propensity to consume.

10. If the economy decides to save more (consume less) at every level of GDP, the equilibrium real GDP will (in-

crease, decrease) _____ and the equilibrium level of saving in the economy will either remain the same

or (increase, decrease) _____.
This consequence of an increased desire to save is called

the _____

11. A recessionary gap exists when equilibrium real GDP

is (greater, less) _____ than the full-employment real GDP; to bring real GDP to the full-employment level, the aggregate-expenditures schedule must (in-

crease, decrease) _____ by an amount

equal to the difference between the equilibrium and the full-employment noninflationary real GDP divided by the

_____

12. When equilibrium nominal GDP is greater than the full-employment real GDP at which prices are stable, there

is a(n) _____ gap; to eliminate this gap

_____ must decrease by _____

_____

divided by the multiplier.

13. When a nation is able to export and import goods and services:

a. Its net exports equal its _____

minus its _____

b. In an open economy:

(1) Aggregate expenditures are equal to consumption

plus planned gross investment plus _____

(2) The equilibrium real GDP is the real GDP which is

equal to _____

14. What would be the effect—increase (+) or decrease (−)—of each of the following upon an open economy's equilibrium real GDP?

a. An increase in its imports _____

b. An increase in its exports _____

c. A decrease in its imports _____

d. A decrease in its exports _____

e. An increasing level of national income among trad-

ing partners _____

f. An increase in trade barriers imposed by trading

partners _____

g. A depreciation in the value of the economy's

currency _____

15. In the aggregate-demand–aggregate-supply model

the price level is a (constant, variable) _____;
in the Keynesian expenditures-output model it is a

_____

a. But if the price level were lower in the Keynesian

model the _____ effect would (raise,

lower) _____ the consumption investment, net exports, and aggregate-expenditures curves; and the equilibrium real GDP would (rise, fall)

_____

b. And if the price level were higher in the Keynesian

model this effect would _____ the consumption investment, net exports, and aggregate-expenditures curves; and the equilibrium real GDP would _____

c. This (direct, inverse) _____ relationship between the price level and the equilibrium real GDP in the Keynesian model is the aggregate (demand, supply) _____ curve (or schedule).

16. If the price level were a constant, a(n)
a. increase in the aggregate-expenditures curve would shift the aggregate-demand curve to the (right, left) _____ by an amount equal to the upward shift in aggregate expenditures times the _____
b. decrease in the aggregate-expenditures curve would shift the aggregate-demand curve to the _____ by an amount equal to the _____

_____

17. Were aggregate demand to increase,
a. the flatter the aggregate-supply curve, the (greater, smaller) _____ is the multiplier effect on the real equilibrium GDP and the _____ is the effect on the equilibrium price level; and
b. the steeper the aggregate-supply curve, the _____ is the multiplier effect on the equilibrium real GDP and the _____ is the effect on the equilibrium price level.

■ **PROBLEMS AND PROJECTS**

1. The table below shows consumption and saving at various levels of real GDP. Assume the price level is constant, the economy is closed and there are no government, no business savings, no depreciation, and no net American income earned abroad.
a. The next table is an investment-demand schedule which shows the net amounts investors plan to invest at different rates of interest. Assume the rate of interest is 6% and complete the gross investment, the consumption-plus-investment, and the unplanned investment (**UI**) columns—showing unplanned investment with a + and unplanned disinvestment with a −.

Interest rate	I_g
10%	$ 0
9	7
8	13
7	18
6	22
5	25
4	27
3	28

b. The equilibrium real GDP will be $_____
c. The value of the marginal propensity to consume in this problem is _____ and the value of the marginal propensity to save is _____
d. The value of the simple multiplier is _____
e. If the rate of interest should fall from 6% to 5%, planned gross investment would increase, decrease) _____ by $_____; and the equilibrium real GDP would, as a result, (increase, decrease) _____ by $_____
f. Suppose the rate of interest were to rise from 6% to 7%. Planned investment would _____ by $_____; and the equilibrium real GDP would _____ by $_____
g. Assume the rate of interest is 6%.
(1) On the graph below, plot **S** and I_g and indicate the equilibrium real GDP.

Real GDP	C	S	I_g	C + I_g	UI
$1300	$1290	$10	$22	$1312	−12
1310	1298	12	22	1320	−10
1320	1306	14	____	____	____
1330	1314	16	____	____	____
1340	1322	18	____	____	____
1350	1330	20	____	____	____
1360	1338	22	____	____	____
1370	1346	24	____	____	____
1380	1354	26	____	____	____
1390	1362	28	22	1384	+6
1400	1370	30	22	1392	+8

0   **Real GDP**

(2) On the following graph, plot **C, C** + **I_g**, and the 45-degree line, and indicate the equilibrium real GDP.

0   **Real GDP**

2. Assume the marginal propensity to consume is 0.8 and the change in gross planned investment is $10. Complete the table below modeled after Table 11-2 in the textbook.

	Change in income	Change in consumption	Change in saving
Increase in gross investment of $10	$ + 10	$ _____	$ _____
Second round	_____	_____	_____
Third round	_____	_____	_____
Fourth round	_____	_____	_____
Fifth round	_____	_____	_____
All other rounds	16.38	13.10	3.28
Totals	_____	_____	_____

3. Below are a saving schedule and an investment schedule (I_g) indicating that planned investment is constant.

Real GDP	S	I_g
$300	$ 5	$15
310	7	15
320	9	15
330	11	15
340	13	15
350	15	15
360	17	15
370	19	15
380	21	15
390	23	15
400	25	15

a. The equilibrium real GDP is $_____

and saving and planned investment are both $_____

b. The marginal propensity to save is _____

and the simple multiplier is _____

c. A $2 rise in the I_g **schedule** will cause real GDP to

rise by $_____

d. Use the investment schedule given in the table and assume a $2 increase in the saving schedule in the table—that is, saving at every real GDP increases by $2.

(1) Equilibrium real GDP will _____ to

$_____ and at this real GDP saving will be

$_____

(2) The effect of the increase in the saving schedule is

to _____ equilibrium real GDP; this is called

the _____

(3) The amount by which real GDP changes depends on the size of the change in the saving schedule and

the size of _____

4. In the table below are consumption and saving schedules for a closed economy. Assume that the level of real GDP at which full employment without inflation is achieved is $590.

Real GDP	C	S
$550	$520	$30
560	526	34
570	532	38
580	538	42
590	544	46
600	550	50
610	556	54
620	562	58
630	568	62

a. The value of the multiplier is _____

b. If planned net investment is $58, the equilibrium

money GDP is $_____ and exceeds the full-employment noninflationary real GDP by

$_____. There is a(n) _____ gap

of $_____

c. If planned investment is $38, the equilibrium real

GDP is $_____ and is less than full-

employment real GDP by $_____

There is a(n) _____

gap of $_____

5. Below is a schedule showing what aggregate expenditures (consumption plus planned gross investment) would be at various levels of real net domestic product in a closed economy.

a. Were this economy to become an open economy the volume of exports would be a constant $90 billion; and the volume of imports would be a constant $86

Possible levels of real GDP (billions)	Aggregate expenditures, closed economy (billions)	Exports (billions)	Imports (billions)	Net exports (billions)	Aggregate expenditures, open economy (billions)
$ 750	$ 776	$90	$86	$_____	$_____
800	816	90	86	_____	_____
850	856	90	86	_____	_____
900	896	90	86	_____	_____
950	936	90	86	_____	_____
1,000	976	90	86	_____	_____
1,050	1,016	90	86	_____	_____

billion. At each of the seven levels of real GDP, net exports would be $_____ billion.

b. Compute aggregate expenditures in this open economy at the seven real GDP levels and enter them in the table.

c. The equilibrium real GDP in this open economy would be $_____ billion.

d. The value of the multiplier in this open economy is equal to _____

e. A $10 billion increase in:

(1) exports would (increase, decrease) _____

the equilibrium real GDP by $_____ billion.

(2) imports would (increase, decrease) _____

the equilibrium real GDP by $_____ billion.

6. The real GDP an economy might produce is shown in column (1) below.

(1) Real GDP	(2) $AE_{1.20}$	(3) $AE_{1.00}$	(4) $AE_{0.80}$
$2100	$2110	$2130	$2150
2200	2200	2220	2240
2300	2290	2310	2330
2400	2380	2400	2420
2500	2470	2490	2510
2600	2560	2580	2600

a. If the price level in this economy were $1.20 the aggregate expenditures (AE) at each real GDP would be those shown in column (2) and the equilibrium real GDP would be $_____

b. But if the price level were $1.00 the aggregate expenditures at each real GDP would be those shown in column (3) and the equilibrium real GDP would be $_____

c. And if the price level were $0.80 the aggregate expenditures at each real GDP would be those shown in column (4) and the equilibrium real GDP would be $_____

d. Show in the schedule below the equilibrium real GDP at each of the three price levels.

Price level	Equilibrium real GDP
$1.20	$___
1.00	___
.80	___

(1) This schedule is the _____ schedule and

(2) in it the equilibrium real GDP is _____ related to the price level.

7. Columns (1) and (2) in the table below are the aggregate-supply schedule of an economy.

a. The economy is in the

(1) classical range when its real GDP is $_____ and the price level is $_____ or higher;

(2) Keynesian range when its real GDP is $_____ or less and its price level is $_____

b. If the aggregate demand in the economy were columns (1) and (3) the equilibrium real GDP would be $_____ and the equilibrium price level would be $_____; and if aggregate demand should increase by $100 to that shown in columns (1) and (4) the equilibrium real GDP would increase by $_____ and the price level would _____

c. Should aggregate demand be that shown in columns (1) and (5) the equilibrium real GDP would be $_____ and the equilibrium price would be $_____; and if aggregate demand should in-

(1) Price level	(2) Real GDP	(3) AD_1	(4) AD_2	(5) AD_3	(6) AD_4	(7) AD_5	(8) AD_6
$2.60	$2390	$ 840	$ 940	$1900	$2000	$2190	$2290
2.40	2390	940	1040	2000	2100	2290	2390
2.20	2390	1040	1140	2100	2200	2390	2490
2.00	2390	1140	1240	2200	2300	2490	2590
1.90	2350	1190	1290	2250	2350	2540	2640
1.80	2300	1240	1340	2300	2400	2590	2690
1.60	2200	1340	1440	2400	2500	2690	2790
1.40	2090	1440	1540	2500	2600	2790	2890
1.20	1970	1540	1640	2600	2700	2890	2990
1.00	1840	1640	1740	2700	2800	2990	3090
1.00	1740	1640	1740	2700	2800	2990	3090
1.00	1640	1640	1740	2700	2800	2990	3090

crease by $100 to that shown in columns (1) and (6) the equilibrium real GDP would increase by $_____

and the price level would rise to $_____
d. And if aggregate demand were that shown in columns (1) and (7) the equilibrium real GDP would be

$_____ and the equilibrium price level would

be $_____; but if aggregate demand increased by $100 to that shown in columns (1) and (8)

the price level would rise to $_____ and the

equilibrium real GDP would _____

■ SELF-TEST

Circle the T if the statement is true; the F if it is false.

1. In the Keynesian model of the economy the price level is constant. **T F**

Questions 2 and 3 are based on the data supplied in the following table.

Real GDP	C
$200	$200
240	228
280	256
320	284
360	312
400	340
440	368
480	396

2. If consumption spending at each level of real GDP increased by $10, the equilibrium level of real GDP would tend to rise by $30. **T F**

3. If planned gross investment was $24, equilibrium real GDP would increase by $28. **T F**

4. The investment schedule is a schedule of planned investment rather than a schedule of actual investment. **T F**

5. Saving and actual gross investment are always equal. **T F**

6. Saving at any level of real GDP equals planned gross investment plus unplanned investment (or minus unplanned disinvestment). **T F**

7. If real GDP were to decline by $40, consumers would reduce their consumption expenditures by an amount less than $40. **T F**

8. A decrease in the rate of interest will, other things remaining the same, result in a decrease in the equilibrium real GDP. **T F**

9. The larger the marginal propensity to consume, the larger the size of the multiplier. **T F**

10. If the slope of a linear consumption schedule is steeper in economy A than economy B, then the MPC is less in economy A than economy B. **T F**

11. The multiplier is based on the idea that any change in income will cause both consumption and saving to vary in the same direction as a change in income and by a fraction of that change in income. **T F**

12. The value of the complex multiplier will usually be greater than the value of the simple multiplier because there will be more injections into the economy. **T F**

13. The paradox of thrift is the idea that if a nation tries to save more, it may wind up saving the same amount. **T F**

14. The equilibrium real GDP is the real GDP at which there is full employment in the economy. **T F**

15. The existence of a recessionary gap in the economy is characterized by the full employment of labor. **T F**

16. The net exports of an economy equal the sum of its exports and its imports of goods and services. **T F**

17. An increase in the volume of a nation's exports, other things being equal, will expand the nation's real GDP. **T F**

18. An increase in the imports of a nation will increase the exports of other nations. **T F**

19. An appreciation of the dollar will increase net exports. **T F**

20. The higher the price level, the smaller are the real balances of consumers, and the lower is the consumption schedule (curve). **T F**

21. An increase in the price level will shift the aggregate-demand curve to the right. **T F**

22. In the Keynesian range on the aggregate-supply curve an increase in aggregate demand will have no effect on the real equilibrium GDP of the economy and will raise its price level. **T F**

23. The greater the increase in the price level that results from an increase in aggregate demand the greater will be the increase in the equilibrium real GDP. **T F**

24. The Keynesian model of the economy does not adequately predict the effects of changes in aggregate expenditures on the equilibrium real GDP if the price level is not constant. **T F**

25. Inflation has no effect on the strength of the multiplier. **T F**

Circle the letter that corresponds to the best answer.

1. The range of the aggregate-supply curve to which the Keynesian model is relevant is:
 (a) the horizontal range
 (b) the intermediate range
 (c) the vertical range
 (d) both the intermediate and the vertical ranges

2. In the Keynesian model in this chapter the equilibrium real GDP is:
 (a) the real GDP at which saving and planned gross investment are equal
 (b) the real GDP at which domestic output and aggregate expenditures are equal
 (c) the real GDP which is equal to consumption plus planned gross investment
 (d) all of the above

Questions 3 and 4 below are based on the consumption schedule preceding true-false questions 2 and 3.

3. If planned gross investment is $60, the equilibrium level of real GDP will be:
 (a) $320
 (b) $360
 (c) $400
 (d) $440

4. If planned gross investment were to increase by $5, the equilibrium real GDP would increase by:
 (a) $5
 (b) $7.14
 (c) $15
 (d) $16.67

5. When the economy's real GDP exceeds its equilibrium real GDP:
 (a) there is unplanned gross investment in the economy
 (b) planned gross investment exceeds saving
 (c) the aggregate expenditures exceed the real domestic output
 (d) there is an inflationary gap

6. If real GDP is $275 billion, consumption $250 billion, and planned gross investment $30 billion, real GDP:
 (a) will tend to remain constant
 (b) will tend to increase
 (c) will tend to decrease
 (d) equals aggregate expenditures

7. Which of the following is an injection?
 (a) investment
 (b) saving
 (c) taxes
 (d) imports

8. If saving is greater than planned gross investment:
 (a) businesses will be motivated to increase their investments

(b) aggregate expenditures will be greater than the real domestic output
 (c) real GDP will be greater than planned gross investment plus consumption
 (d) saving will tend to increase

9. On a graph the equilibrium real GDP is found at the intersection of the 45-degree line and
 (a) the consumption curve
 (b) the investment-demand curve
 (c) the saving curve
 (d) the aggregate-expenditures curve

10. If the value of the marginal propensity to consume is 0.6 and real GDP falls by $25, this was caused by a decrease in the aggregate-expenditures schedule of:
 (a) $10
 (b) $15
 (c) $16⅔
 (d) $20

11. If the marginal propensity to consume is 0.67 and if both planned gross investment and the saving schedule increase by $25, real GDP will:
 (a) increase by $75
 (b) not change
 (c) decrease by $75
 (d) increase by $25

12. The paradox of thrift means that:
 (a) an increase in saving lowers the level of real GDP
 (b) an increase in the average propensity to save lowers or leaves unchanged the level of savings
 (c) an increase in the marginal propensity to save lowers the value of the multiplier
 (d) an increase in real GDP increases investment demand

13. If the economy's full-employment noninflationary real GDP is $1200 and its equilibrium real GDP is $1100 there is a recessionary gap of:
 (a) $100
 (b) $100 divided by the multiplier
 (c) $100 multiplied by the multiplier
 (d) $100 times the reciprocal of the marginal propensity to consume

14. To eliminate an inflationary gap of $50 in an economy in which the marginal propensity to save is 0.1, it will be necessary to:
 (a) decrease the aggregate-expenditures shedule by $50
 (b) decrease the aggregate-expenditures schedule by $5
 (c) increase the aggregate-expenditures schedule by $50
 (d) increase the aggregate-expenditures schedule by $5

Use the data in the table below to answer questions 15, 16, and 17.

Real GDP	C + I_g	Net exports
$ 900	$ 913	$3
920	929	3
940	945	3
960	961	3
980	977	3
1,000	993	3
1,020	1,009	3

15. The equilibrium real GDP is:
(a) $960
(b) $980
(c) $1,000
(d) $1,020

16. If net exports are increased by $4 billion at each level of GDP, the equilibrium real GDP would be:
(a) $960
(b) $980
(c) $1,000
(d) $1,020

17. If the marginal propensity to save in this economy is 0.2, a $10 increase in its net exports would increase its equilibrium real GDP by:
(a) $40
(b) $50
(c) $100
(d) $200

18. Other things remaining constant, which of the following would increase an economy's real GDP and employment?
(a) the imposition of tariffs on goods imported from abroad
(b) a decrease in the level of national income among the trading partners for this economy
(c) a decrease in the exchange rates for foreign currencies
(d) an increase in the exchange rate for foreign currencies

19. An increase in the real GDP of an economy will, other things remaining constant:
(a) increase its imports and the real GDPs in other economies
(b) increase its imports and decrease the real GDPs in other economies
(c) decrease its imports and increase the real GDPs in other economies
(d) decrease its imports and the real GDPs in other economies

Answer the following three questions (20, 21, and 22) on the basis of this table for a private, closed economy. All figures are in billions of dollars.

Expected rate of net profit	Investment	Consumption	GDP
10%	$ 0	$200	$200
8	50	250	300
6	100	300	400
4	150	350	500
2	200	400	600
0	250	450	700

20. If the real rate of interest is 4%, then the equilibrium level of GDP will be:
(a) $300 billion
(b) $400 billion
(c) $500 billion
(d) $600 billion

21. An increase in the interest rate by 4% will:
(a) increase the equilibrium level of GDP by $200 billion
(b) decrease the equilibrium level of GDP by $200 billion
(c) decrease the equilibrium level of GDP by $100 billion
(d) increase the equilibrium level of GDP by $100 billion

22. The multiplier for this economy is:
(a) 2.00
(b) 2.50
(c) 3.00
(d) 3.33

23. The economy is operating at the full-employment level of output. A depreciation of the dollar will most likely result in:
(a) a decrease in exports
(b) an increase in imports
(c) an increase in real GDP
(d) a decrease in real GDP

24. If in an economy a $150 billion increase in investment spending creates $150 of new income in the first round of the multiplier process and $105 billion in the second round, the multiplier and the marginal propensity to consume will be, respectively:
(a) 5.00 and .80
(b) 4.00 and .75
(c) 3.33 and .70
(d) 2.50 and .40

25. If the price level in the Keynesian model were lower the consumption and aggregate-expenditures curves would be:
(a) lower and the equilibrium real GDP would be smaller

(b) lower and the equilibrium real GDP would be larger

(c) higher and the equilibrium real GDP would be larger

(d) higher and the equilibrium real GDP would be smaller

26. An increase in aggregate expenditures in the Keynesian model shifts the aggregate-demand curve to the:

(a) right by the amount of the increase in aggregate expenditures

(b) right by the amount of the increase in aggregate expenditures times the multiplier

(c) left by the amount of the increase in aggregate expenditures

(d) left by the amount of the increase in aggregate expenditures times the multiplier

27. An increase in aggregate demand will increase the equilibrium real GDP if the economy is operating in the:

(a) Keynesian range only

(b) intermediate range only

(c) Keynesian or intermediate ranges

(d) classial range only

28. An increase in aggregate demand will increase both the equilibrium real GDP and the price level if the economy is operating in the:

(a) Keynesian range

(b) intermediate range

(c) intermediate or classical ranges

(d) classical range

29. A decrease in the price level will shift the:

(a) consumption, investment, and net exports curves downward

(b) consumption, investment, and net exports curves upward

(c) consumption and investment curves upward, but the net exports curve downward

(d) consumption and net export curves upward, but the investment curve downward

30. In the aggregate-demand and aggregate-supply model, an increase in the price level will:

(a) increase the marginal propensity to consume

(b) increase the strength of the multiplier

(c) decrease the strength of the multiplier

(d) have no effect on the strength of the multiplier

■ **DISCUSSION QUESTIONS**

1. Why is the price level in the Keynesian model assumed to be constant? How does this Keynesian-model assumption differ from the assumption used in the aggregate-demand–aggregate-supply model?

2. Why is the equilibrium level of real GDP that level of real GDP at which domestic output equals aggregate expenditures and at which saving equals planned gross investment? What will cause real GDP to rise if it is below this level and what will cause it to fall if it is above this level?

3. Explain what is meant by a leakage and by an injection. What are the three major leakages and the three major injections in the flow of income in the American economy? Which leakage and which injection are considered in this chapter? Why is the equilibrium real GDP the real GDP at which the leakages equal the injections?

4. What is meant by "the distinction between saving and investment plans and the actual amounts which households manage to save and businesses to invest"? Is the gross investment schedule planned or actual investment? What adjustment causes planned and actual gross investment to become equal?

5. What is the multiplier effect? ***Why*** does there tend to be a multiplier effect (that is, on what basic economic facts does the multiplier effect depend)? What determines how large the simple multiplier effect will be?

6. What is meant by the paradox of thrift?

7. What relationship is there between the equilibrium level of real GDP and the level of real GDP at which full employment without inflation is achieved?

8. Explain what is meant by a recessionary gap and an inflationary gap. What economic conditions are present in the economy when each of these gaps exists? How is the size of each of these gaps measured?

9. How do exports and how do imports affect aggregate expenditures within a nation? To what is the equilibrium real GDP equal in an open economy (in the Keynesian model)? How does a change in the volume of exports and in the volume of imports affect real GDP and employment in a nation?

10. What are some examples of international economic linkages affecting the domestic level of GDP?

11. How is the aggregate-demand curve used in the aggregate-demand–aggregate-supply model of the economy derived from the Keynesian model?

12. What is the effect of an increase in aggregate expenditures in the Keynesian model (*a*) on the aggregate-demand curve; (*b*) on the equilibrium real GDP and price level in the Keynesian, intermediate, and classical ranges of the aggregate-supply curve; and (*c*) on the size of the multiplier effect on real GDP in each of these three ranges? What is the relationship between the effect of an increase in aggregate expenditures on real GDP and the rise in the price level that accompanies it?

■ ANSWERS

Chapter 11 Equilibrium Domestic Output in the Keynesian Model

FILL-IN QUESTIONS

1. *a.* Keynesian, constant; *b.* real

2. (aggregate)-expenditures–(domestic)-output, leakages-injections

3. *a.* expenditures, output; *b.* consumption, planned gross investment; *c.* 45-degree

4. *a.* saving, gross investment; *b.* (1) taxes, imports; (2) government purchases, exports

5. *a.* less, disinvestment, rise; *b.* greater, investment, fall; *c.* equal to, zero, neither rise nor fall

6. actual; *a.* (1) disinvestment, (2) rise; *b.* (1) investment, (2) fall

7. *a.* the equilibrium real GDP; *b.* marginal propensity to save, the marginal propensity to consume

8. *a.* income; *b.* consumption, marginal propensity to consume

9. increases, decreases; *a.* greater; *b.* directly

10. decrease, decrease; paradox of thrift

11. less, increase, multiplier

12. inflationary, the aggregate-expenditures schedule, the amount by which equilibrium nominal GDP exceeds the full-employment noninflationary real GDP

13. *a.* exports, imports; *b.* (1) net exports, (2) aggregate expenditures

14. *a.* −; *b.* +; *c.* +; *d.* −; *e.* +; *f.* −; *g.* +

15. variable, constant; *a.* wealth, raise, rise; *b.* lower, fall; *c.* inverse, demand

16. *a.* right, multiplier; *b.* left, downward shift in aggregate expenditures times the multiplier

17. *a.* greater, smaller; *b.* smaller, greater

PROBLEMS AND PROJECTS

1. *a.* I_g, 22, 22, 22, 22, 22, 22, 22; $C + I_g$: 1328, 1336, 1344, 1352, 1360, 1368, 1376; *UI:* −8, −6, −4, −2, 0, +2, +4; *b.* 1360; *c.* 0.8, 0.2; *d.* 5; *e.* increase, 3, increase, 15; *f.* decrease, 4, decrease, 20

2. change in income: 8.00, 6.40, 5.12, 4.10, 50,000; change in consumption: 8.00, 6.40, 5.12, 4.10, 3.28, 40.00; change in saving: 2.00, 1.60, 1.28, 1.02, 0.82, 10.00

3. *a.* 350, 15; *b.* 0.20, 5; *c.* 10; *d.* (1) decrease, 340, 15; (2) decrease, paradox of thrift; (3) the multiplier

4. *a.* 2½; *b.* 620, 30, inflationary, 12; *c.* 570, 20, recessionary, 8

5. *a.* $4; *b.* $780, 820, 860, 900, 940, 980, 1,020; *c.* $900; *d.* 5; *e.* (1) increase, $50, (2) decrease, $50

6. *a.* 2200; *b.* 2400; *c.* 2600; *d.* 2200, 2400, 2600, (1) aggregate-demand, (2) inversely

7. *a.* (1) 2390, 2.00, (2) 1840, 1.00; *b.* 1640, 1.00, 100, remain constant; *c.* 2300, 1.80, 2350, 1.90; *d.* 2390, 2.20, 2.40, remain constant

SELF-TEST

1. T, p. 196
2. F, p. 197
3. F, pp. 201–202
4. T, p. 201
5. T, pp. 201–202
6. T, pp. 198–199
7. T, pp. 203–204
8. F, p. 206
9. T, p. 206
10. F, pp. 206–207
11. T, p. 204
12. F, p. 207
13. T, p. 207
14. F, p. 208
15. F, pp. 208–209
16. F, p. 209
17. T, p. 212
18. T, pp. 211–212
19. F, pp. 212–213
20. T, p. 213
21. F, p. 213
22. F, p. 213
23. F, p. 216
24. T, p. 216
25. F, p. 216

1. *a,* p. 196
2. *d,* pp. 197–199
3. *c,* pp. 197–199
4. *d,* pp. 197–199
5. *a,* pp. 197–199
6. *b,* pp. 197–199
7. *a,* p. 200
8. *c,* p. 202
9. *d,* p. 199
10. *a,* pp. 205–206
11. *b,* pp. 207–208
12. *b,* pp. 207–208
13. *b,* pp. 208–209
14. *a,* p. 209
15. *b,* p. 211
16. *c,* p. 211
17. *b,* pp. 206, 211
18. *c,* p. 212
19. *a,* p. 212
20. *c,* pp. 197–199
21. *b,* pp. 197–199
22. *a,* p. 204
23. *b,* p. 212
24. *c,* pp. 204–205
25. *c,* pp. 214–215
26. *b,* pp. 215–216
27. *c,* pp. 215–216
28. *b,* p. 216
29. *b,* pp. 215–216
30. *c,* p. 216

DISCUSSION QUESTIONS

1. pp. 196–197
2. pp. 197–202
3. pp. 199–201
4. pp. 201–202
5. pp. 204–206
6. pp. 207–208
7. pp. 208–209
8. pp. 209–210
9. pp. 210–212
10. p. 212
11. pp. 214–215
12. pp. 214–215

CHAPTER 12
Fiscal Policy

Chapter 12 is really a continuation of the two preceding chapters and is concerned with the chief practical application of the principles discussed in those chapters.

It is worth recalling that principles of economics are generalizations about the way the economy works; and that these principles are studied in order that policies may be devised to solve real problems. Over the past one hundred or so years the most serious problems encountered by the American economy have been those problems that resulted from the business cycle. Learning what determines the real output and price levels of an economy and what causes them to fluctuate will make it possible to discover ways to bring about full employment, maximum output, and stable prices. Economic principles, in short, suggest the policies that will lessen both recession and inflation.

Government spending and taxing have a strong influence on the economy's output and employment and its price level. Federal expenditure and taxation policies designed to expand total production and employment or reduce the rate of inflation are called fiscal policies. (The Federal Reserve Banks are also able to affect these variables by applying monetary policy; but the study of monetary policy must wait until the effect of banks on the operation of the economy is examined in Chapters 13, 14, and 15.)

The brief first section of the chapter makes it clear that Congress in the Employment Act of 1946 committed the Federal government to using fiscal (and monetary) policy to achieve a trio of economic goals—economic growth, stable prices, and full employment. This act also established the Council of Economic Advisers to advise the President and Joint Economic Committee to advise Congress on matters pertaining to national economic policy.

The section entitled "Discretionary Fiscal Policy" is, however, the crucial part of Chapter 12. It introduces government taxing and spending into the analysis of equilibrium real GDP. It is important to note that government purchases of goods and services add to aggregate demand; and that taxation reduces the disposable income of consumers, and thereby reduces both the amount of consumption and the amount of saving that will take place at any level of real GDP. Both "approaches" are again em-

ployed, and you are warned that you must know **what** real GDP will tend to be produced and **why.** Special attention should be directed to the exact effect taxes have upon the consumption and saving schedules and to the multiplier effects of changes in government purchases and taxes.

Once you learn how government purchases and taxing affect the equilibrium real GDP it is fairly easy to understand what fiscal policies will be expansionary and reduce unemployment and what fiscal policies will be contractionary and lessen inflation. In addition to this, you should be aware (1) that if the government has a budget deficit or surplus there are several ways of financing the deficit or disposing of the surplus, and the way the deficit or surplus is handled can affect the economy's operation as much as the size of the deficit or surplus; and (2) that the Federal government has the option of changing its expenditures or altering the taxes it collects when it applies fiscal policy to reduce unemployment or lessen inflation in the economy.

Discretionary fiscal policy requires that Congress take action to change tax rates, transfer payment programs, or purchases of goods and services. **Non**discretionary fiscal policy does not require Congress to take any action; and is a built-in stabilizer of the economy. You should be sure that you understand **why** net taxes increase when the GDP rises and decrease when the GDP falls and **how** this tends to stabilize the economy.

Unfortunately, nondiscretionary fiscal policy by itself may not be able to eliminate any recessionary or inflationary gap that might develop; and discretionary fiscal policy may be necessary if the economy is to produce its full-employment GDP and avoid inflation. And the built-in stabilizers make it more difficult to use discretionary fiscal policy to achieve this goal because they create the illusion that the Federal government's policy is expansionary or contractionary when in fact its policy is just the opposite. Because of the illusions created by the built-in stabilizers, economists developed the full-employment budget and distinguished between a cyclical and structural deficit to enable them to discover whether Federal fiscal policy was actually expansionary or contractionary and to determine what policy should have been followed to move the economy toward full employment or slow the rate of inflation.

In addition to the problems of timing and the political

problems encountered in using fiscal problems in the real world, you will discover in the last major section of the chapter that many economists and other people are concerned by three other important complications. They fear, first of all, that all expansionary fiscal policy which requires the Federal government to borrow in the money market will raise the level of interest rates in the economy and reduce (or crowd out) investment spending; this is called the crowding-out effect and if it is large it will reduce the effect of the expansionary fiscal policy on real GDP and unemployment. A second complication expressed by some economists is that the potential expansionary effects of a budget deficit (public dissaving) are offset by an equal increase in private saving, thereby reducing or eliminating the effects of fiscal policy on the economy. The third problem arises from the connection of the domestic economy to a world economy; aggregate demand shocks from abroad or a net export effect may increase or decrease the effectiveness of a given fiscal policy. The fourth concern is that an expansionary fiscal policy, if the economy is operating in the intermediate range along the aggregate-supply curve, will drive up the price level and have only a small effect on real output and employment. But all is not gloom. The supply-side economists argue that a reduction in tax rates will not only increase aggregate demand but will also (for a number of reasons explained in the text) expand aggregate supply. In this way, they contend, the real equilibrium GDP of the economy can be increased with little or no rise in the price level. This viewpoint will be dealt with in more detail in Chapter 17.

■ **CHECKLIST**

When you have studied this chapter you should be able to:

☐ State the responsibility imposed on the Federal government by the Employment Act of 1946 and the roles of the CEA and JEC in fulfilling this responsibility.
☐ Find the equilibrium real GDP in an economy in which government purchases goods and services and levies net taxes when you are given the necessary data.
☐ Determine the effect on the equilibrium real GDP of a change in government purchases of goods and services and in net taxes.
☐ Explain why the balanced-budget multiplier is equal to one.
☐ Explain when government should pursue an expansionary and a contractionary fiscal policy; what each of these policies might entail; and the effect of each upon the Federal budget.
☐ Describe the best way to finance a government deficit and to dispose of a surplus.
☐ Distinguish between discretionary and nondiscretionary fiscal policy.

☐ Indicate how the built-in stabilizers help to eliminate recession and inflationary pressures.
☐ Describe the relationship between progressive, proportional, and regressive tax systems and the built-in stability of the economy.
☐ Distinguish between the actual budget and the full-employment budget, and between cyclical deficits and structural deficits as indicators of the government's fiscal policy.
☐ Outline the timing and political problems encountered in applying fiscal policy in the real world.
☐ Describe the crowding-out effect of an expansionary fiscal policy and how it may lessen the impact of an expansionary fiscal policy on real output and employment.
☐ Explain the criticism of fiscal policy that arises from the Ricardian equivalence theorem.
☐ Distinguish between the effects of an expansionary fiscal policy in the Keynesian and intermediate ranges of the aggregate-supply curve; and explain how the impact of such a policy is reduced when the economy is in the latter range.
☐ Explain two ways that interdependency with the world economy influences the effectiveness of domestic fiscal policy.
☐ State the effects supply-side economists argue a reduction in tax rates would have on aggregate supply, real GDP, and the price level; and explain why they believe it would have these effects.

■ **CHAPTER OUTLINE**

1. Fiscal policy is the manipulation by the Federal government of its expenditures and tax receipts in order to expand or contract aggregate expenditures in the economy; and by doing so either increase its real output (and employment) or decrease its rate of inflation.

2. The Employment Act of 1946 set the goals of American fiscal policy and provided for a Council of Economic Advisers to the President and the Joint Economic Committee.

3. Discretionary fiscal policy involves deliberate changes in tax rates and government spending to offset cyclical fluctuations and to increase economic growth.

    a. Six assumptions are made in order to simplify the explanation of the effects of government spending and taxes on the equilibrium real GDP.

    b. Government purchases of goods and services add to the aggregate-expenditures schedule and increase equilibrium real GDP; and an increase in these purchases has a multiplier effect upon equilibrium real GDP.

    c. Taxes decrease consumption and the aggregate-expenditures schedule by the amount of the tax times the MPC (and decrease saving by the amount of the tax times the MPS); and an increase in taxes has a negative multiplier effect on the equilibrium real GDP.

When government both taxes and purchases goods and services, the equilibrium GDP is the GDP at which (1) aggregate expenditures (consumption + planned gross investment + net exports + government purchases of goods and services) = the real domestic output (consumption + saving + taxes); or (2) using the leakages-injections approach, at which planned gross investment + exports + government purchases of goods and services = saving + imports + taxes.

d. Equal increases (decreases) in taxes and in government purchases increase (decrease) equilibrium real GDP by the amount of the change in taxes (or in expenditures).

e. The elimination of the inflation (recession) is accomplished by contractionary (expansionary) fiscal policy and by increasing (decreasing) taxes, decreasing (increasing) purchases and incurring budget surpluses (deficits).

f. In addition to the size of the deficit or surplus, the manner in which government finances its deficit or disposes of its surplus affects the level of total spending in the economy.

g. Whether government purchases or taxes should be altered to reduce recession and inflation depends to a large extent upon whether an expansion or a contraction of the public sector is desired.

4. In the United States economy net tax revenues (tax revenues minus government transfer payments) are not a fixed amount or lump sum; they increase as the GDP rises and decrease as the GDP falls.

a. This net tax system serves as a built-in stabilizer of the economy because it reduces purchasing power during periods of inflation and expands purchasing during periods of recession.
(1) As GDP increases, the average tax rates will increase in progressive systems, remain constant in proportional systems, and decrease in regressive systems; there is more built-in stability for the economy in progressive tax systems.
(2) Mainstream economists contend that built-in stabilizers can only reduce and cannot eliminate economic fluctuations.

b. The full-employment budget is a better index than the actual budget of the direction of government fiscal policy because it indicates what the Federal budget deficit or surplus would be if the economy were to operate at full employment. In the case of a budget deficit, the full employment budget:
(1) removes the cyclical portion that is produced by swings in the business cycle; and
(2) reveals the size of the structural deficit, indicating how expansionary fiscal policy was that year.

5. Certain problems and complications arise in enacting and applying fiscal policy.
a. There will be problems of timing because it requires

time to recognize the need for fiscal policy; to take the appropriate steps in the Congress; and for the action taken there to affect output and employment, and the rate of inflation in the economy.

b. There will also be political problems because:
(1) the economy has goals other than full employment and stable prices;
(2) there is an expansionary bias (for budget deficits and against surpluses);
(3) there may be a political business cycle (if politicians lower taxes and increase expenditures before and then do the opposite after elections).

c. An expansionary fiscal policy may, by raising the level of interest rates in the economy, reduce (or crowd out) investment spending and weaken the effect of the policy on real GDP; but this crowding-out effect may be small and can be offset by an expansion in the nation's money supply.

d. The Ricardian equivalence theorem suggests that borrowing to finance a budget deficit (public dissaving) is offset by an increase in private saving as people save in anticipation of higher taxes in the future; thus, the effects of deficit spending (or an expansionary fiscal policy) are offset by the effects of an equal increase in private saving.

e. The effect of an expansionary fiscal policy on the real GDP will also be weakened to the extent that it results in a rise in the price level (inflation).

f. Aggregate-demand and aggregate-supply curves can be used to show how crowding out and inflation weaken the effects of an expansionary fiscal policy on real GDP.

g. The connection of the domestic economy to a world economy means that fiscal policy may be inappropriate or less effective because of aggregate-demand shocks from the world economy or a net export effect that counteracts or reinforces domestic fiscal policy.

h. But an expansionary fiscal policy that includes a reduction in taxes (tax rates) may, by increasing aggregate supply in the economy, expand real GDP (and employment), and reduce inflation.

■ **IMPORTANT TERMS**

Fiscal policy

Employment Act of 1946

Council of Economic Advisers

Joint Economic Committee

Discretionary fiscal policy

Lump-sum tax

Balanced-budget multiplier

Expansionary fiscal policy

Contractionary fiscal policy

Nondiscretionary fiscal policy

Net taxes

Built-in stabilizers

Progressive, proportional, and regressive tax systems

Actual budget

Full-employment budget

Cyclical deficit

Structural deficit

Political business cycle

Crowding-out effect

Ricardian equivalence theorem

Net export effect

Supply-side fiscal policy

■ **FILL-IN QUESTIONS**

1. The use of monetary and fiscal policy to reduce inflation and recession became national economic policy in the _____ Employment _____ Act of 1946. This act also established the Council of ___Economic___ ___Advisors___ to the President and the ___Joint Economic___ Committee in Congress.

2. Taxes tend to reduce consumption at each level of real GDP by an amount equal to the taxes multiplied by the ___MPC___; saving will decrease by an amount equal to the taxes multiplied by the ___MPS___

_____

3. In an economy in which government both taxes and purchases goods and services, the equilibrium level of real GDP is the real GDP at which:

   a. aggregate ___expenditure___ equal the domestic ___output___;

   b. GDP is equal to ___Consumption___ plus ___planned Investment___ plus ___net export___ plus ___Government Expenditure.___

   c. In the leakages-injection approach ___planned investment___ ___export___ plus ___Government___ plus _____ **equals** ___Saving___ plus ___import___ plus ___Taxes.___

4. Equal reductions in taxes and government purchases will (increase, decrease) ___decrease___ real GDP by an amount equal to ___amount of___ ___change in Taxes.___

5. In order to increase real GDP during a recession, taxes should be (increased, decreased) ___decreased___ and government purchases should be ___increased___; to decrease the rise in the price level during a period of inflation taxes should be ___increase___ and government purchases should be ___decrease___

6. If fiscal policy is to have a countercyclical effect, it will probably be necessary for the Federal government to incur a budget (surplus, deficit) ___deficit___ during a recession and a budget ___surplus___ during inflation.

✗ 7. The two principal means available to the Federal government for financing budget deficits are ___borrow from Public___ and ___create new money___; and the (former, latter) ___latter___ is more expansionary.

✗ 8. Those economists who wish to expand the public sector of the economy during a period of **inflation** would most likely advocate a(n) (increase, decrease) ___increase___ in (government purchases, taxes) ___Tax or tax___; and those economists who wish to contract the public sector during a **recession** would most likely advocate a(n) ___decrease___ in ___Taxes___

9. Net taxes:

   a. equal ___Tax___ minus ___transfer Payment___
   b. in the United States will (increase, decrease) ___increase___ as the GDP rises and will ___decrease___ as the GDP falls.

10. When net tax receipts are directly related to the GDP the economy has some ___built in___ stability because:

   a. when the GDP rises, leakages (increase, decrease) ___↑___ and the budget surplus will (increase, decrease) ___↑___ (or the budget deficit will ___↓___);

   b. when the GDP falls, leakages ___↓___ and the budget deficit will ___↑___ (or the budget surplus will ___↓___)

✗ 11. As GDP increases, the average tax rates will increase in (progressive, proportional, regressive) ___progressive___ systems, remain constant in ___proportional___ systems, and decrease in ___regressive___ systems; there is (more, less) ___more___ built-in stability for the economy in progressive tax systems.

12. The full-employment budget:

   a. indicates what the Federal ___deficit/surplus___

would have been if the economy had operated at ___full employment___ during the year;

b. tells us whether the Federal budget was in fact ___expansionary___ or ___contractionary___.

c. A deficit produced by swings in the business cycle is (structural, cyclical) ___cyclical___, whereas a deficit produced through government taxation and spending decisions is ___structural___. The full-employment budget indicates the size of the ___structural___ deficit.

13. There is a problem of timing in the use of discretionary fiscal policy because of the ___recognition___, ___administrative___, and ___operational___ lags.

14. Political problems arise in the application of discretionary fiscal policy to stabilize the economy because government has ___other___ goals; because voters have a bias in favor of budget (surpluses, deficits) ___deficit___; and because politicians use fiscal policies in a way that creates a ___political___ business cycle.

15. When the Federal government employs an expansionary fiscal policy to increase real GDP and employment in the economy it usually has a budget (surplus, deficit) ___deficit___ and (lends, borrows) ___borrows___ in the money market.

  a. This will (raise, lower) ___raise___ interest rates in the economy and (contract, expand) ___contract___ investment spending.

  b. This change in investment spending is the ___crowding-out___ effect of the expansionary fiscal policy and it tends to (weaken, strengthen) ___weaken___ the impact of the expansionary fiscal policy on real GDP and employment.

16. The idea that public dissaving by borrowing to finance a budget deficit is offset by an increase in private saving to pay for expected taxes in the future is associated with the ___Ricardian equivalence Theory___. This idea suggests that fiscal policy may be (less, more) ___less___ effective than originally thought.

17. An expansionary fiscal policy when the economy is operating in the intermediate range of the aggregate-supply curve will increase the real GDP and employment in the economy and (raise, lower) ___raise___ the price level. This change in the price level will (weaken, strengthen) ___weaken___ the impact of the expansionary fiscal policy on output and employment in the economy.

18. Fiscal policy is subject to further complications from ___mutual dependence___ with the world economy.

  a. The economy can be influenced by ___aggregate demand___ shocks that might reinforce or retard fiscal policy; or

  b. from a ___net export___ effect that results from an expansionary or contractionary fiscal policy:
  (1) When fiscal policy is expansionary, it tends to (increase, decrease) ___increase___ interest rates, which in turn tends to ___increase___ the value of the dollar and ___decrease___ net exports.
  (2) When fiscal policy is contractionary, it tends to (increase, decrease) ___decrease___ interest rates, which in turn tends to ___decrease___ the value of the dollar, and ___increase___ net exports.

19. If an expansionary fiscal policy is the result of reduction in taxes, the supply-side effects of the policy may be to (increase, decrease) ___↑___ aggregate supply, to ___↑___ productivity capacity of the economy, to ___↑___ _____ real GDP and employment, to ___decrease___ the rate of inflation, and to (weaken, strengthen) ___strengthen___ the impact of the fiscal policy on output and employment.

■ **PROBLEMS AND PROJECTS**

1. Consumption and saving schedules are shown at the top of the next page.

  a. Assume government levies a lump-sum tax of $100. Also assume that imports are $5.
  (1) Because the marginal propensity to consume in this problem is _____, the imposition of this tax will reduce consumption at all levels of real GDP by $_____. Complete the C_a column to show consumption at each real GDP after the levying of this tax.
  (2) Because the marginal propensity to save in this problem is _____, this tax will reduce saving at all levels of real GDP by $_____. Complete the S_a column to

Real GDP	C	S	C_a	S_a	$S_a + M + T$	$I_g + X + G$	$C_a + I_g + X_n + G$
$1500	$1250	$250	$____	$____	$____	$____	$____
1600	1340	260	____	____	____	____	____
1700	1430	270	____	____	____	____	____
1800	1520	280	____	____	____	____	____
1900	1610	290	____	____	____	____	____
2000	1700	300	____	____	____	____	____
2100	1790	310	____	____	____	____	____

show saving at each real GDP after this tax has been levied.

b. Compute the (after-tax) saving-plus-imports-plus-taxes at each real GDP and put them in the $S_a + M + T$ column.

c. Suppose that planned gross investment is $150, exports are $5, and government purchases of goods and services equal $200. Complete the investment-plus-exports-plus-government-purchases column ($I_g + X + G$) and the (after-tax) consumption-plus-investment-plus-net-exports-plus-government-purchases column ($C_a + I_g + X_n + G$).

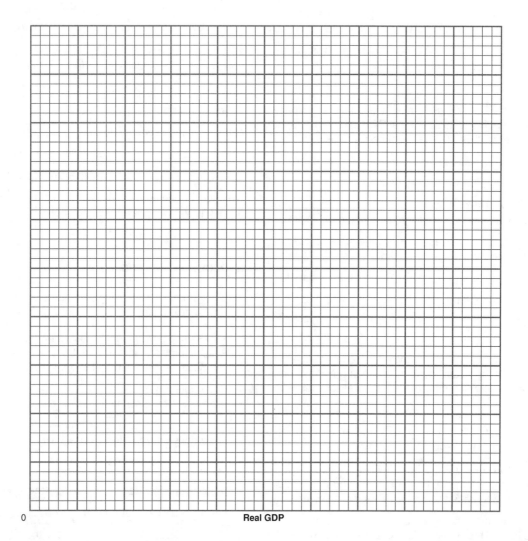

0   **Real GDP**

d. The equilibrium real GDP is $_____
e. On the graphs on page 128 and below plot:
(1) C_a, $I_g + X_n + G$, $C_a + I_g + X_n + G$, and the 45-degree line. Show the equilibrium real GDP.
(2) $S_a + M + T$ and $I_g + X + G$. Show the real equilibrium GDP. (To answer the questions below it is *not* necessary to recompute C, S, $S + M + T$, $I + X + G$, or $C + I_g + X_n + G$. They can be answered by using the multipliers.)
f. If taxes remained at $100 and government purchases rose by $10, the equilibrium real GDP would

(rise, fall) _____ by $_____
g. If government purchases remained at $200 and the lump-sum tax increased by $10, the equilibrium real

GDP would _____ by $_____
h. The combined effect of a $10 increase in government purchases *and* a $10 increase in taxes is to

_____ real GDP by $_____

2. In the table in the next column are seven real GDPs and the net tax revenues of government at each real GDP.

Real GDP	Net tax revenues	Government purchases	Government deficit/surplus
$ 850	$170	$_____	$_____
900	180	_____	_____
950	190	_____	_____
1000	200	_____	_____
1050	210	_____	_____
1100	220	_____	_____
1150	230	_____	_____

a. Looking at the two columns on the left of the table, it can be seen that:
(1) when real GDP increases by $50, net tax revenues

(increase, decrease) _____ by $_____
(2) when real GDP decreases by $100, net tax reve-

nues _____ by $_____
(3) the relation between real GDP and net tax reve-

nues is (direct, inverse) _____

0   Real GDP

b. Assume the investment multiplier has a value of 10 and that investment spending in the economy decreases by $10.

(1) *If* net tax revenues remained constant, the equilibrium real GDP would decrease by $_____

(2) But when real GDP decreases, net tax revenues also decrease; and this decrease in net tax revenues will tend to (increase, decrease) _____ the equilibrium real GDP.

(3) And, therefore, the decrease in real GDP brought about by the $10 decrease in investment spending will be (more, less) _____ than $100.

(4) The direct relationship between net tax revenues and real GDP has (lessened, expanded) _____ the impact of the $10 decrease in investment spending on real GDP.

c. Suppose the government purchases multiplier is also 10 and government wishes to increase the equilibrium real GDP by $50.

(1) *If* net tax revenues remained constant, government would have to increase its purchases of goods and services by $_____

(2) But when real GDP rises, net tax revenues also rise; and this rise in net tax revenues will tend to (increase, decrease) _____ the equilibrium real GDP.

(3) The effect, therefore, of the $5 increase in government purchases will also be to increase the equilibrium real GDP by (more, less) _____ than $50.

(4) The direct relation between net tax revenues and real GDP has (lessened, expanded) _____ the effect of the $5 increase in government purchases; and to raise the equilibrium real GDP by $50 government will have to increase its purchases by (more, less) _____ than $5.

d. Imagine that the full-employment real GDP of the economy is $1150 and that government purchases of goods and services are $200.

(1) Complete the table on page 129 by entering the government purchases and by computing the budget deficit or surplus at each of the real GDPs. (Show a government deficit by placing a minus sign in front of the amount by which expenditures exceed net tax revenues.)

(2) The full-employment surplus equals $_____

(3) Were the economy in a recession and producing a real GDP of $900, the budget would show a (surplus, deficit) _____ of $_____

(4) This budget deficit or surplus makes it appear that government is pursuing a(n) (expansionary, contractionary) _____ fiscal policy; but this deficit or surplus is not the result of countercyclical fiscal policy but the result of the _____

(5) If government did not change its net tax *rates* it could increase the equilibrium real GDP from $900 to the full-employment real GDP of $1150 by increasing its purchases by (approximately) $70. At the full-employment real GDP the budget would show a (surplus, deficit) _____ of $_____

(6) If government did not change its purchases it would increase the equilibrium real GDP from $900 to the full-employment real GDP of $1150 by decreasing net tax revenues at all real GDPs by a lump sum of (approximately) $80. The full-employment budget would have a (surplus, deficit) _____ of $_____

3. a. Complete the table below by computing the average tax rates, given the net tax revenue data in columns (2), (4), and (6). Calculate the average tax rate in percentage to one decimal place (for example, 5.4%)

b. As real GDP increases in column (1), the average tax rate (increases, decreases, remains the same) _____ in column (3), _____, in column (5), and _____ in column (7). The tax system is (progressive, proportional, regressive) _____ in column (2), _____ in column (4), and _____ in column (6).

c. Now graph the real GDP, net tax revenue, and government spending data given in columns (1), (2), (4),

(1) Real GDP	(2) Net tax revenue	(3) Average tax rate	(4) Net tax revenue	(5) Average tax rate	(6) Net tax revenue	(7) Average tax rate	(8) Government spending
$1000	$100	____%	$100	____%	$100	____%	$120
$1100	$120	____	$110	____	$108	____	$120
$1200	$145	____	$120	____	$115	____	$120
$1300	$175	____	$130	____	$120	____	$120
$1400	$210	____	$140	____	$123	____	$120

(6), and (8) in the graph below. Tax revenue system with the steepest slope is found in column _____ and it is (progressive, proportional, regressive) _____

while the one with the flattest slope is found in column _____ and it is _____

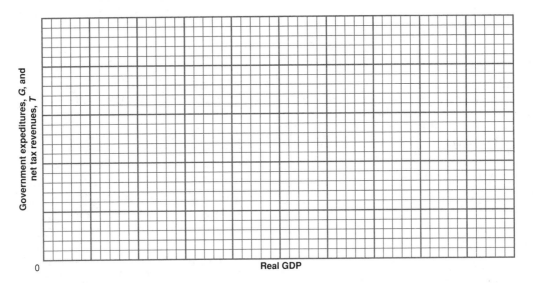

Government expenditures, G, and net tax revenues, T

Real GDP

0

4. a. Complete the table below by stating whether the direction of discretionary fiscal policy was contractionary, expansionary, or had no effect, given the hypothetical budget data for an economy.

(1) Year	(2) Actual budget surplus (+) or deficit (−)	(3) Full-employment budget budget surplus (+) or deficit (−)	(4) Direction of fiscal policy
1	−$ 10 billion	+$ 10 billion	_____
2	+$ 10 billion	−$ 20 billion	_____
3	−$ 20 billion	+$ 0 billion	_____
4	−$120 billion	−$120 billion	_____
5	−$150 billion	−$130 billion	_____

b. The best gauge of the direction of fiscal policy is the (actual, full-employment) _____ budget deficit or surplus because it removes the (cyclical, structural)

_____ component from the discussion of the budget situation.

c. (1) In which years is there is cyclical deficit and what was the size of the cyclical deficit in each of those

years? _____

_____

(2) In what years were there structural deficits and what was the size of the structural deficits in each of

those years? _____

5. Columns (1) and (2) in the table below are the aggregate-supply schedule and columns (1) and (3) are the aggregate-demand schedule.

(1) Price level	(2) Real GDP$_1$	(3) AD$_1$	(4) AD$_2$	(5) Real GDP$_2$
220	2390	2100	2200	2490
200	2390	2200	2340	2490
190	2350	2250	2350	2450
180	2300	2300	2400	2400
160	2200	2400	2500	2300

a. The equilibrium real GDP is $_____

and the price level is _____

b. Suppose that an expansionary fiscal policy increases aggregate demand from that shown in columns (1) and (3) to that shown in columns (1) and (4).
(1) If the price level remained constant the equilibrium

real GDP would increase to $_____
(2) But the increase in aggregate demand does raise

the price level to _____; and this rise in the price level results in real GDP increasing to only

$_____
c. If the expansionary fiscal policy that increased aggregate demand also has supply-side effects and increased aggregate supply from that shown in columns (1) and (2) to that shown in columns (1) and (5):
(1) The equilibrium real GDP would increase to

$_____; and

(2) the price level would _____

■ **SELF-TEST**

Circle the T if the statement is true; the F if it is false.

1. The Employment Act of 1946 committed the Federal government to using monetary and fiscal policy to achieve economic stability. **T** (**F**)

2. The purposes of discretionary fiscal policy are to reduce the rate of inflation, to reduce unemployment, and to stimulate economic growth. (**T**) **F**

0.7 · MPC = 1 − 0.3 = 0.7

3. If the MPS were 0.3 and taxes were levied by the government so that consumers paid $20 in taxes at each level of real GDP, consumption expenditures at each level of real GDP would be $14 less. 20 × 7/10 (**T**) **F**

0.6

4. If taxes are reduced by only $10 at all levels of real GDP and the marginal propensity to save is 0.4, equilibrium real GDP will rise by $25. 6 × **T** (**F**)
10 × 0.6 = 6
MPS = 0.4
6 × MPC = 0.6 · Multiply = MPS.

5. Even a balanced budget can be a weapon in fighting depression and inflation. (**T**) **F**

6. A full-employment budget deficit is contractionary. **T** (**F**)

7. A reduction in taxes and an increase in government spending during a recession would tend to contract the public sector of the economy. **T** (**F**)

8. Built-in stabilizers are not sufficiently strong to prevent recession or inflation, but they can reduce the severity of a recession or inflation. (**T**) **F**

9. The automatic (or built-in) stabilizers also increase the sizes of the government expenditures and investment multipliers. **T** (**F**)

10. The full-employment budget indicates how much government must spend and tax if there is to be full employment in the economy. cause by business cycle **T** (**F**)

11. A cyclical deficit is the result of countercyclical actions by government to stimulate the economy. (**T**) **F**

12. If an economy had achieved a full-employment level of output, but tax revenues were less than government expenditures, then a structural deficit is created. (**T**) **F**

13. Recognition, administrative, and operational lags in the timing of Federal fiscal policy make fiscal policies more effective in reducing the rate of inflation and decreasing unemployment in the economy. **T** (**F**)

14. The fiscal policies of state and local governments have tended to assist and reinforce the efforts of the Federal government to mitigate depression and inflation. **T** (**F**)

15. The spending and taxing policies of the Federal government are designed solely to reduce unemployment and limit inflation in the economy. **T** (**F**)

16. It is generally easier to induce U.S. Senators and Representatives to vote for decreases in tax rates and for increases in government purchases than for increased taxes and decreased purchases. (**T**) **F**

17. Economists who see evidence of a political business cycle argue that members of Congress tend to increase taxes and reduce expenditures before and to reduce taxes and increase expenditures after elections. **T** (**F**)

18. For a domestic economy, there are gains for specialization and trade but also complications from the interdependency with the world economy. (**T**) **F**

19. A net export effect may partially offset an expansionary fiscal policy. (**T**) **F**

20. Supply-side economists maintain that reductions in tax rates decrease aggregate supply and are, therefore, inflationary. **T** (**F**)

Circle the letter that corresponds to the best answer.

1. Which of the following was instrumental in assigning to the Federal government the basic responsibility for promoting economic stability in the American economy?
(**a**) the Employment Act of 1946
(**b**) the Tax Reform Act of 1986
(**c**) the Ricardian equivalence theorem
(**d**) the balanced-budget multiplier

$$MPC = \frac{8}{10} \quad MPC = 0.8$$
$$MPS = 1 - 0.8 = 0.2$$

The next four questions (2, 3, 4, and 5) are based on the consumption schedule below. Investment figures are for planned investment.

$C + I + X + G$

Income

Real GDP	C
$300	$290 286
310	298 294
320	306 302
330	314 310
340	322 318
350	330 326
360	338 334

8 < (bracket on C column)   >10

2. If taxes were zero, government purchases of goods and services $10, and investment $6, and net exports are zero, equilibrium real GDP would be:

(a) $310
(b) $320
(c) $330
(d) $340

$5 \times \frac{8}{10} = 4$

3. If taxes were $5, government purchases of goods and services $10, and investment $6, and net exports are zero, equilibrium real GDP would be:

(a) $300
(b) $310
(c) $320
(d) $330

$310 = 288 + 16$

$40 \times \frac{8}{10}$

4. Assume investment is $42, taxes are $40, net exports are zero, and government purchases of goods and services zero. If the full-employment level of real GDP is $340, the gap can be eliminated by reducing taxes by:

(a) $8
(b) $10
(c) $13
(d) $40

$42 - 32 = 10$

$X \times \frac{8}{10} = 8$ $332 - 340$
$x = 10$ $= 8$

5. Assume that investment is zero, that taxes are zero, net exports are zero, and the government purchases of goods and services are $20. If the full-employment-without-inflation level of real GDP is $330, the gap can be eliminated by decreasing government expenditures by:

(a) $4
(b) $5
(c) $10
(d) $20

6. If the marginal propensity to consume is 0.67 and both taxes and government purchases of goods and services increase by $25, real GDP will:

(a) fall by $25
(b) rise by $25
(c) fall by $75
(d) rise by $75

7. Which of the following policies would do the *most* to reduce inflation?

(a) increase taxes by $5 billion
(b) reduce government purchases of goods and services by $5 billion
(c) increase taxes and government expenditures by $5 billion
(d) reduce both taxes and government purchases by $5 billion

$MPC = 0.9 \cdot 30 \times \frac{9}{10}$ (27)

8. If APS is .2 and MPS is .10, a simultaneous increase in both taxes and government spending of $30 billion will:

(a) reduce consumption by $27 billion, increase government spending by $27 billion, and increase GDP by $30 billion   30
(b) reduce consumption by $27 billion, increase government spending by $27 billion, and increase GDP by $27 billion
(c) reduce consumption by $24 billion, increase government spending by $30 billion, and increase GDP by $30 billion
(d) reduce consumption by $24 billion, increase government spending by $24 billion, and increase GDP by $24 billion

Answer the next three questions (9, 10 and 11) on the basis of the following diagram.

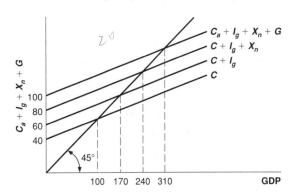

9. The size of the multiplier associated with changes in government spending in this economy is approximately:

(a) .29
(b) 1.50
(c) 2.50
(d) 3.50

$\frac{70}{20}$

10. If this was an open economy without a government sector, the level of GDP would be:

(a) $100
(b) $170
(c) $240
(d) $310

11. In this diagram it is assumed that investment, net exports, and government expenditures:

(a) vary inversely with GDP

(b) vary directly with GDP
(c) are independent of GDP
(d) are all negative

12. If the MPC in an economy is .75, government could eliminate a recessionary gap of $50 billion by decreasing taxes by:
(a) $33.3 billion
(b) $50 billion
(c) $66.7 billion
(d) $80 billion

$50 = 0.75 \lor \%$ 66.
$50 = \frac{3}{4} \times \%$ $\frac{43}{2}\big|\frac{250}{2}$
$5 \lor \frac{9}{3}$

13. In which of the following situations for an open mixed economy will the level of GDP contract?
(a) when $C_a + S + M$ is less than $I_g + X + T$
(b) when $I_g + M + T$ is less than $C + X + S$
(c) when $S_a + M + T$ is less than $I_g + X + G$
(d) when $I_g + X + G$ is less than $S_a + M + T$

14. If the government wishes to increase the level of real GDP, it might:
(a) reduce taxes
(b) reduce its purchases of goods and services
(c) reduce transfer payments
(d) reduce the size of the budget deficit

15. Which of the following by itself is the most expansionary (least contractionary)?
(a) redemption of government bonds held by the public
(b) borrowing from the public to finance a budget deficit
(c) a build-up in the size of the government's checking account in the central banks
(d) issuing new money to finance a budget deficit

16. Which of the following by itself is the most contractionary (least expansionary)?
(a) redemption of government bonds held by the public
(b) borrowing from the public to finance a budget deficit
(c) a build-up in the size of the government's checking account in the central banks
(d) issuing new money to finance a budget deficit

17. If the economy is to have built-in stability, when real GDP falls:
(a) tax revenues and government transfer payments both should fall
(b) tax revenues and government transfer payments both should rise
(c) tax revenues should fall and government transfer payments should rise
(d) tax revenues should rise and government transfer payments should fall

18. A direct relation between net tax revenues and real GDP:
(a) automatically produces budget surpluses during a recession
(b) makes it easier for discretionary fiscal policy to

move the economy out of a recession and toward full employment
(c) makes it easier to maintain full employment in a growing economy
(d) reduces the effect of a change in planned investment spending upon the domestic output and employment

*Answer the next three questions (**19, 20,** and **21**) on the basis of the following diagram.*

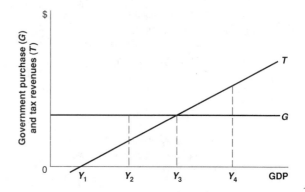

19. If the slope of the line **T** was steeper, there would be:
(a) more in-built stability for the economy
(b) less in-built stability for the economy
(c) no change in the in-built stability for the economy
(d) the need for more emphasis on discretionary fiscal policy

20. If the slope of the line **T** was flatter, there would be:
(a) larger cyclical deficits produced as GDP moved from Y_3 to Y_2
(b) smaller cyclical deficits produced as GDP moved from Y_3 to Y_2
(c) larger structural deficits produced as GDP moved from Y_3 to Y_2
(d) smaller structural deficits produced as GDP moved from Y_3 to Y_2

21. Actions by the Federal government to "index" personal income taxes and lower marginal tax rates would tend to:
(a) flatten the slope of line **T** and increase in-built stability
(b) flatten the slope of line **T** and decrease in-built stability
(c) steepen the slope of line **T** and increase in-built stability
(d) steepen the slope of line **T** and decrease in-built stability

22. With a proportional tax system, as the level of income increases in an economy, the average tax rate will:
(a) increase
(b) decrease

(c) remain the same
(d) either increase or decrease

23. If the full employment budget shows a deficit of about $200 billion and the actual budget shows a deficit of about $230 billion over a several-year period, it can be concluded that fiscal policy is:
  (a) expansionary and that there is both a structural and a cyclical deficit
  (b) expansionary and that there is a structural but not a cyclical deficit
  (c) expansionary and that there is a cyclical but not a structural deficit
  (d) contractionary and that there is cyclical but not a structural deficit

24. The length of time it takes for the fiscal action taken by Congress to affect output, employment, or the price level is referred to as the:
  (a) administrative lag
  (b) operational lag
  (c) recognition lag
  (d) fiscal lag

25. The crowding-out effect of an expansionary (deficit) fiscal policy is the result of government borrowing in the money market which:
  (a) increases interest rates and net investment spending in the economy
  (b) increases interest rates and decreases net investment spending
  (c) decreases interest rates and increases net investment spending
  (d) decreases interest rates and net investment spending

26. Which situation would best illustrate the ideas expressed in the Ricardian equivalence theorem as it is applied to the aggregate-expenditures model? A rise in government spending or decline in tax that produces a budget deficit that is expected to increase in aggregate expenditures will actually be offset by:
  (a) an upward shift in the consumption schedule and downward shift in the saving schedule
  (b) a downward shift in the consumption schedule and an upward shift in the saving schedule
  (c) an upward shift in the investment schedule and a downward shift in the net exports
  (d) a downward shift in the investment schedule and an upward shift in net exports

27. Suppose that the economies of trading partners for the United States improved substantially and at the same time the United States had adopted an expansionary fiscal policy. What would most likely happen in the United States?
  (a) there would a rise net exports, a rise in aggregate demand, and the potential for demand-pull inflation

  (b) there would be a fall in interest rates, a rise in aggregate demand, and the potential for a recession
  (c) there would be a rise in the incomes of trading partners, less demand for United States goods, and the potential for recession
  (d) there would be a rise in the employment in other nations, a fall in net exports, and the potential for demand-pull inflation.

28. If the United States pursued a contractionary fiscal policy, then what would be the likely effects?
  (a) there would be a lower domestic interest rate and an increase in the demand for dollars that would partially offset the policy
  (b) there would be a depreciation in the value of the dollar and a decrease in net exports that would partially reinforce the policy
  (c) there would be an increase in net exports and an increase in aggregate demand that would partially offset the policy
  (d) there would be a decrease in net exports and a decrease in aggregate demand that would partially reinforce the policy

29. The effect of an expansionary (deficit) fiscal policy on the real GDP of an economy operating in the Keynesian range on the aggregate-supply curve is lessened by:
  (a) increases in aggregate supply
  (b) the crowding-out effect
  (c) increases in the price level
  (d) both *b* and *c*

30. The effect of an expansionary (deficit) fiscal policy on the real GDP of an economy operating in the intermediate range on the aggregate-supply curve is lessened by:
  (a) increases in aggregate supply
  (b) the crowding-out effect
  (c) increases in the price level
  (d) both *b* and *c*

■ **DISCUSSION QUESTIONS**

  1. What is meant by fiscal policy?

  2. In the Employment Act of 1946, (*a*) what responsibility was given to the Federal government; (*b*) what tasks were assigned to the Council of Economic Advisers and the Joint Economic Committee; and (*c*) what specific kinds of policy were to be used to achieve the goals established by the act?

  3. What is the exact effect which taxes will have on the consumption schedule? On the saving schedule?

  4. Explain why, with government taxing and spending, the equilibrium real GDP is the real GDP at which real GDP equals consumption plus planned investment plus net exports plus government purchases of goods and services;

and saving plus imports plus taxes equals planned investment plus exports plus government purchases. What will cause GDP to move to its equilibrium level?

5. If both taxes and government purchases increase by equal amounts, real GDP will increase by that amount. Why?

6. What three things might the Federal government do if its fiscal policy were to be (a) expansionary and if it were to be (b) contractionary? When would it invoke each of these two kinds of policy and what would be their effects on the Federal budget?

7. What are the alternative means of financing deficits and disposing of surpluses available to the Federal government? What is the difference between these methods insofar as their expansionary and contractionary effect is concerned?

8. Explain the fiscal policy that would be advocated during a recession and during a period of inflation (a) by those who wish to expand the public sector and (b) by those who wish to contract the public sector.

9. What is the difference between discretionary and nondiscretionary fiscal policy? How do the built-in stabilizers work to reduce rises and falls in the level of nominal GDP?

10. Explain why a tax system in which net tax revenues vary directly with the level of nominal GDP makes it difficult to achieve and sustain full employment.

11. Supply a definition of a progressive, proportional, and regressive tax system. What are the implications of the type of tax system for the built-in stability of the economy?

12. What is the full-employment budget? What was the problem which the use of the full-employment budget was designed to solve?

13. Explain the distinction between a cyclical deficit and structural deficit. Which type of deficit provides the best indication of the direction of fiscal policy? Why?

14. Explain the three kinds of time lags that make it difficult to use fiscal policy to stabilize the economy.

15. What are three political problems that complicate the use of fiscal policy to stabilize the economy?

16. How do (a) crowding out and (b) inflation reduce the effect of an expansionary (deficit) fiscal policy on real GDP and employment?

17. Explain how the Ricardian equivalence theorem can be applied to government budget deficits and fiscal policy. What conclusions would be drawn about fiscal policy based on this theorem? What criticisms have been leveled against this type of analysis?

18. What complications for fiscal policy arise from inter-

dependency with the world economy? Explain how aggregate demand shocks from abroad and the net export effect influence fiscal policy.

19. What might be the supply-side effects of a reduction in tax rates on the capacity output of the economy, the equilibrium levels of real GDP and employment, and the price level?

■ **ANSWERS**

Chapter 12 Fiscal Policy

FILL-IN QUESTIONS

1. Employment, Economic Advisers, Joint Economic

2. marginal propensity to consume, marginal propensity to save

3. a. expenditures, output; b. consumption, planned gross investment, net exports, government purchases of goods and services; c. planned gross investment, exports, government purchases of goods and services, saving, imports, net taxes

4. decrease; the decreases in taxes and government purchases

5. decreased, increased, increased, decreased

6. deficit, surplus

7. borrowing from the public, creating new money, latter

8. increase, taxes, decrease, taxes

9. a. taxes, transfer payments; b. increase, decrease

10. built-in; a. increase, increase, decrease; b. decrease, increase, decrease

11. progressive, proportional, regressive, more

12. a. budget surplus or deficit, full employment; b. expansionary, contractionary; c. cyclical, structural, structural

13. recognition, administrative, operational

14. other, deficits, political

15. deficit, borrows; a. raise, contract; b. crowding-out, weaken

16. Ricardian equivalence theorem, less

17. raise, weaken

18. mutual interdependency; a. aggregate demand; b. net export, (1) increase, increase, decrease, (2) decrease, decrease, increase

19. increase, increase, increase, decrease, strengthen

PROBLEMS AND PROJECTS

1. a. (1) 0.9, 90, C_a: 1160, 1250, 1340, 1430, 1520, 1610, 1700, (2) 0.1, 10, S_a: 240, 250, 260, 270, 280, 290, 300; b. $S_a + M + T$: 345, 355, 365, 375, 385, 395, 405; c. $I_g + X + G$: 355, 355, 355, 355, 355, 355, 355; $C_a + I_g + X_n + G$: 1510, 1600, 1690, 1780, 1870, 1960, 2050; d. 1600; f. rise, 100; g. fall, 90; h. raise, 10

2. *a.* (1) increase, $10, (2) decrease, $20, (3) direct; *b.* (1) $100, (2) increase, (3) less, (4) lessened; *c.* (1) $5, (2) decrease, (3) less, (4) lessened, more; *d.* (1) government expenditures are $200 at all GDPs, government surplus or deficit: −30, −20, −10, 0, 10, 20, 30, (2) $30, (3) deficit, $20, (4) expansionary, recession, (5) deficit, $40, (6) deficit, $50

3. *a.* column 3: 10.0, 10.9, 12.1, 13.5, 15.0; column 5: 10.0 at each GDP level; column 7: 10.0, 9.8, 9.6, 9.2, 8.8; *b.* increases, remains the same, decrease; progressive, proportional, regressive; *c.* 2, progressive, 6, regressive

4. *a.* contractionary, expansionary, no effect, expansionary, expansionary; *b.* full-employment, cyclical; *c.* (1) year 1 ($10 billion); year 3 ($20 billion); year 5 ($20 billion); (2) year 2 ($20 billion); year 4 ($120 billion); year 5 ($130 billion)

5. *a.* 2300, 180; *b.* (1) 2400, (2) 190, 2350; *c.* (1) 2400, (2) remain constant

SELF-TEST

1. T, p. 222
2. T, p. 222
3. T, p. 225
4. F, p. 225
5. T, p. 227
6. F, p. 231
7. F, p. 228
8. T, p. 231
9. F, p. 230
10. F, p. 231
11. F, pp. 231–232
12. T, pp. 231–232
13. F, pp. 232–233
14. F, p. 233
15. F, p. 233
16. T, p. 233
17. F, p. 233
18. T, p. 236
19. T, pp. 236–237
20. F, pp. 237–238

1. *a,* p. 222
2. *c,* p. 223
3. *b,* pp. 223–235
4. *b,* pp. 223–235
5. *a,* pp. 223–235
6. *b,* pp. 223–235
7. *b,* p. 227
8. *a,* pp. 223–227
9. *d,* p. 223
10. *c,* p. 223
11. *c,* p. 223
12. *c,* pp. 225–227
13. *d,* pp. 225–227
14. *a,* p. 225
15. *d,* p. 229
16. *c,* p. 229
17. *c,* p. 230
18. *d,* p. 230
19. *a,* p. 230
20. *b,* p. 230
21. *b,* pp. 230–231
22. *c,* p. 230
23. *a,* pp. 231–232
24. *b,* p. 233
25. *b,* p. 228
26. *b,* p. 234
27. *a,* pp. 236–237
28. *c,* pp. 236–237
29. *b,* pp. 235–236
30. *d,* pp. 235–236

DISCUSSION QUESTIONS

1. p. 222
2. p. 222
3. pp. 225–227
4. pp. 222–226
5. p. 227
6. pp. 227–228
7. pp. 228–229
8. pp. 228–229
9. pp. 229–231
10. pp. 230–231
11. pp. 230–231
12. pp. 231–232
13. pp. 231–232
14. pp. 232–233
15. pp. 233–234
16. pp. 235–237
17. pp. 234–235
18. pp. 236–237
19. pp. 237–239

CHAPTER 13

Money and Banking

By and large, Chapter 13 is descriptive and factual. It contains only a brief explanation of how the financial system affects the operation of the economy. The purpose of this chapter is, however, to prepare you for a more detailed explanation (in Chapters 14 and 15).

Of special importance in this chapter are the many terms and definitions which will be new to you. These must be learned if the following two chapters and their analysis of how the financial system affects performance of the economy are to be understood. Chapter 13 also contains a factual description of the institutions which compose the American financial system—the Board of Governors of the Federal Reserve System, the Federal Reserve Banks, the commercial banks, and the "thrifts"—and the functions of these four institutions.

You will do well to pay particular attention to the following: (1) what money is and the functions it performs, what types of money exist in the American economy and their relative importance, and how the three measures of the money supply (M1, M2, and M3) are defined; (2) what gives value to or "backs" American money; (3) why people want to have money in their possession and what determines how much money they want to have on hand at any time; (4) how the total demand for money and the money supply together determine the equilibrium rate of interest; and (5) the four principal institutions of the American financial system and their functions.

Several points are worth repeating here because so much depends upon their being fully understood. First, money is whatever performs the three functions of money, and in the United States money consists largely of the debts (promises to pay) of the Federal Reserve Banks and depository institutions. In the United States, this money is "backed" by the goods and services for which its owners can exchange it and not by gold.

Second, because money is used as a medium of exchange, consumers and business firms wish to have money on hand to use for transaction purposes; and the quantity of money they demand for this purpose is directly related to the size of the economy's nominal (or money) gross domestic product. This means that when either the price level or the real gross domestic product increases

they will want to have more money on hand to use for transactions. But money is also used as a store of value: consumers and firms who own assets may choose to have some of their assets in the form of money (rather than in stocks, bonds, goods, or property). There is, therefore, also an asset demand for money. Holding money, however, imposes a cost on those who hold it. This cost is the interest they lose when they own money rather than (say) bonds. This means that people will demand less money for asset purposes when the rate of interest (the cost of holding money) is high and more when the rate of interest is low: the quantity of money demanded for this purpose is inversely related to the interest rate. The total demand for money is the sum of the transactions demand and the asset demand and, therefore, depends upon the nominal GDP and the rate of interest. This total demand and the money supply determine interest rates in the economy.

Third, the central bank in the United States is the twelve Federal Reserve Banks and the Board of Governors of the Federal Reserve System which oversees their operation. These banks, while privately owned by the commercial banks, are operated more or less as an agency of the Federal government not for profit, but primarily to regulate the nation's money supply in the best interests of the economy as a whole and secondarily to perform other services for the banks, the government, and the economy. They are able to perform their primary function because they are bankers' banks where depository institutions (commercial banks and the "thrifts") can deposit and borrow money. They do not deal directly with the public.

Fourth, these depository institutions accept deposits and make loans, but they also are literally able to create money by lending checkable deposits. Because they are able to do this, they have a strong influence on the size of the money supply and the value of money. The Federal Reserve Banks exist primarily to regulate the money supply and its value by influencing and controlling the amount of money depository institutions create.

The final section of Chapter 13 discusses bank and thrift failures of the 1980s and early 1990s. These events are important because banks and thrifts are critical for the sound financial health of the economy and because there is a high long-term cost for taxpayers from bailing out financial institutions, especially the many insolvent savings and loan institutions. As you will learn, the reasons for the savings and loan collapse involve many factors, including deregulation of the banking industry, more competition among financial institutions, higher level of deposit insurance, loan defaults, and fraud. The failure of many financial institutions led the government to institute new reforms in the banking industry that should be felt throughout the 1990s.

■ CHECKLIST

When you have studied this chapter you should be able to:

☐ List the three functions of money; and explain the meaning of each function.
☐ Define the money supply, *M*1.
☐ Identify the four kinds of checkable deposits; and the principal kinds of depository institutions.
☐ Explain the meaning of near-money and identify the principal near-monies; and then define *M*2 and *M*3.
☐ Present three reasons why near-monies are important.
☐ Distinguish between credit cards and money.
☐ Explain why money in the American economy is debt; and whose debts paper money and checkable deposits are.
☐ Present three reasons why currency and checkable deposits are money and have value.
☐ Indicate the precise relationship between the value of money and the price level.
☐ Explain what is meant by stabilizing the value of money.
☐ Enumerate the two devices government utilizes to try to stabilize the value of money.
☐ Identify the two demands for money and the determinant of each of these demands.
☐ Explain the relationship between each of the two demands from money and its determinant.
☐ Describe what determines the equilibrium rate of interest.
☐ Explain how changes in nominal GDP and in the money supply affect the interest rate.
☐ Explain how disequilibrium in the money market is corrected through changes in bond prices.
☐ Describe the structure of the American financial system.
☐ Explain why the Federal Reserve Banks are central, quasi-public, bankers' banks.
☐ Enumerate the five functions of the Federal Reserve System; explain the meaning of each of these functions; and indicate which is the most important.
☐ State two reasons why the bank and thrift failures of the 1980s and early 1990s were important.

☐ State several reasons why many savings and loan institutions collapsed in recent years.
☐ Explain what actions were taken by government to help the recent problems with financial institutions.

■ CHAPTER OUTLINE

1. Money is whatever performs the three basic functions of money: a medium of exchange, a measure of value, and a store of value.

2. In the American economy money is whatever is generally used as a medium of exchange; and consists of the debts of the Federal government and of commercial banks and other financial institutions.
  a. The narrowly defined money supply is called *M*1 and has two principal components.
  (1) The smaller component is currency: coins which are token money and paper money largely in the form of Federal Reserve Notes.
  (2) The larger and more important component is checkable deposits in commercial banks and savings institutions.
  (3) These checkable deposits include demand deposits (checking accounts), negotiable order of withdrawal (NOW) accounts, automatic transfer service (ATS) accounts, and share draft accounts, all of which give the depositor the ability to write checks.
  (4) Currency and checkable deposits owned by the Federal government, commercial banks and savings institutions, and the Federal Reserve Banks are not, however, included in *M*1 or any of the more broadly defined money supplies.
  b. *M*2 and *M*3 are the more broadly defined money supplies; and include not only the currency and checkable deposits in *M*1 but such near-monies as noncheckable savings deposits and time deposits in commercial banks and savings institutions.
  (1) *M*2 includes *M*1 plus noncheckable savings deposits plus small time deposits (less than $100,000) plus money market deposit accounts (MMDA) plus money market mutual funds (MMMF).
  (2) *M*3 includes *M*2 plus large time deposits ($100,000 or more).
  (3) There are advantages to each of the different measures of money, but since *M*1 is included in all the definitions and the principles that apply to it are applicable to the other measure, that narrow definition is used for the textbook discussion unless noted otherwise.
  c. Near-monies held by the public are important because they affect spending habits, serve as a stabilizing force in economic activity, and provide different definitions of money for the conduct of monetary policy.
  d. Credit cards are not money but are a device by

which the cardholders obtain a loan (credit) from the issuer of the card.

3. In the United States:

   a. Money is the promise of a commercial bank, a savings (thrift) institution, or a Federal Reserve Bank to pay; but these debts cannot be redeemed for anything tangible.

   b. Money has value only because people can exchange it for desirable goods and services.

   c. The value of money is inversely related to the price level.

   d. Money is "backed" by the confidence which the public has that the value of money will remain stable; and the Federal government can use monetary and fiscal policy to keep the value of money relatively stable.

4. Business firms and households wish to hold and, therefore, demand money for two reasons.

   a. Because they use money as a medium of exchange they have a transactions demand which is directly related to the nominal gross domestic product of the economy.

   b. Because they also use money as a store of value they have an asset demand which is inversely related to the rate of interest.

   c. Their total demand for money is the sum of the transactions and asset demands.

   d. This total demand for money along with the supply of money determine the equilibrium interest rate in the money market of the economy.

   e. Disequilibrium in the money market is corrected through changes in bond prices:

   (1) lower bond prices increase interest rates; and

   (2) higher bond prices decrease interest rates.

5. The financial sector of the American economy has changed dramatically in the past two decades; for example, the Depository Institutions Deregulation and Monetary Control Act of 1980 narrowed the earlier differences between a commercial bank and the various thrift institutions.

   a. But, despite the trend toward deregulation, the financial system remains centralized and regulated by government because the absence of centralization in the past led to an inappropriate supply of money, a multitude of different kinds of money, and a mismanagement of the money supply.

   b. In the Federal Reserve System:

   (1) The Board of Governors exercises control over the supply of money and the banking system. Two important bodies help the Board of Governors in establishing and conducting policy—the Federal Open Market Committee (FOMC), which establishes policy over the buying and selling of government bonds, and the Federal Advisory Council, which provides advice on banking policy.

   (2) The Federal Reserve Banks are central, quasi-public, bankers' banks.

   (3) About 13,700 commercial banks exist in the American financial system; and some of them are state banks and some are national banks. But since 1980 the distinctions between state and national banks and between commercial banks and thrift institutions have all but been eliminated.

   (4) The thrift institutions, like all commercial banks, are subject to the reserve requirements imposed by and may borrow from the Federal Reserve Banks; but they are also subject to the rules imposed upon them by other regulatory agencies. Both they and the commercial banks, by performing the two essential functions of holding deposits and making loans, expand the supply of money.

   c. The Board of Governors and the Federal Reserve Banks perform five functions aimed at providing certain essential services, supervision of the member commercial banks, and the regulation of the supply of money.

6. Bank and thrift failures in the 1980s and early 1990s have been of concern because they affect the financial health of the economy and because of the high long-term cost of bailing out insolvent institutions, especially in the savings and loan industry.

   a. Commercial bank problems resulted largely from economic problems in the agricultural and energy-producing regions of the economy in the 1980s, but the national recession that began in 1990 contributed to more bank failures.

   b. The collapse of the savings and loan industry was due to many factors, such as deregulation, intense competition, a moral hazard problem caused by higher levels of deposit insurance, increased loan defaults, and fraud.

   c. The cost of bailing out the thrifts may total $500 billion over a forty-year period. The savings and loan collapse and other bank problems have led to the passage of the Financial Institutions Reform, Recovery, and Enforcement Act (FIRREA), which may be only the first step in a major government reform of the banking industry.

■ **IMPORTANT TERMS**

Medium of exchange	**Token money**
Measure of value	**Intrinsic value**
Store of value	**Federal Reserve Note**
Money supply	**Checkable deposit**
_M_1 _M_2 _M_3	**Demand deposit**
Currency	**NOW account**
Paper money	**Share draft account**

ATS account

Commercial bank

Thrift (savings) institution

Savings and loan association

Mutual savings bank

Credit union

Near-monies

Monies

Noncheckable savings account

Time deposit

MMDA (money market deposit account)

MMMF (money market mutual fund)

Legal tender

Fiat money

Value of money

Transactions demand for money

Asset demand for money

Total demand for money

Money market

Bonds

Depository institution

Depository Institutions Deregulation and Monetary Control Act

Board of Governors

Federal Open Market Committee

Federal Advisory Committee

Federal Reserve Bank

Central bank

Quasi-public bank

Bankers' bank

Commercial banks

State bank

National bank

Member bank

Federal Deposit Insurance Corporation

Moral hazard problem

Resolution Trust Corporation

Financial Institutions Reform, Recovery, and Enforcement Act

■ FILL-IN QUESTIONS

1. Three functions of money are:

a. _Medium of exchange_

b. _Measure of Value_

c. _Store of value_

2. M1 is the sum of:

a. _currency_ which consists of _coin_ and paper _Money_;

b. and (time, checkable) _Checkable_ deposits in (commercial banks, thrift institutions, depository institutions) _____

c. not owned by depository institutions, the _Federal Reserve_ Banks, or the _Federal_ government.

3. In addition to:

a. commercial banks, the principal depository institutions in the American economy are _Saving and Loan_ associations, _mutual savings_ banks, and _Credit_ unions.

b. Checkable deposits include demand deposits, _Now_ and _ATS_ accounts, and _share_ drafts.

4. In the American economy:

a. M2 is equal to M1 plus

(1) (checkable, noncheckable) _noncheckable_ _____ savings deposits

(2) (small, large) _small_ time deposits

(3) and money market (deposit, mutual funds) _mutual fund_ accounts and money market _deposit_

b. M3 is equal to M2 plus (small, large) _large_ time deposits

c. Large time deposits are mainly _Certificate_ of deposits which have a face value of $_100,000_ or more.

5. Near-money in the United States includes not only noncheckable savings and time deposits:

a. but such government securities as _Treasury_ bills and U.S. government savings _bonds._

b. all of which can be easily converted into _currency_ or _checkable_ deposits without the risk of financial _loss_

6. List three reasons why the existence of near-money is important.

a. _Saving - Consuming habit_

b. _stability_

c. _monetary policy_

7. Money in the United States consists largely of the debts of _depository_ institutions and the _Federal Reserve_ Banks.

8 In the United States currency and checkable deposits:

a. (are, are not) _are not_ "backed" by gold and silver;

b. are money because they are used as a medium of _exchange_, they are in some cases _legal_ tender, and they are relatively (abundant, scarce) _scarce_

9. Money has value because it can be exchanged for _goods and Services_ and its value varies

(directly, inversely) ___*inversely*___ with changes in the ___*price*___ level.

10. The total demand for money is the sum of:

   a. the transactions demand which depends (directly inversely) ___*directly*___ on the *nominal* ___GDP___

   b. and the asset demand which depends on the ___*interest Rate*___

11. The total demand for money and the ___*Supply*___ of money determine the equilibrium ___*interest*___ rate in the ___*money*___ market.

   a. When the quantity of money demanded exceeds the quantity of money supplied, bond prices (increase, decrease) ___*decrease*___ and interest rates ___*increase*___

   b. When the quantity of money demanded is less than the quantity of money supplied, bond prices (increase, decrease) ___*increase*___ and interest rates ___*decrease*___

12. Many of the historical distinctions between commercial banks and the different thrift institutions were eliminated in the ___*DIDMCA*___ of 1980. This act permitted all depository institutions to offer (checkable, time) ___*Checkable*___ deposit accounts. Despite this recent (regulation, deregulation) ___*deregulation*___, depository institutions continue to be subject to central monetary control by the ___*Government F.R.*___ *Federal open Market Committee*

13. Two groups which help the Board of Governors of the Federal Reserve System to formulate its policies are the ___*FOMC*___ and the ___*FAC Federal Advisory Council*___

14. The three principal characteristics of the Federal Reserve Banks are:

   a. ___*They are Central Bank*___

   b. ___*quasi - public Bank*___

   c. ___*Bankers Bank.*___

15. If a bank is a bankers' bank it means that it accepts the ___*deposit*___ of and makes ___*loan*___ to (households, business firms, depository institutions, the public sector) ___*depository institution*___

16. Both commercial banks and thrift institutions perform two essential functions for the economy: they hold the ___*deposit*___ of and make ___*loan*___

to the public; and in performing these functions they (increase, decrease) ___*increase*___ money supply.

17. The five major functions of the Federal Reserve Banks are:

   a. ___*holding the deposit of Banks and thrifts*___

   b. ___*supervising member banks.*___

   c. ___*providing for the Collection of Checks.*___

   d. ___*Fiscal agent for Fed Government*___

   e. ___*regulary money Supply.*___

The most important of the functions which the Federal Reserve Banks perform is that of ___*Regulating Money Supply*___

18. In the 1980s and early 1990s, the failure of institutions in the banking and thrift industries were of special concern because of they created (more, less) ___*less*___ stability in the monetary system, and because of the (high, low) ___*high*___ cost of these events to taxpayers.

   a. The reasons for failures in the savings and loans industry are related to: (regulation, deregulation) ___*deregulation*___; (more, less) ___*more*___ competition in the industry; (an ethical, a moral hazard) ___*moral hazard*___ problem resulting from (lower, higher) ___*higher*___ levels of deposit insurance and (risky, safe) ___*risky*___ loans; and (legal, illegal) ___*illegal*___ activity.

   b. To correct some of the problems, the Financial Institutions Reform, Recovery, and Enforcement Act (FIRREA) established the ___*Resolution Trust Corporation*___ to oversee the closing and sale of insolvent thrifts, and place deposit insurance for banks and thrifts under the control of the ___*Federal Deposit Insurance Corporation*___.

■ **PROBLEMS AND PROJECTS**

1. From the figures in the table below it can be concluded that:

Item	Billions of dollars
Small time deposits	630
Large time deposits	645
Money market deposit accounts	575
Money market mutual funds	425
Checkable deposits	448
Noncheckable savings deposits	300
Currency held by public	170

a. *M*1 is equal to the sum of $_____

and $_____; and totals $_____
billion.

b. *M*2 is equal to *M*1 plus $_____ and $_____

and $_____ and $_____; and totals $_____
billion.

c. *M*3 is equal to *M*2 plus $_____; and

totals $_____ billion.

2. Complete the following table showing the relationship between a percentage change in the price level and the percentage change in the value of money. Calculate the percentage change in the value of money to one decimal place.

Change in price level	Change in value of money
a. *rise* by:	
5%	− ____ . __ %
10%	− ____ . __
15%	− ____ . __
20%	− ____ . __
25%	− ____ . __
b. *fall* by:	
5%	+ ____ . __
10%	+ ____ . __
15%	+ ____ . __

3. The total demand for money is equal to the transaction plus the asset demand for money.
  a. Assume each dollar held for transaction purposes is spent (on the average) four times per year to buy final goods and services.
  (1) This means that transaction demand for money will

be equal to (what fraction or percent) _____
of the nominal GDP; and
  (2) If the nominal GDP is $2000 billion, the transaction

demand will be $_____ billion.
  b. The table at the top of the next column shows the number of dollars demanded for asset purposes at each rate of interest.
  (1) Given the transactions demand for money in (*a*), complete the table.
  (2) On the graph on the next page plot the *total* demand for money (*D*ₘ) at each rate of interest.
  c. Assume the money supply (*S*ₘ) is $580 billion.
  (1) Plot this money supply on the graph which you drew on page 145.

Interest rate	Amount of money demanded (billions)	
	For asset purposes	Total
16%	$ 20	$____
14	40	____
12	60	____
10	80	____
8	100	____
6	120	____
4	140	____

  (2) Using either the graph or the table, the equilibrium

rate of interest is _____%.
  d. Should the money supply:
  (1) increase to $600 billion the equilibrium interest rate

would (rise, fall) _____ to _____%.
  (2) decrease to $540 billion the equilibrium interest

rate would _____ to _____%.
  e. If the nominal GDP:
  (1) increased by $80 billion, the total demand for

money would (increase, decrease) _____

by $_____ billion at each rate of interest and the equilibrium rate of interest would (rise,

fall) _____ by _____%.
  (2) decreased by $120 billion, the total demand for

money would _____ by $_____
billion at each rate of interest and the equilibrium inter-

est rate would _____ by _____%.

4. Suppose a bond with no expiration date pays a fixed $500 annually and sells for its face value of $5,000.
  a. Complete the table below, calculate the interest rate (to one decimal place) that would be obtained from the bond when the bond price is given, or calculate the bond price when the interest rate is given.

Bond price	Interest rate
$4,000	____ . __ %
$____	11.0
$5,000	____ . __
$5,500	____ . __
$____	8.0

  b. Based on the results of the table, as the price increases on a bond with a fixed annual payment, the interest yield on the bond (decreases, increases)

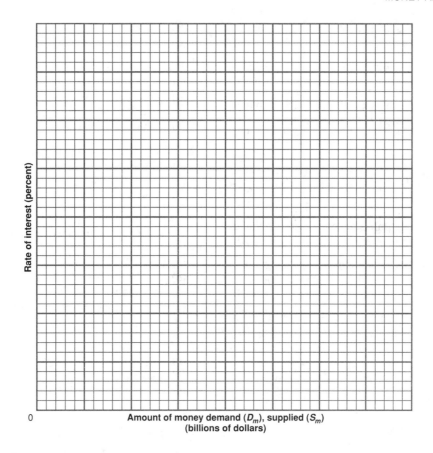

Rate of interest (percent)

0   **Amount of money demand (D_m), supplied (S_m)**
(billions of dollars)

_____, but when the price of a bond decreases, the interest yield _____. Given this situation in an economy, you can conclude that a higher price for bonds _____ interest rates and that a lower price for bonds _____ interest rates.

■ SELF-TEST

Circle the T if the statement is true; the F if it is false.

1. The money supply designated *M*1 is the sum of currency and noncheckable deposits.   T **(F)**

2. The currency component of *M*1 includes both coins and paper money.   **(T)** F

3. If a coin is "token money," its face value is less than its intrinsic value.   **(T)** F

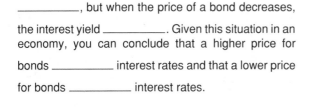

4. Both commercial banks and thrift institutions accept checkable deposits.   **(T)** F

5. The checkable deposits of the Federal government at the Federal Reserve Banks are a component of *M*1.   T **(F)**

6. *M*2 exceeds *M*1 by the amount of noncheckable savings, small time deposits, and money market deposit accounts and money market mutual funds.   **(T)** F

7. A ***small*** time deposit is one that is less than $100,000.   **(T)** F

8. *M*2 is less than *M*3 by the amount of small time deposits in depository institutions.   T **(F)**

9. Economists and public officials are in general agreement on how to define the money supply in the United States.   T **(F)**

10. A near-money is a medium of exchange.   T **(F)**

11. The larger the volume of near-monies owned by consumers, the larger will be their average propensity to save.   T **(F)**

12. Currency and checkable deposits are money because they are acceptable to sellers in exchange for goods and services.   **(T)** F

13. If money is to have a fairly stable value, its supply must be limited relative to the demand for it.   T **(F)**

14. There is a transactions demand for money because

households and business firms use money as a store of value.   T (F)

15. An increase in the price level would, ***ceteris paribus***, increase the transactions demand for money.   (T) F

16. An increase in the nominal GDP, other things remaining the same, will increase both the total demand for money and the equilibrium rate of interest in the economy.   (T) F

17. The Board of Governors of the Federal Reserve System is appointed by the President of the United States and confirmed by the Senate.   (T) F

18. The Federal Reserve Banks are owned and operated by the United States government.   T (F)

19. Federal Reserve Banks are bankers' banks because they make loans to and accept deposits from depository institutions.   (T) F

20. The most important function of the Federal Reserve Banks is the control of the size of the economy's money supply.   (T) F

Circle the letter that corresponds to the best answer.

1. Which of the following is ***not*** one of the functions of money?
 (a) a factor of production
 (b) a medium of exchange
 (c) a store of value
 (d) a measure of value

2. Checkable deposits are:
 (a) all deposits in commercial banks
 (b) demand deposits in commercial banks
 (c) deposits in thrift institutions on which checks may be written
 (d) the sum of *b* and *c* above

3. The largest element of the currency component of *M*1 is:
 (a) coins
 (b) United States Notes
 (c) silver certificates
 (d) Federal Reserve Notes

4. Which of the following constitutes the largest element in the *M*1 money supply?
 (a) currency
 (b) Federal Reserve Notes
 (c) time deposits
 (d) checkable deposits

5. Checkable deposits are money because they are:
 (a) legal tender
 (b) fiat money

 (c) a medium of exchange
 (d) token money

6. Which of the following is ***not*** called a thrift institution?
 (a) a commercial bank
 (b) a savings and loan association
 (c) a credit union
 (d) a mutual savings bank

7. Which of the following is ***not*** a checkable deposit?
 (a) a NOW account
 (b) a time deposit
 (c) an ATS account
 (d) a share draft

8. The supply of money *M*1 consists almost entirely of the debts of:
 (a) the Federal government
 (b) the Federal Reserve Banks
 (c) depository institutions
 (d) the Federal Reserve Banks and depository institutions

9. Which of the following is ***not*** a near-money?
 (a) a noncheckable savings account
 (b) a time deposit
 (c) a credit card
 (d) a money market mutual fund

*Use the following table to answer the next three questions (**10, 11,** and **12**) about the money supply, given the following hypothetical data for the economy.*

Item	Billions of Dollars
Checkable deposits	1,775
Small time deposits	345
Currency held by public	56
Large time deposits	1,230
Noncheckable savings deposits	945
Money market deposit accounts	256
Money market mutual funds	587

10. The size of the *M*1 money supply is:
 (a) $1,775
 (b) $1,831
 (c) $2,176
 (d) $3,019

11. The size of the *M*2 money supply is:
 (a) $2,176
 (b) $3,146
 (c) $3,964
 (d) $4,532

12. The size of the *M*3 money supply is:
 (a) $4,532
 (b) $5,194

(c) $5,339
(d) $6,007

13. Which of the following **best** describes the "backing" of money in the United States?
(a) the gold bullion stored at Fort Knox, Kentucky
(b) the belief of holders of money that it can be exchanged for desirable goods and services
(c) the willingness of banks and the government to surrender something of value in exchange for money
(d) the faith and confidence of the public in the ability of government to pay its debts

14. If the price level increases 20%, the value of money decreases:
(a) 14.14%
(b) 16.67%
(c) 20%
(d) 25%

15. To keep the value of money fairly constant the Federal government and Federal Reserve:
(a) utilize price and wage controls
(b) employ fiscal policy
(c) control the money supply
(d) do both b and c above

16. The total quantity of money demanded is:
(a) directly related to nominal GDP and the rate of interest
(b) directly related to nominal GDP and inversely related to the rate of interest
(c) inversely related to nominal GDP and directly related to the rate of interest
(d) inversely related to nominal GDP and the rate of interest

17. There is an asset demand for money because money is:
(a) a medium of exchange
(b) a measure of value
(c) a store of value
(d) a standard of deferred payment

18. If the dollars held for transactions purposes are, on the average, spent five times a year for final goods and services, then the quantity of money people will wish to hold for transactions is equal to:
(a) five times the nominal GDP
(b) 20% of the nominal GDP
(c) five divided by the nominal GDP
(d) 20% divided by the nominal GDP

19. An increase in the rate of interest would increase:
(a) the opportunity cost of holding money
(b) the transactions demand for money

(c) the asset demand for money
(d) the prices of bonds

Use the table below to answer questions 20 and 21.

Interest rate	Asset demand (billions)
14%	$100
13	150
12	200
11	250

20. Suppose the transactions demand for money is equal to 10% of the nominal GDP, the supply of money is $450 billion, and the asset demand for money is that shown in the table. If the nominal GDP is $3,000 billion, the equilibrium interest rate is:
(a) 14%
(b) 13%
(c) 12%
(d) 11%

3000 × 10% = 300
450 − 300 = 150

21. If the nominal GDP remains constant an increase in the money supply from $450 billion to $500 billion would cause the equilibrium interest rate to:
(a) rise to 14%
(b) fall to 11%
(c) fall to 12%
(d) remain unchanged

22. The stock of money is determined by the Federal Reserve System and does not change when the interest rate changes, so therefore the:
(a) supply of money curve is downward sloping
(b) demand for money curve is downward sloping
(c) supply of money curve is upward sloping
(d) supply of money curve is vertical

23. If the legal ceiling on the interest rate was set below equilibrium, then the:
(a) quantity of money demanded would be greater than the quantity of money supplied
(b) quantity of money demanded would be less than the quantity of money supplied
(c) supply of money would increase and the demand for money would decrease
(d) demand for money would increase and the supply of money would decrease

24. Which one of the following points would be true?
(a) bond prices and the interest rate are directly related
(b) a lower interest rate raises the opportunity cost of holding money
(c) the supply of money is directly related to the interest rate
(d) the total demand for money is inversely related to the interest rate

Answer the next two questions (25 and 26) on the basis of the following information: Bond price = $10,000; bond fixed annual interest payment = $1,000; bond annual rate of interest = 10%.

25. If the price of this bond decreases by $2,500, the interest rate in effect will:
(a) decrease by 1.1 percentage points
(b) decrease by 1.9 percentage points
(c) increase by 2.6 percentage points
(d) increase by 3.3 percentage points

26. If the price of this bond increases by $2000, the interest rate in effect will:
(a) decrease by 1.7 percentage points
(b) decrease by 2.4 percentage points
(c) increase by 1.1 percentage points
(d) increase by 2.9 percentage points

27. Since the passage of the DIDMC Act in 1980:
(a) both nonmember commercial banks and thrift institutions have been subject to the reserve requirements set by the Federal Reserve Banks
(b) the thrift institutions have been allowed to accept checkable deposits
(c) nonmember commercial banks and the thrifts have been allowed to borrow at the Federal Reserve Banks
(d) all of the above

28. Both commercial banks and thrift institutions:
(a) accept the checkable deposits of the public
(b) make loans to the public
(c) expand the money supply
(d) do all of the above

29. A moral hazard problem is created in the banking industry when:
(a) there is more regulation of the industry by the government
(b) insurance is offered by the government to protect bank deposits
(c) the Federal Reserve System exercises less supervision of banking institutions
(d) the Resolution Trust Corporation sells off more failed thrifts

30. One of major reasons for the failure of many savings and loan associations during the 1980s and early 1990s was:
(a) less intensive competition among depository institutions
(b) lower levels of deposit insurance for customers
(c) deregulation of the financial industry
(d) a reduction in loan losses as the economy moved out of recession

■ **DISCUSSION QUESTIONS**

1. How would you define money? What are the components of the *M*1 supply of money in the United States? Which of these components is the larger?

2. What is (a) a checkable deposit; (b) a noncheckable deposit; (c) a thrift (or savings) institution; (d) a depository institution?

3. What is a near-money? What are the more important near-monies in the American economy? Define *M*2 and *M*3 and explain why the existence of near-monies is important.

4. For what reasons are checkable deposits included in the money supply?

5. What "backs" the money used in the United States? What determines the value of money? Explain the relationship between the value of money and the price level.

6. What must government do if it is to stabilize the value of money?

7. What are the two reasons people wish to hold money? How are these two reasons related to the "functions" of money?

8. Explain the determinant of each of the two demands for money and how a change in the size of these determinants will affect the amount of money people wish to hold.

9. The rate of interest is a price. Of what good or service is it the price? Explain how demand and supply determine this price.

10. Describe how changes in bond prices correct disequilibrium in the money market. What is the relationship between bond prices and interest rates?

11. Outline the structure of the Federal Reserve System and explain the chief functions of each of the four parts of the system.

12. As briefly as possible outline the three characteristics of the Federal Reserve Banks and explain the meaning of these characteristics.

13. What are the chief functions which the Federal Reserve Banks perform? Explain briefly the meaning of each of these functions. Which of the chief functions is the most important?

14. Why did banks and savings and loan associations fail during the 1980s and 1990s? What reforms have been instituted to correct the problems? What is the estimated cost to taxpayers?

15. Explain why the provision of deposit insurance creates a "moral hazard" problem. How does this problem contribute to the potential for failure of financial institutions?

■ **ANSWERS**

Chapter 13 Money and Banking

FILL-IN QUESTIONS

1. *a.* medium of exchange; *b.* measure of value; *c.* store of value

2. *a.* currency, coins, money; *b.* checkable, depository institutions; *c.* Federal Reserve, Federal

3. *a.* savings and loan, mutual savings, credit; *b.* NOW, ATS (either order), share

4. *a.* (1) noncheckable, (2) small; (3) deposit, mutual fund; *b.* large; *c.* certificates, 100,000

5. *a.* Treasury, bonds; *b.* currency, checkable, loss

6. *a.* their existence influences consuming-saving habits; *b.* conversion from near-money to money or from money to near-money may affect the stability of the economy; *c.* important when monetary policy is to be employed

7. depository, Federal Reserve

8. *a.* are not; *b.* exchange, legal, scarce

9. desirable goods and services, inversely, price

10. *a.* directly, nominal GDP; *b.* inversely, rate of interest

11. supply, interest, money; *a.* decrease, increase; *b.* increase, decrease

12. Depository Institutions Deregulation and Monetary Control (DIDMCA), checkable, deregulation, Federal Reserve System

13. Federal Open Market Committee, Federal Advisory Council

14. *a.* they are central banks; *b.* they are quasi-public banks; *c.* they are bankers' banks

15. deposits, loans, depository institutions

16. deposits, loans, increase

17. *a.* holding the deposits (reserves) of banks and thrifts; *b.* providing for the collection of checks; *c.* acting as fiscal agents for the Federal government; *d.* supervising member banks; *e.* regulating the money supply; regulating the money supply

18. less, high; *a.* deregulation, more, a moral hazard, higher, risky, illegal; *b.* Resolution Trust Corporation, Federal Deposit Insurance Corporation

PROBLEMS AND PROJECTS

1. *a.* 170, 448 (either order), 618; *b.* 300, 1,630, 575, 425 (either order), 2,548; *c.* 645, 3,193

2. *a.* 4.8, 9.1, 13, 16.7, 20; *b.* 5.3, 11.1, 17.6

3. *a.* (1) ¼ (25%), (2) 500; *b.* (1) 520, 540, 560, 580, 600, 620, 640; *c.* (2) 10; *d.* (1) fall, 8, (2) rise, 14; *e.* (1) increase, 20, rise, 2, (2) decrease, 30, fall, 3

4. *a.* 12.5%, $4545, 10.0%, 9.1%, $6250; *b.* decreases, increases, decreases, increases

SELF-TEST

1. F, p. 244	11. F, p. 247
2. T, p. 245	12. T, pp. 248–249
3. F, p. 245	13. T, p. 249
4. T, p. 246	14. F, p. 251
5. F, p. 246	15. T, p. 251
6. T, p. 247	16. T, pp. 253–254
7. T, p. 247	17. T, p. 255
8. F, p. 247	18. F, pp. 256–257
9. F, p. 247	19. T, pp. 257–258
10. F, p. 246	20. T, p. 258

1. *a,* p. 244	16. *b,* p. 253
2. *d,* pp. 244–246	17. *c,* pp. 252–253
3. *d,* p. 245	18. *b,* p. 253
4. *b,* p. 246	19. *a,* p. 254
5. *c,* pp. 248–249	20. *b,* pp. 252–253
6. *a,* p. 246	21. *c,* pp. 252–253
7. *b,* p. 246	22. *d,* p. 253
8. *d,* p. 248	23. *a,* pp. 253–254
9. *c,* pp. 247–248	24. *d,* pp. 253–254
10. *b,* p. 246	25. *d,* p. 254
11. *c.* p. 247	26. *a,* p. 254
12. *b,* p. 247	27. *d,* p. 255
13. *b,* pp. 248–249	28. *d,* p. 255
14. *b,* p. 248	29. *b,* p. 260
15. *d,* pp. 250–251	30. *c,* p. 259

DISCUSSION QUESTIONS

1. pp. 244–245	9. pp. 253–254
2. pp. 245–246	10. pp. 253–254
3. pp. 246–247	11. pp. 255–256
4. pp. 245–246	12. pp. 256–258
5. pp. 248–249	13. p. 258
6. pp. 249–251	14. pp. 258–261
7. pp. 251–253	15. pp. 260–261
8. pp. 251–253	

CHAPTER 14
How Banks Create Money

Chapter 13 explained the institutional structure of banking in the United States today, the functions which banks and the other depository institutions and money perform, and the composition of the money supply. Chapter 14 explains how banks literally create money—checking account money—and the factors which determine and limit the money-creating ability of commercial banks. Even though the other depository institutions also create checkable deposits, this chapter focuses its attention on the commercial banks because they have created and will continue to create a very large part of the total amount of money created by all depository institutions in the United States. But where the term **commercial bank** (or bank) appears it is legitimate to substitute depository **institution;** and it is permissible to substitute **checkable deposit** for **demand deposit** (or checking account).

The device (and a most convenient and simple device it is) employed to explain commercial banking operations and money creation is the balance sheet. All banking transactions affect this balance sheet, and the first step to understanding how money is created is to understand how various simple and typical transactions affect the commercial bank balance sheet.

In reading this chapter you must analyze for yourself the effect upon the balance sheet of each and every banking transaction discussed. The important items in the balance sheet are demand deposits and reserves, because demand deposits **are** money, and the ability of a bank to create new demand deposits is determined by the amount of reserves the bank has. Expansion of the money supply depends upon the possession by commercial banks of excess reserves. Excess reserves do not appear explicitly in the balance sheet but do appear there implicitly because excess reserves are the difference between the actual reserves and the required reserves of commercial banks.

Two cases—the single commercial bank and the banking system—are presented in order to help you build an understanding of banking and money creation. It is important here to understand that the money-creating potential of a single commercial bank differs in an important way from the money-creating potential of the entire banking system; it is equally important to understand how the

money-creating ability of many single commercial banks is **multiplied** and results in the money-creating ability of the banking system as a whole.

Certain assumptions are used throughout most of the chapter to analyze money-creating ability; in certain instances these assumptions may not be completely realistic and may need to be modified. The chapter concludes with a discussion of how the earlier analysis must be modified—but not changed in its essentials—to take account of these slightly unrealistic assumptions.

■ CHECKLIST

When you have studied this chapter you should be able to:

☐ Define the basic items in a bank's balance sheet.
☐ Recount the story of how goldsmiths came to issue paper money and became bankers who created money and held fractional reserves.
☐ Explain the effects of the deposit of currency in a checking account on the composition and size of the money supply.
☐ Compute a bank's required and excess reserves when you are given the needed balance-sheet figures.
☐ Explain why a commercial bank is required to maintain a reserve; and why this reserve is not sufficient to protect the depositors from losses.
☐ Indicate how the deposit of a check drawn on one commercial bank in a second commercial bank will affect the reserves and excess reserves of the two banks.
☐ Show what happens to the money supply when a commercial bank makes a loan (or buys securities); and what happens to the money supply when a loan is repaid (or a bank sells securities).
☐ Explain what happens to a commercial bank's reserves and demand deposits after it has made a loan, a check has been written on the newly created demand deposit, deposited in another commercial bank and cleared; and what happens to the reserves and demand deposits of the commercial bank in which the check was deposited.

☐ Describe what would happen to a commercial bank's reserves if it made loans (or bought securities) in an amount that exceeded its excess reserves.

☐ State the money-creating potential of a commercial bank (the amount of money a commercial bank can safely create by lending or buying securities).

☐ Explain how the Federal funds market helps reconcile the goals of profits and liquidity for commercial banks.

☐ State the money-creating potential of the banking system.

☐ Explain how it is possible for the banking system to create an amount of money which is a multiple of its excess reserves when no individual commercial bank ever creates money in an amount greater than its excess reserve.

☐ Compute the size of the monetary multiplier and the money-creating potential of the banking system when you are provided with the necessary data.

☐ List the two leakages which reduce the money-creating potential of the banking system.

☐ Explain why the size of the money supply needs to be controlled.

■ **CHAPTER OUTLINE**

1. The balance sheet of the commercial bank is a statement of the assets, liabilities, and net worth (capital stock) of the bank at a specific time; and in the balance sheet the bank's assets equal its liabilities plus its net worth.

2. The history of the early goldsmiths illustrates how paper money came into being, how they became bankers when they began to make loans and issue money in excess of their gold holdings, and how the presently used fractional reserve system with its two significant characteristics were developed.

3. By examining the ways in which the balance sheet of the commercial bank is affected by various transactions, it is possible to understand how a single commercial bank in a multibank system can create money.

   a. Once a commercial bank has been founded,
   (1) by selling shares of stock and obtaining cash in return;
   (2) and acquired the property and equipment needed to carry on the banking business;
   (3) the deposit of cash in the bank does not affect the total money supply; it only changes its composition by substituting demand deposits for currency in circulation;
   (4) three reserve concepts are vital to an understanding of the money-creating potential of a commercial bank.
   (a) The **legal reserve deposit** (required reserve) which a bank **must** maintain at its Federal Reserve Bank (or as vault cash—which can be ignored) equals the reserve ratio multiplied by the deposit liabilities of the commercial bank;
   (b) the **actual reserves** of a commercial bank are its deposits at the Federal Reserve Bank (plus the vault cash which is ignored);
   (c) the **excess reserves** equal to the actual reserves less the required reserve.
   (5) The writing of a check upon the bank and its deposit in a second bank results in a loss of reserves and deposits for the first and a gain in reserves and deposits for the second bank.

   b. When a single commercial bank lends or buys government securities it increases its own deposit liabilities and, therefore, the supply of money by the amount of the loan or security purchase. But the bank only lends or buys securities in an amount equal to its excess reserves because it fears the loss of reserves to other commercial banks in the economy.

   c. When a single commercial bank receives loan repayments or sells government securities, its deposit liabilities and, therefore, the supply of money are described by the amount of the loan repayments or securities sale.

   d. An individual commercial bank balances its desire for profits (which result from the making of loans and the purchase of securities) with its desire for liquidity or safety (which it achieves by having excess reserves or vault cash).

   e. The Federal funds market allows banks with excess reserves to lend funds overnight to banks which are short of reserves. The interest rate paid on the overnight loans is the Federal funds rate.

4. The ability of a banking system composed of many individual commercial banks to lend and to create money is a multiple (greater than one) of its excess reserves; and is equal to the excess reserves of the banking system multiplied by the demand-deposit (or monetary) multiplier.

   a. The banking system as a whole can do this even though no single commercial bank ever lends an amount greater than its excess reserve because the banking system, unlike a single commercial bank, does not lose reserves.

   b. The monetary (or demand-deposit) multiplier is equal to the reciprocal of the required reserve ratio for demand deposits; and the maximum expansion of demand deposits is equal to the excess reserves in the banking system times the monetary multiplier.

   c. The potential lending ability of the banking system may not be fully achieved if there are leakages because borrowers choose to have additional currency or bankers choose to have excess reserves.

   d. If bankers lend as much as they are able during periods of prosperity and less than they are able during recessions, they add to the instability of the economy;

and to reduce this instability the Federal Reserve Banks must control the size of the money supply.

■ **IMPORTANT TERMS**

Balance sheet

Assets

Liabilities

Net worth

Fractional reserve system of banking

Vault cash (till money)

Legal (required) reserve (deposit)

Reserve ratio

Fractional reserve

Actual reserve

Excess reserve

Federal Deposit Insurance Corporation

The lending potential of an individual commercial bank

Federal funds rate

Commercial banking system

Monetary (demand-deposit) multiplier

The lending potential of the banking system

Leakage

■ **FILL-IN QUESTIONS**

1. The balance sheet of a commercial bank is a statement of the bank's ___*assets*___ ___*liabilities*___ and ___*net worth (capital)stock*___ at some specific point in time.

2. The coins and paper money which a bank has in its possession are called ___*Vault*___ cash or ___*Till*___ money.

3. When a person deposits cash in a commercial bank and receives a demand deposit in return, the size of the money supply has (increased, decreased, not changed) ___*not changed*___

4. The legal reserve deposit of a commercial bank (ignoring vault cash) must be kept at the ___*Fed Reserve*___ and must equal (at least) its ___*deposit liability*___ multiplied by the ___*legal reserve required reserve ratio*___

5. The excess reserves of a commercial bank equal its ___*actual Reserve*___ less its ___*required Reserve*___

6. If commercial banks are allowed to accept (or create) deposits in excess of their reserves, the banking system is operating under a system of ___*fractional*___ reserves.

7. When a check is drawn upon bank X, deposited in bank Y, and cleared, the reserves of bank X are (increased, decreased, not changed) ___*decrease*___ and the reserves of bank Y are ___*increase*___; deposits in bank X are ___*decrease*___ and deposits in bank Y are ___*increase*___

8. A single commercial bank in a multibank system can safely make loans or buy government securities equal in amount to the ___*excess reserve*___ of that commercial bank.

9. When a commercial bank makes a new loan of $10,000, it (increases, decreases) ___*increase*___ the supply of money by $___*10,000*___; but when this loan is repaid, the supply of money ___*decrease*___ by $___*1000*___

10. When a commercial bank sells a $2000 government bond to a securities dealer the supply of money (increases, decreases) ___*decrease*___ by $___*2000*___; but when a commercial bank buys a $2000 government bond from a securities dealer the supply of money ___*increase*___ by $___*2000*___

11. A bank ordinarily pursues two conflicting goals; they are ___*profit*___ and ___*liquidity*___

12. When a bank lends temporary excess reserves held at the ___*Federal Reserve*___ banks to other commercial banks that are temporarily short of legally required reserves, it is participating in the ___*Fed Funk*___ market. The interest rate paid on these overnight loans is the ___*Fed Fund*___ rate.

13. The banking system can make loans (or buy government securities) and create money in an amount equal to its excess reserves multiplied by the ___*monetary multiplier*___. Its lending potential per dollar of excess reserves is greater than the lending potential of a single commercial bank because it does not lose ___*reserve*___ to other banks.

14. The greater the reserve ratio is, the (larger, smaller) ___*smaller*___ is the monetary multiplier.

15. If the required reserve ratio is 16⅔%, the banking system is $6 million short of reserves, and the banking system is unable to increase its reserves, the banking sys-

tem must ___decrease___ the money supply by
$___36 mil.___

16. The money-creating potential of the commercial banking system is lessened by the withdrawal of ___currency___ from banks and by the decisions of bankers to keep ___excess___ reserves.

17. Commercial banks in the past:
   a. have kept considerable excess reserves during periods of (prosperity, recession) ___recession___ and have kept few or no excess reserves during periods of ___prosperity___
   b. and by behaving in this way have made the economy (more, less) ___more___ unstable.

a. A check for $50 is drawn by one of the depositors of the bank, given to a person who deposits it in another bank, and cleared (column a).
b. A depositor withdraws $50 in cash from the bank, and the bank restores its vault cash by obtaining $50 in additional cash from its Federal Reserve Bank (column b).
c. A check for $60 drawn on another bank is deposited in this bank and cleared (column c).
d. The bank sells $100 in government bonds to the Federal Reserve Bank in its district (column d).

2. Below are five balance sheets for a single commercial bank (columns 1a–5a). The required reserve ratio is 20%.
   a. Compute the required reserves (A); ignoring vault cash, the excess reserves (B) of the bank (if the bank is short of reserves and must reduce its loans or obtain additional reserves, show this by placing a minus sign in front of the amounts by which it is short of reserves); and the amount of new loans it can extend (C).

	(1a)	(2a)	(3a)	(4a)	(5a)
Assets:					
Cash	$ 10	$ 20	$ 20	$ 20	$ 15
Reserves	40	40	25	40	45
Loans	100	100	100	100	150
Securities	50	60	30	70	60
Liabilities and net worth:					
Demand deposits	175	200	150	180	220
Capital stock	25	20	25	50	50
A. Required reserve	$___	$___	$___	$___	$___
B. Excess reserve	___	___	___	___	___
C. New loans	___	___	___	___	___

■ PROBLEMS AND PROJECTS

1. The table below is the simplified balance sheet of a commercial bank. Assume that the figures given show the bank's assets and demand-deposit liabilities **prior to each of the following four transactions.** Draw up the balance sheet as it would appear after each of these transactions is completed and place the balance-sheet figures in the appropriate column. **Do not** use the figures you place in columns a, b, and c when you work the next part of the problem; start all parts of the problem with the printed figures.

		(a)	(b)	(c)	(d)
Assets:					
Cash	$100	$___	$___	$___	$___
Reserves	200	___	___	___	___
Loans	500	___	___	___	___
Securities	200	___	___	___	___
Liabilities and net worth:					
Demand deposits	900	___	___	___	___
Capital stock	100	100	100	100	100

b. Draw up for the individual bank the five balance sheets as they appear after the bank has made the new **loans** that it is capable of making (columns 1b–5b).

	(1b)	(2b)	(3b)	(4b)	(5b)
Assets:					
Cash	$___	$___	$___	$___	$___
Reserves	___	___	___	___	___
Loans	___	___	___	___	___
Securities	___	___	___	___	___
Liabilities and net worth:					
Demand deposits	___	___	___	___	___
Capital stock	___	___	___	___	___

3. In the table at the top of the next page are several reserve ratios. Compute the monetary multiplier for each of the reserve ratios and enter the figures in column 2. In column 3 show the maximum amount by which a single commercial bank can increase its loans for each dollar's worth of excess reserves it possesses. In column 4 indicate the maximum amount by which the banking system can increase its loans for each dollar's worth of excess reserves in the system.

(1)	(2)	(3)	(4)
12½%	$____	$____	$____
16⅔%	____	____	____
20%	____	____	____
25%	____	____	____
30%	____	____	____
33⅓%	____	____	____

4. Shown below is the simplified consolidated balance sheet for *all* commercial banks in the economy. Assume that the figures given show the banks' assets and liabilities *prior to each of the following three transactions* and

that the reserve ratio is 20%. *Do not* use the figures you placed in columns 2 and 4 when you begin parts *b* and *c* of the problem: start parts *a, b,* and *c* of the problem with the printed figures.

a. The public deposits $5 in cash in the banks and the banks send the $5 to the Federal Reserve, where it is added to their reserves. Fill in column 1. If the banking system extends the new loans it is capable of extending, show in column 2 the balance sheet as it would then appear.

b. The banking system sells $8 worth of securities to the Federal Reserve. Complete column 3. Assuming the system extends the maximum amount of credit of which it is capable, fill in column 4.

c. The Federal Reserve lends $10 to the commercial banks; complete column 5. Complete column 6 showing the condition of the banks after the maximum amount of new loans which the banks are capable of making is granted.

		(1)	(2)	(3)	(4)	(5)	(6)
Assets:							
Cash	$ 50	$____	$____	$____	$____	$____	$____
Reserves	100	____	____	____	____	____	____
Loans	200	____	____	____	____	____	____
Securities	200	____	____	____	____	____	____
Liabilities and net worth:							
Demand deposits	500	____	____	____	____	____	____
Capital stock	50	50	50	50	50	50	50
Loans for Federal Reserve	0	____	____	____	____	____	____
Excess reserves		____	____	____	____	____	____
Maximum possible expansion of the money supply		____	____	____	____	____	____

■ **SELF-TEST**

Circle the T if the statement is true; the F if it is false.

1. The balance sheet of a commercial bank shows the transactions in which the bank has engaged during a given period of time. T **F**

2. A commercial bank's assets plus its net worth equal the bank's liabilities. T **F**

3. Goldsmiths increased the money supply when they accepted deposits of gold and issued paper receipts to the depositors. T **F**

4. Roberta Lynn, the music star, deposits a $30,000 check in a commercial bank and receives a demand deposit in return; an hour later the Manfred Iron and Coal Company borrows $30,000 from the same bank. The

money supply has increased $30,000 as a result of the two transactions. **T** F

5. A commercial bank may maintain its legal reserve either as a deposit in its Federal Reserve Bank or as government bonds in its own vault. **T** F

6. The legal reserve which a commercial bank maintains must equal at least its own deposit liabilities multiplied by the required reserve ratio. **T** F

7. The actual reserves of a commercial bank equal excess reserves plus required reserves. **T** F

8. The reserve of a commercial bank in the Federal Reserve Bank is an asset of the Federal Reserve Bank. T **F**

9. A check for $1000 drawn on bank X by a depositor

and deposited in bank Y will increase the excess reserves of bank Y by $1000.   T (F)

10. A single commercial bank can safely lend an amount equal to its excess reserves multiplied by the required reserve ratio.   T (F)

11. When a borrower repays a loan of $500, either in cash or by check, the supply of money is reduced by $500.   (T) F

12. The granting of a $5000 loan and the purchase of a $5000 government bond from a securities dealer by a commercial bank have the same effect on the money supply.   (T) R

13. A commercial bank seeks both profits and liquidity; but these are conflicting goals.   (T) F

14. If the banking system has $10 million in excess reserves and if the reserve ratio is 25%, it can increase its loans by $40 million.   (T) F

15. While a single commercial bank can increase its loans only by an amount equal to its excess reserves, the entire banking system can increase its loans by an amount equal to its excess reserves multiplied by the reciprocal of the reserve ratio.   (T) F

16. When borrowers from a commercial bank wish to have cash rather than demand deposits, the money-creating potential of the banking system is increased.   T (F)

17. The Federal funds rate is the interest rate at which the Federal government lends funds to commercial banks.   T (F)

18. Modern banking systems use gold as the basis for the fractional reserve system.   T (F)

19. The selling of a government bond by a commercial bank will increase the money supply.   T (F)

20. There is a need for the Federal Reserve System to control the money supply because profit-seeking banks tend to make changes in the money supply that are pro-cyclical.   (T) F

Circle the letter that corresponds to the best answer.

1. The goldsmiths became bankers when:
(a) they accepted deposits of gold for safe storage
(b) they issued receipts for the gold stored with them
(c) their receipts for deposited gold were used as paper money
(d) they issued paper money in excess of the amount of gold stored with them

2. When cash is deposited in a demand-deposit account in a commercial bank there is:
(a) a decrease in the money supply
(b) an increase in the money supply

(c) no change in the composition of the money supply
(d) a change in the composition of the money supply

3. A commercial bank has actual reserves of $9000 and deposit liabilities of $30,000; and the required reserve ratio is 20%. The excess reserves of the bank are:
(a) $3000
(b) $6000
(c) $7500
(d) $9000

4. A commercial bank is required to have a deposit at its Federal Reserve Bank in order:
(a) to protect the deposits in the commercial bank against losses
(b) to provide the means by which checks drawn on the commercial bank and deposited in other commercial banks can be collected
(c) to add to the liquidity of the commercial bank and protect it against a "run" on the bank
(d) to provide the Board of Governors of the Federal Reserve System with a means of controlling the lending ability of the commercial bank

5. A depositor places $750 in cash in a commercial bank, and the reserve ratio is 33⅓%; the bank sends the $750 to the Federal Reserve Bank. As a result, the **reserves** and the **excess reserves** of the bank have been increased, respectively, by:
(a) $750 and $250
(b) $750 and $500
(c) $750 and $750
(d) $500 and $500

6. A commercial bank has no excess reserves, but then a depositor places $600 in cash in the bank, and the bank adds the $600 to its reserves by sending it to the Federal Reserve Bank. The commercial bank then lends $300 to a borrower. As a consequence of these transactions the size of the money supply has:
(a) not been affected
(b) increased by $300
(c) increased by $600
(d) increased by $900

7. A commercial bank has excess reserves of $500 and a required reserve ratio of 20%; it grants a loan of $1000 to a borrower. If the borrower writes a check for $1000 which is deposited in another commercial bank, the first bank will be short of reserves, after the check has been cleared, in the amount of:
(a) $200
(b) $500
(c) $700
(d) $1000

8. A commercial bank sells a $1000 government security to a securities dealer. The dealer pays for the bond in

cash, which the bank adds to its vault cash. The money supply has:

(a) not been affected
(b) decreased by $1000
(c) increased by $1000
(d) increased by $1000 multiplied by the reciprocal of the required reserve ratio

25000

9. A commercial bank has deposit liabilities of $100,000, reserves of $37,000, and a required reserve ratio of 25%. The amount by which a **single commercial bank** and the amount by which the **banking system** can increase loans are, respectively:

(a) $12,000 and $48,000
(b) $17,000 and $68,000
(c) $12,000 and $60,000
(d) $17,000 and $85,000

37000
−2500
1200

10. If the required reserve ratio were 12½% the value of the monetary multiplier would be:

(a) 5
(b) 6
(c) 7
(d) 8

$\frac{1}{3}$

11. The commercial banking system has excess reserves of $700 and makes new loans of $2100 and is just meeting its reserve requirements. The required reserve ratio is:

(a) 20%
(b) 25%
(c) 30%
(d) 33⅓%

12. The commercial banking system, because of a recent change in the required reserve ratio from 20% to 30%, finds that it is $60 million short of reserves. If it is unable to obtain any additional reserves it must decrease the money supply by:

(a) $60 million
(b) $180 million
(c) $200 million
(d) $300 million

$60 \times \frac{10}{3}$

$80000 \times \frac{4}{5}$
$= 64000$

13. Only one commercial bank in the banking system has an excess reserve, and its excess reserve is $100,000. This bank makes a new loan of $80,000 and keeps an excess reserve of $20,000. If the required reserve ratio for all banks is 20%, the potential expansion of the money supply is:

(a) $80,000
(b) $100,000
(c) $400,000
(d) $500,000

Total excess Res
in system

20000 +
newly created deposit
80000 (5×64000)

14. The money-creating potential of the banking system is reduced when:

(a) bankers choose to hold excess reserves
(b) borrowers choose to hold none of the funds they have borrowed in currency

(c) the Federal Reserve lowers the required reserve ratio
(d) bankers borrow from the Federal Reserve

15. The excess reserves held by banks tend to:

(a) rise during periods of prosperity
(b) fall during periods of recession
(c) rise during periods of recession
(d) fall when interest rates in the economy fall

16. Unless controlled, the money supply will:

(a) fall during periods of prosperity
(b) rise during periods of recession
(c) change in a procyclical fashion
(d) change in an anticyclical fashion

*Use the following balance sheet for the First National Bank in answering the next five questions (**17, 18, 19, 20,** and **21**). Assume the required reserve ratio is 20%.*

Assets		Liabilities and Net Worth	
Reserves	$ 50,000	Demand Deposits	$150,000
Loans	70,000	Capital Stock	100,000
Securities	30,000		
Property	100,000		

17. This commercial bank has excess reserves of:

(a) $10,000
(b) $20,000
(c) $30,000
(d) $40,000

18. This bank can safely expand its loans by a maximum of:

(a) $50,000
(b) $40,000
(c) $30,000
(d) $20,000

19. Using the original bank balance sheet, assume that the bank makes a loan of $10,000 and has a check cleared against it for the amount of the loan, then its reserves and demand deposits will now be:

(a) $40,000 and $140,000
(b) $40,000 and $150,000
(c) $30,000 and $150,000
(d) $60,000 and $140,000

20. Using the original bank balance sheet, assume that the bank makes a loan of $15,000 and has a check cleared against it for the amount of the loan, then it will have excess reserves of:

(a) $5,000
(b) $10,000
(c) $15,000
(d) $20,000

21. If the original bank balance sheet was for the commercial banking **system,** rather than a single bank, loans

and deposits could have been expanded by a maximum of:
- (a) $50,000
- (b) $100,000
- (c) $150,000
- (d) $200,000

22. The claims of the owners of the bank against the bank assets is the bank's:
- (a) net worth
- (b) liabilities
- (c) balance sheet
- (d) fractional reserves

23. The selling of government bonds by commercial banks is most similar to the:
- (a) making of loans by banks because both actions increase the money supply
- (b) making of loans by banks because both actions decrease the money supply
- (c) repayment of loans to banks because both actions decrease the money supply
- (d) repayment of loans to banks because both actions increase the money supply

Answer the next two questions (24 and 25) on the basis of the following consolidated balance sheet for the commercial banking system. All figures are in billions. Assume that the required reserve ratio is 12.5%.

Assets		Liabilities and Net Worth	
Reserves	$ 40	Demand Deposits	$200
Loans	80	Capital Stock	120
Securities	100		
Property	200		

24. The maximum amount by which this commercial banking system can expand the supply of money by lending is:
- (a) $120 billion
- (b) $240 billion
- (c) $350 billion
- (d) $440 billion

25. If there is a deposit of $20 billion of new currency into checking accounts in the banking system, excess reserves will increase by:
- (a) $16.5 billion
- (b) $17.0 billion
- (c) $17.5 billion
- (d) $18.5 billion

■ **DISCUSSION QUESTIONS**

1. How did the early goldsmiths come to issue paper money and then become bankers? Explain the difference between a 100% and a fractional reserve system of bank-

ing and why the latter system is subject to "runs" and requires public regulation.

2. Commercial banks seek both profits and safety. Explain how the balance sheet of the commercial banks reflects the desires of bankers for profits and for liquidity. Discuss how the Federal funds market helps banks reconcile the two goals of profits and liquidity.

3. Do the reserves held by commercial banks satisfactorily protect the bank's depositors? Are the reserves of commercial banks needed? Explain your answers.

4. Explain why the granting of a loan by a commercial bank increases the supply of money. Why does the repayment of a loan decrease the supply of money?

5. How does the buying or selling of government securities by commercial banks influence the money supply?

6. The owner of a sporting goods store writes a check on his account in a Kent, Ohio, bank and sends it to one of his suppliers who deposits it in his bank in Cleveland, Ohio. How does the Cleveland bank obtain payment from the Kent bank? If the two banks were in Kent and New York City, how would one bank pay the other? How are the excess reserves of the two banks affected?

7. Why is a single commercial bank able to lend safely only an amount equal to its excess reserves?

8. No one commercial bank ever lends an amount greater than its excess reserve, but the banking system as a whole is able to extend loans and expand the money supply by an amount equal to the system's excess reserves multiplied by the reciprocal of the reserve ratio. Explain why this is possible and how the multiple expansion of deposits and money takes place.

9. On the basis of a given amount of excess reserves and a given reserve ratio, a certain expansion of the money supply may be possible. What are two reasons why the potential expansion of the money supply may not be fully achieved?

10. Why is there a "need for monetary control" in the American economy?

■ **ANSWERS**

Chapter 14 How Banks Create Money

FILL-IN QUESTIONS

1. assets, liabilities, net worth (capital)

2. vault, till

3. not changed

4. Federal Reserve Bank in its district, deposit liabilities, reserve ratio

5. actual reserves, required reserves

6. fractional

7. decreased, increased, decreased, increased

8. excess reserves

9. increases, 10,000, decreases, 10,000

10. decreases, 2000, increases, 2000

11. profits, liquidity (safety)

12. Federal Reserve, Federal funds, Federal funds rate

13. monetary multiplier (reciprocal of the reserve ratio), reserves

14. smaller

15. decrease, 36 million

16. currency (cash), excess

17. *a.* recession, prosperity; *b.* more

PROBLEMS AND PROJECTS

1.

	(a)	(b)	(c)	(d)
Assets:				
Cash	$100	$100	$100	$100
Reserves	150	150	260	300
Loans	500	500	500	500
Securities	200	200	200	100
Liabilities and net worth:				
Demand deposits	850	850	960	900
Capital stock	100	100	100	100

2.

a.

	(1a)	(2a)	(3a)	(4a)	(5a)
A. Required reserve	$35	$40	$30	$36	$44
B. Excess reserve	5	0	−5	4	1
C. New loans	5	0	*	4	1

b.

	(1b)	(2b)	(3b)	(4b)	(5b)
Assets:					
Cash	$ 10	$ 20	$20	$ 20	$ 15
Reserves	40	40	25	40	45
Loans	105	100	*	104	151
Securities	50	60	30	70	60
Liabilities and net worth:					
Demand deposits	180	200	*	184	221
Capital stock	25	20	25	50	50

* If an individual bank is $5 short of reserves it must either obtain additional reserves of $5 by selling loans, securities, or its own IOUs to the reserve bank or contract its loans by $25.

3. column 2: 8, 6, 5, 4, 3⅓, 3; column 3: 1,1,1,1,1,1; column 4: 8, 6, 5, 4, 3⅓, 3

4.

	(1)	(2)	(3)	(4)	(5)	(6)
Assets:						
Cash	$ 50	$ 50	$ 50	$ 50	$ 50	$ 50
Reserves	105	105	108	108	110	110
Loans	200	220	200	240	200	250
Securities	200	200	192	192	200	200
Liabilities and net worth:						
Demand deposits	505	525	500	540	500	550
Capital stock	50	50	50	50	50	50
Loans from Federal Reserve	0	0	0	0	10	10
Excess reserves	4	0	8	0	10	0
Maximum possible expansion of the money supply	20	0	40	0	50	0

SELF-TEST

1. F, pp. 264–265
2. F, p. 265
3. F, p. 265
4. T, p. 265
5. F, p. 267
6. T, p. 267
7. T, p. 268
8. F, p. 269
9. F, p. 269
10. F, p. 272

11. T, p. 272
12. T, p. 273
13. T, p. 273
14. T, p. 276
15. T, p. 276
16. F, p. 277
17. F, pp. 273–274
18. F, p. 265
19. F, p. 273
20. T, pp. 278–279

1. *d*, p. 265
2. *d*, pp. 266–267
3. *a*, p. 268
4. *d*, pp. 268–269
5. *b*, pp. 267–268
6. *b*, p. 271
7. *b*, p. 272
8. *b*, p. 273
9. *a*, p. 276
10. *d*, p. 276
11. *d*, p. 276
12. *c*, p. 277
13. *c*, p. 277

14. *a*, p. 277
15. *c*, pp. 278–279
16. *c*, pp. 277–278
17. *b*, pp. 267–268
18. *d*, p. 274
19. *b*, pp. 269–270
20. *a*, pp. 271–272
21. *b*, p. 276
22. *a*, p. 265
23. *c*, p. 273
24. *a*, p. 276
25. *c*, p. 268

DISCUSSION QUESTIONS

1. p. 265
2. pp. 273–274
3. pp. 268–269
4. pp. 271–273
5. p. 273

6. pp. 269–270
7. pp. 267–268
8. pp. 274–276
9. p. 277
10. pp. 278–279

CHAPTER 15

The Federal Reserve Banks and Monetary Policy

Chapter 15 is the third chapter dealing with money and banking. It explains how the Board of Governors of the Federal Reserve System and the Federal Reserve Banks affect output, income, employment, and the price level of the economy. Central-bank policies designed to affect these variables are called monetary policies, the goal of which is full employment without inflation.

You should have little difficulty with this chapter if you have understood the material in Chapter 14. In the first half of Chapter 15 attention should be concentrated on the following: (1) the important items on the balance sheet of the Federal Reserve Banks; (2) the three major controls available to the Federal Reserve Banks, and how the employment of these controls can affect the reserves, excess reserves, the actual money supply, and the money-creating potential of the banking system; (3) the actions the Federal Reserve would take if it were pursuing a tight money policy to curb inflation, and the actions it would take if it were pursuing an easy money policy to reduce unemployment; and (4) the relative importance of the three major controls which the Federal Reserve Banks use or have used to influence the economy.

In order to acquire a thorough knowledge of the manner in which each of the Federal Reserve transactions affects reserves, excess reserves, the actual money supply, and the potential money supply, you must study very carefully each of the sets of balance sheets which are used to explain these transactions. On these balance sheets the items to watch are again reserves and demand deposits! Be sure that you know why each of the balance sheet changes is made and are able, **on your own,** to make the appropriate balance-sheet entries to trace through the effects of any transaction.

Following the examination of "The Tools of Monetary Policy" Professors McConnell and Brue explain how the demand for and the supply of money determine the interest rate (in the "money market"); how the interest rate and the investment-demand schedule determine the level of planned investment in the economy; and how planned investment and the saving schedule together determine the equilibrium GDP. How an easy money policy and a tight money policy work through this cause-effect chain is illus-

trated with examples and summarized in Table 15-3, which you should study.

This explanation of the traditional or Keynesian view of monetary policy makes it clear that the effect of a change in the money supply depends upon just how steep or flat the down-sloping demand-for-money and investment-demand curves are. Professors McConnell and Brue also use the aggregate-supply and the aggregate-demand curves to show you how changes in the money supply affect national output and the price level in the three stages along the aggregate-supply curve.

The strengths and shortcomings of monetary policy in reducing unemployment (and expanding domestic output) and in reducing inflation are examined in the next-to-last major section of the chapter. Here you will also encounter the dilemma faced by the Fed: it cannot simultaneously control both the money supply and the level of interest rates in the economy. You will also learn that monetary policy is further complicated by linkages with the international economy.

The last section of Chapter 15 is a summary of Chapters 7 through 15. It will restate for you the main outline of the Keynesian theory of employment and the principal public policies that may be used to promote full employment without creating inflation. They will help you to see that the various principles discussed in the previous chapters are **not** separate theories but are, in fact, connected parts of the one mainstream or Keynesian theory; and that the public policies discussed in earlier chapters are **not** really separate policies but are alternative means of achieving the goal of economic stabilization.

This one theory of employment and the alternative means of achieving this one goal are summarized for you in Figure 15-4. This is probably the single most important figure in the textbook.

■ **CHECKLIST**

When you have studied this chapter you should be able to:

☐ State the fundamental objective of monetary policy.

☐ List the important assets and liabilities of the Federal Reserve Banks.

☐ Identify the three tools of monetary policy.

☐ Explain how the Federal Reserve expands or contracts the money supply by buying or selling government bonds.

☐ Describe how changes in reserve ratios or the discount rate by the Federal Reserve affect the money supply.

☐ Prescribe the three specific monetary policies the Federal Reserve should utilize to reduce unemployment; and the three specific policies it should employ to reduce inflationary pressures in the economy.

☐ State which of the three monetary-policy tools is the most effective.

☐ Draw the demand-for-money and the supply-of-money curves and use them to show how a change in the supply of money will affect the interest rate.

☐ Draw an investment-demand curve to explain the effects of changes in the interest rate on investment spending.

☐ Construct a leakages-injections graph to show the effects of a change in planned investment on the equilibrium GDP.

☐ Explain, using the traditional or Keynesian cause-effect chain, the links between a change in the money supply and a change in the equilibrium GDP when there is an easy money policy and when there is a tight money policy.

☐ State precisely how the steepness of the demand-for-money and of the investment-demand curves affects the impact of a change in the money supply on the equilibrium GDP.

☐ Use the aggregate-demand and aggregate-supply curves to show the effects of changes in the money supply on national output and the price level in the Keynesian, classical, and intermediate ranges of aggregate supply.

☐ List three strengths and three shortcomings of monetary policy.

☐ State the target (or policy) dilemma confronted by the Fed; and explain why it faces this dilemma.

☐ Give three examples of how the Federal Reserve pursued a flexible approach to the target dilemma in recent years.

☐ Describe the relationship between the prime interest rate, the Federal funds rate, and monetary policy.

☐ Describe how the effectiveness of an easy money policy or a tight money policy is influenced by net exports and how these policies affect international trade deficits.

☐ Summarize the Keynesian theory of employment and the policies that may be utilized to promote a full-employment noninflationary GDP.

■ **CHAPTER OUTLINE**

1. The objective of monetary policy is full employment without inflation. The Federal Reserve Banks can accomplish this objective by exercising control over the amount of excess reserves held by commercial banks and thereby influencing the size of the money supply and the level of aggregate expenditures.

2. By examining the consolidated balance sheet and the principal assets and liabilities of the Federal Reserve Banks, an understanding of the ways in which the Federal Reserve can control and influence the reserves of commercial banks and the money supply can be obtained.

    a. The principal assets of the Federal Reserve Banks (in order of size) are U.S. government securities and loans to commercial banks.

    b. Their principal liabilities are Federal Reserve Notes, the reserve deposits of commercial banks and U.S. Treasury deposits.

3. The Federal Reserve Banks employ three principal tools (techniques or instruments) to control the reserves of banks and the size of the money supply.

    a. The Federal Reserve can buy and sell government securities in the open market.

    (1) Buying securities in the open market from either banks or the public increases the reserves of banks.

    (2) Selling securities in the open market to either banks or the public decreases the reserves of banks.

    b. It can raise or lower the reserve ratio.

    (1) Raising the reserve ratio decreases the excess reserves of banks and the size of the monetary (demand-deposit) multiplier.

    (2) Lowering the reserve ratio increases the excess reserves of banks and the size of the monetary multiplier.

    c. And it can also lower the discount rate to encourage banks to borrow reserves from the Fed and raise it to discourage them from borrowing reserves from the Fed.

    d. An easy money policy can be implemented by actions of the Federal Reserve to buy government bonds in the open market, decrease the discount rate, or decrease the reserve ratio.

    e. A tight money policy can be implemented by actions of the Federal Reserve to sell government bonds in the open market, increase the discount rate, or increase the reserve ratio.

4. To state the effects of monetary policy on the equilibrium GDP from the mainstream or Keynesian view:

    a. In the money market the demand-for- and the supply-of-money curves determine the real interest rate; the investment-demand curve and this rate of interest determine planned investment; and planned investment along with the saving curve determine the equilibrium GDP.

    b. If unemployment and deflation is the problem, the Federal Reserve takes policy actions to increase the money supply, causing the interest rate to fall and investment spending to increase, thereby increasing the real GDP by a multiple of the increase in investment.

    c. But if inflation is the problem, the Federal Reserve uses its tools to decrease the money supply, causing the interest rate to rise and investment spending to decrease, and thereby reducing inflation.

d. There are refinements and feedback effects to monetary policy that must be considered:

(1) The steeper the demand-for-money curve and the flatter the investment-demand curve the greater will be the effect on the equilibrium GDP of a change in the money supply.

(2) Changes in the equilibrium GDP that result from a change in the money supply will alter the demand for money and dampen the effect of the change in the money supply on the GDP.

e. Stated in terms of the aggregate-demand–aggregate-supply model:

(1) An increase (decrease) in the money supply decreases (increases) interest rates, increases (decreases) investment spending, and ultimately increases (decreases) aggregate demand.

(2) The flatter (steeper) the aggregate-supply curve is, the greater (smaller) is the effect of a change in the money supply on real domestic output and employment and the smaller (greater) is the effect on the price level.

5. Whether monetary policy is effective in promoting full employment without inflation is a debatable question because monetary policy has both strengths and shortcomings in fighting recession and inflation.

a. Its strengths are that it can be more quickly changed than fiscal policy; it is more isolated from political pressure than fiscal policy; and (some economists believe) it is the key determinant of economic activity and, therefore, more effective than fiscal policy.

b. Its weaknesses are that it is more effective in fighting inflation than it is in curbing recession; it can be offset by changes in the velocity of money; and it may not have a significant impact on investment spending in the economy.

c. A most difficult problem for the Fed is its inability to control both the money supply and the level of interest rates at the same time.

(1) If the Fed's policy target is the stabilization of interest rates, an increase in the nominal GDP (and the resulting increase in the demand for money) will require it to increase the money supply; and if its policy target is the stabilization of the money supply, an increase in the nominal GDP (and the demand for money) will force interest rates upward.

(2) The Federal Reserve has used a flexible approach to the interest rate or money supply dilemma as is evident in actions taken to deal with the stock market crash of 1987, changes in the measurement of the money supply in the 1980s, and the lowering of interest rates to combat recession in 1991.

(3) The prime interest rate is the rate that banks charge their most credit-worthy customers; it tends to rise and fall with the Federal funds rate, or the rate that banks charge other banks for overnight loans of excess re-

serves held at the Federal Reserve banks. When the Fed buys bonds, it becomes cheaper for banks to borrow excess reserves overnight because the Federal funds rate falls; conversely, when the Fed sells bonds, the Federal funds rate rises and it becomes more expensive for banks to borrow funds.

6. There are international linkages to monetary policy:

a. An easy money policy to bring the economy out of recession or slow growth will tend to lower domestic interest rates and cause the dollar to depreciate. In this situation, net exports will increase, thus increasing aggregate demand and reinforcing the effect of the easy money policy.

b. A tight money policy to reduce inflation will tend to raise domestic interest rates and cause the dollar to appreciate. These events will decrease net exports and reduce aggregate demand, thereby strengthening the tight money policy.

c. An easy policy is compatible with the goal of correcing a balance of trade deficit, but a tight money policy conflicts with this economic goal.

7. The income, employment, output, and prices of an economy in traditional or Keynesian theory are positively related to the level of aggregate expenditures, which has four principal components.

a. These four components are consumption spending which depends upon the stable consumption schedule and the income of the economy; investment spending which is more unstable; government spending which depends partly on the level of spending needed to achieve full employment and price stability; and net exports which are influenced by exchange rates and the levels of domestic and foreign GDP.

b. To achieve economic stability, government employs both fiscal and monetary policy; but to be effective these two types of policy must be coordinated.

■ **IMPORTANT TERMS**

Monetary policy	Feedback effects
Open-market operations	Velocity of money
Discount rate	Target dilemma
Easy money policy	Prime interest rate
Tight money policy	Net export effect
Money market	

■ **FILL-IN QUESTIONS**

1. The objective of monetary policy in the United States is a _____ level of total output. Responsibility for these monetary policies rests with the _____ of the Federal Reserve System;

and they are put into effect by the twelve Federal Reserve

_____

2. The two important assets of the Federal Reserve Banks are _____ and _____. Their three major liabilities are _____, _____, and _____

3. The three tools (or instruments) employed by the monetary authority to control the money supply are _____, changing _____, and changing _____

4. The Federal Reserve Banks buy and sell government securities in the open market in order to change the amount of new _____ commercial banks are able to create and the rate of _____ in the economy.

5. If the Federal Reserve Banks were to sell $10 million in government bonds to the **public** and the reserve ratio were 25%, the supply of money would immediately be reduced by $_____, the reserves of commercial banks would be reduced by $_____, and the excess reserves of the banks would be reduced by $_____. But if these bonds were sold to the commercial banks, the supply of money would immediately be reduced by $_____, the reserves of the banks would be reduced by $_____, and the excess reserves of the banks would be reduced by $_____

6. Changes in the reserve ratio affect the ability of commercial banks to create money in two ways: they affect the amount of _____ held by the commercial banks and the size of the monetary _____

7. If the Federal Reserve Banks were to lower the discount rate commercial banks would tend to borrow (more, less) _____ from them; and this would (increase, decrease) _____ their excess reserves.

8. To increase the supply of money, the Federal Reserve Banks should (raise, lower) _____ the reserve ratio, (buy, sell) _____ securities in the open market, and/or (increase, decrease) _____ the discount rate.

9. An easy money policy would be characterized by actions of the Federal Reserve to (increase, decrease) _____ the discount rate, _____ reserve ratios, and (buy, sell) _____ government bonds; whereas a tight money policy would include actions taken to (increase, decrease) _____ the discount rate, to _____ reserve ratios, and (buy, sell) _____ government bonds.

10. The most effective and often-used monetary control is _____. A change in the _____ may have an important "announcement effect" about the direction of monetary policy, but it is relatively weak because it does not affect much borrowing of bank reserve; conversely, the _____ are rarely changed because the impact on bank reserves is so powerful, blunt, and immediate.

11. Graphically, in an economy in which government neither purchases goods and services nor collects net taxes and which neither exports nor imports goods and services:
   a. the equilibrium real interest rate is determined by the demand-for- and the supply-of-_____ curves;
   b. this equilibrium interest rate and the _____ curve determine the level of planned investment;
   c. and the level of planned investment, using the leakages-injections approach, and the _____ _____ curve determine the equilibrium GDP;
   d. but when the supply-of-money curve increases (shifts to the right), the real interest rate will (increase, decrease) _____, planned investment will _____, and the equilibrium GDP will _____

12. To eliminate inflationary pressures in the economy the traditional view holds that the monetary authority should seek to (increase, decrease) _____ the reserves of commercial banks; this would tend to _____ the money supply and to _____ the rate of interest; and this in turn would cause investment spending, aggregate expenditures, and GDP to _____. This action by monetary authorities would be considered a(n) _____ policy.

13. If there was a serious problem with unemployment in the economy, the traditional view would be that the

Federal Reserve should pursue a(n) _____ policy, in which case the Federal Reserve would (buy, sell) _____ government bonds as a way of (increasing, decreasing) _____ the money supply, and thereby _____ interest rates; these events would have the effect of _____ investment spending and thus _____ real GDP.

14. The effect of a $1 billion increase or decrease in the money supply upon the equilibrium GDP is greater the (flatter, steeper) _____ the demand-for-money curve and the _____ the investment-demand curve.

15. An increase in the money supply will shift the aggregate (supply, demand) _____ curve to the (right, left) _____

a. In the Keynesian (or depression) range along the aggregate-supply curve this increase in the money supply will have a (small, large) _____ effect on real domestic output and a _____ effect on the price level.

b. In the classical range along the aggregate-supply curve this increase in the money supply will have a _____ effect on real domestic output and a _____ effect on the price level.

c. In the intermediate range along the aggregate-supply curve the effect of an increase in the money supply on the real domestic output is greater the (steeper, flatter) _____ the aggregate-supply curve, and the effect on the price level is greater the _____ the aggregate-supply curve.

16. The:

a. strengths of monetary policy are that it is more _____, more isolated from _____, and (in the view of the monetarists) more _____ than fiscal policy;

b. weaknesses of monetary policy are that it is more effective in curbing (recession, inflation) _____ than _____, can be ineffective if the _____ of money changes in the (same, opposite) _____ direction as the money supply, and will not be effective if changes in the interest rate have little or no effect on _____ spending in the economy.

17. The target dilemma faced by the Fed is that it is (able, unable) _____ to control both the money supply and the level of interest rates simultaneously.

a. If it is to stabilize the interest rate it must (increase, decrease) _____ the money supply when the nominal GDP rises.

b. And if it stabilizes the money supply it must allow the interest rate to _____ when the nominal GDP rises.

18. An easy money policy (increases, decreases) _____ net exports; a tight money policy _____ net exports. The net export effect from an easy money policy thus (strengthens, weakens) _____ domestic monetary policy and the net export effect from a tight money policy _____ it. Also, an easy money policy is (compatible, incompatible) _____ with the economic goal of reducing a balance of trade deficit, but a tight money policy is _____ with this economic goal.

19. In the Keynesian theory the levels of output, employment, income, and prices depend on the level of aggregate _____ which in turn depend upon the amounts of _____, _____, _____, and _____ spending in the economy.

20. Government seeks to bring about a full-employment noninflationary GDP by employing both _____ and _____ policies.

■ **PROBLEMS AND PROJECTS**

1. Assume that the consolidated balance sheet below is for all commercial banks. Assume also that the required reserve ratio is 25% and that cash is **not** a part of the commercial banks' legal reserve.

Assets		Liabilities	
Cash	$ 50	Demand deposits	$400
Reserves	100	Loans from Federal	
Loans	150	Reserve	25
Securities	200	Net worth	75
	$500		$500

a. To **increase** the supply of money by $100, the Federal Reserve Banks could **either:**

(1) (increase, decrease) _____ the re-

serve ratio to _____%

(2) *or* (buy, sell) _____ securities worth

$_____ in the open market.

b. To *reduce* the supply of money by $50, the Federal Reserve Banks could *either:*

(1) _____ the reserve ratio to _____%

(2) *or* _____ securities worth

$_____ in the open market.

2. Shown below are the consolidated balance sheets of the Federal Reserve and of the commercial banks. Assume that the reserve ratio for commercial banks is 25%, that cash is *not* a part of a bank's legal reserve, and that the figures in column 1 show the balance sheets of the Federal Reserve and the commercial banks *prior to each of the following five transactions.* Place the new balance-sheet figures in the appropriate columns and complete A, B, C, D, and E in these columns. *Do not* use the figures you place in columns (2) through (5) when you work the next part of the problem; start all parts of the problem with the printed figures in column (1).

	(1)	(2)	(3)	(4)	(5)	(6)
		Federal Reserve Banks				
Assets:						
Gold certificates	$ 25	$___	$___	$___	$___	$___
Securities	30	___	___	___	___	___
Loans to commercial banks	10	___	___	___	___	___
Liabilities						
Reserves of commercial banks	50	___	___	___	___	___
Treasury deposits	5	___	___	___	___	___
Federal Reserve Notes	10	___	___	___	___	___
		Commercial Banks				
Assets:						
Reserves	$ 50	$___	$___	$___	$___	$___
Securities	70	___	___	___	___	___
Loans	90	___	___	___	___	___
Liabilities						
Demand deposits	200	___	___	___	___	___
Loans from Federal Reserve	10	___	___	___	___	___
A. Required reserves		___	___	___	___	___
B. Excess reserves		___	___	___	___	___
C. How much has the money supply changed?		___	___	___	___	___
D. How much *more* can the money supply change?		___	___	___	___	___
E. What is the total of C and D?		___	___	___	___	___

a. The Federal Reserve Banks sell $3 in securities to the public, which pays by check (column 2).
b. The Federal Reserve Banks buy $4 in securities from the commercial banks (column 3).
c. The Federal Reserve Banks lower the required reserve ratio for commercial banks to 20% (column 4).
d. The U.S. Treasury buys $5 worth of goods from American manufacturers and pays the manufacturers by checks drawn on its accounts at the Federal Reserve Banks (column 5).

e. Because the Federal Reserve Banks have raised the discount rate, commercial banks repay $6 which they owe to the Federal Reserve (column 6).

3. On the graph at the top of the left column on the next page, is the demand-for-money curve which shows the amounts of money consumers and firms wish to hold at various rates of interest (when the nominal GDP in the economy is given).

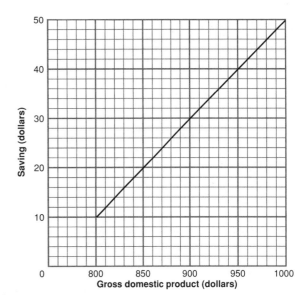

a. Suppose the supply of money is equal to 300.
(1) Draw on this graph the supply-of-money curve.
(2) The equilibrium rate of interest in the economy is

_____%.

b. On the graph below is an investment-demand curve which shows the amounts of planned investment at various rates of interest. Given your answer to (2) above, how much will investors plan to spend for capital

goods? $_____

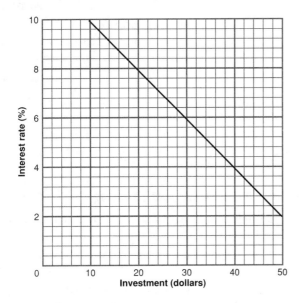

c. On the following graph is the saving curve in an economy in which the only leakage from the GDP is saving. (There are no taxes collected and no imports of goods and services.)

(1) On this graph plot the investment curve when planned investment is the amount given by you in your answer to (b) above.
(2) If the only injection into this economy is investment spending (that is, if there is no government spending for and no exports of goods and services), the equilib-

rium GDP wil be $_____
d. Assume the money supply increases to $400. On the first graph plot the new supply-of-money curve. The new:

(1) Equilibrium interest rate is _____%;

(2) Level of planned investment is $_____;

(3) Equilibrium GDP is $_____
e. Suppose the full-employment noninflationary GDP in this economy is $875.
(1) At this GDP saving would be $_____
(2) For this GDP to be the equilibrium GDP, investment

would have to be equal to $_____
(3) For investment to be at this level the rate of interest

would have to be _____%.
(4) And for the interest rate to be at this level the supply

of money would have to be equal to $_____
f. In this economy:
(1) the marginal propensity to save is equal to _____ and the multiplier has, therefore, a value equal to

_____;

(2) a one percentage point decrease in the interest

rate will (increase, decrease) _____

planned investment by $_____ and will,

therefore, (increase, decrease) _____

the equilibrium GDP by $_____;
(3) but for the interest rate to decrease by one percentage point the money supply must (increase, decrease) _____ by $_____

4. Columns (1) and (2) of the table below are the aggregate-supply schedule. (The price level is a price index and real domestic output is measured in billions of dollars.)

(1) Price level	(2) Real output	(3) AD$_1$	(4) AD$_2$	(5) AD$_3$	(6) AD$_4$	(7) AD$_5$	(8) AD$_6$
.30	$1500	$1600	$1700	$2070	$2400	$2920	$3020
.30	1600	1600	1700	2070	2400	2920	3020
.30	1700	1600	1700	2070	2400	2920	3020
.40	1790	1500	1600	1970	2300	2820	2920
.50	1870	1400	1500	1870	2200	2720	2820
.60	1940	1300	1400	1770	2100	2620	2720
.70	2000	1200	1300	1670	2000	2520	2620
.80	2050	1100	1200	1570	1900	2420	2520
.90	2090	1000	1100	1470	1800	2320	2420
1.00	2120	900	1000	1370	1700	2220	2320
1.10	2120	800	900	1270	1600	2120	2220
1.20	2120	700	800	1170	1500	2020	2120

a. The Keynesian range on this aggregate-supply schedule is from a real domestic output of zero to $_____ billion.
b. The classical range on this aggregate-supply curve is at the real domestic output of $_____ billion.
c. If the aggregate-demand schedule were that shown in columns (1) and (3) the equilibrium real domestic output would be $_____ billion and the price level would be _____
d. If the aggregate-demand schedule increased from that shown in columns (1) and (3) to the one shown in columns (1) and (4) the equilibrium real domestic output would _____ and the price level would _____
e. If the aggregate-demand schedule increased from that shown in columns (1) and (5) to the one shown in columns (1) and (6) the equilibrium real domestic output would _____ and the price level would _____
f. And if the aggregate-demand schedule increased from that shown in columns (1) and (7) to the one shown in columns (1) and (8) the equilibrium real domestic output would _____ and the price level would _____

5. Columns (1) and (2) in the following table show the money supply and column (3) shows the demand for money. (Dollar figures are in billions and the interest rate is a percentage.)

(1) Supply of money	(2) Interest rate	(3) Demand for money	(4) Demand for money
$400	.08	$100	$200
400	.07	200	300
400	.06	300	400
400	.05	400	500
400	.04	500	600
400	.03	600	700
400	.02	700	800

a. The equilibrium interest rate is _____%.
b. Suppose the Fed wishes to stabilize the interest rate at this level; but the nominal GDP produced by the economy increases, and as a result the demand for money in the economy increases from that shown in column (3) to that shown in column (4). The Fed will have to (increase, decrease) _____ the supply of money to $_____ billion.
c. But if the Fed stabilizes the supply of money at $400 billion and the nominal GDP increases to increase the demand for money from that shown in column (3) to that shown in column (4) the interest rate will (rise, fall) _____ to _____%.
d. If the Fed stabilizes the interest rate it must (increase, decrease) _____ the supply of money when the nominal GDP rises and _____ it when the nominal GDP falls; and if it holds the supply of money constant the interest rate will (rise, fall) _____ when the nominal GDP increases and _____ when the nominal GDP decreases.

■ **SELF-TEST**

Circle the T if the statement is true; the F if it is false.

1. The fundamental goal of monetary policy is to stabilize interest rates. T **F**

2. The securities owned by the Federal Reserve Banks are almost entirely U.S. government bonds. **T** F

3. If the Federal Reserve Banks buy $15 in government securities from the public in the open market, the effect will be to increase the excess reserves of commercial banks by $15. **T** F

4. When the Federal Reserve sells bonds in the open market, the price of these bonds falls. **T** F

5. A change in the <u>reserve ratio</u> will affect the multiple by which the banking system can create money, but it will not affect the actual or excess reserves of member banks.   T **F**

6. If the reserve ratio is lowered, some required reserves are turned into excess reserves.   **T** F

7. When commercial banks borrow from the Federal Reserve Banks they increase their excess reserves and their money-creating potential.   **T** F

8. If the monetary authority wished to follow a tight money policy, it would sell government bonds in the open market.   **T** F

9. An increase in the required reserve ratio tends to reduce the profits of banks.   **T** F

10. The equilibrium rate of interest is found at the intersection of the demand-for-money and the supply-of-money curves.   **T** F

11. An increase in the equilibrium GDP will shift the demand-for-money curve to the left and increase the equilibrium interest rate.   T **F**

12. Consumer spending is more sensitive to changes in the rate of interest than is investment demand.   T **F**

13. Monetary policy is more effective in fighting depression than it is in curbing inflation.   T **F**

14. In an economy in which the GDP is either rising or falling the Fed is unable to control both the money supply and interest rates.   **T** F

15. When the economy is at or near full employment an increase in the money supply tends to be inflationary.   **T** F

16. It is generally agreed that fiscal policy is more effective than monetary policy in controlling the business cycle because fiscal policy is more flexible.   T **F**

17. The prime interest rate is the rate that banks charge other banks for overnight loans of excess reserves at Federal Reserve banks.   T **F**

18. An easy money policy decreases net exports.   T **F**

19. A tight money policy will tend to cause the dollar to appreciate.   **T** T

20. A tight money policy is compatible with the goal of correcting a trade deficit.   T **F**

Circle the letter that corresponds to the best answer.

1. The agency directly responsible for monetary policy in the United States is:
(a) the twelve Federal Reserve Banks
(b) the Board of Governors of the Federal Reserve System

(c) the Congress of the United States
(d) the U.S. Treasury

2. The largest single asset in the Federal Reserve Banks' consolidated balance sheet is:
(a) securities
(b) the reserves of commercial banks
(c) Federal Reserve Notes
(d) loans to commercial banks

3. The largest single liability of the Federal Reserve Banks is:
(a) securities
(b) the reserves of commercial banks
(c) Federal Reserve Notes
(d) loans to commercial banks

4. Assuming that the Federal Reserve Banks sell $20 million in government securities to commercial banks and the reserve ratio is 20%, then the effect will be:
(a) to reduce the actual supply of money by $20 million
(b) to reduce the actual supply of money by $4 million
(c) to reduce the potential money supply by $20 million
(d) to reduce the potential money supply by $100 million

5. Which of the following acts would **not** have the same general effect upon the economy as the other three?
(a) the Federal Reserve Banks sell bonds in the open market
(b) the Federal Reserve increases the discount rate
(c) the Federal Reserve eases credit for the purchase of consumer durables
(d) the Federal Reserve raises the reserve ratio

6. Which of the following is the most important control used by the Federal Reserve Banks to regulate the money supply?
(a) changing the reserve ratio
(b) open-market operations
(c) changing the discount rate
(d) changing the Federal funds rate

7. Assume that there is a 20% reserve ratio and that the Federal Reserve buys $100 million worth of government securities. If the securities are purchased from the public, then this action has the potential to increase bank lending by a maximum of:
(a) $500 million, but only by $400 million if the securities are purchased directly from commercial banks
(b) $400 million, but by $500 million if the securities are purchased directly from commercial banks
(c) $500 million, and also by $500 million if the securities are purchased directly from commercial banks
(d) $400 million, and also by $400 million if the securities are purchased directly from commercial banks

8. A newspaper headline reads: "Fed Cuts Discount Rate for Third Time This Year." This headline indicates that the Federal Reserve is most likely trying to:

(a) reduce inflationary pressures in the economy
(b) increase the Federal funds rate
(c) reduce the cost of credit and stimulate the econ-omy
(d) increase the value of the dollar

9. A change in the money supply has the *least* effect on the equilibrium GDP when:
(a) both the demand-for-money and the investment-demand curves are steep
(b) both the demand-for-money and the investment-demand curves are flat
(c) the demand-for-money curve is flat and the invest-ment-demand curve is steep
(d) the demand-for-money curve is steep and the in-vestment-demand curve is flat

10. An increase in the money supply will have little or no effect on the real domestic output and employment in:
(a) the horizontal range on the aggregate-supply curve
(b) the intermediate range along the aggregate-supply curve
(c) the classical range on the aggregate-supply curve
(d) any of the three ranges on the aggregate-supply curve

11. In the traditional or Keynesian chain of cause and ef-fect between changes in the excess reserves of commer-cial banks and the resulting changes in output and em-ployment in the economy:
(a) an increase in excess reserves will decrease the money supply
(b) a decrease in the money supply will increase the rate of interest
(c) an increase in the rate of interest will increase ag-gregate expenditures
(d) an increase in aggregate expenditures will de-crease output and employment

12. Which of the following is more likely to be affected by changes in the rate of interest?
(a) consumer spending
(b) investment spending
(c) the spending of the Federal government
(d) the exports of the economy

13. An increase in the money supply will have little or no effect on the price level in:
(a) the Keynesian range
(b) the intermediate range
(c) the classical range
(d) any of the three ranges

Use the graph below to answer the next three questions (14, 15, and 16).

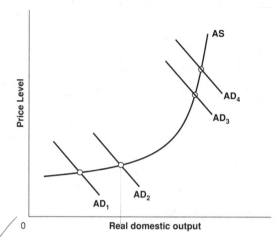

14. A shift from AD$_1$ to AD$_2$ would be most consistent with:
(a) an increase in the prime interest rate
(b) an increase in the discount rate by the Federal Re-serve
(c) the buying of securities by the Federal Reserve
(d) the selling of securities by the Federal Reserve

15. Which shift would be most consistent with the poten-tial effects of tight money policy in an inflationary period in an economy where prices are flexible?
(a) AD$_1$ to AD$_2$
(b) AD$_3$ to AD$_4$
(c) AD$_4$ to AD$_3$
(d) AD$_2$ to AD$_1$

16. If the Federal Reserve adopted an easy money policy in a period of high unemployment, the situation can best be characterized by a shift from:
(a) AD$_1$ to AD$_2$
(b) AD$_3$ to AD$_4$
(c) AD$_4$ to AD$_3$
(d) AD$_2$ to AD$_1$

17. An increase in the money supply is *least* effective in stimulating aggregate expenditures when the velocity of money:
(a) falls as the money supply increases
(b) remains constant
(c) rises as the money supply increases
(d) is equal to 5

18. The Fed:
(a) can stabilize both the interest rate and the money supply
(b) cannot stabilize the interest rate
(c) cannot stabilize the money supply
(d) cannot stabilize both the interest rate and the money supply

expansionary ↑ interest Rate : demand ↑

19. The prime rate of interest is the rate that:
(a) banks charge for overnight use of excess reserves held at the Federal Reserve banks
(b) banks charge for loans to the most credit-worthy customers
(c) the Federal Reserve charges for short-term loans to commercial banks
(d) government bonds are sold at in the open-market operations of the Federal Reserve

20. When the Federal Reserve uses open-market operations to reduce the federal funds rate it is pursuing an:
(a) easy money policy and targeting interest rates
(b) easy money policy and targeting the money supply
(c) tight money policy and targeting interest rates
(d) tight money policy and targeting the money supply

21. Which of the following are coordinated policies?
(a) an increase in government expenditures and in the money supply
(b) a decrease in personal tax rates and in the money supply
(c) an increase in transfer payments and a decrease in the money supply
(d) an increase in corporate tax rates and in the money supply

22. When the Federal Reserve Banks decide to buy government bonds, the demand for government bonds will:
(a) decrease, bond prices will decrease, and the interest rate will decrease
(b) increase, bond prices will increase, and the interest rate will decrease
(c) increase, bond prices will increase, and the interest rate will increase
(d) decrease, bond prices will increase, and the interest rate will decrease

23. A tight money policy in the United States is most likely to:
(a) increase domestic interest rates and cause the value of the dollar to depreciate
(b) decrease domestic interest rates and cause the value of the dollar to appreciate
(c) increase domestic interest rates and cause the value of the dollar to appreciate
(d) decrease domestic interest rates and cause the value of the dollar to depreciate

24. Which policy combination would tend to reduce net exports? *↑ interest rate*
(a) tight money policy and expansionary fiscal policy
(b) easy money policy and expansionary fiscal policy
(c) tight money policy and contractionary fiscal policy
(d) easy money policy and contractionary fiscal policy

25. A tight money policy that is used to reduce inflation in the domestic economy:
(a) is best conducted by reducing the required reserve ratios at commercial banks

(b) increases net exports and the effectiveness of the policy
(c) conflicts with the economic goal of correcting a trade deficit
(d) causes the dollar to depreciate

■ DISCUSSION QUESTIONS

1. What is the basic goal of monetary policy? What actions are taken to achieve this goal during recession or during a period of high inflation?

2. What are the important assets and liabilities of the Federal Reserve Banks?

3. Explain how the monetary-policy tools of the Federal Reserve Banks would be used to contract the supply of money. How would they be used to expand the supply of money?

4. What is the difference between the effects of the Federal Reserve's buying (selling) government securities in the open market from (to) commercial banks and from (to) the public?

5. Which of the monetary-policy tools available to the Federal Reserve is most effective? Why is it more effective than other tools?

6. Using mainstream or Keynesian theory and three graphs, explain what determines (a) the equilibrium interest rate; (b) planned investment; and (c) the equilibrium GDP. Now employ these three graphs to show the effects of a decrease in the money supply upon the equilibrium GDP.

7. Utilizing your answers to the question above, (a) what determines how large the effect of the decrease in the money supply on the equilibrium GDP will be; and (b) how would the change in the equilibrium GDP affect the demand-for-money curve, the interest rate, planned investment, and the GDP itself?

8. Explain from a traditional or Keynesian viewpoint how the Board of Governors and the Federal Reserve Banks can influence income, output, employment, and the price level. In your explanation, employ the following concepts: reserves, excess reserves, the supply of money, the availability of bank credit, and the rate of interest.

9. Why are changes in the rate of interest more likely to affect investment spending than consumption and saving?

10. How does a change in the money supply affect the aggregate-demand curve? How will a change in the money supply and the resulting shift in the aggregate-demand curve affect the real domestic output and the price level in (a) the Keynesian range, (b) the classical range, and (c) the intermediate range along the aggregate-supply curve?

11. What are the strengths and shortcomings of monetary policy?

12. Why is monetary policy more effective in controlling inflation than in reducing unemployment?

13. What is the target or policy dilemma of the Federal Reserve? What approach has the Fed taken in recent years to resolve this dilemma? Cite three examples.

14. What is the prime interest rate and how is it related to the Federal funds rate? What happens to the Federal funds rate when the Federal Reserve expands or contracts the money supply through open-market operations?

15. Suppose the nominal GDP in the American economy is increasing or decreasing. Why is the Federal Reserve unable to keep both interest rates and the size of the money supply from changing?

16. Explain how the net export effect influences the effectiveness of a tight or an easy money policy.

17. What type of monetary policy would you recommend to correct a balance of trade deficit? Why?

18. Explain as briefly as possible what mainstream or Keynesian economists believe determines the level of national output in the American economy.

19. Distinguish between fiscal and monetary policy and explain how we may use each of them to achieve reasonably full employment and relatively stable prices.

■ **ANSWERS**

Chapter 15 the Federal Reserve Banks and Monetary Policy

FILL-IN QUESTIONS

1. full-employment noninflationary, Board of Governors, Banks

2. securities, loans to commercial banks (either order), reserves of commercial banks, Treasury deposits, Federal Reserve Notes (any order)

3. open-market operations, reserve ratio, the discount rate (any order)

4. money, interest

5. 10 million, 10 million, 7.5 million, 0, 10 million, 10 million

6. excess reserves, multiplier

7. more, increase

8. lower, buy, decrease

9. decrease, decrease, buy, increase, increase, sell

10. open-market operation, discount rate, reserve ratios

11. *a.* money; *b.* investment-demand; *c.* saving; *d.* decrease, increase, increase

12. decrease, decrease, increase, decrease, tight money

13. easy money, buy, increasing, decreasing, increasing, increasing

14. steeper, flatter

15. demand, right; *a.* large, small; *b.* small, large; *c.* flatter, steeper

16. *a.* flexible, political pressure, effective; *b.* inflation, recession, velocity, opposite, investment

17. unable; *a.* increase; *b.* increase

18. increases, decreases, strengthens, weakens, compatible, incompatible

19. expenditures, consumption, investment, government, net export

20. fiscal, monetary (either order)

PROBLEMS AND PROJECTS

1. *a.* (1) decrease, 20, (2) buy, 25; *b.* (1) increase, $28^4/_7$, (2) sell, $12^1/_2$

2.

	(2)	(3)	(4)	(5)	(6)
		Federal Reserve Banks			
Assets:					
Gold certificates	$ 25	$ 25	$ 25	$ 25	$ 25
Securities	27	34	30	30	30
Loans to commercial banks	10	10	10	10	4
Liabilities:					
Reserves of commercial banks	47	54	50	55	44
Treasury deposits	5	5	5	0	5
Federal Reserve Notes	10	10	10	10	10
		Commercial Banks			
Assets:					
Reserves	$ 47	$ 54	$ 50	$ 55	$ 44
Securities	$ 70	66	70	70	70
Loans	90	90	90	90	90
Liabilities:					
Demand deposits	197	200	200	205	200
Loans from Federal Reserve	10	10	10	10	4
A. Required reserves	49.25	50	40	51.25	50
B. Excess reserves	−2.25	4	10	3.75	−6
C. How much has the money supply changed?	−3	0	0	+5	0
D. How much *more* can the money supply change?	−9	+16	+50	+15	−24
E. What is the total of C and D?	−12	+16	+50	+20	−24

3. *a.* (2) 8: *b.* 20; *c.* (2) 850; *d.* (1) 6, (2) 30, (3) 900; *e.* (1) 25, (2) 25, (3) 7, (4) 350; *f.* (1) 0.20, 5, (2) increase, 5, increase, 25, (3) increase, 50

4. *a.* 1700; *b.* 2120; *c.* 1600, .30; *d.* rise to $1700 billion, remain constant; *e.* rise from $1870 billion to $2000 billion, rise from .50 to .70; *f.* remain constant at $2120 billion, rise from 1.10 to 1.20

5. *a.* 5; *b.* increase, 500; *c.* rise, 6; *d.* increase, decrease, rise, fall

SELF-TEST

1. F, p. 282
2. T, p. 282
3. F, p. 285
4. T, pp. 286–287
5. F, p. 287
6. T, p. 287
7. T, p. 288
8. T, p. 289
9. T, p. 289
10. T, p. 290
11. F, p. 290
12. F, p. 290
13. F, p. 294
14. T, p. 295
15. T, p. 293
16. F, p. 294
17. F, p. 296
18. F, pp. 296–297
19. T, pp. 296–297
20. F, p. 297

1. *b,* p. 282
2. *a,* pp. 282–283
3. *c,* pp. 285–286
4. *d,* pp. 288–289
5. *c,* p. 289
6. *b,* pp. 283–285
7. *b,* p. 288
8. *c,* p. 292
9. *c,* pp. 293–294
10. *c,* p. 290
11. *b,* p. 290
12. *b,* pp. 293–294
13. *a,* p. 294
14. *c,* pp. 293–294
15. *c,* pp. 293–294
16. *a,* pp. 293–294
17. *a,* pp. 294–295
18. *d,* p. 295
19. *b,* p. 296
20. *a,* pp. 299–300
21. *a,* pp. 299–300
22. *b,* pp. 296–297
23. *c,* pp. 296–297
24. *a,* pp. 296–297
25. *c,* p. 297

DISCUSSION QUESTIONS

1. p. 282
2. pp. 282–283
3. pp. 283–286
4. pp. 283–286
5. pp. 289–290
6. pp. 290–293
7. pp. 290–291
8. pp. 290–292
9. pp. 290–291
10. pp. 293–294
11. pp. 294–295
12. p. 294
13. pp. 295–296
14. p. 296
15. p. 295
16. pp. 296–297
17. p. 297
18. pp. 297–298
19. pp. 299–300

CHAPTER 16

Alternative Views:
Monetarism and Rational Expectations

Now that you understand the basic ideas behind fiscal and monetary policy from the Keynesian perspective you are ready to learn about different theories of how the economy functions and you are prepared to explore controversial issues to expand your understanding of macroeconomics. Chapter 16, therefore, begins a first of a four-chapter section of the text that examines "Problems and Controversies in Macroeconomics." This chapter focuses on alternative views to the Keynesian position on monetary policy and stabilization policy for the economy. Chapter 17 explores reasons for the simultaneous occurrence of inflation and unemployment in the economy and discusses supply-side economics. In Chapter 18, the problems with the Federal budget deficit and the national debt are examined. Finally, Chapter 19 deals with the topic of economic growth and the long-term performance of the economy.

Economics has always been an arena in which conflicting theories and policies opposed each other. This field of intellectual combat, in major engagements, has seen Adam Smith do battle with the defenders of a regulated economy. It witnessed the opposition of Karl Marx to the orthodox economics of his day. In more recent times it saw Keynes in conflict with the classical economists. Around the major engagements have been countless minor skirmishes between opposing viewpoints. Out of these major and minor confrontations have emerged not winners and losers but the advancement of economic theory and the improvement of economic policy.

Monetarism and (more recently) rational-expectations theory are the latest challengers to enter this intellectual arena. The opponent is the reigning champion, Keynesianism, which bested classical economics in the same arena during the 1940s. Monetarists and rational-expectations theorists wish to free the economy from what they see as the destabilizing effects of discretionary fiscal and monetary policies. They view the Keynesians as the proponents of government intervention and see themselves as the defenders of *laissez-faire*.

Chapter 16 examines both monetarism and rational-expectations theory; but it directs most of its attention toward monetarism. But this chapter is more than a comparison of the attitudes of Keynesians and monetarists to-

ward the role of government in the economy. And it is more than a comparison of the basic equations of the two schools of thought. The basic equation of the Keynesians and the equation of exchange of the monetarists say pretty much the same thing. The equation of exchange ($MV = PQ$) is another way of saying that the economy will produce the GDP which is equal to the aggregate quantity of goods and services demanded.

The issue is whether the velocity of money—the V in the equation of exchange—is stable or unstable. If it is stable, as the monetarists contend, then the only kind of policy that can be used to control (to increase or decrease) nominal GDP is monetary policy; and fiscal policy cannot expand or contract nominal GDP. But if V is unstable, as the Keynesians argue, then fiscal policy is the only effective means and monetary policy is an ineffective means of controlling nominal GDP. The issue of whether V is stable or unstable becomes an issue of whether the size of the money supply matters very much or very little. Monetarists argue that the M in the equation of exchange is the only thing that matters and their Keynesian rivals contend that it doesn't matter very much.

The emphasis in Chapter 16 is on monetarism because earlier chapters have emphasized Keynesianism. You are not expected, however, to determine which of the two groups is correct. But you should see that monetarism is an alternative to Keynesianism; that the economic issue is the stability of V; that the political issue is whether monetary or fiscal policy is more effective; and that the policy issue is whether rules or discretion should be used to conduct monetary policy.

Rational-expectations theorists take a more extreme position in the debate over the relative effectiveness of monetary and fiscal policies. Their position is that the economy tends to produce its full-employment output and that neither of the two types of policy can expand real output and employment in either the short run or the long run: the only effect on the economy of an expansionary monetary or fiscal policy is inflation. They are modern-day (or the new) classical economists who argue that neither the size of the money supply nor the fiscal policies of government has any effect on real output and employment. While this extreme position will be strange to those who have come to believe government can bring about full employment without inflation in the economy, advocates of the rational-expectations theory are careful to explain how they reach these conclusions; and you should be sure you understand the assumptions they make in order to reach their unusual conclusions before you dismiss their extreme position.

Economic theory has been changed by the debate among Keynesians, monetarists, and rational expectationists, as has been the case with similar debates over macroeconomics in the past. In particular, there is now recognition that "money matters" and that both the money supply and monetary policy have a significant effect on the economy. More attention is also being given to the coordination of fiscal and monetary policy, and to the influence of expectations on markets and the economy. These debates have caused economists to reconsider the basic aspects of macroeconomics and have resulted in the incorporation of new ideas into mainstream thinking about the macroeconomics.

■ **CHECKLIST**

When you have studied this chapter you should be able to:

☐ Compare the positions of Keynesian and monetarist economists on the competitiveness of a capitalistic economy and its inherent stability and on the role government should play in stabilizing it.
☐ Write the equation of exchange and define each of the four terms in the equation.
☐ Show how the basic Keynesian equation is "translated" into the equation of exchange.
☐ Compare the monetarist and Keynesian views on the functions of money; on why households and firms demand money; and on what determines the quantity of money demanded.
☐ Explain why the monetarists believe nominal GDP is directly and predictably linked to M.
☐ Write a brief scenario which explains what monetarists believe will happen to change the nominal GDP and to V when M is increased.
☐ Construct a scenario which explains why Keynesians believe will happen to the interest rate and to V and nominal GDP if M is increased.
☐ Discuss empirical evidence about velocity from a monetarist or Keynesian perspective.
☐ Explain why Keynesians favor and monetarists reject the use of fiscal policy to stabilize the economy.
☐ State the monetary rule of the monetarists, and the two reasons why they propose a rule instead of discretionary monetary policy.
☐ Use the aggregate demand-aggregate supply models

of the Keynesians and the monetarists to compare and contrast the effects of an expansionary monetary or fiscal policy on the real domestic output and the price level.
☐ Clarify the debate over the monetarist call for a monetary rule using the aggregate demand-aggregate supply model.
☐ State the two basic assumptions of the rational-expectations theory (RET).
☐ Explain how RET advocates believe firms, workers, and consumers react to the announcement of an expansionary monetary or fiscal policy to frustrate the achievement of the goal of the policy.
☐ Use aggregate demand and aggregate supply to show the effects of an expansionary monetary or fiscal policy on real output and the price level in the RET.
☐ Write a brief scenario to explain why rational-expectations theorists believe discretionary monetary and fiscal policies are ineffective.
☐ State what type of government policy is advocated by RET theorists.
☐ Present three criticisms of the RET.
☐ Cite three examples of how ideas from monetarism and rational expectations have been absorbed into mainstream thinking about macroeconomics.

■ **CHAPTER OUTLINE**

1. Monetarism and rational-expectations theory (RET) are alternatives to the Keynesian macroeconomic theory and policy recommendations; and while this chapter examines both of these alternatives, it stresses monetarism.

2. Keynesians and monetarists differ over the inherent stability of capitalistic economies and ideologically over the role government should play in the economy.

    a. Keynesians believe that, because many markets in a capitalistic economy are noncompetitive, it is unstable, that government should intervene to stabilize the economy, and that fiscal policy is a more effective stabilizer than monetary policy.

    b. Monetarists believe that because markets in a capitalistic economy are competitive the economy would be stable if it were not for government interference, that government intervention destabilizes the economy, and that government should not use either discretionary fiscal or monetary policy to try to stabilize it.

3. In the Keynesian model the equilibrium output of the economy is the output at which

$$C_a + I_g + X_n + G = \text{GDP}$$

    a. In the monetarist model the basic equation is the equation of exchange.

$$MV = PQ$$

but because MV (total spending) $= C_a + I_g + X_n +$

G and *PQ* = **GDP** the equations are different ways of stating the same relationship.

b. While Keynesians assign a secondary role to money because they believe the links in the cause-effect chain are loose ones, monetarists, believing *V* in the equation of exchange is stable, find that while a change in *M* may affect *Q* in the short run it will in the long run affect only *P*. These competing views of the monetary transmission mechanism are illustrated for you in Figure 16-1 of the textbook.

4. Whether *V* in the equation of exchange is stable or unstable is a critical question because if it is stable *PQ* is closely linked to *M*; and if it is unstable the link between *PQ* and *M* is loose and uncertain.

   a. Reasoning that people have a stable desire to hold money relative to holding other assets or to making purchases, monetarists conclude that the quantity of money demanded is a stable percentage of GDP (that GDP/*M* is constant); that an increase (a decrease) in *M* will leave firms and households with more (less) money than they wish to have; that they will, therefore, increase (decrease) spending for consumer and capital goods; and that this will cause the GDP and the amount of money they wish to hold for transactions purposes to rise (fall) until their demand for money is equal to *M* and GDP/*M* = *V*.

   b. But Keynesians argue that consumers and business firms also have an asset demand for money as well as a transactions demand for money; that this asset demand for money is inversely related to the rate of interest; and that an increase (a decrease) in *M* will decrease (increase) the interest rate, increase (decrease) the amount of money people wish to hold as an asset, lower (raise) *V*, and leave the effect on GDP uncertain.

   c. Empirical evidence confirms neither the contention of the monetarists that *V* is stable nor the contention of the Keynesians that it is variable (or unstable).

5. Because their theories (their views on the stability of *V*) differ, Keynesians and monetarists disagree over the effectiveness of fiscal and monetary policies in stabilizing the economy.

   a. Keynesians favor the use of fiscal policy to stabilize the economy because they believe it is a more powerful stabilizer; but the monetarists argue that the use of fiscal policy is both harmful and ineffective because of the crowding-out effect it has on investment expenditures in the economy.

   b. Arguing that discretionary changes in *M* have produced monetary mismanagement and macroeconomic instability, the monetarists have proposed the monetary rule that *M* be increased at the same annual rate as the potential annual rate of increase in the real GDP.

   c. In the aggregate demand-aggregate supply model the monetarists see an aggregate-supply curve that is very steep (or vertical) and in which an increase in aggregate demand has little (or no) effect on real domestic output and increases the price level by a relatively large amount; but the Keynesians see an aggregate-supply curve that is nearly flat (or horizontal) and in which an increase in aggregate demand has little (or no) effect on the price level and increases the real domestic output by a relatively large amount. At the full employment level of output, where the aggregate-supply curve is vertical, both Keynesians and monetarists would agree that expansionary policies would lead to demand-pull inflation.

   d. The debate over the call for a monetary rule by the monetarist is also illustrated in the aggregate demand-aggregate supply model.

   (1) From the monetarist perspective, a monetary rule would shift aggregate demand rightward to match a shift in the aggregate-supply curve because of economic growth, thus keeping the price level stable.

   (2) From the Keynesian view, the loose link between changes in money and aggregate demand mean that a monetary rule might produce too great a shift in aggregate demand (and demand-pull inflation) or too small a shift (and deflation) to match the shift in aggregate supply, and therefore such a rule would contribute to price instability.

6. The RET, developed since the mid-1970s and called the new classical economics, is an alternative to Keynesian economics and to monetarism.

   a. Economists who advocate the RET make two basic assumptions:

   (1) business firms, consumers, and workers understand how the economy works so that they can anticipate the effect on the economy of an economic event or a change in economic policy, and use all available information to make decisions in a way to further their own self-interests; and

   (2) all markets in the economy are so competitive that equilibrium prices and quantities quickly adjust to these events and changes in public policy.

   b. From these assumptions the proponents of the RET conclude that the response of the public to the expected inflationary effect of an expansionary monetary (or fiscal) policy will cancel the intended effect on output and employment in the economy.

   c. In an aggregate demand-aggregate supply model of the RET the aggregate supply curve is vertical; and any monetary or fiscal policy that increases or decreases aggregate demand affects only the price level, and has no effect on real output or employment, real wages, or real interest rates in either the short or the long run.

   d. Rational-expectations theorists argue that discretionary monetary and fiscal policies are ineffective, and would (like the monetarist) replace discretionary monetary policies with rules; however, rational expectation-ists argue for monetary rules because the actions and knowledge of the public will counteract the intent of the policies, but monetarists argue for rules because monetary authorities do not have sufficient information to correct for time lags and other problems.

e. The appeal of the RET comes from the inability of Keynesian economics to explain and to develop poli-cies to correct simultaneous inflation and unemploy-ment, and from the long-sought connection between micro- and macroeconomics; but RET has been sub-jected to three basic criticisms.

(1) One criticism is that people are not so well informed on the workings of the economy and the effect of eco-nomic policy on it as the rational-expectations theorists assume.

(2) A second criticism is that many markets in the economy are not so competitive as assumed in the RET, and do not, therefore, adjust their prices as rap-idly as assumed.

(3) And the third criticism is that monetary and fiscal policies have worked in the past to expand real output and employment in the economy.

f. The controversies in macroeconomics in the past two decades have led to the incorporation of several ideas from monetarism and rational expectations into mainstream thinking about macroeconomics. Three ex-amples illustrate this point: first, changes in the money supply and monetary policy are given more importance than in the past; second, there is recognition of the need to coordinate fiscal and monetary policy and to prevent crowding-out of economic activity; and third, more attention is given to the effects of expectations on markets and the economy. As in the past, debates in macroeconomics have changed the views about ma-croeconomic theory and policy.

■ **IMPORTANT TERMS**

Keynesianism

Monetarism

Equation of exchange

Income (or circuit) velocity
of money

Crowding-out effect

Monetary rule

Rational-expectations
theory

■ **FILL-IN QUESTIONS**

1. Keynesians believe that capitalism is inherently (sta-ble, unstable) _____ because many of its markets are (competitive, noncompetitive) _____, advocate (government intervention,

laissez-faire) _____, and favor (monetary, fiscal) _____ over _____ policy.

2. Monetarists argue that capitalism is inherently _____ because most of its markets are _____, advocate _____ and favor the use of (discretionary, nondiscretionary) _____ (monetary, fiscal) _____ policy.

3. The basic equation of the monetarists is _____ = _____

   a. This equation is called the _____ _____

   b. Indicate below what each of the four letters in this equation represents.

   (1) **M**: _____

   (2) **V**: _____

   (3) **P**: _____

   (4) **Q**: _____

4. The basic equation of the Keynesians is $C_a + I_g + X_n + G = $ GDP.

   a. $C_a + I_g + X_n + G$ is _____ and in the equation of exchange is equal to _____

   b. Nominal GDP is equal to _____ in the equation of exchange.

5. Monetarists argue that
   a. any increase in **M** will (increase, decrease) _____ **PQ**;
   b. in the **short run** any increase in **M** will (increase, decrease) _____ both **P** and **Q**; but
   c. in the **long run** any increase in **M** will (increase, decrease) _____ only (**P, Q**) _____

6. In the debate on the stability of **V**:
   a. monetarists argue that people have a (stable, unstable) _____ desire to hold money relative to holding other assets or to making purchases, that the amount of money people will want to hold will de-pend on the level of _____ and that **V** is, therefore, _____
   b. Keynesians contend that, in addition to a transac-tions demand for money, there is also a(n) _____ demand for money, that this demand is inversely re-

lated to the _____, and that **V** is, there-

fore, _____

7. An increase in **M**:
  a. to the monetarist's way of thinking will

  (1) leave the public with (more, less) _____
  money than it wishes to have,
  (2) induce the public to (increase, decrease)
  _____ its spending for consumer and
  capital goods,

  (3) which will result in a(n) _____ in
  nominal GDP

  (4) until the nominal GDP (or **MV**) is equal to _____

  times _____
  b. to the Keynesian's way of thinking will

  (1) result in a(n) _____ in the rate of interest,

  (2) which will _____ the demand for money

  (3) and _____ **V**
  (4) and the effect on nominal GDP will be

  _____

8. In short, it is the view of the:
  a. monetarists that **V** (in the equation of exchange) is
  stable and that there is a direct relationship between

  _____ and _____

  b. Keynesians that **V** is (directly, inversely) _____
  related to the interest rate; that the interest rate (in-

  creases, decreases) _____ when **M** increases;
  and that, therefore, **M** and **V** are (directly, inversely)

  _____ related to each other.

9. The empirical evidence about velocity (**V**) is mixed
and can support two positions:

  a. The fact that there is a (strong, weak) _____
  correlation between the money supply (**M**) and nominal
  domestic output (**PQ**) suggest that velocity (**V**) is (sta-

  ble, unstable) _____. This evidence tends to sup-

  port the (Keynesian, monetarist) _____ position.

  b. In contrast, (Keynesians, monetarists) _____

  calculate **V** by dividing **M** by _____ and find that **V**

  is (stable, unstable) _____. A plot of **V** with

  the interest rate also shows a (strong, weak) _____
  correlation, which suggests that **V** is (stable, unstable)

  _____. Another criticism is that the (Keynesians,

monetarists) _____ were forced to change to
an (**M**1, **M**2) _____ definition of velocity to correct
past problems with velocity.

10. In the debate on the use of fiscal policy:
  a. the Keynesians contend that the more effective
  tool for stabilizing the economy is (fiscal, monetary)

  _____ policy; but
  b. the monetarists reply that government borrowing to

  finance a budget deficit will (raise, lower) _____

  the rate of interest and have a _____
  effect on investment spending.

11. Monetarists would have the supply of money increase
at the same annual rate as the potential rate of growth of

_____ and this is a rate of from _____

to _____%.

12. Monetarists proposed the adoption of the "Monetary
Rule" because they believe that discretionary monetary

policy tends to (stabilize, destabilize) _____
the economy. Two important sources of the problem are

irregular _____ for monetary policy to take effect and

a focus on the wrong policy target of _____.

13. In the:
  a. Keynesian model of the economy the aggregate

  supply curve is relatively (steep, flat) _____
  and an increase in aggregate demand will have a rela-

  tively (large, small) _____ effect on the

  price level and a relatively _____ effect
  on the real domestic output.
  b. monetarist model the aggregate-supply curve is

  relatively _____ and an increase in ag-

  gregate demand will have a relatively _____

  effect on price level and a relatively _____
  effect on real domestic output.
  c. From the monetarist perspective, a monetary
  rule would keep the price level (stable, unstable)

  _____ because a rightward shift in the
  aggregate supply from economic growth would be

  (greater than, less than, or equal to) _____
  the rightward shift of aggregate demand, but Keynesians would argue that the shift in aggregate demand

  with a monetary rule might be _____ or

  _____ the shift in aggregate supply, there-

  fore, making the price level (stable, unstable) _____

14. In the rational-expectations theory:
   a. Individuals correctly anticipate the effects of any economic event or a change in public policy on the economy and make decisions based on their anticipations to maximize their own _____;
   b. the markets in the economy are (noncompetitive, purely competitive) _____ and prices in these markets are perfectly (inflexible, flexible) _____; and as a result,
   c. an expansionary monetary or fiscal policy will lead the public to expect (inflation, a recession) _____ _____ and they will react in a way that results in (an increase, a decrease, no change) _____ in the real output of the economy and _____ in the price level.

15. The aggregate supply curve in the RET is (vertical, horizontal) _____ and a change in aggregate demand brings about a change in (the price level, the real output) _____ and no change in _____ of the economy.

16. Proponents of the RET:
   a. contend that discretionary monetary and fiscal policies are (effective, ineffective) _____; and
   b. like the monetarists, favor (policy rules, discretionary policy) _____
   c. however, the problems of time lags and information that reduce the ability monetary authorities to conduct monetary policy are the reasons (monetarists, rational expectationists) _____ favor rules, whereas _____ favor them because the reaction of the public can counteract or change the intended effects of monetary policy.

17. The critics of the RET maintain that people are (less well, better) _____ informed than assumed in the theory; markets are (more, less) _____ competitive than assumed in the theory and prices are, therefore, (sticky, flexible) _____; and monetary and fiscal policies have been employed in the past to (stabilize, destabilize) _____ the economy and to expand its (real, nominal) _____ output.

18. Many ideas from monetarism and rational expectations have been absorbed into mainstream thinking about macroeconomics. For example, there is more recognition that the money supply and monetary policy are (important, unimportant) _____, that there needs to be (less, more) _____ coordination between monetary and fiscal policy, and that _____ or the reactions of the public affect economic policies that are established for the economy.

■ PROBLEMS AND PROJECTS

1. You must imagine that you are a monetarist in this problem and assume that **V** is stable and equal to 4. In the table below is the aggregate supply schedule: the real output **Q** which producers will offer for sale at seven different price levels **P**.

P	Q	PQ	MV
$1.00	100	$_____	$_____
2.00	110	_____	_____
3.00	120	_____	_____
4.00	130	_____	_____
5.00	140	_____	_____
6.00	150	_____	_____
7.00	160	_____	_____

   a. Compute and enter in the table above the seven values of **PQ**.
   b. Assume **M** is $90. Enter the values of **MV** on each of the seven lines in the table. The equilibrium
   (1) nominal domestic output (**PQ** or **MV**) is $_____
   (2) price level is $_____
   (3) real domestic output (**Q**) is $_____

   c. When **M** increases to $175, **MV** at each price level is $_____; and the equilibrium
   (1) nominal domestic output is $_____
   (2) price level is $_____
   (3) real domestic output is $_____

2. In this problem you are a Keynesian. The left side of the table on the next page shows the amounts of money firms and households wish to have for transactions at different levels of nominal GDP. The right side of the table shows the amounts of money they want to have as assets at different rates of interest.
   a. Suppose the nominal GDP is $500, the interest is 7%, and the supply of money is $125.

Nominal GDP	Transactions demand	Interest rate	Asset demand
$ 500	$ 50	7.0%	$ 75
600	60	6.8	80
700	70	6.6	85
800	80	6.4	90
900	90	6.2	95
1000	100	6.0	100

(1) The amount of money demanded for transactions

is $_____

(2) The amount of money demanded as an asset is

$_____

(3) The total amount of money demanded for both purposes is $_____

(4) The amount of money firms and households wish to have is (greater than, less than, equal to)

_____ the amount of money they actually have.

(5) The velocity of money (equal to nominal GDP divided by the supply of money) is _____

b. Assume the Federal Reserve Banks expand the supply of money to $160 by purchasing securities in the open market; and that as a result the rate of interest falls to 6% and the nominal GDP rises to $600.

(1) The amount of money demanded for transactions

is now $_____ and the amount demanded

as an asset is now $_____

(2) The total amount of money demanded is

$_____ and the amount of money the

public wishes to have is _____ the amount of money they actually have.

(3) The velocity of money is _____

c. Suppose the Federal government pursues an expansionary fiscal policy which raises the nominal GDP from $600 to $800 and the interest rate from 6% to 6.8%, and the money supply remains at $160.

(1) The transactions demand for money is

$_____, the asset demand

is $_____, and the total de-

mand is $_____

(2) The velocity of money is _____

d. The effect of the easy money policy was to (increase, decrease) _____ the velocity of money and the effect of the expansionary fiscal policy was to _____ it.

3. On the graph that follows are three aggregate-supply curves: S_1, S_2, and S_3.

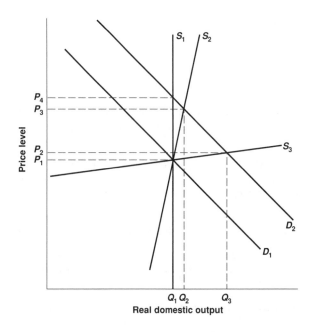

a. S_1 is the (Keynesian, monetarist, rational-expectations) _____ supply curve, S_2 is

the _____ supply curve, and S_3 is

the _____ supply curve.

b. Regardless of which is the economy's supply curve, if the aggregate-demand curve is D_1, the equilibrium

real domestic output is _____ and

the equilibrium price level is _____

c. Should aggregate demand increase from D_1 to D_2 in the

(1) monetarist model the equilibrium real domestic output would (increase, decrease, remain constant)

_____ to (at) _____ and the equilibrium price level would (increase, decrease, remain constant) _____

to (at) _____;

(2) Keynesian model the equilibrium real domestic out-

put would _____ to (at)

_____ and the equilibrium price level

would _____ to (at)

_____;

(3) rational-expectations model the equilibrium real do-

mestic output would _____ to

(at) _____ and the equilibrium price

level would _____ to (at)

_____

■ **SELF-TEST**

Circle the T if the statement is true; the F if it is false.

1. The chief exponent of the monetarist position is Milton Friedman. **T   F**

2. The basic equations of the Keynesians and the monetarists are no more than two different ways of stating the same relationship. **T   F**

3. Most monetarists believe that an increase in the money supply will have no effect on real output and employment in either the short run or the long run. **T   F**

4. Keynesians contend that changes in the money supply will have little or no effect on the rate of interest. **T   F**

5. Keynesians also maintain that relatively small changes in the interest rate have relatively large effects on investment spending. **T   F**

6. Monetarists argue that *V* in the equation of exchange is stable and that a change in *M* will bring about a direct and proportional change in *P*. **T   F**

7. In the monetarists' analysis the demand for money is directly related to nominal GDP. **T   F**

8. From the monetarist viewpoint, the economy is in equilibrium when the amount of money firms and households want to hold is equal to the money supply. **T   F**

9. Keynesians contend that the velocity of money is unstable. **T   F**

10. In the Keynesians' analysis the demand for money is directly related to the rate of interest. **T   F**

11. Keynesians argue that a decrease in the rate of interest will decrease the velocity of money. **T   F**

12. Statistical evidence reveals that the velocity of money has remained almost constant from one year to the next. **T   F**

13. An expansionary fiscal policy will, the Keynesians contend, decrease the velocity of money. **T   F**

14. Monetarists conclude that discretionary monetary policy has resulted in macroeconomic instability. **T   F**

15. Monetarists and Keynesians would agree that expansionary stabilization policies will produce demand-pull inflation in the classical range of the aggregate-supply curve. **T   F**

16. According to Keynesians, a monetary rule would help promote price stability in the economy. **T   F**

17. Rational-expectations theory assumes that both product and resource markets are uncompetitive and that wages and prices are "sticky." **T   F**

18. Economists who have advanced the rational-expectations theory argue that discretionary fiscal and monetary policies have helped to stabilize the economy. **T   F**

19. Most economists are proponents of the rational-expectations theory. **T   F**

20. A legacy of rational expectations is that economists and policy makers are more sensitive about how expectations might affect the outcome of a policy change. **T   F**

Circle the letter that corresponds to the best answer.

1. Keynesians:
(a) believe capitalism is inherently stable
(b) believe the markets in a capitalistic economy are highly competitive
(c) argue against the use of discretionary monetary policy
(d) contend that government intervention in the economy is desirable

2. Monetarists:
(a) argue for the use of discretionary monetary policy
(b) contend that government policies have reduced the stability of the economy
(c) believe a capitalistic economy is inherently unstable
(d) believe the markets in a capitalistic economy are largely noncompetitive

3. Which of the following is *not* true?
(a) *MV* is total spending
(b) *PQ* is the real GDP
(c) *PQ* is nominal GDP
(d) $MV = C_a + I_g + X_n + G$

4. If *V* in the equation of exchange is constant, an increase in *M* will necessarily increase:
(a) *P*
(b) *Q*
(c) both *P* and *Q*
(d) *P* times *Q*

5. When nominal gross domestic product (GDP) is divided by the money supply (*M*), then you will obtain the:
(a) income velocity of money
(b) monetary multiplier
(c) equation of exchange
(d) monetary rule

6. Monetarists argue that velocity is stable and that the amount of money the public will want to hold depends primarily on the level of:
(a) nominal GDP
(b) investment
(c) consumption
(d) prices

7. From the monetarist viewpoint, an increase in the supply of money will:
   (a) raise the rate of interest
   (b) increase spending for consumer and capital goods
   (c) increase the asset demand for money
   (d) increase the demand for government securities

8. Keynesians argue that:
   (a) the only demand for money is the asset demand
   (b) the only demand for money is the transactions demand
   (c) there is no transactions demand
   (d) there is both a transactions and an asset demand for money

9. From the Keynesian viewpoint, an increase in supply of money will:
   (a) raise the rate of interest
   (b) decrease spending for consumer and capital goods
   (c) increase the asset demand for money
   (d) decrease the demand for government securities

10. Which of the following would be considered as evidence for the monetarist position that velocity is stable?
   (a) a strong correlation between the velocity of money and the interest rate
   (b) a strong correlation between the money supply and nominal domestic output
   (c) the use of $M2$ to define velocity rather than $M1$
   (d) cyclical and secular changes in velocity as the economy changes

11. The crowding-out effect is the effect of borrowing funds to finance a government deficit on:
   (a) imports into the economy
   (b) the money supply
   (c) investment spending
   (d) consumer expenditures

12. Keynesians contend that borrowing to finance a government deficit incurred in order to increase employment and output in the economy will:
   (a) have little or no effect on the rate of interest
   (b) have little or no effect on investment spending
   (c) have a significant effect on Q in the equation of exchange
   (d) have all of the above effects

13. From a monetarist perspective, two important sources of monetary mismanagement are:
   (a) cyclical variations and secular trends in the economy
   (b) monetary rules and a constant velocity
   (c) irregular time lags and interest rates as the wrong policy target
   (d) a flat demand for money cure and a steep investment demand curve

14. The rule suggested by the monetarists is that the money supply should be increased at the same rate as:
   (a) the price level
   (b) the interest rate
   (c) the velocity of money
   (d) the potential growth in real GDP

15. In the monetarist model:
   (a) the aggregate-supply curve is very steep and an increase in aggregate demand will have little or no effect on the price level
   (b) the aggregate-supply curve is nearly flat and an increase in aggregate demand will have little or no effect on the price level
   (c) the aggregate-supply curve is very steep and an increase in aggregate demand will have a large effect on the price level
   (d) the aggregate-supply curve is nearly flat and an increase in aggregate demand will have a large effect on the price level

16. In the Keynesian model:
   (a) the aggregate-supply curve is very steep and an increase in aggregate demand will have a large effect on real domestic output
   (b) the aggregate-supply curve is nearly flat and an increase in aggregate demand will have a large effect on real domestic output
   (c) the aggregate-supply curve is very steep and an increase in aggregate demand will have little or no effect on real domestic output
   (d) the aggregate-supply curve is nearly flat and an increase in aggregate demand will have little or no effect on real domestic output

17. Which perspective would be most closely associated with the view that discretionary monetary policy is ineffective because of policy errors and timing problems?
   (a) monetarism
   (b) Keynesianism
   (c) rational expectations
   (d) new classical economics

18. In the rational-expectations theory:
   (a) individuals understand how the economy works and can correctly anticipate the effects of an event or a change in public policy on the economy
   (b) the markets in the economy are purely competitive
   (c) individuals to maximize their own self-interests respond to any expansionary fiscal or monetary policy in a way that prevents an increase in real output and fosters an increase in the price level
   (d) all of the above are true

19. In the rational-expectations model, an increase in aggregate demand will:
   (a) increase the price level and have no effect on real domestic output

(b) increase real domestic output and have no effect on the price level
(c) increase both the price level and the real domestic output
(d) have none of the above effects

20. To stabilize the economy rational-expectations theorists favor the use of:
(a) price controls
(b) discretionary fiscal policy
(c) discretionary monetary policy
(d) policy rules

21. The contention that changes in the money supply cause direct and predictable changes in aggregate demand and therefore changes in nominal GDP would be most closely associated with the view of:
(a) Keynesians
(b) monetarists
(c) new classical economists
(d) rational-expectations economists

22. Proponents of rational expectations argue that people:
(a) are not as rational as they are assumed to be by monetarists
(b) tend to make perfect forecasts, which frustrates policy makers
(c) have considerable knowledge about policy decisions and their impacts, which limits the effects of policies
(d) do not respond quickly to changes in wages and prices, causing a misallocation of resources in the economy

23. The idea that the Federal Reserve should follow a monetary rule would find the most support from which combination?
(a) Keynesians and monetarists
(b) RET economists and Keynesians
(c) RET economists and monetarists
(d) classical economists and Keynesians

24. A distinguishing feature of the rational expectations in the aggregate demand-aggregate supply model would be an aggregate:
(a) demand curve that is downward sloping
(b) demand curve that is vertical
(c) supply curve that is vertical
(d) supply curve that is horizontal

25. Which of the following would be an example of an idea from monetarism or rational expectations which has been absorbed into mainstream macroeconomics?
(a) the importance of government spending, taxation, and fiscal policy
(b) the importance of the money supply and monetary policy

(c) the building of macro foundations for microeconomics
(d) the emphasis on discretion rather than rules for guiding economic policy

■ **DISCUSSION QUESTIONS**

1. How do the views of Keynesians and monetarists on the competitiveness of capitalistic economies, their stability, and the need for government intervention in the economy differ?

2. What is the basic equation of the Keynesians and the basic equation of the monetarists? Define all terms in both equations and explain how the Keynesian equation can be converted to the monetarist equation.

3. Why do Keynesians believe that monetary policy is an "uncertain, unreliable and weak stabilization tool as compared to fiscal policy"?

4. Explain how a change in M in the equation of exchange will, to the monetarist way of thinking, affect
(a) P times Q,
(b) P and Q in the short run, and
(c) P and Q in the long run.

5. Explain the differences between the monetarist and Keynesian views on why firms and households demand money (or liquid balances); on what determines the demand for money; and the stability, therefore, of the velocity of money.

6. Suppose firms and households, because of an increase in the money supply, find themselves with more money than they wish to have. What do the monetarists believe they will do with this excess money? What effect will this have on the velocity of money and nominal GDP?

7. Suppose the supply of money increases. What do Keynesians believe will happen to the rate of interest, the amount of money firms and households will wish to hold, planned investment spending, and to the nominal GDP?

8. What empirical evidence is there to support the Keynesian contention that V is unstable or the monetarist contention that it is relatively stable?

9. Why do the Keynesians advocate and the monetarists reject the use of fiscal policy to stabilize the economy?

10. What is the monetary rule? Why do monetarists suggest this rule to replace discretionary monetary policy?

11. How do the aggregate demand-aggregate supply models of the Keynesians and monetarists differ? What effect will an expansionary monetary or fiscal policy have upon real domestic output and the price level in each of these models?

12. Use the aggregate demand-aggregate supply model to explain monetarist and Keynesian views of the use of a monetary rule for an expanding economy.

13. In as few words as possible, explain how and why rational-expectations theorists believe firms, workers, and consumers will respond to an expansionary monetary or fiscal policy; and how these responses make the policy ineffective and promote economic instability.

14. How will an expansionary monetary or fiscal policy affect real domestic output and the price level in the rational-expectations theorists' aggregate demand-aggregate supply model? Why does it have these effects?

15. What criticisms have been made of the RET by its opponents?

16. What influence has monetarism and rational expectations had on mainstream macroeconomic theory and policy? Give three examples of ideas that have changed mainstream thinking.

■ **ANSWERS**

Chapter 16 Alternative Views: Monetarism and Rational Expectations

FILL-IN QUESTIONS

1. unstable, noncompetitive, government intervention, fiscal, monetary

2. stable, competitive, laissez-faire, nondiscretionary, monetary

3. $MV = PQ$; a. equation of exchange; b. (1) the money supply, (2) the (income or circuit) velocity of money, (3) the average price of each unit of physical output, (4) the physical volume of goods and services produced

4. a. total spending (aggregate demand), MV; b. PQ

5. a. increase; b. increase; (c) increase, P

6. a. stable, nominal GDP, stable; b. asset, interest rate, unstable

7. a. (1) more, (2) increase, (3) increase, (4) P, Q; b. (1) decrease, (2) increase, (3) decrease, (4) uncertain

8. a. M, PQ; b. directly, decreases, inversely

9. a. strong, stable, monetarists; b. Keynesian, GDP, unstable, strong, unstable, monetarists, $M2$

10. a. fiscal; b. raise, crowding-out

11. real GDP, 3, 5

12. destabilize, time lags, interest rates

13. a. flat, small, large; b. steep, large, small; c. stable, equal to, less than, greater than (either order), unstable

14. a. self-interests; b. purely competitive, flexible; c. inflation, no change, an increase

15. vertical, the price level, the real output

16. a. ineffective; b. policy rules; c. monetarists, rational expectationists

17. less well, less, sticky, stabilize, real

18. important, more, expectations

PROBLEMS AND PROJECTS

1. a. 100, 220, 360, 520, 700, 900, 1120; b. 360, 360, 360, 360, 360, 360, 360, (1) 360, (2) 3.00, (3) 130; c. 700, (1) 700, (2) 5.00, (3) 140

2. a. (1) 50, (2) 75, (3) 125, (4) equal to, (5) 4; b. (1) 60, 100, (2) 160, equal to, (3) 3.75; c. (1) 80, 80, 160, (2) 5; d. decrease, increase

3. a. rational-expectations, classical, Keynesian; b. Q_1, P_1; c. (1) increase, Q_2, increase, P_3, (2) increase, Q_3, increase, P_2, (3) remain constant, Q_1, increase, P_4

SELF-TEST

1. T, p. 305	**8.** T, p. 309	**15.** T, pp. 315–316
2. T, p. 307	**9.** T, p. 309	**16.** F, p. 316
3. F, p. 307	**10.** F, p. 310	**17.** F, p. 317
4. T, pp. 307–308	**11.** T, p. 310	**18.** F, p. 317
5. F, p. 307	**12.** F, p. 310	**19.** F, p. 319
6. F, p. 309	**13.** F, p. 313	**20.** T, p. 321
7. T, p. 309	**14.** T, p. 313	

1. d, p. 306	**10.** b, pp. 310–311	**18.** d, p. 317
2. b, p. 306	**11.** c, pp. 312–313	**19.** a, p. 317
3. b, p. 307	**12.** d, p. 313	**20.** d, p. 318
4. d, p. 308	**13.** c, p. 314	**21.** b, p. 309
5. a, p. 310	**14.** d, p. 314	**22.** c, pp. 317–318
6. a, p. 309	**15.** c, p. 315	**23.** c, p. 318
7. b, p. 309	**16.** b, p. 315	**24.** c, p. 318
8. d, p. 309	**17.** a, pp. 313–314	**25.** b, p. 320
9. c, pp. 309–310		

DISCUSSION QUESTIONS

1. p. 306	**7.** pp. 309–310	**12.** p. 316
2. pp. 306–307	**8.** pp. 310–311	**13.** p. 317
3. pp. 307–308	**9.** pp. 312–313	**14.** p. 318
4. p. 309	**10.** p. 314	**15.** p. 319
5. pp. 309–310	**11.** pp. 314–315	**16.** pp. 319–321
6. p. 309		

CHAPTER **17**

The Inflation-Unemployment Relationship

This chapter continues the discussion of alternative perspectives of macroeconomic theory and policy by examining the explanations for the simultaneous presence of unemployment and inflation in the United States economy. The mainstream or Keynesian views of the relationship between unemployment and inflation during the past three decades as embodied in the Phillips Curve are contrasted with new classical economics, with its the natural rate hypothesis and the distinction made between the short-run and long-run aggregate-supply curve. The chapter also presents other policy options for dealing with inflation and unemployment and introduces the perspective of supply-side economics.

In the early 1960s most economists believed that it was possible for the American economy to have both full employment and stable prices. This belief was based on the assumption that the price level would not rise until the labor force was fully employed. All that was necessary for full employment without inflation was just the right level of aggregate expenditures. Fiscal and monetary policy, thought Keynesian economists, could be used to assume that aggregate demand was adequate but not excessive.

But the assumption underlying this simplest Keynesian model was not realistic. The price level can rise before full employment is achieved; and the closer the economy moves to full employment the greater the rate at which prices rise. This observation became the basis for the concept of an unemployment-inflation rate tradeoff and its menu of policy choices as described in the supposedly stable Phillips Curve. According to Keynesians, the reason for inflation before full employment and for the Phillips Curve is that some types of labor become fully employed before other types of labor, and possibly also the market power of businesses and unions to raise prices and wages.

While this apparent unemployment-inflation rate tradeoff created a policy dilemma for economists of the 1960s, the situation and the problem became much more complicated in the 1970s and early 1980s. The problem was stagflation, with rising prices and rising unemployment rates. Keynesians explained stagflation of the period by citing events that produced aggregate-supply shocks, de-creasing the aggregate-supply curve and driving up the price level and reducing real output and employment. The leftward shift in the aggregate-supply curve caused the Phillips Curve to move to the right; hence the occurrence of both rising prices and unemployment. The events of the 1982–1989 period shifted the aggregate-supply curve rightward again and the Phillips Curve to the left, or so the Keynesian view went.

An alternative explanation of the events of the 1970s and 1980s came from the natural rate hypothesis of new classical economics. The two variants of this hypothesis were those of adaptive-expectations and rational-expectations theorists. Both adaptive- and rational-expectations theorists contend that the downsloping Phillips Curve is a figment of Keynesian imagination; that it is actually a vertical line; and that government attempts to reduce the unemployment rate below the rate at which the vertical Phillips Curve meets the horizontal axis produce a higher rate of inflation. The major difference between the adaptive expectationists and rational expectationists is that the former believe that expansionary monetary or fiscal policies can bring about a temporary decline in the unemployment rate; the latter argue that such policies do not even reduce unemployment temporarily, and any short-term instability in the macro economy is a product of price-level surprises.

New classical economists also distinguish between a short-run and a long-run aggregate-supply curve. In the short run, nominal wages are fixed so an increase in the price level increases business profits and real output. In the long run, nominal wages are flexible so business profits and employment return to their original level, making the long-run aggregate supply curve vertical at the potential level of real output. Keynesians question the speed of these adjustments because of the downward inflexibility of wages and prices and hold that there are opportunities for the use of stabilization policies to reduce the high cost of unemployment or inflation.

The distinction between the short-run and long-run aggregate-supply curve requires a reinterpretation of demand-pull and cost-push inflation. Although demand-pull inflation will increase the price level and real output in the short run, once nominal wages increase, the temporary increase in output will be gone, but the price level will be higher at the potential level of output for the economy. Cost-push inflation will increase the price level and decrease real output in the short run, but again, once nominal wages fall, output and the price level will return to the original level. If policy makers try to counter cost-push inflation by increasing aggregate demand, they may make matters worse by increasing the price level and causing the short-run aggregate-supply curve to decrease again.

Other solutions for stagflation have been sought by the United States and other mixed market economies. Discussed in the chapter are market policies and wage-price policies that were used in the 1960s and 1970s to correct aspects of the unemployment and inflation problem. Of more recent appeal, however, was supply-side economics, which gained visibility during the Reagan administration (1981–1989). Supply-side economists pointed to the role of the Federal government in causing the slump in productivity and economic growth in the economy during the 1970s. The solutions, which became the program of Reaganomics, were to come from massive reduction in personal and corporate income taxes, reduced government regulation, cuts in social and welfare spending by government, and control over the rate of growth of the money supply. Despite its successes, this program and supply-side economics have been criticized, especially for the failure of the large cuts in the tax rates to increase significantly the aggregate-supply curve beyond its historical level.

The chapter concludes with a recap of the alternative macroeconomic theories and policies presented in this and the previous chapter. You should take time to study Table 17-1 in detail so that you understand and can explain the different viewpoints.

■ **CHECKLIST**

When you have studied this chapter you should be able to:

☐ Explain how early Keynesian analysis was able to conclude that the economy could achieve both full employment and stable prices; and what was needed to reach these two goals simultaneously.
☐ Draw a traditional Phillips Curve (after properly labeling the two axes); and explain how to derive this curve by using the aggregate demand–aggregate supply model.
☐ State the two basic causes of the inflation shown on the Phillips Curve.
☐ Explain and use the Phillips Curve to illustrate the stabilization policy dilemma.
☐ Define stagflation; and contrast stagflation with the relationship shown by a Phillips Curve.

☐ Enumerate the supply-side shocks experienced by the American economy in the 1970s and early 1980s; and use the aggregate demand—aggregate supply model to explain why these shocks led to stagflation.
☐ List the events that contributed to stagflation's demise during the 1982–1989 period.
☐ Describe the Keynesians view of the Phillips Curve from 1960 to 1989.
☐ Explain the natural rate hypothesis and the two variants of this hypothesis—adaptive expectations and rational expectations.
☐ Use the adaptive expectations model to explain the process of inflation and disinflation in the economy.
☐ Compare and contrast how adaptive expectations and rational expectations theorists view the Phillips Curve.
☐ Distinguish the short-run aggregate-supply curve from the long-run aggregate-supply curve.
☐ Compare and contrast Keynesian and new classical perspectives of stabilization policy.
☐ Apply the distinction between the short-run and long-run aggregate-supply curve to explain demand-pull and cost-push inflation.
☐ State the two kinds of market policies that might be used to combat stagflation.
☐ Distinguish between wage-price guideposts and wage-price controls; and explain why they are called income policies.
☐ Explain what the advocates of supply-side economics saw as the three tax-transfer disincentives in the American economy.
☐ Explain the hypothesized relationship between tax rates and tax revenues as suggested by the Laffer Curve.
☐ State three criticisms of the Laffer Curve.
☐ Describe two other tenants of supply-side economics.
☐ Explain the four economic policies proposed by the Reagan administration to deal with stagflation.
☐ Evaluate the program of the Reagan administration (Reaganomics) and the effectiveness of that program.
☐ Summarize the alternative macroeconomic theories and policies of various issues.

■ **CHAPTER OUTLINE**

1. In the simple Keynesian model of aggregate demand and aggregate supply, an assumption is made that the aggregate-supply curve is shaped as a reverse "L" with a horizontal (Keynesian) range and a vertical (classical) range.
   a. With this basic model, the economy may realize either unemployment or inflation, but not both problems simultaneously. The stagflation episodes of the 1970s showed this conclusion to be incorrect.
   b. The model can be revised to account for the events

of the 1970s by including an upsloping portion in the intermediate range of the aggregate-supply curve and by allowing the aggregate-supply curve to shift left.

2. If aggregate supply is constant and the economy is operating in the intermediate range on the aggregate-supply curve, the greater the rate of increase in aggregate demand the greater is the rate of increase in the price level and in real output, and the lower is the rate of unemployment (and **vice versa**); and there is, therefore, an inverse relationship (or tradeoff) called the Phillips Curve between the inflation rate and the unemployment rate.

   a. There are at least two reasons why inflation occurs before the economy reaches full employment.

   (1) Scarcities of some kinds of labor develop before the economy's entire labor force is fully employed; and these scarcities increase wage rates, production costs, and prices.

   (2) Labor unions and business firms have market power and they raise wage rates and prices as the economy approaches full employment.

   b. While fiscal and monetary policy can be employed to manage aggregate demand and to affect unemployment and the rate of inflation, the nation faces a serious policy dilemma: full employment without inflation and price stability without unemployment are impossible and the nation must choose one of the combinations of inflation and unemployment that lies on the Phillips Curve.

   c. Events in the 1960s seemed to confirm the inverse relationship between the unemployment and inflation rates.

3. Events of the 1970s and 1980s, however, called into question the stability of the Phillips Curve:

   a. In the 1970s and early 1980s the American economy experienced both higher rates of inflation and greater unemployment rates; and this stagflation suggests either that there is no dependable relationship between the inflation and unemployment rates or that the Phillips Curve had shifted to the right.

   (1) During these years six cost- or supply-side shocks decreased aggregate supply (moved the aggregate-supply curve left) to increase both prices and unemployment in the United States; and the experiences of the American economy suggest that the Phillps Curve is not a stable relationship and cannot be used as the basis for economic policy.

   (2) The demise of stagflation came in the 1982–1989 period because of a variety of factors; but unemployment and inflation moved in the same direction at times, not in the opposite direction implied by the Phillips Curve of the 1960s.

   b. The Keynesian view is that a tradeoff between unemployment and inflation does exist; the explanation for the data problems were the supply shocks that produced a rightward shift in the Phillips Curve during the 1971–1982 period, and changes in the economy that produced a leftward shift during the 1982–1989 period.

4. The natural rate hypothesis questions the existence of a downsloping Phillips Curve and views the economy as stable in the long run at the natural rate of unemployment. There are two variants to this hypothesis:

   a. The theory of adaptive expectations suggests that an increase in aggregate demand sponsored by government may temporarily reduce unemployment as the price level increases and profits expand, but the actions also set into motion other events:

   (1) The increase in the price level reduces the real wages of workers who demand and obtain higher nominal wages; these actions return unemployment to its original level.

   (2) Back at the original level, there is now a higher actual and expected rate of inflation for the economy, so the short-run Phillips Curve has shifted upward.

   (3) The process is repeated when government tries again to reduce unemployment and the rise in the price level accelerates as the short-run Phillips Curves shift upward.

   (4) In the long run, the Phillips Curve is stable only as a vertical line at the natural rate of unemployment; there is no tradeoff between unemployment and inflation.

   b. Rational expectations theory assumes that workers fully anticipate that government policies to reduce unemployment will also be inflationary, and they increase their nominal wage demands to offset the expected inflation; thus there will not even be a temporary decline in unemployment, or even a short-run Phillips Curve.

5. The aggregate-supply curve has short- and long-run characteristics, and implications for policy:

   a. In the short run, where nominal wages are fixed, the aggregate-supply curve is upward sloping: an increase in the price level will increase profits and cause a rise in real output; in contrast, when the price level decreases, profits are reduced and so is real output.

   b. In the long run, where nominal wages are variable, the aggregate-supply curve is vertical at the potential level of output: increases in the price level will increase in nominal wages and cause a shift to the left in the short-run aggregate-supply curve; or declines in the price level reduce nominal wages and shift the short-run aggregate-supply curve to the right; but in either case, although the price level changes, output returns to its potential level, so the long-run aggregate supply curve is vertical.

   c. Proponents of new classical economics subscribe to the view that the flexible nominal wages the economy is basically stable at the full-employment level of output in the long run, and thus there no need for policy actions; modern Keynesians contend that nominal wages may be slow to adjust to price level changes and support the use of stabilization policies to reduce unemployment or inflation costs to the economy.

6. Knowledge of the short- and long-run features of aggregate supply provide insights into these types of inflation:

a. Demand-pull inflation will shift the aggregate-demand curve, which increases the price level and causes a temporary increase in real output; but in the long run, nominal wages will increase and the short-run aggregate supply will shift to the left, resulting in an even higher price level with real output returning to its previous level.

b. Cost-push inflation will shift the short-run aggregate supply curve left:

(1) this action increases the price level and temporarily decreases real output;

(2) the resulting recession will reduce nominal wages, shifting the short-run aggregate supply to its original position;

(3) but if government takes actions to counter the cost-push inflation and recession by shifting aggregate demand, the price level will move to an even higher level.

c. The aggregate supply curve is vertical in the long run.

7. Because of the ineffectiveness of demand-management policies in coping with stagflation, the American economy has sought other kinds of policies to prevent decreases in or to increase aggregate supply (to shift the Phillips Curve to the left).

a. Market policies try to eliminate the causes of premature inflation and include:

(1) employment and training policies to reduce the scarcities of particular kinds of labor that occur before the labor force is fully employed;

(2) pro-competition policies to reduce the power of labor unions and business firms to raise wage rates and prices.

b. Wage-price (or incomes) policies restrict increases in wages and prices by utilizing either guideposts or controls.

(1) Wage-price guideposts are voluntary restraints. The Kennedy-Johnson guideposts restricted nominal wage increases in all industries to the rate at which the productivity of labor in the economy had increased; and allowed an industry to increase the price of its product by an amount equal to the increase in its unit labor cost.

(2) Wage-price controls are mandatory (or legal) restraints; and were employed in 1971 to deal with stagflation in the American economy.

(3) Whether to employ wage-price policies has been a vigorously debated issue; and the proponents and opponents have based their arguments on the questions of workability and compliance and allocative efficiency.

8. Supply-side economists argue that mainstream economics has overemphasized aggregate demand and neglected aggregate supply in explaining changes in the price level and unemployment.

a. They argue that high marginal tax rates and a widespread system for public transfer payments reduce incentives to work, and that high taxes also reduce incentives to save and to invest; these policies lead to a misallocation of resources, less productivity, and a decrease in aggregate supply.

b. To increase aggregate supply, and thus decrease inflation and increase employment, supply-side economists call for a cut in marginal tax rates.

(1) The Laffer Curve suggests in theory that it is possible to lower tax rates and increase tax revenues, thus avoiding a budget deficit because the policies will result in less tax evasion and reduced transfer payments.

(2) Critics of supply-side economics and the Laffer Curve suggest that the policy of cutting tax rates will not work because:

(a) it has only a small or uncertain effect on incentives to work (on aggregate supply);

(b) it would increase aggregate demand relative to aggregate supply and thus reinforce inflation when there is full-employment and also add to an existing budget deficit;

(c) the expected tax revenues from tax rate cuts depend on assumptions about the position on the Laffer Curve; if tax cuts reduce tax revenues, it only contributes to problems with an existing budget deficit.

c. There are two other tenets of supply-side economics:

(1) Taxes are a "wedge" between the cost of resources and the price of a product. This cost ultimately get passed on to consumers in the form of higher prices, and shifts the aggregate-supply curve to the left.

(2) Overregulation of the economy by government has decreased productivity and led to higher costs.

d. The economic program of the Reagan administration (1981–1989) or "Reaganomics" was based on supply-side ideas:

(1) The program called for a reduction in almost all government spending (except defense expenditures), less government regulation of private businesses, restricting the growth in the money supply to prevent inflation, and cuts in personal and corporate income tax rates.

(2) The record shows that by the late 1980s there was a reduction in inflation and interest rates, an economic expansion, and the achievement of full employment, but most economists do not attribute this success to supply-side economics but to other factors and they point to other problems with the program.

(a) The reduction in inflation came not from tax cuts and other supply-side policies but from a tight monetary policy of the Federal Reserve in the 1980s that produced a severe recession in the 1980–1982 (reducing aggregate demand), and from a drop in oil prices in the mid-1980s.

(b) The tax cuts of the 1980s increased the budget deficit and stimulated economic expansion from the demand side; they also crowded-out investment and caused problems in exporting and importing industries. (c) Little evidence is found that the tax cuts increased saving or investment, or provided strong incentives to work, and thus did not shift aggregate supply.

9. Table 17-1 contains a recap of the differences among Keynesianism, monetarism, rational expectations, and supply-side economics on various issues discussed in this chapter and previous chapters.

■ IMPORTANT TERMS

Phillips Curve	New classical economics
Stagflation	Price-level surprises
Aggregate-supply shocks	Demand-pull inflation
Inflationary expectations	Cost-push inflation
Natural-rate hypothesis	Market policies
Adaptive expectations theory	Wage-price guideposts
Rational-expectations theory	Wage-price controls
Disinflation	Incomes policies
Short-run aggregate-supply curve	Supply-side economics
Long-run aggregate-supply curve	Tax-transfer disincentives
	Laffer Curve
	Tax "wedge"
	Reaganomics

■ FILL-IN QUESTIONS

1. In the simplest Keynesian view, the price level of the economy would not increase until the economy reached _____ and inflation was the result of (excess, insufficient) _____ aggregate demand; and the economy can have (either, both) _____ unemployment and/or inflation.

2. In the aggregate demand–aggregate supply model, when the economy is producing in the intermediate range along the aggregate-supply curve:
a. An increase in aggregate demand will (increase, decrease) _____ real output and employment.
b. A decrease in aggregate supply will _____ real output and employment.

3. If aggregate supply remains constant, along the intermediate range of aggregate supply:
a. the greater the increase in aggregate demand, the (greater, smaller) _____ will be the increase in the price level, the _____ will be the increase in real output, and the _____ will be the unemployment rate;
b. there will be a(n) (direct, inverse) _____ relationship between the rate of inflation and the unemployment rate.

4. When prices rise before _____ _____, this is the result of the market power of _____ and _____ and of imbalances or bottlenecks in _____ markets.

5. The Phillips Curve:
a. is the relation between the annual rate of increase in the _____ and the _____ rate;
b. has a (positive, negative) _____ slope.

6. The stabilization policy dilemma faced by the American economy is that:
a. to have full employment it must also have _____ and to have stable prices it must tolerate _____.
b. to reduce the unemployment rate, the rate of inflation must (increase, decrease) _____ and to reduce the rate of inflation the unemployment rate must _____.

7. Policies to manage aggregate demand can be used to (shift the, select a point on the) _____ Phillips Curve, but such policies do not improve the "unemployment rate-inflation rate" _____.

8. List the six factors (supply-side shocks) that shifted the Phillips Curve to the right after 1972 according to Keynesian economists.
a. _____
b. _____
c. _____
d. _____
e. _____
f. _____

9. In the equation that relates unit labor costs to nominal wage rates and the productivity of labor:
a. If the rate at which nominal wages increase is greater than the rate at which productivity increases,

unit labor costs will (increase, decrease) _____

b. If the productivity of labor decreases and nominal wage rates are constant, unit labor costs will

_____

10. The expectation of inflation by workers and employers leads to (higher, lower) _____ wage rates and in turn to a (rise, fall) _____ in production costs, to a(n) (increase, decrease) _____ in aggregate supply, to a (higher, lower) _____ price level, and to a _____ rate of unemployment in the economy.

11. The rising unemployment rates and the sharp inflation following the supply-side shocks can be understood by using the aggregate demand–aggregate supply model.

a. The shocks (increased, decreased) _____ aggregate supply.

b. Which in turn increased both the _____ level and the _____ rate.

c. And these two events when they occur simultaneously are called _____

12. List four factors that contributed to stagflation's demise during the 1982–1989 period:

a. _____

b. _____

c. _____

d. _____

13. During the 1960s, the empirical data indicate that unemployment and inflation moved in the (same, opposite) _____ direction; in 1973–1974, 1978–1980, and in some years during the 1982–1989 period, unemployment and inflation moved in the _____ direction.

14. There is much debate among economists about the Phillips Curve:

a. Keynesian economists contend that during the stagflation of the 1970s, the Phillips Curve shifted (right, left) _____; during the demise of stagflation from 1982–1989, the Phillips Curve shifted _____

b. Other economists associated with new classical thinking conclude that the downsloping Phillips Curve does not _____ in the long run and sub-

scribe to the _____ hypothesis, for which there are two variants—_____ and _____ expectations.

c. The theory of adaptive expectations suggests that people form their expectations of _____ based on experience and (immediately, gradually) _____ change expectations over time.

d. With this theory:

(1) the (short-run, long-run) _____ Phillips Curve may be downsloping, but the _____ Phillips Curve is vertical at the _____

_____

(2) attempts by government to reduce the unemployment rate bring about a rate of inflation that (increases, decreases) _____

e. The rational expectations theory suggests that:

(1) attempts by government to reduce the unemployment rate lead workers to anticipate the amount of _____ this will cause and to keep their (real, nominal) _____ wages constant they obtain a(n) (increase, decrease) _____ in their _____ wages; and

(2) this brings about (a rise, a fall, no change) _____ in the price level and _____ in the unemployment rate.

15. With the aggregate-supply curve:

a. In the short run, the curve is (upsloping, vertical) _____ and in the long run the curve is _____;

b. In the short run, nominal wages are (fixed, variable) _____, and in the long run, nominal wages are _____.

c. Proponents of new classical economics think that wages and prices are (flexible, inflexible) _____ and that the economy is (stable, unstable) _____ in the long run at the full employment level of real output; policy changes by government (will, will not) _____ be anticipated in advance and _____ influence the economy in the short run; only _____ surprises produce temporary changes in real output.

d. Modern Keynesians accept the distinction between short- and long-run aggregate supply, but contend that wages and prices are (flexible, inflexible)

_____ downward, and therefore they advocate a(n) (active, hand-offs) _____ policy by government in the short run to reduce the (low, high) _____ cost of inflation and unemployment.

16. Demand-pull inflation will shift the aggregate-demand curve (right, left) _____, which will (decrease, increase) _____ the price level and temporarily _____ real output. As a consequence, the (short-run, long-run) _____ aggregate-supply curve will shift left because of a rise in (real, nominal) _____ wages, producing a (lower, higher) _____ price level at the original level of real output.

17. Cost-push inflation will shift the short-run aggregate-supply curve (right, left) _____, thus the price level will (increase, decrease) _____ and real output will temporarily _____; if government takes no actions to counter the cost-push inflation, the resulting recession will _____ nominal wages, and shift the short-run aggregate-supply curve back to its original position; yet, if the government tries to counter the cost-push inflation and recession with a(n) _____ in aggregate demand, the price level will move even higher.

18. Three kinds of economic policies might be used to deal with stagflation.

  a. These three policies are _____ policies, _____-_____ policies, and the policies identified with _____ economics.
  b. If effective, these policies would move the Phillips Curve to the (right, left) _____

19. Market policies to reduce unemployment include:
  a. those designed to reduce bottlenecks in labor markets and are called _____ policies; and
  b. those aimed at reducing the market power of business firms and labor unions and are called pro-_____ policies.

20. Wage-price policies:

  a. are sometimes called _____ policies;
  b. involve either;

  (1) wage-price (controls, guideposts) _____ which rely upon the voluntary cooperation of labor unions and business firms

  (2) or wage-price _____ which have the force of law to make them effective.

21. The wage-price guideposts for curbing inflation during the Kennedy-Johnson administrations limited **wage** increases in an industry to the overall rate of increase in the _____ of labor and limited **price** increases to an amount equal to the increase in _____ costs in that industry.

22. It is the view of supply-side economists that:

  a. high marginal tax rates reduce _____ to work, save, invest, and take risks;
  b. the remedy for stagflation is a substantial (increase, decrease) _____ in marginal tax rates; and
  c. a cut in tax rates would significantly shift the (aggregate-demand, aggregate-supply) _____ curve (leftward, rightward) _____ and make the economy grow at a pace greater than historical experience.

23. The Laffer Curve depicts the relationship between tax rates and tax revenues. In theory, as the tax rates increase from 0%, tax revenues will (increase, decrease) _____ to some maximum level, after which tax revenues will _____ as the tax rates increase; or, as tax rates are reduced from 100%, tax revenues will _____ to some maximum level, after which tax revenues will _____ as tax rates decrease.

24. The criticisms of the Laffer Curve are that the effects of a cut in tax rates on incentives to work, save, and invest are (large, small) _____; that the tax cuts generate an increase in aggregate (demand, supply) _____ that outweigh any increase in aggregate _____ and in a full employment situation will lead to _____; and that tax cuts can produce (gain, loss) _____ in tax revenues that only adds to or creates a budget deficit.

25. Two other supply-side tenets are that business costs and product prices have increased because government has raised taxes and these taxes are a business _____ and a tax "_____" between the price of a product and the cost of resources; and that the productivity of business have been decreased by _____ of industry by government.

26. The four principal elements of Reaganomics were:

a. _____

b. _____

c. _____

d. _____

27. The evidence suggests that supply-side economics ideas (did, did not) _____ work as proposed in Reaganomics.

a. Although inflation fell in the 1980s, it was because of a (tight, easy) _____ money policy of the Federal Reserve, the effects of a severe _____ in 1980–1982, and because of a (rise, fall) _____ in oil prices in the mid-1980s.

b. The cut in tax rate primarily (increased, decreased) _____ aggregate demand and sparked an economic expansion in the 1980s, but the tax cuts also _____ tax revenues contributing to increasing budget _____

c. The impact of tax cuts on saving, investment, and productivity was (minimal, substantial) _____ deficit, and thus the pace of economic growth was (greater than, less than, about the same as) _____ the historical experience.

■ **PROBLEMS AND PROJECTS**

1. In the next column is a traditional Phillips Curve.

a. At full employment (a 4% unemployment rate) the price level would rise by _____% each year.

b. If the price level were stable (increasing by 0% a year) the unemployment rate would be _____%.

c. Which of the combinations along the Phillips Curve would you choose for the economy? _____ Why would you select this combination? _____ _____

2. In columns (1) and (2) of the table below is a portion of an aggregate-supply schedule. Column (3) shows the number of full-time workers (in millions) that would have to be employed to produce each of the seven real domestic outputs (in billions) in the aggregate-supply schedule.

The labor force is 80 million workers and the full-employment output of the economy is $_____

a. If the aggregate-demand schedule were that shown by columns (1) and (4):

(1) The price level would be _____ and the real output would be $_____

(2) the number of workers employed would be _____, the number of workers unemployed would be _____, and the unemployment *rate* would be _____%.

(1) Price level	(2) Real output supplied	(3) Employment (in millions)	(4) Real output demanded	(5) Real output demanded	(6) Real output demanded
130	$ 800	69	$2300	$2600	$1900
140	1300	70	2200	2500	1800
150	1700	72	2100	2400	1700
160	2000	75	2000	2300	1600
170	2200	78	1900	2200	1500
180	2300	80	1800	2100	1400
190	2300	80	1700	2000	1300

b. If aggregate demand were to increase to that shown in columns (1) and (5) and aggregate supply remained constant:

(1) the price level would rise to _____

and the real output would rise to $_____

(2) employment would increase by _____

_____ workers and the unemployment

rate would fall to _____%.

(3) the price level has increased by and the rate of

inflation has been _____%.

c. If aggregate demand were to decrease to that shown in columns (1) and (6) and aggregate supply remained constant:

(1) the price level would fall to _____

and the real output would fall to $_____

(2) employment would decrease by _____
compared with situation a, and workers and the un-

employment rate would rise to _____%.

(3) the price level has decreased and the rate of infla-

tion has been (positive, negative) _____

3. Below is an adaptive expectations model of the short- and long-run Phillips Curve.

a. Suppose you begin at point X_1; then an assumption is made that nominal wages are set on the original expectation that a 3% rate of inflation will continue in the economy.

(1) If government invokes expansionary monetary and fiscal policy to reduce the unemployment rate from 6% to 3%, then the actual rate of inflation will move to

_____%. The higher product prices will lift profits of firms and they will hire more workers; thus in the short run the economy will temporarily move to point

_____

(2) If workers then demand and receive higher wages to compensate for the loss of purchasing power from higher than expected inflation, then business profits will fall from previous levels and firms will reduce employment. Therefore, employment will move from point

_____ to point _____ on the graph.

The short-run Phillips Curve has shifted from _____

to _____ on the graph.

(3) If government again tries to stimulate aggregate demand with monetary and fiscal policy to reduce the unemployment rate from 6% to 3%, then prices will rise before nominal wages, and output and employment will increase, so that there will be a move from point

_____ to point _____ on the graph.

(4) But when workers get nominal wage increases, profits fall, and employment moves from point

_____ at _____% to point

_____ at _____%. The short-run

Phillips Curve has now shifted from _____

to _____ on the graph.

(5) The long-run Phillips Curve is the line _____

_____

b. Suppose you begin at point X_3, where the expected and actual rate of inflation is 9% and the unemployment rate is 6%.

(1) If there should be a decline in aggregate demand because of a recession and if the actual rate of inflation should fall to 6%, well below the expected rate of 9%, then business profits will fall and the unemployment rate will decrease to 9% as shown by the movement

from point X_3 to point _____

(2) If firms and workers adjust their expectation to the 6% rate of inflation, then nominal wages will fall, profits will rise, and the economy will move from point

_____ to point _____. The short-run

Phillips Curve has shifted from _____ to

_____

(3) If this process is repeated, the long-run Phillips

Curve will be traced as line _____

4. Below is an aggregate-demand and aggregate-supply model. Assume that the economy is initially in equilibrium at AD₁ and AS₁. The price level will be _____ and the real domestic output will be _____

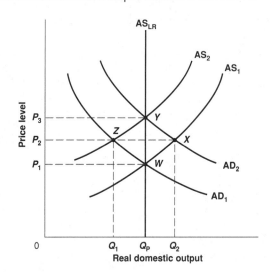

a. If there is demand-pull inflation, then:
(1) in the short run, the new equilibrium is at point _____, with the price level at _____ and real output at _____;
(2) in the long run, nominal wages will rise so the aggregate-supply curve will shift from _____ to _____. The equilibrium will be at point _____ with the price level at _____ and real output at _____; and so the increase in aggregate demand has only moved the economy along its _____ curve.
b. Now assume that the economy is initially in equilibrium at point **W**, where AD₁ and AS₁ intersect. If there is cost-push inflation, then:
(1) In the short run, the new equilibrium is at point _____, with the price level at _____ and real output at _____
(2) If the government tries to counter the cost-push inflation with expansionary monetary and fiscal policy, then aggregate demand will shift from _____ to _____, with the price level becoming _____ and real output _____; but this policy has a trap because the price level has shifted from _____ to _____ and the new level of inflation might shift _____ leftward.
(3) If government does not counter the cost-push infla-

tion, the price level will eventually move to _____ and real output to _____ as the recession reduces nominal wages and shifts the aggregate-supply curve from _____ to _____

5. Assume that the overall rate of increase in the productivity of labor in the economy is 4% per year.
 a. The general level of wages in the economy can increase by _____% a year without increasing unit labor costs and inducing cost-push inflation.
 b. If the wage rate were increased by this percentage,
 (1) in an industry in which the productivity of labor had increased 3%, labor costs per unit would (increase, decrease) _____ by _____%; and the application of the Kennedy-Johnson price guidepost would permit the price of the product produced by this industry to (rise, fall) _____ by _____%.
 (2) In an industry in which the productivity of labor had increased by 6%, labor costs per unit would _____ by _____%; and the price guidepost would permit the price of the product to _____ by _____%.
 (3) In an industry in which the productivity of labor had **decreased** by 2%, labor costs per unit would _____ by _____%; and the price guidepost would permit the price of the product to _____ by _____%.

■ **SELF-TEST**

Circle the T if the statement is true; the F if it is false.

1. In the simplest Keynesian model the aggregate-supply curve has no intermediate range.   **T F**

2. The simple Keynesian model provides a reasonably satisfactory explanation of the macroeconomic behavior of the American economy between 1930 and 1970, but does not explain the stagflation of the 1970s and early 1980s.   **T F**

3. When aggregate supply is constant, higher rates of inflation àre accompanied by higher rates of unemployment.   **T F**

4. According to the conventional Phillips Curve the rate of inflation increases as the level of unemployment decreases.   **T F**

5. Labor market imbalances and market power are explanations offered by Keynesians to explain the intermediate range of the aggregate supply curve.   **T F**

6. According to Keynesian economists, as the economy approaches full employment, some type of labor become fully employed before all the labor force is fully employed. **T F**

7. Policies to manage aggregate supply can be used to choose a point on the Phillips Curve, but these policies do not improve the "unemployment rate-inflation rate" trade-off reflected in the Phillips Curve **T F**

8. Stagflation refers to a situation in which both the price level and the unemployment rate are rising. **T F**

9. Keynesian economists contend that the Phillips Curve shifted left during the 1973–1982 period and shifted right during the 1982–1989 period. **T F**

10. Expectations of inflation induce workers to demand a higher nominal wage and their employers to pay them higher wages. **T F**

11. When the nominal wage rate increases at a rate greater than the rate at which the productivity of labor increases, unit labor cost will rise. **T F**

12. The demise of stagflation and a decline in unit labor costs will tend to shift the aggregate-supply curve rightward and the Phillips curve leftward. **T F**

13. The natural rate hypothesis suggests that there is a natural rate of inflation for the economy. **T F**

14. The theory of adaptive expectations indicates that there may be a short-run tradeoff between inflation and unemployment, but no long-run tradeoff. **T F**

15. From the adaptive expectations perspective, when the actual rate of inflation is higher than expected, the unemployment rate will rise. **T F**

16. Adaptive expectation theorists believe that they are able to explain disinflation in the economy. **T F**

17. The theory of rational expectations maintains that if workers believe expansionary monetary and fiscal policies will be inflationary and therefore lower their real wages, then the reaction of the workers to these expectations results in higher nominal wages, higher labor costs, and no change in employment in the economy. **T F**

18. Natural rate theorists conclude that demand-management policies cannot influence real output and employment in the long run, but only the price level. **T F**

19. The long-run aggregate supply curve is upsloping at the potential level of real national output. **T F**

20. New classical economists hold that price level surprises produce short-run fluctuations in the economy, but in the long run the economy is stable at the full-employment level of output. **T F**

21. Keynesian economists contend that nominal wages are inflexible upward and therefore they advocate a hands-off approach to stabilization policy. **T F**

22. Demand-pull inflation will increase the price level and real output in the short run, but in the long run, only the price level will increase. **T F**

23. An inflationary spiral is likely to result from the use of stabilization policies to maintain full employment when the economy is experiencing cost-push inflation. **T F**

24. Of the policies that might be employed to deal with stagflation, wage-price policies were designed to move the Phillips Curve to the right. **T F**

25. Voluntary restraint by business and labor leaders is not apt to be effective in preventing price and wage increases because such restraint requires them to abandon their major goals. **T F**

26. The wage-price guideposts of the Kennedy-Johnson administrations for preventing cost-push inflation were to limit wage increases to the overall rate of increase in labor productivity in the economy. **T F**

27. Supply-side economists contend that Keynesian economics is unable to explain stagflation because costs and aggregate supply play an "active" role in the Keynesian model. **T F**

28. The tax "wedge" to which supply-side economists refer is the difference between the price of a product and the cost of economic resources required to produce it. **T F**

29. If the economy were at point **A** on the Laffer Curve shown below, a decrease in tax rates would increase tax revenues. **T F**

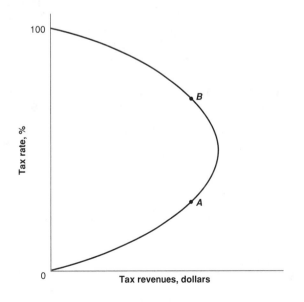

30. The supply-side economists believe that the economy is at a point such as point **B** on the Laffer Curve on the previous page, and that a substantial reduction in tax rates would both increase tax revenues and increase incentives to work, invest, innovate, and take risks.   **T   F**

Circle the letter that corresponds to the best answer.

1. In the Keynesian expenditures-output model it is impossible for the economy to experience:
(a) full employment
(b) inflation
(c) unemployment and inflation
(d) full employment and stable prices

2. As long as aggregate supply remains constant and the economy operates along the intermediate range of the aggregate-supply curve, the greater the increase in aggregate demand:
(a) the greater is the increase in the price level
(b) the greater is the increase in the unemployment rate
(c) the smaller is the increase in real output
(d) the smaller is the increase in employment

3. The conventional Phillips Curve:
(a) shows the inverse relation between the rate of increase in the price level and the unemployment rate
(b) makes it possible for the economy to achieve full employment and stable prices
(c) indicates that prices do not rise until full employment has been achieved
(d) slopes upward from left to right

4. Labor-market adjustments do not eliminate bottleneck problems when there is less than full employment in the economy. Which of the following is *not* one of the reasons for these labor-market imbalances?
(a) unemployed workers often lack the skills or training needed for a new occupation
(b) the demand for workers in the markets in which there are labor shortages is inadequate
(c) there are artificial restrictions which prevent unemployed workers from filling the job openings
(d) unemployed workers do not know of the shortages of workers in other labor markets in the economy

5. If inflation during periods of less than full employment is to be explained by market power, it must be assumed that:
(a) only unions possess considerable market power
(b) only employers possess considerable market power
(c) both unions and employers possess considerable market power
(d) neither unions nor employers possess considerable market power

6. The stabilization policy dilemma illustrated by a Phillips Curve is the mutual inconsistency of:
(a) more employment and price stability
(b) a higher unemployment rate and price stability
(c) inflation and more employment
(d) inflation and a lower unemployment rate

7. Demand-management (monetary and fiscal) policies can be employed to:
(a) shift the Phillips Curve to the right
(b) shift the Phillips Curve to the left
(c) achieve full employment without inflation
(d) reduce the unemployment rate

8. Which of the following was one of the supply-side shocks to the American economy during the 1970s and early 1980s?
(a) the removal of wage and price controls
(b) the appreciation of the dollar
(c) the fall in the price charged by OPEC nations for oil
(d) worldwide agricultural surpluses

9. If the percentage change in the productivity of labor is 2% and the percentage change in nominal-wage rates is 5%, the percentage change in unit labor costs is:
(a) 1%
(b) 3%
(c) 7%
(d) 10%

10. Suppose the overall rate of increase in the productivity of labor in the economy is 4%. If the productivity of labor in a particular industry has increased at a rate of only 3%, the Kennedy-Johnson wage-price guideposts would have allowed this industry:
(a) to increase both the wage rate and the price of its product by 3%
(b) to increase the wage rate by 3% and would have allowed no increase in price
(c) to increase the wage rate by 4% and would have allowed no increase in price
(d) to increase the wage rate by 4% and to increase price by about 1%

11. Supply shocks which cause a leftward shift in the aggregate-supply curve, aggregate demand remaining constant, will:
(a) decrease the price level
(b) decrease the unemployment rate
(c) increase real output
(d) increase both the price level and the unemployment rate

12. Which one of the following would be a factor contributing to the demise of stagflation during the 1982–1989 period?
(a) a lessening of foreign competition

(b) a strengthening of the monopoly power of OPEC

(c) a recession brought on largely by a tight monetary policy

(d) an increase in regulation of airline and trucking industries

13. According to the Keynesian view, the collapse of the traditional unemployment rate-inflation rate tradeoff and the likely shift in the Phillips Curve during the 1980s were the consequence of a:

(a) rightward shift in aggregate demand

(b) rightward shift in aggregate supply

(c) leftward shift in aggregate demand

(d) leftward shift in aggregate supply

14. The natural rate hypothesis suggests that the economy is stable only in the:

(a) short run at the natural rate of unemployment

(b) short run at the natural rate of inflation

(c) long run at the natural rate of unemployment

(d) long run at the natural rate of inflation

15. The theory of adaptive expectations suggests that if increases in nominal wage rates lag behind increases in the price level, and government attempts to reduce unemployment by using fiscal and monetary policies, then employment:

(a) and the price level increase in the long run

(b) remains constant and the price level increases in the short run

(c) increases and the price level remains constant in the short run

(d) remains constant and the price level increases in the long run

16. The rational expectations theorists contend that when government attempts to reduce unemployment by using monetary and fiscal policies, unemployment decreases:

(a) temporarily and the price level rises

(b) permanently and the price level rises

(c) both temporarily and permanently and the price level rises

(d) neither temporarily nor permanently and the price level rises

17. In the view of natural rate theorists, the long-run Phillips Curve is:

(a) horizontal

(b) vertical

(c) upsloping

(d) downsloping

18. Disinflation, or reductions in the rate of inflation, can be explained based on the natural rate conclusion that when the:

(a) actual rate of inflation is lower than the expected rate, the unemployment rate will rise to bring the expected and actual rates into balance

(b) expected rate of inflation is lower than the actual rate, the unemployment rate will rise to bring the expected and actual rates into balance

(c) actual rate of inflation is higher than the expected rate, the unemployment rate will fall to bring the expected and actual rates into balance

(d) expected rate of inflation is higher than the actual rate, the unemployment rate will fall to bring the expected and actual rates into balance

19. The natural rate theory suggests that the aggregate-supply curve:

(a) is stable in the short run so long as nominal wages do not increase in the short run in response to the increase in the price level

(b) unstable in the long run because real wages are continually changing

(c) will shift to the right when the price of capital increases

(d) will shift to the right when nominal wages increase

20. According to new classical thinking, fully anticipated changes in the price level do **not** change the:

(a) level of real output

(b) level of prices

(c) inflexibility of wages and prices

(d) effectiveness of stabilization policy

21. In the short run, demand-pull inflation:

(a) is caused by a rightward shift in the Phillips Curve

(b) is the result of a decrease in aggregate demand

(c) produces an increase in real output

(d) creates price level surprises

22. In the long run, demand-pull inflation will:

(a) decrease the unemployment rate

(b) decrease the level of nominal wages

(c) increase the level of prices

(d) increase real national output

23. A likely result of treating unemployment associated with cost-push inflation by stimulating aggregate demand with monetary and fiscal policies is:

(a) an inflationary spiral

(b) a price level surprise

(c) disinflation

(d) a recession

24. Which of the following is **not** one of the employment and training policies that might help relieve the problem of stagflation?

(a) application of antimonopoly laws to labor unions

(b) removal of discrimination as an obstacle to employment

(c) improvement of the flow of job information between workers without jobs and employers with unfilled positions

(d) expansion of programs that provide job training

25. From the viewpoint of supply-side economists, stagflation is the result of
(a) excessive taxation
(b) government deregulation
(c) a shifting Phillips Curve
(d) unanticipated inflation

26. Supply-side economists of the 1980s thought that the American system of taxes reduced:
(a) unemployment, but increased inflation
(b) incentives to work, save, and invest
(c) transfer payments to the poor and homeless
(d) the effectiveness of wage-price guideposts for the economy

For multiple-choice question 27 refer to the graph used for true-false question 29.

27. A cut in the tax rate from 100% to point **B** on the Laffer curve would tend to:
(a) decrease tax revenues and support the view of supply-side economists
(b) increase tax revenues and support the views of supply-side economists
(c) increase tax revenues and support the views of Keynesian economists
(d) decrease tax revenues and support the views of Keynesian economists

28. In the case of cuts in the tax rates, most mainstream economists take the position that:
(a) the demand-side effects outweigh the supply-side effects
(b) the supply-side effects outweigh the demand-side effects
(c) the demand-side and supply-side effects offset each other
(d) there are only supply-side effects

29. Which one of the following was an element in the Reaganomics program for reducing stagflation in the American economy?
(a) a reduction in defense expenditures
(b) a reduction in personal income tax rates
(c) an increase in rate of growth of the money supply
(d) an increase in the regulation of private business firms

30. One general criticism of supply-side economics during the 1980–1988 period was that:
(a) the growth of the money supply was not slowed to a more moderate rate
(b) all sectors of the economy failed to achieve optimal efficiency from increased regulation by government
(c) the productive capacity of the economy did not expand at a pace faster than historical experience
(d) there was a significant increase in the inflation rate over the period

■ **DISCUSSION QUESTIONS**

1. Why does the simplest Keynesian model imply that the economy may have either unemployment or inflation but will not experience unemployment and inflation simultaneously?

2. What is a Phillips Curve? Explain how a Phillips Curve with a negative slope may be derived by holding aggregate supply constant and mentally increasing aggregate demand.

3. What factors do Keynesian economists point to that underlie the Phillips Curve? How are those factors related to the intermediate range of the aggregate-supply curve?

4. What is the stabilization policy dilemma illustrated by the traditional Phillips Curve? Does the manipulation of aggregate demand through monetary and fiscal policy move the Phillips Curve or cause a movement along the Phillips Curve?

5. Were the rates of inflation and of unemployment consistent with the Phillips Curve in the 1950s and 1960s? What do these two rates suggest about the curve in the 1970s and early 1980s?

6. What were the supply-side shocks to the American economy during the 1970s and early 1980s? How did these shocks affect aggregate supply and the Phillips Curve in the United States?

7. How do expectations of inflation and declines in the productivity of labor affect aggregate supply and the Phillips Curve?

8. When do increases in nominal-wage rates increase unit labor costs, decrease aggregate supply, and increase the price level in the economy?

9. Describe the factors that contributed to stagflation's demise during the 1982–1989 period. What do mainstream economists contend happened to the Phillips Curve during this period compared to the 1970s and early 1980s?

10. Explain the natural rate hypothesis and briefly describe the two variants of the interpretation of the unemployment-inflation rate data of 1960–1991.

11. What does "adaptive" refer to in the theory of adaptive expectations? Illustrate how this theory is used to explain both inflation and disinflation in the economy.

12. What are the views of the adaptive expectationists on:
(a) the effects of expansionary monetary and fiscal policy on employment in the short run and on the short-run Phillips Curve; and,
(b) the long-run Phillips Curve? How do they reach these conclusions?

13. How do rational expectationists believe expansionary monetary and fiscal policy affects the price level and employment in the short run and the long run? What assumptions do they make to reach this conclusion?

14. Compare and contrast the theories of rational expectations and adaptive expectations in terms of views on inflationary expectations, the interpretation of the Phillips Curve, and the effectiveness of demand-management policies.

15. Identify the basic difference between a short-run and a long-run aggregate-supply curve. Explain what happens to aggregate supply when an increase in the price level results in an increase in nominal wages.

16. How do Keynesian economists and new classical economists view wage and price flexibility in the economy? What implications does each group draw about economic policy for the economy?

17. Describe the process of demand-pull inflation in the short run and in the long run. How does demand-pull inflation influence the aggregate-supply curve?

18. What are two generalizations that emerge from the analysis of cost-push inflation? Describe the two scenarios that provide the basis for the generalizations.

19. What are the two kinds of market policies that might be employed to shift the Phillips Curve to the left? Within each of these two categories, what specific things might be done to reduce the causes of inflation?

20. Explain
(a) what is meant by wage-price policy;
(b) why wage-price policy is often called incomes policy; and
(c) the difference between wage-price guideposts and wage-price controls.

21. What
(a) was the wage guidepost and
(b) the price guidepost of the Kennedy-Johnson administrations? Why would adherence to these guideposts by labor and management have limited the rate of inflation?

22. What wages and prices were controlled during the Nixon administration? Why did it seem necessary to control them?

23. State the cases *for* and ***against*** the use of wage-price (or incomes) policy to limit inflation. Build each case upon the two points on which the wage-price policy debate has centered.

24. Why do supply-side economists criticize mainstream or Keynesian economics? Discuss three ways that supply-side economists contend there are tax and transfer payment disincentives in the economy.

25. Draw a Laffer Curve showing the relationship between tax rates and tax revenues. Explain the position of supply-side economists and Keynesian economists using the curve. Outline the three criticisms of the ideas expressed in Laffer Curve.

26. What were the four major steps the Reagan administration proposed to increase employment and reduce inflation in the American economy?

27. Criticize and defend the contention that Reaganomics worked well to reduce stagflation in the United States. Did supply-side economics accomplish its goals under Reaganomics?

28. Summarize the major aspects of competing macroeconomic theories and policy perspectives.

■ **ANSWERS**

Chapter 17 The Inflation-Unemployment Relationship

FILL-IN QUESTIONS

1. full employment, excess, either
2. *a.* increase; *b.* decrease
3. *a.* greater, greater, smaller; *b.* inverse
4. full employment is reached; business firms, labor unions, labor
5. *a.* price level, unemployment; *b.* negative
6. *a.* inflation, unemployment; *b.* increase, increase
7. select a point on the; tradeoff
8. *a.* the dramatic rise in the oil prices of OPEC; *b.* agricultural shortfalls throughout the world (higher agricultural prices); *c.* the devaluation of the dollar; *d.* the abandonment of wage-price controls; *e.* the fall in the rate of growth of labor productivity; *f.* inflationary expectations
9. *a.* increase; *b.* increase
10. higher, rise, decrease, higher, higher
11. *a.* decreased; *b.* price, unemployment; *c.* stagflation
12. (any order) *a.* recession of 1981–1982 with tight monetary policy; *b.* intensive foreign competition suppressed some wages and prices; *c.* deregulation in some industries depressed wages; *d.* a decline in the monopoly power of OPEC
13. opposite, same
14. *a.* right, left; *b.* exist, natural rate, adaptive, rational (either order for last two); *c.* inflation, gradually; *d.* (1) short-run, long-run, natural rate of unemployment, (2) increases; *e.* (1) inflation, real, increase, nominal, (2) a rise, no change
15. *a.* upsloping, vertical; *b.* fixed, variable; *c.* flexible, stable, will, will not, price level; *d.* inflexible, active, high
16. right, increase, increase, short-run, nominal, higher

17. left, increase, decrease, decrease, increase

18. *a.* market, wage, price, supply-side; *b.* left

19. *a.* employment and training; *b.* competition

20. *a.* incomes; *b.* (1) guideposts, (2) controls

21. productivity, unit labor

22. *a.* incentives; *b.* decrease, aggregate supply, rightward

23. increase, decrease, increase, decrease

24. small, demand, supply, inflation, loss

25. cost, wedge, overregulation

26. *a.* substantial reduction in Federal expenditures except those for defense; *b.* reduction in government regulation of private business; *c.* limitation of the rate of growth in the money supply; *d.* sharp reduction in personal and corporate income tax rates

27. *a.* did not, tight, recession, fall; *b.* increased, decreased, deficits; *c.* minimal, about the same as

PROBLEMS AND PROJECTS

1. *a.* 20; *b.* 9; *c.* (it's your choice)

2. 2300; *a.* (1) 160, 2000, (2) 75, 5, 6.25; *b.* (1) 170, 2200, (2), 3, 2.5, (3) 6.25; *c.* (1) 150, 1700, (2) 3, 10, (3) negative

3. *a.* (1) 6, Y_1; (2) Y_1, X_2, PC_1, PC_2, (3) X_2, Y_2, (4) Y_2, 3, X_3, 6, PC_2, PC_3, (5) PC_{LR}; *b.* (1) Z_2, (2) Z_2, X_2, PC_3, PC_2, (3)PC_{LR}

4. P_1, Q_p; *a.* (1) X, P_2, Q_2, (2) AS_1, AS_2, Y, P_3, Q_p, AS_{LR}; *b.* (1) Z, P_2, Q_1, (2) AD_1, AD_2, P_3, Q_p, P_2, P_3, AS_2, (3) P_1, Q_p, AS_2, AS_1

5. *a.* 4; *b.* (1) increase, 1, rise, 1; (2) decrease, 2, fall, 2; (3) increase, 6, rise, 6

SELF-TEST

1. T, p. 324
2. T, p. 325
3. F, p. 325
4. T, p. 325
5. T, pp. 326–327
6. T, p. 326
7. F, p. 327
8. T, p. 327
9. F, pp. 327–328
10. T, p. 329
11. T, p. 329
12. T, p. 330
13. F, p. 330
14. T, p. 331
15. F, p. 331
16. T, p. 332
17. T, p. 333
18. T, p. 333
19. F, p. 335
20. T, p. 336
21. F, p. 336
22. T, p. 336
23. T, p. 338
24. F, p. 338
25. T, p. 340
26. T, p. 340
27. F, p. 341
28. F, pp. 343–344
29. F, pp. 342–343
30. T, p. 341

1. *c*, p. 324
2. *a*, p. 325
3. *a*, pp. 325–326
4. *b*, pp. 326–327
5. *c*, p. 327
6. *a*, p. 327
7. *d*, p. 327
8. *a*, pp. 328–329
9. *b*, p. 329
10. *d*, p. 340
11. *d*, pp. 329–330
12. *c*, p. 330
13. *b*, p. 330
14. *c*, p. 330
15. *d*, pp. 331–332
16. *d*, p. 333
17. *b*, pp. 331–332
18. *a*, p. 333
19. *a*, p. 334
20. *a*, p. 335
21. *c*, p. 336
22. *c*, p. 336
23. *a*, pp. 337–338
24. *a*, pp. 338–339
25. *a*, p. 341
26. *b*, p.341
27. *b*, p. 342
28. *a*, p. 343
29. *b*, p. 344
30. *c*, pp. 344–345

DISCUSSION QUESTIONS

1. pp. 324–325
2. pp. 325–326
3. pp. 326–327
4. p. 327
5. pp. 325–326
6. pp. 327–329
7. p. 327
8. p. 329
9. p. 330
10. pp. 330–333
11. pp. 331–332
12. pp. 331–332
13. p. 333
14. pp. 331–332
15. pp. 334–335
16. pp. 335–336
17. p. 336
18. p. 338
19. pp. 338–340
20. pp. 339–341
21. p. 340
22. pp. 340–341
23. pp. 340–341
24. pp. 341–342
25. pp. 342–343
26. p. 344
27. pp. 344–345
28. p. 345

CHAPTER 18

Budget Deficits and the Public Debt

Over the past thirty years, the Federal government has had budget deficits in all but one year. In the past decade these budget deficits have grown quite large and have caused problems for the American economy. Chapter 18, therefore, looks at data and the issues surrounding budget deficits and the related public debt.

The Federal government can operate with a budget deficit, a budget surplus, or with a balanced budget during a year. Any budget surplus or deficit affects the size of the public (sometimes called national) debt; surpluses decrease it and deficits increase it. After defining a budget deficit and the public debt, three budget philosophies are discussed. You should be aware that the philosophies adopted by the Federal government have a significant impact on output and employment in the economy *and* on the public debt.

The chapter then discusses how three major factors—wars, recessions, and tax cuts—have contributed to increases in the public debt since 1929. The increased public debt resulting from these factors is placed into perspective for you with a quantitative description of the size of the public debt (and interest payments for it) relative to the size of the economy (GDP), and how the public debt in the United States compares with that found in other industrial nations, and measurement problems caused by accounting and inflation.

The two middle sections of the chapter examine the economic implications or consequences of the public debt and deficits. These economic problems do not include bankrupting the Federal government because the government has three ways that it can meet its obligations. Nor does the public debt simply shift the economic burden to future generations because the public debt is all a public credit for the many people who hold that debt in the form of government bonds. Rather, the public debt and payment of interest on the debt contribute to four important problems: increased inequality in income; reduced incentives for work and production; decreased standard of living when part of the debt is paid to foreigners; and less capital investment.

The crowding-out of investment in plant and equipment in the United States is probably the most serious of these four problems. You should understand how crowding-out works and how it may impose a burden on future generations by reducing the growth of the nation's capital stock. Whether it does impose a burden on a future generation depends on how the increased government spending is financed. Raising taxes to pay for increased spending imposes a burden on the current taxpayers, whereas government borrowing to finance increased spending tends to reduce private investment and the future capital stock.

The final section of the chapter is an extensive discussion of the macroeconomic problems with the Federal deficits of the past decade. The recent deficits are of great concern because of their relative large size, high interest cost, and the problems they pose for domestic macroeconomic and trade policy. Be sure that you study each link in the chain of events that lead to the contractions of output and employment in the United States economy as a result of large deficits. There is not any new economic theory in this discussion, just an application of theory you have learned in previous chapters. The chapter then concludes with an explanation of four different policy responses to eliminate or reduce our persistent Federal budget deficits.

■ **CHECKLIST**

When you have studied this chapter you should be able to:

☐ Define a budget deficit (and surplus) and the public debt; and explain how the latter is related to the former.
☐ Explain each of the three budget philosophies.
☐ Identify the three principal causes of the public debt.
☐ Describe the absolute and relative sizes of the public debt and interest payments on it since 1929.
☐ Compare the relative size of the public debt of the United States to public debts in other industrial nations.
☐ Explain how adjusting the size of the nominal public debt for inflation affects the real size of the debt and the real size of a budget deficit; and why the accounting procedures employed by the Federal government do not accurately reflect its financial condition.

☐ Give three reasons why a large public debt will not bankrupt the government.

☐ Discuss whether the public debt imposes a burden on future generations; and why the public debt is for the most part also a public credit.

☐ Enumerate the four real issues related to the public debt.

☐ Compare the effects of an internal debt with the effects of an external debt on the economy.

☐ Describe the crowding-out effect of borrowing to finance an increase in government expenditures and the burden this method of financing expenditures places on future generations.

☐ Compare the burden imposed on future generations by borrowing to finance expenditures with the burden placed on them if the increased expenditures are financed by increased taxation; and qualify in two ways this comparison.

☐ Discuss five concerns with the deficits and the public debt in the past decade.

☐ Trace the effects of borrowing to finance an increase in government expenditures on interest rates, the attractiveness of American securities to foreigners, the international debts of the United States, the international value of the dollar, American exports and imports, and output and employment in the United States.

☐ Contrast the mainstream analysis of recent budget deficits with the analysis by economists who adhere to the Ricardian equivalence theorem.

☐ List four policy responses to the budget deficits of the Federal government and to the public debt of the United States.

☐ Describe the features and history of legislative actions in Congress since 1985 to reduce budget deficits.

☐ Identify two examples of other proposals that have been suggested for use in reducing budget deficits.

☐ Explain why increasing debt is necessary in a growing economy if the economy is to remain at full employment and when it is necessary for the public debt to expand.

■ **CHAPTER OUTLINE**

1. The budget deficit of the Federal government is the amount by which its expenditures exceed its revenues in any year; and the public debt at any time is the sum of the Federal government's previous annual deficits (less any annual surpluses).

2. If the Federal government utilizes fiscal policy to combat recession and inflation its budget is not likely to be balanced in any particular year. Three budgetary philosophies may be adopted by the government; and the adoption of any of these philosophies will affect employment, real output, and the price level of the economy.

   a. Proponents of an annually balanced budget would have government expenditures and tax revenues equal

in every year; such a budget is pro- rather than counter-cyclical; but conservative economists favor it to prevent the expansion of the public sector (and the contraction of the private sector) of the economy without the increased payment of taxes by the public.

   b. Those who advocate a cyclically balanced budget propose matching surpluses (in years of prosperity) with deficits (in depression years) to stabilize the economy; but there is no assurance that the surpluses will equal the deficits over the years.

   c. Advocates of functional finance contend that deficits, surpluses, and the size of the debt are of minor importance; that the goal of full employment without inflation should be achieved regardless of the effects of the necessary fiscal policies upon the budget and the size of the public debt.

3. Any government deficit increases the size of the public debt; and the public debt has grown substantially since 1929.

   a. The growth of the debt is the result of Federal borrowing during wartime and during recessions (when the built-in stability of economy generates budget deficits automatically); and in the early 1980s the debt grew as a result of reductions in tax rates without matching reductions in government expenditures.

   b. The public debt in 1991 was $3.6 trillion.

   (1) The size of the debt as a percentage of the economys GDP did not grow so rapidly as the absolute size of the debt between 1940 and 1991; but relative to the GDP it has increased significantly since the early 1980s.

   (2) Other industrial nations have relative public debts similar to or greater than the United States.

   (3) Since the 1970s the interest payments on the debt (because of increases in the size of the debt and higher interest rates in the economy) have also increased significantly; and interest payments as a percentage of the economy's GDP have grown dramatically.

   (4) About one-fourth of the public debt is owed to government agencies and the Federal Reserve Banks and three-fourths to others; but, more importantly, about 12% of it is owed to foreign citizens, firms, and governments.

   (5) Because the accounting system used by the Federal government records its debts but not its assets the public debt is not a true picture of its financial position; and when adjusted for inflation, the decrease in the real value of its debt can exceed its nominal deficit and result in a real budget surplus.

4. The contentions that a large debt will eventually bankrupt the government and that borrowing to finance expenditures passes the cost on to future generations are false.

   a. The debt cannot bankrupt the government

(1) because the government need not retire (reduce) the debt and can refund (or refinance) it;

(2) because the government has the constitutional authority to levy and collect taxes; and

(3) because the government can always print (or create) money to pay both the principal and the interest on it.

b. The debt cannot shift the burdens of the debt to future generations because the debt is largely internally held, and repayment of any portion of the principal and the payment of interest on it does not reduce the wealth or purchasing power of Americans.

5. But the debt does create real and potential problems in the economy.

a. The payment of interest on the debt probably increases the extent of income inequality.

b. The payment of taxes to finance these interest payments may also reduce the incentives to bear risks, to innovate, to invest, and to save, and so slow economic growth in the economy.

c. The portion of the debt that is externally held requires the repayment of principal and the payment of interest to foreign citizens and institutions and transfers a part of the real output of the American economy to them.

d. An increase in government spending may or may not impose a burden on future generations.

(1) If the increase in government spending is financed by increased personal taxes, the burden of the increased spending is on the present generation whose consumption is reduced; but if it is financed by an increased public debt, the increased borrowing of the Federal government will raise interest rates, crowd-out investment spending, and future generations will inherit a smaller stock of capital goods.

(2) The burden imposed on future generations is lessened if the increase in government expenditures is for real or human capital or if the economy were initially operating at less than full employment (and it stimulates an increase in investment demand).

6. In the 1980s the Federal government incurred deficits and the public debt rose.

a. This caused concern because:

(1) the deficits and the increases in the public debt have grown larger;

(2) recent budget deficits may be understated because surpluses from social security are being used to offset current government spending;

(3) interest costs of the debt have risen;

(4) the deficits have taken place in an economy operating close to full employment, which means there is great potential for the "crowding out" of real private investment and for demand-pull inflation; and

(5) large budget deficits make it difficult for a nation to achieve a balance in its international trade.

b. These large deficits have produced a cause-and-effect chain of events: they have increased interest rates; higher interest rates have crowded-out real private investment and made financial investment by foreigners in the United States more attractive; the latter increased the external debt of the United States and raised the international value of the dollar; and the latter reduced U.S. exports, expanded U.S. imports, and had a contractionary effect on employment and output in the American economy, which softened the overall expansionary impact of a deficit.

c. There are three loose ends to the complex chain of events as described in *b* above:

(1) The inflow of foreign funds helped keep interest rates lower than would otherwise be the case and diminished the size of the crowding-out effect;

(2) High interest rates in the United States resulting from large deficits placed an increased burden on less developed countries, thereby contributing to the world debt problem and banking problems in the United States; and

(3) The unfavorable trade balance meant that the United States had to borrow heavily from other nations and to sell assets to foreign investors, thereby affecting the course of economic growth in the future.

d. The mainstream analysis is contested by some economists who use the Ricardian equivalence theorem to study the effects of budget deficits. They conclude that interest rates will not increase as a result of large Federal deficits because people will increase private saving in anticipation of higher future taxes. The increased saving offsets the increased government borrowing in the money market, and thus the interest rate does not change.

e. A number of policy responses have been suggested to lessen the deficits and the increases in the public debt.

(1) One suggested remedy is an amendment to the U.S. Constitution that would require Congress to balance the Federal budget each year.

(2) In December of 1985, Congress passed the Gramm-Rudman-Hollings (GRH) Act which required it to reduce the deficits annually and to balance the budget by 1991 and which mandated automatic reductions in spending when Congress and the President cannot agree on how to achieve the targeted deficit reductions. This act was revised in 1987 to achieve a balanced budget by 1993.

(3) The Budget Reconciliation Act of 1990 replaced the GRH legislation with a package of tax increases and spending cuts for reducing the budget deficits from 1991 to 1996 by $500 billion. In addition, the Budget Enforcement Act of 1990 required that new legislation that increased spending or decreased taxes must be "paid for" by legislative actions to decrease other government spending or increase other taxes.

(4) And several other proposals have been considered, such as the privatization of some government assets and programs by selling them to private business firms, or giving the President the power to veto spending measures on a line-item basis.

f. Despite the problems associated with deficits and the public debt, private and public debt has an important role to play: it absorbs the saving from a growing economy at full employment and sustains the aggregate expenditures of consumers, businesses, and governments at the full-employment level; and if consumers and firms do not borrow sufficient amounts, the public debt must be increased to maintain full employment and economic growth in the economy.

■ **IMPORTANT TERMS**

Budget deficit	Gramm-Rudman-Hollings (GRH) Act
Public debt	
Annually balanced budget	Budget Reconciliation Act of 1990
Cyclically balanced budget	Budget Enforcement Act of 1990
Functional finance	Privatization
External debt	Line-item veto
Crowding-out effect	
Balanced Budget Amendment	

■ **FILL-IN QUESTIONS**

1. The budget deficit of the Federal government in any year is equal to its (expenditures, revenues) _____ less its _____ in that year; and the public debt is equal to the sum of the Federal government's past budget _____ less its budget _____.

2. An annually balanced budget is (pro-, counter-) _____ cyclical because governments tend to (raise, lower) _____ taxes and to _____ their purchases of goods and services during a recession (and to do just the opposite during an inflation).

3. A cyclically balanced budget suggests that to ensure full employment without inflation, the government incur deficits during periods of _____ and surpluses during periods of _____ with the deficits and surpluses equaling each other over the business cycle.

4. Functional finance has as its main goal the achievement of _____; and would regard budget _____ and increases in the _____ as of secondary importance.

5. The principal causes of the public debt are past _____ and _____ and recent discretionary reductions in tax _____.

6. There are several quantitative aspects to the public debt:

a. In 1991, it is equal to about $_____ trillion and to about _____% of GDP, and the annual interest charges on this debt are about $_____ billion and equal to about _____% of GDP.

b. The public debt as a percentage of GDP was (higher, lower) _____ in Japan and Canada, and _____ in Germany and the United Kingdom.

c. Federal government agencies and our central banks hold about (one-fourth, three-fourths) _____ of the debt, and commercial banks, financial institutions, and private individuals hold about _____ of the debt.

d. The majority of the public debt is (internal, external) _____ because foreigners hold only about _____% of the public debt.

e. The public debt and budget deficits are subject to measurement problems because the accounting procedures used by the Federal government reflect (assets, debts) _____ but do not reflect its _____.

f. Robert Eisner demonstrated that if the Federal government used a capital budget which included depreciation costs, then the Federal budget deficit would be (increased, decreased) _____; and, if the Federal budget was adjusted for the effects of inflation, the budget deficit would be _____.

7. The possibility that the Federal government will go bankrupt is a false issue. It need not (reduce, refinance) _____ its debt; and it can retire maturing securities by _____ them or by creating _____. The government can also levy and collect _____ to pay its debts.

8. As long as the government expenditures which lead

to the increase in the public debt are not financed by borrowing from foreigners, the public debt of the United States is also an _____ of the American people who own government securities; and the cost of a government program financed by borrowing from the American public is equal to their decreased _____ of goods and services and is a burden on (the present, a future) _____ generation.

9. The public debt is a burden on an economy if it is (internally, externally) _____ held. It and the payment of interest on it may, however (increase, decrease) _____ income inequality in the economy, dampen the _____ to work, take risks, save, and invest in the economy, and have a _____ effect on investment.

10. A public debt which is internally held imposes a burden on future generations if the borrowing done to finance an increase in government expenditures (increases, decreases) _____ interest rates, _____ investment spending, and leaves future generations with a smaller stock of _____ goods.
   a. But if the increased government expenditures are financed by an increase in the taxes on personal income, the present generation will have fewer _____ goods and the burden of the increased government expenditures will be on the _____ generation.
   b. These generalizations are subject to two qualifications: The size of the burden of increased government expenditures financed by borrowing on future generations is weakened if the government expenditures finance increases in physical or human _____ or if the economy had been operating at (full, less than full) _____ employment.

11. The increased concern of the public with Federal deficits and the expanding public debt in the 1980s is the result of the large _____ of these deficits, the use of _____ surpluses that offset and understate the deficit, the rising interest _____ of the public debt, inappropriate macroeconomic _____ for dealing with the deficit, and the difficulty of achieving a _____ in international trade.

12. Large deficits during times of full employment raise two problems. First, there is great potential for the _____ of real private investment. Second, the stimulus to the economy from the deficits may create the conditions for _____

13. Large budget deficits tend to increase _____ and decrease _____ to create an unfavorable trade balance. This trade imbalance has contributed to making the United States a (creditor, debtor) _____ nation and (increased, decreased) _____ the selling of domestic assets to foreign investors.

14. The deficits of the Federal government tend to (increase, decrease) _____ interest rates in the money markets.
   a. This change in interest rates (expands, contracts) _____ private investment spending and makes financial investments by foreigners in the U.S. (more, less) _____ attractive.
   b. This change in the financial investments of foreigners in the U.S. (increases, decreases) _____ the external debts of the U.S. and (raises, lowers) _____ the international value of the dollar.
   c. This change in the international value of the dollar (expands, contracts) _____ American exports, _____ American imports, and _____ *net* exports.
   d. This change in American net exports has a(n) (expansionary, contractionary) _____ effect on real output and employment in the United States.
   e. The overall expansionary effect of a budget deficit may be reduced somewhat by the _____ effect and the _____ effect.

15. There are other points to be considered in the chain of events from the budget deficits of the 1980s. First, the inflow of funds from abroad (raised, lowered) _____ domestic interest rates than would otherwise be the case and therefore (strengthened, weakened) _____ the crowding-out effect. Second, the high interest rates in the United States placed greater burden on (developed, underdeveloped) _____ countries and created debt problems for the _____ system. Third, the value of imports became (greater than, less than) _____, so the United States had to borrow from foreigners and sold more assets.

16. A few economists disagree with mainstream analysis of the problems caused by budget deficits. From their perspective:

    a. financing a deficit by borrowing is the same as financing a deficit through tax increases because of their use of the _____ theorem;

    b. and they think that with a budget deficit interest rate (will, will not) _____ increase because and private saving will increase in anticipation of higher future taxes, and this saving increase will (increase, offset) _____ the borrowing demands of government in credit markets.

17. Two policy responses to the problems of large budget deficits of the Federal government are a _____ admendment to balance the budget, and the _____ Act of 1985 that set deficit reduction targets.

18. In 1990, Congress sought to trim $500 billion from the 1991–1996 deficits with the passage of the _____ Act. This legislation was supplemented by the _____ Act that established a "pay-as-you-go" test for financing increased government spending or reducing taxes.

19. Other policy responses related to the deficit problem have been considered. Two topics that have received attention are the _____ of government assets and programs, and granting the President the power to use _____ on spending proposals by the Congress.

20. Public and private debts play a positive role if they absorb a sufficient amount of _____ to enable an economy that is (stationary, growing) _____ to remain at _____

■ PROBLEMS AND PROJECTS

1. The table below gives data on the public debt and the GDP for selected five-year periods from 1961–1991. Data for the public debt and the GDP are in billions of dollars.

    a. Calculate the ratio of the public debt to GDP expressed as a percentage of GDP. Enter the numbers into the column of the table below.

Year	Debt	GDP	Debt/GDP
1961	$ 292.6	$ 531.8	_____%
1966	328.5	769.8	_____
1971	408.2	1097.2	_____
1976	629.0	1768.4	_____
1981	994.3	3030.6	_____
1986	2120.1	4268.6	_____
1991	3559.0	5671.8	_____

    b. On the graph below, plot the year on the horizontal axis and plot the public debt as a percentage of GDP on the vertical axis.

    c. Explain what happened to the public debt as a percentage of GDP over the thirty-year period.

_____

_____

_____

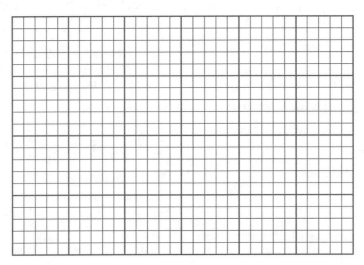

2. The table below gives data on interest rates and investment demand in a hypothetical economy.

Interest rate	I_{d1}	I_{d2}
10%	$250	$300
8	300	350
6	350	400
4	400	450
2	450	500

a. Use the I_{d1} schedule. Assume that the government needs to finance a budget deficit and this public borrowing increases the interest rate from 4% to 6%. How much crowding-out of private investment will occur?

_____

b. Now assume that the deficit is used to improve the performance of the economy, and that as a consequence, the investment-demand schedule changes from I_{d1} to I_{d2}. At the same time, the interest rate rises from 4% to 6% as the government borrows money to finance the deficit. How much crowding out of private

investment will occur in this case? _____

c. Graph the two investment-demand schedules on the graph below and show the difference between the two events. Put the interest rate on the vertical axis and the quantity of investment demanded on the horizontal axis.

3. Columns (1) and (2) in the table below are the investment-demand schedule and show planned investment (_I_) at different rates of interest (_i_). Assume the marginal propensity to consume in the economy is 0.8.

(1) _i_	(2) _I_	(3) _I'_
.08	$115	$125
.07	140	150
.06	165	175
.05	190	200
.04	215	225

a. If the Federal government were to spend an additional $20 for goods and services the equilibrium real

GDP would (increase, decrease) _____ by

$_____

b. If the Federal government had obtained the additional $20 by
(1) increasing taxes by $20 the equilibrium real GDP

would have (increased, decreased) _____ a total of

$_____;
(2) borrowing $20 in the money market and this borrowing had increased the interest rate from 5% to 6%, (a) planned investment spending would have (in-

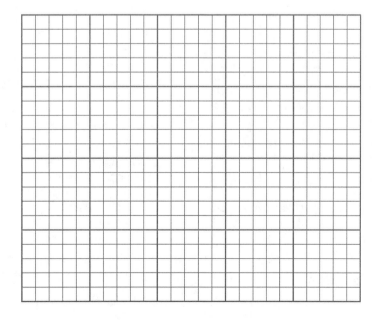

creased, decreased) _____ by $_____,

(b) the equilibrium real GDP would have _____

by $_____, and

(c) the net effect of the increased government spending of the $20 borrowed in the money market would

have been to _____ the equilibrium real

GDP by $_____

c. But if the government deficit-spending had improved business profit expectations and shifted the investment-demand schedule to the one shown in columns (1) and (3) in the table above the total effect of the increased government spending of the $20 borrowed in the money market would have been to

_____ the equilibrium real GDP by $_____

■ SELF-TEST

Circle the T if the statement is true; the F if it is false.

1. The budget deficit of the Federal government in any year is equal to its revenues less its expenditures. T (F)

2. There is no assurance that a nation can both use fiscal policy to promote full employment and balance its budget cyclically. (T) F

3. Proponents of functional finance argue that a balanced budget, whether it is balanced annually or over the business cycle, is of minor importance when compared with the objective of full employment without inflation. (T) F

4. The primary reason for the increase in the public debt since 1929 has been because of government spending associated with recessions. 3.6 trillion (T) (F)

5. The public debt was about $1800 billion in 1991. T (F)

6. Between 1940 and the present both the public debt and the interest charges on this debt as percentages of GDP have decreased. T (F)

7. About one-tenth of the public debt is currently held by foreigners and about three-fourths of it is held by agencies of the Federal government and the American central banks. T (F)

8. Inflation increases the **real** value of the **nominal** public debt. (T) (F)

9. A large public debt will bankrupt the Federal government. T (F)

10. The public debt is a public credit. (T) F

11. Selling government securities to foreigners to finance increased expenditures by the Federal government imposes a burden on future generations. (T) F

12. The crowding-out effect is caused by a rise in interest rates resulting from an increase in government borrowing in the money market to finance government expenditures. (T) F

13. Financing increased government expenditures by increasing personal taxes imposes a burden on future generations. T (F)

14. Crowding-out shifts the investment-demand curve to the left. 3 5 6 (T) (F)

15. Higher interest rates in the United States not only crowd-out real investment but make financial investment by foreigners in the United States less attractive. T (F)

16. Increases in the international value of the dollar tend to have an expansionary effect on output and employment in the United States. T (F)

17. New classical economists who use the Ricardian equivalence theorem in their analysis believe that large Federal deficits have significant stimulative effects on the economy. T (F)

18. The Gramm-Rudman-Hollings Act that was revised in 1987 was an attempt to set deficit targets to achieve a balanced budget by 1993. (T) F

19. The Budget Reconciliation Act of 1990 is a constitutional amendment that requires a balanced Federal budget by 1996. (T) F

20. Privatization would allow the Federal government to acquire the assets of profitable privately owned business firms in order to increase the revenues and reduce the budget deficits of the Federal government. T (F)

21. The amount of saving done at full employment increases in a growing economy. (T) F

22. To maintain full employment in a growing economy it is necessary for the total of public and private debt to increase. (T) F

Circle the letter that corresponds to the correct answer.

1. The public debt is the sum of all previous:
(a) expenditures of the Federal government
(b) budget deficits of the Federal government
(c) budget deficits less the budget surpluses of the Federal government
(d) budget surpluses less the current budget deficit of the Federal government

2. Which of the following would involve reducing government expenditures and increasing tax rates during a recession?
(a) an annually balanced budget policy

(b) functional finance

(c) a cyclically balanced budget policy

(d) a policy employing built-in stability

3. What three factors largely explain why the public debt has increased since 1929?

(a) interest payments on the public debt, spending for social security, and depreciation of the dollar

(b) deficit spending to finance a war, effects of automatic stabilizers on the budget during recessions, and tax cuts not offset by spending cuts

(c) deficit spending caused by depressions, borrowing funds from other nations, and increased government spending to cover economic problems such as the saving and loan bailout

(d) interest payments on the public debt, government spending for welfare programs, and the crowding-out of investment spending

4. Since the 1980s, the public debt relative to GDP has:

(a) increased and interest payments relative to GDP has increased

(b) decreased and interest payments relative to GDP have decreased

(c) decreased, but interest payments relative to GDP have decreased

(d) increased, but interest payments relative to GDP have decreased

5. As a percentage of the gross domestic product, the public debt and interest on the debt were in 1991, respectively, about:

(a) 49% and 1%

(b) 49% and 2%

(c) 53% and 2%

(d) 63% and 3%

6. Which nation has the larger public debt relative to its domestic output in 1990?

(a) United States

(b) German

(c) United Kingdom

(d) Japan

7. The annual interest payments on the public debt in 1991 were about:

(a) $188 billion

(b) $119 billion

(c) $100 billion

(d) $89 billion

8. The accounting procedures used by the Federal government record:

(a) only its assets

(b) only its debts

(c) both its assets and debts

(d) its net worth

9. Inflation is a tax on:

(a) the holders of the public debt, and it reduces the real size of the public debt.

(b) the holders of the public debt, and expands the real size of the public debt.

(c) the Federal government, and reduces the real size of the public debt.

(d) the Federal government, and expands the real size of the public debt.

10. The public debt cannot bankrupt the Federal government because the Federal government:

(a) has the power to levy taxes

(b) is able to refinance the debt.

(c) can create money to repay the debt and pay the interest on it

(d) all of the above

11. Incurring an internal debt to finance a war does not pass the cost of the war on to future generations because:

(a) the opportunity cost of the war is borne by the generation that fights it

(b) the government need not pay interest on internally held debts

(c) there is never a need for government to refinance the debt

(d) wartime inflation reduces the relative size of the debt

12. Which of the following would be a consequence of the retirement of the internally held portion of the public debt?

(a) a reduction in the nation's productive capacity

(b) a reduction in the nation's standard of living

(c) a redistribution of the nation's wealth among its citizens

(d) an increase in aggregate expenditures in the economy

13. Which of the following is an important consequence of the public debt of the United States?

(a) it increases incentives to work and invest

(b) it transfers a portion of the American output of goods and services to foreign nations

(c) it reduces income inequality in the United States

(d) it leads to greater saving at every level of disposable income

14. The crowding-out effect of borrowing in the money market to finance an increase in government expenditures:

(a) reduces current private investment expenditures

(b) decreases the rate at which the privately owned stock of real capital increases

(c) imposes a burden on future generations

(d) does all of the above

15. The crowding-out effect of government borrowing to finance its increased expenditures is reduced:

(a) when the economy is operating at less than full employment

(b) when the expenditures expand human capital in the economy

(c) when the government's deficit financing improves the profit expectations of business firms

(d) when any one or more of the above are true

16. Which one of the following is **not** one of the sources of the concern with the deficits of the Federal government and the growth of the public debt during the 1980s?

(a) the large increases in the size of the deficits and in the public debt

(b) the operation of the economy substantially below full employment throughout the decade

(c) the rising interest costs of the debt

(d) problems with the balance of trade

17. Deficits in the early 1990s were primarily increased by:

(a) an increase in spending for social security

(b) a recession and a bailout of the savings and loan industry

(c) an increased demand by foreigners for government securities

(d) an easy money policy of the Federal Reserve

18. The increased foreign demand for American securities that results from higher interest rates in the United States during the 1980s:

(a) increases the external debts of the United States and the international value of the dollar

(b) increases the external debts of the United States and decreases the international value of the dollar

(c) decreases the external debts of the United States and increases the international value of the dollar

(d) decreases the external debts of the United States and the international value of the dollar

19. When the international value of the dollar rises:

(a) American exports tend to increase

(b) American imports tend to decrease

(c) American net exports tend to decrease

(d) all of the above tend to occur

20. High interest rates in the United States which were related to Federal budget deficits of the 1980s tended to:

(a) contribute to the debt burden of underdeveloped nations that traded with the United States

(b) reduce the flow of funds from foreign nations to the United States

(c) increase the long-term economic growth and domestic investment of foreign nations that transferred funds to the United States

(d) enable the United States to become a major creditor nation for the first time in many decades

21. Some economists use the Ricardian equivalence theorem to argue that recent Federal deficits have:

(a) had desirable effects on the economy because of the fiscal policy stimulus

(b) had little effect on the economy because households respond to budget deficits by increasing their present saving in anticipation of higher future taxes

(c) created a sizable trade imbalance with other nations and contributed to the selling of United States assets to foreigners

(d) caused interest rates to rise and crowded-out private investment

22. The Gramm-Rudman-Hollings Act of 1985 and its revision in 1987 require that:

(a) the sizes of the Federal budget deficits be reduced annually

(b) the Federal budget be balanced by 1993

(c) the expenditures of the Federal government be automatically reduced if Congress and the President cannot agree on how to reach the targeted reductions in the budget deficits

(d) all of the above

23. The Budget Reconciliation Act of 1990 was:

(a) a failed attempt by Congress to balance the 1990 budget

(b) a package of tax increases and spending cuts designed to reduce budget deficits by $500 billion between 1991 and 1996

(c) a cut in marginal tax rate from 50% to 28% that was enacted to stimulate work, investment, and saving

(d) an accord between Congress and the Federal Reserve to finance the borrowing needs of the Federal government

24. Two serious proposals that have been suggested to help reduce the Federal budget deficit are:

(a) privatization and the line-item veto

(b) changes in accounting practices and use of social security surpluses

(c) a moratorium on interest payments on the public debt and a reduction in interest rates

(d) using countercyclical fiscal policy and increasing the supply of money

■ DISCUSSION QUESTIONS

1. What is the difference between the (Federal) budget deficit and the public debt?

2. Explain why an annually balanced budget is not "neutral" and how it can intensify, rather than reduce, the tendencies for GDP to rise and fall.

3. How does a cyclically balanced budget philosophy differ from the philosophy of functional finance? Why do advocates of functional finance argue that budget deficits and a mounting national debt are of secondary importance?

4. How big is the public debt of the United States absolutely and relative to the GDP? How large are the interest payments on this debt absolutely and relative to the GDP? What has happened to the size of the debt and the interest payments on it absolutely and relatively since 1930 and since 1980? Why have these changes occurred?

5. In what way do the accounting procedures of the Federal government misstate its actual financial position (its net worth)? How does inflation affect the *real* size of the public debt and the real size of the Federal government's budget deficits?

6. Why can't the public debt result in the bankruptcy of the Federal government?

7. Explain the difference between an internally held and an externally held public debt. If the debt is internally held government borrowing to finance a war does not pass the cost of the war on to future generations? Why?

8. How does the public debt and the payment of interest on this debt affect:
  (a) the distribution of income and
  (b) incentives?

9. Who owns the public debt? What percentage is held by the two major groups? What percentage of the public debt is held by foreigners? What are the economic implications of the portion of the public debt held by foreigners?

10. How can deficit financing impose a burden on future generations? Why don't increases in government expenditures financed by increased personal taxes impose the same burden on future generations? What will lessen the burden on future generations of deficit financing?

11. What heightened the concern of the public over recent budget deficits and the increase in the public debt?

12. How do budget deficits (and the increase in the public debt) affect:
  (a) interest rates;
  (b) planned domestic investment in real capital and the financial investment of foreigners in American securities;
  (c) the external debts of the United States and the international value of the dollar;
  (d) American exports and imports of goods and services; and
  (e) employment and real output in the American economy?

13. Discuss other deficit-related effects on interest rates and crowding out, interest rates and the international debt crisis, and the trade imbalance and the borrowing needs of the United States.

14. Explain how an economist would use the Ricardian

equivalence theorem to explain the effects of large budget deficits on the economy.

15. Explain the policy responses that have been suggested for the Federal budget deficits and the increasing public debt. What were the chief provisions of the Gramm-Rudman-Hollings Act of 1985? How was the act revised in 1987? Explain the key features of the Budget Reconciliation Act of 1990 and the Budget Enforcement Act of 1990.

16. How would privatization or a line-item veto help reduce budget deficits?

17. What tends to happen to the amount of saving done at full employment as the full-employment real GDP grows? Why, in a growing economy, must debt increase in order to maintain full employment and economic growth?

■ **ANSWERS**

Chapter 18 Budget Deficits and the Public Debt

FILL-IN QUESTIONS

1. expenditures, revenues, deficits, surpluses

2. pro-, raise, lower

3. recession, inflation

4. full employment without inflation, deficits, public debt

5. wars, recessions, rates

6. *a.* $3.6, 63, 188, 3.3; *b.* higher, lower; one-fourth, three-fourths; *d.* internal, 12; *e.* debts, assets; *f.* decreased, decreased

7. reduce, refinancing, money, taxes

8. asset, consumption, the present

9. externally, increase, incentives, crowding-out

10. increases, decreases, capital; *a.* consumer, present; *b.* capital, less than full

11. size, social security, cost, policies, balance

12. crowding-out, demand-pull inflation

13. imports, exports, debtor, increased

14. increase; *a.* contracts, more; *b.* increases, raises; *c.* contracts, expands, contracts; *d.* contractionary; *e.* crowding-out, net export (either order)

15. lowered, weakened, underdeveloped, banking, greater than

16. Ricardian equivalence, will not, offset

17. constitutional amendment, Gramm-Rudman-Hollings (GRH)

18. Budget Reconciliation, Budget Enforcement

19. privatization, line-item veto

20. saving, growing, full employment

PROBLEMS AND PROJECTS

1. *a.* 55, 43, 37, 36, 33, 50, 63; *c.* The debt as a percent of GDP fell from 1961 to 1981 and then rose substantially from 1981 to 1991.

2. *a.* $50 billion; *b.* none

3. *a.* increase, 100; *b.* (1) increased, 20, (2) (a) decreased, 25, (b) decreased, 125, (c) decrease, 25; *c.* increase, 25

SELF-TEST

1. F, p. 349
2. T, pp. 350–351
3. T, p. 351
4. T, p. 351
5. F, p. 352
6. F, pp. 353; 362
7. F, p. 353
8. F, p. 353
9. F, p. 354
10. T, p. 354
11. T, p. 355
12. T, pp. 355–356
13. F, p. 356
14. F, p. 356
15. F, p. 359
16. F, p. 359
17. F, p. 360
18. T, pp. 360–361
19. F, p. 361
20. F, p. 361
21. T, p. 362
22. T, p. 362

1. *c,* p. 349
2. *a,* p. 350
3. *b,* p. 351
4. *a,* pp. 352–353
5. *d,* p. 352
6. *d,* p. 353
7. *a,* p. 352
8. *b,* p. 353
9. *a,* p. 353
10. *d,* p. 354
11. *a,* p. 354
12. *c,* p. 355
13. *b,* p. 355
14. *d,* pp. 355–356
15. *d,* pp. 356–357
16. *b,* pp. 357–358
17. *b,* p. 357
18. *a,* p. 359
19. *c,* p. 359
20. *a,* pp. 359–360
21. *b,* p. 360
22. *d,* pp. 360–361
23. *b,* p. 361
24. *a,* pp. 361–362

DISCUSSION QUESTIONS

1. pp. 349–350
2. p. 350
3. pp. 350–351
4. pp. 352–353
5. p. 353
6. p. 354
7. pp. 354–355
8. p. 355
9. pp. 353–354
10. p. 356
11. pp. 357–358
12. pp. 358–359
13. pp. 359–360
14. p. 360
15. pp. 360–361
16. p. 361
17. p. 362

CHAPTER 19

Economic Growth

Chapter 19 is the last of four chapters that discuss macro-economic issues and problems. While the previous chapters focused primarily on short-term instability in output and the price level, this chapter looks at the longer-term problem of economic growth.

After briefly defining and explaining the significance of growth, the text analyzes the six factors that make growth possible. The four **supply** factors increase the output potential of the economy. Whether the economy actually produces its full potential—that is, whether the economy has both full employment and full production—depends upon two other factors: the level of aggregate expenditures (the **demand** factor) and the efficiency with which the economy reallocates resources (the **allocative** factor).

The next section of the chapter places the factors contributing to economic growth in graphical perspective with the use of two familiar models. The production possibilities model was originally presented in Chapter 2 and is now used to discuss how the two major supply factors—labor input and labor productivity—shift the production possibilities curve outward. The second model is the aggregate-demand and aggregate-supply framework that was first explained in Chapter 9 and was discussed in more detail in Chapter 17. Here you learn how both the short-run and the long-run shifts in aggregate supply combined with shifts in aggregate demand (and the supply and demand factors underlying those shifts) affect the output and the price level.

The growth record of the United States has been impressive both in terms of increases in real GDP and in real GDP per capita. What accounts for this long-term economic growth of the United States? First, the American population and the size of its labor force have grown. Second and more important, the productivity of the labor force in the United States has increased. The increase in the productivity of labor is the result of technological advances; the expansion of the stock of capital goods in the American economy; the improved education and training of its labor force; economies of scale; the reallocation of resources; the generous quantities of natural resources with which the American economy was endowed; and its social, cultural, and political environment. (Note, however,

that the regulations of government tend to slow the rates at which the productivity of labor and the output of the economy grow.) But in addition to the increases in the ability of the economy to produce goods and services made possible by the supply and allocative factors, aggregate expenditures have expanded sufficiently (though unsteadily) to bring about most of the actual growth made possible by the increases in the quantity and the productivity of labor.

The rate of increase in labor productivity was less in the 1970s and 1980s compared with previous decades, and also less when compared with some of our major trading partners. This slowdown in labor productivity is significant for several reasons related to our standard of living, inflation, the competitiveness of the United States in world markets. As you will learn, the decline stems from at least five major problems experienced by the economy in the past two decades. Although productivity growth has increased modestly in recent years, the resurgence may be transitory and low productivity may continue to limit the long-term potential for economic growth in the American economy.

The latter part of Chapter 19 asks an important question—whether further economic growth is **desirable** in the already affluent American economy. The controversy over whether growth should be a social goal with a high priority in the United States has, of course, two sides to it. The case in defense of and the case against growth are both considered. You will have to decide for yourself which case is the stronger and whether the social benefits from growth are worth the costs. And should you think that economic growth is desirable, the final section of the chapter outlines three policy approaches for achieving growth.

Actually, Chapter 19 contains very little that is really new. It uses a few of the ideas, terms, and theories found in earlier chapters to explain what makes an economy capable of growing (that is, what increases the size of its full-employment or capacity output) and what is necessary if it is actually to grow (that is, if it is to produce all which its expanding capital allows). You also are presented with historical data on the United States economy to place economic growth in a long-run perspective. With careful reading you should have little or no trouble with Chapter 19, providing you have done a good job on the earlier chapters.

■ CHECKLIST

When you have studied this chapter you should be able to:

☐ Distinguish between employment theory and growth economics.
☐ Define economic growth in two different ways.
☐ Explain why economic growth is important to any economy.
☐ Use the "rule of 70" to demonstrate how different growth rates affect real domestic output over time.
☐ Identify four supply factors in economic growth.
☐ Explain demand and allocative factors in economic growth.
☐ Illustrate graphically how economic growth affects supply and demand curves.
☐ State the two fundamental means by which an economy can increase its real GDP.
☐ Show graphically how economic growth shifts the production possibilities curve.
☐ Describe the growth record of the American economy since 1940 and its rates of economic growth since World War II.
☐ Compare the relative importance of the two major means of increasing the real GDP in the United States since 1929.
☐ Enumerate the several sources of the growth of the productivity of labor in the United States since 1929; and state their relative importance in the growth of its real national income.
☐ Identify the chief detriment to the increase in labor productivity; and state by how much it and other factors have slowed the growth of real national income in the United States since 1929.
☐ Explain why the actual rate of growth in the United States has been less than its potential rate of growth and why it has been unstable.
☐ Give three reasons why the slowdown in productivity is significant.
☐ Enumerate the five principal causes of the slowdown in the rate of labor productivity in the United States.
☐ Discuss whether there has been a resurgence of productivity.
☐ Present the case against more economic growth in the United States.
☐ Defend more economic growth.
☐ Outline the three types of economic policies that might be utilized to stimulate growth in the United States.

■ CHAPTER OUTLINE

1. While employment theory and stabilization policy are concerned with the short run and an economy with a fixed productive capacity, growth economics deals with the long run and changes in productive capacity over time.
  a. Economic growth means an increase in either the total or the per capita real output of an economy; and is measured in terms of the annual percentage rate of growth of either total or per capita real output.
  b. Economic growth is important because it lessens the burden of scarcity; it provides the means of satisfying existing wants more fully and fulfilling new wants.
  c. One or two percentage point differences in the rate of growth result in substantial differences in annual increases in the economy's output.

2. Whether economic growth *can* occur depends on supply, demand, and allocative factors:
  a. supply factors include the quantity and quality of resources (natural, human, and capital), and technology;
  b. demand factors influence the level of aggregate demand in the economy that is important for sustaining full employment of resources;
  c. allocative factors affect the efficient use of resources to obtain maximum production of goods and services that are valued by society.

3. Two familiar economic models can be used for the analysis of economic growth.
  a. In the production possibilities model, economic growth shifts the production possibilities curve outward because of improvement in supply factors that:
  (1) increase real output by increasing the labor inputs and by increasing the productivity of labor (in equation terms: total output = worker-hours × labor productivity);
  (2) however, whether the economy operates on the frontier of the curve depends on demand factors affecting the full employment of resources and allocative factors affecting full production.
  b. In the aggregate-demand and aggregate-supply model, economic growth is also affected by these supply, demand, and allocative factors.
  (1) Supply factors that contribute to economic growth shift the vertical long-run aggregate supply to the right in the model.
  (2) But since the price level has increased over time, this suggests that the increase in potential output has been accompanied by an even greater shift in aggregate demand (and its underlying demand and allocative factors).

4. Over the last sixty years, the growth record of the American economy has been impressive; but economic growth in America has been less impressive than the record of many advanced industrialized nations in recent decades.

a. Economic well-being may be understated by economic growth figures because the figures do not take into account improvements in product quality or increases in leisure time.

b. But growth may have adverse effects on the environment or the quality of life that are not reflected in growth figures, thus the figures may overstate the benefits of growth.

5. Denison estimates that between 1929 and 1982 the real national income in the United States grew at an average annual rate of 2.9%.

a. Two-thirds of this growth was the result of the increased productivity of labor, and one-third of it was the result of the increased quantity of labor employed in the economy.

b. During this period the American population and its labor force expanded; and despite decreases in the length of the workweek and birthrates, the increased participation of women in the labor force and the growth of its population continue to expand the size of the labor force by two million workers a year.

c. Technological advance is combining given amounts of resources in new ways that result in a larger output; and during the 1929–1982 period it accounted for 28% of the increase in real national income.

d. Saving and investment have expanded the American economy's stock of capital; increased the quantity of tools, equipment, and machinery with which each worker has to work; and accounted for 19% of the increase in real national income between 1929 and 1982.

e. Increased investment in human capital (in the training and education of workers) expands the productivity of workers; and accounted for 14% of the 1929–1982 increase in real national income.

f. Economies of scale and the improved allocation of resources also expand the productivity of workers; and in the American economy 9% and 8%, respectively, of the increase in real national income between 1929 and 1982 can be attributed to them.

g. But such detriments (or deterrents) to the growth of productivity as the government regulation of industry, of pollution, and of worker health and safety divert investment away from productivity-increasing additions to capital; and they accounted for a negative 9% of the increased real national income in the 1929–1982 period.

h. Such difficult-to-quantify factors as its general abundance of natural resources and social-cultural-political environment have also contributed to economic growth in the United States

i. While actual growth in real national income during the 1929–1982 period averaged 2.9% a year, it would have been (an estimated) 3.2% a year if aggregate demand had not at times fallen below its full-employment levels.

j. Increases in the productivity of labor have been more important than increases in the quantity of labor employed in expanding real national income in the American economy; but these increases in productivity cannot be taken for granted, are not automatic, and are the results of the changes in the economy described above.

6. The annual rates of growth in labor productivity in the United States declined substantially during the 1970s, and rose only modestly during the 1980s and early 1990s. Productivity rates achieved in the United States are also less than those found in other major industrial nations such as Japan or Germany.

a. The slowdown in the growth of labor productivity is significant.

b. The suggested causes of the productivity slowdown have included:

(1) labor quality—a decline in the quality (education, training, and experience) of the American labor force;

(2) less technological progress—a decline in research and development expenditures as a percentage of GDP;

(3) low investment—reduced investment in capital goods as a percentage of GDP than in previous periods stemming from low saving rates, import competition, regulation, and less spending for infrastructure;

(4) high energy prices—higher prices in 1973–1975 and 1978–1980 increased production costs and had inflationary and adverse macro policy effects on the economy.

(5) adversarial labor relations—worker and management relations can be adversial rather than cooperative, especially when compared with the Japanese.

c. Productivity improved in the 1981–1990 period when compared with the 1973–1981 period, but it is not known if this modest "resurgence" is permanent or transitory.

7. Americans today debate whether economic growth is or is not desirable.

a. Those opposed to rapid economic growth contend that

(1) it pollutes the environment;

(2) it is not needed to resolve domestic problems;

(3) it makes people more anxious and insecure; and

(4) while providing more goods and services, it does not result in a better life.

b. Those in favor of growth argue that

(1) it results in a higher standard of living and lessens the burden of scarcity;

(2) it is not the cause of pollution;

(3) it is the easiest way to reduce poverty and to bring about a more equitable distribution of income; and

(4) ending or slowing growth will not improve the quality of life.

8. Three types of policies have been discussed for achieving more economic growth in the American economy. Demand-side policies focus on the use of monetary and fiscal policies to affect aggregate demand and maintain the full employment of resources. Supply-side policies to expand the economy's output potential often involve recommendation for changes in taxes to increase investment, saving, work effort, and risk taking. Some economists have also advocated an industrial policy that would shape the structure and composition of industry to target it at the best possibilities for the economic growth in the nation.

■ **IMPORTANT TERMS**

Economic growth	Labor productivity
Supply factor	Productivity slowdown
Demand factor	Infrastructure
Allocative factor	Industrial policy

■ **FILL-IN QUESTIONS**

1. Employment theory assumes the productive capacity of the economy is (fixed, variable) _____ while growth economics is concerned with an economy whose productive capacity (increases, remains constant) _____ over time.

2. Economic growth can mean an increase in either the _____ or the _____ of an economy.

3. A rise in output per capita (increases, decreases) _____ the standard of living and _____ the burden of scarcity in the economy.

4. Assume an economy has a GDP of $3600 billion. If the growth rate is 5%, GDP will increase by $_____ billion a year; but if the rate of growth is only 3%, the annual increase in GDP will be $_____ billion. A two percentage point difference in the growth rate results in a $_____ billion difference in the annual increase in GDP.

5. The four supply factors in economic growth are

_____,

_____,

_____, and

_____.

The other two growth factors are the _____ _____ factor and the _____ factor.

6. In the production possibilities model, economic growth increases primarily because of (demand, supply) _____ factors that shift the production possibilities curve to the (left, right) _____; but the economy may not realize its potential because there may be less than full _____ and full _____

7. The real GDP of any economy in any year is equal to the _____ of labor employed **multiplied** by the _____ of labor.

 a. The former is measured by the number of (workers, hours of labor) _____ employed.

 b. The latter is equal to the real GDP per _____ per _____

8. The quantity of labor employed in the economy in any year depends on the size of the employed _____ force and the _____ of the average workweek. The size element depends upon the size of the working-age _____ and the labor-force _____ rate.

9. In the aggregate-demand and aggregate-supply framework, economic growth is illustrated by an (increase, decrease) _____ in the long-run aggregate-supply curve; and when the price level also increases, it indicates that the aggregate-demand curve has increased (more, less) _____ rapidly than the long-run aggregate supply.

10. Since 1948, the average rates of growth in real GDP and real GDP per capita in the United States have been _____% and _____%, respectively, but they were _____% and _____% in Japan, and _____% and _____% in Germany.

11. Edward Denison studied economic growth in the United States from 1929–1982 and found that the increase in the quantity of labor accounted for (one-third, two-thirds) _____ of economic growth and increases in labor productivity accounted for _____ of economic growth. Factors contributing to labor productivity include:

a. technological _____;

b. increases in the quantity of _____ employed and in the quantity employed per _____;

c. the improved _____ and _____ of workers;

d. economies of _____; and

e. the improved _____ of resources.

12. An increase in the stock of capital of a nation is the result of saving and _____. In the United States the stock of capital has historically grown (more, less) _____ rapidly than the quantity of labor employed.

13. Technological progress means that we learn how to employ given quantities of resources to obtain greater _____; and, more often than not, this progress requires _____ in new machinery and equipment.

14. The principal detriment to growth of real national income in the 1929–1982 period seems to have been government _____ which diverted (consumption, investment) _____ spending away from uses that would have increased the _____ of labor.

15. Two other factors that have led to economic growth in the United States are its abundant _____ resources and its social-cultural-political _____

16. Denison's analysis is designed to explain (actual, potential) _____ real national income. When there is a deficiency of aggregate demand the _____ rate of economic growth falls short of the _____. Denison estimates that the rate would have been higher at _____% per year, if the economy's (actual, potential) _____ had been achieved year after year.

17. The annual rates of increase in the productivity of labor, between the middle 1960s and 1981, (rose, fell, remained constant) _____

_____

This resulted in a (rise, fall) _____ in the

rates at which the standard of _____ and the (nominal, real) _____ wages of labor increased, in a (rise, fall) _____ in unit labor costs and (inflation, deflation) _____ in the United States, and the loss of international markets to (American, foreign) _____ producers of goods and services.

18. The slowdown in productivity growth as a result of problems with _____ quality, less _____ progress, relatively low levels of _____ spending as a percent of GDP, high _____ prices in certain years, adversarial _____ relations. Some of these problems have lessened in the past decade, and as a consequence, there has been a resurgence in _____, but it is not known whether the change is permanent or _____.

19. Influential economists arguing against the need for growth in the United States believe that growth _____ the environment, does not lead to the solution of _____, breeds _____ and _____, and does not result in the _____.

20. Those who favor growth for the American economy argue that it is the basic way to raise the standard of _____ and lessen the _____ _____ dilemma, that economic growth does not necessarily result in _____, that growth is the only practical way of obtaining a more _____ distribution of _____, and that limiting growth will not bring about _____.

21. Three types of growth policies have been suggested for stimulating economic growth in the United States. (Supply, Demand) _____-side policies involve the use of monetary and fiscal policies to sustain and expand the full employment of resources in the economy, whereas _____-side policies focus primarily on tax changes to stimulate saving, investment, and entrepreneurship, and thereby expand capacity output. Shaping the structure and composition of American industry is the target of _____ policies for economic growth.

■ PROBLEMS AND PROJECTS

1. The table below shows the quantity of labor (measured in hours) and the productivity of labor (measured in real GDP per hour) in a hypothetical economy in three different years.

Year	Quantity of labor	Productivity of labor	Real GDP
1	1000	$100	$_____
2	1000	105	_____
3	1100	105	_____

a. Compute the economy's real GDP in each of the three years and enter them in the table.

b. Between years 1 and 2, the quantity of labor remained constant; but

(1) the productivity of labor increased by _____%; and

(2) as a consequence, real GDP increased by _____%.

c. Between years 2 and 3, the productivity of labor remained constant; but

(1) the quantity of labor increased by _____%; and

(2) as a consequence, real GDP increased by _____%.

d. Between years 1 and 3

(1) real GDP increased by _____%; and

(2) this rate of increase is approximately equal to the sum of the rates of increase in the _____

and the _____ of labor.

2. Suppose the real GDP and the population of an economy in seven different years were those shown in the next table.

a. How large would the real per capita GDP of the

Year	Population, million	Real GDP, billions of dollars	Per capita real GDP
1	30	$ 9	$ 300
2	60	24	____
3	90	45	____
4	120	66	____
5	150	90	____
6	180	99	____
7	210	105	____

economy be in each of the other six years? Put your figures in the table.

b. What would have been the size of the optimum population of this economy? _____

c. What was the *amount* of growth in real GDP between year 1 and year 2? $_____

d. What was the *rate* of growth in real GDP between year 3 and year 4? _____%

Year	Population, million	Real GDP, billions of dollars	Per capita real GDP
1	30	$ 9	$ 300
2	60	24	____
3	90	45	____
4	120	66	____
5	150	90	____
6	180	99	____
7	210	105	____

3. Given the hypothetical data in the table below, calculate the average annual rates of growth in real GDP and real per capita GDP over the period given. (Note: Remember to adjust rate of growth for the number of years in the period so you get average annual rates. Real GDP is in billions.)

Year	Real GDP	Annual growth in %	Real GDP per capita	Annual growth in %
1970	$2,416	____	$11,785	____
1975	2,695	____	12,593	____
1980	3,187	____	13,978	____
1985	3,618	____	15,139	____
1988	3,995	____	16,240	____
1991	4,545	____	17,110	____

■ SELF-TEST

Circle the T if the statement is true; the F if it is false.

1. Growth economics concerns an economy in which productive capacity is not fixed.   **T F**

2. The better of the two definitions of economic growth is an increase in the per capita real output of the economy.   **T F**

3. Suppose two economies both have GDPs of $500 billion. If the GDPs grow at annual rates of 3% in the first and 5% in the second economy, the difference in their amounts of growth in one year is $10 billion.   T F

4. If the rate of growth in real GDP averages 2.5% a year, it will take about 28 years for real GDP to double.   T F

5. The potential of an enhanced productive capacity in an economy will not be completely realized unless there is full employment of resources and full production in the economy.   T F

6. An increase in economic growth will increase the long-run aggregate supply curve and the short-run aggregate supply curve, but decrease the aggregate demand curve.   T F

7. The demand factor in economic growth refers to the ability of the economy to expand its production as the demand for products grows.   T F

8. The allocative factor in economic growth refers to the ability of the economy to move resources from one use to another as the productive capacity of the economy grows.   T F

9. The real GDP of an economy in any year is equal to its input of labor divided by the productivity of labor. T F

10. Real GDP has tended to increase more rapidly than real per capita GDP in the United States.   T F

11. Growth and rates-of-growth estimates generally attempt to take account of changes in the quality of goods produced and in the amount of leisure members of the economy enjoy.   T F

12. Increased labor productivity has been more important than increased labor inputs in the growth of the American economy since 1929.   T F

13. Since 1929 improved technology has accounted for about 28% of the increase in labor productivity in the United States.   T F

14. More often than not technological progress requires the economy to invest in new machinery and equipment.   T F

15. The single most important source of the growth of labor productivity in the United States since 1929 has been the increase in the size of the American labor force. T F

16. The regulation of industry, the pollution of the environment, and increase regulation of the health and safety of workers by government tend to reduce the rate at which labor productivity grows.   T F

17. The availability of natural resources in the United States has been a significant factor in the growth of the American economy.   T F

18. Over the past sixty years, the American social, cultural, and political environment has slowed the economic growth of the United States.   T F

19. Increases in labor productivity can, at least in the American economy, be taken pretty much for granted because the rate of increase has been nearly constant for well over half a century.   T F

20. Between the mid-1960s and 1981 the productivity of labor in the United States fell.   T F

21. Productivity growth is a major factor contributing to increases in real wage rates and the standard of living in a nation.   T F

22. There was a significant improvement in the education, employment training, and work experience of workers in the 1970s and 1980s that contributed to increased labor productivity in those decades.   T F

23. During the 1970s and 1980s the United States invested a larger percentage of its GDP in capital goods.   T F

24. Adversarial industrial relations between managers and their employees in the United States can slow the rate at which the productivity of labor increases.   T F

25. Supply-side economists favor increasing taxes to stimulate saving, investment, and economic growth in the economy.   T F

Circle the letter that corresponds to the best answer.

1. Which of the following is a benefit of real economic growth to a society?
 (a) everyone enjoys a greater nominal income
 (b) the standard of living increases
 (c) the burden of scarcity increases
 (d) the society is less able to satisfy new wants

2. If the real output of an economy were to increase from $2000 billion to $2100 billion in one year the rate of growth of real output during that year would be:
 (a) 0.5%
 (b) 5%
 (c) 10%
 (d) 50%

3. Suppose an economy has a real GDP of $700 billion and an annual growth rate of 5%. Over a *two*-year period real GDP will increase by:
 (a) $14 billion
 (b) $35 billion
 (c) $70 billion
 (d) $71¾ billion

4. If a nation's real GDP is growing by 2% per year, then approximately how many years will it take for real GDP to double?

(a) 25 years
(b) 30 years
(c) 35 years
(d) 40 years

Use the following graph to answer the next two questions (5 and 6).

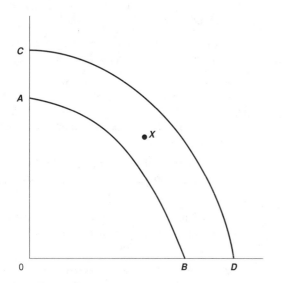

5. If the production possibilities curve of an economy shifts from **AB** to **CD**, it is most likely caused by:
(a) supply factors
(b) demand factors
(c) allocative factors
(d) industrial policy

6. If the production possibilities curve for an economy at **CD** but the economy is operating at point **X**, the reasons are most likely to be because of:
(a) supply and environmental factors
(b) demand and allocative factors
(c) labor inputs and labor productivity
(d) technological progress

7. Which of the following is **not** a supply factor in economic growth?
(a) an expansion in purchasing power
(b) an increase in the economy's stock of capital goods
(c) more natural resources
(d) technological progress

Use the graph in the next column to answer the next two questions (8 and 9).

8. A shift from Q_1 to Q_2 is caused by a shift in the:
(a) level of prices
(b) aggregate demand curve
(c) short-run aggregate supply curve
(d) long-run aggregate supply curve

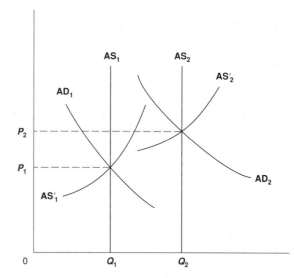

9. Which combination would best explain a shift in the price level from P_1 to P_2 and an increase in real domestic output from Q_1 to Q_2?
(a) an increase in the long-run aggregate supply (AS_1 to AS_2) and in short-run aggregate supply (AD_1 to AD_2).
(b) an increase in aggregate demand (AD_1 to AD_2) and an increase in aggregate supply (AD_1 to AD_2).
(c) an increase in the long-run aggregate supply (AS_1 to AS_2), an increase in aggregate demand (AD_1 to AD_2), and an increase in short-run aggregate supply (AS_1 to AS_2).
(d) a decrease in the long-run aggregate supply (AS_2 to AS_1), a decrease in aggregate demand (AD_2 to AD_1), and a decrease in short-run aggregate supply (AS_2 to AS_1).

10. Since 1940 real GDP in the United States has increased about:
(a) twofold
(b) threefold
(c) fourfold
(d) fivefold

11. The real GDP of the American economy between 1948 and 1988 increased at an average **annual** rate of about:
(a) .5%
(b) 2.1%
(c) 3.3%
(d) 5.4%

12. Real GDP per capita in the United States between 1948 and 1988 increased at an average annual rate of about:
(a) 1%
(b) 2%
(c) 3%
(d) 4%

13. Data on real GDP, real GDP per capita, and the respective growth rates for those measure in the United States take into account:
 (a) improvement in product quality
 (b) increases in available leisure time
 (c) environmental problems
 (d) changes in domestic output

14. About what fraction of the growth in the real national income of the United States since 1929 has been due to increases in the quantity of labor employed?
 (a) one-fourth
 (b) one-third
 (c) one-half
 (d) two-thirds

15. The factor accounting for the greatest increase in the productivity of labor in the United States between 1929 and 1982 was:
 (a) economies of scale
 (b) technological advance
 (c) the improved education and training of the labor force
 (d) the expanded quantity of capital

16. Approximately what percentages of the labor force have completed high school and four years of college?
 (a) 45% and 8%
 (b) 44% and 13%
 (c) 60% and 8%
 (d) 80% and 20%

17. The average rate of growth in labor productivity in the United States:
 (a) fell from 1966 to 1981, and has risen modestly from 1981 to 1990
 (b) rose from 1966 to 1981, and has risen modestly from 1981 to 1990
 (c) fell from 1996 to 1981, and has continued to fall from 1981 to 1990
 (d) rose from 1966 to 1981, and rose again from 1981 to 1990

18. The decline in the rate of productivity of labor from 1966–1981 in the United States led to:
 (a) a fall in the relative prices of American goods in world markets
 (b) a rise in the standard of living in the United States
 (c) a rise in unit labor costs and inflation in the United States
 (d) a fall in energy prices

19. Which factor has contributed to the slowdown in the growth of productivity in recent decades?
 (a) more cooperative rather than competitive relationships between workers and management
 (b) an increase in the rate of technological progress

 (c) an increase in the amount of investment in capital goods
 (d) a work force that was less experienced and less prepared for employment

20. Which of the following best explains why there has been a lower level of capital investment in the United States in the past two decades?
 (a) less regulation of business practices
 (b) less competition from imported goods
 (c) higher level of spending for infrastructure
 (d) a lower rate of saving

21. Which of the following is *not* a part of the case against economic growth?
 (a) growth produces pollution
 (b) growth impedes the increased production of consumer goods
 (c) growth prevents the attainment of a better life
 (d) growth is not needed to provide us with the means of solving domestic social problems

22. Which of the following is *not* a part of the case in defense of economic growth?
 (a) growth lessens the unlimited wants–scarce resources problem
 (b) growth lessens the extent of anxiety and insecurity
 (c) growth need not be accompanied by the pollution of the environment
 (d) growth is the only practical way to reduce poverty

23. Which situation would be viewed by most economists as a limitation of the market system stemming from spillover or external costs, and therefore would not be viewed as a reason to limit economic growth?
 (a) environmental pollution
 (b) poverty
 (c) income inequality
 (d) adversarial industrial relations

24. The active use of monetary and fiscal policy to eliminate or reduce the severity of recession would be an example of:
 (a) industrial policy
 (b) demand-side policy
 (c) supply-side policy
 (d) investment policy

25. What type of policy is being suggested by the person who makes this statement: "What this nation needs is a comprehensive plan developed by government and business to direct economic activity to those opportunities that have the best chance of creating more economic growth for the nation"?
 (a) a demand-side policy
 (b) a supply-side policy
 (c) an industrial policy
 (d) an investment policy

■ **DISCUSSION QUESTIONS**

1. How does growth economics differ from the theory of employment and stabilization policy?

2. What is meant by economic growth? Why should the citizens of the United States be concerned with economic growth?

3. What are the six basic ingredients of economic growth? What is the essential difference between the supply factors and the other two factors? Is there any relationship between the strength of the supply factors and the strength of the demand factor?

4. What is the relationship between the real GDP produced in any year and the quantity of labor employed and labor productivity?

5. In what units are the quantity of labor and the productivity of labor measured? What:
  (a) are the two principal determinants of the quantity of the labor input;
  (b) determines the size of the labor force?

6. How does economic growth affect production possibilities? What demand and allocative assumptions are necessary to achieve maximum productive potential?

7. Describe how economic growth can be illustrated in an aggregate-demand and aggregate-supply framework. What has happened to aggregate demand compared to long-run aggregate supply when the price level and real domestic output both increase?

8. What has been the growth record of the American economy? Compare recent American growth rates with those in other nations.

9. What have been the sources of the growth of the real national income in the United States since 1929? What has tended to slow the increase in labor productivity and in real national income?

10. What changes have occurred in the size of the American population and labor force since 1929? What factor has slowed the rate of growth of the former and what factor has speeded the growth of the latter?

11. What is the relationship between investment and the stock of capital? By how much has capital per worker expanded since 1889? What is the connection between increases in the capital stock and the rate of economic growth.

12. What is technological advance and why are technological advance and capital formation closely related processes.

13. What is meant by and, therefore, tends to increase the "quality" of labor? How is this quality usually measured?

14. What are the economic consequences if aggregate demand increases less than productive capacity increases? What are the long-term consequences of this macroeconomic instability?

15. By how much did the annual increases in the productivity of labor decline in the United States between the mid-1960s and 1981? What have been:
  (a) the five major causes; and
  (b) the three consequences of this decline?

16. How might changes in labor quality dampen productivity growth? What factors in the United States have contributed to this situation?

17. What is the relationship between the capital investment and productivity growth? What four conditions in the United States have affected the relative level of investment?

18. Has economic growth resurged since 1981? What long-term problems does productivity growth pose for the economy of the United States?

19. What arguments can be presented on both sides of the question of whether growth in the United States is desirable?

20. What are the basic differences between demand-side, supply-side, and industrial policies that are designed to stimulate economic growth?

■ **ANSWERS**

Chapter 19 Economic Growth

FILL-IN QUESTIONS

1. fixed, increases

2. real output (GDP), real output (GDP) per capita

3. increases, decreases

4. 180, 108, 72

5. quantity and quality of natural resources, quantity and quality of human resources, the supply or stock of capital goods, technology, demand, allocative

6. supply, right, employment, production (either order for last two)

7. quantity, productivity; *a.* hours of labor; *b.* worker, hour (either order)

8. labor, length, population, participation

9. increase, more

10. 3.3, 1.9, 7.1, 5.9, 5.0, 4.2

11. one-third, two-thirds; *a.* progress (advance); *b.* capital, worker; *c.* education, training; *d.* scale; *e.* allocation

12. investment, more

13. output (production), investment

14. regulations, investment, productivity

15. natural, environment

16. actual, actual, potential, 3.2, potential

17. fell; fall, living, real, rise, inflation, foreign

18. labor, technological, investment, energy, industrial, productivity

19. pollutes, domestic problems, anxiety, insecurity, good life

20. living, unlimited wants-scarce resources, pollution, equitable, income, a better life

21. Demand, supply, industrial

PROBLEMS AND PROJECTS

1. *a.* 100,000, 105,000, 115,500; *b.* (1) 5, (2), 5; *c.* (1) 10, (2) 10; *d.* (1) 15.5, (2) quantity, productivity

2. *a.* 400, 500, 550, 600, 550, 500; *b.* 150 million; *c.* $15 billion; *d.* 46.7%

3. real GDP: 1970–75 2.3; 1975–80 3.7; 1980–85 2.7; 1985–88 3.5; 1988–1991, 4.6; real GDP per capita: 1970–75 1.4; 1975–80 2.2; 1980–85 1.7; 1985–88 2.4; 1988–1991, 1.8

SELF-TEST

1. T, p. 365

2. F, p. 366

3. T, p. 366

4. T, p. 366

5. T, p. 367

6. F, p. 368

7. F, p. 367

8. T, p. 367

9. F, p. 368

10. T, p. 369

11. F, p. 370

12. T, p. 370

13. F, p. 371

14. T, p. 371

15. F, p. 371

16. T, p. 373

17. T, pp. 373–374

18. F, p. 374

19. F, pp. 374–375

20. F, p. 375

21. T, p. 375

22. F, p. 375

23. F, p. 376

24. T, p. 377

25. F, p. 379

1. *b,* p. 366

2. *b,* p. 366

3. *d,* p. 366

4. *c,* p. 366

5. *a,* p. 367

6. *b,* p. 367

7. *a,* pp. 366–367

8. *d,* pp. 368–369

9. *c,* pp. 368–369

10. *d,* p. 369

11. *c,* p. 370

12. *b,* p. 370

13. *d,* pp. 369–370

14. *b,* p. 370

15. *b,* p. 371

16. *d,* p. 372

17. *a,* pp. 374–375

18. *c,* p. 375

19. *d,* pp. 375–376

20. *d,* p. 376

21. *b,* p. 378

22. *b,* pp. 378–379

23. *a,* p. 378

24. *b,* p. 379

25. *c,* p. 380

DISCUSSION QUESTIONS

1. pp. 365–366

2. p. 366

3. pp. 366–367

4. p. 368

5. p. 368

6. pp. 367–368

7. p. 368

8. pp. 369–370

9. pp. 370–371

10. pp. 372–373

11. pp. 371–372

12. p. 371

13. p. 372

14. p. 374

15. p. 375

16. pp. 375–376

17. p. 376

18. p. 377

19. pp. 377–379

20. p. 379–380

CHAPTER 20

Demand and Supply: Elasticities and Applications

In this chapter the text shifts from the study of *macro*economics to the study of *micro*economics; from the analysis of domestic output and the price level to analysis of the outputs and prices of firms and industries; from an examination of the economy as a whole to an examination of the parts of the economy. The focus is no longer how much total output is to be produced or on the level of employment of resources in an economy. Rather, the focus shifts to four other questions—what goods and services are to be produced, how are the goods and services to be produced, who is to receive income generated by production, and how can the economy adapt to change.

You learned in previous chapters that it is the market system in the American economy that answers the last four fundamental questions. You also found that in a competitive market, supply and demand determine the price and quantity of a good or service that this bought and sold in the market.

Chapter 20 is basically a continuation of Chapter 4, as you might have guessed from the chapter title. In the earlier part of the book, it was necessary only for you to have an elementary knowledge of supply and demand. Now the economic principles, problems, and policies to be studied require a more detailed examination and analysis of supply and demand. Therefore, before you start to read Chapter 20 you are urged—you would be commanded if this were possible—to read and study Chapter 4 again. It is absolutely essential that you master Chapter 4 if the new material in this chapter is to be understood.

The concept of price elasticity of demand, to which the major portion of Chapter 20 is devoted, is of great importance for studying material found in the remainder of the text. It is essential that you understand (1) what price elasticity measures; (2) how the price-elasticity formula is applied to measure the price elasticity of demand; (3) the difference between price elastic, price inelastic, and unitary price elastic demand; (4) how total revenue varies by the type of price elasticity of demand; (5) the meaning of perfect price elasticity and perfect price inelasticity of demand; (6) the four major determinants of price elasticity of

demand; and (7) the practical application of the concept to many economic issues.

When you have become thoroughly acquainted with the price elasticity of demand concept, you will find that you have very little trouble understanding the elasticity of **supply**. The transition requires no more than the substitution of the words "quantity supplied" for the words "quantity demanded." Here attention should be concentrated on the meaning of price elasticity of supply and the effect of time on it.

The chapter also introduces you to two other elasticity concepts. The **cross elasticity of demand** measures the sensitivity of a change in the quantity demanded for one product due to a change in the price of another product. This concept is especially important to identifying substitute, complementary, or independent goods. The **income elasticity of demand** assesses the change in the quantity demanded of a product resulting from a change in consumer incomes. It is useful for categorizing products as superior, normal, or inferior.

The final section of the chapter discusses **price ceilings** and **price floors** that are created when legal prices are imposed on the competitive market by government. You should note that these ceilings and floors prevent supply and demand from determining the equilibrium price and quantity of a commodity in the market. The economic consequence of this interference in the market will be shortages of surpluses of the commodity. Among the applications presented in this section to illustrate the economic effects of price ceilings or price floors are: (1) price controls during World War II; (2) rent controls; (3) limits on interest rates for credit cards; and (4) price supports for agricultural products.

The concepts of demand and supply, which have been expanded in Chapter 20 to include discussion of elasticity and price ceilings and price floors, are the foundations of the next ten chapters in the text. If you master the topics in Chapter 20, you will be prepared to understand the material in these chapters.

227

■ CHECKLIST

When you have studied this chapter you should be able to:

☐ Define price elasticity of demand and compute the coefficient for it when you are given the demand data.

☐ State two reasons why the formula for price elasticity of demand uses percentages rather than absolute amounts in measuring consumer responsiveness.

☐ Explain the meaning of elastic, inelastic, and unitary price elasticity of demand.

☐ Define and illustrate graphically the concepts of perfectly price elastic and perfectly price inelastic demand.

☐ State the midpoint formula for price elasticity of demand and explain how it refines the original formula for price elasticity.

☐ Describe the relationship between price elasticity of demand and the price range for most demand curves.

☐ Explain why the slope of the demand curve is *not* a sound basis for judging price elasticity.

☐ Apply the total-revenue test to determine whether demand is elastic, inelastic, or unitary elastic.

☐ Illustrate graphically the relationship between price elasticity of demand and total revenue.

☐ List the four major determinants of the price elasticity of demand; and explain how each determinant affects price elasticity.

☐ Describe seven practical applications of the concept of price elasticity of demand.

☐ Define the price elasticity of supply and compute the coefficient for it when given the relevant data.

☐ Explain the effect of time on price elasticity of supply.

☐ Define cross elasticity of demand and compute the coefficient for it when given relevant data.

☐ Define income elasticity of demand and compute the coefficient for it when given relevant data.

☐ Explain the economic consequences of price ceilings and give four examples of the use of price ceilings.

☐ Describe how price floors affect the price and quantity of a product in a market.

■ CHAPTER OUTLINE

1. It is necessary to review the analysis of supply and demand and the concepts found in Chapter 4 before studying this chapter.

2. Price elasticity of demand is a measure of the sensitivity of quantity demanded to changes in the price of a product; and when quantity demanded is relatively sensitive (insensitive) to a price change demand is said to be elastic (inelastic).

a. The exact degree of elasticity can be measured by using a formula to compute the elasticity coefficient.

(1) The changes in quantity demanded and in price are comparisons of consumer responsiveness to price changes of different products.

(2) Because price and quantity demanded are inversely related to each other the price elasticity of demand coefficient is a negative number; but economists ignore the minus sign in front of the coefficient and focus their attention on its absolute value.

(3) Demand is elastic (inelastic, unit elastic) when the percentage change in quantity is greater than (less than, equal to) the percentage change in price and the elasticity coefficient is greater than (less than, equal to) 1.

(4) Perfectly inelastic demand means that a change in price results in no change in quantity demanded of a product, whereas perfectly elastic demand means that a small change in price causes buyers to purchase all they desire of a product.

b. In measuring the percentage changes in quantity and in price the average of the two quantities and the average of the two prices are used as the reference points. It is important to note that graphically the elasticity of demand:

(1) is not the same at all prices and that demand is typically elastic at higher and inelastic at lower prices;

(2) cannot be judged from the slope of the demand curve.

c. The way in which total revenue changes (increases, decreases, or remains constant) when price changes is a test of the elasticity of demand for a product.

(1) When demand is *elastic*, a decrease in price will increase total revenue, and a decrease in price will increase total revenue.

(2) When demand is *inelastic*, a decrease in price will decrease total revenue, and an increase in price with increase total revenue.

(3) When demand is *unit elastic*, an increase or decrease in price will not affect total revenue.

d. The price elasticity of demand for a product depends upon the number of good substitutes for the product, its relative importance in the consumer's budget, whether it is a necessity or a luxury, and the period of time under consideration.

e. Price elasticity of demand is of practical importance in matters of public policy and in the setting of prices by the individual business firm. The concept is relevant to wage bargaining, bumper crops in agriculture, automation, airline deregulation, excise taxes, heroin and street crime, and minimum wage laws.

3. Price elasticity of supply is a measure of the sensitivity of quantity supplied to changes in the price of a product.

a. There is both a general formula and a midpoint formula that is similar to those for the price elasticity of demand, but "quantity supplied" replaces "quantity demanded."

b. The price elasticity of supply depends primarily on the amount of time sellers have to adjust to a price change; supply will tend to be more price inelastic in the short run than in the long run.

c. There is no total-revenue test for price elasticity of supply because price and total revenue move in the same direction regardless of the degree of price elasticity of supply.

4. There are two other elasticity concepts of importance.
a. The cross elasticity of demand measures the degree to which the quantity demanded of one product is affected by a change in the price of another product; cross elasticities of demand are positive for substitute goods, negative for complementary goods, and essentially zero for independent goods.
b. The income elasticity of demand measures the effect of a change in income on the quantity demanded of a product; income elasticities of demand are positive for normal or superior goods, and negative for inferior goods.

5. Supply and demand analysis and the elasticity concepts have many important applications.
a. Legal price ceilings and price floors prevent price from performing its rationing function.
(1) A price ceiling results in a shortage of the commodity; may bring about formal rationing by government and a black market; and causes a misallocation of resources.
(2) A price floor creates a surplus of the commodity; and may induce government to undertake measures either to increase the demand for or to decrease the supply of the commodity.
b. There are many examples of price ceilings and shortages created by legal prices:
(1) Price controls were imposed on many commodities during World War II;
(2) Rent controls have been established by cities in an attempt to restrain rent increases in housing markets; and
(3) Bills have been introduced in Congress to restrict the interest rate that can be charged to holders of credit cards.
c. Pricing below the equilibrium price is not just practiced by government. Businesses may price a product below the market-clearing price to generate excess demand. For example, rock stars may price concert tickets below the market-clearing price to generate publicity and enthusiasm for the concert.
d. There are also illustrations of price floors resulting from legal prices set by government to support the price of some agricultural products.

■ **IMPORTANT TERMS**

Price elasticity of demand	Inelastic supply
Elastic demand	Market period
Inelastic demand	Short run
Unit elasticity	Long run
Perfect inelasticity of demand	Increasing-cost industry
	Constant-cost industry
Perfect elasticity of demand	Cross elasticity of demand
Total-revenue test	Income elasticity of demand
Price elasticity of supply	Price ceiling
Elastic supply	Price floor

Note: Before answering the Fill-in, Self-test, and Discussion questions and working out the Problems and Projects, you should return to Chapter 4 in this study guide and review the important terms, answer the questions, and rework the problems.

■ **FILL-IN QUESTIONS**

1. The efficient use of an economy's available resources requires that these resources be ___fully___ employed and that they be ___allocated___ among alternative uses in an efficient way.
a. The present chapter begins the study of the (latter, former) ___latter___ aspect of the efficient use of resources and the study of (macro-, micro-) ___micro___ economics.
b. This requires an analysis of the ___market___ system and how individual ___prices___ are determined in various kinds of markets in the economy.

2. If a relatively large change in price results in a relatively small change in quantity demanded, demand is ___inelastic___; if a relatively small change in price results in a relatively large change in quantity demanded, demand is ___elastic___

3. The price elasticity formula is based on ___percentages___ rather than absolute amounts because it avoids the problems caused by the arbitrary choice of units, and because it permits a meaningful ___comparison___ of consumer responsiveness to changes in the prices of different products.

4. If a change in price causes no change in quantity demanded, demand is perfectly (elastic, inelastic)

_____inelastic_____ and the demand curve is (horizontal, vertical) _____vertical_____; if an extremely small change in price results in an extremely large change in quantity demanded, demand is _____perfectly elastic_____ and the demand curve is _____horizontal_____

5. The midpoints formula for the price elasticity of demand uses the _____average_____ of the two quantities as a reference point in calculating the percentage change in quantity and the _____average_____ of the two prices as a reference point in calculations of the percentage change in price.

6. Two characteristics of the price elasticity of a linear demand curve are that elasticity (is constant, varies) _____varies_____ over the different price ranges, and the slope is a(n) (sound, unsound) _____unsound_____ basis for judging its elasticity.

7. If the price of a commodity declines,
   a. When demand is inelastic the loss of revenue due to the lower price is _____greater than_____ the gain in revenue due to the greater quantity demanded.
   b. When demand is elastic the loss of revenue due to the lower price is _____less than_____ the gain in revenue due to the greater quantity demanded.
   c. When demand is of unitary elasticity the loss of revenue due to the lower price is _____equal to_____ the gain in revenue due to the greater quantity demanded.

8. If demand is elastic, price and total revenue are (directly, inversely) _____inversely_____ related; if demand is inelastic, they are _____directly_____ related.

9. Complete the summary table below.

If demand is	The elasticity coefficient is	If price rises, total revenue will	If price falls, total revenue will
Elastic	> 1	decrease	Increase
Inelastic	< 1	Increase	decrease
Of unitary elasticity	1	Remain	Unchanged

10. List four determinants of the price elasticity of demand:
   a. _____Substitutability_____
   b. _____% Income_____
   c. _____Luxury or Necessity_____
   d. _____Time_____

11. The price elasticity of supply measures the percentage change in (price, quantity supplied) _____quantity supplied_____ divided by the percentage change in _____price_____

12. The most important factor affecting the price elasticity of supply is _____the amount of time seller has to respond_____ Typically, the price elasticity of supply is (more, less) _____less_____ elastic in the short run than in the long run.

13. The measure of the sensitivity of the consumption of one product given a change in the price of another product is the _____cross_____ elasticity of demand. The measure of the responsiveness of consumer purchases to changes in income is the _____income_____ elasticity of demand.

14. When the cross elasticity of demand is positive, two products are (complements, substitutes, independent) _____substitute_____, but when the cross elasticity of demand is negative, they are _____Complements_____. A zero cross elasticity suggest that two products are _____independent_____.

15. If consumers increase purchases of a product as consumer incomes increase, then a good is classified as (inferior, normal, or superior) _____normal or superior_____; if consumers decrease purchases of a product as consumer incomes increase, then a good is classified as _____inferior_____

16. If the demand and supply schedules for a certain product are those given in the table, answer the following questions.

Quantity demanded	Price	Quantity supplied
12,000	$10	18,000
13,000	9	17,000
14,000	8	16,000
15,000	7	15,000
16,000	6	14,000
17,000	5	13,000
18,000	4	12,000

   a. The equilibrium price of the product is $_____7_____ and the equilibrium quantity is _____15000_____
   b. If the government imposes a price ceiling of $5 on this product, there would be a (shortage, surplus) _____shortage_____ of _____4000_____ units.
   c. If the government supports a price of $8, there would be a _____surplus_____ of _____2000_____ units.

17. Price ceilings imposed by the United States government have usually occurred during _____ War periods, result in _____ shortages _____ of the commodities, and require that the government institute _____ rationing

18. The two most common examples of government imposed minimum prices are _____ minimum wages _____ agricultural price support

and _____

19. A minimum price imposed by the government on a commodity causes a _____ surplus _____ of the commodity and requires that the government either _____ attempt to reduce supply or increase demand. purchase the surplus or _____ to eliminate this, and store or dispose of it

20. Price ceilings and price floors prevent prices from performing their _____ rationing _____ function.

■ **PROBLEMS AND PROJECTS**

1. In the following table, using the demand data given, complete the table by computing total revenue at each of the seven prices and the six price elasticity coefficients between each of the seven prices, and indicate whether demand is elastic, inelastic, or of unitary elasticity between each of the seven prices.

Price	Quantity demanded	Total revenue	Elasticity coefficient	Character of demand
$1.00	300	$ ____		
.90	400	____	____	____
.80	500	____	____	____
.70	600	____	____	____
.60	700	____	____	____
.50	800	____	____	____
.40	900	____	____	____

2. Use the data from the table above for this problem. On the first graph in the next column, plot the demand curve (price and quantity demanded) and indicate the elastic, unitary, and inelastic portions of the demand curve. On the second graph in the next column, plot the total revenue on the vertical axis and the quantity demanded on the horizontal axis. (**Note:** The scale for quantity demanded that

you plot on horizontal axis of each graph should be the same on both graphs.)

0

0

a. As price decreases from $1.00 to $0.70, demand is (elastic, inelastic, unitary) _____ and total revenue (increases, decreases, remains the same)

_____

b. As price decreases from $.070 to $0.60, demand is (elastic, inelastic, unitary) _____ and total revenue (increases, decreases, remains the same) _____

c. As price decreases from $0.60 to $0.40, demand is (elastic, inelastic, unitary) _____ and total revenue (increases, decreases, remains the same) _____

3. Using the supply data in the schedule shown below, complete the table by computing the six price elasticity of supply coefficients between each of the seven prices, and indicate whether supply is elastic or of unitary elasticity.

Price	Quantity supplied	Elasticity coefficient	Character of supply
$1.00	800		
.90	700	_____	_____
.80	600	_____	_____
.70	500	_____	_____
.60	400	_____	_____
.50	300	_____	_____
.40	200	_____	_____

4. On the following graph are three different supply curves (**S_1**, **S_2**, and **S_3**) for a product bought and sold in a competitive market.

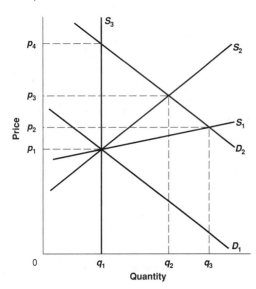

a. The supply curve for the:

(1) market period is the one labeled _____

(2) short run is the one labeled _____

(3) long run is the one labeled _____

b. No matter what the period of time under consideration, if the demand for the product were **D_1**, the equilibrium price of the product would be _____

and the equilibrium quantity would be _____
(1) in the market period the equilibrium price would increase to _____ and the equilibrium

quantity would _____
(2) in the short run the price of the product would in-

crease to _____ and the quantity would

increase to _____
(3) in the long run the price of the product would be

_____ and the quantity would be

_____

d. The longer the period of time allowed to sellers to

adjust their outputs the (more, less) _____
elastic is the supply of the product.
e. The more elastic the supply of a product, the

(greater, less) _____ is the effect on

equilibrium price and the _____ is the effect on equilibrium quantity of an increase in demand.

5. For the following three cases, use a midpoints formula to calculate the coefficient for the cross elasticity of demand and identify the relationship between the two goods (complement, substitute, or independent).
a. The quantity demanded for good A increases from 300 to 400 as the price of good B increases from $1.00

to $2.00. Coefficient: _____ Relationship: _____
b. The quantity demanded for good J decreases from 2000 to 1500 as the price of good K increases from $10

to $15. Coefficient: _____ Relationship: _____
c. The quantity demanded for good X increases from 100 to 101 units as the price of good Y increases from

$8 to $15. Coefficient: _____ Relationship: _____

6. Use the information in the table below to identify the income characteristic of each product A–E using the following labels: N = normal (or superior); I = inferior.

Product	% change in income	% change in quantity demanded	Income type (N or I)
A	10	10	_____
B	1	15	_____
C	5	−12	_____
D	5	−2	_____
E	10	1	_____

■ **SELF-TEST**

Circle the T if the statement is true; the F if it is false.

1. If the relative change in price is greater than the relative change in quantity demanded, the price elasticity coefficient is greater than one.   T (F)

2. If the quantity demanded for a product increases from 100 to 150 units when the price decreases from $14 to

$$\frac{\Delta Q}{\Delta P} \cdot \frac{\bar{P}}{\bar{Q}} = \frac{50 \times 12}{4 \times 125}$$

$10, the price elasticity of demand for this product in this price range is 1.2.   T **F**

3. A product with a price elasticity of demand equal to 1.5 is described as price inelastic.   T **F**

4. The flatness or steepness of a demand curve is based on absolute changes in price and quantity, while elasticity is based on relative or percentage changes in price and quantity.   **T** F

use %-change $\frac{\Delta Q}{Q} \div \frac{\Delta P}{P}$

5. Demand tends to be _inelastic_ at higher prices and elastic at lower prices.   T **F**

6. Price elasticity of demand and the slope of the demand curve are two different things.   **T** F

7. If the price of a product increases from $5 to $6 and the quantity demanded decreases from 45 to 25, then according to the total revenue test, the product is price inelastic in this price range.   T **F**

$225 > 125$
$(5 \times 45)\ (6 \times 25)$

8. Total revenue will not change when price changes if the price elasticity of demand is unitary.   **T** F

9. When the absolute value of the price elasticity coefficient is greater than 1 and the price of the product decreases, then the total revenue will increase.   **T** F

10. The demand for most agricultural products is inelastic. Consequently, an increase in supply will reduce the total income of producers of agricultural products.   **T** F

11. A state government seeking to increase its excise-tax revenues is more likely to increase the tax rate on restaurant meals than on automobile tires.   T **F**

12. In general, the larger the portion of a household budget required to buy a product, the greater will tend to be the price elasticity of demand for the product.   **T** F

13. An empirical study of commuter rail transportation in the Philadelphia area indicates that the "short-run" commuter response is price elastic, while the "long-run" response is price inelastic.   T **F**

14. If the demand for soybeans is highly inelastic, a bumper crop may reduce farm incomes.   **T** F

15. If an increase in product price results in no change in the quantity supplied, supply is perfectly elastic.   T **F**

16. The immediate market period is a time so short that producers cannot respond to a change in demand and price.   **T** F

17. The price elasticity of supply will tend to be more inelastic in the long run.   T **F**

18. A constant-cost industry has a vertical or near-vertical long-run supply curve.   374   **T** F

19. Cross elasticity of demand is measured by the percentage change in quantity demanded over the percentage change in income.   T **F**

20. A negative cross elasticity of demand for two goods indicates that they are complements.   **T** F

21. Inferior goods have a positive income elasticity of demand.   T **F**

22. If the government imposes a price ceiling below what would be the free-market price of a commodity, a shortage of the commodity will develop.   **T** F

23. A price floor set by government will raise the equilibrium price and quantity in a market.   T **F**

24. If the legal price floor is above the equilibrium price, shortages will develop in the market.   T **F**

25. A legal ceiling on interest rates charged by issuers of bank credit cards would probably lead to actions by the issuers to reduce costs or to increase revenues.   **T** F

Circle the letter that corresponds to the best answer.

1. If when the price of a product rises from $1.50 to $2, the quantity demanded of the product decreases from 1000 to 900, the price elasticity of demand coefficient is:
  (a) 3.00
  (b) 2.71
  (c) 0.37
  (d) 0.33

2. If a 1% fall in the price of a commodity causes the quantity demanded of the commodity to increase 2%, demand is:
  (a) inelastic
  (b) elastic
  (c) of unitary elasticity
  (d) perfectly elastic

3. In the diagram below, D_1 is a:

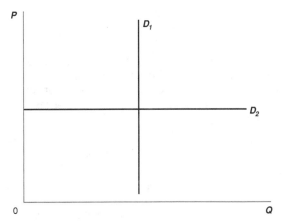

  (a) perfectly elastic demand curve
  (b) perfectly inelastic demand curve

(c) unitary elastic demand curve
(d) a "long-run" demand curve

4. Compared to the lower-right portion, the upper-left portion of most demand curves tends to be:
(a) more inelastic
(b) more elastic
(c) unitary elastic
(d) perfectly inelastic

5. In which range of the demand schedule is demand price inelastic?

Price	Quantity demanded
$11	50
9	100
7	200
5	300
3	400

(a) $11–$9
(b) $9–$7
(c) $7–$5
(d) $5–$3

6. When a business increased the price of its product from $7 to $8 when the price elasticity of demand was inelastic, then:
(a) total revenues decreased
(b) total revenues increased
(c) total revenues remain unchanged
(d) total revenues were perfectly inelastic

7. You are the sales manager for a pizza company and have been informed that the price elasticity demand for your most popular pizza is greater than one. To increase total revenues, you should:
(a) increase the price of the pizza
(b) decrease the price of the pizza
(c) hold pizza prices constant
(d) decrease demand for your pizza

8. Which of the following is **not** characteristic of a commodity the demand for which is elastic?
(a) the price elasticity coefficient is less than unity
(b) total revenue decreases if price rises
(c) buyers are relatively sensitive to price changes
(d) the relative change in quantity is greater than the relative change in price

9. The demand for Nike basketball shoes is more price elastic than the demand for basketball shoes as a whole. This is best explained by the fact that:
(a) Nike basketball shoes are a luxury good, not a necessity
(b) Nike basketball shoes are the best made and widely advertised
(c) there are more complements for Nike basketball shoes than for basketball shoes as a whole

(d) there are more substitutes for Nike basketball shoes than for basketball shoes as a whole

10. Which of the following is **not** characteristic of a good the demand for which is inelastic?
(a) there are a large number of good substitutes for the good for consumers
(b) the buyer spends a small percentage of his total income on the good
(c) the good is regarded by consumers as a necessity
(d) the period of time for which demand is given is very short

11. An empirical study of commuter rail transportation in the Philadelphia area indicated that price elasticity of demand is:
(a) elastic in the "short run" and the "long run"
(b) inelastic in the "short run" and the "long run"
(c) elastic in the "short run" but inelastic in the "long run"
(d) inelastic in the "short run" but elastic in the "long run"

12. If a 5% fall in the price of a commodity causes quantity supplied to decrease by 8%, supply is:
(a) inelastic
(b) of unitary elasticity
(c) elastic
(d) perfectly inelastic

13. In the diagram below, what is the price elasticity of supply between points **A** and **C**?

(a) 1.33
(b) 1.67
(c) 1.85
(d) 2.46

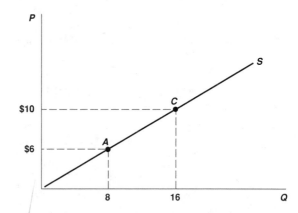

14. If supply is inelastic and demand decreases, the total revenue of sellers will:
(a) increase
(b) decrease
(c) decrease only if demand is elastic
(d) increase only if demand is inelastic

15. The chief determinant of the price elasticity of supply of a product is:
 (a) the number of good substitutes the product has
 (b) the length of time sellers have to adjust to a change in price
 (c) whether the product is a luxury or a necessity
 (d) whether the product is a durable or a nondurable good

16. The long-run supply curve in a constant-cost industry will be:
 (a) perfectly elastic
 (b) perfectly inelastic
 (c) unit elastic
 (d) income elastic

17. The slope of the long-run supply curve in an increasing-cost industry would be:
 (a) vertical
 (b) horizontal
 (c) upsloping
 (d) downsloping

18. If a 5% increase in the price of one good results in a decrease of 2% in the quantity demanded of another good, then it can be concluded that the two goods are:
 (a) complements
 (b) substitutes
 (c) independent
 (d) normal

19. Most goods can be classified as **normal** goods rather than inferior goods. The definition of a normal good means that:
 (a) the percentage change in consumer income is greater than the percentage change in price of the normal good
 (b) the percentage change in quantity demanded of the normal good is greater than the percentage change in consumer income
 (c) as consumer income increases, consumer purchases of a normal good increase
 (d) the income elasticity of demand is negative

20. Based on the information in the table, which product would be an inferior good?

Product	% change in income	% change in quantity demanded
A	− 10	+ 10
B	+ 10	+ 10
C	+ 5	+ 5
D	− 5	− 5

 (a) Product A
 (b) Product B
 (c) Product C
 (d) Product D

21. In the diagram below, a legal price floor of $9.00 will result in:

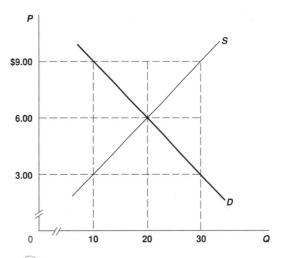

 (a) a surplus of 20 units
 (b) a surplus of 10 units
 (c) a shortage of 20 units
 (d) no shortage or surplus

*The next three questions (**22, 23,** and **24**) relate to the table below that shows a hypothetical supply and demand schedule for a product.*

Quantity demanded (pounds)	Price (per pound)	Quantity supplied (pounds)
200	$4.40	800
250	4.20	700
300	4.00	600
350	3.80	500
400	3.60	400
450	3.40	300
500	3.20	200

22. The equilibrium price and quantity is:
 (a) $4.00 and 600 pounds
 (b) $3.80 and 350 pounds
 (c) $3.60 and 400 pounds
 (d) $3.40 and 300 pounds

23. If a legal price floor is established at $4.20, there will be a:
 (a) shortage of 450 pounds
 (b) surplus of 450 pounds
 (c) shortage of 300 pounds
 (d) surplus of 300 pounds

24. A shortage of 150 pounds of the product will occur if a legal price is established at:
 (a) $3.20
 (b) $3.40
 (c) $3.80
 (d) $4.00

25. Which of the following would be an example of a price floor?
  (a) controls on apartment rent in major cities
  (b) limiting interest charged by credit card companies
  (c) price controls during World War II
  (d) price supports for agricultural products

■ DISCUSSION QUESTIONS

1. Define and explain the price elasticity of demand concept in terms of each of the following:
  (a) the relative sensitiveness of quantity demanded to changes in price;
  (b) the behavior of total revenue when price changes;
  (c) the elasticity coefficient; and
  (d) the relationship between the relative (percentage) change in quantity demanded and the relative (percentage) change in price.

2. What is meant by perfectly elastic demand? By perfectly inelastic demand? What does the demand curve look like when demand is perfectly elastic and when it is perfectly inelastic?

3. In computing the price elasticity coefficient, it usually makes a considerable difference whether the higher price and lower quantity or the lower price and higher quantity are used as a point of reference. What have economists done to eliminate the confusion which would arise if the price elasticity of demand coefficient varied and depended upon whether a price rise or fall were being considered?

4. Demand seldom has the same elasticity at all prices. What is the relationship between the price of most commodities and the price elasticity of demand for them?

5. What is the relationship, if there is a relationship, between the price elasticity of demand and the slope of the demand curve?

6. When the price of a commodity declines, the quantity demanded of it increases. When demand is elastic, total revenue is greater at the lower price; but when demand is inelastic, total revenue is smaller. Explain why total revenue will sometimes increase and why it will sometimes decrease.

7. What are the factors which together determine the price elasticity of demand for a product?

8. Of what practical importance is the price elasticity of demand? Cite examples of its importance to business firms, workers, farmers, and governments.

9. Explain what determines the price elasticity of supply of an economic good or service.

10. Why does the government from time to time impose price ceilings and minimum prices on certain goods and services? What are the consequences of these ceilings and minimums if they are not set at the price which would prevail in the free market?

■ ANSWERS

Chapter 20 Demand and Supply: Elasticities and Applications

FILL-IN QUESTIONS

1. fully, allocated; *a.* latter, micro-; *b.* market, prices

2. inelastic, elastic

3. percentages, comparisons

4. inelastic, vertical, perfectly elastic, horizontal

5. average, average

6. varies, unsound

7. *a.* greater than; *b.* less than; *c.* equal to

8. inversely, directly

9. elastic: greater than 1, decrease, increase; inelastic: less than 1, increase, decrease; of unitary elasticity: equal to 1, remain constant, remain constant

10. *a.* the number of good substitute products available; *b.* the relative importance of the product in the total budget of the buyer; *c.* whether the good is a necessity or a luxury; *d.* the period of time in which demand is being considered

11. quantity supplied, price

12. the amount of time which a seller has to respond to a price change, less

13. cross, income

14. substitutes, complements, independent

15. normal or superior, inferior

16. *a.* 7.00, 15,000; *b.* shortage, 4000; *c.* surplus, 2000.

17. war, shortages, rationing

18. minimum wages, agricultural price supports

19. surplus, attempt to reduce supply or increase demand, purchase the surplus and store or dispose of it

20. rationing

PROBLEMS AND PROJECTS

1. total revenue: $300, 360, 400, 420, 420, 400, 360; elasticity coefficient: $2^5/_7$ (2.71), $1^8/_9$ (1.89), $1^4/_{11}$ (1.36), 1, $^{11}/_{15}$ (0.73), $^9/_{17}$ (0.53); character of demand: elastic, elastic, elastic, unitary elasticity, inelastic, inelastic

2. *a.* elastic, increases; *b.* unitary, remains the same; *c.* inelastic, decreases

3. Elasticity coefficient: $1^4/_{15}$ (1.27), $1^4/_{13}$ (1.31), $1^4/_{11}$ (1.36), $1^4/_9$ (1.44), $1^4/_7$ (1.57), $1^4/_5$ (1.8); character of supply: elastic, elastic, elastic, elastic, elastic, elastic

4. *a.* (1) S_3; (2) S_2; (3) S_1; *b.* p_1, q_1; *c.* (1) p_4, remain at q_1; (2) p_3, q_2; (3) p_2, q_3; *d.* more; *e.* less, greater

5. *a.* .43, substitute; *b.* $-$.71 complement; *c.* .02, independent

6. N, N, I, I, N

SELF-TEST

1. F, p. 384	**14.** T, p. 391
2. T, p. 385	**15.** F, p. 392
3. F, p. 385	**16.** T, p. 392
4. T, p. 386	**17.** F, p. 393
5. F, p. 386	**18.** F, p. 394
6. T, p. 386	**19.** F, p. 394
7. F, pp. 387–388	**20.** T, p. 394
8. T, p. 388	**21.** F, p. 394
9. T, p. 387	**22.** T, p. 395
10. T, p. 391	**23.** F, p. 397
11. F, p. 391	**24.** F, p. 397
12. T, p. 389	**25.** T, p. 396
13. F, pp. 389–390	

1. *c*, p. 384	**14.** *b*, pp. 392–393
2. *b*, p. 385	**15.** *b*, p. 392
3. *b*, p. 385	**16.** *a*, p. 394
4. *b*, p. 386	**17.** *c*, pp. 393–394
5. *d*, pp. 387–388	**18.** *a*, p. 394
6. *b*, p. 387	**19.** *c*, p. 394
7. *b*, p. 387	**20.** *a*, p. 394
8. *a*, p. 389	**21.** *a*, p. 397
9. *d*, pp. 388–389	**22.** *c*, p. 395
10. *a*, pp. 388–389	**23.** *b*, p. 397
11. *d*, pp. 389–390	**24.** *b*, p. 395
12. *c*, p. 392	**25.** *d*, p. 397
13. *a*, p. 392	

DISCUSSION QUESTIONS

1. pp. 383–385	**6.** pp. 387–388
2. p. 385	**7.** pp. 388–389
3. pp. 385–386	**8.** pp. 390–392
4. p. 386	**9.** pp. 392–393
5. p. 386	**10.** pp. 395–397

Consumer Behavior and Utility Maximization

Previous chapters explained that consumers typically buy more of a product as its price decreases and less of a product as its price increases. Chapter 21 looks behind this law of demand to explain why consumers behave in this way.

Two explanations for the law of demand are presented in the chapter. The first explanation is a general and simple one that is based on income and substitution effects. From this perspective, a change in the price of a product changes the amount consumed because of a change in the real income and because of a change in the price of this good relative to other products that could be purchased. The other explanation is more detailed and abstract because it is based on the concept of marginal utility. In this view, the additional satisfaction (or marginal utility) that a consumer obtains from the consumption of each additional unit of a product will tend to decline, and therefore a consumer will only have an incentive to purchase additional units of a product if its price falls. (A third explanation of consumer demand that is more complete than the first two is based on the use of indifference curves, but this more complex discussion is placed in the appendix to the chapter.)

The majority of the chapter presents the marginal-utility view of consumer behavior. This explanation requires that you first understand the concepts and assumptions upon which this theory of consumer behavior rests, and second, do some rigorous reasoning using these concepts and assumptions. It is an exercise in logic, but be sure that you follow the reasoning. To aid you, several problems are provided so that you can work things out for yourself.

Of course no one believes that consumers actually perform these mental gymnastics before they spend their incomes or make a purchase. But the marginal-utility approach to consumer behavior is studied because the consumers behave "as if" they made their purchases on the basis of very fine calculations. Thus, this approach explains what we do in fact observe, and makes it possible for us to predict with a good deal of precision how consumers will react to changes in their incomes and in the prices of products.

The consumption of any good or service requires that

the consumer use scarce and valuable time. The final section of the chapter will show you how the value of the time required for the consumption of a product can be put into the marginal-utility theory; and what the implications of this modification of the theory are.

■ CHECKLIST

When you have studied this chapter you should be able to:

☐ Define and distinguish between the income and the substitution effects of a price change.

☐ Use the income and the substitution effects to explain why a consumer will buy more of a product when its price falls and why a consumer will buy less of a product when its price rises.

☐ Define marginal utility, total utility, and the law of diminishing marginal utility.

☐ Explain the relationship of the law of diminishing marginal utility to demand and to elasticity.

☐ List four assumptions made in the theory of consumer behavior.

☐ State the utility-maximizing rule.

☐ Use the utility-maximizing rule to determine how a consumer would spend his fixed income when you are given the utility and price data.

☐ Derive a consumer's demand for a product from utility, income, and price data.

☐ Explain how the value of time is incorporated into the theory of consumer behavior; and several of the implications of this modification of the theory.

■ CHAPTER OUTLINE

1. The law of consumer demand can be explained by employing either the income-effect and substitution-effect concepts, or the concept of marginal utility.

    a. Consumers buy more of a commodity when its price falls because their money income will go further (the income effect) and because the commodity is now less expensive relative to other commodities (the substitution effect).

b. The essential assumption made in the alternative explanation is that the more the consumer buys of any commodity, the smaller becomes the marginal (extra) utility obtained from it.

2. The assumption (or law) of diminishing marginal utility is the basis of the theory that explains how a consumer will spend his or her income.

a. The typical consumer, it is assumed, is rational, knows his or her marginal-utility schedules for the various goods available, has a limited money income to spend, and must pay a price to acquire each of the goods which yield utility.

b. Given these assumptions, the consumer maximizes the total utility obtained when the marginal utility of the last dollar spent on each commodity is the same for all commodities.

c. Algebraically, total utility is a maximum when the marginal utility of the last unit of a commodity purchased divided by its price is the same for all commodities (that is, marginal utility per dollar is equal for all commodities).

3. To find a consumer's demand for a product the utility-maximizing rule is applied to determine the amount of the product the consumer will purchase at different prices, income, and tastes and the prices of other products remaining constant.

4. The marginal-utility theory includes the fact that consumption takes time and time is a scarce resource.

a. The full price of any consumer good or service is equal to its market price plus the value of time taken to consume it (the income the consumer could have earned had he used that time for work).

b. The inclusion of the value of consumption time in theory of consumer behavior has several significant implications.

■ **IMPORTANT TERMS**

Income effect
Substitution effect
Utility
Marginal utility

Law of diminishing marginal utility
Rational
Budget restraint
Utility-maximizing rule

■ **FILL-IN QUESTIONS**

1. A fall in the price of a product tends to (increase, decrease) _increase_ the **real** income of a consumer, and a rise in its prices tends to _decrease_

real income. This is called the _income_ effect.

2. When the price of a product increases, the product becomes relatively (more, less) _more_ expensive than it was and the prices of other products become relatively (higher, lower) _lower_ than they were; the consumer will, therefore, buy (less, more) _less_ of the product in question and _more_ of the other products. This is called the _substitution_ effect.

3. The law of diminishing marginal utility is that marginal utility will (increase, decrease) _decrease_ as a consumer increases the quantity of a particular commodity consumed.

4. Assuming that all other things are equal, if the marginal utility of a product decreases rapidly as additional units are consumed, then demand is likely to be (elastic, inelastic) _inelastic_, but if marginal utility decreases slowly as consumption increases then it suggests that demand is _elastic_

5. The marginal-utility theory of consumer behavior assumes that the consumer is _rational_ and has certain _preferences_ for various goods.

6. A consumer cannot buy all he or she wishes of every good and service because income is _limited_ and goods and services have _prices_; these two facts are called the _budget restraint_

7. When the consumer is maximizing the utility which his income will obtain for him, the _ratio of the marginal utility of the last unit purchased_ is the same for all the products he buys. _of a product to its price_

8. If the marginal utility of the last dollar spent on one product is greater than the marginal utility of the last dollar spent on another product, the consumer should (increase, decrease) _increase_ her purchases of the first and _decrease_ her purchases of the second product.

9. Assume there are only two products, X and Y, a consumer can purchase with a fixed income. The consumer is maximizing utility algebraically when:

(a) _MU of Product X_ (c) _MU of product Y_

(b) _price of X_ (d) _price of Y_

10. In deriving a consumer's demand for a particular product the two factors (other than the tastes of the consumer) which are held constant are:

a. _the income of Consumer_

b. _the price of other product_

11. The consumption of any product requires _time_

a. This is a valuable economic resource because it is _scarce_.

b. Its value is equal to _the income that can be earned by using the time to work_

c. And the full price to the consumer of any product is, therefore, _Market price_ plus _Value of the consumption time_

■ **PROBLEMS AND PROJECTS**

1. Suppose that when the price of bread is a dollar per loaf, the Robertson family buys six loaves of bread in a week.

a. When the price of bread falls to 80 cents, the Robertson family will increase its bread consumption to seven loaves.

(1) Measured in terms of bread, the fall in the price of bread will _____ their real income by _____ loaves. (**Hint:** How many loaves of bread **could** they now buy without changing the amount they spend on bread?)

(2) Is the Robertsons' demand for bread elastic or inelastic? _____

b. When the price of bread rises from a dollar to $1.20 per loaf, the Robertson family will decrease its bread consumption to four loaves.

(1) Measured in terms of bread, this rise in the price of bread will _____ their real income by _____ loaf.

(2) Is the Robertson's demand for bread elastic or inelastic? _____

2. Assume that Palmer finds only three goods, A, B, and C, are for sale; and that the amounts of utility which their consumption will yield him are as shown in the table below. Compute the marginal utilities for successive units of A, B, and C and enter them in the appropriate columns.

	Good A			Good B			Good C	
Quantity	Utility	Marginal utility	Quantity	Utility	Marginal utility	Quantity	Utility	Marginal utility
1	21	____	1	7	____	1	23	____
2	41	____	2	13	____	2	40	____
3	59	____	3	18	____	3	52	____
4	74	____	4	22	____	4	60	____
5	85	____	5	25	____	5	65	____
6	91	____	6	27	____	6	68	____
7	91	____	7	28.2	____	7	70	____

3. Using the marginal-utility data for goods A, B, and C which you obtained in problem 2, assume that the prices of A, B, and C are $5, $1, and $4, respectively, and that Palmer has an income of $37 to spend.

a. Complete the table at the top of the next page by computing the **marginal utility per dollar** for successive units of A, B, and C.

b. Palmer would **not** buy 4 units of A, 1 unit of B, and 4 units of C because _____

c. Palmer would **not** buy 6 units of A, 7 units of B, and 4 units of C because _____

d. When Palmer is maximizing his utility he will buy:

(1) _____ units of A, (2) _____ units of B, (3) _____ units of C; his total utility will be _____ and the marginal utility of the last dollar spent on each good will be _____

e. If Palmer's income increased by $1, he would spend it on good _____, assuming he can buy fractions of a unit of a good, because _____

	Good A		Good B		Good C
Quantity	Marginal utility per dollar	Quantity	Marginal utility per dollar	Quantity	Marginal utility per dollar
1	___	1	___	1	___
2	___	2	___	2	___
3	___	3	___	3	___
4	___	4	___	4	___
5	___	5	___	5	___
6	___	6	___	6	___
7	___	7	___	7	___

4. Ms. Thompson has an income of $36 to spend each week. The only two goods she is interested in purchasing are H and J. The marginal-utility schedules for these two goods are shown in the table below.

	Good H						Good J	
Quantity	MU	MU/$6	MU/$4	MU/$3	MU/$2	MU/$1.50	MU	MU/$4
1	45	7.5	11.25	15	22.5	30	40	10
2	30	5	7.5	10	15	20	36	9
3	20	3.33	5	6.67	10	13.33	32	8
4	15	2.5	3.75	5	7.5	10	28	7
5	12	2	3	4	6	8	24	6
6	10	1.67	2.5	3.33	5	6.67	20	5
7	9	1.5	2.25	3	4.5	6	16	4
8	7.5	1.25	1.88	2.5	3.75	5	12	3

The price of J does not change from week to week and is $4. The marginal utility per dollar from J is also shown in the table.

But the price of H varies from one week to the next. The marginal utility per dollar from H when the price of H is $6, $4, $3, $2, and $1.50 is shown in the table.

a. Complete the table below to show how much of H Ms. Thompson will buy each week at each of the five possible prices of H.

Price of H	Quantity of H demanded
$6.00	___
4.00	___
3.00	___
2.00	___
1.50	___

b. What is the table you completed in *a* called?

_____

5. Assume that a consumer can purchase only two goods. These two goods are *R* (recreation) and *M* (material goods). The market price of *R* is $2 and the market price of *M* is $1. The consumer spends all her income in such a way that the marginal utility of the last unit of *R* she buys is 12 and the marginal utility of the last unit of *M* she buys is 6.

a. If we ignore the time it takes to consume *R* and *M*, is the consumer maximizing the total utility she obtains from two two goods? _____

b. Suppose it takes 4 hours to consume each unit of *R* and 1 hour to consume each unit of *M*; and the consumer can earn $2 an hour when she works.

(1) The full price of a unit of *R* is $_____

(2) The full price of a unit of *M* is $_____

c. If we take into account the full price of each of the commodities, is the consumer maximizing her total utility? _____ How do you know this? _____

d. If the consumer is not maximizing her utility, should she increase her consumption of *R* or of *M*? _____

Why should she do this? _____

e. Will she use more or less of her time for consuming *R*? _____

■ **SELF-TEST**

Circle the T if the statement is true; the F if it is false.

1. An increase in the real income of a consumer will result from an increase in the price of a product which the consumer is buying. T (F)

2. The income and substitution effects will induce the consumer to buy more of normal good Z when the price of Z increases. T (F)

3. Utility and usefulness are not synonymous. (T) F

4. Marginal utility is the change in total utility from consuming one more unit of a product. (T) F

5. Because utility cannot actually be measured, the marginal-utility theory cannot really explain how consumers will behave. T (F)

6. A consumer's demand curve for a product is down-sloping because total utility decreases as more of the product is consumed. T (F)

7. If total utility is increasing, then marginal utility is positive and may be either increasing or decreasing. (T) F

negative

8. There is a significant, <u>positive</u> relationship between the rate of decrease in marginal utility and the price elasticity of demand. T (F)

9. When marginal utility falls slowly as more of a good is consumed, then demand will tend to be *inelastic*. T (F)

10. The theory of consumer behavior assumes that consumers act rationally to "get the most from their money." (T) F

11. All consumers are subject to the budget restraint. (T) F

12. To find a consumer's demand for a product, the price of the product is varied while tastes and income and the prices of other products remain unchanged. (T) F

405

13. The theory of consumer behavior assumes that consumers attempt to maximize marginal utility. T (F)

14. If the marginal utility per dollar spent on product A is greater than the marginal utility per dollar spent on product B, then to maximize utility the consumer should purchase less of A and more of B. T (F)

ratio

15. When the consumer is maximizing total utility, the marginal utilities of the last unit of every product he buys are identical. T (F)

406-407

16. The marginal utility of product X is 15 and its price is $5, while the marginal utility of product Y is 10 and its price is $2. The utility-maximizing rule suggests that there should be *less* consumption of product Y. T (F)

17. In most cases, a change in incomes will cause a change in the portfolio of goods and service of purchased by consumers. (T) F

18. A consumer can earn $10 an hour when she works. It takes 2 hours to consume a product. The value of the time required for the consumption of the product is $5. T (F)

19. The marginal utility of leisure time appears to decrease as the quantity of available leisure time increases. (T) F

20. A decrease in the productivity of labor will tend over time to increase the value of time. T (F)

Circle the letter that corresponds to the best answer.

1. The reason the substitution effect works to encourage a consumer to buy more of a product when its price decreases is:
   (a) the real income of the consumer has been increased
   (b) the real income of the consumer has been decreased
   (c) the product is now relatively less expensive than it was
   (d) other products are now relatively less expensive than they were

2. Karen Hansen buys only two goods, food and clothing. Both are normal goods for Karen. Suppose the price of food decreases. Karen's consumption of clothing will:
   (a) decrease due to the income effect
   (b) increase due to the income effect
   (c) increase due to the substitution effect
   (d) decrease due to the substitution effect

3. Which of the following best expresses the law of diminishing marginal utility?
   (a) the more a person consumes of a product, the smaller becomes the utility which he receives from its consumption
   (b) the more a person consumes of a product, the smaller becomes the additional utility which he receives as a result of consuming an additional unit of the product
   (c) the less a person consumes of a product, the smaller becomes the utility which he receives from its consumption
   (d) the less a person consumes of a product, the smaller becomes the additional utility which he receives as a result of consuming an additional unit of the product

The table below shows a hypothetical total utility schedule for a consumer of chocolate candy bars.

Number consumed	Total utility
0	0
1	9
2	19
3	27
4	35
5	42

4. This consumer begins to experience diminishing marginal utility when he consumes the:
   (a) first candy bar
   (b) second candy bar
   (c) third candy bar
   (d) fourth candy bar

5. Other things being equal, demand is likely to be **_elastic_** if the marginal utility of a product:
   (a) decreases rapidly as additional units are consumed
   (b) decreases slowly as additional units are consumed
   (c) increases rapidly as additional units are consumed
   (d) increases slowly as additional units are consumed

6. Which of the following is **not** an essential assumption of marginal-utility theory of consumer behavior?
   (a) the consumer has a small income
   (b) the consumer is rational
   (c) goods and services are not free
   (d) goods and services yield decreasing amounts of marginal utility as the consumer buys more of them

7. A consumer is making purchases of products A and B such that the marginal utility of product A is 20 and the marginal utility of product B is 30. The price of product A is $10 and the price of product B is $20. The utility-maximizing rule suggests that this consumer should increase consumption of product:
   (a) B and decrease consumption of product A
   (b) B and increase consumption of product A
   (c) A and decrease consumption of product B
   (d) make no change in consumption of A or B

*Answer the next three questions (**8, 9,** and **10**) based on the table below showing the marginal-utility schedules for goods X and Y for a hypothetical consumer. The price of good X is $1 and the price of good Y is $2. The income of the consumer is $9.*

Good X		Good Y	
Quantity	MU	Quantity	MU
1	8	1	10
2	7	2	8
3	6	3	6
4	5	4	4
5	4	5	3
6	3	6	2
7	2	7	1

8. To maximize utility, the consumer will buy:
   (a) 7X and 1Y
   (b) 5X and 2Y
   (c) 3X and 3Y
   (d) 1X and 4Y

9. When the consumer purchases the utility-maximizing combination of goods X and Y, total utility will be:
   (a) 36
   (b) 45
   (c) 48
   (d) 52

10. Suppose that the consumer's income increased from $9 to $12. What would be the utility-maximizing combination of goods X and Y?
   (a) 5X and 2Y
   (b) 6X and 3Y
   (c) 2X and 5Y
   (d) 4X and 4Y

11. Suppose that the prices of A and B are $3 and $2, respectively, that the consumer is spending his entire income and buying 4 units of A and 6 units of B, and that the marginal utility of both the 4th unit of A and the 6th unit of B is 6. It can be concluded that:
   (a) the consumer is in equilibrium
   (b) the consumer should buy more of A and less of B
   (c) the consumer should buy less of A and more of B
   (d) the consumer should buy less of both A and B

12. A decrease in the price of product Z will:
   (a) increase the marginal utility per dollar spent on Z
   (b) decrease the marginal utility per dollar spent on Z
   (c) decrease the total utility per dollar spent on Z
   (d) cause no change in the marginal utility per dollar spent on Z

13. Robert Woods is maximizing his satisfaction consuming two goods, X and Y. If the marginal utility of X is half that of Y, what is the price of X if the price of Y is $1.00?
   (a) $0.50
   (b) $1.00
   (c) $1.50
   (d) $2.00

14. Summing the marginal utilities of each unit consumed will determine total:
   (a) cost
   (b) revenue
   (c) utility
   (d) consumption

*Answer the next four questions (**15, 16, 17,** and **18**) on the basis of the following total utility data for products A and B. Assume that the prices of A and B are $6 and $8, respectively, and that consumer income is $36.*

6, 4   8

Units of A	Total utility	Units of B	Total utility
1	18	1	32
2	30	2	56
3	38	3	72
4	42	4	80
5	44	5	84

(handwritten annotations around table: 18 4.5, 12 3, 8 2, 4 1, 2; next to A column. 3 2 4, 2 4, 1 6, 8, 4 next to B column)

15. What is the level of total utility for the consumer in equilibrium?

(a) 86
(b) 102
(c) 108
(d) 120

16. How many units of the two products will the consumer buy?

(a) 1 of A and 4 of B
(b) 2 of A and 2 of B
(c) 2 of A and 3 of B
(d) 3 of A and 4 of B

$3 \times 8 = 24 > 36$
$2 \times 6 = 12$

17. If the price of A decreases to $4, then the utility-maximizing combination of the two products is:

(a) 2 of A and 2 of B
(b) 2 of A and 3 of B
(c) 3 of A and 3 of B
(d) 4 of A and 4 of B

18. Which of the following represents the demand curve for A?

(a)		(b)		(c)		(d)	
P	**Q_d**	**P**	**Q_d**	**P**	**Q_d**	**P**	**Q_d**
$6	1	$6	2	$6	2	$6	2
4	4	4	5	4	3	4	4

19. The full price of a product to a consumer is:

(a) its market price
(b) its market price plus the value of its consumption time
(c) its market price less the value of its consumption time
(d) the value of its consumption time less its market price

34

20. A consumer has two basic choices: rent a videotape movie for $4.00 and spend two hours of time watching it, or spend $15 for dinner at a restaurant that takes an hour of time. If the marginal utilities of the movie and the dinner are the same, and the consumer values time at $15 an hour, the rational consumer will most likely:

(a) rent more movies and buy fewer restaurant dinners
(b) buy more restaurant dinners and rent fewer movies
(c) buy fewer restaurant dinners and rent fewer movies
(d) make no change in the consumption of both

■ **DISCUSSION QUESTIONS**

1. Explain, employing the income-effect and substitution-effect concepts, the reasons consumers buy more of a product at a lower price than at a higher price, and vice versa.

2. Why is utility a "subjective concept"? How does the subjective nature of utility limit the practical usefulness of the marginal-utility theory of consumer behavior?

3. What is the relationship of marginal utility to the price elasticity of demand?

4. What essential assumptions are made about consumers and the nature of goods and services in developing the marginal-utility theory of consumer behavior? What is meant by "budget restraint"?

5. When is the consumer in equilibrium and maximizing total utility? Explain why any deviation from this equilibrium will decrease the consumer's total utility.

6. Using the marginal-utility theory of consumer behavior, explain how an individual's demand schedule for a particular consumer good can be obtained. Why does a demand schedule obtained in this fashion almost invariably result in an inverse or negative relationship between price and quantity demanded?

7. Explain how a consumer might determine the value of his or her time. How does the value of time affect the full price the consumer pays for a good or service?

8. What does taking time into account explain that the traditional approach to consumer behavior does not explain?

■ **ANSWERS**

Chapter 21 Consumer Behavior and Utility Maximization

FILL-IN QUESTIONS

1. increase, decrease, income

2. more, lower, less, more, substitution

3. decrease

4. inelastic, elastic

5. rational, preferences

6. limited, prices, budget restraint

7. ratio of the marginal utility of the last unit purchased of a product to its price

8. increase, decrease

9. *a.* MU of product X; *b.* price of X; *c.* MU of product Y; *d.* price of Y

10. *a.* the income of the consumer; *b.* the prices of other products

11. time; *a.* scarce; *b.* the income that can be earned by using the time for work; *c.* market price, value of the consumption time

PROBLEMS AND PROJECTS

1. *a.* (1) increase, $1\frac{1}{2}$; (2) inelastic; *b.* (1) decrease, 1; (2) elastic

2. marginal utility of good A: 21, 20, 18, 15, 11, 6, 0; marginal utility of good B: 7, 6, 5, 4, 3, 2, 1.2; marginal utility of good C: 23, 17, 12, 8, 5, 3, 2

3. *a.* marginal utility per dollar of good A: $4\frac{1}{5}$, 4, $3\frac{3}{5}$, 3, $2\frac{1}{5}$, $1\frac{1}{5}$, 0; marginal utility per dollar of good B: 7, 6, 5, 4, 3, 2, $1\frac{1}{5}$; marginal utility per dollar of good C, $5\frac{3}{4}$, $4\frac{1}{4}$, 3, 2, $1\frac{1}{4}$, $\frac{3}{4}$, $\frac{1}{2}$; *b.* the marginal utility per dollar spent on good B (7) is greater than the marginal utility per dollar spent on good A (3), and the latter is greater than the marginal utility per dollar spent on good C (2); *c.* he would be spending more than his $37 income; *d.* (1) 4; (2) 5; (3) 3; 151, 3; *e.* A, he would obtain the greatest marginal utility for his dollar ($2\frac{1}{5}$)

4. *a.* 2, 3, 4, 6, 8; *b.* the demand schedule (for good H)

5. *a.* yes; *b.* (1) 10, (2) 3; *c.* no, the marginal utility to price ratios are not the same for the two goods; *d.* of M, because its MU/P ratio is greater; *e.* less

SELF-TEST

DISCUSSION QUESTIONS

Appendix to Chapter 21 Indifference Curve Analysis

This brief appendix contains the third explanation or approach to the theory of consumer behavior. In it you are introduced first to the budget line and then to the indifference curve. These two geometrical concepts are next combined to explain when a consumer is purchasing the combination of two products that maximizes the total utility obtainable with his or her income. The last step is to vary the price of one of the products to find the consumer's demand (schedule or curve) for the product.

■ CHECKLIST

When you have studied this appendix you should be able to:

☐ Define the concept of a budget line.
☐ Explain how to measure the slope of a budget line and determine the location of the budget line.
☐ Define the concept of an indifference curve.
☐ State two characteristics of indifference curves.
☐ Explain the meaning of an indifference map.
☐ Given an indifference map, determine which indifference curves bring more or less total utility to consumers.
☐ Use indifference curves to identify which combination of two products maximizes the total utility of consumers.
☐ Derive a consumer's demand for a product using indifference curve analysis.
☐ Compare and contrast the marginal-utility and the indifference curve analyses of consumer behavior.

■ APPENDIX OUTLINE

1. A budget line shows graphically the different combinations of two products a consumer can purchase with a particular money income; and it has a negative slope.
   a. An increase (decrease) in the money income of the consumer will shift the budget line to the right (left) without affecting its slope.
   b. An increase (decrease) in the prices of both products shifts it to the left (right); but an increase (decrease) in the price of the product the quantity of which is measured horizontally (the price of the other product remaining constant) pivots the budget line around a fixed point on the vertical axis in a clockwise (counterclockwise) direction.

2. An indifference curve shows graphically the different combinations of two products which bring a consumer the same total utility.
   a. An indifference curve is downsloping; if utility is to remain the same when the quantity of one product increases the quantity of the other product must decrease.
   b. An indifference curve is also convex to the origin; the more a consumer has of one product the smaller is the quantity of a second product he is willing to give up to obtain an additional unit of the first product.
   c. The consumer has an indifference curve for every level of total utility; and the nearer (farther) a curve is to (from) the origin in this indifference map the smaller (larger) is the utility of the combinations on that curve.

3. The consumer is in equilibrium and purchasing the combination of two products that brings the maximum utility to him where the budget line is tangent to an indifference curve.

4. In the marginal-utility approach to consumer behavior it is assumed that utility is measurable; but in the indifference curve approach it need only be assumed that a consumer can say whether a combination of products has more utility than, less utility than, or the same amount of utility as another combination.

5. The demand (schedule or curve) for one of the products is derived by varying the price of that product and shifting the budget line, holding the price of the other product and the consumer's income constant, and finding the quantity of the product the consumer will purchase at each price when in equilibrium.

■ **IMPORTANT TERMS**

Budget line

Indifference curve

Marginal rate of substitution

Indifference map

Equilibrium position

■ **FILL-IN QUESTIONS**

1. A budget line shows the various combinations of two products that can be purchased with a given _income_; and, when quantities of X are measured horizontally and quantities of Y vertically, it has a slope equal to the ratio of _price of X_ to the _Price of Y_

2. When:
  a. a consumer's income increases the budget line moves to the (right, left) _right_
  b. quantities of E are measured horizontally and quantities of F vertically, an increase in the price of E will fan the budget line (outward, inward) _inward_ around a fixed point on the _F_ axis.

3. An indifference curve shows the various combinations of two products that give a consumer the same _utilities_
  a. An indifference curve slopes (upward, downward) _downward_ and the slope of an indifference curve is equal to the marginal _rate_ of _substitution_ curve or schedule for that product.

MRS

b. It is (concave, convex) _convex_ to the origin.

4. The more a consumer has of one product, the (greater, smaller) _smaller_ is the quantity of a second product he or she will give up to obtain an additional unit of the first product: as a result the marginal rate of substitution of the first for the second product (increases, decreases) _decrease_ as a consumer moves from left to right (or downward) along an indifference curve.

5. The farther from the origin an indifference curve lies, the (greater, smaller) _greater_ is the total utility obtained from the combinations of products on that curve.

6. A consumer obtains the greatest attainable total utility or satisfaction when he or she purchases that combination of two products at which his or her budget line is _tangent to an indifference curve_. At this point the consumer's marginal rate of substitution is equal to _ratio of the Price of X to price of Y._

7. Were a consumer to purchase a combination of two products which lies on her budget line and at which her budget line is steeper than the indifference curve intersecting that point, she could increase her satisfaction by trading (down, up) _up_ her budget line.

8. The marginal-utility approach to consumer behavior requires that we assume utility (is, is not) _is_ numerically measurable; and the indifference curve approach (does, does not) _does not_ require we make this assumption.

9. When quantities of product X are measured along the horizontal axis, a decrease in the price of X:
  a. fans the budget line (inward, outward) _outward_ and to the (right, left) _right_;
  b. puts the consumer, when in equilibrium, on a (higher, lower) _higher_ indifference curve;
  c. and normally induces the consumer to purchase (more, less) _more_ of product X.

10. Using indifference curves and different budget lines to determine how much of a particular product an individual consumer will purchase at different prices makes it possible to derive that consumer's _demand_ curve or schedule for that product.

■ PROBLEMS AND PROJECTS

1. Following are the schedules for three indifference curves.

Indifference schedule 1		Indifference schedule 2		Indifference schedule 3	
A	**B**	**A**	**B**	**A**	**B**
0	28	0	36	0	45
1	21	1	28	1	36
2	15	2	21	2	28
3	10	3	15	3	21
4	6	4	10	4	15
5	3	5	6	5	10
6	1	6	3	6	6
7	0	7	1	7	3
		8	0	8	1
				9	0

a. On the graph below, measure quantities of A along the horizontal axis (from 0 to 9) and quantities of B along the vertical axis (from 0 to 45).

(1) Plot the 8 combinations of A and B from indifference schedule 1 and draw through the 8 points a curve which is in no place a straight line. Label this curve IC 1.

(2) Do the same for the 9 points in indifference schedule 2 and label it IC 2.

(3) Repeat the process for the 10 points in indifference schedule 3 and label the curve IC 3.

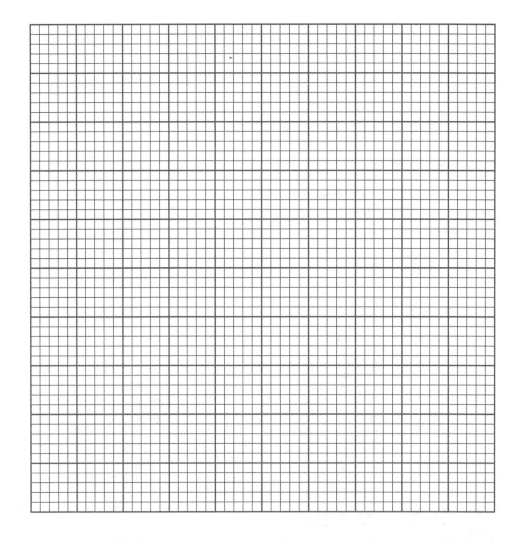

b. Assume the price of A is $12, the price of B is $2.40, and a consumer has an income of $72.

(1) Complete the table below to show the quantities of A and B this consumer is able to purchase.

A	B
0	____
1	____
2	____
3	____
4	____
5	____
6	____

(2) Plot this budget line on the graph you completed in part *a* (above).

(3) This budget line has a slope equal to _____
c. To obtain the greatest satisfaction or utility from his income of $72 this consumer will:

(1) purchase _____ units of A and _____ of B;

(2) and spend $_____ on A and $_____ on B.

2. Shown below is a graph with three indifference curves and three budget lines. This consumer has an income of $100 and the price of Y remains constant at $5.

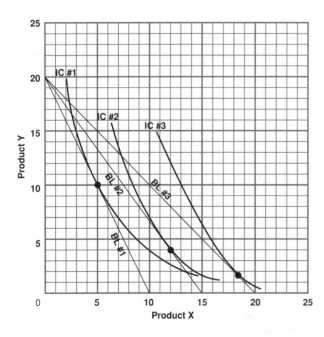

a. When the price of X is $10 the consumer's budget line is BL #1 and the consumer:

(1) purchases _____ X and _____ Y;

(2) and spends $_____ on X and $_____ on Y.
b. If the price of X is $6⅔ the budget line is BL #2 and the consumer:

(1) purchases _____ X and _____ Y;

(2) and spends $_____ for X and $_____ for Y.
c. And when the price of X is $5, the consumer has budget line BL #3 and:

(1) buys _____ X and _____ Y; and

(2) spends $_____ on X and $_____ on Y.
d. On the graph below plot the quantities of X demanded at the three prices.

e. Between $10 and $5 this consumer's demand for X is (elastic, inelastic) _____ and for him products X and Y are (substitutes, complements) _____

■ **SELF-TEST**

Circle the T if the statement is true; the F if it is false.

1. The slope of the budget line when quantities of F are measured horizontally and quantities of G vertically is equal to the price of G divided by the price of F.   **T** (**F**)

2. An increase in the money income of a consumer shifts the budget line to the right.   (**T**) **F**

3. The closer to the origin an indifference curve lies the smaller is the total utility a consumer obtains from the combinations of products on that indifference curve. T **F**

4. If a consumer moves from one combination (or point) on an indifference curve to another combination (or point) on the same curve the total utility obtained by the consumer does not change. T **F**

5. A consumer maximizes total utility when he or she purchases the combination of the two products at which his or her budget line crosses an indifference curve. T **F**

6. A consumer is unable to purchase any of the combinations of two products which lie below (or to the left) of the consumer's budget line. T **F**

7. An indifference curve is concave to the origin. T **F**

8. A decrease in the price of a product normally enables a consumer to reach a higher indifference curve. **T** F

9. It is assumed in the marginal-utility approach to consumer behavior that utility is numerically measurable. **T** F

10. In both the marginal-utility and indifference curve approaches to consumer behavior it is assumed that a consumer is able to say whether the total utility obtained from combination A is greater than, equal to, or less than the total utility obtained from combination B. **T** F

11. The budget line shows all combinations of two products which the consumer can purchase, given money income and the prices of the products. **T** F

12. On an indifference map, the further from the origin, the lower the level of utility associated with each indifference curve. T **F**

13. The marginal rate of substitution shows the rate, at the margin, at which the consumer is prepared to substitute one good for the other so as to remain equally satisfied. **T** F

14. On an indifference map, the consumer's equilibrium position will be where the slope of the highest attainable indifference curve equals the slope of the budget line. **T** F

15. There can be an intersection of consumer indifference curves. T **F**

Circle the letter that corresponds to the best answer.

1. Suppose a consumer has an income of $8, the price of R is $1, and the price of S is $0.50. Which of the following combinations is on the consumer's budget line?
  (a) 8R and 1S
  (b) 7R and 1S

  (c) 6R and 6S
  (d) 5R and 6S

2. If a consumer has an income of $100, the price of U is $10, and the price of V is $20, the maximum quantity of U the consumer is able to purchase is:
  (a) 5
  (b) 10
  (c) 20
  (d) 30

3. When the income of a consumer is $20, the price of T is $5, the price of Z is $2, and the quantity of T is measured horizontally, the slope of the budget line is:
  (a) $\frac{2}{5}$
  (b) $2\frac{1}{2}$
  (c) 4
  (d) 10

4. An indifference curve is a curve which shows the different combinations of two products that:
  (a) give a consumer equal marginal utilities
  (b) give a consumer equal total utilities
  (c) cost a consumer equal amounts
  (d) have the same prices

5. In the schedule for an indifference curve below, how much of G is the consumer willing to give up to obtain the third unit of H?
  (a) 3
  (b) 4
  (c) 5
  (d) 6

Quantity of G	Quantity of H
18	1
12	2
7	3
3	4
0	5

6. The slope of the indifference curve measures the:
  (a) slope of the budget line
  (b) total utility of a good
  (c) space on an indifference map
  (d) marginal rate of substitution

7. To derive the demand curve of a product, the price of the product is varied. For the indifference curve analysis, the:
  (a) budget line is held constant
  (b) money income of the consumer changes
  (c) tastes and preferences of the consumer are held constant
  (d) prices of other products the consumer might purchase changes

The next four questions (*8, 9, 10,* and *11*) are based on the diagram below.

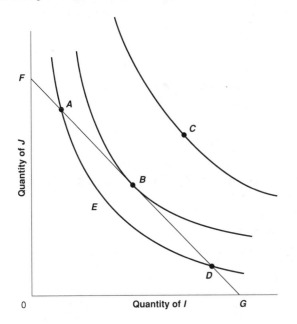

The next four questions (*12, 13, 14,* and *15*) are based on the diagram below.

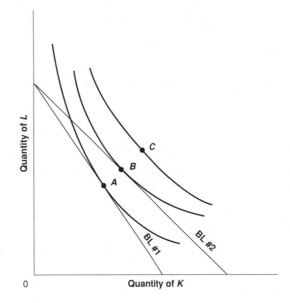

8. The budget line is best represented by line:
(a) *AB*
(b) *AD*
(c) *FG*
(d) *DG*

9. Which combination of goods *I* and *J* will the consumer purchase?
(a) *A*
(b) *B*
(c) *C*
(d) *E*

10. Suppose the price of good *I* increases. The budget line will shift:
(a) inward around a point on the *J* axis
(b) outward around a point on the *J* axis
(c) inward around a point on the *I* axis
(d) outward around a point on the *I* axis

11. If the consumer chooses the combination of goods *I* and *J* represented by point *E*, then the consumer could:
(a) obtain more goods with the available money income
(b) not obtain more goods with the available money income
(c) shift the budget line outward so that it is tangent with point *C*
(d) shift the budget line inward so that it is tangent with point *E*

12. If the budget line shifts from BL #1 to BL #2, it is because the price of:
(a) *K* increased
(b) *K* decreased
(c) *L* increased
(d) *L* decreased

13. If the budget line shifts from BL #2 to BL #1, it is because the price of:
(a) *K* increased
(b) *K* decreased
(c) *L* increased
(d) *L* decreased

14. When the budget line shifts from BL #2 to BL #1, the consumer will buy:
(a) more of *K* and *L*
(b) less of *K* and *L*
(c) more of *K* and less of *L*
(d) less of *K* and more of *L*

15. Point *C* on indifference curve IC #3 can be an attainable combination of products *K* and *L*, if:
(a) the price of *K* increases
(b) the price of *L* increases
(c) money income increases
(d) money income decreases

■ DISCUSSION QUESTIONS

1. Explain why the slope of the budget line is negative and why the slope of an indifference curve is negative and convex to the origin.

2. How will each of the following events affect the budget line?
  (a) A decrease in the money income of the consumer;
  (b) an increase in the prices of both products; and
  (c) a decrease in the price of one of the products.

3. Explain why the budget line can be called "objective" and an indifference curve "subjective."

4. Suppose a consumer purchases a combination of two products that is on his or her budget line but the budget line is not tangent to an indifference curve at that point. Of which product should the consumer buy more and of which should he or she buy less? Why?

5. Explain how the indifference map of a consumer and the budget line are utilized to derive the consumer's demand for one of the products. In deriving demand, what is varied and what is held constant?

6. What is the "important difference between the marginal utility theory and the indifference curve theory of consumer demand"?

■ ANSWERS

Appendix to Chapter 21 Indifference Curve Analysis

FILL-IN QUESTIONS

1. income, the price of X, price of Y

2. *a.* right; *b.* inward, F

3. total satisfaction (utility); *a.* downward, rate, substitution; *b.* convex

4. smaller, decreases

5. greater

6. tangent to an indifference curve, the ratio of the price of the product measured on the horizontal axis to the price of the product measured on the vertical axis

7. up

8. is, does not

9. *a.* outward, right; *b.* higher; *c.* more

10. demand

PROBLEMS AND PROJECTS

1. *b.* (1) 30, 25, 20, 15, 10, 5, 0; (3) 5; *c.* (1) 3, 15; (2) 36, 36

2. *a.* (1) 5, 10; (2) 50, 50; *b.* (1) 12, 4; (2) 80, 20; *c.* (1) 19, 1; (2) 95, 5; *e.* elastic, substitutes

SELF-TEST

1. F, p. 412	**9.** T, p. 415
2. T, p. 412	**10.** T, p. 414
3. T, p. 414	**11.** T, p. 412
4. T, p. 413	**12.** F, p. 414
5. F, p. 414	**13.** T, p. 413
6. F, p. 414	**14.** T, pp. 414–415
7. F, p. 413	**15.** F, p. 414
8. T, p. 414	

1. *d*, p. 412	**9.** *b*, p. 414
2. *b*, p. 412	**10.** *a*, pp. 412–413
3. *b*, p. 412	**11.** *a*, p. 414
4. *b*, p. 413	**12.** *b*, p. 412
5. *c*, p. 413	**13.** *a*, p. 412
6. *d*, p. 413	**14.** *b*, p. 414
7. *c*, pp. 415–416	**15.** *c*, p. 414
8. *c*, p. 412	

DISCUSSION QUESTIONS

1. pp. 412–413	**4.** p. 414
2. pp. 412–413	**5.** pp. 415–416
3. pp. 412–413	**6.** p. 415

The Costs of Production

In previous chapters, the factors which influence the demand for a product purchased by consumers were examined in some detail. Chapter 22 turns to the other side of the market and begins the investigation of the forces which determine the amount of a particular product a business firm will produce and the price it will charge for that product.

The factors that determine the output of a firm and the price of the product are the costs of producing the product **and** the structure of the market in which the product is sold. In addition there is the demand for the product. In the next four chapters you will learn how costs and demand determine price and output in four different kinds of market structures: pure competition, pure monopoly, monopolistic competition, and oligopoly. Because Chapter 22 is an examination of the way in which the costs of the firm change as the output of the firm changes, this chapter is extremely important if the four chapters which follow it are to be understood. For this reason it is necessary for you to master the material dealing with the costs of the firm.

You will probably find that you have some difficulty with the new terms and concepts. Particular attention, therefore, should be given to them. These new terms and concepts are used in the explanation of the costs of the firm and will be used over and over again in later chapters. If you try to learn them in the order in which you encounter them you will have little difficulty because the later terms build on the earlier ones.

After the new terms and concepts are well fixed in your mind, understanding the generalizations made about the relationships between cost and output will be much simpler. Here the important things to note are (1) that the statements made about the behavior of costs are **generalizations** (they do not apply to any particular firm or enterprise, but are more or less applicable to every business firm); and (2) that the generalizations made about the relationships between particular types of cost and the output of the firm are fairly precise generalizations. When attempting to learn these generalizations, you will find it worthwhile to draw rough graphs (with cost on the vertical and output on the horizontal axis) which describe the cost relationships. Try it especially with the following types of costs: **short-run** fixed, variable, total, average fixed, average variable, average total, and marginal costs; and **long-run** average cost.

One last cue: In addition to learning **how** the costs of the firm vary as its output varies, be sure to understand **why** the costs vary the way they do. In this connection note that the behavior of short-run costs is the result of the law of diminishing returns and that the behavior of long-run costs is the consequence of economies and diseconomies of scale.

■ CHECKLIST

When you have studied this chapter you should be able to:

☐ Define economic cost.
☐ Distinguish between an explicit and an implicit cost.
☐ Explain the difference between normal profit and economic profit and why the former is a cost and the latter is not a cost.
☐ Distinguish between the short run and the long run in production.
☐ State the law of diminishing returns and explain its rationale with examples.
☐ Compute marginal and average product when you are given the necessary data.
☐ Explain the relationship between marginal and average product.
☐ Explain the difference between a fixed cost and a variable cost and between average cost and marginal cost.
☐ Compute and graph average fixed cost, average variable cost, average total cost, and marginal cost when you are given total-cost data.
☐ State the relationship between average product and average variable cost and between marginal product and marginal cost.
☐ Explain why cost curves might shift.
☐ Explain the difference between short-run costs and long-run costs.
☐ State why the long-run average cost curve is expected to be U-shaped.

☐ List the causes of the economies and the diseconomies of scale.
☐ Indicate the relationship between long-run average costs and the structure and competitiveness of an industry.
☐ Describe the relevance of economies and diseconomies of scale.
☐ Explain the concept of minimum efficient scale.

■ CHAPTER OUTLINE

1. Because resources are scarce and may be employed to produce many different products, the economic cost of using resources to produce any one of these products is an opportunity cost: the amount of other products that cannot be produced.

a. In money terms, the costs of employing resources to produce a product are also an opportunity cost: the payments a firm must make to the owners of resources to attract these resources away from their best alternative opportunities for earning incomes; and these costs may be either explicit or implicit.

b. *Normal* profit is an implicit cost and is the minimum payment that entrepreneurs must receive for performing the entrepreneurial functions for the firm.

c. *Economic*, or pure, profit is the revenue a firm receives in excess of all its explicit and implicit economic (opportunity) costs. (The firm's accounting profit is its revenue less only its *explicit* costs.)

d. The firm's economic costs vary as the firm's output varies; and the way in which costs vary with output depends upon whether the firm is able to make short-run or long-run changes in the amounts of resources it employs. The firm's plant is a fixed resource in the short run and a variable resource in the long run.

2. In the short run the firm cannot change the size of its plant and can vary its output only by changing the quantities of the variable resources it employs.

a. The law of diminishing returns determines the manner in which the costs of the firm change as it changes its output in the short run.

b. The total short-run costs of a firm are the sum of its fixed and variable costs. As output increases:
(1) the fixed costs do not change;
(2) at first the variable costs increase at a decreasing rate, and then increase at an increasing rate;
(3) and at first total costs increase at a decreasing rate and then increase at an increasing rate.

c. Average fixed, variable, and total costs are equal, respectively, to the firm's fixed, variable, and total costs divided by the output of the firm. As output increases:
(1) average fixed cost decreases;
(2) at first average variable cost decreases and then increases;

(3) and at first average total cost also decreases and then increases.

d. Marginal cost is the extra cost incurred in producing one additional unit of output.
(1) Because the marginal product of the variable resource increases and then decreases (as more of the variable resource is employed to increase output), marginal cost decreases and then increases as output increases.
(2) At the output at which average variable cost is a minimum, average variable cost and marginal cost are equal; and at the output at which average total cost is a minimum, average total cost and marginal cost are equal.
(3) On a graph, marginal cost will always intersect average variable cost at its minimum point, and marginal cost will always intersect average total cost at its minimum point. These intersections will always have marginal cost approaching average variable cost and average total cost from below.
(4) Changes in either resource prices or technology will cause the cost curves to shift.

3. In the long run, all the resources employed by the firm are variable resources, and, therefore, all its costs are variable costs.

a. As the firm expands its output by increasing the size of its plant, average cost tends to fall at first because of the economies of large-scale production; but as this expansion continues, sooner or later, average cost begins to rise because of the diseconomies of large-scale production.

b. The economies and diseconomies encountered in the production of different goods are important factors influencing the structure and competitiveness of various industries.
(1) Minimum efficient scale (MES) is the smallest level of output at which a firm can minimize long-run average costs. This concept explains why relatively large and small firms could coexist in an industry and be viable when there is an extended range of constant returns to scale.
(2) In other industries the long-run average cost curve will decline over a range of output. Given consumer demand, efficient production will be achieved only with a small number of large firms.
(3) When economies of scale extend beyond the market size, the conditions for a natural monopoly are produced, wherein unit costs are minimized by having a single firm produce a product.

■ IMPORTANT TERMS

Economic cost	Implicit cost
Opportunity cost	Economic (pure) profit
Explicit cost	Short run

Long run

Law of diminishing returns

Normal profit

Marginal product

Average product

Fixed resource

Variable resource

Fixed cost

Variable cost

Total cost

Average fixed cost

Average variable cost

Total product

Average (total) cost

Marginal cost

Economies of (large) scale

Diseconomies of (large) scale

Constant returns to scale

Minimum efficient scale (MES)

Natural monopoly

entrepreneurs
entrepreneurs
entrepreneurs

■ **FILL-IN QUESTIONS**

1. The cost of producing a particular product is the quantity of _____ *other* _____ products that cannot be produced. The value or worth of any resource is what it can earn in its best alternative use and is called the (out-of-pocket, opportunity) _____ *opportunity* cost of that resource.

2. The money cost of producing a product is the amount of money the firm must pay to resource owners to _____ *attract* _____ these resources away from alternative employments in the economy; and these costs may be either _____ *implicit* _____ or _____ *explicit* _____ costs.

3. Normal profit is a cost because it is the payment which the firm must make to obtain the services of the _____ *entrepreneur* _____ *entrepreneurs*
   a. Economic profit is not a cost and is equal to the firm's total _____ *revenue* _____ less its total _____ *economic cost*
   b. Accounting profit is equal to the firm's total revenue less its (explicit, implicit) _____ *explicit* _____ costs.

4. In the short run the firm can change its output by changing the quantity of the (fixed, variable) _____ *variable* resources it employs; but it cannot change the quantity of the _____ *fixed* resources. This means that the firm's plant capacity is fixed in the (short, long) _____ *short* _____ run and variable in the _____ *long* _____ run.

5. The law of diminishing returns is that as successive units of a (fixed, variable) _____ *variable* _____ resource are added to a _____ *fix* _____ resource beyond some point the (total, marginal) _____ *marginal* _____ product of the former resource will decrease. The law

assumes that all units of input are of (equal, unequal) _____ *equal* _____ quality.

6. When the total product:
   a. increases at an increasing rate, the marginal product is (rising, falling) _____ *rising* _____;
   b. increases at a decreasing rate, the marginal product is (positive, negative, zero) _____ *positive* _____, but (rising, falling) _____ *falling* _____ before;
   c. is at a maximum, the marginal product is (positive, negative, zero) _____ *zero* _____;
   d. decreases, the marginal product is (positive, negative, zero) _____ *negative*

7. When the marginal product of any input:
   a. exceeds its average product the average product is (rising, falling) _____ *rising* _____;
   b. is less than its average product the average product is _____ *falling* _____;
   c. is equal to its average product the average product is a (minimum, maximum) _____ *maximum*

8. On the graph below sketch the way in which the average product and the marginal product of a resource change as the firm increases its employment of that resource.

9. The short-run costs of a firm are either _____ *variable* costs or _____ *fix* _____ costs, but in the long run all costs are _____ *variable* costs.

10. On the graph on the next page sketch the manner in which fixed cost, variable cost, and total cost change as the output the firm produces in the short run changes.

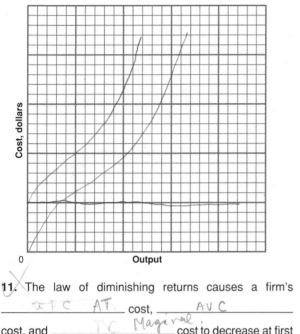

11. The law of diminishing returns causes a firm's

_____ I F C   A T. _____ cost, _____ A V C _____

cost, and _____ T C   Maginal _____ cost to decrease at first
and then to increase as the output of the firm increases.
Sketch these three cost curves on the graph below in such
a way that their proper relationship to each other is shown.

12. Marginal cost is the increase in either _____ T V _____

_____ T C _____ cost or _____
which occurs when the firm increases its output by one
unit.

13. If marginal cost is less than average variable cost,
average variable cost will be (rising, falling, constant)

_____ falling _____ but if average variable cost is less than

marginal cost, average variable cost will be _____ rising _____

14. Assume that labor is the only variable input in the
short run and that the wage rate paid to labor is constant.
   a. When the marginal product of labor is rising, the
   marginal cost of producing a product is (rising, falling)

   _____ falling _____

   b. When the average variable cost of producing a
   product is falling, the average product of labor is

   _____ rising _____

   c. At the output at which marginal cost is a minimum,
   the marginal product of labor is a (minimum, maximum)

   _____ maximum _____

   d. At the output at which the average product of labor
   is a maximum, the average variable cost of producing

   the product is a _____ minimum _____
   e. At the output at which average variable cost is a
   minimum:

   (1) average variable cost and _____ Marginal _____ cost

   are _____ equal _____

   (2) average product and _____ marginal _____ product are

   _____ equal _____

15. The long-run average cost of producing a product is
equal to the lowest of the short-run costs of producing that
product after the firm has had all the time it requires
to make the appropriate adjustments in the size of its

_____ plant. _____

16. Below are the short-run average-cost curves of producing a product with three different sizes of plants, plant
1, plant 2, and plant 3. Draw the firm's long-run average
cost on this graph.

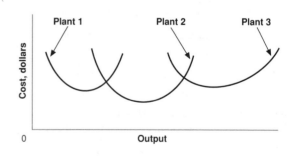

17. List below four important types of economy of large
scale:
   a. _____ labor specialization _____

   b. _____ allocative effect. more efficient plant equipment _____

   c. _____ management efficiency _____

   d. _____ by product. _____

managerial complexity

18. The factor which gives rise to diseconomies of large scale is ___*inefficient management*___.

19. Economies and diseconomies of scale are significant in the American economy because they affect the ___*size*___ and the ___*#*___ of the firms in a particular industry.

MES

20. The smallest level of output at which a firm can minimize long-run average costs is ___*minimum efficient scale*___. Relatively large and small firms could coexist in this type of industry and be equally viable when there is an extended range of ___*constant-return to scale*___
constant-return of scales

21. In some industries, the long-run average cost curve will (increase, decrease) ___*decrease*___ over a long range of output and efficient production will be achieved with only a few (small, large) ___*large*___ firms. The conditions for a ___*natural monopoly*___ are created when unit costs are minimized by having a single firm produce a product, so that (economies, diseconomies) ___*economies*___ of scale extend beyond the market's size.

✱ smallest level of output at which a firm can minimize long-run average cost   MES

■ PROBLEMS AND PROJECTS

1. The table below shows the total production of a firm as the quantity of labor employed increases. The quantities of all other resources employed are constant.
    a. Compute the marginal products of the first through the eighth unit of labor and enter them in the table.
    b. Now compute the average products of the various quantities of labor and enter them in the table.

Units of labor	Total production	Marginal product of labor	Average product of labor
0	0		0
1	80	___	___
2	200	___	___
3	330	___	___
4	400	___	___
5	450	___	___
6	480	___	___
7	490	___	___
8	480	___	___

    c. There are increasing returns to labor from the first through the ___ unit of labor and decreasing returns from the ___ through the eighth unit.
    d. When total production is increasing, marginal product is (positive, negative) ___ and when total production is decreasing, marginal product is ___
    e. When marginal product is greater than average product, then average product will (rise, fall) ___, and when marginal product is less than average product, then average product will ___

2. Assume that a firm has a plant of fixed size and that it can vary its output only by varying the amount of labor it employs. The table at the top of the next page shows the relationships between the amount of labor employed, the output of the firm, the marginal product of labor, and the average product of labor.
    a. Assume each unit of labor costs the firm $10. Compute the total cost of labor for each quantity of labor the firm might employ, and enter these figures in the table.
    b. Now determine the marginal cost of the firm's product as the firm increases its output. Divide the *increase* in total labor cost by the *increase in total output* to find the marginal cost. Enter these figures in the table.
    c. When the marginal product of labor:
    (1) Increases, the marginal cost of the firm's product (increases, decreases) ___
    (2) Decreases, the marginal cost of the firm's product ___
    d. If labor is the only variable input, the total labor cost and total variable cost are equal. Find the average variable cost of the firm's product (by dividing the total labor cost by total output) and enter these figures in the table.
    e. When the average product of labor:
    (1) Increases, the average variable cost (increases, decreases) ___
    (2) Decreases, the average variable cost ___

Quantity of labor employed	Total output	Marginal product of labor	Average product of labor	Total labor cost	Marginal cost	Average variable cost
0	0	—	—	$_____	—	—
1	5	5	5	_____	$_____	$_____
2	11	6	5½	_____	_____	_____
3	18	7	6	_____	_____	_____
4	24	6	6	_____	_____	_____
5	29	5	5⅘	_____	_____	_____
6	33	4	5½	_____	_____	_____
7	36	3	5⅐	_____	_____	_____
8	38	2	4¾	_____	_____	_____
9	39	1	4⅓	_____	_____	_____
10	39	0	3⁹⁄₁₀	_____		_____

3. In the table below you will find a schedule of a firm's fixed cost and variable cost.

   a. Complete the table by computing total cost, average fixed cost, average total cost, and marginal cost.

b. On the first graph on page 259, plot and label fixed cost, variable cost, and total cost.

c. On the second graph on page 259, plot average fixed cost, average variable cost, average total cost, and marginal cost; label the four curves.

Output	Total fixed cost	Total variable cost	Total cost	Average fixed cost	Average variable cost	Average total cost	Marginal cost
$ 0	$200	$ 0	$_____				
1	200	50	_____	$_____	$50.00	$_____	$_____
2	200	90	_____	_____	45.00	_____	_____
3	200	120	_____	_____	40.00	_____	_____
4	200	160	_____	_____	40.00	_____	_____
5	200	220	_____	_____	44.00	_____	_____
6	200	300	_____	_____	50.00	_____	_____
7	200	400	_____	_____	57.14	_____	_____
8	200	520	_____	_____	65.00	_____	_____
9	200	670	_____	_____	74.44	_____	_____
10	200	900	_____	_____	90.00	_____	_____

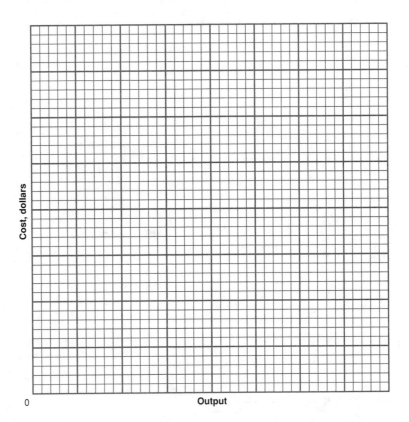

4. Below are the short-run average-total-cost schedules for three plants of different size which a firm might build to produce its product. Assume that these are the only possible sizes of plants which the firm might build.

Plant size A		Plant size B		Plant size C	
Output	ATC	Output	ATC	Output	ATC
10	$ 7	10	$17	10	$53
20	6	20	13	20	44
30	5	30	9	30	35
40	4	40	6	40	27
50	5	50	4	50	20
60	7	60	3	60	14
70	10	70	4	70	11
80	14	80	5	80	8
90	19	90	7	90	6
100	25	100	10	100	5
110	32	110	16	110	7
120	40	120	25	120	10

a. Complete the **long-run** average-cost schedule for the firm in the table below.

Output	Average cost
10	$_____
20	_____
30	_____
40	_____
50	_____
60	_____
70	_____
80	_____
90	_____
100	_____
110	_____
120	_____

b. For outputs between:

(1) _____ and _____, the firm should build plant A.

(2) _____ and _____, the firm should build plant B.

(3) _____ and _____, the firm should build plant C.

■ **SELF-TEST**

Circle the T if the statement is true; the F if it is false.

1. The economic costs of a firm are the payments it must make to resource owners to attract their resources from alternative employments. **(T) F**

2. Economic or pure profit is an explicit cost, while normal profit is an implicit cost. **T (F)**

3. In the short run the size (or capacity) of a firm's plant is fixed. **(T) F**

4. The resources employed by a firm are all variable in the long run and all fixed in the short run. **T (F)**

5. The law of diminishing returns is that as successive amounts of a variable resource are added to a fixed resource, beyond some point total output will diminish. *Marginal* **T (F)**

6. An assumption of the law of diminishing returns is that all units of variable inputs are of equal quality. **(T) F**

7. When total product is increasing at a decreasing rate, marginal product is positive and increasing. **T (F)**

8. When average product is falling, marginal product is greater than average product. **T (F)**

9. When marginal product is negative, total production (or output) is decreasing. **(T) F**

10. The larger the output of a firm, the smaller is the fixed cost of the firm. *average* **T (F)**

11. If the fixed cost of a firm increases from one year to the next (because the premium it must pay for the insurance on the buildings it owns has been increased) while its variable-cost schedule remains unchanged, its marginal-cost schedule will also remain unchanged. **(T) F**

12. Marginal cost is equal to average variable cost at the output at which average variable cost is a minimum. **(T) F**

13. When the marginal product of a variable resource increases, the marginal cost of producing the product will decrease; and when marginal product decreases, marginal cost will increase. **(T) F**

14. If the price of a variable input should increase, the average variable cost, average total cost, and marginal cost curves would all shift upward, but the position of the average fixed cost curve would remain unchanged. **(T) F**

15. One of the explanations of why the long-run average-cost curve of a firm rises after some level of output has been reached is the law of diminishing returns. *diseconomies of* **T (F)**

16. The primary cause of diseconomies of scale is increased specialization of labor. **T (F)**

17. If a firm has constant returns to scale in the long run the total costs of producing its product do not change when it expands or contracts its output. **(T) F**

18. Many firms appear to be larger than is necessary for them to achieve the minimum efficient scale. **(T) F**

19. If a firm increases all its inputs by 30% and its output increases by 20%, the firm is encountering economies of scale. **T (F)**

smaller

20. Minimum efficient scale occurs at the largest level of output at which a firm can minimize long-run average costs. **T (F)**

500,000 - 350,000

Circle the letter that corresponds to the best answer.

x 5

1. Suppose that a firm produces 100,000 units a year and sells them all for $5 each. The explicit costs of production are $350,000 and the implict costs of production are $100,000. The firm has an accounting profit of:
  (a) $200,000 and pure economic profit of $25,000
  (b) $150,000 and pure economic profit of $50,000
  (c) $125,000 and pure economic profit of $75,000
  (d) $100,000 and pure economic profit of $50,000

2. Pure economic profit for a firm is defined as the total revenues of the firm minus its:
  (a) accounting profit
  (b) explict costs of production
  (c) implicit cost of production
  (d) opportunity cost of all inputs ✓

3. The law of diminishing returns is most useful for explaining the:
  (a) shape of the short-run marginal cost curve
  (b) shape of the long-run average cost curve
  (c) decline in average fixed costs as output increases
  (d) decline in total fixed costs as output increases

Use the table below to answer the next two questions (4 and 5). Assume that the only variable resource used to produce output is labor.

Amount of labor	Amount of output
1	3
2	8
3	12
4	15
5	17
6	18

4. The marginal product of the fourth unit of labor is:
  (a) 3 units of output
  (b) 3¾ units of output   *15-12*
  (c) 4 units of output
  (d) 15 units of output

5. When the firm hires four units of labor the average product of labor is:
  (a) 3 units of output
  (b) 3¾ units of output $\frac{15}{4}$ $3\frac{3}{4}$
  (c) 4 units of output
  (d) 15 units of output

6. Because the average product of a variable resource initially increases and later decreases as a firm increases its output:
  (a) average variable cost decreases at first and then increases
  (b) average fixed cost declines as the output of the firm expands
  (c) variable cost at first increases by increasing amounts and then increases by decreasing amounts
  (d) marginal cost at first increases and then decreases

7. Because the marginal product of a resource at first increases and then decreases as the output of the firm increases:
  (a) average fixed cost declines as the output of the firm increases
  (b) average variable cost at first increases and then decreases
  (c) variable cost at first increases by increasing amounts and then increases by decreasing amounts
  (d) total cost at first increases by decreasing amounts and then increases by increasing amounts

For the next three questions (8, 9, and 10) use the data given in the table below. The fixed cost of the firm is $500 and the firm's total variable cost is indicated in the table.

Output	Total variable cost
1	$ 200
2	360
3	500
4	700
5	1,000
6	1,800

8. The average variable cost of the firm when 4 units of output are produced is:
  (a) $175
  (b) $200
  (c) $300
  (d) $700

9. The average total cost of the firm when 4 units of output are being produced is:
  (a) $175
  (b) $200
  (c) $300
  (d) $700

10. The marginal cost of the sixth unit of output is:
  (a) $200
  (b) $300
  (c) $700
  (d) $800

11. Marginal cost and average variable cost are equal at the output at which:
  (a) marginal cost is a minimum
  (b) marginal product is a maximum
  (c) average product is a maximum   *⇒ AVC is min*
  (d) average variable cost is a maximum

12. Average variable cost may be either increasing or decreasing when:
(a) marginal cost is decreasing
(b) marginal product is increasing
(c) average fixed cost is decreasing *Most obvious*
(d) average total cost is decreasing

The next four questions (13, 14, 15, and 16) are based on the following figure.

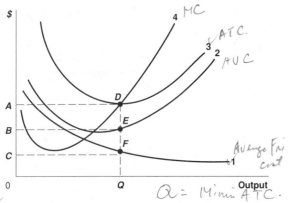

Q = Minim ATC.

13. In the figure, curves 1, 3, and 4, respectively, represent:
(a) average variable cost, marginal cost, and average total cost
(b) average total cost, average variable cost, and marginal cost
(c) avarage fixed cost, average total cost, and marginal cost
(d) marginal cost, average total cost, and average variable cost

14. At output level **Q**, the average fixed cost is measured by vertical distance represented by:
(a) **DE**
(b) **DF**
(c) **DQ**
(d) **EF**

15. As output increases beyond the level represented by **Q**:
(a) marginal product is rising
(b) marginal product is falling
(c) total fixed costs are rising
(d) total costs are falling

16. If the firm is producing at output level **Q**, then the total variable costs of production are represented by area:
(a) 0**QFC**
(b) 0**QEB**
(c) 0**QDC**
(d) **CFEB**

17. At an output of 10,000 units per year, a firm's total

variable costs are $50,000 and its average fixed costs are $2. The total costs per year for the firm are:
(a) $50,000   50000 + 2 × 10000
(b) $60,000
(c) $70,000
(d) $80,000   TFC

18. A firm has total fixed costs of $4,000 a year. The average variable cost is $3.00 for 2000 units of output. At this level of output, its average total costs are:
(a) $2.50
(b) $3.00
(c) $4.50
(d) $5.00

$$AFC = \frac{4000}{2000} = 2.$$
$$AVC = 3 +$$
$$ATC = 3 + 2 =$$

19. If the short-run average variable costs of production for a firm are falling, then this indicates that:
(a) average variable costs are above average fixed costs
(b) marginal costs are below average variable costs
(c) average fixed costs are constant
(d) total costs are falling

20. Which of the following is most likely to be a long-run adjustment for a firm which manufactures jet fighter planes on an assembly-line basis?
(a) an increase in the amount of steel the firm buys
(b) a reduction in the number of "shifts" of workers from three to two
(c) a changeover from the production of one type of jet fighter to the production of a later-model jet fighter
(d) a changeover from the production of jet fighters to the production of sports cars

Answer the next two questions (21 and 22) using the following table. Three short-run cost schedules are given for three plants of different sizes which a firm might build in the long run.

Plant 1		Plant 2		Plant 3	
Output	ATC	Output	ATC	Output	ATC
10	$10	10	$15	10	$20
20	9	20	10	20	15
30	8	30	7	30	10
40	9	40	10	40	8
50	10	50	14	50	9

21. What is the **long-run** average cost of producing 40 units of output?
(a) $7
(b) $8
(c) $9
(d) $10

22. At what output is long-run average cost a minimum?
(a) 20
(b) 30
(c) 40
(d) 50

23. Which of the following is *not* a factor which results in economies of scale?

  (a) more efficient utilization of the firm's plant
  (b) increased specialization in the use of labor
  (c) greater specialization in the management of the firm   *By product*
  (d) utilization of more efficient equipment

24. The long-run average costs of producing a particular product are one of the factors that determine:

  (a) the competition among the firms producing the product
  (b) the number of firms in the industry producing the product
  (c) the size of each of the firms in the industry producing the product
  (d) all of the above   *Cnst a*

25. A firm is encountering constant returns to scale when it increases all of its inputs by 20% and its output increases by:

  (a) 10%
  (b) 15%   *MES*
  (c) 20%
  (d) 25%

■ **DISCUSSION QUESTIONS**

1. Explain the meaning of the opportunity cost of producing a product and the difference between an explicit and an implicit cost. How would you determine the implicit money cost of a resource?

2. What is the difference between normal and economic profit? Why is the former an economic cost? How do you define accounting profit?

3. What type of adjustments can a firm make in the long run that it cannot make in the short run? What adjustments can it make in the short run? How long is the short run?

4. Why is the distinction between the short run and the long run important?

5. State precisely the law of diminishing returns. Exactly what is it that diminishes, and why does it diminish?

6. Distinguish between a fixed cost and a variable cost. Why are short-run total costs partly fixed and partly variable costs, and why are long-run costs entirely variable?

7. Why do short-run variable costs increase at first by decreasing amounts and later increase by increasing amounts? How does the behavior of short-run variable cost influence the behavior of short-run total costs?

8. Describe the way in which short-run average fixed cost, average variable cost, average total cost, and marginal cost vary as the output of the firm increases.

9. What is the connection between marginal product and marginal cost and between average product and average variable cost? How will marginal cost behave as marginal product decreases and increases? How will average variable cost change as average product rises and falls?

10. What is the precise relationship between marginal cost and minimum average variable cost and between marginal cost and minimum average total cost? Why are these relationships necessarily true?

11. What happens to the average total costs, average variable cost, average fixed cost, and marginal cost curves when the price of a variable input increases or decreases? Describe what other factor can cause short-run cost curves to shift.

12. What does the long-run average-cost curve of a firm show? What relationship is there between long-run average cost and the short-run average-total-cost schedules of the different-sized plants which a firm might build?

13. Why is the long-run average-cost curve of a firm U-shaped?

14. What is meant by an economy of scale? What are some of the more important types of such an economy?

15. What is meant by and what causes diseconomies of large scale?

16. Why are the economies and diseconomies of scale of great significance, and how do they influence the size of firms in an industry and the number of firms in an industry?

■ **ANSWERS**

Chapter 22 The Costs of Production

FILL-IN QUESTIONS

  1. other, opportunity

  2. attract, explicit, implicit

  3. entrepreneur(s); *a.* revenues, costs; *b.* explicit

  4. variable, fixed, short, long

  5. variable, fixed, marginal, equal

  6. *a.* rising; *b.* positive, falling; *c.* zero; *d.* negative

  7. *a.* rising; *b.* falling; *c.* maximum

  8. see Figure 22–2(b) of the text

  9. fixed, variable, variable

  10. see Figure 22–3 of the text

  11. average variable, average total, marginal; see Figure 22–6 of the text

  12. total variable, total cost

  13. falling, rising

  14. *a.* falling; *b.* rising; *c.* maximum; *d.* minimum; *e.* (1) marginal, equal, (2) marginal, equal

15. plant

16. see Figure 22–8 of the text

17. *a.* increased specialization in the use of labor; *b.* better utilization of and increased specialization in management; *c.* more efficient productive equipment; *d.* better utilization of by-products

18. managerial complexities (problems)

19. size, number

20. minimum efficient scale, constant returns to scale

21. decrease, large, natural monopoly, economies

PROBLEMS AND PROJECTS

1. *a.* 80, 120, 130, 70, 50, 30, 10, − 10; *b.* 80, 100, 110, 100, 90, 80, 70, 60; *c.* third, fourth; *d.* positive, negative; *e.* rise, fall

2. *a.* $0, 10, 20, 30, 40, 50, 60, 70, 80, 90, 100; *b.* $2.00, 1.67, 1.43. 1.67, 2.00, 2.50, 3.33, 5.00, 10.00; *c.* (1) decreases, (2) increases; *d.* 2.00, 1.82, 1.67. 1.67, 1.72, 1.82, 1.94, 2.11, 2.31, 2.56; *e.* (1) decreases, (2) increases

3. *a.*

Total cost	Average fixed cost	Average total cost	Marginal cost
$ 200	—	—	—
250	$200.00	$250.00	$ 50
290	100.00	145.00	40
320	66.67	106.67	30
360	50.00	90.00	40
420	40.00	84.00	60
500	33.33	83.33	80
600	28.57	85.71	100
720	25.00	90.00	120
870	22.22	96.67	150
1,100	20.00	110.00	230

4. *a.* $7.00, 6.00, 5.00, 4.00, 4.00, 3.00, 4.00, 5.00, 6.00, 5.00, 7.00, 10.00; *b.* (1) 10, 40; (2) 50, 80; (3) 90, 120

SELF-TEST

1. T, p. 418
2. F, p. 419
3. T, p. 420
4. F, p. 420
5. F, p. 420
6. T, p. 421
7. F, pp. 421–422
8. F, p. 422
9. T, p. 422
10. F, p. 423
11. T, p. 428
12. T, p. 427
13. T, pp. 426–427
14. T, p. 428
15. F, p. 429
16. F, p. 432
17. F, p. 432
18. T, p. 433
19. F, p. 432
20. F, p. 433

1. *b,* p. 419
2. *d,* p. 419
3. *a,* p. 420
4. *a,* p. 421
5. *b,* pp. 421–422
6. *a,* pp. 422–423
7. *d,* p. 423
8. *a,* p. 424
9. *c,* p. 425
10. *d,* pp. 425–426
11. *c,* pp. 426–427
12. *c,* p. 425
13. *c,* pp. 425; 427
14. *a,* p. 424
15. *b,* p. 427
16. *b,* pp. 424–425
17. *c,* p. 425
18. *d,* p. 425
19. *b,* p. 427
20. *d,* p. 420
21. *b,* pp. 428–429
22. *b,* pp. 428–429
23. *a,* pp. 430–431
24. *d,* pp. 433–434
25. *c,* p. 432

DISCUSSION QUESTIONS

1. p. 418
2. p. 419
3. p. 420
4. pp. 420–421
5. p. 423
6. pp. 423–424
7. pp. 424–426
8. pp. 426–427
9. p. 427
10. p. 428
11. pp. 428–429
12. p. 429
13. p. 429
14. pp. 429–431
15. p. 432
16. pp. 432–433

Price and Output Determination: Pure Competition

Chapter 23 is the first of four chapters which bring together the demand for a product and the production costs studied in Chapter 22. Each of the four chapters combines demand and production costs in a ***different*** market structure and analyzes and draws conclusions for that particular kind of product market. The questions which are analyzed and for which ***both short-run*** and ***long-run*** answers are sought are the following. Given the costs of the firm, what output will it produce; what will be the market price of the product; what will be the output of the entire industry; what will be the profit received by the firm; and what relationships will exist between price, average total cost, and marginal cost?

In addition to finding the answers to these questions you should learn ***why*** the questions are answered the way they are in each of the market models and in what way the answers obtained in one model ***differ*** from those obtained in the other models.

Actually, the answers are obtained by applying logic to different sets of assumptions. It is important, therefore, to note specifically what the assumptions are and how the assumptions made in one model differ from those of other models. Each model assumes that every firm is guided in making its decisions solely by the desire to maximize its profits, and that the costs of the firm are not materially affected by the type of market in which it ***sells*** its output. The important differences in the models which account for the differing answers involve (1) such characteristics of the market as the number of sellers, the ease of entry into and exodus from the industry, and the kind of product (standardized or differentiated) produced; and (2) the way in which the ***individual firm*** sees the demand for its product.

Chapter 23 begins by describing the three major characteristics of each of the four basic types of market models. From this point on it focuses its attention entirely on the purely competitive model. There are several good reasons for studying pure competition. Not the least of these reasons is that in the long run, pure competition—subject to certain exceptions—results in an ideal or perfect allocation of resources. After obtaining the answers to the questions listed in the first paragraph above, the authors

return at the end of the chapter to explain in what sense competitive resource allocation is ideal and in what cases it may be less than ideal. In Chapters 24 and 25, which concern monopoly and monopolistic competition, respectively, it will be found that in these market situations resource allocation is less than ideal. You, therefore, should pay special attention in Chapter 23 to what is meant by an ideal allocation of resources and why pure competition results in this perfect allocation.

■ CHECKLIST

When you have studied this chapter you should be able to:

☐ List the five characteristics of each of the four basic market models.

☐ Give examples of industries that reflect the characteristics of the four basic market models.

☐ Explain why a purely competitive firm is a "price taker."

☐ Describe the firm's view of the demand for its product and the marginal revenue from the sale of additional units.

☐ Compute average, total, and marginal revenue when you are given the demand schedule faced by a purely competitive firm.

☐ Use the total-revenue and total-cost approach to determine the output that a purely competitive firm will produce in the short run under three different conditions; and explain ***why*** the firm will produce this output.

☐ Use the marginal-revenue and marginal-cost approach to determine the output that a purely competitive firm will produce in the short run under three different conditions; and explain ***why*** the firm will produce this output.

☐ Compare and contrast the total and marginal approaches to the determination of output in the short run.

☐ Find the ***firm's*** short-run supply curve when you are given the firm's short-run cost schedules.

☐ Find the ***industry's*** short-run supply curve (or schedule) when you are given the typical firm's short-run cost schedules.

☐ Determine, under short-run conditions, the price at which the product will sell, the output of the industry, and the output of the individual firm.

☐ Determine, under long-run conditions, the price at which the product will sell, the output of the firm, and the output of the industry.

☐ Explain the role played by the entry and exit of firms in a purely competitive industry in achieving equilibrium in the long run.

☐ Describe the characteristics and rationale for the long-run supply curve in a constant-cost industry, in an increasing-cost industry, and in a decreasing-cost industry.

☐ Distinguish between productive and allocative efficiency.

☐ Explain the significance of (MR) P = AC = MC.

☐ Identify four potential barriers for achieving allocative and productive efficiency in a competitive market.

■ **CHAPTER OUTLINE**

1. The *price* a firm charges for the good or service it produces and its *output* of that product depend not only on the demand for and the cost of producing it but on the character (or structure) of the market (industry) in which it sells the product.

2. The models of the markets in which firms sell their products are pure competition, pure monopoly, monopolistic competition, and oligopoly; and these four models are defined in terms of the number of firms in the industry, whether the product they sell is standardized or differentiated, and how easy it is for new firms to enter the industry.

3. This chapter examines pure competition in which a large number of independent firms, no one of which is able by itself to influence market price, sell a standardized product in a market which firms are free to enter and to leave in the long run. Although pure competition is rare in practice, there are at least three good reasons for studying this "laboratory case."

4. A firm selling its product in a purely competitive industry cannot influence the price at which the product sells; and is a price taker.

  a. The demand for its product is, therefore, perfectly price elastic.

  b. Average revenue (or price) and marginal revenue are equal and constant at the fixed (equilibrium) market price; and total revenue increases at a constant rate as the firm increases its output.

  c. The demand (average revenue) and marginal revenue curves faced by the firm are horizontal and identical at the market price; and the total revenue curve has a constant positive slope.

5. There are two complementary approaches to the analysis of the output that the purely competitive firm will produce in the short run.

  a. Employing the total-revenue-total-cost approach, the firm will produce the output at which total economic profit is the greatest or total loss is the least, provided that the loss is less than the firm's fixed costs (that is, provided that total revenue is greater than total variable cost). If the firm's loss is greater than its fixed cost, it will minimize its loss by producing no output.

  b. Employing the marginal-revenue-marginal-cost approach, the firm will produce the output at which marginal revenue (or price) and marginal cost are equal, provided price is greater than average variable cost. If price is less than average variable cost, the firm will shut down to minimize its loss. The short-run supply curve of the individual firm is that part of its short-run marginal-cost curve which is above average variable cost.

  c. Table 23-8 in the text summarizes the principles which the competitive firm follows when it decides what output to produce in the short run.

  d. The short-run supply curve of the industry (which is the sum of the supply curves of the individual firms) and the total demand for the product determine the short-run equilibrium price and equilibrium output of the industry; and the firms in the industry may be either prosperous or unprosperous in the short run.

6. In the long run the price of a product produced under conditions of pure competition will equal the minimum average total cost, and firms in the industry will neither have economic profits nor suffer economic losses.

  a. If economic profits are being received in the industry during the short run, firms will enter the industry in the long run (attracted by the profits), increase total supply, and thereby force price down to the minimum average total cost, leaving only a normal profit.

  b. If losses are being suffered in the industry during the short run, firms will leave the industry in the long run (seeking to avoid losses), reduce total supply, and thereby force price up to the minimum average total cost, leaving only a normal profit.

  c. If an industry is a constant-cost industry, the entry of new firms will not affect the average-total-cost schedules or curves of firms in the industry.

  (1) An increase in demand will result in no increase in the long-run equilibrium price, and the industry will be able to supply larger outputs at a constant price.

  (2) Graphically, the long-run supply curve in a constant-cost industry is horizontal at the minimum of the average-total-cost curve, indicating that firms make only normal profits, but not economic profits.

  d. If an industry is an increasing-cost industry, the entry of new firms will raise the average-total-cost schedules or curves of firms in the industry.

(1) An increase in demand will result in an increase in the long-run equilibrium price, and the industry will be able to supply larger outputs only at higher prices.

(2) Graphically, the long-run supply curve in an increasing-cost industry is upsloping at the minimum of the average-total-cost curve, indicating that firms make only normal profits, but not economic profits.

e. If an industry is a decreasing-cost industry, the entry of new firms will lower the average-total-cost schedules or curves of firms in the industry.

(1) An increase in demand will result in a decrease in the long-run equilibrium price, and the industry will be able to supply larger outputs only at lower prices.

(2) Graphically, the long-run supply curve in a decreasing-cost industry is downsloping at the minimum of the average-total-cost curve, indicating that firms make only normal profits, but not economic profits.

7. In the long run, each purely competitive firm is compelled by competition to produce that output at which price, marginal revenue, average cost, and marginal cost are equal and average cost is a minimum.

a. An economy in which all industries were purely competitive would use its resources efficiently.

(1) Goods are efficiently **produced** when the average total cost of producing them is at a minimum; buyers benefit most from this efficiency when they are charged a price just equal to minimum average total cost.

(2) Resources are efficiently **allocated** when goods are produced in such quantities that the total satisfaction obtained from the economy's resources is at a maximum; or when the price of each good is equal to its marginal cost.

b. Even in a purely competitive economy, the allocation of resources may not, for at least four reasons, be the most efficient.

(1) The distribution of income provided by the competitive market system may be quite unequal and create distortions in allocation of resources and the production of goods and services.

(2) Spillover costs and benefits and the production of public goods may not be taken into account in the allocation of resources in the competitive market model.

(3) The rate of technological advance may be slower and use of the best-known productive techniques may be less widespread in purely competitive industries.

(4) The range of consumer choice and the development of new products may be restricted in a purely competitive economy.

■ IMPORTANT TERMS

Pure competition	**Oligopoly**
Pure monopoly	**Imperfect competition**
Monopolistic competition	**Price-taker**

Total revenue
Average revenue
Marginal revenue
Total-receipts-total-cost approach
Marginal-revenue-marginal-cost approach
The profit-maximizing case
Break-even point
The loss-minimizing case
The close-down case
MR = MC rule
P = MC rule

The firm's short-run supply curve (schedule)
The competitive industry's short-run supply curve (schedule)
Short-run competitive equilibrium
Long-run competitive equilibrium
Constant-cost industry
Increasing-cost industry
Long-run supply
Productive efficiency
Allocative efficiency

standardized.
oligopoly

■ FILL-IN QUESTIONS

1. The four market models examined in this and the next three chapters:

a. are ___*Pure Competiti.*___,
___*Monopoly*___,
___*monopolistic Competi.*___, and
___*oligopoly*___;

b. differ in terms of ___*#*___ of firms in the industry; whether the product is ___*homogenous*___ or ___*differentiated*___; control over ___*Price*___; how easy or difficult it is for new firms to ___*enter or exit*___ the industry; and nonprice ___*determinant Competition.*___

2. What are the four specific conditions which characterize pure competition?

a. ___*Large # of firms or seller*___

b. ___*sell a standardized product.*___

c. ___*Free to enter and exit industry*___

d. ___*no single firm supply enough to influence Price*___

3. The individual firm in a purely competitive industry is a price-(maker, taker) ___*taker*___; and finds that the demand for its product is perfectly (elastic, inelastic) ___*elastic*___ and that marginal revenue is (less than, greater than, equal to) ___*equal to*___ the price of the product.

4. Economic profit is equal to ___*Total revenue*___ ___*- Economic cost*___

5. The two approaches which may be used to determine the most profitable output for any firm are the _total revenue – total cost_ approach and _Marginal R – Marginal Cost_ approach.

6. A firm should produce in the short run only if it can obtain a _normal profit_ or suffer an economic loss which is no greater than its _Total fix Cost_. Provided it produces any output at all:

  a. It will produce that output at which its profit is a (maximum, minimum) _maximum_ or its loss is a _minimum_.

  b. Or, said another way, the output at which marginal _Revenue_ and marginal _Cost_ are equal.

7. A firm will produce at an economic loss in the short run if the price which it receives is greater than its average (fixed, <u>variable</u>, total) _variable_ cost.

8. In the short run the individual firm's supply curve is _the portion of MC which lies above AVC_; the short-run market supply curve is _Sum of the individual SC_.

9. The short-run equilibrium price for a product produced by a purely competitive industry is the price at which _Total quantity demand_ and _Total quantity supply_ are equal; the equilibrium quantity is _the quantity demanded and supplied at equilibrium price_.

10. In a purely competitive industry in the short run the number of firms in the industry and the sizes of their plants are (fixed, variable) _fixed_; but in the long run they are _variable_.

11. When a purely competitive industry is in long-run equilibrium the price which the firm is paid for its product is equal not only to marginal revenue but to long-run _Average total_ cost and to long-run _Marginal cost_ cost; and long-run average cost is a (maximum, minimum, neither) _minimum_.

12. Firms tend to enter industry in the long run if _the firms are making profit in the SR_ and leave it if _The firms are realizing losses in the SR._

13. If the entry of new firms into an industry tends to raise the costs of all firms in the industry, the industry is said to

be a(n) (constant-, increasing-, decreasing-) _increasing_ cost industry; and its long-run supply curve is (horizontal, downsloping, upsloping) _upsloping_.

14. If an economy is to make the best use of its scarce resources it is necessary that it achieve both _allocativ_ and _productive_ efficiency.

15. The purely competitive economy achieves productive efficiency in the long run because price and _Average_ cost are equal and the latter is a (<u>maximum</u>, minimum) _minimum_.

16. In the long run the purely competitive economy is allocatively efficient because price and _Marginal_ cost are equal.

17. List four reasons why resource allocation in a purely competitive economy may be less than efficient.

  a. _Income distribution_
  b. _Spillover benefit and cost._
  c. _Less technological advances_
  d. _Less consumer Choices_

■ **PROBLEMS AND PROJECTS**

1. Employing the following set of terms, complete the table at the top of page 269 by inserting the appropriate letter or letters in the blanks.

a. one   h considerable
b. few   i. very easy
c. many   j. blocked
d. a very large number   k. fairly easy
e. standardized   l. fairly difficult
f. differentiated   m. none
g. some   n. unique

2. Below is the demand schedule facing the individual firm.

Price	Quantity demanded	Average revenue	Total revenue	Marginal revenue
$10	0	$____	$____	—
10	1	____	____	$____
10	2	____	____	____
10	3	____	____	____
10	4	____	____	____
10	5	____	____	____
10	6	____	____	____

Market characteristics	Market model			
	Pure competition	Pure monopoly	Monopolistic competition	Oligopoly
Number of firms	_____	_____	_____	_____
Type of product	_____	_____	_____	_____
Control over price	_____	_____	_____	_____
Conditions of entry	_____	_____	_____	_____
Nonprice competition	_____	_____	_____	_____

a. Complete the table by computing average revenue, total revenue, and marginal revenue.

b. Is this firm operating in a market which is purely competitive? _____ How can you tell?

c. The coefficient of the price elasticity of demand is the same between every pair of quantities demanded.

What is it? _____

d. What relationship exists between average revenue and marginal revenue? _____

_____

e. On the following graph plot the demand schedule, average revenue, total revenue, and marginal revenue; label each of these curves.

Dollars

0   Quantity

f. The demand, average-revenue, and marginal-revenue curves are all _____ lines at a price of $_____ across all quantities.

g. The total-revenue curve is an upsloping line with a _____ slope because marginal revenue is _____

3. Assume that a purely competitive firm has the schedule of costs given in the table below.

Output	TFC	TVC	TC
0	$300	$ 0	$ 300
1	300	100	400
2	300	150	450
3	300	210	510
4	300	290	590
5	300	400	700
6	300	540	840
7	300	720	1,020
8	300	950	1,250
9	300	1,240	1,540
10	300	1,600	1,900

a. Complete the table below to show the total revenue and total profit of the firm at each level of output the firm might produce. Assume market prices of $55, $120, and $200.

b. Indicate what output the firm would produce and what its profits would be at a:

(1) Price of $55: output of _____ and profit of _____

(2) Price of $120: output of _____ and profit of _____

(3) Price of $200: output of _____ and profit of _____

c. Plot the cost data for total variable cost and total cost in the graph on the opposite page. Then plot the total revenue when the price is $55, $120, and $200. For each price indicate the level of output and the economic profit or loss on the graph.

	Market price = $55		Market price = $120		Market price = $200	
Output	Revenue	Profit	Revenue	Profit	Revenue	Profit
0	$_____	$_____	$_____	$_____	$_____	$_____
1	_____	_____	_____	_____	_____	_____
2	_____	_____	_____	_____	_____	_____
3	_____	_____	_____	_____	_____	_____
4	_____	_____	_____	_____	_____	_____
5	_____	_____	_____	_____	_____	_____
6	_____	_____	_____	_____	_____	_____
7	_____	_____	_____	_____	_____	_____
8	_____	_____	_____	_____	_____	_____
9	_____	_____	_____	_____	_____	_____
10	_____	_____	_____	_____	_____	_____

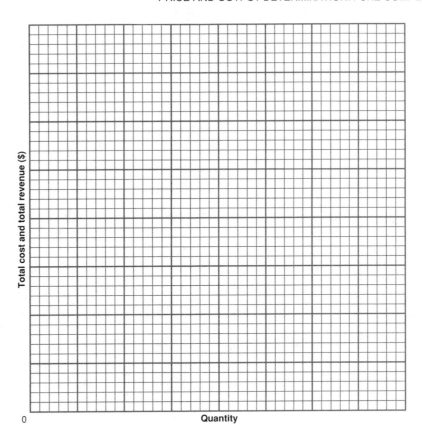

4. Now assume that the same purely competitive firm has the schedule of average and marginal costs given in the table below.

Output	AFC	AVC	ATC	MC
0				
1	$300	$100	$400	$100
2	150	75	225	50
3	100	70	170	60
4	75	73	148	80
5	60	80	140	110
6	50	90	140	140
7	43	103	146	180
8	38	119	156	230
9	33	138	171	290
10	30	160	190	360

a. At a price of $55, the firm would produce _____ units of output. At a price of $120, the firm would pro-

duce _____ units of output. At a price of $200, the

firm would produce _____ units of output. Compare your answers to those you gave in problem 3.

b. The **per unit** economic profit (or loss) is calculated

by subtracting _____ at a particular

level of output from the product price. This **per unit** economic profit is then multiplied by the number of units

of _____ to determine the economic profit for the competitive firm.

(1) At the product price of $200, the average total costs

are $_____, so **per unit** economic profit is $_____. Multiplying this amount by the number of units of output

results in an economic profit of $ _____

(2) At the product price of $120, the average total costs

are $_____, so **per unit** economic losses are

$_____. Multiplying this amount by the number of

units of output results in an economic loss of $_____

(3) Compare your answers to those you gave in problem 3b (2) and 3b (3).
b. Plot the data for average and marginal cost in the graph on the next page. Then plot the marginal revenue when the price is $55, $120, and $200. For each price, indicate the level of output and the economic profit or loss on the graph. Compare your answers and graph to those you gave in problem 3.

嫁　未　玉　小
得　應　階　摘
春　移　曾　人
風　植　待　間
盡　空　探　紫
日　門　重　牡
閒　裡　還　丹

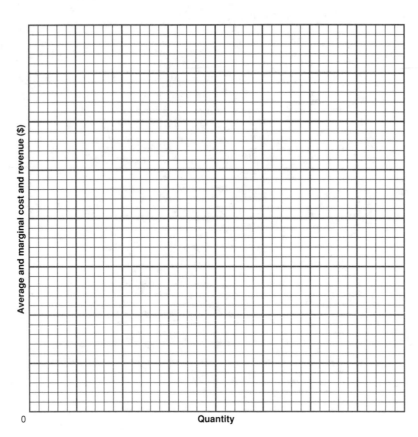

Average and marginal cost and revenue ($)

0   Quantity

5. Use the total cost data in problem 3 or the average and marginal cost data in problem 4 in your work on problem 5.

　a. In the table below, complete the supply schedule for the competitive firm and state what the economic profit will be at each price.

Price	Quantity supplied	Profit
$360	_____	$_____
290	_____	_____
230	_____	_____
180	_____	_____
140	_____	_____
110	_____	_____
80	_____	_____
60	_____	_____

　b. If there are 100 firms in the industry and all have the same cost schedule:

(1) Complete the market supply schedule in the table.

Quantity demanded	Price	Quantity supplied
400	$360	_____
500	290	_____
600	230	_____
700	180	_____
800	140	_____
900	110	_____
1,000	80	_____

(2) Using the demand schedule given in (1):

(a) what will the market price of the product be?

$_____ ;

(b) what quantity will the individual firm produce?

_____ ;

(c) how large will the firm's profit be? $_____ ;

(d) will firms tend to enter or leave the industry in the long run? _____ Why? _____

_____

6. If the total costs assumed for the individual firm in problem 3 were long-run total costs and if the industry were a constant-cost industry:

a. What would be the market price of the product in the long run? $_____

b. What output would each firm produce when the industry was in long-run equilibrium? _____

c. Approximately how many firms would there be in the industry in the long run, given the present demand for the product? _____

d. If the table below was the market demand schedule for the product, how many firms would there be in the long run in the industry? _____

Price	Quantity demanded
$360	500
290	600
230	700
180	800
140	900
110	1,000
80	1,100

e. On the graph below draw a long-run supply curve of
(1) a constant-cost industry
(2) an increasing-cost industry

0

At equilibrium MC= MR=P.

16. If a purely competitive firm is in short-run equilibrium and its marginal cost is grater than is average total cost, then firms will leave the industry in the long run.　T　F

17. Pure competition, if it could be achieved in all industries in the economy, would result in the most efficient allocation of resources.　T　F

18. Under conditions of pure competition, firms are forced to employ the most efficient production methods available to survive.　T　F

19. The marginal costs of producing a product are society's measure of the marginal worth of alternative products.　T　F

20. There is no scientific basis for determining which distribution of total money income results in the greatest satisfaction of wants in the economy.　T　F

Circle the letter that corresponds to the best answer.

1. The four models of the markets (industries) in which business firms sell their products differ in terms of:
(a) the number of firms in the industry
(b) how easy or difficult it is for new firms to enter the industry
(c) whether the product is standardized or differentiated
(d) all of the above

2. Which of the following is *not* characteristic of pure competition?
(a) large number of sellers
(b) differentiated product
(c) easy entry
(d) no advertising

3. If the product produced by an industry is standardized, the market structure can be:
(a) pure competition or monopolistic competition
(b) pure competition or oligopoly
(c) monopolistic competition or oligopoly
(d) pure competition, monopolistic competition, or oligopoly

4. Into which of the following industries is entry least difficult?
(a) pure competition
(b) pure monopoly
(c) monopolistic competition
(d) oligopoly

5. Which of the following industries comes *closest* to being purely competitive?
(a) wheat
(b) shoes
(c) retailing
(d) farm implements

6. In which of the following market models is the individual seller of a product a "price-taker"?
(a) pure competition
(b) pure monopoly
(c) monopolistic competition
(d) oligopoly

7. In a purely competitive industry:
(a) each of the existing firms will engage in various forms of nonprice competition
(b) new firms are free to enter and existing firms are able to leave the industry very easily
(c) individual firms have a "price policy"
(d) each of the firms produces a differentiated (nonstandardized) product

8. The demand schedule or curve confronted by the individual purely competitive firm is:
(a) perfectly inelastic
(b) inelastic but not perfectly inelastic
(c) perfectly elastic
(d) elastic but not perfectly elastic

9. A firm will be willing to produce at a loss in the short run if:
(a) the loss is no greater than its total fixed costs
(b) the loss is no greater than its average fixed costs
(c) the loss is no greater than its total variable costs
(d) the loss is no greater than its average variable cost

10. The individual firm's short-run supply curve is that part of its marginal-cost curve lying above its:
(a) average-total-cost curve
(b) average-variable-cost curve
(c) average-fixed-cost curve
(d) average-revenue curve　　$MC = AC$

11. If a single purely competitive firm's most profitable output in the short run were an output at which it was neither receiving an economic profit nor suffering an economic loss, one of the following would *not* be true. Which one?
(a) marginal cost and average total cost are equal
(b) marginal cost and average variable cost are equal
(c) marginal cost and marginal revenue are equal
(d) marginal cost and average revenue are equal

12. Which one of the following statements is true of a purely competitive industry in short-run equilibrium?
(a) price is equal to average total cost
(b) total quantity demanded is equal to total quantity supplied
(c) profits in the industry are equal to zero
(d) output is equal to the output at which average total cost is a minimum　*long run*

13. Suppose that when 2000 units of output are produced, the marginal cost of the 2001st unit is $5. This amount is equal to the minimum of average total cost, and

marginal cost is rising. If the optimal level of output in the short run is 2500 units, then at that level:
- (a) marginal cost is greater than $5 and marginal cost is less than average total cost
- (b) marginal cost is greater than $5 and marginal cost is greater than average total cost
- (c) marginal cost is less than $5 and marginal cost is greater than average total cost
- (d) marginal cost is equal to $5 and marginal cost is equal to average total cost

14. The Zebra, Inc., is selling in a purely competitive market. Its output is 250 units which sell for $2 each. At this level of output, marginal cost is $2 and average variable cost is $2.25. The firm should:
- (a) produce zero units of output
- (b) decrease output to 200 units
- (c) continue to produce 250 units
- (d) increase output to maximize profits

The next four questions (15, 16, 17 and 18) are based on the following graph.

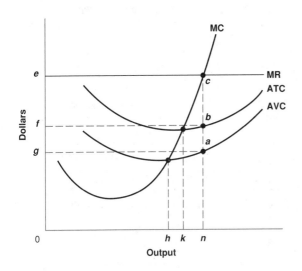

15. If the firm is producing at output level 0*n*, the rectangular area *fecb* is:
- (a) total variable cost
- (b) total fixed costs
- (c) total revenue
- (d) total economic profit

16. At the profit-maximizing output, average fixed cost is:
- (a) *ab*
- (b) *ac*
- (c) *na*
- (d) *nb*

17. At the profit-maximizing output, the total variable costs are equal to the area:
- (a) 0*fbn*
- (b) 0*ecn*
- (c) 0*gan*
- (d) *gfba*

18. The demand curve for this firm is equal to:
- (a) MR, and the supply curve is the portion of the MC curve where output is greater than level *n*
- (b) MR, and the supply curve is the portion of the MC curve where output is greater than level *k*
- (c) MR, and the supply curve is the portion of the MC curve where output is greater than level *h*
- (d) MR, and the supply curve is the portion of the ATC curve where output is greater than level *k*

Answer the next five questions (19, 20, 21, 22, and 23) on the basis of the following cost data for a firm that is selling in a purely competitive market.

Output	AFC	AVC	ATC	MC
1	$300	$100	$400	$100
2	150	75	225	50
3	100	70	170	60
4	75	73	148	80
5	60	80	140	110
6	50	90	140	140
7	43	103	146	180
8	38	119	156	230
9	33	138	171	290
10	30	160	190	360

19. If the market price for the firm's product is $140, the competitive firm will produce:
- (a) 5 units at an economic loss of $150
- (b) 6 units and "break even"
- (c) 7 units and "break even"
- (d) 8 units at an economic profit of $74

20. If the market price for the firm's product is $290, the competitive firm will produce:
- (a) 7 units at an economic profit of $238
- (b) 8 units at an economic profit of $592
- (c) 9 units at an economic profit of $1071
- (d) 10 units at an economic profit of $1700

21. If the product price is $179, then *per unit* economic profit at the profit-maximizing output is:
- (a) $15
- (b) $23
- (c) $33
- (d) $39

22. The total fixed costs are:
- (a) $100
- (b) $200
- (c) $300
- (d) $400

Assume there are 100 identical firms in this industry and total or market demand is shown below.

Price	Quantity demanded
$360	600
290	700
230	800
180	900
140	1000
110	1100
80	1200

23. The equilibrium price will be:
   (a) $140
   (b) $180
   (c) $230
   (d) $290

24. Assume that the market for wheat is purely competitive. Currently, each of the firms growing wheat are experiencing economic losses. In the long run, we can expect this market's:
   (a) supply curve to increase
   (b) demand curve to increase
   (c) supply curve to decrease
   (d) demand curve to decrease

25. The long-run supply curve under pure competition will be:
   (a) downsloping in an increasing-cost industry and upsloping in a decreasing-cost industry
   (b) horizontal in a constant-cost industry and upsloping in a decreasing-cost industry
   (c) horizontal in a constant-cost industry and upsloping in an increasing-cost industry
   (d) upsloping in an increasing-cost industry and vertical in a constant-cost industry

26. Increasing-cost industries find that their costs rise as a consequence of an increased demand for the product because of:
   (a) the diseconomies of scale
   (b) diminishing returns
   (c) higher resource prices
   (d) a decreased supply of the product

27. When a purely competitive industry is in long-run equilibrium, one of the following statements is **not** true. Which one?
   (a) firms in the industry are earning normal profits
   (b) price and long-run average total cost are equal to each other
   (c) long-run marginal cost is at its minimum level
   (d) long-run marginal cost is equal to marginal revenue

28. It is contended that which of the following triple identities results in the most efficient use of resources?
   (a) P = AC = MC
   (b) P = AR = MR

   (c) P = MR = MC
   (d) AC = MC = MR

29. An economy is producing the goods most wanted by society when, for each and every good, its:
   (a) price and average cost are equal
   (b) price and marginal cost are equal
   (c) marginal revenue and marginal cost are equal
   (d) price and marginal revenue are equal

30. The operation of a purely competitive market system accurately measures:
   (a) both spillover costs and spillover benefits
   (b) spillover costs but not spillover benefits
   (c) spillover benefits but not spillover costs
   (d) neither spillover costs nor spillover benefits

■ **DISCUSSION QUESTIONS**

1. What are the four market models (or situations) which economists employ and what are the major characteristics of each type of market?

2. If pure competition is so rare in practice, why are students of economics asked to study it?

3. Explain how the firm in a purely competitive industry sees the demand for the product it produces in terms of
   (a) the price elasticity of demand;
   (b) the relation of average to marginal revenue; and
   (c) the behavior of total, average, and marginal revenues as the output of the firm increases.

4. Why is a firm willing to produce at a loss in the short run if the loss is no greater than the fixed costs of the firm?

5. Explain how the short-run supply of an individual firm and of the purely competitive industry are determined.

6. What determines the equilibrium price and output of a purely competitive industry in the short run? Will economic profits in the industry be positive or negative?

7. Why do the MC = MR rule and MC = P rule mean the same thing under conditions of pure competition?

8. What are the important distinctions between the short run and the long run and between equilibrium in the short run and in the long run in a competitive industry?

9. When is the purely competitive industry in long-run equilibrium? What forces the purely competitive firm into this position?

10. What is a constant-cost industry? What is an increasing-cost industry? Under what economic conditions is each likely to be found? What will be the nature of the long-run supply curve in each of these industries?

11. When has an economy achieved the most efficient use of its scarce resources? What two kinds of efficiency are necessary if the economy is to make the most efficient use of its resources?

12. Why is it said that a purely competitive economy is an efficient economy?

13. What did Adam Smith mean when he said that self-interest and competition bring about results which are in the best interest of the economy as a whole without government regulation or interference?

14. Even if an economy is purely competitive, the allocation of resources may not be ideal. Why?

15. Does pure competition *always* promote both the use of the most efficient technological methods of production and the development of better methods?

■ **ANSWERS**

Chapter 23 Price and Output Determination: Pure Competition   *exodus* .

FILL-IN QUESTIONS

1. *a.* pure competition, pure monopoly, monopolistic competition, oligopoly (any order); *b.* number, standardized, differentiated (either order), price, enter, competition

2. *a.* a large number of independent sellers; *b.* a standardized product; *c.* no single firm supplies enough to influence market price; *d.* no obstacles to the entry of new firms or the exodus of old firms   *obstacles*   *exodu*

3. taker, elastic, equal to   *exodu*

4. total revenue minus total cost   *exodu*

5. total-revenue-total-cost, marginal-revenue-marginal-cost

6. profit, fixed costs; *a.* maximum, minimum; *b.* cost, revenue (either order)

7. variable

8. that portion of the firm's marginal-cost curve which lies above the average-variable-cost curve, the sum of the short-run supply curves of all firms in the industry

9. total quantity demanded, total quantity supplied (either order), the quantity demanded and supplied at the equilibrium price

10. fixed, variable

11. average, marginal (either order), minimum

12. the firms in the industry are realizing profits in the short run, the firms in the industry are realizing losses in the short run

13. increasing-, upsloping

14. productive, allocative (either order)

15. average, minimum

16. marginal

⋆17. *a.* the competitive price system does not necessarily result in an ideal distribution of money income in the economy; *b.* the competitive price system does not accurately measure costs and benefits when spillover costs and benefits are significant or provide social goods; *c.* the competitive price system does not entail the use of the most efficient productive techniques; *d.* the competitive price system may not provide for a sufficient range of consumer choice or for the development of new products

PROBLEMS AND PROJECTS

1. number of firms: d, a, c, b; type of product: e, n, f, e, or f; control over price: m, h, g, g; entry: i, j, k, l; nonprice competition: m, g, h, g or h

2. *a.* average revenue: all are $10.00; total revenue: $0, 10.00, 20.00, 30.00, 40.00, 50.00, 60.00; marginal revenue: all are $10,000; *b.* yes, because price (average revenue) is constant and equal to marginal revenue; *c.* infinity; *d.* they are equal; *e.* see Figure 23-1 of text for an example; *f.* horizontal, $10; *g.* constant, constant

3. *a.* (see table below); *b.* (1) 0, −$300; (2) 5, −$100; (3) 7, $380; *c.* see Figure 23-2 of the text for an example

4. *a.* 0, 5, 7 (same answers as in **3***b*); *b.* average total cost; output; (1) $146 ($200−$146 = $54), ($54 × 7 = $378); (2) $140, ($120 − $140 = −$20), (−$20 × 5 = −$100); (3) same answers but $2 difference in **3***b*(3) and **4***b*(1) due to rounding; *c.* see Figure 23-3 of text for an example

Market price = $55		Market price = $120		Market price = $200	
Revenue	**Profit**	**Revenue**	**Profit**	**Revenue**	**Profit**
$ 0	$ −300	$ 0	$ −300	$ 0	$ −300
55	−345	120	−280	200	−200
110	−340	240	−210	400	−50
165	−345	360	−150	600	90
220	−370	480	−110	800	210
275	−425	600	−100	1,000	300
330	−510	720	−120	1,200	360
385	−635	840	−180	1,400	380
440	−810	960	−290	1,600	350
495	−1,045	1,080	−460	1,800	260
550	−1,350	1,200	−700	2,000	100

5. *a.* see table below

Price	Quantity supplied	Profit
$360	10	$1,700
290	9	1,070
230	8	590
180	7	240
140	6	0
110	5	−150
80	4	−270
60	0	−300

b. (1) quantity supplied: 1000, 900, 800, 700, 600, 500, 400; (2) (*a*) 180; (*b*) 7; (*c*) 240; (*d*) enter, profits in the industry will attract them into the industry

6. *a.* 140; *b.* 6; *c.* 133 = 800 (the total quantity demanded at $140) ÷ 6 (the output of each firm); *d.* 150 = 900 ÷ 6; *e.* (1) the curve is a horizontal line (see Figure 23–10 in the text), (2) the curve slopes upward (see Figure 23–11 in the text)

SELF-TEST

1. F, p. 438	**11.** T, p. 445
2. T, p. 439	**12.** T, p. 450
3. T, p. 439	**13.** F, p. 445
4. T, p. 439	**14.** T, p. 456
5. F, p. 440	**15.** T, p. 454
6. T, p. 441	**16.** F, p. 454
7. F, p. 440	**17.** F, p. 457
8. T, p. 442	**18.** T, p. 457
9. T, p. 451	**19.** T, p. 458
10. T, p. 449	**20.** T, pp. 459−460

1. *d,* p. 439	**16.** *a,* p. 448
2. *b,* p. 439	**17.** *c,* p. 448
3. *b,* p. 439	**18.** *c,* p. 450
4. *a,* p. 439	**19.** *b,* p. 445
5. *a,* p. 439	**20.** *c,* p. 446
6. *a,* p. 439	**21.** *d,* p. 447
7. *b,* pp. 439−440	**22.** *c,* p. 448
8. *c,* p. 440	**23.** *c,* p. 451
9. *a,* p. 442	**24.** *c,* p. 454
10. *b,* p. 450	**25.** *c,* pp. 455−456
11. *b,* p. 451	**26.** *c,* p. 456
12. *b,* pp. 451−452	**27.** *c,* p. 457
13. *b,* pp. 449−450	**28.** *a,* p. 457
14. *a,* pp. 448−449	**29.** *b,* p. 458
15. *d,* p. 447	**30.** *d,* p. 461

DISCUSSION QUESTIONS

1. p. 439	**9.** pp. 452−453
2. p. 440	**10.** pp. 456−457
3. pp. 440−442	**11.** pp. 457−458
4. p. 442	**12.** pp. 457−458
5. pp. 449−451	**13.** p. 459
6. pp. 451−452	**14.** pp. 459−461
7. pp. 451; 458	**15.** pp. 457−461
8. p. 452	

CHAPTER 24

Price and Output Determination: Pure Monopoly

Chapter 24 is the second of the four chapters which deal with specific market models and is concerned with what economists call pure monopoly. Like pure competition, pure monopoly is rarely found in the American economy. But there are industries which are close to being pure monopolies, and these industries produce about 5% of the GDP; an understanding of pure monopoly is helpful in understanding the more realistic situation of oligopoly.

It is only possible for pure monopoly, approximations of pure monopoly, and oligopoly to exist if firms are prevented in some way from entering an industry in the long run. Anything which tends to prevent entry is referred to as a "barrier to entry." The second part of Chapter 24 is devoted to a description of the more important types of barriers to entry. Remember that barriers to entry not only make it possible for monopoly to exist in the economy but also explain why so many markets are oligopolies (which you will study in Chapter 26).

Like the preceding chapter, this chapter tries to answer certain questions about the firm. These are: what output will the firm produce; what price will it charge; what will be the profit received by the firm; and what will be the relationship between price and average cost and between price and marginal cost? In answering these questions for the monopoly firm and in comparing pure competition and pure monopoly note the following:

1. Both the competitive and monopoly firm try to maximize profits by producing that output at which marginal cost and marginal revenue are equal.

2. The individual firm in a perfectly competitive industry sees a perfectly price elastic demand for its product at the going market price because it is but one of many firms in the industry; but the monopolist sees a market demand schedule which is less than perfectly price elastic because the monopolist *is* the industry. The former, therefore, has *only* an output policy and is a price-taker; but the latter is able to determine the price at which it will sell its product and is a price-maker.

3. When demand is perfectly price elastic, price is equal to marginal revenue and is constant; but when demand is less than perfectly price elastic, marginal revenue is less

than price and both decrease as the output of the firm increases.

4. Because entry is blocked in the long run, firms cannot enter a monopolistic industry to compete away profits as they can under conditions of pure competition.

In addition to determining the price the monopolist will charge, the quantity of its product it will produce, and the size of its profits, Chapter 24 has three other goals. It examines the economic effects of monopoly by comparing it with pure competition. Chapter 24 also explains what is meant by price discrimination, the conditions which must prevail if a monopolist is to engage in price discrimination. The final section of Chapter 24 introduces you to the problem a government agency faces when it must determine the maximum price a public utility will be allowed to charge for its product.

■ CHECKLIST

When you have studied this chapter you should be able to:

☐ Define pure monopoly based on five characteristics.
☐ List and explain four potential barriers that would prevent or deter the entry of new firms into an industry.
☐ Describe the demand curve or schedule for the product produced by a pure monopolist and cite three implications.
☐ Compute marginal revenue when you are given the demand for the monopolist's product.
☐ Explain the relationship between the price the monopolist charges and the marginal revenue from the sale of an additional unit of the product.
☐ State the principle which explains what output the monopolist will produce and the price that will be charged.
☐ Determine the profit-maximizing output and price for the pure monopolist when you are given the demand and cost data.
☐ Explain why there is no supply curve for the pure monopolist.
☐ Discuss three popular misconceptions about the pricing behavior of pure monopolists.

☐ Describe the economic effects of monopoly on the price of the product, the quantity of output produced, the allocation of the economy's resources, and the distribution of income.

☐ Explain the complications caused by economies of scale, X-inefficiency, and rent-seeking expenditures in comparing the costs of firms operating in competitive and monopoly industries.

☐ Define technological progress (or dynamic efficiency) and compare technological progress in competitive and monopoly models.

☐ Define price discrimination and list three conditions which are necessary for it to exist.

☐ Explain the economic consequences of price discrimination.

☐ Use graphical analysis to identify the socially optimal price and the fair return price for the regulated monopoly (public utility).

☐ Explain the dilemma of regulation based on your graphical analysis of regulated monopoly.

■ **CHAPTER OUTLINE**

1. Pure monopoly is a market situation in which a single firm sells a product for which there are no close substitutes. While it is rare in practice, the study of monopoly provides an understanding of firms which are "almost" monopolies and is useful in understanding monopolistic competition and oligopoly.

2. Pure monopoly (and oligopoly) can exist in the long run only if potential competitors find there are barriers which prevent their entry into the industry.

    a. There are at least four types of entry barriers: economies of scale; natural monopolies (public utilities); legal barriers (patents and licenses); and ownership of essential resources.

    b. Entry barriers are seldom perfect in preventing the entry of new firms, and efficient production may, in some cases, require that firms be prevented from entering an industry.

3. The demand curve of the monopolist is downsloping because the monopolist is the industry. By contrast, the purely competitive firm has a horizontal (perfectly price elastic) demand curve because it is only one of many small firms in an industry. The implications of the downsloping shape monopolist's demand curve are several:

    a. The monopolist can only increase sales by lowering product price; thus price will exceed marginal revenue for every unit of output but the first.

    b. The monopolist will have a pricing policy, or is a "price-maker"; the purely competitive firm has no price policy and is a "price-taker."

    c. The monopolist will avoid setting price in the inelas-

tic segment of its demand curve because total revenue will be decreasing and marginal revenue will be negative; price will be set in the elastic portion of the demand curve.

4. The output and price determination of the profit-maximizing monopolist entails several considerations:

    a Monopoly power in the sale of a product does not necessarily affect the prices that the monopolist pays for resources or the costs of production; an assumption is made in this chapter that the monopolist hires resources in a competitive market and uses the same technology as competitive firms.

    b. The monopolist produces that output at which marginal cost and marginal revenue are equal, and charges a price at which this profit-maximizing output can be sold.

    c. The monopolist has no supply curve because there is no unique relationship between price and quantity supplied; price and quantity supplied will change when demand and marginal revenue change. By contrast, a purely competitive firm has a supply curve that is the portion of the marginal cost curve above average variable cost, and there is a unique relationship between price and quantity supplied.

    d. Three popular misconceptions about monopolists are that they charge as high a price as is possible, that they seek maximum profit *per unit* of output, and that they are always profitable and never experience losses.

5. The existence of pure monopoly has significant effects on the economy as a whole.

    a. Because it produces smaller outputs and charges higher prices than would result under conditions of pure competition and because price is greater than both average total and marginal cost, monopoly misallocates resources (results in neither productive nor allocative efficiency).

    b. Monopoly contributes to income inequality in the economy.

    c. A monopolist may have lower or higher average costs than a pure competitor producing the same product would have.

    (1) If there are economies of scale in the production of the product, the monopolist is able to produce the good or service at a lower long-run average cost than a large number of small pure competitors could produce it.

    (2) But if a monopolist is more susceptible to X-inefficiency than a purely competitive firm, its long-run average costs at every level of output are higher than what those of a purely competitive firm would be.

    (3) Rent-preserving expenditures in the form of legal fees, lobbying, and public-relations expenses to obtain or maintain a monopoly position add nothing to output, but increase costs.

d. A monopolist may also be more or less efficient over time than pure competitors in developing new lower-cost techniques of producing existing products and in developing new products.

6. To increase profits a pure monopolist may engage in price discrimination by charging different prices to different buyers of the same product (when the price differences do not represent differences in the costs of producing the product).

    a. To discriminate the seller must have some monopoly power; be capable of separating buyers into groups which have different price elasticities of demand; and be able to prevent the resale of the product from one group to another group.

    b. The seller charges each group the highest price that group would be willing to pay for the product rather than go without it. Discrimination increases not only the profits but also the output of the monopolist.

    c. Price discrimination is common in the American economy.

7. The prices charged by monopolists are often regulated by governments to reduce the misallocation of resources.

    a. A ceiling price determined by the intersection of the marginal-cost and demand schedules is the socially optimum price and improves the allocation of resources.

    b. This ceiling may force the firm to produce at a loss; and so government may set the ceiling at a level determined by the intersection of the average-cost and demand schedules to allow the monopolist a fair return.

    c. The dilemma of regulation is that the socially optimum price may cause losses for the monopolist, and that a fair-return price results in a less efficient allocation of resources.

■ **IMPORTANT TERMS**

Pure monopoly	Dynamic efficiency
Barrier to entry	Price discrimination
Natural monopoly	Socially optimal price
X-inefficiency	Fair-return price
Rent-seeking behavior	Dilemma of regulation

■ **FILL-IN QUESTIONS**

1. Pure monopoly is an industry in which a single firm is the sole producer of a product for which are are no (substitutes, close substitutes) _____ and into which entry in the long run is (easy, difficult, blocked) _____

2. What are the four most important types of barrier to entry?

    a. _____

    b. _____

    c. _____

    d. _____

3. If there are substantial economies of scale in the production of a product, a small-scale firm will find it difficult to enter into and survive in an industry because its average costs will be (greater, less) _____ than those of established firms; and a firm will find it difficult to start out on a large scale because it will be nearly impossible to acquire the needed (labor, money capital) _____

4. Public utility companies tend to be _____ _____ monopolies, and they receive their franchises from and are _____ by governments.

5. The demand schedule confronting the pure monopolist is _____ perfectly elastic; this means that marginal revenue is (greater, less) _____ than average revenue (or price) and that both marginal revenue and average revenue (increase, decrease) _____ as output increases.

6. When demand is price elastic, a decrease in price will (increase, decrease) _____ total revenue, but when demand is price inelastic, a decrease in price will _____ total revenue. The demand curve for the purely competitive firm is (horizontal, downsloping) _____, but it is _____ for the monopolist. The profit maximizing monopolist will want to set price in the price (elastic, inelastic) _____ portion of its demand curve.

7. The supply curve for a purely competitive firm is the portion of the (average variable cost, marginal cost) _____ curve that lies above the _____ curve. The supply curve for the monopolist (is the same, does not exist) _____

8. When the profits of a monopolist are a maximum, _____ and _____ are equal; and price (or average revenue) is (greater, less) _____ than marginal cost.

9. Three common fallacies about pure monopoly are that:

a. It charges the _____ price.

b. Its average (or per unit) profit is _____

_____

c. It always receives a _____

10. The output produced by a monopolist is inefficiently *produced* because the average total cost of producing the product is not _____ and resources are not efficiently **allocated** because _____ is not equal to

_____

11. Monopoly seems to result in a greater inequality in the distribution of income because the owners of monopolies are largely in the (upper, middle, lower) _____ income groups.

12. Resources can be said to be more efficiently allocated by pure competition than by pure monopoly only if the purely competitive firm and the monopoly have the same _____ and they will not be the same if the monopolist:

a. by virtue of being a large firm enjoys economies of _____ not available to a pure competitor; or

b. is more susceptible to _____ than pure competitors, and

c. may need to make _____ expenditures to obtain or maintain monopoly privileges granted by government; this expense increases costs.

13. Monopolists are more dynamically efficient than pure competitors if they improve the _____ of producing existing products (and thereby lower the _____ of producing them) and develop new _____ over time more rapidly than pure competitors.

14. There is price discrimination whenever a product is sold at different _____ and these differences are not equal to the differences in the _____ of producing the product.

15. Price discrimination is possible only when the following three conditions are found:

a. _____

b. _____

c. _____

16. The two economic consequences of a monopolist's engagement in price discrimination are a(n) (increase, decrease) _____ in the profits and a(n) _____ in the output of the monopolist.

17. The misallocation of resources that results from monopoly can be **eliminated** if a ceiling price for the monopolist's product is set equal to _____; such a price is, however, usually less than _____

18. If a regulated monopolist is allowed to earn a fair return, the ceiling price for the product is set equal to _____; such a price reduces but does not eliminate the _____ of resources caused by monopoly.

■ **PROBLEMS AND PROJECTS**

1. The demand schedule for the product produced by a monopolist is given in the table below.

a. Complete the table by computing total revenue, marginal revenue, and the price elasticity of demand (use midpoints formula).

Quantity demanded	Price	Total revenue	Marginal revenue	Price elasticity
0	$700	$____		
1	650	____	$____	____
2	600	____	____	____
3	550	____	____	____
4	500	____	____	____
5	450	____	____	____
6	400	____	____	____
7	350	____	____	____
8	300	____	____	____
9	250	____	____	____
10	200	____	____	____
11	150	____	____	____
12	100	____	____	____
13	50	____	____	____
14	0	____	____	____

b. The relationships in the table indicate that:

(1) total revenue rises from $0 to a maximum of

$_____ as price falls from $700 to $_____.
Then, as price falls to zero, total revenue falls from its

maximum to $_____;
(2) the relationship between price and total revenue
suggests that demand is price (elastic, inelastic)

_____ when quantity demanded is between a
zero and 7 units of output, but that demand is price

(elastic, inelastic) _____ when quantity demanded is between 7 units and 14 units;

(3) When demand is price elastic and total revenue
rises from $0 to a maximum, marginal revenue is (nega-

tive, positive) _____, but when demand is price
inelastic and total revenue falls from its maximum, mar-

ginal revenue is _____
c. Use the data in the table on page 282 to plot and
graph the demand curve and the marginal revenue
curve for the monopolist. Indicate the portion of the demand curve that is price elastic and the portion that is
price inelastic.

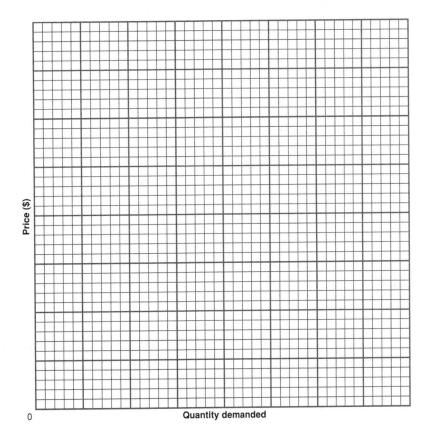

Price ($)

0   **Quantity demanded**

2. In the table on the next page are demand and cost data
for a pure monopolist.
    a. Complete the table by filling in the column for total
revenue, marginal revenue, and marginal cost.
    b. Answer the next three questions using the data you
calculated in the table.
    (1) What output will the monopolist produce?

_____

(2) What price will the monopolist charge?

_____
(3) What total profit will the monopolist receive at the

profit-maximizing level of output? _____

Quantity	Price	Total revenue	Marginal revenue	Total cost	Marginal cost
0	$17	$____		$10	
1	16	____	$____	18	$____
2	15	____	____	23	____
3	14	____	____	25	____
4	13	____	____	27	____
5	12	____	____	28	____
6	11	____	____	32	____
7	10	____	____	40	____
8	9	____	____	50	____
9	8	____	____	64	____
10	7	____	____	80	____

3. Now assume that the pure monopolist in problem 2 is able to engage in price discrimination and sell each unit of the product at a price equal to the maximum price the buyer of that unit of the produce would be willing to pay.

a. Complete the table below by computing total revenue and marginal revenue.

Quantity	Price	Total revenue	Marginal revenue	Total cost	Marginal cost
0	$17	$____		$10	
1	16	____	$____	18	$____
2	15	____	____	23	____
3	14	____	____	25	____
4	13	____	____	27	____
5	12	____	____	28	____
6	11	____	____	32	____
7	10	____	____	40	____
8	9	____	____	50	____
9	8	____	____	64	____
10	7	____	____	80	____

b. From the table it can be seen that:
(1) the marginal revenue which the discriminating monopolist obtains from the sale of an additional unit is equal to the _____

(2) Using the same table of costs, the discriminating monopolist would produce _____ units of the product, charge the buyer of the last unit of product produced a price of $_____, and obtain a total economic profit of $_____

(3) If the pure monopolist is able to engage in price discrimination its profits will be (larger, smaller, the same) _____ and it will produce an output that is (larger, smaller, the same) _____

4. In the table below are cost and demand data for a pure monopolist.

Quantity demanded	Price	Marginal revenue	Average cost	Marginal cost
0	$17.50			
1	16.00	$16.00	$24.00	$24.00
2	14.50	13.00	15.00	6.00
3	13.00	10.00	11.67	5.00
4	11.50	7.00	10.50	7.00
5	10.00	4.00	10.00	8.00
6	8.50	1.00	9.75	8.50
7	7.00	−2.00	9.64	9.00
8	5.50	−5.00	9.34	9.25
9	4.00	−8.00	9.36	9.50

a. An unregulated monopolist would produce _____ units of a product, sell it at a price of $_____, and receive a total profit of $_____

b. If this monopolist were regulated and the maximum price it could charge were set equal to marginal cost, it would produce _____ units of a product, sell it at a price of $_____, and receive a total profit of $_____. Such regulation would either _____ the firm or require that the regulating government _____ the firm.

c. If the monopolist were not regulated and were allowed to engage in price discrimination by charging the maximum price it could obtain for each unit sold it would produce 6 units (because the marginal revenue from the 6th unit and the marginal cost of the 6th unit would both be $8.50). Its total revenue would be $_____, its total costs would be $_____, and its total profit would be $_____

d. If the monopolist were regulated and allowed to charge a fair-return price, it would produce _____ units of product, charge a price of $_____, and receive a profit of $_____

e. From which situation—a, b, or d—does the most efficient allocation of resources result? _____ From which situation does the least efficient allocation result? _____ In practice, government would probably select situation _____

■ **SELF-TEST**

Circle the T if the statement is true; the F if it is false.

1. The pure monopolist produces a product for which there are no substitutes. **T F**

2. The weaker the barriers to entry into an industry, the more competition there will be in the industry, other things being equal. **T F**

3. Barriers to entry are rarely complete for the monopolist. **T F**

4. Monopoly is always undesirable unless it is regulated by the government. **T F**

5. The monopolist can increase the sale of its product if it charges a lower price. **T F**

6. As a monopolist increases its output, it finds that its total revenue at first decreases, and that after some output level is reached, its total revenue begins to increase. **T F**

7. A purely competitive firm is a price-taker but a monopolist is a price-maker. **T F**

8. A monopolist will not voluntarily sell at a price at which the demand for its product is inelastic. **T F**

9. The monopolist determines the profit-maximizing output by producing that output at which marginal cost and marginal revenue are equal and sets the product price equal to marginal cost and marginal revenue at that output. **T F**

10. The monopolist maximizing total profit is also producing that output at which per unit (or average) profit is a maximum. **T F**

11. A monopolist "will charge the highest price it can get." **T F**

12. Pure monopoly guarantees economic profits. **T F**

13. A monopolist seeks maximum total profits, not maximum unit profits. **T F**

14. Resources are misallocated by monopoly because price is not equal to marginal cost. **T F**

15. One of the economic effects of monopoly is less income inequality. **T F**

16. When there are substantial economies of scale in the production of a product, the monopolist may charge a price that is lower than the price that would prevail if the product were produced by a purely competitive industry. **T F**

17. The purely competitive firm is more likely to be affected by X-inefficiency than a monopolist. **T F**

18. Rent-seeking expenditures that monopolists make to obtain or maintain monopoly privilege have no effect on the firm's costs. **T F**

19. Economists are agreed that monopolies are less dynamically efficient than competitive firms. **T F**

20. In a society in which technology is not changing and the economies of scale can be employed by both pure competitors and monopolists, the purely competitive firm will use the more efficient methods of production. **T F**

21. Price discrimination occurs when a given product is sold at more than one price and these price differences are not justified by cost differences. **T F**

22. A discriminating monopolist will produce a larger output than a nondiscriminating monopolist. **T F**

23. The regulated utility is likely to make economic profit when price is set to achieve the most efficient allocation of resources (P = MC). **T F**

24. A "fair return" price for a regulated utility would have price set to equal average cost. **T F**

25. The dilemma of monopoly regulation is that the production by a monopolist of an output that causes no misallocation of resources may force the monopolist to suffer an economic loss. **T F**

Circle the letter that corresponds to the best answer.

1. Which of the following is the *best* example of a pure monopoly?
(a) your neighborhood grocer
(b) the telephone company in your community
(c) the manufacturer of a particular brand of toothpaste
(d) an airline furnishing passenger service between two major cities

2. Which of the following is an important characteristic of a natural monopoly?
(a) economies of scale throughout the range of market demand
(b) competition would be less expensive for the consumer
(c) it is a public utility
(d) it has low fixed costs

3. Monopoly can probably exist over a long period of time only if:
(a) it is based on the control of raw materials
(b) it controls the patents on the product
(c) cut-throat competition is employed to eliminate rivals
(d) government assists the monopoly and prevents the establishment of rival firms

4. Which of the following is true with respect to the demand data confronting a monopolist?
(a) marginal revenue is greater than average revenue
(b) marginal revenue decreases as average revenue decreases

(c) demand is perfectly price elastic
(d) average revenue (or price) increases as the output of the firm increases

5. When the monopolist is maximizing total profits **or** minimizing losses:
(a) total revenue is greater than total cost
(b) average revenue is greater than average total cost
(c) average revenue is greater than marginal cost
(d) average total cost is less than marginal cost

6. At which of the following combinations of price and marginal revenue is the price elasticity of demand less than 1?
(a) price equals $102, marginal revenue equals $42
(b) price equals $92, marginal revenue equals $22
(c) price equals $82, marginal revenue equals $2
(d) price equals $72, marginal revenue equals −$18

7. Monopolists' profits may be positive, negative, or zero:
(a) in the short run
(b) in the long run
(c) in both the short run and long run
(d) where marginal cost equals marginal revenue and where average total cost is less than demand

8. At present ouput a monopolist determines that its marginal cost is $18 and its marginal revenue is $21. The monopolist will maximize profits or minimize losses by:
(a) increasing price while keeping output constant
(b) decreasing price and increasing output
(c) decreasing both price and output
(d) increasing both price and output

Answer the next four questions (9, 10, 11, and 12) based on the demand and cost data for a pure monopolist given in the table below.

Output	Price	Total cost
0	$1,000	$ 500
1	600	520
2	500	580
3	400	700
4	300	1,000
5	200	1,500

9. How many units of output will the profit-maximizing monopolist produce?
(a) 1
(b) 2
(c) 3
(d) 4

10. The profit-maximizing monopolist would set its price at:
(a) $120
(b) $200
(c) $233
(d) $400

11. If the monopolist could sell each unit of the product at the maximum price the buyer of that unit would be willing to pay for it and if the monopolist sold 4 units, total revenue would be:
(a) $1200
(b) $1800
(c) $2000
(d) $2800

12. If the monopolist were forced to produce the socially optimal output by the imposition of a ceiling price, the ceiling price would have to be:
(a) $200
(b) $300
(c) $400
(d) $500

13. The supply curve for a pure monopolist:
(a) is the portion of the marginal cost curve that lies above the average variable cost curve
(b) is perfectly price elastic at the market price
(c) is upsloping
(d) does not exist

14. A monopolist at the equilibrium level of output does not **produce** the product as efficiently as is possible because:
(a) the average total cost of producing it is not a minimum
(b) the marginal cost of producing the last unit is less than its price
(c) it is earning a profit
(d) average revenue is greater than the cost of producing an extra unit of output

15. X-inefficiency means that a firm fails to:
(a) produce an output at the lowest average cost possible
(b) produce an output at the lowest total cost possible
(c) employ resources in their least-cost combination to produce an output
(d) do all of the above

16. Dynamic efficiency refers to:
(a) the achievement of economies of scale in producing products
(b) the development over time of more efficient (less costly) techniques of producing products and the improvement of these products
(c) the avoidance of X-inefficiency
(d) the avoidance of allocative inefficiency

17. Over time monopoly **may** result in greater technological improvement than would be forthcoming under conditions of pure competition for several reasons. Which of the following is **not** one of these reasons?
(a) technological advance will lower the costs and enhance the profits of the monopolist, and these increased profits will not have to be shared with rivals

(b) technological advance will act as a barrier to entry and thus allow the monopolist to continue to be a monopolist

(c) technological advance requires research and experimentation, and the monopolist is in a position to finance them out of profits

(d) technological advance is apt to make existing capital equipment obsolete, and the monopolist can reduce costs by speeding up the rate at which its capital becomes obsolete

18. Which of the following is *not* one of the conditions which must be realized before a seller finds price discrimination is workable?

(a) the buyer must be unable to resell the product
(b) the product must be a service
(c) the seller must have some degree of monopoly power
(d) the seller must be able to segment the market

19. If a monopolist engages in price discrimination rather than charging all buyers the same price its:

(a) profits and its output are greater
(b) profits and its output are smaller
(c) profits are greater and its output is smaller
(d) profits are smaller and its output is greater

*Answer the next four questions (**20, 21, 22,** and **23**) based on the demand and cost data for a pure monopolist given in the table below.*

Quantity demanded	Price	Total cost
0	$700	$ 300
1	650	400
2	600	450
3	550	510
4	500	590
5	450	700
6	400	840
7	350	1,020
8	300	1,250
9	250	1,540
10	200	1,900

20. The profit-maximizing output and price for this monopolist would be:

(a) 5 units and a $450 price
(b) 6 units and a $400 price
(c) 7 units and a $350 price
(d) 8 units and a $300 price

*In answering the next two questions (**21** and **22**), assume this monopolist is able to engage in price discrimination and sell each unit of the product at a price equal to the maximum price the buyer of that unit would be willing to pay.*

21. The marginal revenue that the price discriminating monopolist obtains from the sale of an additional unit is equal to:

(a) total revenue
(b) average cost
(c) unit cost
(d) price

22. The profit maximizing output and price for the price discriminating monopolist would be:

(a) 6 units and a $400 price
(b) 7 units and a $350 price
(c) 8 units and a $300 price
(d) 9 units and a $250 price

23. How much greater would the total economic profits be for the discriminating monopolist than the nondiscriminating monopolist?

(a) $720
(b) $830
(c) $990
(d) $1070

*The next question (**24**) is based on the graph below.*

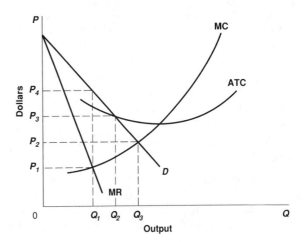

24. The price and output combination for the unregulated profit maximizing monopoly compared with the socially optimal price and output combination for the regulated monopoly would be, respectively:

(a) P_4 and Q_1 versus P_3 and Q_2
(b) P_4 and Q_1 versus P_2 and Q_3
(c) P_3 and Q_2 versus P_4 and Q_1
(d) P_2 and Q_3 versus P_3 and Q_2

25. A monopolist who is limited by the imposition of a ceiling price to a fair return sells the product at a price equal to:

(a) average total cost
(b) average variable cost
(c) marginal cost
(d) average fixed cost

■ DISCUSSION QUESTIONS

1. What is pure monopoly? Why is it studied if it is so rare in practice?

2. What is meant by a barrier to entry? What kinds of such barriers are there? How important are they in pure competition, pure monopoly, monopolistic competition, and oligopoly?

3. Why are the economies of scale a barrier to entry?

4. Why are most natural monopolies also public utilities? What does government hope to achieve by granting exclusive franchises to and regulating such natural monopolies?

5. How do patents and licenses create barriers to entry? Cite examples.

6. Compare the pure monopolist and the individual pure competitor with respect to:
(a) the demand schedule;
(b) the marginal-revenue schedule;
(c) the relationship between marginal revenue and average revenue;
(d) price policy; and
(e) the ability to administer (or set) price.

7. Explain why marginal revenue is always less than average revenue when demand is less than perfectly elastic.

8. Suppose a pure monopolist discovered it was producing and selling an output at which the demand for its product was inelastic. Explain why a decrease in its output would increase its economic profits.

9. What output will the monopolist produce? What price will it charge?

10. Why does the monopolist not charge the highest possible price for the product? Why does the monopolist not set the price for the product in such a way that average profit is a maximum? Why are some monopolies unprofitable?

11. In what sense is resource allocation and production more efficient under conditions of pure competition than under monopoly conditions?

12. How does monopoly allegedly affect the distribution of income in the economy and why does monopoly seemingly have this effect on income distribution in the American economy?

13. What are the three complications that may result in a monopolist having lower or higher average costs than a competitive firm? How do each of these complications affect the average costs of a monopolist and what evidence is there to support the belief that these two complications lower or raise the average costs of a monopolist?

14. Does monopoly, when compared with pure competition, result in more or less dynamic efficiency (technological progress)? What are the arguments on **both** sides of this question? What evidence is there to support the two views?

15. What is meant by price discrimination and what conditions must be realized before it is workable? Explain how a monopolist who discriminates would determine what price to charge for each unit of the product sold (or to charge each group of buyers) and how discrimination would affect the profits and the output of the monopolist.

16. How do public utility regulatory agencies attempt to eliminate the misallocation of resources that results from monopoly? Explain the dilemma that almost invariably confronts the agency in this endeavor; and explain why a fair-return policy only reduces but does not eliminate misallocation.

■ ANSWERS

Chapter 24 Price and Output Determination: Pure Monopoly

FILL-IN QUESTIONS

1. close substitutes, blocked

2. *a.* the economies of scale; *b.* natural monopolies; *c.* patents and licenses; *d.* ownership of essential raw materials

3. greater, money capital

4. natural, regulated

5. less than, less, decrease

6. increase, decrease, horizontal, downsloping, elastic

7. marginal cost, average variable cost, does not exist

8. marginal revenue, marginal cost, greater

9. *a.* highest possible; *b.* a maximum; *c.* pure profit

10. a minimum, price (or average revenue), marginal cost

11. upper

12. costs (or cost schedules); *a.* scale; *b.* X-inefficiency; rent-preserving

13. techniques (technology), costs (or cost schedules), products

14. prices, cost

15. *a.* the seller has some monopoly power; *b.* the seller is able to separate buyers into groups which have different elasticities of demand for the product; *c.* the original buyers cannot resell the product

16. increase, increase

17. marginal cost, average (total) cost

18. average (total) cost, misallocation

PROBLEMS AND PROJECTS

1. *a.* total revenue: $0, 650, 1200, 1650, 2000, 2250, 2400, 2450, 2400, 2250, 2000, 1650, 1200, 650, 0; marginal revenue: $650, 550, 450, 350, 250, 150, 50, −50, −150, −250, −350, −400, −550, −650; price elasticity: 27, 8.33, 4.60, 3.00, 2.11, 1.54, 1.15, .87, .65, .47, .33, .22, .12, .04 *b.* (1) $2450, $350, 0; (2) elastic, inelastic; (3) positive, negative *c.* see Figure 24−2 in the text as an example

2. *a.* total revenue: $0, 16, 30, 42, 52, 60, 66, 70, 72, 72, 70; marginal revenue: $16, 14, 12, 10, 8, 6, 4, 2, 0, −2; marginal cost: $8, 5, 2, 2, 1, 4, 8, 10, 14, 16 *b.* (1) 6; (2) $11; (3) $34 (TR of $66 minus TC of $32)

3. *a.* total revenue: $0, 16, 31, 45, 58, 70, 81, 91, 100, 108, 115; marginal revenue: $16, 15, 14, 13, 12, 11, 10, 9, 8, 7; marginal cost: $8, 5, 2, 2, 1, 4, 8, 10, 14, 16; *b.* (1) price; (2) 7 units; $10; $51 (TR of $91 minus TC of $40); (3) larger, larger

4. *a.* 4, 11.50, 4.00; *b.* 6, 8.50, −7.50, bankrupt, subsidize; *c.* 73.50, 58.50, 15.00; *d.* 5, 10.00, zero; *e.* b, a, d

SELF-TEST

1. F, p. 465
2. T, p. 466
3. T, p. 466
4. F, p. 469
5. T, p. 469
6. F, p. 469
7. T, pp. 465; 471
8. T, p. 471
9. F, pp. 471−473
10. F, p. 474
11. F, p. 474
12. F, p. 474
13. T, p. 474
14. T, p. 475
15. F, p. 476
16. T, p. 476
17. F, pp. 476−477
18. F, p. 477
19. F, p. 478
20. T, p. 478
21. T, p. 479
22. T, p. 480
23. F, p. 481
24. T, p. 481
25. T, pp. 481−482

1. *b*, p. 466
2. *a*, p. 467
3. *d*, p. 469
4. *b*, p. 470
5. *c*, pp. 472−473
6. *d*, p. 471
7. *a*, p. 474
8. *b*, p. 473
9. *c*, pp. 471−473
10. *d*, pp. 471−473
11. *b*, p. 480
12. *b*, p. 481
13. *d*, p. 474
14. *a*, p. 475
15. *d*, pp. 476−477
16. *b*, p. 478
17. *d*, p. 478
18. *b*, p. 479
19. *a*, p. 480
20. *b*, pp. 471−473
21. *d*, p. 480
22. *c*, p. 480
23. *c*, p. 480
24. *b*, p. 481
25. *a*, p. 481

DISCUSSION QUESTIONS

1. pp. 465−466
2. pp. 467−469
3. p. 467
4. pp. 467−468
5. p. 468
6. pp. 469−471
7. pp. 467−470
8. p. 471
9. pp. 471−473
10. p. 474
11. p. 475
12. p. 476
13. pp. 476−477
14. p. 478
15. pp. 479−480
16. pp. 481−482

Price and Output Determination: Monopolistic Competition

Chapter 25 is the third of the four chapters which deal with specific market situations. As its name implies, monopolistic competition is a blend of pure competition and pure monopoly. One of the reasons for studying those relatively unrealistic market situations was to prepare you for this realistic study of monopolistic competition.

It must be pointed out that monopolistic competition is not a description of all markets. The study of it, however, will help you to understand the many markets which are nearly monopolistically competitive. It will also help you to understand, as you will learn in the next chapter, why oligopoly is prevalent in the American economy and how oligopoly differs from monopolistic competition.

The first task is to learn exactly what is meant by monopolistic competition. Next you should examine the demand curve which the monopolistically competitive firm sees for its product and note how and why it differs from the demand curves faced by the purely competitive firm and by the monopolist. In this connection it is also important to understand that as the individual firm changes the character of the product it produces or changes the extent to which it promotes the sale of its product, both the costs of the firm and the demand for its product will change. A firm confronts a different demand curve every time it alters its product or its promotion of the product.

With the product and promotional campaign of the firm *given*, the price-output analysis of the monopolistic competitor is relatively simple. In the short run this analysis is identical with the analysis of the price-output decision of the pure monopolist in the short run. It is only in the long run that the competitive element makes itself apparent: The entry (or exit) of firms forces the price the firm charges down (up) *toward* the level of average cost. This price is not equal either to *minimum* average cost or to marginal cost; and consequently monopolistic competition, on these two scores, can be said to be less efficient than pure competition.

A relatively large part of Chapter 25 is devoted to a discussion of nonprice competition. This explanation is given for very good reasons. In monopolistically competitive industries a part of the competitive effort of individual firms is given over to product differentiation, product de-

velopment, and product advertising. Each firm has three things to manipulate—price, product, and advertising—in trying to maximize its profits. While monopolistic competition may not be as economically efficient as pure competition in terms of a *given* product and the promotion of it, when all the economic effects—good and bad—of differentiation, development, and advertising are considered this shortcoming may or may not be offset. Whether it is actually offset is an unanswerable question.

If Chapter 25 has one central idea it is this: monopolistic competition cannot be compared with pure competition solely on the basis of prices charged at any given moment of time; it must also be judged in terms of whether it results in better products, in a wider variety of products, in better-informed consumers, in lower-priced radio and television programs, magazines, and newspapers, and other socially redeeming features.

The study of monopolistic competition is a realistic study and for that reason it is a difficult study. Many factors have to be considered in explaining how such a group of firms behaves and in appraising the efficiency with which such an industry allocates scarce resources.

■ **CHECKLIST**

When you have studied this chapter you should be able to:

☐ List the four characteristics of monopolistic competition.
☐ Describe the four forms that product differentiation may take in the marketplace.
☐ Compare the firm's demand curve under monopolistic competition with a firm's demand curve in pure monopoly and in pure competition.
☐ Determine the output of and the price charged by a monopolistic competitor (producing a given product and engaged in a given amount of sales promotion) in the short run when you are given the cost and demand data.
☐ Explain why the price charged by a monopolistic competitor (producing a given product and engaged in a given

amount of sales promotion) will in the long run tend to equal average cost.

☐ Identify the "wastes of monopolistic competition" and explain why product differentiation may "offset" these wastes.

☐ Enumerate the three principal types of nonprice competition.

☐ Present the major arguments in the cases for and against advertising.

☐ Discuss the empirical evidence in support of the traditional and new perspective views of advertising.

☐ Explain why monopolistic competition is more complex in practice than is suggested by the graphical analysis represented in the chapter.

■ CHAPTER OUTLINE

1. A monopolistically competitive industry is one in which a fairly large number of independent firms produces differentiated products, in which both price and various forms of nonprice competition occur, and into which entry is relatively easy in the long run. Many American industries approximate monopolistic competition.

2. Assume that the products the firms in the industry produce and the amounts of promotional activity in which they engage are given.

  a. The demand curve confronting each firm will be highly but not perfectly price elastic because each firm has many competitors who produce close but not perfect substitutes for the product it produces.

  (1) Comparing the demand curve for the monopolistic competitor to other market structures suggests that it is not perfectly elastic as is the case with the pure competitor, but it is also more elastic than the demand curve of the pure monopolist.

  (2) The degree of elasticity, however, for each monopolistic competitor will depend on the number of rivals and the extent of product differentiation.

  b. In the short run the individual firm will produce the output at which marginal cost and marginal revenue are equal and charge the price at which that output can be sold; either profits or losses may result in the short run.

  c. In the long run the entry and exodus of firms will **tend** to change the demand for the product of the individual firm in such a way that profits are eliminated (price and average costs are made equal to each other).

3. Monopolistic competition among firms producing a given product and engaged in a given amount of promotional activity results in less economic efficiency and more waste than does pure competition.

  a. The average cost of each firm is equal in the long run to its price, but the industry does not realize allo-

cative efficiency because output is smaller than the output at which marginal cost and price are equal.

  b. The industry does not realize productive efficiency because the output is smaller than the output at which average cost is a minimum.

4. In addition to setting its price and output so that its profit is maximized, each individual firm also attempts to differentiate its product and to promote or advertise it to increase the firm's profit; these additional activities give rise to nonprice competition among firms.

  a. Product differentiation means that the monopolistically competitive firms will offer consumers a wide range of types, style, brands, and quality variants of a product; this expansion of consumer choice may offset the wastes of monopolistic competition.

  b. Product development is an attempt by firms to improve a product, and it serves as a form of nonprice competition; to the extent that improved products contribute to consumer welfare, this type of nonprice competition among monopolistic firms may also offset some of the wastes of competition.

5. Whether the advertising of differentiated products results in economic waste or in greater efficiency is debatable; there are good arguments on both sides of this question and there is no clear answer to it.

  a. The arguments focus on three major questions: whether advertising is persuasion or information, whether advertising promotes economic concentration or competition, and whether advertising contributes to economic waste or economic efficiency.

  b. Empirical evidence on the economic effects of advertising has produced two schools of thought:

  (1) The traditional view argues and presents evidence in support of the idea that advertising reduces active competition among existing firms and serves as a barrier to entry to new firms. Higher prices to consumers and enhanced profits for existing firms result.

  (2) The new perspective view and evidence indicate that advertising acts as a relatively inexpensive means of increasing the number of substitute products known to buyers; thus, this information makes an industry more competitive.

  c. The monopolistically competitive firm tries to adjust its price, its product, and its promotion of the product so that the amount by which the firm's total revenue exceeds the total cost of producing and promoting its product is at a maximum.

■ IMPORTANT TERMS

Monopolistic competition
Product differentiation
Nonprice competition

Wastes of monopolistic competition
Traditional and new perspective views of advertising

■ **FILL-IN QUESTIONS**

1. In a monopolistically competitive market a (few, relatively large number of) _____ producers sell (standardized, differentiated) _____ _____ products; these producers (do, do not) _____ collude; and they engage in both _____ and _____ competition. In the long run entry into the industry is (difficult, fairly easy) _____

2. Because monopolistically competitive firms sell differentiated products each firm has (no, limited, complete) _____ control over the price of its product and there is _____ between the firms.

3. List the four forms that product differentiation may take:

a. _____

b. _____

c. _____

d. _____

4. Given the product being produced and the extent to which that product is being promoted, in the *short run*:

a. The demand curve confronting the monopolistically competitive firm will be (more, less) _____ elastic than that facing a monopolist and _____ elastic than that facing a pure competitor.

b. The elasticity of this demand curve will depend upon _____ and _____

c. The firm will produce the output at which _____ and _____ are equal.

5. In the long run, the *entry* of new firms into a monopolistically competitive industry will (expand, reduce) _____ the demand for the product produced by each firm in the industry and (increase, decrease) _____ the elasticity of that demand.

6. In the long run, *given* the product and the amount of product promotion, the price charged by the individual firm will tend to equal _____, its economic profits will tend to equal _____, and its average cost will

be _____ than the minimum average cost of producing and promoting the product.

7. Although representative firms in monopolistic competition tend to earn (economic, normal) _____ profits in the long run, there can be complications that may result in firms earning _____ profits or losses in the long run.

a. Some firms may achieve a degree of product _____ that cannot be duplicated by other firms that contribute to _____ profits.

b. There may be _____ to entry that prevent penetration of the market by other firms that contribute to _____ profit.

c. Some firms may attempt to maintain a "_____ of life," and consequently experience _____ losses.

8. Given the product and the extent of product promotion, monopolistic competition is wasteful because _____ _____ and because _____

9. In the long run, the monopolistic competitor cannot protect and increase profits by varying the product's price or output but it can try to protect and increase profits by _____ and _____

10. Product differentiation and product development tend to result in the consumer being offered a wider _____ of goods at any given time and an improved _____ of goods over a period of time.

11. The debate over advertising focuses on three critical areas:

a. _____ or _____?

b. _____ or _____?

c. _____ or _____?

12. The traditional view of advertising is that it will alter consumer preferences in favor of a product, or _____ consumers, but the new perspective contends that consumers get important _____ from advertising.

13. The creation of "brand loyalty" is a traditional view of advertising that suggests it promotes economic _____ industries because advertising makes product (demand, supply) _____

(more, less) _____ elastic. The counter

view is that advertising promotes _____
because it makes consumers more aware of substitutes

and decreases (demand, supply) _____ for
a particular product.

14. Advertising has long been thought to be wasteful be-

cause it prevents the realization of _____

and _____ efficiency, but the newer view
of advertising contends that it is efficient because it pro-

vides important _____ for consumer and

reduces _____ costs of consumers.

15. The different case studies of the economic effects
of advertising indicate that in the U.S. it is (procompetitive, anticompetitive, both pro- and anticompetitive)

_____

16. In attempting to maximize its profits the monopolistic

competitor will vary the price, the _____,

and the _____
of the product until the firm feels no further change in these
three variables will result in greater profit.

■ **PROBLEMS AND PROJECTS**

1. Listed below are several industries. Indicate in the
space after each whether you believe it is monopolistically
competitive (MC) or not monopolistically competitive (N).
If you indicate the latter, explain why you think the industry
is not a monopolistically competitive one.
  a. The production of automobiles in the United States.

  _____

  b. The retail distribution of automobiles in the United

  States. _____

  _____

  c. Grocery supermarkets in a city of 500,000 people.

  _____

  _____

  d. The retail sale of gasoline in a city of 500,000 people.

  _____

  _____

  e. The production of low-priced shoes in the United

  States. _____

  _____

  f. The mail-order sale of men's clothes. _____

  _____

  _____

2. Assume that the short-run cost and demand data given
in the table below confront a monopolistic competitor selling a given product and engaged in a given amount of
product promotion.

Output	Total cost	Marginal cost	Quantity demanded	Price	Marginal revenue
0	$ 50		0	$120	
1	80	$____	1	110	$____
2	90	____	2	100	____
3	110	____	3	90	____
4	140	____	4	80	____
5	180	____	5	70	____
6	230	____	6	60	____
7	290	____	7	50	____
8	360	____	8	40	____
9	440	____	9	30	____
10	530	____	10	20	____

  a. Compute the marginal cost and marginal revenue
of each unit of output and enter these figures in the
table.

  b. In the short run the firm will (1) produce _____
units of output, (2) sell its output at a price of

  $_____, and (3) have a total eco-

  nomic profit of $_____
  c. In the long run, (1) the demand for the firm's product

  will _____, (2) until the price of the prod-

  uct equals _____ and (3) the total

  economic profits of the firm are _____

3. Match the following descriptions to the correct graph
on the next page. Indicate on each graph, the area of economic profit or loss, or state if the firm is just making normal
profits.
  a. a purely competitive firm in earning economic profits

  in the short run   Graph _____
  b. a purely competitive firm in long-run equilibrium

                                          Graph _____

  c. a natural monopoly   Graph _____
  d. a monopolistically competitive firm earning eco-

  nomic profits in the short run   Graph _____

e. a monopolistically competitive firm experiencing economic losses in the short run   Graph _____

f. a monopolistically competitive firm in long-run equilibrium   Graph _____

1

2

3

4

5

6

■ **SELF-TEST**

Circle the T if the statement is true; the F if it is false.

1. Monopolistic competitors have no control over the price of their products. **T F**

2. The publisher of McConnell/Brue *Economics* and this *Study Guide* is a monopolistic competitor. **T F**

3. The firm's reputation for servicing or exchanging its product is a form of product differentiation under monopolistic competition. **T F**

4. Entry is relatively easy in pure competition but there are significant barriers to entry in monopolistic competition. **T F**

5. There are thousands of competitors in a monopolistically competitive industry. **T F**

6. The smaller the number of firms in an industry and the greater the extent of product differentiation, the greater will be the elasticity of the individual seller's demand curve. **T F**

7. The demand curve of the monopolistic competitor is most likely to be less elastic than the demand curve of the pure monopolist. **T F**

8. In the short run, firms that are monopolistically competitive may earn economic profits or incur losses. **T F**

9. The long-run equilibrium position in monopolistic competition would be where price is equal to marginal cost. **T F**

10. Representative firms in a monopolistically competitive market earn economic profits in the long run. **T F**

11. One reason why monopolistic competition is wasteful, given the products the firms produce and the extent to which they promote them, is that the average cost of producing the product is greater than the minimum average cost at which the product could be produced. **T F**

12. The wider the range of differentiated products offered to consumers by a monopolistically competitive industry the less excess capacity there will be in that industry. **T F**

13. A firm will improve the quality of its product only if it expects that the additional revenue which it will receive will be greater than the extra costs involved. **T F**

14. Successful product improvement by one firm has little or no effect on other firms under monopolistic competition. **T F**

15. Cash rebates are a common form of nonprice competition. **T F**

16. Through product development and advertising expenditures, a monopolistically competitive firm may strive to increase the demand for its product more than these forms of nonprice competition increase its costs. **T F**

17. Those who contend that advertising contributes to the growth of economic concentration in the economy argue that the advertising by established firms creates barriers to the entry of new firms into an industry. **T F**

18. The new perspective on advertising would be that advertising increases knowledge of available products so that consumers are more aware of substitutes. **T F**

19. There tends to be rather general agreement among both critics and defenders of advertising that advertising increases the average cost of producing and promoting the product. **T F**

20. Empirical evidence clearly indicates that advertising reduces competition and leads to a misallocation of the economy's resources. **T F**

Circle the letter that corresponds to the best answer.

1. Which of the following would be most characteristic of monopolistic competition?
 (a) thousands of firms in the industry
 (b) product standardization
 (c) collusion among firms
 (d) nonprice competition

2. All the following are forms that product differentiation can take in monopolistic competition *except:*
 (a) promotion and packaging of the product
 (b) sale of the homogeneous product at a standard price
 (c) physical or qualitative differences in the products
 (d) services and the conditions involving the sale of the product

3. In the short run, a representative monopolistically competitive firm:
 (a) obtains an economic profit
 (b) breaks even
 (c) suffers an economic loss
 (d) may have an economic profit or loss or break even

4. A monopolistically competitive firm is producing at an output level in the short run where average total cost is $3.50, price is $3.00, marginal revenue is $1.50, marginal cost is $1.50. This firm is operating:
 (a) with an economic loss in the short run
 (b) with an economic profit in the short run
 (c) at the break-even level of output in the short run
 (d) at an inefficient level of output in the short run

5. If firms enter a monopolistically competitive industry, then we would expect the firm's demand curve to:
 (a) increase and the firm's price to increase
 (b) decrease and the firm's price to decrease
 (c) remain the same but the firm's price to increase

(d) remain the same and the firm's price to remain the same

Price	Quantity demanded	Total cost	Output
$10	1	$14	1
9	2	17	2
8	3	22	3
7	4	29	4
6	5	38	5
5	6	49	6

Answer the next four questions (6, 7, 8, and 9) on the basis of the following diagram for a monopolistically competitive firm in short-run equilibrium. Assume the firm is part of an increasing-cost industry.

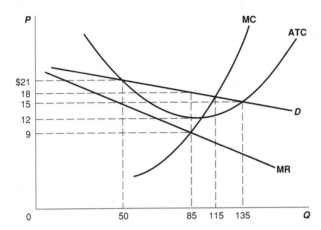

6. The firm's profit maximizing price will be:
(a) $9
(b) $12
(c) $15
(d) $18

7. The equilibrium output for this firm will be:
(a) 50
(b) 85
(c) 115
(d) 135

8. This firm will realize an economic profit of:
(a) $510
(b) $765
(c) $1021
(d) $1170

9. If firms enter this industry in the long run the:
(a) average total cost curve will shift upward and demand will decrease
(b) average total cost curve will shift downward and demand will increase
(c) marginal revenue curve will shift upward and demand will decrease
(d) marginal revenue curve will shift upward and demand will increase

Answer the next three questions (10, 11, and 12) based on the demand and cost schedules for a monopolistic competitor given in the table at the top of the next column.

10. What output will the monopolistic competitor produce?
(a) 2
(b) 3
(c) 4
(d) 5

11. What will be the economic profit or loss for this monopolistic competitor at the profit-maximizing level of output?
(a) −$1
(b) $1
(c) $2
(d) $3

12. *In the long run,* the number of firms in this monopolistic competitive industry will most likely:
(a) stay the same
(b) decrease
(c) increase
(d) cannot be determined from the information

13. Given the product the firm is producing and the extent to which the firm is promoting it, *in the long run:*
(a) the firm will produce that output at which marginal cost and price are equal
(b) the elasticity of demand for the firm's product will be less than it was in the short run
(c) the number of firms in the industry will be greater than it was in the short run
(d) the economic profits being earned by the firms in the industry will tend to equal zero

14. Which of the following is *not* one of the features of monopolistic competition which may offset the wastes associated with such a market structure?
(a) a wider variety of products is offered to consumers
(b) much advertising is self-canceling
(c) the quality of products improves over time
(d) consumers are better informed of the availability and prices of products

15. If an industry is to be economically efficient it is necessary that:
(a) price equal average cost
(b) price equal marginal cost
(c) average cost equal marginal cost
(d) all of the above

16. Were a monopolistically competitive industry in long-run equilibrium a firm in that industry might be able to increase its economic profits by:
(a) increasing the price of its product
(b) increasing the amounts it spends to advertise its product
(c) decreasing the price of its product
(d) decreasing the output of its product

17. The traditional view of advertising argues that advertising:
(a) makes the firm's demand curve less elastic and helps the firm reduce prices to consumers
(b) makes the firm's demand curve less elastic and helps the firm increase profits
(c) gives a new firm an opportunity to overcome barriers to entry created by an established firm
(d) gives consumers information on products to increase the known number of substitutes to buyers

18. Which of the following would be closest to recent empirical evidence supporting the new perspective on advertising? A study that showed that:
(a) above average levels of advertising produced below average rates of increases in output
(b) above average rates of increases in prices produced below average levels of advertising
(c) below average rates of output increases produced above average levels of advertising
(d) above average levels of advertising produced below average rates of increases in prices

19. Which of the following can be fairly concluded with respect to the economic effects of advertising?
(a) advertising helps to maintain a high level of aggregate demand in the economy
(b) evidence on the economic effects of advertising is mixed because of the difficulties of determining cause and effect in studies
(c) advertising in the American economy leads almost invariably to higher product prices
(d) lower unit costs and lower prices result when a firm advertises because advertising increases the size of the firm's market and promotes economies of scale

20. In seeking to maximize its profits the three variables which the monopolistically competitive firm must consider are:
(a) price, product, and promotion
(b) price, publicity, and promotion
(c) price, product, and publicity
(d) product, publicity, and promotion

■ DISCUSSION QUESTIONS

1. What are the chief characteristics of a monopolistic competitive market? In what sense is there competition and in what sense is there monopoly in such a market?

2. What is meant by product differentiation? By what methods can products be differentiated? How does product differentiation affect the kind of competition in, and inject an element of monopoly into, markets?

3. Comment on the elasticity of the demand curve faced by the monopolistically competitive firm in the short run. Assume that the firm is producing a given product and is engaged in a given amount of promotional activity. What two factors determine just how elastic that demand curve will be?

4. What output will the monopolistic competitor produce in the short run, and what price will it charge for its product? What determines whether the firm will earn profits or suffer losses in the short run?

5. In the long run what level of economic profits will the individual monopolistically competitive firm *tend* to receive? Why is this just a tendency? What forces economic profits toward this level, and why will the firm produce a long-run output which is smaller than the most "efficient" output? (Again assume, in answering this question, that the firm is producing a given product and selling it with a given amount of promotional activity.)

6. In what two senses is monopolistic competition wasteful or a misallocation of resources?

7. What methods, other than price cutting, can an individual monopolistic competitor employ to attempt to protect and increase its economic profits in the long run?

8. To what extent and how do product differentiation and product development offset the "wastes" associated with monopolistic competition?

9. Does advertising result in a waste of resources, or does it promote a more efficient utilization of resources? What arguments can be presented to support the contention that it is wasteful and detrimental, and what claims are made to support the view that it is beneficial to the economy?

10. What is the empirical evidence in support of the traditional and new perspective views of advertising? What conclusion can be drawn about the economic effects of advertising?

11. When is a monopolistic competitor in long-run equilibrium not only with respect to the price it is charging but also with respect to the product it is producing and the extent to which it is promoting its product?

■ ANSWERS

Chapter 25 Price and Output Determination: Monopolistic Competition

FILL-IN QUESTIONS

1. relatively large number of, differentiated, do not, price, non-price, fairly easy

2. limited, rivalry

3. *a.* product quality; *b.* services; *c.* location; *d.* promotion and packaging

4. *a.* more, less; *b.* number of rivals the firm has, the degree of product differentiation; *c.* marginal cost, marginal revenue

5. reduce, increase

6. average cost, zero, greater

7. normal, economic; *a.* differentiation, economic; *b.* barriers, economic; *c.* way, economic

8. average cost is greater than minimum average cost, price is greater than marginal cost

9. product differentiation, product promotion

10. variety, quality

11. *a.* persuasion or information; *b.* concentration or competition; *c.* wasteful or efficient

12. persuade (or manipulate), information

13. concentration, demand, less, competition, demand

14. allocative, productive (either order); information, search

15. both

16. product, promotion

PROBLEMS AND PROJECTS

1. *a.* N; *b.* MC; *c.* MC; *d.* MC; *e.* N; *f.* MC

2. *a.* marginal cost: $30, 10, 20, 30, 40, 50, 60, 70, 80, 90; marginal revenue: $110, 90, 70, 50, 30, 10, −10, −30, −50, −70;

b. (1) 4; (2) $80; (3) $180; *c.* (1) decrease; (2) average cost; (3) equal to zero

3. *a.* 2; *b.* 5; *c.* 4; *d.* 6; *e.* 3; *f.* 1

SELF-TEST

1. F, p. 486	**11.** T, p. 489
2. T, p. 486	**12.** F, pp. 489–490
3. T, p. 486	**13.** T, p. 491
4. F, p. 487	**14.** F, p. 491
5. F, pp. 485–486	**15.** F, p. 490
6. F, p. 487	**16.** T, pp. 490–491
7. F, p. 487	**17.** T, p. 492
8. T, p. 486	**18.** T, p. 492
9. F, p. 488	**19.** F, p. 493
10. F, p. 488	**20.** F, p. 493

1. *d*, p. 487	**11.** *c*, p. 488
2. *b*, p. 486	**12.** *c*, p. 488
3. *d*, p. 488	**13.** *d*, pp. 488–489
4. *a*, p. 488	**14.** *b*, p. 489
5. *b*, p. 488	**15.** *d*, p. 489
6. *d*, p. 488	**16.** *b*, p. 491
7. *b*, p. 488	**17.** *b*, p. 492
8. *a*, p. 488	**18.** *d*, pp. 493–494
9. *a*, p. 488	**19.** *b*, p. 493
10. *b*, p. 488	**20.** *a*, p. 495

DISCUSSION QUESTIONS

1. pp. 485–486	**7.** pp. 490–491
2. pp. 486–487	**8.** pp. 489–490
3. p. 487	**9.** pp. 492–493
4. pp. 488–489	**10.** pp. 493–494
5. pp. 488–489	**11.** p. 495
6. p. 489	

CHAPTER 26

Price and Output Determination: Oligopoly

This chapter is the last of four chapters on market structures, and in some ways it is the most difficult. Oligopoly is one of those topics of study in economics that offer few definite conclusions. The ambiguity resulting from the analysis of oligopoly often makes it frustrating for students to study. By contrast, economists do draw fairly definite conclusions and make strong generalizations about price and output determination under conditions of pure competition, pure monopoly, and monopolistic competition, as you have learned in the last three chapters.

Oligopoly, however, is the most realistic market structure that you will examine. Many economists believe that it is the most prevalent type of market structure—or at least the most important—in the American economy. This realism and the different examples of oligopoly that can be found throughout the American economy make the study of oligopoly more difficult and complex than is the case with other market structures. Despite these problems, there are insights about oligopoly that you **can** and **should** learn.

The concept of oligopoly is fairly easy to grasp—a few firms that are mutually interdependent and that dominate the market for a product. The underlying causes of oligopoly are economies of scales, barriers to entry, and mergers, which are subjects you have read about before. Economists use concentration ratios to measure the degree of firm dominance of an industry, but as with most economic measures you have studied in previous chapters, they are subject to several shortcomings.

What is more difficult to grasp is oligopoly behavior. The game theory overview should help you understand **what is meant** by mutual interdependence and **why it exists** in an oligopoly. If you can do this, you will be well on the road to understanding why specific conclusions cannot be reached about the price and output determination of individual firms. You will also see why oligopolists are loath to engage in price competition and why they frequently resort to **collusion** to set prices and sometimes use nonprice competition to determine market share. Collusion does not give firms complete protection from the rigors of competition because there are incentives to cheat on collusive agreements.

There is no standard model of oligopoly because of the diversity of markets and the uncertainty caused by mutual interdependence among firms. Chapter 26, however, does present four variants of oligopoly models that cover the range of market situations. The kinked-demand curve model is the first of these variants. It explains why, in the absence of collusion, oligopolists will not raise or lower their prices even when their costs change. But the kinked-demand curve does not explain what price oligopolists will set; it only explains why price, once set, will be relatively inflexible.

The second model examines how oligopolists resort to collusion to set price. The collusion can be overt, as in a cartel agreement, or the collusion can be covert, as in a gentlemen's agreement. The history of the OPEC international cartel provides a classic example of how covert collusion can work in practice, and how obstacles to collusion can eventually weaken the power of a cartel.

Two other models of oligopoly are also worthy of note. In some industries there is a dominant firm that serves as the price leader for the other firms. In this price leadership model there is no overt collusion, only tacit collusion, among firms involved in setting prices in this industry. The fourth model is based on "cost-plus pricing" where an oligopolist estimates the cost of production and uses a standard percentage "markup" to determine price. This pricing scheme is especially helpful to multiproduct oligopolists.

Whether oligopoly is economically efficient is a difficult question given the various models of oligopoly. Nevertheless, you should take time to evaluate the allocative and productive efficiency of a collusive oligopoly (or cartel) and compare it to pure competition or pure monopoly. A more controversial question, however, is whether oligopoly is desirable in the long run for technological progress. Both the competitive and Schumpeter-Galbraith views are presented on this question along with the empirical evidence.

In the final section of the chapter the American automobile industry is examined to illustrate a real-world oligopoly in action. Here you will see that three firms dominated an industry characterized by high barriers to entry, price-leadership, and nonprice competition in the three decades following World War II. But you will also discover that the American automobile industry, like the Old Gray Mare, "ain't what she used to be." Over the past twenty-five years, foreign competition weakened the oligopolistic structure of the domestic automobile industry; GM, Ford, and Chrysler now account for only about 65% of domestic car sales. The industry responded to this foreign competition by lobbying Congress for import protection and by participating in joint ventures with foreign producers, both actions serving to preserve the market power of the oligopoly as it entered a new era.

■ **CHECKLIST**

When you have studied this chapter you should be able to:

☐ Define oligopoly and distinguish between homogeneous and differentiated oligopolies.
☐ Describe concentration ratios and list five shortcomings of this measure.
☐ Use the Herfindahl index to assess the distribution of market power among dominant firms in an oligopoly.
☐ Identify the three most significant causes of oligopoly and explain how each of these tends to result in oligopolistic industries.
☐ Explain why it is difficult to predict what price will be charged and what output will be produced by an oligopolist.
☐ Describe three characteristics of oligopoly using a game theory perspective.
☐ Employ the kinked demand curve to explain why oligopoly prices tend to be inflexible.
☐ Explain two criticisms of kinked-demand analysis.
☐ Describe the price that would be set and the output that would be produced by oligopolists who were producing a homogeneous product with identical cost and demand curves.
☐ Give examples of overt and covert collusion.
☐ List six obstacles to collusion.
☐ Use the history of OPEC to illustrate how cartels can work to benefit oil producers and how obstacles to collusion eventually weakened OPEC.
☐ Describe the price leadership model of oligopoly and three tactics used by a price leader.
☐ Describe how a firm (such as General Motors) employs cost-plus pricing to determine the prices it will charge for its products.
☐ Explain the role played by nonprice competition in oligopolistic industries and two reasons why oligopolists emphasize nonprice competition.
☐ Compare oligopoly to other market structures in terms of allocative and productive efficiency.
☐ Compare the Schumpeter-Galbraith view with the competitive view of oligopoly, and explain whether the empirical evidence does or does not support each viewpoint.

☐ Describe the American automobile industry in terms of the number of sellers and their market shares, the height and kinds of barriers to entry, the method employed to set prices, the types of nonprice competition, the level of profits, and the rate of technological progress.
☐ Explain the effects of foreign competition on the domestic automobile industry.

■ **CHAPTER OUTLINE**

1. Oligopoly is frequently encountered in the American economy.
  a. It is composed of a few firms that dominate an industry and that sell a standardized or differentiated product.
  b. Concentration ratios are used to measure the degree of market dominance.
  (1) If the top four firms control 40% or more of the total market, the industry is considered to be oligopolistic.
  (2) But concentration ratios have shortcomings and must be interpreted with care because of problems with defining markets, interindustry competition, world trade, the distribution of market power, and actual market performance.
  c. The existence of oligopoly is usually the result of economies of scale, other barriers to entry, and the advantages of merger.

2. Insight into the pricing behavior of oligopolists can be gained by thinking of the oligopoly situation as a game of strategy. This game theory overview leads to three conclusions.
  a. Firms in an oligopolistic industry are "mutually interdependent" and must consider the actions of rivals when they make price decisions.
  b. Oligopoly often leads to overt or covert collusion among the firms to fix prices or to coordinate pricing because competition among oligopolists results in low prices and profits; collusion helps maintain higher prices and profits.
  c. Collusion creates incentive to cheat among oligopolists.

3. The economic analysis of oligopoly is difficult because the "oligopoly" actually covers many different market situations and because mutual interdependence makes it difficult for an oligopolist to estimate a demand curve. Nevertheless, two important characteristics of oligopoly are inflexible prices and simultaneous price changes by oligopolistic firms. An analysis of four oligopoly models helps explain the various pricing practice of oligopolists.
  a. In the kinked-demand curve model there is no collusion.
  (1) Each firm believes that when it lowers its price its rivals will lower their prices; and when it increases its price its rivals will not increase their prices.

(2) The firm is, therefore, reluctant to change its price for fear of decreasing its profits.

(3) But the model has two shortcomings: it does not explain how the going price gets set; prices are not as rigid as implied by the model.

b. The game theory perspective suggests that "mutual interdependence" of oligopolists encourages firms to collude to maintain or to increase prices and profits.

(1) Firms that collude tend to set their prices and joint output at the same level a pure monopolist would set them.

(2) The method of collusion employed by the firms may be covert, as in a cartel agreement, or covert, as in a gentlemen's agreement.

(3) There are at least six obstacles that make it difficult for firms to collude or maintain collusive arrangements: difference in demand and cost among firms; the number of firms in the arrangement; incentives to cheat; changing economic conditions; potential for entry by other firms; and legal restrictions and penalties.

(4) The OPEC cartel provides an example of collusion working to increase price and profits during the 1970s and the obstacles to collusion that reduced the market power of the cartel during the 1980s.

c. Price leadership is a form of covert collusion or gentlemen's agreement in which one firm initiates price changes and the other firms in the industry follow the lead. Three price leadership tactics have been observed.

(1) Price adjustments tend to be made infrequently as cost and demand condition change to a significant degree.

(2) The price leader announces the price change in various ways, through speeches, announcement, or other such activities.

(3) The price set may not maximize short-run profits for the industry, especially if the industry wants to prevent entry by other firms.

d. In the cost-plus pricing model a firm determines its price by adding a percentage markup to its average cost of production.

(1) Actions taken by firms under model are also consistent with outcomes from collusion and price leadership models of oligopoly.

(2) Cost-markup pricing is especially appealing to multiproduct oligopolists who find it difficult and costly to estimate demand on many products.

4. Oligopolistic firms often avoid price competition but engage in nonprice competition to determine each firm's market share for two reasons: price cuts are easily duplicated, but nonprice competition is more unique; oligopolists have greater financial resources to devote to advertising and product development.

5. To compare the efficiency of an oligopolist with that of a pure competitor is difficult.

a. Many economists believe that oligopoly is neither allocatively efficient ($P = MC$) nor productively efficient ($P = $ minimum ATC).

b. The competitive view is that oligopoly has much the same result as monopoly; but Schumpeter and Galbraith believe that oligopoly is needed if there is to be rapid technological progress (dynamic efficiency).

c. While the evidence is not conclusive, it appears that most of the important inventions have not been made by large firms; and the structure of the industry may not affect its technological progress.

6. The automobile industry in the United States is an example of an oligopoly in which are found a few large firms and significant barriers to entry; price leadership; styling competition among the sellers; and significant import competition from foreign producers.

■ IMPORTANT TERMS

Oligopoly	Kinked demand curve
Fewness	Price war
Homogeneous oligopoly	Collusion
Differentiated oligopoly	Cartel
Concentration ratio	Gentlemen's agreement
Interindustry competition	Price leadership
Import competition	Cost-plus pricing
Herfindahl index	Traditional view (of oligopoly)
Game theory model	Schumpeter-Galbraith view (of oligopoly)
Mutual interdependence	
Noncollusive oligopoly	

■ FILL-IN QUESTIONS

1. In an oligopoly a _____ firms produce either a _____ or a _____ product, and entry into such an industry is _____

2. The percentage of the total industry sales accounts for the top four firms in an industry is known as a _____. An industry is generally considered to be oligopolistic when the top four firms control _____% or more of the market. The distribution of market power among the dominant firms, however, is measured by the _____; it is calculated by summing the _____ of each firm in the industry.

3. The three major underlying causes of oligopoly are _____,

_____ , and

_____

4. The basics of the pricing behavior of oligopolists can be understood from a _____ theory perspective that leads to three insights.

   a. Oligopoly consists of a _____ number of firms that are _____. This means that when setting the price of its product each producer must consider the _____ of rivals. The monopolist does not face this problem because it has _____ rivals; and the pure competitor and monopolistic competitor do not face it because they have _____ rivals.

   b. The characteristics of oligopoly create a tendency for _____ among firms to set prices and restrict competition.

   c. But, _____ creates incentive to _____ on agreements to increase market share or profits.

5. Formal economic analysis cannot be easily used to explain the prices and outputs of oligopolists because oligopoly is in fact (one, a small number of, many) _____ specific market situation(s); and when firms are mutually interdependent each firm is (certain, uncertain) _____ about how its rivals will react when it changes the price of its product.

6. Oligopoly prices tend to be (flexible, inflexible) _____ and oligopolists tend to change their prices (independently, simultaneously) _____

7. The kinked demand curve which the individual non-colluding oligopolist sees for its product is highly (elastic, inelastic) _____ at prices above the current or going price and tends to be only slightly _____ or _____ below that price.

8. The kinked demand curve for a noncolluding oligopolist is drawn on the assumption that if the oligopolist raises its price its rivals will _____ and if it lowers its prices its rivals will _____

9. Because the oligopolist who confronts a kinked demand curve finds that there is a _____ in

its marginal-revenue curve, small changes in the marginal-cost curve do not change the _____

_____

10. When oligopolists collude, the prices they set and their combined output tend to be the same as would be set (in a purely competitive industry, by a pure monopolist)

_____

11. A cartel is a formal agreement among sellers in which the _____ and the total _____ of the product and each seller's _____ of the market are specified.

12. A gentlemen's agreement is (a formal, an informal) _____ agreement on _____; each firm's share of the market is determined by _____

13. Six obstacles to collusion among oligopolists are:

   a. _____
   b. _____
   c. _____
   d. _____
   e. _____
   f. _____

14. _____ is an international oil cartel whose market power has declined in recent years because of three obstacles to (kinked-demand, collusion)

_____

   a. One reason for the decline is the (increase, decrease) _____ in oil prices during the 1970s that (attracted, discouraged) _____ new entrants into oil production.

   b. A second reason is the (increase, decrease) _____ in the demand for oil during the early 1980s because of recession and (increased, decreased) _____ use of alternative energy sources.

   c. A third reason is (fair-play, cheating) _____ _____ among the (thirteen, thirty) _____ cartel members and the (similarity, diversity) _____ of economic circumstances among the members.

15. When one firm in an oligopoly is almost always the first to change its price and the other firms change their prices after it has changed its price the oligopoly model is called _____

16. When a firm employs a cost-plus formula to determine the price it will charge for a product it adds a percentage _____ to the _____ cost of producing the product.

17. There tends to be very little (price, nonprice) _____ competition among oligopolists and a great deal of _____ competition which they use to determine each firm's _____
The two reasons for the emphasis on this kind of competition are:

   a. _____
   b. _____

18. Although it is difficult to evaluate the economic efficiency of oligopoly, when comparisons are made to pure competition the conclusion drawn is that there will neither be _____ nor _____ efficiency under oligopoly. The price and output behavior of the oligopolist is more likely to be similar to that found under pure _____

19. The competitive view of oligopoly is that it results in (lower, higher) _____ prices and profits, _____ outputs, and a rate of technological progress that is (slower, faster) _____ than would be found if the industry were more competitive.

20. In the Schumpeter-Galbraith view of oligopoly:

   a. Only oligopolists have both the _____ and the _____ to be technologically progressive;
   b. Over time oligopolists will bring about a more rapid rate of _____, lower _____ and _____, and perhaps greater _____ and _____ than the same industry competitively organized.

21. The empirical evidence seems to indicate that the large oligopolists (have, have not) _____ been the major source of technological progress in the United States.

22. The market structure of the automobile industry in the United States can be characterized as (monopolistic, oligopolistic) _____, with price

_____ and nonprice competition that has focused on _____

   a. In recent decades, (import, export) _____ _____ competition reduced the market power of the domestic industry. The industry responded by lobbying government for _____ _____ quotas on Japanese cars during the early 1980s.
   b. The industry also arranged joint ventures with (domestic, foreign) _____ producers, thereby serving to (increase, decrease) _____ mutual interdependence worldwide among automobile producers.

   c. Foreign competition has also altered the _____ role that was traditionally played by General Motors.

■ **PROBLEMS AND PROJECTS**

1. Consider the following payoff matrix in which the numbers indicate the profit in millions of dollars for a duopoly based either a high-price or a low-price strategy.

		Firm X	
		High-price	Low-price
Firm Y	High-price	X = $200 Y = $200	X = $250 Y = $ 50
	Low-price	X = $ 50 Y = $250	X = $ 50 Y = $ 50

   a. *Situation 1:* Each firm chooses a high-price strategy. *Result:* Each firm will earn $_____ million in profit for a total of $_____ million for the two firms.
   b. *Situation 2:* Firm X chooses a low-price strategy while Firm Y maintains a high-price strategy. *Result:* Firm X will earn $_____ million and Firm Y will earn $_____. Compared to Situation 1, Firm X has an incentive to cut prices because it will earn $_____ million more in profit and Firm Y will earn $_____ million less in profit. Together, the firms will earn $_____ million in profit, which is $_____ less than in Situation 1.
   c. *Situation 3:* Firm Y chooses a low-price strategy while Firm X maintains a high-price strategy. *Result:* Firm Y has an incentive to cut prices because it will earn $_____ million and Firm X will earn $_____. Compared to Situation 1, Firm Y will earn $_____ million more in profit and Firm X will earn $_____ million less in profit.

Together, the firms will earn $_____ million in profit, which is $_____ less than in Situation 1.

d. Situation 4: Each firm chooses a low-price strategy. **Result:** Each firm will earn $_____ million in profit for a total of $_____ million for the two firms. This total is $_____ less than in Situation 1.

e. Conclusions:

(1) The two firms have a strong incentive to collude and adopt the high-price strategy because there is the potential for $_____ million more in profit for the two firms than with a low-price strategy (Situation 4), or the potential for $_____ million more for the two firms than with a mixed-price strategy (Situations 2 or 3).

(2) There is also a strong incentive for each firm to cheat on the agreement and adopt a low-price strategy when the other firm maintains a high-price strategy because this situation will produce $_____ more in profit for the cheating firm compared to honoring a collusive agreement for a high-price strategy.

2. The kinked-demand schedule which an oligopolist believes confronts the firm is given in the table in the next column.

Price	Quantity demanded	Total revenue	Marginal revenue per unit
$2.90	100	$_____	
2.80	200	_____	$_____
2.70	300	_____	_____
2.60	400	_____	_____
2.50	500	_____	_____
2.40	525	_____	_____
2.30	550	_____	_____
2.20	575	_____	_____
2.10	600	_____	_____

a. Compute the oligopolist's total revenue at each of the nine prices, and enter these figures in the table.

b. Also compute marginal revenue **for each unit** between the nine prices and enter these figures in the table.

c. What is the current, or going, price for the oligopolist's product? $_____ How much is it selling? _____

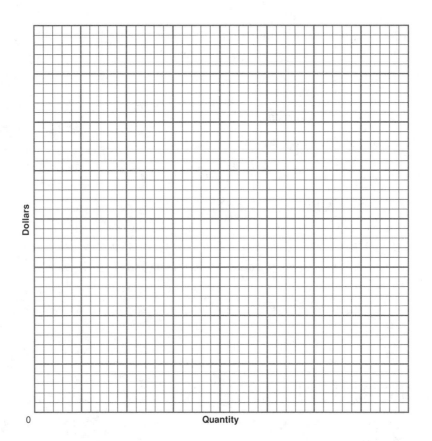

Dollars

0   Quantity

d. On the graph on the previous page, plot the oligopolist's demand curve and marginal-revenue curve. Connect the demand points and the marginal-revenue points with as straight a line as possible. (**Be sure** to plot the marginal-revenue figures at the average of the two quantities involved, that is, at 150, 250, 350, 450, 512½, 537½, 562½, and 587½.)
e. Assume that the marginal-cost schedule of the oligopolist is given in columns (1) and (2) of the table below. Plot the marginal-cost curve on the graph on which demand and marginal revenue were plotted.

(1) Output	(2) MC	(3) MC′	(4) MC″
150	$1.40	$1.90	$.40
250	1.30	1.80	.30
350	1.40	1.90	.40
450	1.50	2.00	.50
512½	1.60	2.10	.60
537½	1.70	2.20	.70
562½	1.80	2.30	.80
587½	1.90	2.40	.90

(1) Given demand and marginal cost, what price should the oligopolist charge to maximize profits?

$_____ How many units of product will it sell

at this price? _____
(2) If the marginal-cost schedule changed from that shown in columns (1) and (2) to that shown in columns

(1) and (3), what price should it charge? $_____

What level of output will it produce? _____
How have profits changed as a result of the change in

costs? _____
Plot the new marginal-cost curve on the graph.
(3) If the marginal-cost curve schedule changed from that shown in columns (1) and (2) to that shown in col-

umns (1) and (4), what price should it charge? $_____

What level of output will it produce? _____
How have profits changed as a result of the change in

costs? _____
Plot the new marginal-cost curve on the graph.

3. An oligopoly producing a homogeneous product is composed of three firms. Assume that these three firms have identical cost schedules. Assume also that if any one of these firms sets a price for the product, the other two firms charge the same price. As long as they all charge the same price they will share the market equally; and the quantity demanded of each will be the same.
At the bottom of the page is the total-cost schedule of one of these firms and the demand schedule that confronts it when the other firms charge the same price as this firm.

a. Complete the marginal-cost and marginal-revenue schedules facing the firm.
b. What price would this firm set if it wished to maxi-

mize its profits? _____
c. How much would:

(1) It sell at this price? _____

(2) Its profits be at this price? $_____
d. What would be the industry's:

(1) Total output at this price? _____

(2) Joint profits at this price? $_____
e. Is there any other price this firm can set, assuming that the other two firms charge the same price, which

would result in a greater joint profit for them? _____

If so, what is that price? $_____
f. If these three firms colluded in order to maximize their joint profit, what price would they charge?

$_____

Output	Total cost	Marginal cost	Price	Quantity demanded	Marginal revenue
0	$ 0		$140	0	
1	30	$_____	130	1	$_____
2	50	_____	120	2	_____
3	80	_____	110	3	_____
4	120	_____	100	4	_____
5	170	_____	90	5	_____
6	230	_____	80	6	_____
7	300	_____	70	7	_____
8	380	_____	60	8	_____

4. A firm producing automobiles has $4 billion invested in capital and its average total cost schedule is shown below.

Output (cars per year)	Average total cost
1,100,000	$14,000
1,200,000	10,000
1,300,000	8,000
1,400,000	7,000
1,500,000	6,500
1,600,000	6,250
1,700,000	6,600
1,800,000	7,200

a. If the objective of the firm is to have an annual return *after* taxes equal to 10% of its invested capital it must earn $_____ million after taxes each year.

b. To earn this amount after taxes when its earnings are taxed at a 50% rate it must earn $_____ million *before* taxes.

c. When the firm estimates that its most likely annual output (its "standard volume") is 1,500,000 automobiles:

(1) to achieve its objective of a 10% after-tax return on its investment it must earn $_____ per automobile. (*Hint*: Divide the required return before taxes by its annual output.)

(2) to earn this amount per automobile it must set the price of an automobile at $_____

(3) the markup is approximately _____%.

■ **SELF-TEST**

Circle the T if the statement is true; the F if it is false.

1. The products produced by the firms in an oligopolistic industry may be either homogeneous (standardized) or differentiated. **T F**

2. Oligopolistic industries contain a few large firms that act independently of one another. **T F**

3. The greeting card industry is an example of a differentiated oligopoly. **T F**

4. Concentration ratios are low in those industries which are oligopolies. **T F**

5. Concentration ratios include adjustments for interindustry competition in measuring concentration in an industry. **T F**

6. The monopoly power of domestic producers is overstated by concentration ratios because import competition from foreign suppliers is not taken into account. **T F**

7. The uncertainty which exists in oligopolies is the uncertainty faced by each firm on how its rivals will react if it changes its price. **T F**

8. The kinked-demand curve is an economic tool which can be used to explain how the current market price of an oligopolistic product is determined. **T F**

9. One of the shortcomings of kinked-demand analysis is that it does not explain how the going oligopoly price was established in the first place. **T F**

10. Collusion occurs when firms in an industry reach an overt or covert agreement to fix prices, divide or share the market, and in some way restrict competition among the firms. **T F**

11. Secret price concessions and other forms of cheating will strengthen collusion. **T F**

12. A cartel is usually a written agreement among firms which sets the price of the product and determines each firm's share of the market. **T F**

13. The practice of price leadership is almost always based on a formal written or oral agreement. **T F**

14. An oligopolist utilizing a cost-plus pricing formula typically adds a percentage markup to what its unit cost would be if it operated at full capacity. **T F**

15. Price competition between firms is an important characteristic of oligopoly. **T F**

16. Nonprice competition is the typical method of determining each oligopolist's share of the total market. **T F**

17. It is often argued that oligopolists typically possess both the means and the incentives for technological progress, and that the means are the substantial profits received by them. **T F**

18. Almost all the important technological advances in the United States between 1880 and 1965 can be attributed to the research and development activities of large business firms. **T F**

19. The American automobile industry is a fairly good example of a differentiated oligopoly. **T F**

20. Foreign competition has altered the price leadership pattern that characterized the American automobile industry in past decades. **T F**

Circle the letter that corresponds to the best answer.

1. The number of firms in an oligopolistic industry is:
   (a) one
   (b) a few
   (c) many
   (d) very many

2. Which of the following products is produced in an industry that best illustrates the concept of a homogeneous oligopoly?
(a) lead
(b) beer
(c) automobiles
(d) breakfast cereal

3. Concentration ratios take into account:
(a) interindustry competition
(b) import competition
(c) the existence of separate local markets for products
(d) none of the above

4. Industry A is dominated by four large firms that hold market shares of 40, 30, 20, and 10. The Herfindahl index for this industry is:
(a) 100
(b) 1000
(c) 3000
(d) 4500

5. Which of the following contributes to the existence of oligopoly in an industry?
(a) low barriers to entry
(b) standardized products
(c) economies of scale
(d) elastic demand

The next three questions (6, 7, and 8) are based on the following payoff matrix for a duopoly in which the numbers indicate the profit in thousands of dollars for a high-price or a low-price strategy.

		Firm A	
		High-price	**Low-price**
Firm B	**High-price**	A = $425 B = $425	A = $525 B = $275
	Low-price	A = $275 B = $525	A = $200 B = $200

6. If both firms collude to maximize joint profits, the total profits for the two firms will be:
(a) $400,000
(b) $800,000
(c) $850,000
(d) $950,000

7. Assume that Firm B adopts a low-price strategy while Firm A maintains a high-price strategy. Compared to the results from a high-price strategy for both firms, Firm B will now:
(a) lose $150,000 in profit and Firm A will gain $150,000 in profit

(b) gain $100,000 in profit and Firm A will lose $150,000 in profit
(c) gain $150,000 in profit and Firm A will lose $100,000 in profit
(d) gain $525,000 in profit and Firm A will lose $275,000 in profit

8. If both firms operate independently and do not collude, the most likely profit is:
(a) $200,000 for Firm A and $200,000 for Firm B
(b) $525,000 for Firm A and $275,000 for Firm B
(c) $275,000 for Firm A and $525,000 for Firm B
(d) $425,000 for Firm A and $425,000 for Firm B

9. Mutual interdependence is only characteristic of:
(a) pure and monopolistic competition
(b) monopolistic competition and oligopoly
(c) pure competition and oligopoly
(d) oligopoly

10. Mutual interdependence means that:
(a) each firm produces a product similar but not identical to the products produced by its rivals
(b) each firm produces a product identical to the products produced by its rivals
(c) each firm must consider the reactions of its rivals when it determines its price policy
(d) each firm faces a perfectly elastic demand for its product

11. The prices of products produced by oligopolies tend to be:
(a) relatively flexible and when firms change prices they are apt to change them at the same time
(b) relatively inflexible and when firms change prices they are not apt to change them at the same time
(c) relatively inflexible and when firms change prices they are apt to change them at the same time
(d) relatively flexible and when firms change prices they are not apt to change them at the same time

12. The demand curve confronting an oligopolist tends to be:
(a) elastic
(b) of unitary elasticity
(c) inelastic
(d) one which depends upon the prices charged by his rivals

13. If an individual oligopolist's demand curve is "kinked," it is necessarily:
(a) inelastic below the going price
(b) inelastic above the going price
(c) elastic above the going price
(d) of unitary elasticity at the going price

Use the following diagram to answer the next question (14).

14. The profit maximizing price and output for this oligopolistic firm is:
(a) P_5 and Q_2
(b) P_4 and Q_2
(c) P_3 and Q_3
(d) P_2 and Q_4

15. Below is the demand schedule confronting an oligopolist. Which one of the eight prices seems to be the "going" price of the product produced by the firm?
(a) $4.50
(b) $4
(c) $3.50
(d) $3

Price	Quantity demanded
$5.00	10
4.50	20
4.00	30
3.50	40
3.00	42
2.50	44
2.00	46
1.00	48

16. Which of the following is *not* a means of colluding?
(a) a cartel
(b) a kinked demand curve
(c) a gentlemen's agreement
(d) price leadership

17. To be successful, collusion requires that oligopolists be able to:
(a) keep prices and profits as low as possible
(b) block or restrict the entry of new producers
(c) reduce legal obstacles that protect market power
(d) keep the domestic economy from experiencing high inflation

18. Oligopolists tend to collude because collusive control over the price they charge permits them to:
(a) increase their profits
(b) decrease their uncertainties

(c) deter the entry of new firms into their industry
(d) do all of the above

19. When oligopolists collude the results are generally:
(a) greater output and higher price
(b) greater output and lower price
(c) smaller output and lower price
(d) smaller output and higher price

20. Which of the following constitutes an obstacle to collusion among oligopolists?
(a) a general business recession
(b) a small number of firms in the industry
(c) a homogeneous product
(d) the patent laws

21. Oligopolistic firms that produce a variety of products and do not wish to estimate demand for products would tend to use which price strategy?
(a) price wars
(b) price leadership
(c) cost-plus pricing
(d) price inflexibility

22. Market shares in oligopolistic industries are usually determined on the basis of:
(a) covert collusion
(b) nonprice competition
(c) gentlemen's agreements
(d) joint profit maximization

23. Many economists would conclude that in a highly oligopolistic market there is:
(a) allocative efficiency, but not productive efficiency
(b) productive efficiency, but not allocative efficiency
(c) both allocative and productive efficiency
(d) neither allocative nor productive efficiency

24. It is the belief of Schumpeter and Galbraith that an industry organized oligopolistically when compared with the same industry organized competitively would over time:
(a) foster more rapid improvement in the quality of the good or service produced
(b) bring about a greater reduction in the average cost of producing the product
(c) lower the price of the product by a larger percentage
(d) all of the above

25. A factor that has increased mutual interdependence in the worldwide automobile industry has been:
(a) lobbying of Congress by United States automobile producers for import quotas on Japanese cars
(b) the creation of a Japanese export cartel after the expiration of import quotas imposed by the United States
(c) joint ownership arrangement and joint ventures between Japanese and United States automobile producers

(d) price competition by Japanese automobile producers to increase market share of the small-car market in the United States

■ DISCUSSION QUESTIONS

1. What are the essential characteristics of an oligopoly? How does it differ from monopolistic competition?

2. Explain how the concentration ratio in a particular industry is computed. What is the relationship between this ratio and fewness?

3. What are the shortcomings of the concentration ratio as a measure of the extent of competition in an industry?

4. What are the underlying causes of oligopoly?

5. How can game theory be used to explain price behavior under oligopoly? What do "mutual interdependence" and "collusion" mean with respect to oligopoly?

6. Why is it difficult to use one standard model to explain the prices charged by and the outputs of oligopolists?

7. Explain what the kinked demand curve is, its most important characteristics, the assumptions upon which it is based, and the kind of marginal-revenue curve to which it gives rise. How can the kinked demand curve be used to explain why oligopoly prices are relatively inflexible? Under what conditions will oligopolists acting independently raise or lower their prices even though their demand curves may be kinked?

8. Why do oligopolists find it advantageous to collude? What are the obstacles to collusion?

9. Suppose a few firms produce a homogeneous product, have identical cost curves, and charge the same price. How will the price they set, their combined output of the product, and their joint profit compare with what would be found in the same industry if it were a pure monopoly with several plants?

10. Explain:
   (a) a cartel;
   (b) a gentlemen's agreement;
   (c) price leadership, and
   (d) cost-plus pricing.

11. Why do oligopolists engage in little price competition and in extensive nonprice competition?

12. Contrast the Schumpeter-Galbraith views on the dynamic economic efficiency of oligopoly with the competitive view.

13. What does the empirical evidence have to say about sources of technological progress in the United States?

14. Using the following criteria, describe the American automobile industry: (1) number of firms and their market shares; (2) the barriers to entry; (3) the means used to establish the prices of automobiles; (4) the role of nonprice competition; (5) profits; and (6) technological progress.

15. Explain the causes of and the effects of foreign competition on the American automobile industry during the past two decades. How has competition in the market for automobiles in the United States been affected?

■ ANSWERS

Chapter 26 Price and Output Determination: Oligopoly

FILL-IN QUESTIONS

1. few, standardized, differentiated, difficult

2. concentration ratio; 40; Herfindahl index, squared market shares

3. the economies of scale, other barriers to entry, the advantages of merger

4. game; *a.* few, mutually interdependent, reactions, no, many; *b.* collusion; *c.* collusion, cheat

5. many, uncertain

6. inflexible, simultaneously

7. elastic, elastic, inelastic

8. not raise their prices, lower their prices

9. gap, price the oligopolist will charge

10. by a pure monopolist

11. price, output, share

12. an informal, prices, the ingenuity of each seller (i.e., nonprice competition)

13. *a.* demand and cost differences; *b.* a large number of firms; *c.* cheating (secret price cutting); *d.* a recession; *e.* potential entry; *f.* legal obstacles (antitrust laws)

14. OPEC (Organization of Petroleum Exporting Countries), collusion; *a.* increase, attracted; *b.* decrease, increased; *c.* cheating, thirteen, diversity

15. price leadership

16. markup, average

17. price, nonprice, share of the market, *a.* price cuts can be quickly matched by rival firms; *b.* oligopolists tend to have the greater financial resources required to engage in nonprice competition

18. allocative, productive, monopoly

19. higher, lower, slower

20. *a.* means, incentives; *b.* product improvement, costs, prices, output, employment

21. have not

22. oligopolistic, leadership, styling and technology; *a.* import, import; *b.* foreign, increase; *c.* price leadership

PROBLEMS AND PROJECTS

1. *a.* 200, 400; *b.* 250, 50, 50, 150, 300, 100; *c.* 250, 50, 50, 150, 300, 100; *d.* 50, 100, 300; *e.* (1) 300, 100; (2) 50

2. *a.* total revenue: 290, 560, 810, 1040, 1250, 1260, 1265, 1265, 1260; *b.* marginal revenue: 2.70, 2.50, 2.30, 2.10, 0.40, 0.20, 0, −0.20; *c.* 2.50, 500; *e.* (1) 2.50, 500; (2) 2.50, 500, they have decreased; (3) 2.50, 500, they have increased.

3. *a.* marginal cost: $30, 20, 30, 40, 50, 60, 70, 80; marginal revenue: $130, 110, 90, 70, 50, 30, 10, −10; *b.* $90; *c.* (1) 5; (2) $280; *d.* (1) 15; (2) $840; *e.* no; *f.* $90

4. *a.* 400; *b.* 800; *c.* (1) 533.33, (2) 7033.33, (3) 8.2

SELF-TEST

1. T, p. 498
2. F, p. 498
3. T, p. 499
4. F, p. 499
5. F, p. 499
6. T, p. 499
7. T, p. 501
8. F, p. 504
9. T, p. 504
10. T, p. 505
11. F, p. 507
12. T, p. 506
13. F, p. 508
14. F, p. 509
15. F, p. 510
16. T, p. 510
17. T, p. 511
18. F, p. 511
19. T, p. 512
20. T, pp. 513–516

1. *b*, p. 498
2. *a*, p. 498
3. *d*, p. 499
4. *c*, pp. 499–500
5. *c*, p. 500
6. *c*, pp. 501–502
7. *b*, pp. 501–502
8. *a*, pp. 501–502
9. *d*, p. 501
10. *c*, p. 501
11. *c*, p. 503
12. *d*, p. 503
13. *c*, p. 503
14. *b*, p. 504
15. *c*, pp. 503–504
16. *b*, p. 503
17. *b*, p. 505
18. *d*, p. 505
19. *d*, p. 505
20. *a*, p. 507
21. *c*, p. 509
22. *b*, p. 510
23. *d*, pp. 510–511
24. *d*, p. 511
25. *c*, p. 516

DISCUSSION QUESTIONS

1. pp. 498–499
2. p. 499
3. p. 499
4. p. 500
5. pp. 501–502
6. pp. 502–503
7. pp. 503–504
8. pp. 505–506
9. p. 510
10. pp. 506–509
11. p. 510
12. pp. 510–511
13. pp. 511–512
14. pp. 512–513
15. pp. 513–516

CHAPTER 27

Production and the Demand for Resources

Chapter 27 is the first of a group of three chapters which examine the markets for resources. Resource markets are markets in which employers of resources (demanders) and the owners of these resources (suppliers) determine the prices at which resources will be employed and the quantities of these resources that will be hired.

These resources—you should recall—are labor, land, capital, and entrepreneurial ability. The prices of resources have particular names. The price paid for labor is called a wage, the price paid for the use of land is rent, the price paid for the use of capital is interest, and the price paid for entrepreneurial ability is profit.

The employers of resources are business firms who use resources to produce their products. When the number of employers and the number of owners of a resource are large the market for that resource is a purely competitive market; and—as you already know—the demand for and the supply of that resource will determine its price and the total quantity of it that will be employed.

Chapter 27 begins the examination of resource markets by looking at the business firm and the demand (or employer) side of the resource market. The material in this chapter is *not* an explanation of what determines the demand for a *particular* resource; but it is an explanation of what determines the demand for *any* resource. In Chapters 28 and 29 the other sides of the resource markets and particular resources are examined in detail.

The list of important terms for Chapter 27 is relatively short, but included in the list are two very important concepts—*marginal revenue product* and *marginal resource cost*—which you must grasp if you are to understand how much of a resource a firm will hire. These two concepts are similar to, but not identical with, the marginal-revenue and marginal-cost concepts employed in the study of product markets and in the explanation of the quantity of output a firm will produce.

Marginal revenue and marginal cost are, respectively, the change in the firm's total revenue and the change in the firm's total cost when it produces and sells an additional unit of *output*; marginal revenue product and marginal resource cost are, respectively, the change in the firms' total revenue and the change in the firm's total cost when it hires an additional unit of an *input*. You should note that the two new concepts deal with changes in revenue and costs as a consequence of hiring more of a *resource*.

When a firm wishes to maximize its profits, it produces that *output* at which marginal revenue and marginal cost are equal. But how much of each resource does it hire if it wishes to maximize its profits? It hires that amount of each *resource* at which the marginal revenue product and the marginal resource cost of that resource are equal. And a firm that employs the amount of each resource that maximizes its profits *also* produces the output that maximizes its profits. (If you doubt this statement, see footnote number 4 in the text.)

There is another similarity between the output and the input markets insofar as the firm is concerned. You will recall that the competitive firm's *supply* curve is a portion of its *marginal-cost* curve. The purely competitive firm's *demand* curve for a resource is a portion of its *marginal-revenue-product* curve. Just as cost is the important determinant of supply, the revenue derived from the use of a resource is the important factor determining the demand for that resource.

■ CHECKLIST

When you have studied this chapter you should be able to:

☐ Present four reasons for studying resource pricing.
☐ Explain why the demand for an economic resource is a derived demand.
☐ Define marginal revenue product.
☐ Determine the marginal revenue product schedule of a resource used to produce a product which is sold in a purely competitive market when you are given the relevant data.
☐ Define marginal resource cost.
☐ State the rule employed by a profit-maximizing firm to determine how much of a resource it will employ.
☐ Apply the MRP = MRC rule to determine the quantity

of a resource a firm will hire when you are given the necessary data.

□ Explain why the marginal revenue product schedule of a resource is the firm's demand for the resource.

□ Find the marginal revenue product schedule of a resource used to produce a product which is sold in an imperfectly competitive market when you are given the necessary data.

□ Derive the market demand for a resource.

□ List the three factors which would change a firm's demand for a resource.

□ Predict the effect of an increase or decrease in each of the three factors affecting resource demand on the demand of a firm for a resource.

□ Enumerate the four determinants of the price elasticity of demand for a resource.

□ Describe how a change in each of the four determinants of the resource price elasticity would change the price elasticity of demand for a resource.

□ State the rule employed by a firm to determine the least-cost combination of resources.

□ Use the least-cost rule to find the least-cost combination of resources for production when you are given the necessary data.

□ State the rule employed by a profit-maximizing firm to determine how much of each of several resources to employ.

□ Apply the profit-maximizing rule to determine the quantity of each resource a firm will hire when you are given the necessary data.

□ Explain the "marginal productivity theory of income distribution."

□ Give two criticisms of the marginal productivity theory of income distribution.

■ **CHAPTER OUTLINE**

1. The study of what determines the prices of resources is important because resource prices: influence the size of individual incomes and the resulting distribution of income; allocate scarce resources; affect the way in which firms combine resources to produce their products; and raise ethical questions about the distribution of income.

2. Economists generally agree upon the basic principles of resource pricing, but the complexities of different resources markets make these principles difficult to apply.

3. The demand for a single resource depends upon (or is derived from) the demand for the goods and services it can produce.

   a. Because resource demand is a derived demand, the demand for a single resource depends upon the marginal productivity of the resource and the market price of the good or service it is used to produce.

   b. Marginal revenue product combines these two fac-

tors—the marginal product of a resource and the market price of the product it produces—into a single useful tool.

   c. A firm will hire a resource up to the quantity at which the marginal revenue product of the resource is equal to its marginal resource cost.

   d. The firm's marginal-revenue-product schedule for a resource is that firm's demand schedule for the resource.

   e. If a firm sells its output in an imperfectly competitive market, the more the firm sells the lower becomes the price of the product. This causes the firm's marginal-revenue-product (resource demand) schedule to be less elastic than it would be if the firm sold its output in a purely competitive market.

   f. The market (or total) demand for a resource is the horizontal summation of the demand schedules of all firms employing the resource.

4. Changes in the demand for the product being produced, changes in the productivity of the resource, and changes in the prices of other resources will tend to change the demand for a resource.

   a. A change in the demand for a product produced by a resource such as labor will change the demand of a firm for labor in the same direction.

   b. A change in the productivity of a resource such as labor (caused by an increase in the quantity of other resources such as capital, technological improvements, and improvement in resource quality) will change the demand of a firm for the resource in the same direction.

   c. A change in the price of a

   (1) *substitute* resource will change the demand for a resource such as labor in the same direction if the substitution effect outweighs the output effect, and in the opposite direction if the output effect outweighs the substitution effect;

   (2) *complementary* resource will change the demand for a resource such as labor in the opposite direction.

5. The price elasticity of resource demand measures the sensitivity of producers to changes in resource prices.

   a. There are four possible factors that affect the price elasticity of resource demand:

   (1) the rate at which the marginal product of the resource declines—the slower the rate, the more elastic the resource demand;

   (2) the ease of substitution of other resources—the more good substitute resources that are available, the more elastic the demand for the resource;

   (3) the elasticity of the demand for the product that the resource produces—the more elastic the product demand, the more elastic the resource demand;

   (4) the ratio of labor cost to total cost—the greater the ratio of labor cost to total cost, the greater the price elasticity of demand for labor.

6. Firms typically employ more than one resource in producing a product.

a. The firm employing resources in purely competitive markets is hiring resources in the least-cost combination when the ratio of the marginal product of a resource to its price is the same for all the resources the firm hires.

b. The firm is hiring resources in the most profitable combination if it hires resources in a purely competitive market when the marginal revenue product of each resource is equal to the price of that resource.

c. A numerical example illustrates the least-cost and profit-maximizing rules for a firm that employs resources in purely competitive markets.

7. The marginal productivity theory of income distribution seems to result in an equitable distribution of income because each unit of a resource receives a payment equal to its marginal contribution to the firm's revenue; but the theory has at least two serious faults.

a. The distribution of income will be unequal because resources are unequally distributed among individuals in the economy.

b. The income of those who supply resources will not be based on their marginal productivities if there is monopsony or monopoly in the resource markets of the economy.

■ **IMPORTANT TERMS**

Derived demand

Marginal revenue product

Marginal resource cost

MRP = MRC rule

Substitution effect

Output effect

Least-cost rule (combination)

Profit-maximizing rule (combination)

Marginal productivity theory of income distribution

■ **FILL-IN QUESTIONS**

1. Resource prices allocate _____ and are one of the factors that determine the (incomes, costs) _____ of households and the _____ of business firms.

2. The demand for a resource is a _____ demand and depends upon the _____ of the resource and the _____ of the product produced from the resource.

3. A firm will find it profitable to hire units of a resource up to the quantity at which the _____

and the _____ of the resource are equal; and if the firm hires the resource in a purely competitive market, the _____ and the _____ of the resource will be equal.

4. A firm's demand schedule for a resource is the firm's _____ schedule for that resource because both indicate the quantities of the resource the firm will employ at various resource _____

5. A producer that sells its product in an imperfectly competitive market finds that the more of a resource it hires, the (higher, lower) _____ becomes the price at which it can sell its product. As a consequence, the marginal-revenue-product (or demand) schedule for the resource is (more, less) _____ elastic than it would be if the output were sold in a purely competitive market.

6. The market demand curve for a resource is obtained by _____

7. The demand for a resource will change if the demand for the _____ changes, if the _____ of the resource changes, or if the _____ of other resources change.

8. In the space to the right of each of the following, indicate whether the change would tend to increase (+) or decrease (−) a firm's demand for a particular resource.

a. An increase in the demand for the firm's product. ____

b. A decrease in the amounts of all other resources the firm employs. ____

c. An increase in the productivity of the resource. ____

d. An increase in the price of a substitute resource when the output effect is greater than the substitution effect. ____

e. A decrease in the price of a complementary resource. ____

9. The output of the firm being constant, a decrease in the price of resource A will induce the firm to hire (more, less) _____ of resource A and _____ of other resources; this is called the _____ effect. But if the decrease in the price of A results in lower total costs and an increase in output, the firm may hire _____ of both resources; this is called the _____ effect.

10. Four determinants of the price elasticity of demand for a resource are the rate at which the

_____ of the resource decreases, the ease with which other resources can be

_____ for it, the _____ of demand for the product which it is used to produce, and the

_____

11. Suppose a firm employs resources in purely competitive markets. If the firm wishes to produce any given amount of its product in the least costly way, the ratio of

the _____ of each resource to its

_____ must be the same for all resources.

12. A firm that hires resources in purely competitive markets is employing the combination of resources which will result in maximum profits for the firm when the

_____ of every resource is equal to its _____

13. When the marginal revenue product of a resource is equal to the price of that resource, the marginal revenue product of the resource divided by its price is equal to

_____

14. In the marginal productivity theory the distribution of income is an equitable one because each unit of each

resource is paid an amount equal to its _____

_____

15. The marginal productivity theory rests on the assumption of (competitive, imperfect) _____ markets. In the real world, there are market imperfections because of monopsony or monopoly power, so wage rates

and other resource prices (do, do not) _____ measure contributions to national output.

■ **PROBLEMS AND PROJECTS**

1. The table at the bottom of the page shows the total production a firm will be able to obtain if it employs varying amounts of resource A while the amounts of the other resources the firm employes remain constant.

a. Compute the marginal product of each of the seven units of resource A and enter these figures in the table.

b. Assume the product the firm produces sells in the market for $1.50 per unit. Compute the total revenue of the firm at each of the eight levels of output and the marginal revenue product of each of the seven units of resource A. Enter these figures in the table at the bottom of the page.

c. On the basis of your computations complete the firm's demand schedule for resource A by indicating in the table below how many units of resource A the firm would employ at the given prices.

Price of A	Quantity of A demanded
$21.00	_____
18.00	_____
15.00	_____
12.00	_____
9.00	_____
6.00	_____
3.00	_____
1.50	_____

2. In the table on the next page are the marginal product data for resource B. Assume that the quantities of other resources employed by the firm remain constant.

a. Compute the total product (output) of the firm for each of the seven quantities of resource B employed and enter these figures in the table.

b. Assume that the firm sells its output in an imperfectly competitive market and that the prices at which

Quantity of resource A employed	Total product	Marginal product of A	Total revenue	Marginal revenue product of A
0	0		$_____	
1	12	_____	_____	$_____
2	22	_____	_____	_____
3	30	_____	_____	_____
4	36	_____	_____	_____
5	40	_____	_____	_____
6	42	_____	_____	_____
7	43	_____	_____	_____

it can sell its product are those given in the table. Compute and enter in the table:
(1) Total revenue for each of the seven quantities of B employed.
(2) The marginal revenue product of each of the seven units of resource B.
c. How many units of B would the firm employ if the market price of B were:

(1) $25: _____

(2) $20: _____

(3) $15: _____

(4) $9: _____

(5) $5: _____

(6) $1: _____

Quantity of resource B employed	Marginal product of B	Total product	Product price	Total revenue	Marginal revenue product of B
0	—	0		$0.00	—
1	22	____	$1.00	____	$____
2	21	____	.90	____	____
3	19	____	.80	____	____
4	16	____	.70	____	____
5	12	____	.60	____	____
6	7	____	.50	____	____
7	1	____	.40	____	____

3. In the table below are the marginal-product and marginal-revenue-product schedules for resource C and resource D. Both resources are variable and are employed in purely competitive markets. The price of C is $2 and the price of D is $3.

Quantity of resource C employed	Marginal product of C	Marginal revenue product of C	Quantity of resource D employed	Marginal product of D	Marginal revenue product of D
1	10	$5.00	1	21	$10.50
2	8	4.00	2	18	9.00
3	6	3.00	3	15	7.50
4	5	2.50	4	12	6.00
5	4	2.00	5	9	4.50
6	3	1.50	6	6	3.00
7	2	1.00	7	3	1.50

a. The least-cost combination of C and D that would enable the firm to produce:

(1) 64 units of its product is _____ C and _____ D.

(2) 99 units of its product is _____ C and _____ D.
b. The profit-maximizing combination of C and D is

_____ C and _____ D.
c. When the firm employs the profit-maximizing combination of C and D, it is also employing C and D in the

least-cost combination because _____

equals _____

d. Examination of the figures in the table reveals that

the firm sells its product in a _____

competitive market at a price of $_____
e. Employing the profit-maximizing combination of C and D, the firm's:

(1) Total output is _____

(2) Total revenue is $_____

(3) Total cost is $_____

(4) Total profit is $_____

■ **SELF-TEST**

Circle the T if the statement is true; the F if it is false.

1. In the resource markets of the economy resources are demanded by business firms and supplied by households.   **T F**

2. The prices of resources are an important factor in the determination of the supply of a product.   **T F**

3. The market demand for a particular resource is the sum of the individual demands of all firms that employ that resource.   **T F**

4. A resource which is highly productive will always be in great demand.   **T F**

5. A firm's demand schedule for a resource is the firm's marginal-revenue-product schedule for the resource.
                                                           T F

6. It will be profitable for a firm to hire additional units of labor resources up to the point where the marginal revenue product of labor is equal to its marginal resource cost.   **T F**

7. A firm with one worker can produce 30 units of a product that sells for $4 a unit, but the same firm with two workers can produce 70 units of that product. The marginal revenue product of the second worker is $400.   **T F**

8. The marginal revenue product of a purely competitive seller will fall because marginal product diminishes and product price falls.   **T F**

9. A producer's demand schedule for a resource will be more elastic if the firm sells its product in a purely competitive market than it would be if it sold the product in an imperfectly competitive market.   **T F**

10. When two resources are substitutes for each other both the substitution effect and the output effect of a decrease in the price of one of these resources operate to increase the quantity of the other resource employed by the firm.   **T F**

11. The output effect of an increase in the price of a resource is to increase the quantity demanded of that resource.   **T F**

12. If two resources are complementary, an increase in the price of one of them will reduce the demand for the other.   **T F**

13. An increase in the price of a resource will cause the demand for the resource to decrease.   **T F**

14. The demand curve for labor will increase when the demand for (and price of) the product produced by that labor increases.   **T F**

15. There is an inverse relationship between the productivity of labor and the demand for labor.   **T F**

16. The faster the rate at which the marginal product of a variable resource declines, the greater will be the price elasticity of demand for that resource.   **T F**

17. The demand for labor will be less elastic when labor is a smaller proportion of the total cost of producing a product.   **T F**

Use the following information as the basis for answering questions 18 and 19. The marginal revenue product and price of resource A are $12 and a constant $2, respectively; and the marginal revenue product and price of resource B are $25 and a constant $5, respectively. The firm sells its product at a constant price of $1.

18. The firm should decrease the amount of A and increase the amount of B it employs if it wishes to decrease its total cost without affecting its total output.   **T F**

19. If the firm wishes to maximize its profits, it should increase its employment of both A and B until their marginal revenue products fall to $2 and $5, respectively.   **T F**

20. The marginal productivity theory of income distribution results in an equitable distribution only if resource markets are competitive.   **T F**

Circle the letter that corresponds to the best answer.

1. The prices paid for resources affect:
  (a) the money incomes of households in the economy
  (b) the allocation of resources among different firms and industries in the economy
  (c) the quantities of different resources employed to produce a particular product
  (d) all of the above

2. The study of the pricing of resources tends to be complex because:
  (a) supply and demand do not determine resource prices
  (b) economists do not agree on the basic principles of resource pricing
  (c) the basic principles of resource pricing must be varied and adjusted when applied to particular resource markets
  (d) resource pricing is essentially an ethical question

3. The demand for a resource is ***derived*** from:
  (a) the marginal productivity of the resource and price of the good or service produced from it
  (b) the marginal productivity of the resource and the price of the resource
  (c) the price of the resource and the price of the good or service produced from it
  (d) the price of the resource and the quantity of the resource demanded

4. As a firm that sells its product in an imperfectly competitive market increases the quantity of a resource it employs, the marginal revenue product of that resource falls because:

(a) the price paid by the firm for the resource falls
(b) the marginal product of the resource falls
(c) the price at which the firm sells its product falls
(d) both the marginal product and the price at which the firm sells its product fall

5. The law of diminishing returns explains why:

(a) the MRP of an input in a purely competitive market decreases as a firm increases the quantity of an employed resource
(b) the MRC of an input in a purely competitive market decreases as a firm increases the quantity of an employed resource
(c) resource demand is a derived demand
(d) there are substitution and output effects for resources

Use the following total-product and marginal-product schedules for a resource to answer the next four questions (6, 7, 8, and 9). Assume that the quantities of other resources the firm employs remain constant.

Units of resource	Total product	Marginal product
1	8	8
2	14	6
3	18	4
4	21	3
5	23	2

6. If the product the firm produces sells for a constant $3 per unit, the marginal revenue product of the 4th unit of the resource is:

(a) $3
(b) $6
(c) $9
(d) $12

7. If the firm's product sells for a constant $3 per unit and the price of the resource is a constant $15, the firm will employ how many units of the resource?

(a) 2
(b) 3
(c) 4
(d) 5

8. If the firm can sell 14 units of output at a price of $1 per unit and 18 units of output at a price of $0.90 per unit, the marginal revenue product of the 3rd unit of the resource is:

(a) $4
(b) $3.60
(c) $2.20
(d) $0.40

9. If the firm can sell 8 units at a price of $1.50, 14 units at a price of $1.00, 18 units at a price of $0.90, 21 units at a price of $0.70, and 23 units at a price of $0.50, then the firm is:

(a) maximizing profits at a product price of $0.50
(b) minimizing its costs at a product price of $1.00
(c) selling in an imperfectly competitive market
(d) selling in a purely competitive market

10. Which of the following would increase a firm's demand for a particular resource?

(a) an increase in the prices of complementary resources used by the firm
(b) a decrease in the demand for the firm's product
(c) an increase in the productivity of the resource
(d) a decrease in the price of the particular resource

11. In finding the substitution effect of a change in the price of a particular resource, which of the following is assumed to be constant?

(a) the total output of the firm
(b) the total expenditures of the firm
(c) the employment of all other resources
(d) the MPs of all resources

12. Suppose resource A and resource B are substitutes and the price of A increases. If the output effect is greater than the substitution effect:

(a) the quantity of A employed by the firm will increase and the quantity of B employed will decrease
(b) the quantity of both A and B employed by the firm will decrease
(c) the quantity of both A and B employed will decrease
(d) the quantity of A employed will decrease and the quantity of B employed will increase

13. Two resource inputs, capital and labor, are complementary and used in fixed proportions. A decrease in the price of capital will:

(a) increase the demand for labor
(b) decrease the demand for labor
(c) decrease the quantity demanded for labor
(d) have no effect because the relationship is fixed

14. Which of the following would result in an increase in the elasticity of demand for a particular resource?

(a) an increase in the rate at which the marginal product of that resource declines
(b) a decrease in the elasticity of demand for the product which the resource helps to produce
(c) an increase in the percentage of the firm's total costs accounted for by the resource
(d) a decrease in the number of other resources which are good substitutes for the particular resource

15. A firm is allocating its expenditure for resources in a way that will result in the least total cost of producing any given output when:

(a) the amount the firm spends on each resource is the same
(b) the marginal revenue product of each resource is the same
(c) the marginal product of each resource is the same
(d) the marginal product per dollar spent on the last unit of each resource is the same

16. A business is employing inputs such that the marginal product of labor is 20 and the marginal product of capital is 45. The price of labor is $10 and the price of capital is $15. If the business wants to minimize costs, then it should:
(a) use more labor and less capital
(b) use less labor and less capital
(c) use less labor and more capital
(d) make no change in resource use

17. Assume that a profit-maximizing computer disk manufacturer is employing resources so that the MRP of the last unit hired for resource X is $240 and the MRP of the last unit hired for resource Y is $150. The price of resource X is $80 and the price of resource Y is $50. The firm should:
(a) hire more of resource X and less of resource Y
(b) hire less of resource X and more of resource Y
(c) hire less of both resource X and resource Y
(d) hire more of both resource X and resource Y

18. A firm that hires resources in a purely competitive market is **not necessarily** maximizing its profits when:
(a) the marginal revenue product of every resource is equal to 1
(b) the marginal revenue product of every resource is equal to its price
(c) the ratio of the marginal revenue product of every resource to its price is equal to 1
(d) the ratio of the price of every resource to its marginal revenue product is equal to 1

Answer the next three questions (19, 20, and 21) on the basis of the information in the following table for a purely competitive market.

Number of workers	Total product	Product price ($)
0	0	4
1	16	4
2	26	4
3	34	4
4	40	4
5	44	4

19. At a wage rate of $15, the firm will choose to employ:
(a) 2 workers
(b) 3 workers
(c) 4 workers
(d) 5 workers

20. At a wage rate of $30, the firm will choose to employ:
(a) 2 workers
(b) 3 workers
(c) 4 workers
(d) 5 workers

21. If the product price increases to a constant $8, then at a wage rate of $30, the firm will choose to employ:
(a) 2 workers
(b) 3 workers
(c) 4 workers
(d) 5 workers

22. The demand for labor would most likely become more inelastic as a result of an increase in the:
(a) elasticity of the demand for the product that the labor produces
(b) time for employers to make technological changes or purchase new equipment
(c) proportion of labor costs to total costs
(d) rate at which marginal revenue product declines

23. Assume that a purely competitive firm uses two resources, labor (L) and capital (C), to produce a product. In which situation would the firm be maximizing profit?

	MRP_L	MRP_C	P_L	P_C
(a)	10	20	30	40
(b)	10	20	10	20
(c)	15	15	10	10
(d)	30	40	10	5

24. In the marginal productivity theory of income distribution when all markets are purely competitive, each unit of each resource receives a money payment equal to:
(a) its marginal product
(b) its marginal revenue product
(c) the needs of the resource-owner
(d) the payments received by each of the units of the other resources in the economy

25. A major criticism of the marginal productivity theory of income distribution is that:
(a) labor markets are often subject to imperfect competition
(b) the theory suggests that there eventually will be equality in incomes
(c) purely competitive firms are only interested in profit maximization
(d) the demand for labor resources are price elastic

■ **DISCUSSION QUESTIONS**

1. Why is it important to study resource pricing?

2. Why is resource demand a derived demand, and upon what two factors does the strength of this derived demand depend?

3. Explain why firms that wish to maximize their profits follow the MRP = MRC rule.

4. What constitutes a firm's demand schedule for a resource? Why? What determines the total, or market, demand for a resource?

5. Why is the demand schedule for a resource less elastic when the firm sells its product in an imperfectly competitive market than when it sells it in a purely competitive market?

6. Explain what will cause the demand for a resource to increase and what will cause it to decrease.

7. Explain the difference between the "substitution effect" and the "output effect."

8. What determines the elasticity of the demand for a resource? Explain the exact relationship between each of these four determinants and elasticity.

9. Assuming a firm employs resources in purely competitive markets, when is it spending money on resources in such a way that it can produce a given output for the least total cost?

10. When is a firm that employs resources in purely competitive markets utilizing these resources in amounts that will maximize the profits of the firm?

11. What *is* the marginal productivity theory of income distribution? What ethical proposition must be accepted if this distribution is to be fair and equitable? What are the two major shortcomings of the theory?

■ **ANSWERS**

Chapter 27 Production and the Demand for Resources

FILL-IN QUESTIONS

1. resources, incomes, costs

2. derived, productivity, value (price)

3. marginal revenue product, marginal resource cost, price, marginal resource cost (either order)

4. marginal revenue product, prices

5. lower, less

6. adding the demand curves for the resource of all the firms hiring the resource

7. product, productivity, prices

8. *a.* +; *b.* −; *c.* +; *d.* −; *e.* +

9. more, less, substitution, more, output

10. marginal product, substituted, price-elasticity, portion of total production costs accounted for by the resource

11. marginal product, price

12. marginal revenue product, price

13. one

14. marginal revenue product (marginal contribution to the firm's revenue)

15. competitive, do not

PROBLEMS AND PROJECTS

1. *a.* marginal product of A: 12, 10, 8, 6, 4, 2, 1; *b.* total revenue: 0, 18.00, 33.00, 45.00, 54.00, 60.00, 63.00, 64.50; marginal revenue product of A: 18.00, 15.00, 12.00, 9.00, 6.00, 3.00, 1.50; *c.* 0, 1, 2, 3, 4, 5, 6, 7

2. *a.* total product: 22, 43, 62, 78, 90, 97, 98; *b.* (1) total revenue: 22.00, 38.70, 49.60, 54.60, 54.00, 48.50, 39.20; (2) marginal revenue product of B: 22.00, 16.70, 10.90, 5.00, −0.60, −5.50, −9.30; *c.* 0, 1, 2, 3, 4, 4

3. *a.* (1) 1, 3; (2) 3, 5; *b.* 5, 6; *c.* the marginal product of C divided by its price, the marginal product of D divided by its price; *d.* purely, $.50; *e.* (1) 114; (2) $57; (3) $28; (4) $29

SELF-TEST

1. T, p. 518	11. F, p. 524
2. T, p. 519	12. T, p. 525
3. T, p. 523	13. F, p. 525
4. F, p. 520	14. T, p. 525
5. T, p. 521	15. F, p. 523
6. T, p. 520	16. F, p. 525
7. F, p. 520	17. T, p. 526
8. F, p. 521	18. F, p. 526
9. T, p. 522	19. T, p. 527
10. F, p. 524	20. F, p. 529

1. *d*, p. 519	14. *c*, p. 526
2. *c*, p. 519	15. *d*, p. 526
3. *a*, pp. 519–520	16. *c*, p. 526
4. *d*, p. 521	17. *d*, p. 527
5. *a*, p. 520	18. *a*, p. 527
6. *c*, p. 520	19. *d*, pp. 520–521
7. *a*, pp. 520–521	20. *b*, pp. 520–521
8. *c*, pp. 521–522	21. *d*, pp. 520–521
9. *c*, pp. 521–522	22. *d*, p. 525
10. *c*, p. 523	23. *b*, p. 527
11. *a*, p. 524	24. *b*, p. 529
12. *b*, p. 524	25. *a*, p. 530
13. *a*, p. 524	

DISCUSSION QUESTIONS

1. p. 519	7 p. 524
2. pp. 519–520	8. pp. 525–526
3. pp. 520–521	9. pp. 526–527
4. p. 521	10. pp. 527–528
5. pp. 521–523	11. pp. 529–530
6. pp. 523–525	

The Pricing and Employment of Resources: Wage Determination

The preceding chapter of the text defined marginal revenue product and marginal resource cost. It also explained what determines the demand for *any* resource. Chapter 28 builds upon these explanations and applies them to the study of a particular resource, labor, and the wage rate, the price paid for labor.

But as you learned in Chapters 23 through 26, it requires more than an understanding of supply and demand to explain the price of a product and the output of a firm and an industry. An understanding of the competitiveness of the market in which the product is sold is also required. It was for this reason that purely competitive, monopolistic, monopolistically competitive, and oligopolistic markets were examined in detail. The same is true of labor markets. The competitiveness of labor markets must be examined if the factors which determine wage rates and the quantity of labor employed are to be understood.

Following comments on the meanings of certain terms, the general level of wages, and the reasons for the high wage level in the United States, Chapter 28 explains how wage rates are determined in particular types of labor markets. Six kinds of labor markets are studied: (1) the competitive market in which the number of employers is large and labor is nonunionized; (2) the monopsony market in which a single employer hires labor under competitive (nonunion) conditions; (3) a market in which a union controls the supply of labor, the number of employers is large, and the union attempts to increase the total demand for labor; (4) a similar market in which the union attempts to reduce the total supply of labor; (5) another similar market in which the union attempts to obtain a wage rate that is above the competitive-equilibrium level by threatening to strike; and (6) the bilateral monopoly market, in which a single employer faces a labor supply controlled by a single union.

It is, of course, important for you to learn the characteristics of and the differences between each of these labor markets. It is also important that you study each of them carefully to see *how* the characteristics of the market affect the wage rate that will be paid in these markets. In the first two types of markets, the wage rate which will be paid is quite definite, and here you should learn exactly what level of wages and employment will prevail.

When unions control the supply of labor, wage and employment levels are less definite. If the demand for labor is competitive, the wage rate and the amount of employment will depend upon how successful the union is in increasing the demand for labor, in restricting the supply of labor, or in setting a wage rate which employers will accept. If there is but a single employer, wages and employment will fall within certain limits; exactly where they occur within these limits will depend upon the bargaining strength of the union and of the firm. You should, however, know what the limits are.

The sections explaining wages in particular labor markets are the more important parts of the chapter. But the sections which examine the effects of minimum wage laws on employment and wage rates, the reasons why different workers receive different wage rates, and pay and performance are also important. You should, therefore, pay attention to (1) the case against, the case for, and the real-world effects of the minimum wage; (2) the several causes of wage differentials; and (3) the principal agent problem and different schemes that are used by employers to prevent shirking or to tie worker pay to performance.

■ CHECKLIST

When you have studied this chapter you should be able to:

☐ Define wages (or the wage rate); and distinguish between nominal and real wages.
☐ Identify two major factors that contribute to the general level of wages in the United States.
☐ List at least five reasons for high productivity in the United States.
☐ Describe the long-run relationship between real wages and productivity in the United States.
☐ Define the difference between a competitive labor market and a monopsonistic labor market.

☐ Use graphs to explain wage rates and the level of employment in competitive labor markets.
☐ Use graphs to explain wage rates and the level of employment in monopolistic labor markets.
☐ List three techniques labor unions use to increase the demand for labor.
☐ Enumerate the ways in which exclusive or craft unions try to decrease the supply of labor.
☐ Explain and illustrate graphically the effects of actions taken by craft unions to decrease the supply of labor on wages and the employment of workers.
☐ Explain and illustrate graphically how the organization of workers by an industrial union in a previously competitive labor market would affect the wage rate and the employment level.
☐ Describe evidence on the effect of unions on wage increases and two reasons that might mitigate unemployment effects from wage increases.
☐ Use a graph to explain why the equilibrium wage rate and employment level is indeterminate when a labor market is a bilateral monopoly; and to predict the range within which the wage rate will be found.
☐ Present the case for, and the case against, a legally established minimum wage.
☐ List the three major factors which explain why wage differentials exist.
☐ Describe two reasons why groups of workers in the labor force with similar characteristics may earn different wages.
☐ Explain the nonmonetary aspect of job differences.
☐ Cite three reasons for labor market imperfections.
☐ Describe the principal agent problem.
☐ Identify five different pay schemes that have been used by employers to prevent shirking or to tie worker pay to performance.

■ **CHAPTER OUTLINE**

1. A wage (or the wage rate) is the price paid per unit of time for any type of labor and can be measured either in money or in real terms. Earnings are equal to the wage multiplied by the amount of time worked.

2. The general (or average) level of real wages in the United States is among the highest in the world because the demand for labor in the United States has been great relative to the supply of labor.
   a. The demand for labor in the United States has been strong because labor has been highly productive; and it has been highly productive for several major reasons—substantial quantities of capital goods and natural resources, technological advancement, improvements in labor quality, and other factors (management

techniques, business environment, and size of the domestic market).
   b. The real hourly wage rate and output per hour of labor are closely and directly related to each other; and real income per worker can increase only at the same rate as output per worker.
   c. The increases in the demand for labor that have resulted from the increased productivity of labor over time have been greater than the increase in the supply of labor in the United States; and as a result the real wage rate in the United States has increased in the long run.

3. The wage rate received by a specific type of labor depends upon the demand for and the supply of that labor, and upon the competitiveness of the market in which that type of labor is hired.
   a. In a purely competitive and nonunionized labor market the total demand for and the total supply of labor determine the wage rate; from the point of view of the individual firm the supply of labor is perfectly elastic at this wage rate (that is, the marginal labor cost is equal to the wage rate) and the firm will hire the amount of labor at which the marginal revenue product of labor is equal to its marginal labor cost.
   b. In a monopsonistic and nonunionized labor market the firm's marginal labor costs are greater than the wage rates it must pay to obtain various amounts of labor; and it hires the amount of labor at which marginal labor cost and the marginal revenue product of labor are equal. Both the wage rate and the level of employment are less than they would be under purely competitive conditions.
   (1) Note that if the firm employs resources in imperfectly competitive markets, it is hiring resources in the least-cost combination when the ratio of the marginal product of a resource to its marginal resource cost is the same for all resources; and,
   (2) it is hiring resources in the most profitable combination when the marginal revenue product of each resource is equal to its marginal resource cost.
   c. In labor markets in which labor unions represent workers, the unions attempt to raise wage rates by
   (1) increasing the demand for labor by increasing the demands for the products produced by the union workers, by increasing the productivity of these workers, and by increasing the prices of resources which are substitutes for the labor provided by the members of the union;
   (2) reducing the supply of labor; or
   (3) imposing upon employers wage rates in excess of the equilibrium wage rate which would prevail in a purely competitive market.
   d. Labor unions are aware that actions taken by them to increase wage rates may also increase the unemployment of their members and may, therefore, limit

their demands for higher wages; but the unemployment effect of higher wages is lessened by increases in and a relatively inelastic demand for labor.

e. In a labor market characterized by bilateral monopoly, the wage rate depends, within certain limits, on the relative bargaining power of the union and of the employer.

f. Whether minimum wage laws reduce poverty is a debatable question; but the evidence suggests that while they increase the incomes of employed workers they also reduce the number of workers employed.

4. Differences in wages exist among workers for three major reasons.

a. Workers are not homogeneous and they can be thought of as falling into many **noncompeting** occupational groups. The wages for each group differs because of:

(1) differences in the abilities or skills possessed by workers, the number of workers in each group, and the demand for those abilities or skills in the labor market; and

(2) investment in human capital by workers through education and training.

b. Jobs also vary in difficulty and attractiveness, and thus higher wages may be necessary to compensate for less desirable aspects of some jobs.

c. Workers are not perfectly mobile because of geographic, institutional, and sociological conditions or situations.

5. Wage payments in labor markets are often more complex in practice and are often designed to make a connection between worker pay and performance.

a. A **principal-agent problem** arises when the interests of agents (workers) diverge from the interest of principal (firms). For example, **shirking** on the job can occur if workers give less than the desired level of performance for pay received.

b. Firms can try to reduce shirking by monitoring worker activity, but this monitoring is costly; therefore, **incentive pay** plans are adopted by firms to tie worker compensation more closely to performance. Among the various incentive schemes are:

(1) piece rate payments, commissions, royalties, bonuses, and profit sharing plans;

(2) seniority pay to give junior workers an incentive to work harder to achieve the benefits of senority; and

(3) efficiency wages that pay workers above-market wages to get greater effort.

b. Wage decisions are often more complex than indicated in the models of wage and employment determination discussed in this chapter; decisions over the most effective incentive scheme directly affect worker performance and the monitoring costs of employers.

■ IMPORTANT TERMS

Wage (rate)
Earnings
Nominal wage (rate)
Real wage (rate)
Marginal resource (labor) cost
Competitive labor market
Monopsony
Oligopsony
Exclusive unionism
Craft union
Occupational licensure

Inclusive unionism
Industrial union
Bilateral monopoly
Minimum wage
Wage differential
Noncompeting groups
Equalizing differences
Human capital investment
Principal-agent problem
Shirking
Incentive pay plan

■ FILL-IN QUESTIONS

1. A wage rate is the price paid for labor per unit of _____ and the earnings of labor are equal to the _____ multiplied by _____; nominal wages are an amount of money, while real wages are _____ _____

2. The general level of wages is higher in the United States than in most foreign countries because:

a. The demand for labor in the U.S. is (strong, weak) _____ relative to the supply of labor;

b. American labor tends to be highly productive, among other reasons, because it has relatively large amounts of _____ and _____ with which to work and employs a generally superior _____ to produce goods and because of the high _____ of the American labor force.

3. In a competitive labor market:

a. the supply curve slopes upward from left to right because it is necessary for employers to pay higher _____ to attract workers from _____. The market supply curve rises because it is an _____ curve.

b. the demand is the sum of the _____ _____ of all firms hiring this type of labor;

c. the wage rate will equal the rate at which the

_____ and the

_____ are equal.

4. Insofar as an individual firm hiring labor in a competitive market is concerned, the supply of labor is

_____ elastic because the individual firm is

unable to affect the _____ it must pay.

5. The individual employer who hires labor in a competitive market hires that quantity of labor at which the

_____ of labor is equal to the

_____ or the _____.

6. A monopsonist employing labor in a market which is competitive on the supply side will hire that amount of labor

at which _____

_____ and

_____ are equal. And because

the marginal labor cost is (greater, less) _____

_____ than the wage rate in such a market the

employer will pay a wage rate which is less than both the

_____ of labor and the marginal

_____

a. It is employing the combination of resources that enables it to produce any given output in the least

costly way when the _____ of every resource

divided by its _____ is the same for all resources.
b. It is employing the combination of resources that

maximizes its profits when the _____ of

every resource is equal to its _____ (or

when the _____ of each resource di-

vided by its _____ is equal to _____)

7. When compared with a competitive labor market, a market dominated by a monopsonist results in (higher,

lower) _____ wage rates and in (more,

less) _____ employment.

8. The basic objective of labor unions is to

_____; they

attempt to accomplish this goal either by increasing the

_____ for labor, restricting

the _____ of labor, or imposing

_____ wage rates on employers.

9. Craft unions typically try to increase wages by

_____ while industrial unions

try to increase wages by _____
a. If they are successful, employment in the craft or industry is (decreased, increased, not affected)

_____

b. This effect on the employment of their members

may lead unions to (increase, decrease) _____
their wage demands.
c. But unions will not worry too much about the effect on employment of higher wage rates if the economy is

(growing, contracting, stationary) _____
or if the demand for labor is relatively (elastic, inelastic)

_____

10. Labor unions can increase the demand for the services of their members by increasing the demand for

_____, by increasing the _____

of their members, and by increasing the _____
of resources which are substitutes for the services supplied by their members.

11. In a labor market which is a bilateral monopoly, the monopsonist will not pay a wage greater than

_____; the union will ask for some wage

greater than the _____.
Within these limits the wage rate will depend on

_____

12. The effect of the imposition of effective minimum wage rates, ignoring any shock effects, in:
a. competitive labor markets is to (increase, decrease)

_____ the wage rate and to _____
employment.

b. monopsonistic labor markets is to _____

the wage rate and to _____ employment.

13. After a minimum wage increase workers will (in-

crease, decrease) _____ their income, but the em-

ployment of certain groups will _____, and the in-

comes of these workers will _____. It is estimated

that a _____% increase in the minimum wage will re-

duce employment of teenage workers by 1 to 3%. An in-

crease in the minimum wage will also tend to reduce em-

ployment among _____ adults, _____, and

_____ because they are employed in a dispropor-

tionate share of low-wage occupations. The antipoverty

effect of the minimum wage is a _____ one for the economy.

14. Actual wage rates received by different workers tend to differ because workers are not _____, because jobs vary in _____, and because labor markets are _____.

15. The total labor force is composed of a number of _____ groups of workers. Wages differ among these groups as a consequence of differences in innate _____ and because of different investments in _____ through training and education.

16. Within each of these noncompeting groups, some workers receive higher wages than others to compensate these workers for the less desirable _____ aspects of a job. These wage differentials are called

_____.

17. Another reason that workers performing identical jobs often receive different wages is due to _____, which are of three basic types: _____, _____, and _____.

18. Parties, such as workers, who are hired to advance the firm's interests can be regarded as the firm's _____, and firms may be regarded as _____, or parties who hire others to achieve their objectives. The objective of a firm is to maximize _____ and workers help a firm achieve that objective in return for _____, but when the interests of a firm and the workers diverge, a _____ problem is created.

19. An example of this type of problem is _____, a situation where workers provide less than the agreed amount of work effort on the job. To prevent this situation, firms can closely _____ job performance, but this is costly; therefore, firms offer different _____ plans. Examples of such plans include _____ rate payments, _____ and royalties, and bonuses and _____ sharing.

20. Two other pay plans used by firms are _____ pay, which is designed to give the young worker an incentive to work hard for job tenure, and _____ wages, which means that workers are paid above equilibrium wages to encourage greater work effort.

■ **PROBLEMS AND PROJECTS**

1. Suppose a single firm has for a particular type of labor the marginal revenue product schedule given in the following table.

Number of units of labor	MRP of labor
1	$15
2	14
3	13
4	12
5	11
6	10
7	9
8	8

a. Assume there are 100 firms with the same marginal-revenue-product schedules for this particular type of labor. Compute the total or market demand for this labor by completing column 1 in the table below.

(1) Quantity of labor demanded	(2) Wage rate	(3) Quantity of labor supplied
____	$15	850
____	14	800
____	13	750
____	12	700
____	11	650
____	10	600
____	9	550
____	8	500

b. Using the supply schedule for labor given in columns 2 and 3:

(1) What will be the equilibrium wage rate? $_____

(2) What will be the total amount of labor hired in the market? _____

c. The individual firm will:

(1) have a marginal labor cost of $_____

(2) employ _____ units of labor.

(3) pay a wage of $_____

d. On the graph on the next page plot the market demand and supply curves for labor and indicate the equilibrium wage rate and the total quantity of labor employed.

0   Quantity of labor

(1) Number of labor units	(2) MRP of labor	(3) Wage rate	(4) Total labor cost	(5) Marginal labor cost
0		$ 2	$_____	
1	$36	4	_____	$_____
2	32	6	_____	_____
3	28	8	_____	_____
4	24	10	_____	_____
5	20	12	_____	_____
6	16	14	_____	_____
7	12	16	_____	_____
8	8	18	_____	_____

a. Compute the firm's total labor costs at each level of employment and the marginal labor cost of each unit of labor, and enter these figures in columns 4 and 5.

b. The firm will:

(1) hire _____ units of labor.

(2) pay a wage of $_____

(3) have a marginal revenue product for labor of

$_____ for the last unit of labor employed.

c. Plot the marginal revenue product of labor, the supply curve for labor, and the marginal-labor-cost curve on the following graph and indicate the quantity of labor the firm will employ and the wage it will pay.

e. On the graph below plot the individual firm's demand curve for labor, the supply curve for labor, and the marginal-labor-cost curve which confronts the individual firm; and indicate the quantity of labor the firm will hire and the wage it will pay.

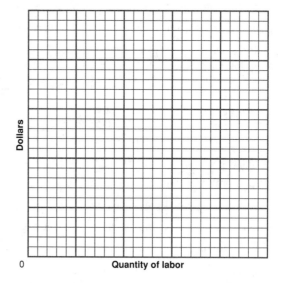

0   Quantity of labor

f. The imposition of a $12 minimum wage rate would change the total amount of labor hired in this market to

_____

2. In the table at the top of the page, assume a monopsonist has the marginal-revenue-product schedule for a particular type of labor given in columns 1 and 2 and that the supply schedule for labor is that given in columns 1 and 3.

d. If this firm hired labor in a competitive labor market,

it would hire at least _____ units and pay a wage of at least $_____

3. Assume that the employees of the monopsonist in problem 2 organize a strong industrial union. The union demands a wage rate of $16 for its members, and the monopsonist decides to pay this wage because a strike would be too costly.

a. In the table below compute the supply schedule for labor which now confronts the monopsonist by completing column 2.

(1) Number of labor units	(2) Wage rate	(3) Total labor cost	(4) Marginal labor cost
1	$_____	$_____	
2	_____	_____	$_____
3	_____	_____	_____
4	_____	_____	_____
5	_____	_____	_____
6	_____	_____	_____
7	_____	_____	_____
8	_____	_____	_____

b. Compute the total labor cost and the marginal labor cost at each level of employment and enter these figures in columns 3 and 4.

c. The firm will:

(1) hire _____ units of labor.

(2) pay a wage of $_____

(3) pay total wages of $_____

d. As a result of unionization the wage rate has _____, the level of employment has _____, and the earnings of labor have _____

e. On the graph below plot the firm's marginal revenue product of labor schedule, the labor supply schedule, and the marginal-labor-cost schedule. Indicate also the wage rate the firm will pay and the number of workers it will hire.

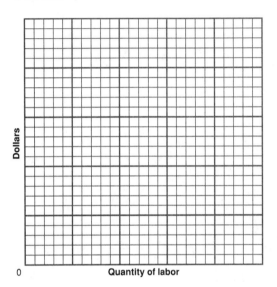

4. Match the following descriptions to the correct graph below.

    a. A bilateral monopoly.   Graph _____
    b. The supply and demand for labor for a purely competitive firm.   Graph _____
    c. The labor strategy used by a craft union to raise wages.   Graph _____

    d. A monopsonistic labor market.   Graph _____
    e. The strategy used by an industrial union to raise wages above a competitive level.   Graph _____
    f. A strategy used by a union to get people to "buy union made products."   Graph _____

1

2

3

4

5

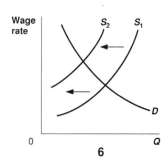

6

■ **SELF-TEST**

Circle the T if the statement is true; the F if it is false.

    1. The general level of real wages is higher in the United States than in many foreign countries because the supply of labor is large relative to the demand for it.   **T F**

    2. The average real income per workers and the average real output per worker in an economy are two names for the same thing.   **T F**

    3. If an individual firm employs labor in a competitive market, it finds that its marginal labor cost is equal to the wage rate in that market.   **T F**

4. Given a purely competitive employer's demand for labor, a lower wage will result in more workers being hired. **T F**

5. Both monopsonists and firms hiring labor in purely competitive markets hire labor up to the quantity at which the marginal revenue product of labor and marginal labor cost are equal. **T F**

6. Increasing the productivity of labor will tend to increase the demand for labor. **T F**

7. One strategy used by unions to bolster the demand for union workers is to lobby against a higher minimum wage for nonunion workers. **T F**

8. Restricting the supply of labor is a means of increasing wage rates more commonly used by craft unions than by industrial unions. **T F**

9. Occupational licensure has been one of the principal means employed by the Federal government to increase the number of blacks and Hispanics in certain skilled occupations and trades. **T F**

10. The imposition of an above-equilibrium wage rate will cause employment to fall off more when the demand for labor is inelastic than it will when the demand is elastic. **T F**

11. Union members are paid wage rates which on the average are greater by 10% or more than the wage rates paid to nonunion members. **T F**

12. The actions of both exclusive and inclusive unions that raise the wage rates paid to them by competitive employers of labor also cause, other things remaining constant, an increase in the employment of their members. **T F**

13. In a bilateral monopoly the negotiated wage will be below the competitive equilibrium wage in that labor market. **T F**

14. If a labor market is purely competitive, the imposition of an effective minimum wage will increase the wage rate paid and decrease employment in that market. **T F**

15. When an effective minimum wage is imposed upon a monopsonist the wage rate paid by the firm will increase and the number of workers employed by it may also increase. **T F**

16. An increase in the minimum wage rate in the American economy tends to increase the unemployment of teenagers and of others in low-wage occupations. **T F**

17. Actual wage rates received in different labor markets tend to differ because the demands for particular types of labor relative to their supplies differ. **T F**

18. Wage differentials that are used to compensate workers for unpleasant aspects of a job are called efficiency wages. **T F**

19. "Ben Robbins is a skilled artisan of a particular type, is unable to obtain membership in the union representing that group of artisans, and is, therefore, unable to practice his trade." This is an example of institutional immobility. **T F**

20. Shirking is an example of a principal-agent problem. **T F**

Circle the letter that corresponds to the best answer.

1. Real wages would decline if the:
(a) prices of goods and services rose more rapidly than money-wage rates
(b) prices of goods and services rose less rapidly than money-wage rates
(c) prices of goods and services and wage rates both rose
(d) prices of goods and services and wage rates both fell

2. Which of the following has *not* led to the generally high productivity of American workers?
(a) the high level of real wage rates in the United States
(b) the superior quality of the American labor force
(c) the advanced technology utilized in American industries
(d) the large quantity of capital available to assist the average worker in the United States

3. A characteristic of a purely competitive labor market would be:
(a) firms hiring different types of labor
(b) workers supplying labor under a union contract
(c) "wage taker" behavior by the firms
(d) "price maker" behavior by the firms

4. The supply curve for labor in a purely competitive market rises because:
(a) it is an opportunity cost curve
(b) the marginal resource cost is constant
(c) the wage rate paid to workers falls
(d) the marginal revenue product rises

5. The individual firm which hires labor under purely competitive conditions faces a supply curve for labor which:
(a) is perfectly inelastic
(b) is of unitary elasticity
(c) is perfectly elastic
(d) slopes upward from left to right

6. All of the following are characteristics of a monopsonist *except*:
(a) the firm's employment is a large portion of the total employment of that type of labor
(b) the type of labor is relatively immobile
(c) the wage rate it must pay workers varies directly with the number of workers it employs
(d) the supply curve is the marginal resource cost curve

7. A monopsonist pays a wage rate which is:
(a) greater than the marginal revenue product of labor
(b) equal to the marginal revenue product of labor
(c) equal to the firm's marginal labor cost
(d) less than the marginal revenue product of labor

8. If a firm employs resources in imperfectly competitive markets, to maximize its profits the marginal revenue product of each resource must equal:
(a) its marginal product
(b) its marginal resource cost
(c) its price
(d) one

9. Compared with a purely competitive labor market, a monopsonistic market will result in:
(a) higher wage rates and a higher level of employment
(b) higher wage rates and a lower level of employment
(c) lower wage rates and a higher level of employment
(d) lower wage rates and a lower level of employment

10. The labor market for nurses in a small community that has two hospitals would be best described as:
(a) monopolistically competitive
(b) a bilateral monopoly
(c) an oligopsony
(d) an oligopoly

11. Higher wage rates and a higher level of employment are the usual consequences of:
(a) inclusive unionism
(b) exclusive unionism
(c) an above-equilibrium wage rate
(d) an increase in the productivity of labor

12. Which of the following would *not* increase the demand for a particular type of labor?
(a) an increase in the productivity of that type of labor
(b) an increase in the prices of those resources which are substitutes for that type of labor
(c) an increase in the prices of those resources which are complements to that type of labor
(d) an increase in the demand for the products produced by that type of labor

13. Occupational licensing laws have the economic effect of
(a) increasing the demand for labor
(b) decreasing the supply of labor
(c) strengthening the bargaining position of an industrial union
(d) weakening the bargaining position of a craft union

14. Industrial unions typically attempt to increase wage rates by:
(a) imposing an above-equilibrium wage rate upon employers
(b) increasing the demand for labor

(c) decreasing the supply of labor
(d) forming a bilateral monopoly

Answer the next three questions (15, 16, and 17) using the data in the table below.

Wage rate	Quantity of labor supplied	Marginal labor cost	Marginal revenue product of labor
$10	0	—	$18
11	100	$11	17
12	200	13	16
13	300	15	15
14	400	17	14
15	500	19	13
16	600	21	12

15. If the firm employing labor were a monopsonist the wage rate and the quantity of labor employed would be, respectively:
(a) $14 and 300
(b) $13 and 400
(c) $14 and 400
(d) $13 and 300

16. But if the market for this labor were purely competitive the wage rate and the quantity of labor employed would be, respectively:
(a) $14 and 300
(b) $13 and 400
(c) $14 and 400
(d) $13 and 300

17. If the firm employing labor were a monopsonist and the workers were represented by an industrial union, the wage rate would be:
(a) between $13 and $14
(b) between $13 and $15
(c) between $14 and $15
(d) below $13 or above $15

Answer the next four questions (18, 19, 20, and 21) on the basis of the following labor market diagram, where D is the demand curve for labor, S is the supply curve for labor, and MRC is the marginal resource (labor) cost.

18. If this were a purely competitive labor market, the number of workers hired and the wage rate in equilibrium would be:
(a) 4000 and $14
(b) 4000 and $8
(c) 6000 and $10
(d) 8000 and $12

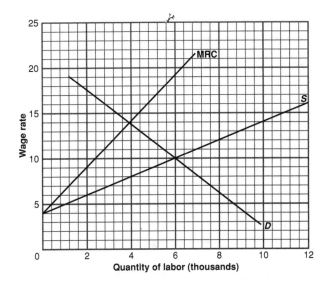

24. Shirking can be considered to be principal-agent problem because:

   (a) work objectives of the principals (the workers) diverge from the profit objectives of the agent (the firm)

   (b) profit objectives of the principal (the firm) diverge from the work objectives of the agents (the workers)

   (c) the firm is operating in an oligopsonistic labor market

   (d) the firm pays efficiency wages to workers in a labor market

25. A firm pays an equilibrium wage of $10.00 an hour and the workers produce 10 units of output an hour. If the firm adopts an efficiency wage and it is successful, then the wage rate for these workers will:

   (a) rise and output will fall

   (b) fall and output will rise

   (c) rise and output will rise

   (d) fall and output will fall

19. If this were a monopsonistic labor market, the number of workers hired and the wage rate in equilibrium would be:

   (a) 4000 and $14

   (b) 4000 and $8

   (c) 6000 and $10

   (d) 8000 and $12

20. An inclusive union seeks to maximize the employment of workers with the monopsonist. If successful, the number of workers employed and the wage rate would be:

   (a) 4000 and $14

   (b) 6000 and $12

   (c) 6000 and $10

   (d) 8000 and $12

21. If the market was characterized as a bilateral monopoly, the number of workers hired and the wage rate in equilibrium would be:

   (a) 6000 and $10

   (b) 4000 and $14

   (c) 4000 and $8

   (d) indeterminant

22. The fact that a baseball player receives a wage of $4,000,000 a year can **best** be explained in terms of:

   (a) noncompeting labor groups

   (b) equalizing differences

   (c) labor immobility

   (d) imperfections in the labor market

23. The fact that unskilled construction workers receive higher wages than gas-station attendants is **best** explained in terms of:

   (a) noncompeting labor groups

   (b) equalizing differences

   (c) labor immobility

   (d) imperfections in the labor market

■ **DISCUSSION QUESTIONS**

1. Why is the general level of real wages higher in the United States than in most foreign nations? Why has the level of real wages continued to increase even though the supply of labor has continually increased?

2. Explain why the productivity of the American labor force increased in the past to its present high level.

3. In the competitive model what determines the market demand for labor and the wage rate? What kind of supply situation do all firms as a group confront? What kind of supply situation does the individual firm confront? Why?

4. In the monopsony model what determines employment and the wage rate? What kind of supply situation does the monopsonist face? Why? How does the wage rate paid and the level of employment compare with what would result if the market were competitive?

5. In what sense is a worker who is hired by a monopsonist "exploited" and one who is employed in a competitive labor market "justly" rewarded? Why do monopsonists wish to restrict employment?

6. When supply is less than perfectly elastic, marginal labor cost is greater than the wage rate. Why?

7. What basic methods do labor unions employ to try to increase the wages received by their members? If these methods are successful in raising wages, what effect do they have upon employment?

8. What three methods might labor employ to increase the demand for labor? If these methods are successful, what effects do they have upon wage rates and employment?

9. When labor unions attempt to restrict the supply of labor to increase wage rates, what devices do they employ to do this for the economy as a whole and what means do they use to restrict the supply of a given type of worker?

10. How do industrial unions attempt to increase wage rates, and what effect does this method of increasing wages have upon employment in the industry affected?

11. Both exclusive and inclusive unions are able to raise the wage rates received by their members. Why might unions limit or temper their demands for higher wages? What two factors determine the extent to which they will or will not reduce their demands for higher wages?

12. What is bilateral monopoly? What determines wage rates in a labor market of this type?

13. What is the effect of minimum wage laws upon wage rates and employment in:
   (a) competitive labor markets;
   (b) monopsony labor markets; and
   (c) the economy as a whole?

14. How:
   (a) do the wage rates paid to union members differ from those paid to nonunion employees; and
   (b) do minimum wage rates affect the employment of workers in high- and low-wage occupations?

15. What is meant by the term "noncompeting" groups in a labor market? What two factors tend to explain wage differentials in noncompeting groups?

16. How are wages used to equalize differences in the characteristics of jobs? Give examples.

17. Describe three types of immobilities that give rise to imperfections in labor markets. Discuss how these immobilities contribute to wage differentials.

18. Explain what is meant by the principal-agent problem and relate it to shirking. What are the different pay incentive plans that are correct for shirking on the job. How does seniority pay reduce shirking? What is the reason for efficiency wages?

■ **ANSWERS**

   Chapter 28 The Pricing and Employment of Resources: Wage Determination

FILL-IN QUESTIONS

1. time, wage rate, the amount of time worked, the goods and services nominal wages will purchase

2. a. strong; b. capital equipment, natural resources, technology, quality

3. a. wages, alternative employment, opportunity cost; b. marginal-revenue-product (demand) schedules; c. total quantity of labor demanded, total quantity of labor supplied (either order)

4. perfectly, wage rate

5. marginal revenue product, wage rate, marginal labor cost

6. marginal revenue product, marginal labor cost, greater, marginal revenue product, labor cost; a. marginal product, marginal resource cost; b. marginal revenue product, marginal resource cost, marginal revenue product, marginal resource cost, one

7. lower, less

8. increase wages, demand, supply, above-equilibrium

9. restricting the supply of labor, imposing above-equilibrium wage rates; a. decreased; b. decrease; c. growing, inelastic

10. products they produce, productivity, prices

11. marginal revenue product of labor, competitive and monopsonistic equilibrium wage, the relative bargaining strength of the union and the monopsonist

12. a. increase, decrease; b. increase, increase

13. increase, decrease, increase, 10, young, blacks, women, mixed (or ambivalent)

14. homogeneous (the same), attractiveness, imperfect

15. noncompeting, abilities, human capital

16. nonmonetary, equalizing differences

17. immobilities, geographic, institutional, sociological

18. agents, principals, profits, wages (or income), principal-agent

19. shirking, monitor, incentive pay, piece, commissions, profit

20. seniority, efficiency

PROBLEMS AND PROJECTS

1. a. quantity of labor demanded: 100, 200, 300, 400, 500, 600, 700, 800; b. (1) 10.00; (2) 600; c. (1) 10.00; (2) 6; (3) 10.00; f. 400

2. a. total labor cost: 0, 4.00, 12.00, 24.00, 40.00, 60.00, 84.00, 112.00, 144.00; marginal labor cost: 4.00, 8.00, 12.00, 16.00, 20.00, 24.00, 28.00, 32.00; b. (1) 5; (2) 12.00; (3) 20.00; d. 6, 14.00

3. a. wage rate: 16.00, 16.00, 16.00, 16.00, 16.00, 16.00, 16.00, 18.00; b. total labor cost: 16.00, 32.00, 48.00, 64.00, 80.00, 96.00, 112.00, 144.00; marginal labor cost: 16.00, 16.00, 16.00, 16.00, 16.00, 16.00, 16.00; c. (1) 6; (2) 16.00; (3) 96.00; d. increased, increased, increased

4. a. 5; b. 3; c. 6; d. 2; e. 4; f. 1

SELF-TEST

1. F, p. 534	**6.** T, p. 541
2. T, p. 535	**7.** F, p. 541
3. T, p. 536	**8.** T, p. 541
4. T, pp. 536–537	**9.** F, pp. 541–542
5. T, p. 539	**10.** F, p. 543

11. T, p. 543
12. F, p. 543
13. F, pp. 543–544
14. T, p. 544
15. T, p. 544

1. *a*, p. 534
2. *a*, p. 534
3. *c*, p. 535
4. *a*, p. 536
5. *c*, p. 537
6. *d*, p. 537
7. *d*, p. 539
8. *b*, p. 539
9. *d*, p. 539
10. *c*, p. 538

16. T, pp. 544–545
17. T, pp. 545–546
18. F, p. 546
19. T, p. 547
20. T, p. 549

11. *d*, pp. 534–535
12. *c*, pp. 540–541
13. *b*, p. 541
14. *a*, p. 542
15. *d*, p. 539
16. *c*, p. 536
17. *b*, pp. 543–544
18. *c*, p. 536
19. *b*, p. 538
20. *c*, p. 542

21. *d*, p. 543
22. *a*, p. 545
23. *b*, p. 546

24. *b*, pp. 548–549
25. *c*, p. 550

DISCUSSION QUESTIONS

1. p. 534
2. pp. 534–535
3. pp. 535–536
4. pp. 537–539
5. pp. 536–539
6. p. 538
7. pp. 540–543
8. pp. 540–543
9. pp. 541–543

10. pp. 542–543
11. p. 543
12. pp. 543–544
13. p. 544
14. pp. 543–544
15. pp. 545–546
16. p. 546
17. pp. 545–547
18. pp. 548–550

The Pricing and Employment of Resources: Rent, Interest, and Profits

Chapter 29 concludes the study of the prices of resources by examining rent, interest, and profits. Compared with the study of wage rates in Chapter 28, each of the first three major sections in Chapter 29 is considerably briefer and a good deal simpler. You might do well to treat these sections as if they were actually three minichapters.

There is nothing especially difficult about Chapter 29. By now you should understand that the marginal revenue product of a resource determines the demand for that resource and that this understanding can be applied to the demand for land and capital. It will be on the supply side of the land market that you will encounter whatever difficulties there are. The supply of land is unique because it is perfectly *inelastic*: changes in rent do not change the quantity of land which will be supplied. Demand, given the quantity of land available, is thus the sole determinant of rent. Of course land varies in productivity and can be used for different purposes, but these are merely the factors which explain why the rent on all lands is not the same.

Capital, as the economist defines it, means capital goods. Is the rate of interest, then, the price paid for the use of capital goods? No, not quite. Capital is not one kind of good; it is many different kinds. In order to be able to talk about the price paid for the use of capital goods there must be a simple way of adding up different kinds of capital goods. The simple way is to measure the quantity of capital goods in terms of money. The rate of interest is, then, the price paid for the use of money (or of financial capital). It is the demand for and the supply of money that determine the rate of interest in the economy. Business firms and households wish to hold—that is, demand—money for two principal reasons. Like the demand for any other good or service, the greater the price of using money (the interest rate) the smaller is the amount of money firms and households will wish to hold. And like other *normal* goods and services, the greater the economy's income, the greater will be the demand for money.

On the supply side, the Federal Reserve Banks, the monetary authority in the American economy, determine how much money will be available. At any time the supply of money is a fixed quantity. This means that the quantity of money available does not rise or fall as a result of

changes in the interest rate; and the supply of money is said to be perfectly inelastic. It is this perfectly inelastic supply and the demand for money that determine the equilibrium interest rate. Like other commodities a change in either the supply of or the demand for money will cause this equilibrium interest rate to change.

This theory of interest will be familiar to you if you have previously studied Chapters 10, 13, and 15 in the macroeconomic-principles parts of the text; but you may wish to review the relevant parts of those chapters. If you have not yet studied these chapters you should probably examine them. Footnote number 2 in Chapter 29 of the text tells you which sections of these three chapters should be read by you.

When it comes to profits, supply and demand analysis fails the economist. Profits are not merely a wage for a particular type of labor; rather they are rewards for taking risks and the gains of the monopolist. Such things as "the quantity of risk taken" or "the quantity of effort required to establish a monopoly" simply can't be measured; consequently it is impossible to talk about the demand for or the supply of them. Nevertheless, profits are important in the economy. They are largely rewards for doing things that have to be done if the economy is to allocate resources efficiently and to progress and develop; they are the lure or the bait which makes people willing to take the risks that result in efficiency and progress.

The final section of Chapter 29 answers two questions about the American economy. What part of the national income goes to workers and what part goes to capitalists—those who provide the economy with land, capital goods, and entrepreneurial ability? And have the shares going to workers and to capitalists changed in the past eighty or so years? The student may be surprised to learn that the lion's share—about 80%—of the national income goes to workers today and went to workers at the beginning of the century; and that capitalists today and in 1900 got about 20%. There is, in short, no evidence to support the belief that workers get less and capitalists more or the opposite belief that workers obtain a greater part and capitalists a smaller part of the national income today than they did about ninety years ago in the United States.

■ CHECKLIST

When you have studied this chapter you should be able to:

☐ Define economic rent and explain what determines the amount of economic rent paid.

☐ Explain why economic rent is a surplus (or unearned income).

☐ State the means Henry George and the socialists would use to recover this surplus.

☐ Explain why the owners of land do not all receive the same economic rent.

☐ Explain why, if economic rent is a surplus, a firm must pay rent.

☐ Define interest and state two aspects about it.

☐ Identify the two demands for money and explain what determines the amount of money that will be demanded for each of these two purposes.

☐ Determine the equilibrium rate of interest in the economy when you are given information on the supply (or stock) of money.

☐ State how much money (or financial capital) an individual business firm will tend to borrow at the equilibrium interest rate.

☐ Distinguish between the nominal and the real interest rate; and explain how the latter is related to the former.

☐ Explain why interest rates differ.

☐ Explain how the real interest rate affects investment spending and the equilibrium real domestic output; and the allocation of capital goods among firms (the composition of the production of real capital).

☐ Define economic profit and distinguish between economic profit and normal profit.

☐ Identify the potential sources of profit for firms.

☐ Explain the functions of profits in the American economy.

☐ State the current relative size of labor's and of capital's share of the national income and describe what has happened to these shares in the U.S. economy since 1900.

■ CHAPTER OUTLINE

1. Economic rent is the price paid for the use of land or natural resources whose supply is perfectly inelastic.

a. Demand is the active determinant of economic rent because changes in the level of economic rent do not change the quantity of land supplied; and economic rent is, therefore, a payment which in the aggregate need not be paid to ensure that the land will be available.

b. Some people have argued that land rents are unearned incomes, and that either land should be nationalized or rents should be taxed away; and the single

tax advocated by Henry George would have no effect on resource allocation in the economy.

(1) Thus the case for taxing land can be made on the basis of equity and efficiency considerations.

(2) But critics have pointed out four disadvantages of such a tax.

c. Economic rents on different types of land vary because land differs in its productivity.

d. Land has alternative uses; and rent is a cost to a firm because it must pay rent to lure land away from alternative employments.

2. The interest rate is the price paid for the use of money.

a. The transaction demand for money is directly related to the level of money GDP and the asset demand is inversely related to the rate of interest; and these two demands along with the supply of money (controlled by the monetary authority) determine the equilibrium rate of interest.

(1) The quantity of real capital demanded in the economy and the quantities of real and financial capital demanded by individual firms is inversely related to the equilibrium interest rate.

(2) But it is the real interest rate (the nominal interest rate less the rate of inflation) that determines the quantities of capital demanded.

b. While it is convenient to speak as if there were but a single interest rate there are actually a number of different rates of interest. The rates vary because of four loan factors—risk, maturity, size, and taxability—and because of market imperfections.

c. The interest rate plays two roles.

(1) Because of the inverse relationship between the interest rate and total investment, the level of the interest rate affects the total output of capital goods and the equilibrium real domestic output of an economy.

(2) The interest rate rations (allocates) financial and real capital among competing firms and determines the composition of the total output of capital goods.

3. Economic profit is what remains of the firm's revenues after all its explicit and implicit opportunity costs have been deducted.

a. Profit is a payment for entrepreneurial ability, which involves combining and directing the use of resources in an uncertain and innovating world.

b. Profits are:

(1) rewards for assuming the risks in an economy in which the future is uncertain and subject to change;

(2) rewards for assuming the risks and uncertainties inherent in innovation; and

(3) surpluses which business firms obtain from the exploitation of monopoly power.

c. The expectation of profits motivates business firms to innovate, and profits (and losses) guide business firms to produce products and to use resources in the way desired by society.

4. National income date for the American economy indicate the following.

a. In the period 1982–1990 wages and salaries were 74% of the national income, but using a broader definition of labor income (wages and salaries plus proprietors' income—which is mostly a payment for labor), labor's share was about 80% and capital's share (rent, interest, and corporate profits) was about 20% of national income.

b. Since the years 1900–1909 wages and salaries have increased from 55 to about 74%.

(1) But labor's share, employing the broader definition of labor income, has remained at about 80% and capital's share at about 20% of the national income because of the structural changes which occurred in the American economy.

(2) The growth of labor unions in the United States does not explain the increases in the wages and salaries received by workers.

■ **IMPORTANT TERMS**

Economic rent	Asset demand (for money)
Incentive function	Nominal interest rate
Single-tax movement	Real interest rate
Truth in Lending Act	Normal profit
The (*or* pure) rate of interest	Economic (pure) profit
	Static economy
The theory of interest	Insurable risk
Transaction demand (for money)	Uninsurable risk

■ **FILL-IN QUESTIONS**

1. Rent is the price paid for the use of _____ _____ and _____ and their total supply is _____

2. The active determinant of rent is (demand, supply) _____ and the passive determinant is _____. Because rent does **not** perform a(n) (rationing, incentive) _____ function economists consider it to be a _____ _____

3. Socialists argue that land rents are (earned, unearned) _____ incomes and that land

should be _____ so that these incomes can be used for the good of society as a whole. Proponents of the _____ argue that economic rent could be completely taxed away without affecting the amount of land available for productive purposes.

4. Rents on different pieces of land are not the same because _____ _____. And while rent from the viewpoint of the economy as a whole is a surplus, rent is a cost to _____ users of land which must be paid because land has _____

5. Interest is the price paid for the use of _____ _____; and interest is typically stated as a _____ of the amount of money borrowed. Money (is, is not) _____ an economic resource because money _____ productive.

6. There are two components in the demand for money.

a. The _____ demand is directly related to the _____

b. And the _____ demand is inversely related to the _____

7. In the American economy:

a. At any moment the money supply is an amount determined by _____

b. The equilibrium interest rate is the rate at which the _____ is equal to _____

8. Were the Federal Reserve Banks to increase the money supply, the equilibrium rate of interest would (increase, decrease) _____ and investment spending would _____. As a result the equilibrium real domestic output would _____

9. As far as the individual business firm is concerned:

a. The supply of financial and real capital at the equilibrium rate of interest is perfectly (elastic, inelastic) _____

b. All investment projects whose expected rate of net profits exceed _____ will be undertaken.

10. The (nominal, real) _____ interest

rate is equal to the _____ interest rate minus the rate of _____; and it is the _____ interest rate that is crucial in determining how much business firms will invest.

11. Give five reasons for why the interest rates on different loans would differ.

a. _____

b. _____

c. _____

d. _____

e. _____

12. In the American economy the interest rate is an "_____ price"; but it performs two important functions. It helps to determine how much _____ will occur in the economy and then _____ it among various firms and industries.

13. Normal profits are a payment for the resource called (land, labor, capital, entrepreneurial ability) _____ and this resource performs four functions: It combines the other _____ to produce goods and services, makes (routine, nonroutine) _____ decisions for the firm, (invents, innovates) _____ new products and production processes, and bears the economic (costs, risks, criticisms) _____ associated with the other three functions.

14. When the future is _____, businesses necessarily assume risks, some of which are _____ and some of which are _____. The risks which businesses cannot avoid arise either because the _____ is changing or because the firm itself deliberately engages in _____

15. Profits:
a. Are important in the American economy because the expectation of profits stimulates firms to innovate, and the more innovation there is, the higher will be the levels of _____,

and _____ in the economy;

b. and losses promote the efficient _____ of resources in the economy unless the profits are the result of (competition, monopoly) _____

16. Defining labor income broadly to include both wages and salaries and proprietors' income:
a. Labor's share of the national income is today about _____%;

b. The capitalists' share is the sum of _____

_____, _____, and

_____; and is today about _____% of the national income;

c. Since the beginning of the twentieth century:
(1) Labor's share has (increased, decreased, remained constant) _____

(2) Capital's share has _____

■ **PROBLEMS AND PROJECTS**

1. Assume that the quantity of a certain type of land available is 300,000 acres and the demand for this land is that given in the table below.

Pure land rent, per acre	Land demanded, acres
$350	100,000
300	200,000
250	300,000
200	400,000
150	500,000
100	600,000
50	700,000

a. The pure rent on this land will be $_____

b. The total quantity of land rented will be _____ acres.

c. On the graph at the top of page 341, plot the supply and demand curves for this land and indicate the pure rent for land and the quantity of land rented.

d. If landowners were taxed at a rate of $250 per acre for their land, the pure rent on this land after taxes would be $_____ but the number of acres rented would be _____

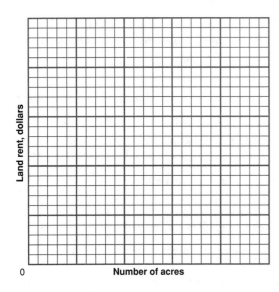

2. The schedule below shows the asset demand for money.

Interest rate	Asset demand for money
8%	$ 60
7	80
6	100
5	120
4	140
3	160
2	180

a. Plot this schedule on the graph below. (The interest rate is measured along the vertical axis and the demand for money is measured along the horizontal axis.)

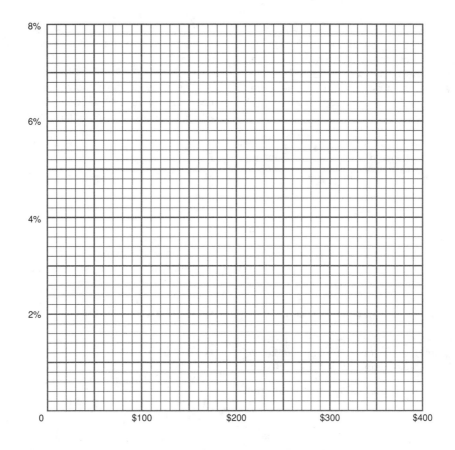

b. Below is a schedule which shows the transactions demand for money. Suppose the GDP is $850.

GDP	Transactions demand for money
$ 750	$160
800	170
850	180
900	190
950	200
1000	210
1050	220

(1) The transactions demand for money is $_____
(2) Plot this demand for money on the graph on the previous page. (The curve will be a vertical line.)
c. In the table below show the total (transactions and asset) demand for money at each of the seven interest rates when the GDP is $850; and plot this demand for money on the graph on the previous page.
d. Suppose the money supply is a fixed amount and equal to $280.
(1) Plot the money supply curve on the graph on the previous page. (It will be a vertical line.)
(2) Enter the supply of money at each of the seven interest rates in the next column in the table.
(3) Using either the money demand and supply curves or schedules, the equilibrium interest rate when GDP is $850 is _____%.

Interest rate	Demand for money	Supply of money
8%	$_____	$_____
7	_____	_____
6	_____	_____
5	_____	_____
4	_____	_____
3	_____	_____
2	_____	_____

e. If a firm had the marginal revenue product of capital schedule (a demand for capital) given in the table below, it would at the equilibrium rate of interest wish to employ $_____ of financial and real capital.

Quantity of capital	Marginal revenue product of capital
$100,000	8%
200,000	7
300,000	6
400,000	5
500,000	4
600,000	3
700,000	2

f. Suppose the GDP remains at $850.
(1) If the money supply were to increase to $300:
(a) the rate of interest would (rise, fall) _____
to _____%;
(b) and the firm in *e* (above) would (increase, decrease) _____ the amount of capital it wishes to employ to $_____
(2) if the money supply were to decrease to $240;
(a) the rate of interest would _____
_____
(b) and the firm in *e* (above) would _____
_____

3. What would the
a. real rate of interest be if the nominal interest rate were 14% and the annual rate of inflation were 8%?
_____%
b. the nominal rate of interest be if the real interest rate were 4% and the annual rate of inflation were 6%?
_____%

4. The following table shows estimated wages and salaries, proprietors' income, corporate profits, interest, rent, and the national income of the United States in 1990.

Wages and salaries	$3290 billion
Proprietors' income	373 billion
Corporate profits	319 billion
Interest	490 billion
Rent	− 13 billion
National income	4460 billion

a. Wages and salaries were _____% of the national income.
b. Labor's share of the national income was _____% and capital's share was _____%.

■ SELF-TEST

Circle the T if the statement is true; the F if it is false.

1. Rent is the price paid for the use of land and other property resources. **T F**

2. The determination of economic rent for land and other natural resources is based on a demand curve that is perfectly inelastic. **T F**

3. Rent is a surplus because it does not perform an incentive function. **T F**

4. Rent is unique because it is not determined by demand and supply. **T F**

5. Henry George argued in *Progress and Poverty* that the increasing land rents would produce more unearned income for landowners which could then be taxed by government. **T F**

6. Critics of the single tax on land argue that it would bring in too much revenue for the government. **T F**

7. For individual producers, rental payments are a surplus, but for society they are a cost. **T F**

8. Money is an economic resource and the interest rate is the price paid for this resource. **T F**

9. The transactions demand for money is directly related to the level of nominal GDP. **T F**

10. The asset demand for money is inversely related to the interest rate. **T F**

11. A decrease in the money supply would tend to increase the interest rate and to decrease investment spending and the equilibrium GDP. **T F**

12. It is the nominal rather than the real interest rate that determines the amounts invested by business firms in additional capital. **T F**

13. Other things equal, long-term loans usually command lower rates of interest than do short-term loans. **T F**

14. The pure rate of interest is best approximated by the interest paid on long-term bonds with very low risk, such as the thirty-year U.S. Treasury bond. **T F**

15. A normal profit is the minimum payment the entrepreneur must expect to receive to induce him or her to provide a firm with entrepreneurial ability. **T F**

16. If the economists' definition of profits were used, total profit in the economy would be greater than they would be if the accountants' definition were used. **T F**

17. The expectation of profits is the basic motive for innovation, while actual profits and losses aid in the efficient allocation of resources. **T F**

18. The increasing importance of the corporation in the American economy is a part of the explanation of why wages and salaries have increased as shares of the national income. **T F**

19. The growth of labor unions is the main cause of the expansion of wages and salaries as a share of the national income. **T F**

20. Over the past ninety years there has been a shift from labor-intensive to capital- and land-intensive production. **T F**

Circle the letter that corresponds to the best answer.

1. Which of the following is considered by economists to be a productive economic resource?

(a) money capital
(b) capital goods
(c) interest
(d) profit

2. The price paid for a natural resource that is completely fixed in supply is:
(a) profit
(b) interest
(c) rent
(d) a risk payment

3. In total, the supply of land is:
(a) perfectly inelastic
(b) of unitary elasticity
(c) perfectly elastic
(d) elastic but not perfectly elastic

4. Which of the following is *not* characteristic of the tax proposed by Henry George?
(a) it would be equal to 100% of all land rent
(b) it would be the only tax levied by government
(c) it would not affect the supply of land
(d) it would reduce rents paid by the amount of the tax

5. A single tax on land in the United States would:
(a) bring in tax revenues sufficient to finance all current government spending
(b) be impractical because it is difficult to distinguish between payments for the use of land and those for the use of capital
(c) tax all "unearned" incomes in the economy at a rate of 100%
(d) be or do all of the above

6. Which of the following is *not* true?
(a) the greater the demand for land, the greater will be the economic rent paid for the use of land
(b) a "windfall profits" tax on the increases in the profits of petroleum producers which have resulted from the rise in oil prices is an example of a tax on economic rent
(c) individual users of land have to pay a rent to its owners because that land has alternative uses
(d) the less productive a particular piece of land is, the greater will be the rent its owner is able to earn from it

7. The economic rent from land will increase, *ceteris paribus*, whenever the:
(a) price of land decreases
(b) demand for land increases
(c) demand for land decreases
(d) supply curve for land increases

8. When the supply curve for land lies entirely to the right of the demand curve:
(a) landowners will receive an economic rent
(b) landowners will not receive an economic rent
(c) the interest rate on land will increase
(d) the interest rate on land will decrease

9. Which of the following would tend to result in a lower interest rate?
(a) the greater the risk involved
(b) the shorter the length of the loan
(c) the smaller the amount of the loan
(d) the greater the imperfections in the money market

10. What is the most likely reason why a lender would prefer a high-quality municipal bond that pays a 6% rate of interest as compared to a high-quality corporate bond paying 8%?
(a) the municipal bond is tax-exempt
(b) the municipal bond is a long-term investment
(c) the corporate bond is safer than the municipal bond
(d) the municipal bond is easier to purchase than a corporate bond

11. If the nominal interest rate were 10% and the annual rate of inflation were 4%, the real interest rate would be:
(a) 14%
(b) 6%
(c) 2½%
(d) −6%

12. Changes in the rate of interest do *not*:
(a) affect the total amount of investment in the economy
(b) affect the amount of investment occurring in particular industries
(c) guarantee that the demand for and the supply of money will be equal
(d) guarantee that there will be full employment in the economy

13. If the annual rate of interest were 18% and the rate of net profit a firm expects to earn annually by building a new plant were 20%, the firm would:
(a) not build the new plant
(b) build the new plant
(c) have to toss a coin to decide whether to build the new plant
(d) not be able to determine from these figures whether to build the plant

14. If the interest rate is 13%:
(a) $300 billion of investment will be undertaken
(b) $360 billion of investment will be undertaken
(c) $430 billion of investment will be undertaken
(d) $500 billion of investment will be undertaken

15. An increase in the interest rate from 15% to 17% would:
(a) increase investment by $40 billion
(b) increase investment by $50 billion
(c) decrease investment by $50 billion
(d) decrease investment by $40 billion

16. Which of the following is an economic cost?
(a) uninsurable risk
(b) normal profit
(c) economic profit
(d) monopoly profit

17. Which of the following would *not* be a function of the entrepreneur?
(a) the introduction of a new product on the market
(b) the making of decisions in a static economy
(c) the incurring of unavoidable risks
(d) the combination and direction of resources in an uncertain environment

18. Business firms obtain economic profits because:
(a) not all risks are insurable
(b) not all markets are competitive
(c) the economy is dynamic
(d) all of these

19. The monopolists who obtain an economic profit are able to do so because:
(a) they are innovators
(b) all their risks are insurable
(c) uncertainty has been reduced to the minimum
(d) most of their decisions are nonroutine

20. Since around 1900:
(a) capital's share of national income has increased
(b) labor's share has increased
(c) labor's share has decreased
(d) capital's share has been almost constant

The next two questions (14 and 15) refer to the following data.

Expected rate of net profit	Amount of capital goods investment (in billions)
19%	$220
17	250
15	300
13	360
11	430
9	500

■ **DISCUSSION QUESTIONS**

1. Explain what determines the economic rent paid for the use of land. What is unique about the supply of land?

2. Why is land rent a "surplus"? What economic difficulties would be encountered if the government adopted Henry George's single tax proposal as a means of confiscating this surplus? What do the critics think of the concept of a single tax on land?

3. Even though land rent is an economic surplus it is also an economic cost for the individual user of land. Why and how can it be both an economic surplus and an economic cost?

4. What is the interest rate? What is the difference between the nominal and real interest rate, and why is the real interest rate the determinant of investment spending by individual firms in the economy?

5. Why are there actually many different rates in the economy at any given time?

6. Explain what determines:
  (a) the amount of money firms and households wish to hold for transaction purposes;
  (b) the amount they wish to have for asset purposes;
  (c) amount of money available for these purposes; and
  (d) the equilibrium rate of interest.

7. How would a change in the money supply affect:
  (a) the interest rate;
  (b) investment spending; and
  (c) the equilibrium real domestic output

8. What two important functions does the rate of interest perform in the economy?

9. What are profits? For what resource are they a payment, and what tasks does this resource perform?

10. Why would there be no economic profits in a purely competitive static economy?

11. "The risks which an entrepreneur assumes arise because of uncertainties which are external to the firm and because of uncertainties which are developed by the initiative of the firm itself." Explain.

12. What two important functions do profits or the expectation of profits perform in the economy? How does monopoly impede the effective performance of these functions?

13. Monopoly results in profits and reduces uncertainty. Is it possible that monopolists may undertake more innovation as a result? Why?

14. What part of the American national income is wages and salaries and what part is labor income? Why do your answers to these questions differ? What part of the national income is the income of capitalists? What kinds of income are capitalist income?

15. What have been the historical trends in the shares of national income that are wages and salaries, labor income, and capitalist income? What changes in the American economy can account for these trends?

16. Explain why the growth of labor unions is not a good explanation of the expanding share of the national income going for wages and salaries.

■ ANSWERS

Chapter 29 The Pricing and Employment of Resources: Rent, Interest, and Profits

FILL-IN QUESTIONS

1. land, natural resources, fixed (perfectly inelastic)

2. demand, supply, incentive, surplus

3. unearned, nationalized, single tax

4. land differs in productivity (quality), individual, alternative uses

5. money; percentage, is not, is not

6. *a.* transactions, nominal GDP; *b.* asset, rate of interest

7. *a.* the monetary authority (the Federal Reserve Banks); *b.* quantity of money demanded, the money supply (stock) (either order)

8. decrease, increase, increase

9. *a.* elastic; *b.* the equilibrium rate of interest

10. real, nominal, inflation, real

11. *a.* risk; *b.* length of loan; *c.* amount of loan; *d.* tax status of loan (or investment); *e.* market imperfections

12. administered, investment, rations

13. entrepreneurial ability, resources, nonroutine, innovates, risks

14. uncertain, insurable, uninsurable, economy as a whole, innovation

15. *a.* investment, employment, output; *b.* allocation, monopoly

16. *a.* 80; *b.* rent, interest, corporate profit, 20; *c.* (1) remained constant, (2) remained constant

PROBLEMS AND PROJECTS

1. *a.* 250; *b.* 300,000; *d.* 0, 300,000

2. *b.* (1) 180; *c.* 240, 260, 280, 300, 320, 340, 360; *d.* (2) 280, 280, 280, 280, 280, 280, 280, (3) 6; *e.* 300,000; *f.* (1) (*a*) fall, 5 (*b*) increase, 400,000, (2) (*a*) rise to 8%, (*b*) decrease the quantity of capital demanded to $100,000

3. *a.* 6; *b.* 10

4. *a.* 73.8; *b.* 81.3, 18.7

SELF-TEST

1. F, p. 553	11. T, p. 557
2. F, p. 554	12. F, p. 557
3. T, pp. 554–555	13. F, p. 558
4. F, p. 554	14. T, p. 558
5. T, p. 555	15. T, p. 560
6. F, p. 555	16. F, p. 559
7. F, p. 556	17. T, pp. 561–562
8. F, p. 557	18. T, p. 564
9. T, p. 557	19. F, p. 564
10. T, p. 557	20. F, p. 564

1. *b*, p. 557
2. *c*, p. 553
3. *a*, p. 554
4. *d*, p. 555
5. *b*, p. 555
6. *d*, p. 554
7. *b*, p. 554
8. *b*, p. 554
9. *b*, p. 558
10. *a*, p. 558

11. *b*, p. 557
12. *d*, p. 559
13. *b*, p. 559
14. *b*, p. 559
15. *c*, p. 559
16. *b*, p. 560
17. *b*, p. 560
18. *d*, pp. 560–561
19. *c*, p. 561
20. *d*, p. 564

DISCUSSION QUESTIONS

1. pp. 553–554
2. pp. 554–555
3. p. 556
4. p. 557
5. p. 558
6. pp. 556–557
7. pp. 557–559
8. p. 559
9. pp. 559–560
10. p. 560
11. pp. 560–561
12. pp. 561–562
13. p. 561
14. pp. 562–564
15. p. 564
16. p. 564

CHAPTER 30

General Equilibrium: The Market System and Its Operation

Chapter 30 provides a conclusion to the previous ten chapters and ties together many of the things you have already learned about microeconomics. By this time you have read a large amount of material concerning the operation of supply and demand in product and resource markets and under different market conditions. You may have lost sight of the fact—emphasized in Chapter 5—that the American economy is a *system* of markets and prices. This means that *all* prices and *all* markets are linked together.

The chief purpose of Chapter 30 is to help you understand why and how these markets are linked together, connected, and interrelated. The theory which explains the relationships between different markets and different prices is called *general* equilibrium analysis. (By way of contrast, the theory which explains a single product or resource market and the price of the one good or service bought and sold in that market is called *partial* equilibrium analysis.) An understanding of general equilibrium is necessary in order to understand how the market system as a whole operates to allocate its scarce resources.

Three approaches are used to enable the student to grasp the essentials and the importance of general equilibrium analysis. First, the chapter illustrates how general equilibrium works using supply and demand analysis in product and resource markets. Here you learn what the effects are of an increase in the demand for hypothetical product X accompanied by a decrease in the demand for product Y. This explanation includes a description of the short- and long-run effects on the products X and Y, and a discussion of the effects on the markets in which the producers employ resources. There are other adjustments that stem from the initial change. These further adjustments involve the markets for complementary and substitute products, the markets in which resources are used to produce these other products, and the distribution of income in the economy. You should also note that, although the competitive market system tends to promote economic efficiency and maximize consumer satisfaction, in the real world there are complications for the achievement of those objectives because markets may be imperfectly competitive.

Second, to help you understand the interrelationships between the different sectors of the economy, an input-output table is used. The table lists the producing sectors and the total output from each sector. It also shows how many inputs are required by each sector to produce its level of output. The interdependent nature of sectors in the economy is demonstrated by following the repercussions of a change in the output of a commodity with the aid of an input-output table.

Third, the chapter makes general equilibrium analysis more concrete by describing two recent examples of how one change in the economy leads to many other changes. The first example focuses on both the domestic and worldwide implications of a significant increase in the price of oil during the 1970s. This economic event had ramifications for many product and resource markets that are interrelated through the market system. You should spend time trying to understand through this example how a change in the price of a product in one market had a "ripple" effect on other markets and on the overall performance of the United States and world economy.

The second example illustrates how a change in the characteristics of our population, not just a change in price, sets off other changes in product and resource markets. The greater longevity and declining birth rates means that the American population is growing older. This important development increases the demand for various medical care—doctors, nursing homes, and prescription drugs—and also reduces the demand for products that would be bought by younger adults—housing, education, and children's household goods. In the resource markets, there is likely to be a slowing in the growth of the labor force, which has other implications for macroeconomic factors such as unemployment rates and microeconomic factors such as the demand for older workers.

What you should learn from this chapter, and the examples it presents, is that general equilibrium analysis is valuable because it provides a deeper and more analytical understanding of a variety of changes in our society. Many interrelations among markets and prices do exist in both the domestic and world economy, and it is important for you to see the connections. To be able to do this means that you must trace the total effect of a change in price or in economic policy throughout the economy, or you must investigate the full consequences of a change in such factors as consumer tastes, population, the availability of resources, or technology on the society.

When you finish Chapter 30, you are ready to examine economic issues or problems related to government and the operation of the market system. This discussion will give you more insight into the problems encountered in allocating scarce resources in our economic system whether it be by government or by the private sector. These topics are examined in the next six chapters which make up Part 6 of the text.

■ **CHECKLIST**

When you have studied this chapter you should be able to:

☐ Distinguish between partial and general equilibrium analysis.

☐ Identify the four concepts which underlie the demand and supply curves in the product and resource markets of the economy.

☐ Explain, using graphs if you wish, both the immediate and secondary effects of a change in tastes, technology, or the availability of resources upon equilibrium prices and quantities in the product and resource markets; and upon the distribution of income in the economy.

☐ State three reasons why the competitive market system makes efficient use of resources.

☐ Identify three potential complications with the efficient operation of the competitive market economy in the real world.

☐ Specify what is shown along the left side, along the top, and in each of the boxes of an input-output table.

☐ Find the effects, when you are given an input-output table, of a change in the output of one industry upon the outputs of other industries in the economy.

☐ Cite examples of how the increase in the price of oil during the 1970s led to changes in resource and product markets in the United States economy.

☐ Describe the effects from the increase in the price of oil during the 1970s on world economy.

☐ Explain the product market implications of an aging population for the United States.

☐ Identify two reasons for the project decline in the growth of the labor force.

☐ Make five predictions about the labor market in the United States based on the projected decline in the growth of the labor force.

■ **CHAPTER OUTLINE**

1. Partial equilibrium analysis is the study of equilibrium prices and quantities in specific product and resource markets which form the price-market system. General equilibrium analysis is the study of the interrelations among these markets.

2. To understand the effects of an increase in consumer demand for product X accompanied by a decrease in consumer demand for product Y, imagine that the industry producing X uses only type A labor and that the industry producing Y uses only type B labor.

    a. Assume also that the demand curve for each product has a negative slope because of diminishing marginal utility and the supply curve has a positive slope because of increasing marginal cost; and assume that the demand curve for each type of labor has a negative slope because of diminishing marginal product and the supply curve has a positive slope because of the work-leisure preferences of workers.

    b. Beginning with all markets in long-run equilibrium, the short-run effects are an increased (decreased) output and price and economic profits (losses) in industry X (Y), an increased (decreased) derived demand for type A (type B) labor, and increased (decreased) wage rates and employment for type A (type B) labor.

    c. The long-run adjustments are the entry (exit) of firms in industry X (Y); an increase (decrease) in the supply of X (Y); a higher (lower) price than existed initially in industry X (Y), assuming increasing-cost industries; an increase (decrease) in the supply of A (B); and higher (lower) wage rates for A (B) than initially existed.

    d. In addition to these adjustments there will also be:

    (1) An increase (decrease) in the demand for and the prices and outputs of products which are substitutes (complements) for X or complements (substitutes) for Y; and an increased (decreased) demand for the resources used to produce those products whose outputs increase (decrease).

    (2) An increase (decrease) in the demand for the other resources used along with A (B).

    (3) A redistribution of income from workers and entrepreneurs in industry Y to those in industry X.

    e. In summary, any initial change in tastes, in the supply of resources, or in technology will not only have an immediate effect upon equilibrium price and quantity in a specific market, but will also have secondary effects in other markets and upon other equilibrium prices and quantities.

    f. There are also implications for economic efficiency in competitive markets:

    (1) In the ideal case, competitive markets will produce an allocation of an economy's resources and output of goods and services that is allocatively efficient, productively efficient, and that maximizes the satisfactions of

consumers, given the distribution of income and free choice by consumers.

(2) In the real world, however, there can be complications from:

(a) the underproduction of public goods and goods with spillover benefits, or the overproduction of goods with spillover costs;

(b) a distribution of income that may not be viewed as just or equitable; and

(c) markets that may be only imperfectly competitive, and therefore less efficient and slow to respond to change.

3. The input-output table indicates the specific relationships that exist among the outputs of the various sectors of the economy.

a. The outputs of each sector are the inputs of the other sectors; and the inputs of each sector are the outputs of the other sectors.

b. Because of this interdependence, any change in the output of one sector will alter the outputs of the other sectors.

4. Oil prices rose during the 1970s because of the actions taken by the OPEC cartel. This change in the price of one resource had a significant effect on many other resource and product markets beyond just the oil market. This example illustrates the difference between partial equilibrium analysis, which considers the impact on just the oil market, and general equilibrium, which considers the repercussions on markets for many oil-related products and resources.

a. In the product market, for example, the increase in the price of oil:

(1) increased the demand for substitute products that were energy-efficient, such as fuel-efficient automobiles or insulation, and decreased the demand for complementary goods and services that require gasoline consumption, such as recreational vehicles or automobile travel (tourism); and

(2) decreased the supply of some products, such as gasoline or fertilizer, because of higher oil costs to produce these products, and increased the supply of other products, such as energy-conserving equipment, because productivity improved in firms making this type of equipment.

b. In the resource market, for example, the increase in the price of oil:

(1) increased the demand for alternative energy sources such as coal or natural gas, and decreased the demand for capital goods that required oil-related energy; and

(2) decreased the supply of labor in the Snow Belt and increased it in the Sun Belt.

c. There were national and international effects from the increase in oil prices.

(1) The national economy experienced a rising tide of imports from fuel-efficient vehicles and more expensive oil that contributed to a decline in net exports and spendable income, thereby reducing aggregate demand; the oil price "shocks" also shifted aggregate supply, leading to cost-push inflation and less domestic output.

(2) On the international level, the increase in oil prices made the United States trade deficits worse, thereby reducing the international value of the dollar and contributing to domestic inflation; less-developed countries that did not produce oil suffered less favorable terms of trade that retarded economic growth.

5. The increase in the average age of the population in the United States has many economic consequences in both the product market and the labor market.

a. In the product market, there will be an increase in the demand for health-related goods and services, and a decrease in demand for child-related goods and services; and the rate of saving is likely to increase because the relative level of consumption and debt is less among an older population that a younger population that is raising children.

b. In the labor market, there will be a decline in the growth of the labor force caused by a drop in the birth rate during the 1960s and 1970s after the "baby boom" years, and by a slowing in the expected rate of participation of women in the work force. These developments are the basis for five predictions about the labor market—lower unemployment rates, higher real wages, retention of older workers, increased immigration, and more emphasis on the growth of productivity.

■ **IMPORTANT TERMS**

Market system	Input-output analysis
Partial equilibrium analysis	Input-output table
General equilibrium analysis	

■ **FILL-IN QUESTIONS**

1. Partial equilibrium analysis is concerned with prices and outputs in _____ markets in the economy, and general equilibrium analysis is concerned with the _____ among markets and prices.

2. General equilibrium exists in an economy where there is _____ in all the _____ and _____ markets in the economy.

3. When studying the markets for products and for resources, we assume that the demand curves slope

_____ and the supply curves slope

_____

   a. The slope of the demand curve for:

(1) products is due to _____

(2) resources is due to _____

   b. The slope of the supply curve for:

(1) products is due to _____

(2) labor is due to _____

4. Assume the demand for consumer good P increases while the demand for consumer good Q decreases. In the short run:

   a. The price and output of P will (increase, decrease)

_____ and the price and output of Q will

_____

   b. Profits in industry _____ will

increase and profits in industry _____
will decrease.

   c. If the only resource used in industry P is type C labor and the only resource used in industry Q is type D labor, the demand for C will (increase, decrease)

_____ and the demand for D

will _____

   d. Wage rates and the quantity of labor employed in

the market for _____ will increase while

those in the market for _____ will
decrease.

5. Using the same assumptions made in **4** above, if the two industries are increasing-cost industries, the increase in the demand for P along with the decrease in the demand for Q will in the long run:

   a. Cause firms to enter industry _____

and to leave industry _____

   b. Cause the supply of P to (increase, decrease)

_____ and the supply of Q

to _____

   c. Bring about a(n) _____ in the price

of P and a(n) _____ in the price of Q.

   d. Increase the supply of type _____

labor and decrease the supply of type _____
labor.

   e. _____ the employment of type C

labor and _____ the employment of
type D labor.

6. Still using the assumptions made in **4** and **5** above, the increase in the price of P and the decrease in the price of Q will:

   a. Increase the demand for products which are (sub-

stitutes, complements) _____ for P and

decrease the demand for _____

   b. (Increase, Decrease) _____ the demand for those resources used along with type C labor

and _____ the demand for those resources used along with type D labor.

   c. Redistribute income from workers and entrepre-

neurs in industry _____ to those in

industry _____

7. The economic changes or disturbances which may set off a complex economic chain reaction are of three

basic types: changes in _____,

changes in _____,

and changes in _____

8. Given the distribution of income, purely competitive product and resource markets bring about the production of a combination of goods and services which maximizes

the _____ of the consumers of the
economy.

9. The ability of a purely competitive price system to allocate resources efficiently is open to question for three reasons:

   a. It fails to take into account the _____

_____ and the

_____ of the goods and services
produced and it neglects or ignores the production of

_____ goods.

   b. It does not necessarily result in an ideal

_____ of income.

   c. Product and resource markets in the real world are

actually _____ competitive. As a result

the allocation of resources is less than _____
and adjustments to changes in tastes, technology, and

the availability of resources are _____

and _____

10. Listed down the left side of an input-output table are

the _____ sectors of the economy and

listed across the top of the table are the _____

sectors. The output of any sector is a(n) _____ of other sectors; and the inputs of any sector are the

_____ of other sectors.

11. Assuming constant returns to scale, if industry X sells 30% of its product to industry Y and if industry Y increases its production by 25%, then industry X will have to increase

its production by _____%.

12. According to the partial equilibrium analysis, the actions of the OPEC cartel to reduce the output of oil caused

the supply of oil to (increase, decrease) _____,

equilibrium price to _____,

and equilibrium output to _____

13. From a general equilibrium perspective, however, the change in oil prices produced changes in product and resource markets and in the national economy:

   a. In the product market, the demand for large,

domestic automobiles (increased, decreased) _____; the demand for fuel-efficient foreign automobiles

_____. The demand for recreational travel

and resorts _____; the demand for insulation

and weather stripping _____
   b. The prices of products derived from oil (increased,

decreased) _____ contributing to (higher,

lower) _____ prices for producers that used these products as inputs.
   c. In the resource markets, the demand for labor in domestic automobile production (increased, de-

creased) _____; the demand for labor

in the energy conservation industry _____.
The supply of capital goods requiring substantial en-

ergy inputs for production _____
   d. For the national economy, net exports and aggregate demand showed a(n) (increase, decrease)

_____ and aggregate supply showed a(n)

_____, causing the price level to

_____ and domestic output

to _____
   e. For the world economy, the rise in oil prices (in-

creased, decreased) _____ the trade

deficit of the United States, _____ the

international value of the dollar, and _____ the

debts of less-developed countries that do not produce oil.

14. The aging of the American population has many economic consequences in both the product market and in the labor market:
   a. In the product market, there will be (an increase, a

decrease) _____ in the demand for health-

related goods and services, and _____ in demand for child-related goods and services; the rate

of saving is likely to show _____ because

there is usually _____ in the rate consumption and debt as adults finish raising families.

   b. In the labor market, there will be _____ in the growth of the labor force caused by a drop in the birth rate and a slowing of growth in the labor force participation of women.

15. The slowing in the growth of the labor force sets the basis for five predictions about future labor markets. There

will be (higher, lower) _____ unemployment rates,

_____ real wages, (less, more) _____ reten-

tion of older workers, _____ immigration, and

_____ emphasis on the growth of productivity in the economy.

■ PROBLEMS AND PROJECTS

1. Below are three types of economic change which can occur in the economy. In the spaces allotted following each change, indicate what you think the effect will be— increase (+), decrease (−), no change (0), or an indeterminate change (?)—on demand or supply, price, and output or employment in the markets affected by the initial change.

   No answers to this problem will be found in the "Answers" section because the answer to each question depends upon such things as whether the short run or the long run is considered, whether the industry is an increasing- or constant-cost industry, and whether you consider only the "immediate-secondary effect" of the initial change. The purpose of this exercise is to get you to *attempt* to trace through the economy the full effect of an initial change and to see the extent and complexity of price-market interrelations.
   a. Decrease in the demand for consumer good X but no *initial* change in the demand for other consumer goods.
   (1) Effect on the price of and the quantity of good X

produced.   _____

(2) Effect on the demand for, the price of, and the output of goods which are substitutes for good X. _____

(3) Effect on the demand for, the price of, and the output of goods which are complements for good X.

_____

(4) Effect on the demand for, the price of, and the employment of resources used in the production of good X. _____

(5) Effect on the supply of, the price of, and the output of goods which employ the same resources used in the production of good X. _____

(6) Effect on the demand for, the price of, and the employment of resources which are substitutes for the resources used to produce good X. _____

b. Decrease in the supply of resource Y.

(1) Effect on the price of and the employment of resource Y. _____

(2) Effect on the supply of, the price of, and the output of goods which employ resource Y in the production process. _____

(3) Effect on the demand for, the price of, and the employment of resources which are complementary to resource Y. _____

(4) Effect on the demand for, the price of, and the output of those goods which are substitutes for the goods produced with resource Y. _____

(5) Effect on the demand for, the price of, and the output of those goods which are complements for goods produced with resource Y. _____

(6) Effect on the demand for, the price of, and the employment of resources which are substitutes for resource Y. _____

c. Improvement in the technology of producing good Z.

(1) Effect on the supply of, the price of, and the output of good Z. _____

(2) Effect on the demand for, the price of, and the output of goods which are substitutes for good Z. _____

(3) Effect on the demand for, the price of, and the output of goods which are complements for good Z.

_____

(4) Effect on the demand for, the price of, and the employment of resources used to produce good Z. _____

(5) Effect on the supply of, the price of, and the output of those goods which also employ the resources used to produce good Z. _____

2. Below is an incomplete input-output table for an economy with five sectors. All the figures in the table are physical units rather than dollars.

Producing sectors	Using sectors					Total outputs
	A	**B**	**C**	**D**	**E**	
A	100	150	75	—	25	425
B	30	20	70	80	200	—
C	10	60	—	20	20	110
D	205	35	40	10	—	300
E	—	140	60	35	80	390

a. Complete the table by computing (by addition or subtraction) the missing input-output figures.

b. Assume that sector B wishes to expand its output by 100 units. By what percentage does sector B wish to expand its output? _____%

c. Assuming constant returns to scale in all sectors of the economy, by how many **units** will each of the following sectors of the economy have to expand its output if sector B is to expand its output by 100 units?

(1) Sector A: _____

(2) Sector C: _____

(3) Sector D: _____

(4) Sector E: _____

d. By what **percentage** will each of these sectors have to expand its output?

(1) Sector A: _____%

(2) Sector C: _____%

(3) Sector D: _____%

(4) Sector E: _____%

e. What further adjustments in the outputs of the various sectors of the economy will follow those given in (c) and (d) above?

_____

_____

■ **SELF-TEST**

Circle the T if the statement is true; the F if it is false.

1. General equilibrium analysis is the same thing as macroeconomics.   **T F**

2. The study of the effect of an increase in the demand for product C, other things remaining equal, upon the price and the output of product C is an example of partial equilibrium analysis.   **T F**

3. General equilibrium analysis gives a broader picture of the economic consequences of economic changes and economic policies than partial equilibrium analysis even though some of these consequences turn out to be insignificant.   **T   F**

4. The demand curve for labor is downsloping because of diminishing marginal utility.   **T   F**

5. The supply curve for a product slopes upward in the short run because of the diminishing marginal productivity of variable resources and increasing marginal cost. **T   F**

Use the following data for the next three questions (6, 7, and 8) and for multiple-choice questions 7 and 8. Initially there is general equilibrium, and then the demand for consumer good W increases and the demand for consumer good Z decreases. Both industries are increasing-cost industries in the long run. Industry W employs only type G labor, and Z employs only type H labor.

6. In the short run, price, output, and profits will increase in industry Z and decrease in industry W.   **T   F**

7. In the long run, the quantity of type G labor employed will increase and the quantity of type H labor employed will decrease.   **T   F**

8. Income will be redistributed from workers and entrepreneurs in industry Z to those in industry W.   **T   F**

9. A change in demand, a change in technology, or a change in resource supply can set off a chain reaction of economic changes in the economy.   **T   F**

10. Given the distribution of income in the economy, purely competitive product and resource markets lead to the production of a collection of products which maximizes the satisfaction of consumer wants.   **T   F**

11. In the real world, product and resource markets tend to be purely competitive.   **T   F**

12. In an input-output table, the inputs of each sector are the outputs of the other sectors.   **T   F**

13. An input-output table is constructed so that a change in one sector will not produce a change in another sector.   **T   F**

14. Higher price for oil during the 1970s increased the demand for domestic cars.   **T   F**

15. The use of capital goods is not affected by higher energy prices because they have already been produced.   **T   F**

16. The short-term demand for gasoline is price elastic.
                                                                  T   F

17. During the 1970s, the increased expenditure by the United States for imported oil increased the supply of dollars relative to demand in foreign exchange markets.
                                                                  T   F

18. The aging of the American population will tend to cause a decrease in the demand for prescription drugs.
                                                                  T   F

19. The level of consumption and consumer debt is likely to increase with the increase in the average age of the population in the United States.   **T   F**

20. One prediction that can be made based on the aging of the American population is that less emphasis will need to be given to productivity in the economy.   **T   F**

Circle the letter that corresponds to the best answer.

1. An economist that studies the economic effects of an increase in a tariff on imported automobiles on producers and consumers, both foreign and domestic, and on national and foreign economies would best be described as conducting:
  (a) partial equilibrium analysis
  (b) general equilibrium analysis
  (c) resource market analysis
  (d) product market analysis

2. The concept of increasing marginal cost serves to explain the:
  (a) downward slope of the product demand curve
  (b) downward slope of the resource demand curve
  (c) upward slope of the product supply curve
  (d) upward slope of the labor supply curve

3. The downward slope of the demand curve for a product is the result of:
  (a) diminishing marginal utility
  (b) diminishing marginal productivity
  (c) increasing marginal cost
  (d) the work-leisure preferences of workers

4. The upward slope of the supply curve of labor is the result of:
  (a) diminishing marginal utility
  (b) increasing marginal productivity
  (c) decreasing marginal cost
  (d) rising opportunity cost

5. If the demand for consumer good A increased, which one of the following would **not** be a possible consequence?
  (a) increase in the price of A
  (b) increase in the demand for resources used to produce A
  (c) increase in the supply of those goods which are substitutes for A
  (d) increase in the prices of other goods which employ the same resources used to produce A

6. If the supply of resource B increased, which one of the following would **not** be a possible consequence?
  (a) decrease in the price of B
  (b) decrease in the demand for those goods produced from B
  (c) decrease in the demand for those resources which are substitutes for resource B
  (d) decrease in the demand for those goods which are substitutes for the goods produced with resource B

*Use the data preceding true-false question **6** to answer the following two questions (**7** and **8**).*

7. When the new long-run general equilibrium is reached:
  (a) the wage rate for type G labor will be higher than it was originally
  (b) the wage rate for type G labor will be lower than it was originally
  (c) wage rates in both labor markets will be the same as they were originally
  (d) it is impossible to tell what will have happened to wage rates

8. As a result of the changes in the demands for W and Z:
  (a) the demand for products which are substitutes for Z will have increased
  (b) the demand for products which are complements for W will have increased
  (c) the demand for products which are substitutes for Z will have decreased
  (d) the demand for products which are complements for Z will have decreased

9. A highly complex chain reaction of economic events can be set off in the economy by an initial change in:
  (a) demand
  (b) technology
  (c) resource supply
  (d) all of the above

10. Which of the following is a disadvantage with purely competitive product and resource markets?
  (a) the maximization of consumer satisfaction
  (b) spillover costs and benefits
  (c) allocative efficiency
  (d) productive efficiency

11. In the construction of an input-output table:
  (a) the outputs of each sector are the outputs of the other sectors
  (b) the inputs of each sector are the inputs of the other sectors

  (c) the outputs of each sector are the inputs of the other sectors
  (d) the input of each sector is equal to the output of each sector

*Use the following input-output table to answer the next two questions (**12** and **13**).*

Producing	Using sectors					Total
sectors	A	B	C	D	E	outputs
A	20	15	35	25	60	155
B	45	55	90	10	20	220
C	40	15	80	10	5	150
D	65	10	25	20	40	160
E	100	75	80	45	10	310

12. If sector C were to decrease its output by 50 units, and assuming constant returns to scale in all sectors, the **initial** impact on sector B would be a decrease in its output of:
  (a) 5 units
  (b) 13⁶⁄₇ units
  (c) 26⅔ units
  (d) 30 units

13. If sector C is to increase its output by 50 units, and assuming constant returns to scale, sector E's output will have to increase initially by:
  (a) 8.6%
  (b) 19.4%
  (c) 20%
  (d) 37.5%

14. When the price of oil rose during the 1970s, it resulted in what changes in the **resource** market?
  (a) less demand for domestic cars and more demand for fuel-efficient foreign cars
  (b) more demand for Thermopane windows for homes and less demand for recreational travel
  (c) more demand for labor in the installation of insulation and less demand for labor in the production of domestic cars
  (d) less demand for motor oil by consumers and more demand for public transportation

15. The price elasticity of demand for gasoline is estimated to be about .20 to .40. This means that:
  (a) a 10% increase in price will result in a 2 to 4% increase in consumption
  (b) a 10% increase in price will result in a 2 to 4% decrease in consumption
  (c) a 1% increase in price will result in a 2 to 4% decrease in consumption

(d) a 2 to 4% increase in price will result in a 10% increase in consumption

16. The best example of an international effect from the increase in oil prices during the 1970s is:

(a) a boom in the economies of oil-producing states in the United States

(b) an increase in the debts of less developed countries that did not produce oil

(c) an increase in the demand for energy-efficient capital goods made in China

(d) a decrease in the imports of fuel-efficient cars from Japan

17. Larger expenditures by the United States for imported oil during the 1970s caused the international value of the United States dollar to:

(a) depreciate because of an increase in the supply of dollars relative to demand

(b) depreciate because of an increase in the demand for dollars relative to the supply

(c) appreciate because of an increase in the supply of dollars relative to the demand

(d) appreciate because of an increase in the demand for dollars relative to the supply

18. The trend toward an older population in the United States will tend to:

(a) increase demand for starter homes and decrease demand for toys

(b) increase demand for consumer credit and increase demand for rental apartments

(c) decrease demand for nurses and increase the demand for furniture

(d) decrease demand for jeans and increase the demand for prescription drugs

19. The aging of the American population suggests that in future labor markets there will be:

(a) an increase in unemployment rates

(b) an increase in real wages

(c) a decrease in emphasis on productivity

(d) a decrease in immigration from other nations

20. Which statements would be the best example of the type of insight provided by general equilibrium analysis?

(a) a decrease in the supply of oil will raise the price of oil and reduce the equilibrium output

(b) tariff-inspired expansion of the auto industry will entail a contraction in the production of many other goods in a full-employment economy

(c) input-output analysis guarantees that planned production targets will be met in less-developed nations

(d) partial equilibrium analysis shows the "little ripples" whereas general equilibrium shows the "big splash" from an oil price increase

■ DISCUSSION QUESTIONS

1. Explain the difference between partial equilibrium and general equilibrium analysis.

2. Why is general equilibrium analysis so important?

3. Suppose the demand for television sets decreases at the same time that the demand for airline travel increases. What would be:

(a) the short-run effects of these changes in the markets for television-set production workers and airline workers;

(b) the long-run effects in these markets;

(c) the long-run effects in the markets for complementary and substitute products and in the markets for other resources; and

(d) the effect upon the distribution of income?

4. Imagine that the availability of iron ore used to produce steel increased or the technology of steel making improved. What would be the short- and long-run effects upon:

(a) the steel industry;

(b) steelworkers;

(c) the automobile industry;

(d) the aluminum industry;

(e) the machine tool industry; and

(f) the coal industry?

5. Why is a purely competitive price system "conducive to an efficient allocation of resources"?

6. When a market system is less than purely competitive, what are the economic consequences?

7. Explain precisely what an input-output table is and the kind of information it contains.

8. In addition to indicating the interrelationships between the various sectors of the economy, an input-output table can be used for what purposes?

9. Describe the multitude of effects on product and resource markets in the United States from the significant increase in oil prices created by the OPEC cartel during the 1970s. How does this event illustrate the value of general equilibrium analysis compared with a partial equilibrium analysis?

10. What was the impact of the oil price increases during the 1970s on the international economy? Give examples of economic events.

11. What changes in the product market and in consumption and saving will result from an increase in the average age of the population.

12. What two factors have contributed to the slowdown in the growth of the labor force? What predictions about labor markets are suggested by this development?

■ ANSWERS

Chapter 30 General Equilibrium: The Market System and Its Operation

FILL-IN QUESTIONS

1. specific, interrelationships

2. equilibrium, product, resource

3. downward, upward: *a.* (1) diminishing marginal utility, (2) diminishing marginal productivity; *b.* (1) increasing marginal cost, (2) rising opportunity cost

4. *a.* increase, decrease; *b.* P, Q; *c.* increase, decrease; *d.* C, D

5. *a.* P, Q; *b.* increase, decrease; *c.* increase, decrease; *d.* C, D; *e.* increase, decrease

6. *a.* substitutes, complements; *b.* increase, decrease; *c.* Q, P

7. tastes, availability of resources, technology

8. satisfaction or utility

9. *a.* spillover costs, spillover benefits, public; *b.* distribution; *c.* imperfectly, ideal, incomplete, slow

10. producing, consuming (using), input, outputs

11. 7.5

12. decrease, increase, decrease

13. *a.* decreased, increased, decreased, increased; *b.* increased, higher; *c.* decreased, increased, decreased; *d.* decrease, decrease, increase, decrease; *e.* increased, decreased, increased

14. *a.* increase, decrease, decrease, increase; *b.* decrease

15. lower, lower, more, more, more

PROBLEMS AND PROJECTS

2. *a.* From left to right: 75, 0, 75, 10, 400; *b.* 25; *c.* (1) 37.5; (2) 15; (3) 8.75; (4) 35; *d.* (1) 8.8; (2) 13.6; (3) 2.9; (4) 8.97; *e.* each sector will have to increase its inputs in order to increase its output, and this will require still further increases in the outputs of the various sectors

SELF-TEST

1. F, pp. 567–568	**11.** F, p. 571
2. T, p. 567	**12.** T, pp. 571–572
3. T, p. 568	**13.** F, p. 572
4. F, p. 568	**14.** F, p. 573
5. T, p. 568	**15.** F, p. 573
6. F, pp. 568–569	**16.** F, p. 573
7. T, p. 570	**17.** T, p. 574
8. T, p. 570	**18.** F, p. 575
9. T, p. 570	**19.** F, p. 575
10. T, p. 571	**20.** F, pp. 576–577

1. *b,* p. 568	**11.** *c,* p. 572
2. *c,* p. 568	**12.** *d,* p. 572
3. *a,* p. 568	**13.** *a,* p. 572
4. *d,* p. 568	**14.** *c,* p. 573
5. *c,* p. 570	**15.** *b,* p. 573
6. *b,* p. 570	**16.** *b,* p. 574
7. *d,* p. 570	**17.** *a,* p. 574
8. *c,* p. 570	**18.** *d,* p. 575
9. *d,* p. 570	**19.** *b,* p. 576
10. *b,* p. 571	**20.** *b,* pp. 567–568

DISCUSSION QUESTIONS

1. pp. 567–568	**7.** pp. 571–572
2. p. 568	**8.** p. 572
3. pp. 568–570	**9.** pp. 573–574
4. pp. 568–570	**10.** p. 574
5. p. 571	**11.** pp. 574–575
6. p. 571	**12.** pp. 575–576

CHAPTER 31

Government and Market Failure: Public Goods, the Environment, and Information Problems

This chapter is the first of two chapters that takes a more extensive look at the economic role of government that was introduced in Chapters 6 and 8. The primary focus of this chapter is **market failures** that occur in our economy. These failures often result in government intervention in the economy to provide public goods and services, to address externality problems such as pollution, and to improve the quality and amount of information for buyers and sellers in private markets.

The chapter begins by reviewing the characteristics of public goods. You should recall from Chapter 6 that a private good is divisible and subject to the exclusion principle, whereas a public good is indivisible and not subject to exclusion. What is new in Chapter 31 is that you are shown how the demand curve and schedule for a public good are constructed and how the optimal allocation of a public good is determined. You should also note how the demand and supply curves for a public good are related to collective marginal benefits and marginal costs.

Governments employ benefit-cost analysis to determine whether they should or should not undertake some specific action—a particular project or program. This type of analysis forces government to estimate both the marginal costs and the marginal benefits of the project or program; to expand its activities only where the additional benefits exceed the added costs; and to reduce or eliminate programs and projects when the marginal costs exceed the marginal benefits. This analysis, however, depends on the ability to measure benefits and costs with some degree of accuracy. This may not be possible in some cases, thereby limiting the application of benefit-cost analysis.

The second topic of the chapter is externalities, a situation where a cost is incurred or a benefit is obtained by a party that was not involved in the market transactions. You learned in Chapter 6 that one role of government is to reduce the spillover costs to society from negative externalities and to increase the spillover benefits to society from positive externalities. This general point is now modified by the **Coase theorem** that suggests that there are situations where government intervention is not required. Individual bargaining can settle most externality problems

when there is clear ownership of property rights, the number of people involved is small, and the costs of bargaining are minimal. When these conditions do not hold, then government action with direct controls or specific taxes may be necessary to solve the problem. You discover that it may even be possible for the government to create a **market** for externality rights, and that there is a rule for the optimal reduction of an externality.

Pollution is a prime example of a negative externality and it is the focus of a case study. There are many types of pollution, but their causes stem from the **law of conservation of matter and energy**. The production of goods and services uses resources that ultimately become waste (matter or energy) that our environment is not able to reabsorb. Over the years, the government has developed a number of antipollution policies. In this chapter you will learn about two national ones—the Superfund law of 1980 and the Clean Air Act of 1990. You will also discover how the market forces of supply and demand in the recycling market help to reduce some of the demands for the dumping of solid waste in landfills.

The third major type of failure that you will encounter in this chapter is information. You probably never thought about the role of information in the functioning of markets, but in this last section of the chapter you will discover how important information is to both buyers and sellers. For example, buyers need some assurance about the measurement standards or quality of products that they purchase, be it gasoline or medical care. The government may intervene in some markets to ensure that this information is made available.

Inadequate information in markets creates problems for sellers, too. In certain markets, such as insurance, sellers experience a **moral hazard problem** because buyers change their behavior and become less careful, and the change in behavior makes it more costly to sellers. There is also an **adverse selection** problem in the insurance market because those buyers most likely to benefit (higher-risk buyers) are more likely to purchase the insurance, and therefore this group imposes higher costs on sellers than if the riskers were more widely spread among the population. Actions of sellers to screen buyers means

that fewer people will be covered by insurance, and it creates a situation that may lead to the provision of social insurance by government. Government may also provide better information about workplace safety or enforce safety standards to address information problems in resource markets.

You should not finish this chapter with the sole thought that all market failures require government intervention and direct control. Some problems do require a specific government action, but other problems may be handled in a more efficient or optimal way through individual negotiations, through lawsuits or through the use of market incentives. What is important for you to understand is the range of solutions to different market and information failures, and the rationale for government intervention to correct them.

■ **CHECKLIST**

When you have studied this chapter you should be able to:

☐ Compare the characteristics of a public good with a private good.
☐ Calculate the demand for a public good when given tabular data.
☐ Explain how marginal costs and marginal benefits are reflected in the demand for or the supply of a public good.
☐ Identify on a graph where there is an overallocation, an underallocation, and an optimal allocation of a public good.
☐ Use benefit-cost analysis to determine the extent to which government should apply resources to a project or program when you are given the cost and benefit data.
☐ Define and give examples of positive and negative externalities (spillovers).
☐ State the conditions that are necessary for the Coase theorem and give an example of its use.
☐ Explain how liability rules and lawsuits are used to resolve externality problems.
☐ Identify two means used by government to achieve allocative efficiency when there are negative externalities.
☐ Determine the price a government agency should charge in a market for pollution rights when you are given the necessary data.
☐ Compare the advantages of a market for pollution rights to direct controls.
☐ Explain and illustrate with a graph a rule for determining the optimal reduction of a negative externality.
☐ Describe the dimensions of the pollution problem.
☐ Cite four major causes of the pollution problem.
☐ Discuss the purpose of the Superfund law of 1980.
☐ Identify five major provisions of the Clean Air Act of 1990.
☐ Explain how pollution rights are traded under the Clean Air Act.

☐ Describe the solid waste disposal problem and the reason for interest in recycling.
☐ Define the meaning of "information failures."
☐ Explain how inadequate information about sellers can cause market failures and give two examples of ways that the government resolves these problems.
☐ Describe how inadequate information about buyers can cause moral hazard, adverse selection, and workplace safety problems and give examples.
☐ Cite an example of a way that information difficulties are overcome without government intervention.

■ **CHAPTER OUTLINE**

1. The characteristics of a private good are that it is divisible and subject to the exclusion principle, where those who are unable to pay for the good or service are excluded from enjoying the benefits of the provision of the good or service; in contrast, a public (collective) good such as national defense is indivisible and not subject to exclusion—once it is provided for one person it is available for all.
   a. The demand for a public good is determined by summing the prices that people are willing to pay collectively for the last unit of the public good at each quantity demanded, whereas the demand for a private good is determined by summing the quantities demanded at each price.
   b. In the market for public goods:
   (1) The demand curve is downsloping because of the law of diminishing marginal utility; it reflects the monetary value of the perceived benefits of additional units that are equally available to people for joint consumption.
   (2) The supply curve is upsloping because of the law of diminishing returns; additional units supplied reflect increasing marginal costs.
   (3) The optimal allocation is determined by the intersection of the supply and demand curves:
   (*a*) if the marginal benefit exceeds the marginal cost, there is an underallocation of a public good;
   (*b*) but if the marginal benefit exceeds the marginal cost there will be an overallocation.
   (*c*) Only when the marginal benefits equal the marginal costs is there an optimal allocation of public goods.
   c. Benefit-cost analysis may be employed by government to determine whether it should employ resources for a project and to decide on the total quantity of resources it should devote to a project.
   (1) Additional resources should be devoted to a project only so long as the marginal benefit to society from using the additional resources for the project exceeds the marginal costs to society of the additional resources, or where the total benefits minus the total costs are at a maximum.

(2) Government encounters the problem of accurately measuring the benefits and the costs in this type of analysis.

2. Market failure can arise from externalities or spillovers, where a third party bears a portion of the cost associated with the production or consumption of a good or service. Negative externalities result in the overallocation of resources to a commodity and positive externalities lead to an underallocation of resources.

a. Individual bargaining can be used to correct negative externalities or to encourage positive externalities. The **Coase theorem** suggests that private negotiations rather than government intervention should be the course of action if there is clear ownership of the property, the number of people involved is small, and the costs of bargaining is minimal. When these conditions do not hold, however, it may be necessary for government intervention.

b. It is possible to resolve disputes that arise from externalities through the legal system. This system defines property rights and specifies liability rules that can be used for lawsuits to cover externality disputes. This method also has limitations because of expense, length of time to resolve the dispute, and the uncertainty of the outcomes.

c. When there is the potential for severe harm to common resources, such as air or water, and when the situation involves a large number of people, two types of government intervention may be necessary.
(1) Direct controls uses legislation to ban or to limit the activities that produce a negative externality. These actions reduce the supply of the products that create the negative externalities to levels that are allocatively efficient.
(2) Specific taxes are also applied to productive activity that create negative externalities. These taxes increase the cost of production, and thus decrease the supply to levels that are allocatively efficient.

d. Another solution has been to create a market for externality rights, or to internalize the spillover cost or benefit in a private market. For example, with a pollution problem in a region:
(1) The government (a pollution-control agency) might set the limit for the amount of pollution permitted, which means that the supply curve is perfectly inelastic (vertical) at some level of pollution;
(2) The demand curve would reflect the willingness of polluters to pay for the right to pollute at different prices for pollution rights;
(3) and the price for pollution rights would be determined by the intersection of the demand and supply curves.
(4) Given a fixed supply curve, an increase in demand, because of economic growth in the region, would increase the price of pollution rights.

e. In most cases, it is not allocatively efficient to eliminate completely the production of goods that create negative externalities. From society's perspective, the optimal reduction of a negative externality occurs where the marginal cost to society and the marginal benefit of reducing the externality are equal (**MB = MC**). Over time, there may be shifts in the marginal cost and marginal benefit curves that change the optimal level.

3. Pollution provides a prime example of a major negative externality for our industrial society.
a. The dimensions of the problem are extensive, and include air pollution, water pollution, toxic waste, solid-waste disposal, oil spills, and potential changes to the climate.
b. The causes of the pollution problem relate to the **law of conservation of matter and energy**. Matter used for production of goods and services ultimately gets transformed into waste (in the form of matter or energy) after it is consumed. The waste creates a problem if there is an imbalance between it and the capacity of the environment to reabsorb the waste. Population density, rising income, changing technology, and economic incentives are all factors contributing to the pollution problem.
c. Antipollution policy in the United States is complex.
(1) The **Superfund law of 1980** uses direct controls and specific taxes to correct the toxic waste problem.
(2) The **Clean Air Act of 1990** uses direct controls through uniform emission standards to limit the amount of air pollution. The act covers toxic chemicals, urban smog, motor vehicle emissions, ozone depletion, and acid rain. The act also permits some trading of pollution rights to reduce acid rain.
d. Solid waste is usually deposited in garbage dumps or it is incinerated. Dumps and incinerators, however, create negative externalities, and they are becoming increasingly expensive. The situation has created a market for recycled items to help reduce this pollution problem. Government can use either demand or supply incentives to encourage recycling as an alternative to dumping or incineration of solid waste.

4. Economic inefficiency from information failures can occur in markets.
a. When information about sellers is incomplete, inaccurate, or very costly, then there will be market failures. For example, in the market for gasoline, consumers need accurate information about the amount and quality of gasoline they purchase. In the market for medical service, it is important that consumers have some assurances about the credentials of physicians. These information failures are remedied by government through such actions as the establishment measurement standards, and by testing and licensing.

b. Inadequate information about buyers creates market failures.

(1) A market may produce less than the optimal amount of goods and services from society's perspective because of a moral hazard problem. This problem results when buyers alter their behavior and increase the costs of sellers. For example, the provision of insurance may cause the insured to be less cautious.

(2) There is also an adverse selection problem that occurs in many markets. In the case of insurance, the buyers most likely to need or benefit from insurance are the ones most likely to purchase it. These higher-risk buyers impose higher costs on sellers. Sellers then screen out the higher-risk buyers, but this action reduces the population covered by insurance in the private market. In some cases, government may establish a social insurance system that is designed to cover a much broader group of the population than would be covered by the private insurers, such as with social security.

(3) Market failures occur in resource markets when there is inadequate information for workers about the health hazards or safety of a workplace. Government can act to correct these problems by publishing health and safety information, or by forcing businesses to provide more information. The more typical approach to this problem has been the enforcement of standards for health and safety on the job.

c. Government does not always need to intervene in the private market to address information problems. Businesses can adopt policies to correct these problems, and some firms or other organizations can specialize in providing important market information for buyers or sellers.

■ **IMPORTANT TERMS**

Public good

Benefit-cost analysis

Marginal cost equals
marginal benefit rule

Positive or negative
externality (spillover)

Coase theorem

Market for externality
rights

Optimal amount of
externality reduction

Law of conservation of
matter and energy

Superfund law of 1980

Clean Air Act of 1990

Moral hazard problem

Adverse selection problem

■ **FILL-IN QUESTIONS**

1. A public good:

a. is one which is _____ and for which
the _____ principle does not apply; and

b. has a market demand curve that will either be

_____ or significantly _____
because people will not make voluntary payments for
public goods in the marketplace;

c. but, if you knew people's preferences for a public
good, you could determine the demand for it by adding

the _____ people collectively are willing
to pay for the last unit of the public good at each quantity demanded.

2. The demand curve for a public good slopes downward because of the law of diminishing marginal (returns,

utility) _____; the supply curve for a public
good is upsloping because of the law of diminishing mar-

ginal _____. The collective demand
curve is based on perceived marginal (benefits, costs)

_____ that are equally available to people
for joint consumption; the supply curve for a public good

reflects marginal _____.

3. The optimal quantity of a public good will be shown

by the _____ of the collective demand
curve and the supply curve for a public good, which means

that _____ equals _____.
When the perceived marginal benefit for a public good is
greater than the marginal cost, there will be an (overallo-

cation, underallocation) _____ of the public
good; but when the perceived marginal benefit is less than

the marginal cost, there will be an _____ of
the public good.

4. In applying benefit-cost analysis, government should
employ more resources in the production of public goods

if the marginal (costs, benefits) _____ from
the additional public goods exceed the marginal

_____ that result from having fewer private

goods. The _____ rule will determine
which plan from a benefit-cost analysis will result in the

(maximum, minimum) _____ net benefit to
society.

5. When government employs benefit-cost analysis, it

often finds it difficult to _____ the benefits
and costs of a program, which means that the analysis
can be difficult to apply.

6. One of the objectives of government is to correct for

externalities or _____ that result in a
cost or a benefit for an individual or a group that is a
third party to a market transaction. When negative

_____ are present there will be an (over-allocation, underallocation) _____ of resources going to the production of that good, whereas there will be an _____ of resources for the production of that good with positive _____ _____.

7. The _____ theorem suggests when there are negative or positive _____ in situations where the _____ of property is defined, the number of people involved is _____, and the costs of bargaining are _____, then government intervention (is, is not) _____ required.

8. This legal system is also important for settling externality disputes between individuals because settling it defines _____ rights and specifies _____ rules that can be used for lawsuits. This method has limitations because of the dollar _____, the length of time, and _____ of the result.

9. Government may intervene to resolve externality problems by using direct _____ in the form of legislation that restricts business activity. In other cases, the government may impose specific _____ or _____ charges.

10. One solution to a negative externality problem such as pollution is to create a _____ for externality rights.
   a. For example, in a region there might be a set amount of air pollution accepted, so the supply curve for the air pollution rights would be perfectly (elastic, inelastic) _____ _____.
   b. The demand curve for air pollution rights would be _____ sloping and would intersect the supply curve to determine the _____ for the right to pollute the air in that area.
   c. If the demand for air pollution rights increased over time, then _____ would rise but the quantity supplied would _____

11. Reducing negative externalities comes at a "_____" and therefore society must decide how much of a decrease it wants to "_____." The optimal reduction of a negative externality occurs where the society's marginal _____ is equal to society's marginal _____.

12. The pollution problem stems from the law of _____.
Matter used for production of goods and services ultimately gets transformed into _____, which is another form of matter or energy that the environment may not be able to re-_____. This pollution problem is the result of increases in population _____, rising _____, changes in _____, and the absence of economic _____ to refrain from polluting.

13. To correct a toxic waste problem, Congress passed the _____ law of 1980. The _____ Act of 1990 imposes uniform _____ standards to limit the amount of air pollution. The act also permits some _____ of pollution rights to reduce acid rain.

14. An alternative to the dumping or incineration of solid waste is _____. Government policies can be enacted to provide incentives on the _____-side or the _____-side of the market.

15. Markets can produce information failures when information about sellers is incomplete or obtaining the information is very _____. For example, in a market for gasoline, the government establishes _____ for measurement or quality. In the medical market, the government protects consumers by _____ physicians.

16. Inadequate information about buyers can lead to two problems. First, if a market situation arises where buyers alter their behavior and increase the cost to sellers, then a moral _____ problem has been created. Second, if buyers withhold information from sellers that would impose a large cost on sellers, then an adverse _____ problem has been created. The first problem occurs (at the same time, after) _____ a person makes a purchase, but the second problem occurs _____ the buyer makes a purchase.

17. Another example of information failure occurs in labor markets where there is incomplete or inadequate information about workplace _____. The government will

intervene in these situations to publish _____ or to enforce _____

18. Private businesses overcome some information problems about the reliability or quality through such actions as _____ for products, or the _____ of businesses that makes them more uniform. Some businesses and organizations also collect and _____ product information that is useful for buyers. Despite these actions, there may still be need for government actions to correct information problems and to promote an _____ allocation of society's scarce resources.

■ PROBLEMS AND PROJECTS

1. Data on two individuals' preferences for a public good are reflected in the table below. P_1 and P_2 represent the prices individuals 1 and 2, the only two people in the society, are willing to pay for each quantity.

Quantity	P_1	P_2
1	$6	$6
2	5	5
3	4	4
4	3	3
5	2	2
6	1	1

a. Complete the table below showing the collective demand for the public good in this society.

Q_d	Price	Q_s
1	$_____	7
2	_____	6
3	_____	5
4	_____	4
5	_____	3
6	_____	2

b. Given the supply schedule for this public good as shown by the Q_s column, the optimal quantity of this public good is _____ units and the optimal price is $_____

c. When 3 units of this public good are produced, the perceived marginal benefit is $_____ and the marginal cost is $_____; there will be an (overallocation, underallocation) _____ of resources to this public good.

d. When 6 units of this public good are produced, the perceived marginal benefit is $_____ and the marginal cost is $_____; there is an (underallocation, overallocation) _____ of resources to this public good.

2. Imagine that a state government is considering the construction of a new highway to link its two largest cities. Its estimate of the total costs and the total benefits of building 2, 4, 6, and 8 lane highways between the two cities are shown in the table at the bottom of the page. (All figures are in millions of dollars.)

a. Compute the marginal cost and the marginal benefit of the 2, 4, 6, and 8 lane highways.

b. Will it benefit the state to allocate resources to construct a highway? _____

c. If the state builds a highway:

(1) It should be a _____ lane highway.

(2) The total cost will be $_____

(3) The total benefit will be $_____

(4) The **net** benefit to the state will be $_____

3. Assume the atmosphere of Cuyahoga County, Ohio (the Cleveland metropolitan area), is able to reabsorb 1500 tons of pollutants per year. The schedule at the top of the next page shows the price polluters would be willing to pay for the right to dispose of 1 ton of pollutants per year and the total quantity of pollutants they would wish to dispose of at each price.

a. If there were no emission fee, polluters would put _____ tons of pollutants in the air each year; and this quantity of pollutants would exceed the

Project	Total cost	Marginal cost	Total benefit	Marginal benefit
No highway	$ 0		$ 0	
2 lane highway	500	$_____	650	$_____
4 lane highway	680	_____	750	_____
6 lane highway	760	_____	800	_____
8 lane highway	860	_____	825	_____

Price (per ton of pollutant rights)	Total quantity of pollutant rights demanded (tons)
$ 0	4,000
1,000	3,500
2,000	3,000
3,000	2,500
4,000	2,000
5,000	1,500
6,000	1,000
7,000	500

ability of nature to reabsorb them by _____ tons.

b. To reduce pollution to the capacity of the atmosphere to recycle pollutants, an emission fee of

$_____ per ton should be set.

c. Were this emission fee set, the total emission fees

set would be $_____

d. Were the quantity of pollution rights demanded at each price to increase by 500 tons, the emission fee

could be increased by $_____ and total

emission fees collected would increase by $_____

■ **SELF-TEST**

Circle the T if the statement is true; the F if it is false.

1. The exclusion principle applies to public goods but it does not apply to private goods.   **T   F**

2. When determining the demand for a public good you add the prices people are willing to pay collectively for the last unit of the public good at each quantity demanded.
                                                                 T   F

3. When the marginal benefit of a public good exceeds the marginal cost there will be an overallocation of resources to that public good use.   **T   F**

4. The optimal allocation of a public good is determined by the rule that marginal cost (MC) equals marginal revenue (MR).   **T   F**

5. Reducing government spending is the same as economy in government.   **T   F**

6. In practice is it usually quite simple to estimate the costs and benefits of a project financed by government.
                                                                 T   F

7. There is an overallocation of resources to the production of a commodity when negative externalities are present.   **T   F**

8. The Coase theorem suggests that government inter-

vention is required whenever there are negative or positive externalities.   **T   F**

9. Lawsuits and liability rules create externality problems instead of helping to resolve them.   **T   F**

10. Taxes that are imposed on businesses which create an externality will lower the marginal cost of production and increase supply.   **T   F**

11. One solution to the negative externalities caused by pollution is to create a market for pollution rights where the social costs of pollution are turned into private costs.
                                                                 T   F

12. In the market for pollution rights, if a government agency sets a fixed level for pollution, the supply curve of pollution rights will be perfectly elastic.   **T   F**

13. If a society has marginal costs for pollution abatement of $10 and the marginal benefit of pollution abatement is $8, then to achieve an optimal amount of the pollution it should increase the amount of pollution abatement.
                                                                 T   F

14. Pollution is caused almost exclusively by profit-seeking business firms.   **T   F**

15. The Superfund law of 1980 uses direct controls and specific taxes to address the problem of toxic waste.
                                                                 T   F

16. The Clean Air Act of 1990 permits the trading of emission credits between electric utilities and the trading of pollution rights between polluters.   **T   F**

17. If the government provides a subsidy to producers of recycled paper products, then the demand for recycled paper **products** should increase.   **T   F**

18. The inspection of meat products by the Federal government for quality is justified on the grounds that it reduces the costs of obtaining information in the market for meat.   **T   F**

19. If the provision of government health insurance encourages people to take more health risks, then it has created a moral hazard.   **T   F**

20. Adverse selection problems primarily result when the government begins enforcing standards for safety in the workplace.   **T   F**

Circle the letter that corresponds to the best answer.

1. How do public goods differ from private goods? Public goods:
   (a) are divisible
   (b) are subject to the exclusion principle
   (c) are divisible and subject to the exclusion principle
   (d) are **not** divisible and **not** subject to the exclusion principle

Answer the next four questions (2, 3, 4, and 5) on the basis of the following information for a public good. P₁ and P₂ represent the prices individuals 1 and 2, the only two people in the society, are willing to pay for each quantity of a public good. Qₛ represents the supply curve for the public good in the society.

Quantity	P_1	P_2	Q_s
0	$5	$6	6
1	4	5	5
2	3	4	4
3	2	3	3
4	1	2	2
5	0	1	1
6	0	0	0

2. This society is willing to pay what amount for the third unit of the public good?
  (a) $5
  (b) $6
  (c) $7
  (d) $8

3. This society is willing to pay what amount for the first unit of the public good?
  (a) $11
  (b) $10
  (c) $9
  (d) $8

4. Given the supply curve Q_s, the optimal price and quantity of the public good in this society will be:
  (a) $9 and 5 units
  (b) $5 and 3 units
  (c) $5 and 4 units
  (d) $3 and 2 units

5. If this good were a private good instead of a public good, the total quantity demanded at the $4 price would be:
  (a) 3 units
  (b) 4 units
  (c) 5 units
  (d) 6 units

Answer the next three questions (6, 7, and 8) for a public good on the basis of the graph at the top of the next column.

6. Where the marginal benefits equal the collective marginal costs is represented by point:
  (a) *b*
  (b) *c*
  (c) *d*
  (d) *e*

7. Which line segment would indicate the amount by which the marginal benefit of this public good is less than the marginal cost?
  (a) *ab*
  (b) *bc*

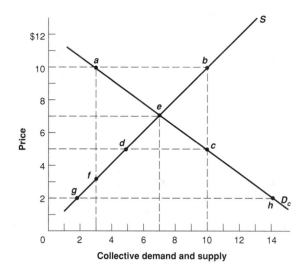

Collective demand and supply

  (c) *fa*
  (d) *gh*

8. If 3 units of this public good are produced there will be an:
  (a) overallocation of resources to this public good because the marginal cost of $10 is greater than the marginal benefit of $3
  (b) overallocation of resources to this public good because the marginal cost of $10 is greater than the marginal benefit of $5
  (c) underallocation of resources to this public good because the marginal benefit of $10 is greater than the marginal cost of $5
  (d) underallocation of resources to this public good because the marginal benefit of $10 is greater than the marginal benefit of $3

9. Assume that a government is considering a new anti-pollution program and it may choose to include in this program any number of four different projects. The marginal cost and the marginal benefits of each of the four projects are given below. What total amount should this government spend on the antipollution program?
  (a) $2 million
  (b) $7 million
  (c) $17 million
  (d) $37 million

Project	Marginal cost	Marginal benefit
# 1	$ 2 million	$ 5 million
# 2	5 million	7 million
# 3	10 million	9 million
# 4	20 million	15 million

10. One condition for the Coase theorem to hold is that there be:
  (a) clear ownership of the property rights
  (b) a large number of people involved in the dispute

(c) active government intervention to solve the externality problem

(d) a sizeable cost for bargaining to settle the dispute between the private parties

11. Which of the following would be the most effective strategy for addressing a problem such as acid rain which stems from the pollution of coal-burning electric utilities?

(a) private negotiations between property owners and the utilities

(b) lawsuits filed against the utilities by property owners

(c) asking consumers to reduce electricity consumption

(d) government taxes on utility emissions

12. If government were to sell pollution rights, an increase in the demand for pollution rights will:

(a) increase both the quantity of pollutants discharged and the market price of pollution rights

(b) increase the quantity discharged and have no effect on the market price

(c) have no effect on the quantity discharged and increase the market price

(d) have no effect on either the quantity discharged or the market price

Use the following table to answer the next three questions (13, 14, and 15). The data in the table show the marginal costs and marginal benefits to a city for five different levels of pollution abatement.

Quantity of pollution abatement	Marginal cost	Marginal benefit
500 tons	$500,000	$100,000
400 tons	300,000	150,000
300 tons	200,000	200,000
200 tons	100,000	300,000
100 tons	50,000	400,000
0 tons	25,000	800,000

13. If the city seeks an optimal reduction of the externality, then it will select how many tons of pollution abatement?

(a) 0

(b) 300

(c) 400

(d) 500

14. If the marginal benefit of pollution abatement increased by $150,000 at each level because of the community's desire to attract more profitable and cleaner industry, then the optimal level of pollution abatement in tons would be:

(a) 200

(b) 300

(c) 400

(d) 500

15. What would cause the optimal level of pollution abatement to be 200 tons?

(a) technological improvement in production that decreases marginal costs by $150,000 at each level

(b) an increase in the health risk from this pollution that increases marginal benefits by $200,000 at each level

(c) the need to replace old pollution monitoring equipment with new equipment that increases marginal costs by $200,000 at each level

(d) reduction in the public demand for pollution control that decreases marginal benefits by $100,000 at each level

16. Which of the following has **not** contributed to the pollution problem in the United States?

(a) increasing population density

(b) rising prices for gasoline and oil

(c) an improved standard of living

(d) more use of plastic and aluminum containers

17. Results from the Superfund law of 1980 indicate that it:

(a) reduced major sources of pollution by 20%, but the fund is now exhausted and reauthorization is uncertain

(b) raised $10 billion from the chemical industry to treat toxic waste, but progress is slow and legal negotiations over dump sites drain funds

(c) made recycling the most economical method for handling waste in many communities, but citizen compliance is limited and depends on economic incentives

(d) established uniform emission standards that are being paid for out of the fund, but legal action is sometimes necessary to get cooperation from companies

18. The acid-rain provisions of the Clean Air Act of 1990:

(a) permit the exchange of pollution rights within firms and between firms in an area

(b) set stricter limits on the discharge of chlorofluorocarbons (CFCs) for the 1990s

(c) fund research on applications of the law of conservation of matter and energy

(d) force companies to install "maximum achievable control technologies" by the year 2000

19. Which of the following would tend to increase the demand for recycled paper?

(a) an increase in the price of regular paper

(b) an increase in taxes on all paper production

(c) a decrease in interest in protecting the environment

(d) a decrease in subsidies for all paper production

20. If Congress adopted an increase in government insurance on bank deposits, this action would create a moral hazard problem because it may:

(a) lead to careful screening of depositors and the source of their funds

(b) restrict the amount of deposits made by bank customers

(c) encourage bank officers to make riskier loans

(d) reduce bank investments in real estate

■ DISCUSSION QUESTIONS

1. What are the basic characteristics of public goods? How do public goods differ from private goods? Contrast how you construct the demand curve for a public good with the procedure for constructing the demand curve for a private good using individual demand schedules.

2. Explain the relationship between the marginal cost and benefit of a public good when there is an underallocation, an overallocation, and an optimal allocation of resources for the provision of the public good.

3. Describe benefit-cost analysis and state the rules used to make decisions from a marginal and a total perspective. What is the major problem encountered when benefit-cost analysis is utilized by government?

4. What are externalities and spillovers? Give examples of positive externalities and negative externalities.

5. Under what conditions might it be worthwhile for the government to intervene or not to intervene to settle a spillover problem? Should the government intervene in an externality dispute between two property owners over the use of one party's land? Should government intervene in the case of acid rain?

6. How do lawsuits and liability rules resolve externality problems? What type of actions would the government take to reduce externalities? How would these actions be justified?

7. How do you create a market for externality rights in the case of pollution? What are some advantages and limitations of this approach to the pollution problem?

8. What rule can society use to determine the optimal level of pollution abatement? What are the problems with this approach?

9. Outline the dimensions of the pollution problem in the United States. Why has this problem developed? What is the specific cause of the pollution problem?

10. Discuss the major features of the Superfund law of 1980 and the Clean Air Act of 1990. What features of a market for externalities are built into the Clean Air Act?

11. Why is solid waste disposal of national concern? How does recycling serve as a partial alternative to it? How does a market for recyclable items work?

12. Describe how inadequate information about sellers creates market problems for buyers. Give examples.

13. Explain what is meant by a "moral hazard problem" and describe how it affects sellers. What are some examples of the application of this problem?

14. How can the market for insurance result in an adverse selection problem? What actions might government take to correct this information problem?

15. In what way does workplace safety become an information problem? How might this problem be resolved by government or by businesses?

■ ANSWERS

Chapter 31 Government and Market Failure: Public Goods, the Environment, and Information Problems

FILL-IN QUESTIONS

1. *a.* indivisible, exclusion; *b.* nonexistent, understated; *c.* prices

2. utility, returns, benefits, costs

3. intersection, marginal benefit, marginal cost (either order); underallocation, overallocation

4. benefits, costs, marginal benefit–marginal cost, maximum

5. measure

6. spillovers, externalities (spillovers), overallocation, underallocation, externalities

7. Coase, externalities (spillovers), ownership, small, negligible (minor), is not

8. property, liability, cost, uncertainty

9. controls, taxes, emissions

10. market, *a.* inelastic; *b.* down, price; *c.* price, remain constant (stays the same)

11. price, buy, benefit, cost (either order for last two)

12. conservation of matter and energy, waste, absorb, density, incomes, technology, incentives

13. Superfund, Clean Air, emission, trading

14. recycling, demand, supply (either order for last two)

15. costly, standards, licensing

16. hazard, selection, after, at the same time

17. safety, information, standards

18. warranties, franchising, publish, efficient

PROBLEMS AND PROJECTS

1. *a.* $12, 10, 8, 6, 4, 2; *b.* 4, 6; *c.* 8, 4, underallocation; *d.* 2, 10, overallocation

2. *a.* marginal cost: $500, $180, $80, $100; marginal benefit: $650, $100, $50, $25; *b.* yes; *c.* (1) 2, (2) $500, (3) $650, (4) $150

3. *a.* 4,000, 2,500; *b.* 5,000; *c.* 7,500,000; *d.* 1,000, 1,500,000

SELF-TEST

1. F, p. 580
2. T, pp.580–581
3. F, p. 581
4. F, p. 581
5. F, p. 582
6. F, p. 583
7. T, p. 583
8. F, p. 583
9. F, p. 584
10. F, p. 585

11. T, p. 585
12. F, p. 585
13. F, p. 587
14. F, p. 589
15. T, p. 589
16. T, p. 590
17. F, p. 592
18. T, p. 593
19. T, p. 594
20. F, p. 594

1. *d*, p. 580
2. *a*, pp. 580–581
3. *c*, pp. 580–581
4. *b*, p. 581
5. *a*, p. 580
6. *d*, p. 582
7. *b*, p. 582
8. *d*, p. 582
9. *b*, p. 582
10. *a*, p. 583

11. *d*, p. 584
12. *c*, p. 586
13. *b*, p. 587
14. *c*, p. 587
15. *c*, p. 587
16. *b*, p. 588
17. *b*, p. 589
18. *a*, p. 590
19. *a*, p. 591
20. *c*, p. 594

DISCUSSION QUESTIONS

1. p. 580
2. pp. 581–582
3. pp. 580–583
4. p. 583
5. pp. 583–584
6. pp. 584–585
7. pp. 585–586
8. pp. 586–587

9. pp. 588–589
10. pp. 589–590
11. pp. 590–592
12. p. 593
13. p. 594
14. pp. 594–595
15. p. 595

Public Choice Theory and Taxation

Although both Chapters 31 and 32 analyze the role of government in the economy, the two chapters look at government from an opposite perspective. Chapter 31 discussed market failure issues and what actions government takes to correct these market problems. Chapter 32 now examines government failure, or why government makes inefficient use of the scarce resources. For this explanation, you will first be introduced to **public choice theory**, or the economic analysis of public decision making. Later in the chapter you will learn more about **public finance**, which covers such topics as the principles of taxation and the economic effects of specific taxes.

Many public decisions are made by majority voting, but this decision-making procedure may distort the true preferences of society. In the first section of the chapter you will find out how majority voting may lead to inefficient outcomes in the provision of public goods. In some choices, the benefits of a public good are greater than the costs, but the majority votes against it. In other choices, the benefits outweigh the costs, but the provision of the public good is supported by the majority vote. Although actions by interest groups and the use of logrolling may tend to reduce inefficiencies created by majority rule, the final result depends on the circumstances of the decision.

There is also a paradox from majority voting that you should note. Depending on how a vote or election is arranged, it is possible for majority rule to produce choices that are inconsistent with the ranking of preferences among voters. You should spend time working through the example in the textbook so you understand how opposing outcomes can result from majority rule. You should also learn why the median voters strongly influence the result of a vote or an election when there is majority rule. In fact, the median-voter model is very useful for explaining why the middle position on issues is often adopted in public decisions.

The second section of Chapter 32 discusses other reasons for inefficiencies by government. Here you will learn that: (1) special-interest effects and rent-seeking behavior impair public decisions; (2) politicians often have a strong incentive to adopt an economic policy that has clear benefits to voters, but hidden or uncertain costs; (3) public choice is more limited and less flexible than private choice

because it entails voting for or accepting a "bundle" of programs, some good and some bad; and (4) bureaucratic inefficiencies in the public sector arise from the lack of the economic incentives and competitive pressures found in the private sector.

Chapter 32 then switches from public choice theory to public finance for further insights about government, and, in particular, about taxation. In the third section of the chapter you learn the economic principles used in levying taxes. You also learn about the regressive, progressive, and proportional classifications for taxes, and how the major taxes of the United States fit into this classification scheme.

The incidence and efficiency loss of a tax are described in the fourth section of the chapter. Incidence means "who ends up paying the tax." As you will discover, the elasticities of demand and of supply determine how much of the tax will be paid by buyers and how much of it will be paid by sellers. No matter who pays the tax, however, there is an efficiency loss to society from the tax, the size of which is also affected by the elasticities of demand and of supply. With this knowledge, you are now ready to study the probable incidence of five taxes—personal income, corporate income, sales, excise, and property—that are used to raise most of the tax revenue for government in the United States.

The fifth and sixth sections of the chapter discuss the American tax structure and explore the question of whether an increase in the size of the role of government reduces or expands the freedoms of individuals. The authors present the conservative case of those who argue that expanded government reduces personal freedom and the liberal case of those who contend that it may create individual freedom.

■ **CHECKLIST**

When you have studied this chapter you should be able to:

☐ Explain the purpose of public choice theory and the topics it covers.

□ Illustrate how majority voting procedures can produce inefficient outcomes either when the vote is "yes" or the vote is "no."

□ Describe how interest groups and political logrolling affect the efficiency of outcomes from voting.

□ Give an example of the paradox of voting.

□ Describe the median-voter model, its applicability to the real world, and two implications of the model.

□ Explain the meaning of the phrase "public sector failure" and cite examples.

□ Give an example of a special-interest effect and an example of rent-seeking behavior.

□ Describe the economic problem that arises when there are clear benefits and hidden costs to a political decision.

□ Compare the type of choices made by consumers in the private market with the type of choices made by citizens.

□ Contrast the incentives for economic efficiency in private business with those found in the public agencies and bureaucracies.

□ Distinguish between the ability-to-pay principle of taxation and the benefits-received principle of taxation.

□ Determine whether a tax is regressive, progressive, or proportional when you are given the necessary data.

□ Describe the progressivity, regressivity, and proportionality of the five major kinds of taxes used in the United States.

□ Illustrate with the use of a supply and demand graph how the price elasticity of demand and supply affect tax incidence.

□ Describe the efficiency loss of a tax using a supply and demand graph.

□ Explain the effects of price elasticity of demand or supply on the efficiency loss of a tax.

□ Evaluate the probable incidence of the personal income, corporate income, sales and excise, and property taxes.

□ Describe recent estimates of the tax burden in the American economy, the progressivity of the tax structure, and the effect of changes in the tax system on the distribution of income.

□ Explain two major tax issues that have been discussed in recent years.

□ Present the case for and present the case against the proposition that an expanded public sector reduces personal freedom.

■ **IMPORTANT TERMS**

Public choice theory	**Public sector failure**
Public finance	**Special-interest effect**
Logrolling	**Rent-seeking behavior**
Paradox of voting	**Benefits-received principle**
Median-voter model	**Ability-to-pay principle**

Average tax rate	Property tax
Progressive tax	Elasticity
Regressive tax	Tax incidence
Proportional tax	Excess burden of a tax
Personal income tax	Tax Reform Act (TRA) of 1986
Sales tax	
Excise tax	Value-added tax (VAT)
Corporate income tax	Fallacy of limited decisions
Payroll tax	

■ **CHAPTER OUTLINE**

1. Critics of the government argue that it has failed to find solutions for many problems of society and that it is very inefficient in its use of society's scarce resources. This chapter first analyzes economic decisions made by government from a *public choice* perspective, and then turns to the issue of *public finance*, and examines the economics of taxation.

2. Most decisions about government activity are made collectively through majority voting, but the procedure is not without problems:

a. Voting outcomes may be economically inefficient in cases where voters reject a public good whose total benefits exceed total costs, or fail to reject a public good whose total costs are greater than the total benefits. These inefficiencies can be resolved sometimes by:

(1) the formation of special interest groups that work to overcome inefficient outcomes,

(2) or, through the use of logrolling, where votes are traded to secure a favorable and efficient decision;

(3) but logrolling can also lead to inefficient decisions.

b. The paradox of voting suggests that the public may not be able to make consistent choices that reflect its preferences.

c. Based on the median-voter model it is suggested that the person or groups holding the middle position on an issue will likely determine the outcome from a majority rule election. Public decisions tend to reflect the median view.

3. Public choice theory suggests that the public sector has failed because the process it uses to make decisions is inherently weak and results in an economically inefficient allocation of resources.

a. The weakness of the decision-making process in the public sector and the resulting inefficient allocation of resources is often the result of pressures exerted on Congress and the bureaucracy by special interests and may be fostered by a system which might encourage rent-seeking behavior, whereby wealth is transferred to one group at the expense of another group or to society as a whole.

b. Those seeking election to public office frequently favor (oppose) programs whose benefits (costs) are clear and immediate and whose costs (benefits) are uncertain and deferred, even when the benefits are less (greater) than the costs.

c. When the citizen must vote for candidates who represent different but complete programs, the voter is unable to select those parts of a program which he or she favors and to reject the other parts of the program.

d. It is argued that the public sector (unlike the private sector) is inefficient because those employed there are offered no incentive to be efficient; and because there is no way to measure efficiency in the public sector.

e. Just as the private or market sector of the economy does not allocate resources perfectly, the public sector does not perform its functions perfectly; and the imperfections of both sectors make it difficult to determine which sector will provide a particular good or service more efficiently.

4. The financing of public goods and services through taxation also raises an important question about how the tax burden is allocated among people.

a. The benefits-received principle and the ability-to-pay principle are widely employed to determine how the tax bill should be apportioned among the economy's citizens.

(1) The benefits-received principle suggests that those people who benefit most from public goods should pay for them.

(2) The ability-to-pay principle states that taxes for the support of public goods should be tied to the income and wealth of people, or their ability to pay.

b. Taxes can be classified as progressive, regressive, or proportional according to the way in which the average tax *rate* changes as incomes change.

(1) The average tax rate increases as income increases with a progressive tax, it decreases as income increases with a regressive tax, and it remains the same as income increases with a proportional tax.

(2) In the United States, the personal income tax tends to be mildly progressive, the corporate income tax is proportional, and the payroll and property taxes are regressive.

5. Tax incidence and the efficiency loss of a tax are also important in discussion of public finance.

a. The price elasticities of demand and supply determine the incidence of a sales or excise tax.

(1) The imposition of such a tax on a commodity decreases the supply of the commodity and increases its price. The amount of the price increase is the portion of the tax paid by the buyer; the seller pays the rest.

(2) The price elasticities of demand and supply affect the portions paid by buyers and sellers: the more elastic (inelastic) the demand for the commodity, the greater (smaller) is the portion paid by the seller; the more elas-

tic (inelastic) the supply of the commodity, the greater (smaller) is the portion paid by the buyer.

b. There is an efficiency loss from taxation. This loss occurs because there is a reduction in output, despite the fact that the marginal benefits of that output are greater than the marginal cost. Thus, the consumption and production of the taxed commodity has been reduced below the optimal level by the tax.

(1) The degree of the efficiency loss of a sales or an excise tax depends on the elasticities of supply and demand: other things equal, the greater the elasticity of supply and demand, the greater the efficiency loss of a sales or an excise tax; consequently, the total tax burden to society may not be equal even though two taxes produce equal tax revenue.

c. A tax levied upon one person or group of persons may be shifted partially or completely to another person or group; and to the extent that a tax can be shifted or passed on through lower prices paid or higher prices received, its incidence is passed on. The incidence of the four major types of taxes is only probable and is not known for certain.

d. Because some taxes levied in the American economy and progressive and some are regressive it appears that the American tax system is only slightly progressive, has very little effect on the distribution of income in the United States, and has become less progressive over the past 20 years; but estimates of the progressivity of the tax system depend on the assumed incidence of the various taxes; and the transfer payments made by governments do reduce income inequality in the United States.

6. In recent years two tax-related issues have been debated in the United States.

a. How to "reindustrialize" the American economy by significantly increasing spending for modern machinery is the first of these issues; and it has been suggested that the corporate income tax be reduced and a *value-added tax* on consumer goods be levied.

b. Whether higher tax rates or new taxes are required to reduce large and persistent Federal budget deficits is the second tax-related issue.

7. The nature and amount of government activity and the extent of individual freedom may be related to each other.

a. Conservatives argue that the cost of government entails not only the economic cost from a growing public sector, but also a cost in terms of reduced economic freedom for the individual because government now makes more of the decisions over economic activity.

b. Liberals counter that the conservative position is subject to the fallacy of limited decisions. If government activity expands, that does not necessarily mean that there is less private decision making because the range of choices can be expanded by increased governmental activity.

■ FILL-IN QUESTIONS

1. The economic analysis of government decisions and the economic problems created by the public sector are topics studied under the theory of public (finance, choice)

_____, while the study of public spending and tax-

ation would be the subject of public _____

2. Many collective decisions are made on the basis of majority voting, which has two problems:

    a. This system of voting leads to economic

_____, where there might be an

_____ or a _____ de-
voted to a particular public good; but the problem might

be resolved through the influence of _____

groups or possibly through _____;

    b. the other problem is the _____,
a situation where the public may not be able to rank its
preferences with consistency.

3. There are also insights into majority voting based on

the _____ model, where the person holding

the _____ position is likely to determine the
outcome from an election.

4. When governments use resources to attempt to solve
social problems and the employment of these resources
does not result in solutions to these problems there has

been _____ sector _____

5. Four possible reasons for inefficiency in the public
sector are:

    a. that government instead of promoting the general
interests (or welfare) of its citizens may promote the

_____ interest of small groups in the

economy and may promote _____
behavior;

    b. that the benefits from a program or project are often

(clear, hidden) _____ and its costs are

frequently _____;

    c. that individual voters are unable to _____

_____ the particular quantities of each
public good and service they wish the public sector to
provide;

    d. that there are weak _____
to be efficient in the public sector and no way to

_____ the efficiency of the public sector.

6. Despite the recognition of inefficiency in the public
sector:

    a. It should be recognized that there is also ineffi-

ciency in the _____ of the economy;

    b. the institutions employed in both sectors to allocate

resources are _____

    c. It is, therefore, difficult to determine to which sector
the production of a particular good or service should be

_____

7. The two philosophies of apportioning the tax burden
which are most evident in the American economy are the

_____ principle and the

_____ principle.

8. As income increases: if a tax is proportional the aver-

age tax rate _____; if it is progressive the

average rate _____; and if it is regressive

the average rate _____

9. Indicate in the space to the right of each of the following taxes whether that tax (as applied in the United States)
is regressive (R) or progressive (P) or whether it is uncertain (U) which it is.

    a. Personal income tax   _____

    b. Sales tax   _____

    c. Payroll tax   _____

    d. Property tax   _____

    e. Corporation income tax   _____

10. When an excise tax is levied on a commodity the
amount of the tax borne by buyers of the commodity is

equal to the amount the _____ of the com-
modity rises as a result of the tax. The incidence of such
a tax depends on the price elasticity of demand and of
supply.

    a. The buyer's portion of the tax is larger the (more,

less) _____ elastic the demand and the

_____ elastic the supply.

    b. The seller's portion of the tax is larger the

_____ elastic the demand and the _____
elastic the supply.

11. When an excise tax reduces the consumption and
production of the taxed product below their allocatively ef-

ficient levels, there is an _____ of the
tax. Other things equal, the greater the elasticity of supply

and demand, the (greater, less) _____ the _____ of the tax.

12. What is the probable incidence of each of the following taxes?

   a. Personal income tax: _____

   b. Sales and excise tax: _____

   c. Corporate income tax: _____

   d. Property tax: _____

_____

13. The American tax structure is mildly (regressive, progressive) _____

   a. As a result it has a (small, great) _____ effect on the distribution of income in the United States.

   b. But these conclusions depend on the assumed _____ of the various taxes used in the American economy.

   c. Over the last 20 years the American tax structure has become (more, less) _____ progressive.

   d. Income inequality in the United States is, however, reduced by the system of _____ payments made by governments.

14. The Tax Reform Act of 1986 (increased, decreased) _____ the number of tax brackets, (raised, lowered) _____ tax rates, and (narrowed, broadened) _____ the tax base of the Federal personal income tax.

15. In recent years, two major issues related to taxes have been:

   a. reindustrializing the U.S. economy and increasing the _____ of American workers.

   (1) This would require that consumption be (increased, decreased) _____ and investment be _____

   (2) This might be accomplished by lowering the (personal, corporate) _____ income tax and establishing a _____ tax on consumption;

   b. whether there should be (higher, lower) _____ tax rates or new taxes to contain large and persistent Federal budget deficits. One option is to introduce _____; the other option is to increase the progressivity of the personal _____

16. Many conservatives argue that a larger public sector also diminishes _____.
Liberals counter that to believe that more governmental activity necessarily decreases private decision-making and economic activity is an example of the fallacy of

_____

■ PROBLEMS AND PROJECTS

1. In the table below are the demand and supply schedules for copra in the New Hebrides Islands.

Quantity demanded (pounds)	Price (per pound)	Before-tax quantity supplied (pounds)	After-tax quantity supplied (pounds)
150	$4.60	900	_____
200	4.40	800	_____
250	4.20	700	_____
300	4.00	600	_____
350	3.80	500	_____
400	3.60	400	_____
450	3.40	300	0
500	3.20	200	0
550	3.00	100	0

a. Before a tax is imposed on copra, its equilibrium price is $_____

b. The government of New Hebrides now imposes an excise tax of $.60 per pound on copra. Complete the after-tax supply schedule in the right-hand column of the table.

c. After the imposition of the tax, the equilibrium price of copra is $_____

d. Of the $.60 tax, the amount borne by

(1) the buyer is $_____ or _____%

(2) the seller is $_____ or _____%

2. On the graph below draw a perfectly elastic demand curve and a normal upsloping supply curve for a commodity. Now impose an excise tax on the commodity, and draw the new supply curve that would result.

0

a. As a consequence of the tax, the price of the commodity has _____

b. It can be concluded that when demand is perfectly elastic, the buyer bears _____ of the tax and the seller bears _____ of the tax.

c. Thus the *more* elastic, the demand, the _____ _____ is the portion of the tax borne by the buyer and the _____ is the portion borne by the seller.

d. But the *less* elastic the demand, the _____ _____ is the portion borne by the buyer and

the _____ is the portion borne by the seller.

3. On the graph below draw a perfectly elastic supply curve and a normal downsloping demand curve. Impose an excise tax on the commodity and draw the new supply curve.

0

a. As a result of the tax, the price of the commodity has _____

b. From this it can be concluded that when supply is perfectly elastic, the buyer bears _____ of the tax and the seller bears _____ of the tax.

c. Thus the *more* elastic the supply, the _____ _____ is the portion of the tax borne by the buyer and the _____ is the portion borne by the seller.

d. But the *less* elastic the supply, the _____ _____ is the portion borne by the buyer and the _____ is the portion borne by the seller.

4. In the table at the top of the next page are five levels of taxable income and the amount that would be paid at each of the five levels under three tax laws: A, B, and C. Compute for each of the three tax laws the *average* rate of taxation at each of the four remaining income levels and indicate whether the tax is regressive, proportional, progressive, or some combination thereof.

Income	Tax A		Tax B		Tax C	
	Tax paid	Av. tax rate %	Tax paid	Av. tax rate %	Tax paid	Av. tax rate %
$ 1,500	45.00	3 %	30.00	2 %	135.00	9 %
3,000	90.00	_____	90.00	_____	240.00	_____
5,000	150.00	_____	150.00	_____	350.00	_____
7,500	225.00	_____	187.50	_____	450.00	_____
10,000	300.00	_____	200.00	_____	500.00	_____
Type of tax:	_____		_____		_____	

5. Assume a state government levies a 4% sales tax on all consumption expenditures. Consumption expenditures at six income levels are shown in the table below.

Income	Consumption expenditures	Sales tax paid	Average tax rate, %
$35,000	$5,000	$200	4.0
6,000	5,800	232	3.9
7,000	6,600	_____	_____
8,000	7,400	_____	_____
9,000	8,200	_____	_____
10,000	9,000	_____	_____

a. Compute the sales tax paid at the next four incomes.
b. Compute the average tax rate at these incomes.
c. Using income as the tax base, the sales tax is a

_____ tax.

■ **SELF-TEST**

Circle the T if the statement is true; the F if it is false.

1. Majority voting may produce outcomes that are economically inefficient because it fails to take into account the strength of preferences of the individual voter. **T F**

2. Logrolling will always diminish economic efficiency in government. **T F**

3. The paradox of voting is that majority voting will result in consistent choices that reflect the preferences of the public. **T F**

4. The proposition that the person holding the middle position on an issue will likely determine the outcome of an election is suggested by the median-voter model. **T F**

5. There is a failure in the public sector whenever a governmental program or activity has been expanded to the level at which the marginal social cost exceeds the marginal social benefit. **T F**

6. The special-interests effect, it is argued by those concerned with public choice theory, tends to reduce public sector failures because the pressures exerted on government by one special-interest group are offset by the pressures brought to bear by other special-interest groups. **T F**

7. When the costs of programs are hidden and the benefits are clear vote-seeking politicians tend to reject economically justifiable programs. **T F**

8. The limited choice of citizens refers to the inability of individual voters to select the precise bundle of social goods and services that best satisfies the citizen's wants when he or she must vote for a candidate and the candidate's entire program. **T F**

9. The chief difficulty in applying the benefits-received principle of taxation is determining who receives the benefit of many of the goods and services which government supplies. **T F**

10. The state and Federal taxes on gasoline are good examples of taxes levied on the benefits-received principle. **T F**

11. A tax is progressive when the average tax rate decreases as income increases. **T F**

12. A general sales tax is considered to be a proportional tax with respect to income. **T F**

13. When an excise tax is placed on a product bought and sold in a competitive market, the portion of the tax borne by the seller equals the amount of the tax less the rise in the price of product due to the tax. **T F**

14. The more elastic the demand for a good, the greater will be the portion of an excise tax on the good borne by the seller. **T F**

15. The efficiency loss of an excise tax is the gain in net benefits for the producers from the increase in the price of the product. **T F**

16. The degrees of efficiency loss from an excise tax varies from market to market and depends on the elasticities of supply and demand. **T F**

17. Estimates of the overall structure of the American tax system depend on the assumed incidence of taxes. **T　F**

18. A value-added tax is a tax on the difference between the value of goods sold by a firm and the value of the goods it purchased from other firms. **T　F**

19. Advocates of "reindustrializing" the American economy have proposed increasing the tax rate imposed by the Federal government on corporate incomes to force corporations to be more efficient. **T　F**

20. Both liberals and conservatives agree that the expansion of government's role in the economy has reduced personal freedom in the United States. **T　F**

Circle the letter that corresponds to the best answer.

1. Deficiencies in the processes used to make collective decisions in the public sector and economic inefficiencies caused by government are the primary focus of:
(a) public finance
(b) public choice theory
(c) the study of tax incidence
(d) the study of tax shifting

2. The trading of votes to secure favorable outcomes on decisions which otherwise would be adverse is referred to as:
(a) logrolling, and it increases economic efficiency
(b) logrolling, and it may increase or decrease economic efficiency
(c) rent-seeking behavior and it decreases economic efficiency
(d) rent-seeking behavior and it may increase or decrease economic efficiency

Answer the next four questions (3, 4, 5, and 6) on the basis of the following table which shows the rankings of the public goods by three voters: A, B, and C.

Public good	Voter A	Voter B	Voter C
Dam	1	2	3
School	3	1	2
Road	2	3	1

3. In a choice between a dam and the school:
(a) a majority of voters favor the dam
(b) a majority of voters favor the school
(c) a majority of voters favor both the dam and the school
(d) there is not a majority of votes for either the dam or the school

4. In a choice between a road and a dam:
(a) a majority of voters favor the dam
(b) a majority of voters favor the road
(c) a majority of voters favor both the dam and the road

(d) there is not a majority of votes for either the road or the dam

5. In a choice between a school and a road:
(a) a majority of voters favor the road
(b) a majority of voters favor the school
(c) a majority of voters favor both the road and the school
(d) there is not a majority of votes for either the road or the school

6. What do the rankings in the table indicate about choices made under majority rule? Majority voting:
(a) reflects irrational preferences
(b) produces inconsistent choices
(c) produces consistent choices in spite of irrational preferences
(d) results in economically efficient outcomes because they have been influenced by special interests

7. The idea that the person holding the middle position will in a sense determine the outcome of an election is suggested by the:
(a) rent-seeking behavior
(b) paradox of voting
(c) median-voter model
(d) fallacy of limited decisions

8. Which of the following is *not* one of the reasons for the alleged greater efficiency of the private sector?
(a) the least efficient workers in the economy gravitate to the public sector
(b) strong incentives to be efficient are largely absent in the public sector
(c) there is no simple way to measure or test efficiency in the public sector
(d) there is a tendency in the public sector to increase the budgets of agencies that have failed to perform efficiently

9. It is difficult to determine whether provision for a particular good or service should be assigned to the private or public sector of the economy because:
(a) the institutions in both sectors function efficiently
(b) the markets function efficiently and the agencies of government perform imperfectly
(c) the markets are faulty and government agencies function with much greater efficiency
(d) the institutions in both sectors are imperfect

10. Which of the following is true of the ability-to-pay principle as applied in the United States?
(a) it is less widely applied than the benefits-received principle
(b) tax incidence is generally taken as the measure of the ability to pay
(c) gasoline taxes are based on this principle
(d) as the tax base increases, taxes paid increase both absolutely and relatively

11. Taxing people according the principle of ability-to-pay would be most characteristic of:
   (a) a payroll tax
   (b) a value-added tax
   (c) a general sales tax
   (d) a progressive income tax

12. When the income of a taxpayer increases and a tax is regressive, the amount of the tax paid by the taxpayer:
   (a) increases
   (b) decreases
   (c) remains unchanged
   (d) may do any of the above

13. Which of the following tends to be a progressive tax in the United States?
   (a) income tax
   (b) property tax
   (c) sales tax
   (d) payroll tax

14. In a competitive market the portion of an excise tax borne by a buyer is equal to:
   (a) the amount the price of the product rises as a result of the tax
   (b) the amount of the tax
   (c) the amount of the tax less the amount the price of the product rises as a result of the tax
   (d) the amount of the tax plus the amount the price of the product rises as a result of the tax

15. Which of the following statements is correct?
   (a) the more elastic the supply, the greater the portion of an excise tax borne by the seller
   (b) the more elastic the demand, the greater the portion of an excise tax borne by the seller
   (c) the more inelastic the supply, the greater the portion of an excise tax borne by the buyer
   (d) the more inelastic the demand, the greater the portion of an excise tax borne by the seller

Answer the next four questions (16, 17, 18, and 19) based on the graph of an excise tax imposed by government, as shown in the next column.

16. What is the amount of the excise tax paid by the seller in terms of price per unit sold?
   (a) $1.00
   (b) $2.00
   (c) $3.00
   (d) $4.00

17. The amount of the excise tax paid by the consumer is:
   (a) $2.00
   (b) $6.00
   (c) $12.00
   (d) $16.00

18. The tax revenue for government is represented by area:
   (a) *abde*
   (b) *abgf*
   (c) *fgde*
   (d) *abcde*

19. The efficiency loss of the tax is represented by area:
   (a) *bgc*
   (b) *bdc*
   (c) *abcf*
   (d) *hbci*

20. The efficiency loss of an excise tax is:
   (a) greater, the greater the elasticity of supply and demand
   (b) greater, the less the elasticity of supply and demand
   (c) less, the greater the elasticity of supply and demand
   (d) not affected by the elasticity of supply and demand

21. Which of the following taxes can be least easily shifted?
   (a) personal income tax
   (b) corporation income tax
   (c) sales tax
   (d) business property tax

22. A recent study of the American tax structure shows it to be:
   (a) very progressive
   (b) slightly progressive
   (c) slightly regressive
   (d) very regressive

23. The advocates of "reindustrializing" the American economy argue that:
   (a) the production of consumer goods must be increased

(b) the productivity of American workers must be improved

(c) corporate income taxes should be increased

(d) the production of investment goods needs to be reduced by a substantial amount

24. A value-added tax as used by many countries would basically tax a firm's:

(a) revenues from the sale of a product

(b) purchases of resources to produce the product

(c) revenue from the firm's sales less the resource cost

(d) capital goods and land held by the firm

25. The statement that "government extends the range of free choice for members of a society when it provides public goods and services" would serve to illustrate:

(a) rent-seeking behavior

(b) the median-voter model

(c) the benefits-received principle

(d) the fallacy of limited decisions

■ DISCUSSION QUESTIONS

1. Explain the difference between public choice theory and public finance. Why has there been dissatisfaction with government decisions?

2. What is the relationship between majority voting and the efficiency of outcomes from an election? How do special interest groups or the use of logrolling influence the efficiency of outcomes?

3. Why is there a paradox with majority voting? Do the outcomes from majority voting suggest that voters are irrational in their preferences?

4. Describe how median voters influence the election results and debates over public issues? What factors make the median voter model imperfect?

5. Explain what is meant by "public sector failure." Is it related to market failure and externalities?

6. Public choice theory suggests that there are a number of reasons for public sector failures. What are the reasons? Explain how each would tend to result in the inefficient allocation of the economy's resources.

7. It is generally agreed that "national defense must lie in the public sector while wheat production can best be accomplished in the private sector." Why isn't there agreement on where many other goods or services should be produced?

8. What are the two basic philosophies for apportioning the tax burden in the United States? Explain each. What are the difficulties encountered in putting these philosophies into practice?

9. Explain the differences among progressive, regressive, and proportional taxes. Which taxes fall into each of these three categories?

10. Explain the effect which the imposition of an excise tax has on the supply of a commodity bought and sold in a competitive market. How do you find what part of the tax is passed on to the buyer and what part is borne by the seller? What determines the division of the tax between the buyer and the seller?

11. What is the relationship between the price elasticity of demand for a commodity and the portion of an excise tax on a commodity borne by the buyer and by the seller? What is the relationship between the price elasticity of supply and the incidence of the tax?

12. How does an excise tax produce an efficiency loss for society? How is this efficiency loss affected by the elasticity of supply or demand? All else equal, shouldn't the total tax burden be equal for two taxes that produce equal revenues?

13. Which of the following taxes tends to be shifted?

(a) personal income tax

(b) corporate income tax

(c) sales and excise taxes

(d) property tax

From whom is the tax shifted and upon whom is the tax incidence?

14. What can be said about the progressivity or regressivity of the overall structure of the American tax system?

15. What does the term "reindustrialize" mean when applied to the American economy? Why do the proponents of reindustrialization feel the economy is in need of it and what steps would they take to accomplish it?

16. Why might higher tax rates or new taxes be needed for the Federal government? What options might be considered?

17. Do you think government limits or expands personal freedom? Do you think that government's role in the economy should be increased or decreased? What is meant by the "fallacy" of limited decisions?

■ ANSWERS

Chapter 32 Public Choice Theory and Taxation

FILL-IN QUESTIONS

1. choice, finance

2. *a.* inefficiency, overallocation, underallocation, special interest, logrolling; *b.* paradox of voting

3. median-voter, middle

4. public, failure

5. *a.* special, rent-seeking; *b.* clear, hidden; *c.* select; *d.* incentives, test (measure)

6. *a.* private sector; *b.* imperfect; *c.* assigned

7. benefits-received, ability-to-pay

8. is constant, increases, decreases

9. *a.* P; *b.* R; *c.* R; *d.* R; *e.* U

10. price; *a.* less, more; *b.* more, less

11. efficiency loss, greater, efficiency loss

12. *a.* the persons upon whom it is levied; *b.* those who buy the taxed product; *c.* either the firm or its customers; *d.* owners when they occupy their own residences, tenants who rent residences from the owners, consumers who buy the products produced on business property

13. progressive; *a.* small; *b.* incidence; *c.* less; *d.* transfer

14. decreased, lowered, broadened

15. *a.* productivity, (1) decreased, increased, (2) corporate, value-added; *b.* higher, VAT, income tax.

16. economic freedom, limited decisions

PROBLEMS AND PROJECTS

1. *a.* $3.60; *b.* (reading down) 600, 500, 400, 300, 200, 100; *c.* $4.00; *d.* (1) $.40, 67; (2) $.20, 33

2. *a.* not changed; *b.* none, all; *c.* smaller, larger; *d.* larger, smaller

3. *a.* increased by the amount of the tax; *b.* all, none; *c.* larger, smaller; *d.* smaller, larger

4. Tax A: 3, 3, 3, 3, proportional; Tax B: 3, 3, 2.5, 2, combination; Tax C: 8, 7, 6, 5, regressive

5. *a.* $264, 296, 328, 360; *b.* 3.8, 3.7, 3.64, 3.6; *c.* regressive

SELF-TEST

1. T, p. 601
2. F, p. 601
3. F, p. 602
4. T, p. 603
5. T, p. 604
6. F, p. 604
7. F, p. 605
8. T, p. 605
9. T, p. 607
10. T, p. 607

11. F, p. 608
12. F, p. 608
13. T, pp. 609–611
14. T, p. 611
15. F, pp. 611–612
16. T, p. 612
17. T, p. 612
18. T, p. 614
19. F, p. 614
20. F, pp. 615–616

1. *b*, p. 600
2. *b*, p. 601
3. *b*, p. 602
4. *a*, p. 602
5. *a*, p. 602
6. *b*, pp. 602–603
7. *c*, p. 603
8. *a*, p. 605
9. *d*, p. 606
10. *d*, p. 607
11. *d*, p. 608
12. *d*, p. 608
13. *a*, p. 608

14. *a*, p. 610
15. *b*, p. 610
16. *b*, pp. 609–610
17. *c*, pp. 609–610
18. *a*, p. 611
19. *b*, p. 611
20. *a*, p. 612
21. *a*, p. 612
22. *b*, p. 613
23. *b*, p. 613
24. *c*, pp. 614–615
25. *d*, pp. 616–617

DISCUSSION QUESTIONS

1. pp. 599–600
2. pp. 600–601
3. p. 602
4. p. 603
5. p. 604
6. p. 604
7. pp. 605–606
8. pp. 607–608
9. p. 608

10. pp. 609–610
11. p. 610
12. pp. 611–612
13. pp. 612–613
14. pp. 613–614
15. p. 614
16. p. 615
17. pp. 615–617

CHAPTER 33

Antitrust and Regulation

This is the third of six chapters which deal with government and current problems in the American economy and is one of the two chapters which concern the monopoly problem. Chapter 33 examines the monopoly problem in output markets, and Chapter 36 examines the monopoly problem in labor markets. It should be noted that the term "monopoly" as used here does **not** mean pure or absolute monopoly; instead it means control of a large percentage of the total supply by one or a few suppliers—industrial concentration. Actually there is no such thing as pure monopoly, just degrees of industrial concentration.

Whether industrial concentration is a real threat to efficient resource allocation and technological progress in the United States is certainly a debatable question. It is a question that will be argued from time to time by the American people and their representatives in Congress. Chapter 33 does not attempt to answer the question. It is important, however, for you to see that it is a debatable question and to see that there are good and plausible arguments on both sides of the question.

A part of Chapter 33 is devoted to an examination of the ways in which the Federal government has attempted to reduce industrial concentration and to limit the use of monopoly power. In this section you will find a discussion of a number of Federal laws, and the question which a student almost always raises is, "Am I expected to know these laws?" The answer is yes, you should have a general knowledge of these laws. Another question which students often raise with respect to these laws is, "What good is there in knowing them anyhow?" In examining any important current problem it is important to know how the problem arose, what steps have already been taken to solve it, how successful the attempts were, and why the problem is still not solved. A more general answer to the same question is that an informed citizenry is necessary if a democracy is to solve its problems. And most of these laws continue in force and are enforced; many of you will work for business firms which are subject to their provisions.

After looking at the case for and the defense of industrial concentration and at the antitrust laws enacted by the Federal government, Chapter 33 presents the two major issues that have arisen in the interpretation of the antitrust laws; asks how effective these laws have been; and ob-serves that the Federal government has in several ways promoted and fostered industrial concentration and restricted competition in the United States.

In addition to restricting and to fostering industrial concentration, the Federal government has also undertaken to regulate, beginning with the railroads in 1887, industries that appeared to be natural monopolies. This regulation by agencies and commissions has, however, at least three serious problems of which you should be aware. One of these problems is that some of the regulated industries may not be natural monopolies at all and would be competitive industries if they were left unregulated. From this problem comes the legal cartel theory of regulation: many industries desire to be regulated so that competition among the firms in the industry will be reduced and the profits of these firms increased. A consequence of the problems encountered in regulating industries has been the trend in recent years to deregulate a few of the industries previously regulated by agencies or commissions. One of the industries which has been deregulated in the United States is the airline industry; and the case of the airlines is examined in a section of the text. Here you will see that despite the predictions of the critics of deregulation, deregulation has been generally beneficial for consumers and the economy.

Beginning in the early 1960s a host of new agencies and commissions began to engage in regulation which is different from the regulation of the prices charged by and the services offered by specific industries. Critics of social regulation contend that it is costly, and that the marginal costs exceed the benefits. Although social regulation does increase product prices and indirectly reduces worker productivity, supporters of this type of regulation argue that the social benefits over time will exceed the costs. You should spend time understanding both sides of this issue.

When you finish this chapter, you should conclude that antitrust, industrial regulation, and social regulation are trouble spots for the American economy. Antitrust and regulation raise important issues and questions about the role of government maintaining competition and restricting certain business practices in a market economy. How we deal with the issues or answer the questions will affect how good or bad our lives are now and will be in the future.

■ CHECKLIST

When you have studied this chapter you should be able to:

☐ Define the term industrial concentration and explain how it is used in this chapter.

☐ Cite four arguments in the case against industrial concentration.

☐ State four arguments in defense of industrial concentration.

☐ Outline the major provisions of each of the following:
- Sherman Act
- Clayton Act
- Federal Trade Commission Act
- Wheeler-Lea Act
- Celler-Kefauver Act

☐ Contrast the behavior and structural approaches to the enforcement of antitrust laws for judging the competitiveness of an industry.

☐ Explain the importance of market definition in the interpretation of antitrust laws.

☐ Generalize about the application of antitrust laws to existing market structure, mergers, and price fixing.

☐ Distinguish between a horizontal, vertical, and conglomerate merger.

☐ Explain the use the Herfindahl index for merger guidelines.

☐ Cite recent examples of price fixing and two major consequences of price fixing.

☐ List three groups which have been exempted from the provisions of the antitrust laws, and list two laws or policies which tend to restrict competition in the United States.

☐ Define a natural monopoly; and explain how it is related to the public interest theory of regulation.

☐ State the three problems that have been encountered in the economic regulation of industries by agencies and commissions.

☐ Distinguish between the public interest and legal cartel theories of regulation.

☐ Describe the principal economic effects of the deregulation of the airline industry in the United States; and compare these effects with the effects predicted by the critics of deregulation.

☐ Contrast industrial (or economic) regulation with social regulation; and state the principal concerns and the three distinguishing features of the latter.

☐ Present the case against social regulation made by its critics.

☐ Describe three economic implications of social regulation.

☐ Make the case for social regulation by discussing the benefits and citing data.

■ CHAPTER OUTLINE

1. The term "industrial concentration," as used in this chapter, means a situation in which a small number of firms control all or a substantial percentage of the total output of a major industry. Business firms may be large in either an absolute or a relative sense, and in many cases they are large in both senses. Chapter 33 is concerned with firms large in both senses.

2. Whether industrial concentration is beneficial or detrimental to the American economy is debatable. A case can be made against industrial concentration; but industrial concentration can also be defended.

   a. Many argue that industrial concentration results in a misallocation of resources; it is not needed for firms to achieve the economics of mass production and it does not lead to technological progress; it contributes to income inequality in the economy; and it is politically dangerous.

   b. But others argue that industrial concentration is often faced by interindustry and foreign competition; that it offers superior products; that large firms are necessary if they are to achieve the economies of scale in producing goods and services; and that monopolistic or concentrated industries promote a high rate of technological progress.

3. Government policies toward industrial concentration have not been clear and consistent; legislation and policy, however, have for the most part been aimed at restricting concentration and promoting competition.

   a. Following the Civil War, the expansion of the American economy brought with it the creation of trusts (or industrial concentration) in many industries; and the fear of the trusts resulted in the enactment of antitrust legislation.

   b. The Sherman Antitrust Act of 1890 was the first antitrust legislation and made monopolization and restraint of trade criminal offenses.

   c. In 1914 the Clayton Antitrust Act outlawed a number of specific techniques by which monopolies or oligopolies had been created.

   d. During the same year Congress passed the Federal Trade Commission Act which established the Federal Trade Commission to investigate unfair practices that might lead to the development of monopoly power; and in 1938 it amended this act by passing the Wheeler-Lea Act to prohibit deceptive practices (including false and misleading advertising and misrepresentation of products).

   e. And in 1950 passage of the Celler-Kefauver Act plugged a loophole in the Clayton Act and prohibited mergers that might lead to a substantial reduction in competition.

4. The effectiveness of the antitrust laws in preventing monopoly and maintaining competition has depended upon the zeal with which the Federal government has enforced the laws and upon the interpretation of these laws by the Federal courts; and two major issues have arisen in the interpretation of the antitrust laws.

a. The first of these issues is whether an industry should be judged on the basis of its highly concentrated structure or on the basis of its market behavior; and this issue has resulted in controversy and in two different approaches to the application of the antitrust laws.

b. The second issue is whether to define the market in which firms sell their products narrowly or broadly.

c. Whether the antitrust laws have been effective is a difficult question to answer. The application of the laws to existing market structures, to the three types of mergers, and to price fixing has ranged from lenient to strict:

(1) for existing market structures, it has been lenient;

(2) for horizontal, vertical, or conglomerate mergers, it usually varies by the type of merger and the particulars of a case, but merger guidelines are based on the Herfindahl index (the sum of the squared values of market shares within an industry);

(3) for price fixing, it has been strict, and as a consequence it is now often done in secret or through the use of informal collusion in the form of price leadership or cost-plus pricing.

d. The United States government has also restricted competition:

(1) by exempting labor unions, agricultural cooperatives, and certain occupational groups (at the state and local levels) from the provisions of the antitrust laws;

(2) by granting monopoly power to the producers of patented products; and

(3) by imposing tariffs and other trade barriers to protect American producers in some industries from foreign competition.

5. In addition to the enactment of the antitrust laws, government has undertaken to regulate natural monopolies.

a. If a single producer can provide a good or service at a lower average cost (because of economies of scale) than several producers, then competition is not economical and a natural monopoly exists. Government may either produce the good or service or (following the public interest theory) regulate private producers of the product for the benefit of the public.

b. The effectiveness of the regulation of business firms by regulatory agencies has been criticized for three principal reasons.

(1) Regulation, it is argued, increases costs and leads to an inefficient allocation of resources and higher prices.

(2) The regulatory agencies, it is also contended, have been "captured" by the regulated industries and protect them rather than the public.

(3) And some of the regulated industries, it can be argued, are not natural monopolies and would be competitive if they were not regulated.

c. The legal cartel theory of regulation is that potentially competitive industries want and support the regulation of their industries in order to increase the profits of the firms in the industries by limiting competition among them.

6. The three criticisms of the regulation of industries and the legal cartel theory of regulation led during the 1970s and 1980s to the deregulation of a number of industries in the United States. In particular, the deregulation of the airlines in 1978 had a number of economic effects:

a. Air fares rose less than the general level of prices and are lower than before deregulation because of increased competition among airlines to reduce unit labor costs.

b. Air service to most communities, even smaller ones, was maintained or expanded, but there have been delays on some routes because of the nature of the "spoke and hub" system; although deregulation raised concerns about air safety, the evidence is at worst mixed.

c. The number of air carriers initially increased, but recent consolidation of the industry has raised new concerns about concentration in the industry; also airport congestion and the competitive practices of airlines make the entry of new firms difficult.

d. Overall, airline deregulation contributed about $100 billion in net benefit to the economy during the 1980s, but growing concentration in the industry will need monitoring and possibly antitrust actions.

7. Beginning in the early 1960s, social regulation developed and resulted in the creation of additional regulatory agencies.

a. This regulation differed in several ways from the older regulation of specific industries and aimed to improve the quality of life in the United States.

b. While the objectives of the new regulation are desirable, the overall costs for both program administration and compliance costs can be high; most of the costs, however, are compliance costs which are about 20 times administrative costs.

c. Critics argue that the marginal costs of this regulation exceed its marginal benefit and it is, therefore, inefficient because:

(1) regulatory standards and objectives are poorly drawn and targeted;

(2) the rules and regulations are made based on limited and inadequate information;

(3) there are unintended secondary effects from the regulation that boost product costs;

(4) regulatory agencies tend to attract "overzealous" workers who believe in regulation.

d. The economic consequences of social regulation are that it increases product prices, it may slow the rate of product innovation, and it may lessen competition.

e. The defenders of social regulation contend that it is needed to fight serious and neglected problems, such as job and auto safety or environment pollution; and that the social benefits, if they can be measured, will over time exceed the costs.

■ IMPORTANT TERMS

Industrial concentration	Rule of reason
Big business	Alcoa case
Interindustry competition	DuPont Cellophane case
Foreign competition	Horizontal merger
Potential competition	Vertical merger
Regulatory agency	Conglomerate merger
Sherman Act	Per se violations
Treble damages	Patent laws
Clayton Act	Natural monopoly
Tying agreement	Public utility
Interlocking directorate	Public interest theory of regulation
Federal Trade Commission Act	
Federal Trade Commission	Legal cartel theory of regulation
	Airline Deregulation Act
Cease-and desist order	Industrial (economic) regulation
Wheeler-Lea Act	
Celler-Kefauver Act	Social regulation
U.S. Steel case	

■ FILL-IN QUESTIONS

1. As used in this chapter, industrial concentration means that (many firms, a few firms) _____ control all or a substantial portion of the output of a major industry; and this chapter is concerned with firms that are large (absolutely, relatively, both absolutely and relatively)

_____

2. Those who argue the case against industrial concentration assert that it results in a _____ of resources, (slows, speeds) _____ the rate of technological progress, contributes to the _____ distribution of income, and creates political _____ in the United States.

3. Those who defend industrial concentration contend that the monopoly power was the result of offering _____ to the market, that their power is limited by _____ and _____ competition, that large firms are necessary to achieve economies of _____, and that the large firms are conducive to a rapid rate of _____

_____

4. Federal legislation and policies have mostly attempted to maintain (competition, monopoly) _____ _____, but at times they have fostered the development of _____

5. The Sherman Act of 1890 made it illegal to _____-ize or to restrain _____ between the states or between nations.

6. The Clayton Act of 1914 prohibited such practices as price _____, acquisition of the _____ of competing corporations, _____ contracts, and _____ directorates.

7. The Federal Trade Commission was set up under the act of that name in 1914 to investigate _____ competitive practices, hold public _____ on such complaints, and to issue _____ orders.

8. The _____ Act had the effect of prohibiting false and misleading advertising.

9. The _____ Act banned the acquisition of the assets of one firm by another, and the _____ Act prohibited the acquisition of the *stock* of one firm by another when the result would be reduced competition.

10. The two basic issues in applying the antitrust laws are whether the extent of industrial concentration in a particular industry should be judged on the basis of that industry's behavior or its _____; and whether the size of the market in which a firm sells its products should be defined _____ or _____

a. The courts judged the steel industry on the basis of its behavior in 1920 when they applied the rule of _____ in the U.S. Steel case; but used the other method of judging an industry in 1945 in the _____ case.

b. In 1956 they ruled that although DuPont sold nearly all the Cellophane produced in the United States it did not dominate the market for flexible _____

11. A merger between two competitors selling similar products in the same market is a (vertical, horizontal, conglomerate) _____ merger. A _____ merger occurs among firms at different stages in the production process of the same industry. A _____

merger results when a firm in one industry is purchased by a firm in an unrelated industry. The _____ index is used as a guideline for mergers.

12. The Federal government promotes the growth of monopoly and restricts competition when it exempts certain industries or practices from the provisions of the

_____ laws.

   a. Federal legislation has exempted _____

_____ and _____ cooperatives.

   b. The _____ laws have the effect of granting inventors legal monopolies on their prod-

ucts; and _____ and other barriers to trade shelter American producers from foreign competition.

13. When a single firm is able to supply the entire market at a lower average cost than a number of competing firms,

there is a _____ monopoly. In the United States many of these monopolies are controlled by

regulatory _____ or _____

14. The three major criticisms of regulation of industries by an agency or commission are
   a. The reguated firms have no incentive to reduce their

_____ because the commission will then require them to lower their prices; and, because the prices they are allowed to charge are based on the value of their capital equipment, firms tend to make uneconomical substitutions of (labor, capital)

_____ for _____
   b. The regulatory commission has been "captured" or

is controlled by _____
   c. Regulation has been applied to industries which are

not _____ monopolies and which in the

absence of regulation would be _____

15. The public interest theory of regulation assumes that the objective of regulating an industry is to protect society

from abuses of _____ power; but an alternative theory assumes that the firms wish to be regulated because it enables them to form, and the commission helps them to create, a profitable and legal

_____

16. Airline deregulation (increased, decreased)

_____ airfares in the 1980s in part because

competition _____ costs. There were

_____ concerns about airline safety because airport congestion _____.
Since deregulation, the number of air carriers initially

_____ but they have now _____,

which _____ concerns about industrial concentration in the airline industry. Overall, the deregu-

lation of airlines _____ the net benefit to society by about $100 billion during the 1980s.

17. The basic reason for social regulation and the creation and growth of the regulatory agencies has been the

desire to improve the (quantity, quality) _____ of life in the United States.

   a. It is concerned with the _____ under which goods and services are produced, the impact of

their production upon _____, and the

physical _____ of the goods.
   b. And it differs in several ways from the older form of

regulation which is labeled _____

or _____ regulation.

18. The costs of social regulation include _____

_____ costs, such as salaries paid to employees of regulatory agencies, and _____
costs incurred by businesses and state and local governments in meeting the requirements of the regulatory laws. The latter costs have been estimated to be about

_____ times those of the former. Critics of social legislation contend that its marginal costs are

(greater, less) _____ than its marginal benefits.

19. The economic effects of social regulation are several:

it tends to (increase, decrease) _____

product prices and tends to _____ worker

productivity; it also may _____ the rate of

innovation and may _____ competition in the economy.

20. Supporters of social regulation hold that there are

serious and substantial _____ that must be dealt with by society; that the relevant economic test is

whether the _____
if social regulation is to be judged as worthwhile; and that

_____ tend to be taken for granted or are difficult to measure, or may require time to accrue.

21. The dispute over social regulation (is, is not) _____ over whether the regulation should occur.

It _____ over how and when regulation should be used and it _____ over how we can improve the system of regulation.

■ **PROBLEMS AND PROJECTS**

1. Below is a list of Federal laws. Following this list is a series of provisions found in Federal laws. Match each of the laws with the appropriate provision by placing the appropriate capital letter after each of the provisions.

   A. Sherman Act
   B. Clayton Act
   C. Federal Trade Commission Act
   D. Wheeler-Lea Act
   E. Celler-Kefauver Act

   a. Established a commission to investigate and prevent unfair methods of competition. _____

   b. Made monopoly and restraint of trade illegal and criminal. _____

   c. Prohibited the acquisition of the assets of a firm by another firm when such an acquisition will lessen competition. _____

   d. Had the effect of prohibiting false and misleading advertising and the misrepresentation of products.

   _____

   e. Clarified the Sherman Act and outlawed specific techniques or devices used to create monopolies and restrain trade. _____

2. Indicate with the letter L for **leniently** (or permissively) and the letter S for **strictly** how the antitrust laws tend to be applied to each of the following.

   a. Vertical mergers in which each of the merging firms sells a small portion of the total output of its industry

   _____

   b. Price fixing by a firm in an industry _____

   c. Conglomerate mergers _____

   d. Existing market structures in which no firm sells 60% or more of the total output of its industry _____

   e. Horizontal mergers in which the merged firms would sell a large portion of the total output of their industry and no one of the firms is on the verge of bankruptcy

   _____

   f. Action by firms in an industry to divide up sales

   _____

   g. Horizontal mergers where one of the firms is on the verge of bankruptcy _____

3. In the table below are data on five different industries and the market shares for each of the firms in the industry. Assume that there is no foreign competition, entry into the industry is difficult, and that no firm in each industry is on the verge of bankruptcy.

Industry	Market share of firms in industry						Herfindahl index
	1	2	3	4	5	6	
A	35	25	15	11	10	4	_____
B	30	25	25	20	—	—	_____
C	20	20	20	15	15	10	_____
D	60	25	15	—	—	—	_____
E	22	21	20	18	12	7	_____

   a. In the column to the right of the table, calculate the Herfindahl index.

   b. The industry with the most monopoly power is Industry _____ and the industry with the least monopoly power is Industry _____

   c. If the **sixth** firm in Industry A sought to merge with the **fifth** firm in that industry, then the government (would, would not) _____ be likely to challenge the merger. The Herfindahl index for this industry is _____, which is higher than the merger guideline of _____ points used by the government, but the merger increases the index by only _____ points.

   d. If the **fourth** firm in Industry B sought to merge with the **third** firm in that industry, then the government (would, would not) _____ be likely to challenge the merger. The Herfindahl index for this industry is _____, which is higher than the merger guideline of the government, and the merger increases the index by _____ points.

   e. A **conglomerate** merger between the **fourth** firm in Industry C and the **fourth** firm in Industry E (would, would not) _____ likely be challenged by the government. The Herfindahl index would (increase, remain the same) _____ with this merger.

   f. If a **vertical** merger between the **first** firm in Industry B with the **first** firm in Industry D lessened competition in each industry, then the merger (would, would not) _____ likely be challenged by the government, but the merger _____ likely be challenged if it did not lessen competition in each industry.

■ **SELF-TEST**

Circle the T if the statement is true, the F it is false.

1. The term "industrial concentration" in this chapter is taken to mean a situation in which a single firm or a small number of firms control the major portion of the output of an important industry. **T F**

2. It is clear that on balance, industrial concentration is detrimental to the functioning of the American economy. **T F**

3. Those who defend industrial concentration contend that it is technologically more progressive than smaller firms. **T F**

4. Potential competition acts as a restraint on the price and output decisons of firms possessing market power. **T F**

5. The Federal government has consistently passed legislation and pursued policies designed to maintain competition. **T F**

6. Industrial concentration and "trusts" developed in the American economy during the two decades preceding the American Civil War. **T F**

7. The courts in 1920 applied the rule of reason to the U.S. Steel Corporation and decided that the corporation possessed monopoly power and had unreasonably restrained trade. **T F**

8. Those who believe an industry should be judged on the basis of its structure contend that any industry with a monopolistic structure must behave like a monopolist. **T F**

9. The market for DuPont's product was broadly defined by the courts in the DuPont Cellophane case of 1956. **T F**

10. The Reagan and Bush administrations were committed to a more vigorous enforcement of the antitrust laws in the areas of market structure and mergers. **T F**

11. To gain a conviction under **per se violations**, the party making the charge must show that the conspiracy to fix prices actually succeeded or caused damage. **T F**

12. Occupational licensure and patent have been most beneficial in promoting competition in markets. **T F**

13. Public ownership rather than public regulation has been the primary means utilized in the United States to ensure that the behavior of natural monopolists is socially acceptable. **T F**

14. The rationale underlying the public interest theory of regulation of natural monopolies is to allow the consumers of their goods or services to benefit from the economies of scale. **T F**

15. Regulated firms, because the prices they are allowed to charge are set to enable them to earn a "fair" return over their costs, have a strong incentive to reduce their costs. **T F**

16. From the perspective of the legal cartel theory of regulation, firms want to be regulated by government. **T F**

17. The deregulation of airlines in the United States generally lowered prices to consumers of airline services during the 1980s. **T F**

18. Those who favor social regulation believe that it is needed in order to improve the quality of life in the United States. **T F**

19. Critics of the social regulation argue that its marginal costs exceed its marginal benefits. **T F**

20. Social regulation tends to lower product prices and raise worker productivity. **T F**

Circle the letter that corresponds to the best answer.

1. "Industrial concentration" in this chapter refers to which one of the following?
(a) firms that are absolutely large
(b) firms that are relatively large
(c) firms that are either absolutely or relatively large
(d) firms that are both absolutely and relatively large

2. Which of the following is **not** a part of the case **against** industrial concentration?
(a) highly concentrated industries are larger than they need to be to benefit from economies of scale
(b) highly concentrated industries earn economic profits which they use for research and technological development
(c) monopoly power leads to the misallocation of resources
(d) monopoly power leads to greater income inequality

3. An essential part of the defense of industrial concentration is that the power of big business is limited by:
(a) interindustry competition
(b) foreign competition
(c) potential competition from new firms in the industry
(d) all of the above

4. Which one of the following laws stated that contracts and conspiracies in restraint of trade, monopolies, attempts to monopolize, and conspiracies to monopolize are illegal?
(a) Sherman Act
(b) Clayton Act
(c) Federal Trade Commission Act
(d) Wheeler-Lea Act

5. Which one of the following acts specifically outlawed tying contracts and interlocking directorates?
(a) Sherman Act
(b) Clayton Act
(c) Federal Trade Commission Act
(d) Wheeler-Lea Act

6. Which one of the following acts has given the Federal Trade Commission the task of preventing false and misleading advertising and the misrepresentation of products?
(a) Sherman Act
(b) Clayton Act
(c) Federal Trade Commission Act
(d) Wheeler-Lea Act

7. Which of the following acts banned the acquisition of the assets of a firm by a competing firm when the acquisition would tend to reduce competition?
(a) Celler-Kefauver Act
(b) Wheeler-Lea Act
(c) Clayton Act
(d) Federal Trade Commission Act

8. The argument that an industry which is highly concentrated will behave like a monopolist and the Alcoa court case of 1945 suggest that the application of antitrust laws should be based on industry:
(a) behavior
(b) structure
(c) efficiency
(d) rule of reason

9. The merger of a firm in one industry with a firm in an unrelated industry is called a:
(a) horizontal merger
(b) vertical merger
(c) secondary merger
(d) conglomerate merger

10. Toward which of the following has the application of the antitrust laws been the most strict in recent years?
(a) existing market structures
(b) conglomerate mergers
(c) mergers in which one of the firms is on the verge of bankruptcy
(d) price fixing

11. An industry has four firms, each with a market share of 25%. There is no foreign competition, entry into the industry is difficult, and no firm is on the verge of bankruptcy. If two of the firms in the industry sought to merger, this action would most likely be opposed by the government because the Herfindahl index for the industry is:
(a) 2000 and the merger would increase the index by 1000
(b) 2500 and the merger would increase the index by 1000

(c) 2500 and the merger would increase the index by 1250
(d) 3000 and the merger would increase the index by 1250

12. When the government or other party making the charge can show that there was a conspiracy to fix prices, even if the conspiracy did not succeed, then this would be an example of:
(a) a tying contract
(b) a per se violation
(c) the rule of reason
(d) the legal cartel theory

13. Which of the following does **not** restrict competition in the American economy?
(a) the exemption of labor unions and agricultural cooperatives from the antitrust laws
(b) protective tariffs and other barriers to international trade
(c) the difficulties many new firms encounter in obtaining charters that allow them to become corporations
(d) American patent laws

14. An example of industrial or economic regulation would be the:
(a) Federal Communications Commission
(b) Food and Drug Administration
(c) Occupational Safety and Health Administration
(d) Environmental Protection Agency

15. Legislations designed to regulate "natural monopolies" would be based on which theory of regulation?
(a) cartel
(b) public interest
(c) X-inefficiency
(d) public ownership

16. Those who oppose the regulation of industry by regulatory agencies contend that:
(a) many of the regulated industries are natural monopolies
(b) the regulatory agencies have been "captured" by the firms they are supposed to regulate
(c) regulation contributes to an increase in the number of mergers in industries
(d) regulation helps to moderate costs and improves efficiency in the production of a good or service produced by the regulated industry

17. The legal cartel theory of regulation:
(a) would allow the forces of demand and supply to determine the rates (prices) of the good or service
(b) would attempt to protect the public from abuses of monopoly power
(c) assumes that the regulated industry wishes to be regulated

(d) assumes that both the demand for and supply of the good or service produced by the regulated industry are perfectly inelastic

18. Critics of the deregulation of industry argue that (among other things) deregulation will lead to:
  (a) higher prices for the products produced by the industry
  (b) the monopolization of the industry by a few large firms
  (c) a decline in the quantity or the quality of the product produced by the industry
  (d) all of the above

19. Deregulation of airlines in the United States has resulted in:
  (a) higher air fares
  (b) the monopolization of the airline industry by two large firms
  (c) a reduction in the availability of air services in the larger communities
  (d) lower wage rates for airline employees

20. The contestability of markets in the airline industry was probably:
  (a) increased by the use of "frequent flyer" programs by airlines
  (b) increased by the improvement in safety and airline regulation
  (c) decreased in the short term by a lack of airport capacity
  (d) decreased in the short term by a reduction in the quality of airline service

21. Which of the following is **not** a concern of the social regulation?
  (a) the prices charged for goods
  (b) the physical characteristics of goods produced
  (c) the conditions under which goods are manufactured
  (d) the impact upon society of the production of goods

22. Those costs incurred by businesses and state and local government in meeting the requirement of regulatory commissions are referred to as:
  (a) administrative costs
  (b) compliance costs
  (c) containment costs
  (d) per unit costs

23. Which one of the following is engaged in social regulation?
  (a) the Federal Trade Commission
  (b) the Interstate Commerce Commission
  (c) the Environmental Protection Agency
  (d) the Federal Energy Regulatory Commission

24. Which of the following is one of the major criticisms leveled against social regulation by its opponents?

  (a) it is procompetitive
  (b) it will decrease the rate of innovation in the economy
  (c) it will increase the amount of price fixing among businesses
  (d) it will require too long a time for it to achieve its objectives

25. Supporters of social regulation contend that:
  (a) there is a pressing need to reduce the number of mergers in American business
  (b) the presence of natural monopoly requires strong regulatory action by government
  (c) the social benefits will over time exceed the social costs
  (d) administrative and compliance costs are often exaggerated

■ **DISCUSSION QUESTIONS**

1. Explain the difference between the way the term "monopoly" is used in this chapter and the way it is used in Chapter 24. How is "industrial concentration" defined? How is the expression used in this chapter?

2. What are the chief arguments in the case against industrial concentration? In what two ways is the term **unprogressive** used in these arguments?

3. What are the chief arguments advanced in defense of industrial concentration?

4. What are the historical background to and the main provisions of the Sherman Act?

5. The Clayton Act and the Federal Trade Commission Act amended or elaborated the provisions of the Sherman Act, and both aimed at preventing rather than punishing monopoly. What were the chief provisions of each of these acts, and how did they attempt to prevent monopoly? In what two ways is the FTC Act important?

6. What loophole in the Clayton Act was plugged by the Celler-Kefauver Act in 1950 and how did it alter the coverage of the antitrust laws with respect to mergers?

7. Contrast the two different approaches to the application of the antitrust laws that are illustrated by the decisions of the courts in the U.S. Steel and Alcoa cases.

8. Why is defining the market an important issue in the application of the antitrust laws? How did the courts define the market in the case brought against DuPont for monopolizing the market for Cellophane?

9. How are the antitrust laws applied today to (*a*) existing market structures; (*b*) horizontal mergers; (*c*) vertical mergers; (*d*) conglomerate mergers; and (*e*) price fixing? What are the guidelines used for mergers?

10. In what ways has the Federal government restricted competition and fostered monopoly in the American economy?

11. What is a natural monopoly and what are the two alternative ways that can be used to ensure that it behaves in a socially acceptable fashion?

12. Explain the three major criticisms leveled against public interest regulation as it is practiced by commissions and agencies in the United States.

13. What is the legal cartel theory of regulation? Contrast it with the public interest theory of regulation.

14. Why were a number of industries in the American economy deregulated in the 1970s and 1980s? What did the proponents and the critics of deregulation predict would be the economic effects of deregulation?

15. How has deregulation affected the airline industry in terms of fares, service, safety, and industry structure? Why might antitrust enforcement be needed in this industry?

16. How does the social regulation differ from the industrial (or economic) regulation? What is the objective of this type of regulation, its three principal concerns, and its three distinguishing features?

17. What are the two types of costs of regulation? How do these costs compare?

18. Why do critics of regulation argue that the marginal costs exceed the marginal benefits?

19. What are three economic implications of social regulation?

20. What arguments do supporters of social regulation give?

■ **ANSWERS**

Chapter 33 Antitrust and Regulation

FILL-IN QUESTIONS

1. a few firms, both absolutely and relatively

2. misallocation, slows, unequal, dangers

3. superior products, interindustry, foreign (either order), scale, technological progress

4. competition, monopoly

5. monopol-, trade

6. discrimination, stock, tying, interlocking

7. unfair, hearings, cease-and-desist

8. Wheeler-Lea

9. Celler-Kefauver, Clayton

10. structure, narrowly, broadly (either order); *a.* reason, Alcoa; *b.* packaging materials

11. horizontal, vertical, conglomerate, Herfindahl

12. antitrust; *a.* (labor) unions, agricultural; *b.* patent, tariffs

13. natural, agencies, commissions (either order)

14. *a.* costs, capital, labor; *b.* the industry (firms) it is supposed to regulate; *c.* natural, competitive

15. monopoly, cartel

16. decreased, decreased, increased, increased, increased, decreased, increased, increased

17. quality; *a.* conditions, society, character; *b.* industrial, economic (either order)

18. administrative, compliance, 20, greater

19. increase, decrease, decrease, decrease

20. problems, benefits exceed the costs, benefits

21. is not, is, is

PROBLEMS AND PROJECTS

1. *a.* C; *b.* A; *c.* E; *d.* D; *e.* B

2. *a.* L; *b.* S; *c.* L; *d.* L; *e.* S; *f.* S; *g.* L

3. *a.* 2312, 2550, 1750, 4450, 1842; *b.* D, C; *c.* would not, 2312, 1800, 80; *d.* would, 2550, 1000; *e.* would not, remain the same; *f.* would, would not

SELF-TEST

1. T, pp. 619–620	6. F, p. 622	11. F, p. 625	16. T, p. 628
2. F, p. 620	7. F, p. 623	12. F, p. 626	17. T, p. 629
3. T, p. 621	8. T, p. 623	13. F, p. 627	18. T, p. 631
4. T, p. 621	9. T, p. 624	14. F, p. 627	19. T, pp. 631–632
5. F, p. 622	10. F, p. 626	15. F, p. 628	20. F, pp. 632–633

1. *d*, p. 620	8. *b*, p. 623	14. *a*, pp. 627; 631	20. *c*, p. 630
2. *b*, p. 620	9. *d*, p. 624	15. *b*, p. 627	21. *a*, p. 631
3. *d*, p. 621	10. *d*, p. 625	16. *b*, p. 628	22. *b*, p. 631
4. *a*, p. 622	11. *c*, p. 625	17. *c*, p. 628	23. *c*, p. 631
5. *b*, p. 622	12. *b*, p. 625	18. *d*, p. 629	24. *b*, p. 633
6. *d*, p. 623	13. *c*, p. 626	19. *d*, p. 630	25. *c*, p. 633
7. *a*, p. 623			

DISCUSSION QUESTIONS

1. pp. 619–620	6. p. 623	11. p. 627	16. p. 631
2. p. 620	7. pp. 623–624	12. p. 628	17. pp. 631–632
3. p. 621	8. p. 624	13. pp. 627–628	18. p. 632
4. pp. 621–622	9. pp. 624–626	14. p. 629	19. pp. 632–633
5. pp. 622–623	10. p. 626	15. pp. 629–630	20. p. 633

CHAPTER 34

Agriculture: Economics and Policy

Agriculture is a large and vital part of the American and world economy, and therefore it merits the special attention it receives in Chapter 34. As you will learn, the economics of agriculture and farm policies of the Federal government are of concern not only to those directly engaged in farming, but also to American consumers and businesses who purchase farm products, and to American taxpayers who subsidize farm incomes. Agriculture is also important in the world economy because each nation must find a way to feed its population, and because domestic farm policies designed to enhance farm incomes often lead to distortions in world trade and economic inefficiency in world agricultural production.

The chapter begins by examining both the short-run and the long-run problem in American agriculture. The short-run problem is that farm prices and incomes have fluctuated sharply from year to year. The long-run problem is that agriculture is a declining industry, and as a consequence farm incomes fell over time. To understand the causes of each of these problems you will have to make use of the concept of inelastic demand and to employ your knowledge of how demand and supply determine price in a competitive market. The effort which you put into the study of these tools in previous chapters will now pay a dividend: understanding the causes of a real-world problem and the policies designed to solve the problem.

The agricultural policies of the Federal government have been directed at enhancing and stabilizing farm incomes by supporting farm prices. In connection with the support of farm prices you are introduced to the concept of parity. Once you understand parity and recognize that the parity price has in the past been above what the competitive price would have been you will come to some important conclusions. Consumers paid higher prices for and consumed smaller quantities of the various farm products; and at the prices supported by the Federal government there were surpluses of these products. The Federal government bought these surpluses to keep the price above the competitive market price. The purchases of the surpluses were financed by American taxpayers. To eliminate these surpluses, government looked for ways to increase the demand for or to decrease the supply of these com-

modities. Programs to increase demand and decrease supply were put into effect, but they failed to eliminate the annual surpluses.

Over the past half century, farm policies have not worked well and have been criticized for several reasons. First, the policies confuse the **symptions** of the problem (low farm prices and incomes) with the **causes** of the problem (resource allocation). Second, the costly farm subsidizes are also misguided because they tend to benefit the high-income instead of the low-income farmer. Third, some policies of the Federal government contradict or offset other policies designed to help farmers. Fourth, changes in the scale of farming and in domestic and world markets contribute to the declining effectiveness of domestic agricultural programs.

Despite the many reasons for criticizing farm policy, you will also learn that a public choice perspective provides insights into why costly farm programs have been subsidized by the Federal government over the years. Government subsidies for agriculture, however, are likely to decline in the future because of a falling farm population and less effective farm lobby, pressures to balance the Federal budget, negative public opinion about farm subsidies, and efforts to develop world agricultural policies.

In recent years, negotiations have been started to reduce world trade barriers to agricultural products. In this section of the chapter you will learn that a high level of domestic support for the price of farm products has severe negative effects on international trade and the economic efficiency in agricultural production worldwide. Although the United States has taken steps to reduce these trade barriers through international negotiations and recent changes in domestic farm policy, much remains to be done.

In the long run, it may be futile to try to enhance farm incomes in an economy in which the basic problem is too many farmers; and it may be better to allow farm prices and farm incomes to drift downward toward their long-run equilibrium levels in a free market. This would accelerate the movement of farmers out of agriculture and improve the allocation of the economy's resources. But to prevent unstable farm prices and farm incomes, the Federal government should try to stabilize farm prices in the short run as they move toward their long-run free market (or competitive) levels. This could be accomplished by the proposed free-market stabilization policy examined in the text.

The final section surveys what the pessimists and the optimists say about the possibility of worldwide shortages of agricultural products (that is, food) in the next century. The question is one of feast or famine during the years in which you will live the greater part of your life.

■ CHECKLIST

When you have studied this chapter you should be able to:

☐ Give five reasons for studying the economics of American agriculture.

☐ Explain the four causes of the short-run problem in agriculture.

☐ Identify two major factors contributing to long-run problems in agriculture.

☐ Use a supply and demand graph to illustrate the long-run problem in agriculture.

☐ Give cost estimates of the size of farm subsidies in the United States in recent years.

☐ Present several arguments which are made in support of Federal assistance to agriculture.

☐ Define the parity ratio and explain its significance to agricultural policy.

☐ Use a supply and demand graph to identify the economic effects of price supports for agricultural products on output, farm income, consumer and taxpayer expenditures, economic efficiency, and international trade.

☐ Give examples of how the Federal government restricts supply and bolsters demand for farm products.

☐ Present four criticisms of American agricultural policy.

☐ Use four insights from public choice theory to discuss the politics of agricultural legislation and expenditures by the Federal government for farm programs.

☐ Give four reasons to support a prediction that farm subsidies will decline in the future.

☐ Explain the effects of agricultural policy in the European Community (EC) and in the United States on world trade in agricultural products.

☐ List three proposals of the United States in the negotiations of the General Agreement on Tariffs and Trade (GATT).

☐ Identify three objectives of the Farm Act of 1990.

☐ Describe the characteristics, operation, and advantages of a market-oriented policy designed to stabilize farm product prices and farm income.

☐ List the contentions of the pessimists and the responses of the optimists on the issue of whether the world will be able to feed itself fifty years from now.

■ CHAPTER OUTLINE

1. The economic analysis of American agriculture is important for at least five reasons: it is the nation's largest industry; it is a real-world example of the purely competitive model; it illustrates the economic effects of government intervention in markets; it reflects changes in global markets; and it highlights aspects of public choice theory.

2. The farm problem is both a short-run and a long-run problem: the short-run problem is the frequent sharp changes in the incomes of farmers from one year to the next; the long-run problem is the tendency for farm prices and incomes to lag behind the upward trend of prices and incomes in the rest of the economy.

   a. The causes of the short-run (income-instability) problem are the inelastic demand for farm products, fluctuations in the output of agricultural products, fluctuations in the domestic demand, and the unstable foreign demand which result in relatively large changes in agricultural prices and farm incomes.

   b. The causes of the long-run problem (low farm income and farm prices) stem from two basic factors:

   (1) the supply of agricultural products increased significantly over most of this century because of technological advance in agriculture; and

   (2) the demand for agricultural products failed to match the large increase in supply even though there were large increases in income (and population) because the demand for agricultural products is *income* inelastic (that is, increases in income lead to less than proportionate increases in expenditures on farm products).

3. Since the 1930s, farmers have been able to obtain various forms of public aid, but the primary purpose of the Federal government programs has been to enhance and stabilize farm prices and incomes.

   a. Federal government support of agricultural programs is costly (estimated to be $40 to $55 billion from 1990–1994); several arguments are used to justify these expenditures, such as the poor incomes of farmers, the importance of the "family farm," the hazards of farming, and market power problems.

   b. The cornerstone of Federal policy to raise farm prices is the concept of parity (or the parity price) which would give the farmer year after year the same real income per unit of output.

   c. Historically farm policy supported farm prices at some percentage of the parity price. But because the supported price was almost always above the market price, government had to support the price by purchasing and accumulating surpluses of agricultural products; and while farmers gained from this policy, there were losses for consumers and for society, and problems were created in the international sector. To reduce the annual and accumulated surpluses, government attempted:

(1) to reduce the output (or supply) of farm products by acreage-allotment and soil bank programs; and
(2) to expand the demand for farm products by finding new uses for farm products, expanding domestic demand, and increasing the foreign demand for agricultural commodities.

4. Agricultural policies designed to stabilize farm income and prices have not worked well over the past half century, and are subject to four major criticisms.

   a. Farm programs have confused the *symptoms* of the problem (low farm product and low farm incomes) with the *causes* of the problem (resource allocation), and have encouraged people to stay in agriculture.

   b. The major benefits from farm programs are misguided because low-income farmers often receive small government subsidies while high-income farmers often receive large government subsidies; price supports also affect land values and become a subsidy for owners of farm land who rent their land and do not farm.

   c. The various farm programs of the Federal government have often offset or contradicted each other.

   d. Domestic farm policy is becoming less effective in its goal of enhancing farm incomes because of the increased size of farm operations, and because of the significant effects on farm incomes from changes in interest rates or the international value of the dollar.

5. The politics of farm policy explain why costly and extensive farm programs have persisted in the United States despite a decline in the farm population and in the farm vote.

   a. Four insights from public choice theory serve to explain this development: *rent-seeking behavior* by farm groups; the *special-interest effect* that impairs public decision-making; political *logrolling* to turn negative outcomes into a positive outcomes; and the *clear benefits and hidden costs* of farm programs.

   b. But farm subsidies are likely to decline in the future because of continuing declines in the farm population, pressures to balance the Federal budget, the excesses and negative publicity from farm subsidies, and conflicts between domestic and world agricultural policies.

6. The move to reduce trade barriers to agricultural products on a worldwide basis is a significant development of recent years.

   a. Increased domestic support for the price of farm products often has negative effects on trade.

   (1) For example, price support policies by the European Community led to higher trade barriers (tariffs or quotas) to restrict the agricultural imports, gave incentives for domestic overproduction led to demands for export subsidies, and caused problems for American farmers.

   (2) From a world perspective, trade barriers for agricultural products are economically inefficient, distort the patterns of world trade, create frictions in international relations, and are costly (about $35 billion per year).

   b. The United States government proposed a reduction in agricultural tariffs, export subsidies for farm products, and domestic farm supports that distort world trade in recent negotiations of the *General Agreements on Tariffs and Trade* (GATT), but no progress has been made because of opposition from other nations.

   c. The *Farm Act of 1990* has sought to reduce the cost of farm subsidies through reductions in acreage covered by farm programs and by increasing the role of the market in determining farm product prices.

   d. In the long run, it is likely that farm policy will shift from the goal of *enhancing* farm income to the goal of *stabilizing* farm incomes by such government actions as buying farm products when they fall below the long-run trend in the market, or by selling accumulated surpluses when prices rise above the long-run trend; several advantages are cited by proponents of this *market-oriented income stabilization policy*.

7. The American economy has produced agricultural surpluses over the years, but other nations have been plagued by chronic shortages of food; a pessimistic or an optimistic answer can be given to the question of whether the world will be able to feed itself in the future.

■ **IMPORTANT TERMS**

Short-run farm problem	Acreage allotment programs
Long-run farm problem	
Agricultural Adjustment Act of 1933	Soil bank program
	Food for Peace program
Parity concept	Farm Act of 1990
Parity ratio	Market-oriented income stabilization
Price support	

■ **FILL-IN QUESTIONS**

   1. It is important to study the economics of American agriculture for at least five reasons: it is the _____ industry in the nation; it provides a real-world example of the _____ model; it demonstrates the effects of government _____; it reflects the _____ agricultural markets; and it illustrates aspects of _____ theory.

   2. The basic cause of the short-run problem in agriculture is the _____ demand for farm products. This demand occurs because farm products have few good _____, and because of rapidly diminishing

_____

3. The inelastic demand for farm products contributes to unstable farm prices and incomes because relatively (large, small) _____ changes in the output of farm products results in relative _____ changes in prices and incomes; and because relatively _____ changes in domestic or foreign demand result in relatively _____ changes in prices and incomes.

4. From a long-run perspective, the (demand for, supply of) _____ agricultural products increased greatly over the past twenty-five years because of technological progress, but the _____ agricultural products did not increase by as much, in large part because food demand is income (elastic, inelastic) _____ and because the rate of population increase has not matched the increase in production.

5. Since the 1930s, the Federal government has primarily developed programs to enhance or to stabilize the _____ and _____ of farmers. Federal support for agricultural programs is estimated to cost $_____ to $_____ billion under the five-year farm bill adopted in 1990.

6. Four arguments used to justify these expenditures are: the _____ income of farmers; the importance to the "_____" farm as an American institution; the "_____" of farming from many natural disasters; and the fact that the farmers sell their output in (purely competitive, imperfectly competitive) _____ markets, and purchase their inputs in _____ markets.

7. If farmers were to receive a parity price for a product, year after year a given output would enable them to acquire a (fixed, increased) _____ amount of goods and services.

8. If the government supports farm prices at an above-equilibrium level, the result will be (shortages, surpluses) _____ which the government must _____ in order to maintain prices at their support level.

   a. Farmers benefit from this price-support program because it increases their _____

   b. But consumers are hurt by it because they must pay

higher _____ and consume (more, less) _____ of the product.

   c. Society (gains, loses) _____ because taxpayers will pay (higher, lower) _____ taxes to finance the purchase of the surplus by government; and because there is economic _____ _____ from the (overallocation, underallocation) _____ of resources to agriculture.

   d. There are also _____ costs from distortion in worldwide supply and demand for agricultural products, the increased potential for _____ barriers, and a (positive, negative) _____ effect on less developed countries.

9. To bring the equilibrium level of prices in the market up to their support level, government has attempted to (increase, decrease) _____ the demand for and to _____ the supply of farm products.

10. Two types of programs that have been used by the Federal government to reduce agricultural production are acreage-_____ and _____ programs. The Federal government has also attempted to find new _____ for agricultural commodities, and to increase domestic and foreign _____ for agricultural products through the domestic food _____ program or the foreign _____ program.

11. Agricultural policies to stabilize farm income and prices (have, have not) _____ worked well over the past sixty years for at least four reasons:

   a. They have confused the _____ of the farm problem (low prices and incomes) with the _____ of the problem (misallocation of resources);

   b. Much of the benefits from farm subsidies go to (high, low) _____-income farmers instead of _____-income farmers;

   c. Farm programs of the Federal government have offset or _____ each other;

   d. Domestic farm policy is (increasing, decreasing) _____ in its effectiveness in enhancing farm incomes because of the _____ scale of farm operations; and because of the significant effects on farm incomes from changes in domestic _____ rates

or the international value of the _____

12. Despite these criticisms, farm policies have received strong support in Congress over the years, the result of which can be explained by insights from _____

theory. Farm groups are exhibiting _____ behavior when they lobby for programs that transfer in-

come to them. There is also a _____ effect because the costs to individual taxpayers is (large, small)

_____ but the benefits to farmers is _____ from farm programs. Agricultural groups or farm-state politicians can turn negative outcomes into positive outcomes

by political _____. The benefits of farm pro-

grams are (clear, hidden) _____, but the costs are

_____

13. Farm subsidies are likely to decline in the future be-

cause of declines in the farm _____, pressures to

balance the Federal _____, negative publicity from

the excesses of farm _____, and domestic and world

agricultural _____ conflicts.

14. The effects of higher supports for the prices of agricultural products by the European Community have

been (increased, decreased) _____ trade barriers,

_____ incentives for domestic production in the

member nations, _____ export subsidies

for farm products in member nations, and _____ sales of American agricultural products to the European Community.

15. World barriers to free trade in agricultural products

_____ trade and contribute to economic

_____ in the allocation of world resources to ag-

riculture. The estimate benefits from free trade in world

agriculture are $_____ billion per year.

16. The American proposals in recent negotiations under

the General Agreements on _____

called for (an increase, a decrease) _____ in agri-

cultural tariffs, _____ export subsidies for farm

products, and _____ domestic price supports for agricultural commodities that distort world trade, but the

negotiations collapsed because of strong opposition from other nations.

17. The *Farm Act of 1990* aimed to decrease the cost of

farm subsidies through reductions in _____ covered by farm programs, and by making more use of the

_____ to determine prices for agricultural commod-

ities.

18. The market-oriented income stabilization policy:
   a. would have the Federal government (buy, sell)

_____ agricultural commodities when their

market prices fell below and _____ agri-

cultural commodities when their market prices rose above their long-run trends of prices.
   b. would, its proponents contend, (expand, contract)

_____ government involvement in

agriculture, improve the _____ of resources in the long run, reduce the costs of the farm

programs to _____, and stimulate

the _____ of agricultural commodities.

19. There is a global dimension to farm problems:
   a. The pessimistic view is one of possible famine as

(supply, demand) _____ outpaces

_____ because:

(1) the quantity of arable land is _____

and its quality is _____;
(2) urban sprawl reduces the availability of (agricul-

tural, nonagricultural) _____ land;
(3) the underground water system is being depleted by

increasing _____;
(4) world _____ continues to increase; and
(5) future agricultural production may be affected by

long-run changes in the _____
   b. Optimists contend global famine is not a serious prospect because:

(1) the arable land for production can be _____

_____;

(2) agricultural _____ continues to rise,

especially in _____ countries;

(3) the rate of world _____ growth is di-

minishing; and
(4) any food shortages would produce adjustments in

_____ system.

■ PROBLEMS AND PROJECTS

1. In columns 1 and 2 in the following table is a demand schedule for agricultural product X.

(1) Price	(2) Bushels of X demanded	(3) Bushels of X demanded
$2.00	600	580
1.80	620	600
1.60	640	620
1.40	660	640
1.20	680	660
1.00	700	680
.80	720	700
.60	740	720

a. Is demand elastic or inelastic in the price range given? _____

b. If the amount of X produced should increase from 600 to 700 bushels, the income of producers of X would

_____ from $_____ to

$_____; an increase of _____% in the amount of X produced would cause income to

_____ by _____%.

c. If the amount of X produced were 700 bushels and the demand for X decreased from that shown in columns 1 and 2 to that shown in columns 1 and 3, the

price of X would _____ from $_____

to $_____; the income of farmers would

_____ from $_____ to $_____

d. Assume that the government supports a price of $1.80, that the demand for X is that shown in columns 1 and 2, and that farmers grow 720 bushels of X.

(1) At the supported price there will be a surplus of

_____ bushels of X.

(2) If the government buys this surplus at the support price the cost to the taxpayers of purchasing the sur-

plus is $_____

(3) The total income of the farmers producing product X when they receive the support price of $1.80 per bush-

el for their entire crop of 720 bushels is $_____

(4) Had farmers to sell the crop of 720 bushels at the free-market price, the price of X would be only

$_____ per bushel; and the total income

of these farmers would be $_____

(5) The gain to farmers producing X from the price-

support program is, therefore, $_____

(6) In addition to the cost to taxpayers of purchasing

the surplus, consumers pay a price that is $_____

greater than the free-market price and receive a quan-

tity of X that is _____ bushels less than they would have received in a free market.

2. The following table gives the index of prices farmers paid in three different years. The price farmers received in year 1, the base year, for a certain agricultural product was $3.50 per bushel.

a. Compute the parity price of the product in years 2 and 3 and enter them in the table.

Year	Index of prices paid	Parity price	Price received	Parity ratio
1	100	$3.50	$3.50	100%
2	120	_____	3.78	____%
3	200	_____	5.25	____%

b. The prices received for the product in each year are also shown in the table. Complete the table by computing the parity *ratio* in years 2 and 3. (*Hint*: It is *not* necessary to construct an index of prices received in order to compute the parity ratio. This ratio can be computed by dividing the price received by the parity price.)

3. The demand schedule for agricultural product Y is given in columns 1 and 2 of the following table.

(1) Price	(2) Bales of Y demanded	(3) Bales of Y demanded
$5.00	40,000	41,000
4.75	40,200	41,200
4.50	40,400	41,400
4.25	40,600	41,600
4.00	40,800	41,800
3.75	41,000	42,000
3.50	41,200	42,200

a. If farmers were persuaded by the government to reduce the size of their crop from 41,000 to 40,000

bales, the income of farmers would _____

from $_____ to $_____
b. If the crop remained constant at 41,000 bales and the demand for Y increased to that shown in columns

1 and 3, the income of farmers would _____

from $_____ to $_____

4. Suppose the demand for sow jowls during a certain period of time was that shown in the table on the next page, and the Federal government wished to stabilize the price of sow jowls at $.70 a pound.

Price (per pound)	Quantity demanded (pounds)
$1.00	1000
.90	1020
.80	1040
.70	1060
.60	1080
.50	1100
.40	1120

a. If the output of sow jowls were 1100 pounds during that period of time, the market price of sow jowls would be $_____ and the Federal government would (buy, sell) _____ (how many) _____ pounds of sow jowls.

b. But if the output were 1000 pounds during that period of time, the market price of sow jowls would be $_____ and the Federal government would _____ (how many) _____ pounds of sow jowls.

■ **SELF-TEST**

Circle the T if the statement is true; the F if it is false.

1. The short-run farm problem is the sharp year-to-year fluctuations in farm prices and farm incomes that frequently occur.   **T   F**

2. The demand for farm products is price elastic.   **T   F**

3. The quantities of agricultural commodities produced tend to be fairly *insensitive* to changes in agricultural prices because a large percentage of farmers' total costs are variable.   **T   F**

4. The foreign demand for farm products is relatively stable.   **T   F**

5. Appreciation of the dollar will tend to increase the demand for farm products.   **T   F**

6. The supply of agricultural products has tended to increase more rapidly than the demand for these products in the United States.   **T   F**

7. Most of the recent technological advances in agriculture have been initiated by farmers.   **T   F**

8. The demand for farm products is income elastic.   **T   F**

9. The long-run farm problem is that the incomes of farmers have been low relative to incomes in the economy as a whole.   **T   F**

10. The size of the farm population in the United States has declined in both relative and absolute terms since about 1930.   **T   F**

11. The major aim of agricultural policy in the United States has been to enhance and stabilize farm prices and farm incomes.   **T   F**

12. Federal expenditures for farm price and income support programs are relatively small and cost only $1 billion a year.   **T   F**

13. If the prices paid by farmers were 500% higher than in the base year and the price received by farmers were 400% higher than in the base year, the parity ratio would be 125%.   **T   F**

14. Application of the parity concept to farm prices causes farm prices to decline and results in agricultural surpluses.   **T   F**

15. When government supports farm prices at above-equilibrium levels it can reduce the annual surpluses of agricultural commodities either by increasing the supply or by decreasing the demand for them.   **T   F**

16. The acreage-allotment and soil bank programs were designed to decrease the supply of farm products.   **T   F**

17. Restricting the number of acres which farmers employ to grow agricultural products has not been a very successful method of reducing surpluses because farmers tend to cultivate their land more intensively when the acreage is reduced.   **T   F**

18. Public policy has been effective in alleviating the resource allocation problem in agriculture.   **T   F**

19. The price-income support programs for agriculture have most benefited those farmers who least need the government assistance.   **T   F**

20. A farm organization lobbying Congress for an increase in farm subsidies is an example of political *logrolling*.   **T   F**

21. One reason to predict that farm subsidies will decline in the future is that there is a declining farm population.   **T   F**

22. Domestic agricultural support programs are not harmful to world agricultural trade and contribute to the efficiency allocation of worldwide resources to agriculture.   **T   F**

23. The Farm Bill of 1990 called for an increase in farm subsidies and reduced reliance on markets to determine the prices of agricultural products.   **T   F**

24. A market-oriented income stabilization policy would shift the goal of farm policy from enhancing to stabilizing farm incomes.   **T   F**

25. There are no strong counterarguments to the position that "unless the nations of the world adopt new agricultural policies there will be a worldwide famine fifty years from now." **T   F**

Circle the letter that corresponds to the best answer.

1. If the demand for agricultural products is price inelastic, a relatively small increase in supply will result in:
(a) a relatively small increase in farm prices and incomes
(b) a relatively small decrease in farm prices and a relatively large increase in farm incomes
(c) a relatively large decrease in farm prices and incomes
(d) a relatively large increase in farm prices and a relatively small decrease in farm incomes

2. The year-to-year instability of farm prices and farm incomes is the result of fluctuations in:
(a) the outputs of farmers
(b) the domestic demand for farm products
(c) the foreign demand for agricultural commodities
(d) all of the above

3. If over time increases in the supply of farm products are much greater than the increases in demand for farm products, then the supply and demand model for farm products would suggest that price:
(a) and quantity will both increase
(b) and quantity will both decrease
(c) will increase, but the quantity will decrease
(d) will decrease, but the quantity will increase

4. Which one of the following is *not* a reason why the increases in demand for agricultural commodities have been relatively small?
(a) the population of the United States has not increased so rapidly as the productivity of agriculture
(b) the increased per capita incomes of American consumers have resulted in less than proportionate increases in their expenditures for farm products
(c) the demand for agricultural products is inelastic
(d) the standard of living in the United States is well above the level of bare subsistence

5. The market system has failed to solve the long-run problem of low farm incomes because:
(a) the demand for agricultural products is relatively inelastic
(b) the supply of agricultural products is relatively elastic
(c) agricultural products have relatively few good substitutes
(d) agricultural resources are relatively immobile

6. The farm bill passed in 1990 is expected to cost, over a five-year period, about:

(a) $5 billion
(b) $20 billion
(c) $40–$55 billion
(d) $100–$115 billion

7. Which of the following is *not* one of the arguments used in support of public aid for agriculture in the United States?
(a) farmers are relative poor and need help to maintain a "way of life"
(b) farmers are subject to hazards to which other industries are not subject
(c) farmers sell their products in highly competitive markets and buy resources in highly imperfect markets
(d) farmers are more affected by competition from foreign producers than other parts of the economy

8. Farm parity means that:
(a) the real income of the farmer remains constant
(b) a given output will furnish the farmer with a constant amount of real income
(c) the purchasing power of the farmer's nominal income remains constant
(d) the nominal income of the farmer will buy a constant amount of goods and services

9. If the index of prices paid by farmers was 1000 and the prices received by farmers was 600, then the parity ratio would be:
(a) 2.1
(b) 1.7
(c) 0.6
(d) 0.4

10. The necessary consequence of the government's supporting farm prices at an above-equilibrium level is:
(a) a surplus of agricultural products
(b) increased consumption of agricultural products
(c) reduced production of agricultural products
(d) the destruction of agricultural products

11. Another consequence of having government support farm prices at an above-equilibrium level is that consumers pay higher prices for farm products and:
(a) consume more of these products and pay higher taxes
(b) consume less of these products and pay higher taxes
(c) consume more of these products and pay lower taxes
(d) consume less of these products and pay lower taxes

Use the diagram on the next page to answer the next three questions (12, 13, and 14). D is the demand for and S is the supply of a certain product.

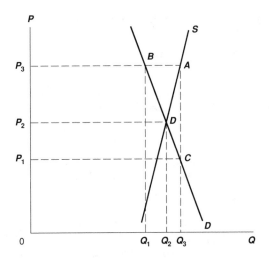

12. If the Federal government supported the price of this product at P_3, the total amount it would have to spend to purchase the surplus of the product would be:
- **(a)** $0Q_3AP_3$
- **(b)** Q_1Q_3AB
- **(c)** P_1CAP_3
- **(d)** $0Q_1BP_3$

13. With a support price of P_3, the total income of producers of the product will be:
- **(a)** $0Q_3AP_3$
- **(b)** $0Q_1BP_3$
- **(c)** $0Q_3CP_1$
- **(d)** $0Q_2DP_2$

14. With a support price of P_3, the amount spent by consumers will be:
- **(a)** $0Q_3AP_3$
- **(b)** $0Q_1BP_3$
- **(c)** $0Q_2DP_2$
- **(d)** Q_1Q_3AB

Answer the next three questions (15, 16, and 17) on the basis of the demand and supply schedules for agricultural product Z as shown below.

Pounds of Z demanded	Price	Pounds of Z supplied
850	$1.30	1150
900	1.20	1100
950	1.10	1050
1000	1.00	1000
1050	.90	950
1100	.80	900
1150	.70	850

15. If the Federal government supports the price of Z at $1.30 a pound, then at this price, there is:
- **(a)** a surplus of 200 pounds of Z
- **(b)** a surplus of 300 pounds of Z

- **(c)** a surplus of 400 pounds of Z
- **(d)** a shortage of 400 pounds of Z

16. With a Federal price support of $1.30 a pound, consumers spend:
- **(a)** $1,040, the Federal government spends $410, and farmers receive income from product Z of $1,450
- **(b)** $1,105, the Federal government spends $390, and farmers receive income from product Z of $1,495
- **(c)** $1,296, the Federal government spends $240, and farmers receive income from product Z of $1,320
- **(d)** $1,045, the Federal government spends $110, and farmers receive income from product Z of $1,155

17. If instead of supporting the price the Federal government took actions to increase demand by 150 units at each price and to decrease supply by 150 units at each price, then the equilibrium price would be:
- **(a)** $1.00 and the income of farmers would be $1000
- **(b)** $1.10 and the income of farmers would be $1320
- **(c)** $1.20 and the income of farmers would be $1260
- **(d)** $1.30 and the income of farmers would be $1300

18. Which one of the following is *not* a reason why farm programs have generally failed to accomplish their aims?
- **(a)** the farm programs have not eliminated the basic cause of the problem
- **(b)** restricting agricultural output increases farm prices but reduces farm income when demand is inelastic
- **(c)** the farm program has become increasingly more costly and less effective
- **(d)** the principal beneficiaries of government aid have been farmers with high, not low, incomes

19. Which of the following can diminish the effectiveness of farm programs?
- **(a)** changes in interest rates in the economy
- **(b)** changes in the international value of the dollar
- **(c)** the accessibility of foreign markets to farmers
- **(d)** all of the above

20. When farmers and farm organizations lobby Congress for a larger appropriation for agricultural price and income programs, then according to public choice theory this action would be an example of:
- **(a)** confusing symptoms with causes
- **(b)** misguided subsidies
- **(c)** rent-seeking behavior
- **(d)** political logrolling

21. Which of the following has been a consequence of protective trade barriers for agriculture established by the nations of the European Community (EC)?
- **(a)** restriction of exports of EC farm products
- **(b)** subsidization of imports of U.S. farm products
- **(c)** overproduction of farm products in the EC
- **(d)** underproduction of farm products in the EC

22. The goal of a market-oriented income stabilization policy would be:

(a) to prevent farm prices and incomes from falling in the long run

(b) to prevent sharp fluctuations in farm prices and incomes from one year to the next

(c) to increase farm prices and incomes in the long run

(d) to prevent both sharp year-to-year fluctuations and falling long-run farm prices and incomes

23. In a market-oriented income stabilization policy the Federal government would:

(a) sell surplus farm commodities when their prices fall below their long-run trend of prices

(b) buy surplus farm commodities when their prices rise above their long-run trend of prices

(c) sell surplus farm commodities when their prices rise above their long-run trend

(d) buy surplus farm commodities when their market prices fall

24. Which of the following is *not* one of the advantages its proponents see in a market-oriented income stabilization policy?

(a) an expansion in the employment of resources in the agricultural sector of the economy

(b) an expansion in the exports of the agricultural sector of the ecoomy

(c) a reduction in the costs to taxpayers of the farm program

(d) a reduction in government involvement in agriculture

25. A good reason for an optimistic view of the capacity of the world to feed itself fifty years from now would be that:

(a) the population of the world is increasing

(b) the climate of the world is changing

(c) agricultural productivity is rising

(d) land is being put to more productive uses in urban areas

■ **DISCUSSION QUESTIONS**

1. Why are the economics of agriculture and agriculture policy important topics for study?

2. What is the short-run farm problem and what are its causes?

3. Why does the demand for agricultural products tend to be inelastic? What are the implications for agriculture?

4. What have been the specific causes of the large increases in the supply of agricultural products since World War I?

5. Why has the demand for agricultural products failed to increase at the same rate as the supply of these products?

6. Explain why the farm population tends to be relatively immobile.

7. What is meant by "the farm program"? What particular aspect of the farm problem has traditionally received the major attention of farmers and their representatives in Congress?

8. Why do agricultural interests claim that farmers have a special right to aid from the Federal government?

9. Explain the concept of parity and the parity ratio.

10. Why is the result of government-supported prices invariably a surplus of farm commodities? How do supported prices affect consumers and farmers?

11. What programs has the government used to try to restrict farm production? Why have these programs been relatively unsuccessful in limiting agricultural production?

12. How has the Federal government tried to increase the demand for farm products?

13. Why has farm policy not been successful in preventing falling farm prices and incomes, surpluses, and the disparity in farm incomes?

14. What insights does public choice theory provide about the persistence of Federal government support for farm programs?

15. What are the reasons to suggest that the Federal government support for farm programs will decline in the future?

16. Explain the economic effects of high trade barriers for agricultural products on a domestic economy and on the world economy using the nations of the European Community as the example of a domestic economy. What are the estimated costs to the world economy of trade barriers in agriculture?

17. Discuss the proposal of the United States in the agricultural trade negotiations of the General Agreements on Tariffs and Trade (GATT).

18. What is the direction of farm policy in the United States as reflected in the Farm Act of 1990?

19. Explain

(a) how the market-oriented income stabilization policy would shift the emphasis from enhancing to stabilizing farm prices and incomes

(b) how the Federal government would stabilize farm prices and incomes if it adopted this policy

(c) what advantages the proponents of this policy believe it would have

20. What are the arguments of the pessimists and of the optimists on the issue of whether the world will be able to feed itself in the next century?

■ ANSWERS

Chapter 34 Agriculture: Economics and Policy

FILL-IN QUESTIONS

1. largest, purely competitive, policies, globalization, public choice

2. inelastic, substitutes, marginal utility

3. small, large, small, large

4. supply of, demand for, inelastic

5. prices, income (either order), 40, 55

6. low (or poor), family, hazards, purely competitive, imperfectly competitive

7. fixed

8. surpluses, purchase; *a.* incomes; *b.* prices, less; *c.* loses, higher, inefficiency, overallocation; *d.* international, trade, negative

9. increase, decrease

10. allotments, soil bank, uses, demand, stamps, Food for Peace

11. have not, *a.* symptoms, causes; *b.* high, low; *c.* contradicted; *d.* decreasing, large, interest, dollar

12. public choice, rent-seeking, special interest, small, large, logrolling, clear, hidden

13. population, budget, subsidies, policy

14. increased, increased, increased, decreased

15. distort, inefficiency, 35

16. Tariffs and Trade, a decrease, a decrease, a decrease

17. acreage, market

18. *a.* buy, sell; *b.* contract, allocation, taxpayers, export

19. *a.* demand, supply; (1) fixed, poor, (2) agricultural, (3) irrigation, (4) population, (5) climate; *b.* (1) increased, (2) productivity, less developed, (3) population, (4) price (market)

PROBLEMS AND PROJECTS

1. *a.* inelastic; *b.* decrease, 1,200.00, 700.00, 16⅔, decrease, 41⅔; *c.* fall, 1.00, 0.80, fall, 700.00, 560.00; *d.* (1) 100, (2) 180, (3) 1296, (4) 0.80, 576, (5) 720, (6) 1.00, 100

2. *a.* 420, 7.00; *b.* 90, 75

3. *a.* increase, 153,750.00, 200,000.00; *b.* increase, 153,750.00, 205,000.00

4. *a.* .50, buy, 40; *b.* 1.00, sell, 60

SELF-TEST

1. T, p. 638	**14.** F, p. 644
2. F, pp. 638–639	**15.** F, p. 644
3. F, p. 639	**16.** T, p. 645
4. F, p. 640	**17.** T, p. 645
5. F, p. 640	**18.** F, p. 646
6. T, pp. 640–641	**19.** T, p. 646
7. F, p. 641	**20.** F, p. 647
8. F, p. 641	**21.** T, p. 648
9. T, pp. 641–642	**22.** F, p. 648
10. T, p. 642	**23.** F, p. 649
11. T, p. 642	**24.** T, p. 649
12. F, p. 642	**25.** F, p. 651
13. F, p. 644	

1. *c*, p. 639	**14.** *b*, p. 644
2. *d*, pp. 639–640	**15.** *b*, p. 644
3. *d*, p. 641	**16.** *b*, p. 644
4. *c*, p. 641	**17.** *d*, pp. 644–645
5. *d*, p. 642	**18.** *b*, p. 646
6. *c*, p. 642	**19.** *d*, p. 647
7. *d*, p. 643	**20.** *c*, p. 647
8. *b*, p. 643	**21.** *c*, p. 648
9. *c*, p. 644	**22.** *b*, p. 649
10. *a*, p. 644	**23.** *c*, pp. 649–650
11. *b*, p. 644	**24.** *a*, p. 650
12. *b*, p. 644	**25.** *c*, p. 651
13. *a*, p. 644	

DISCUSSION QUESTIONS

1. p. 638	**11.** p. 645
2. pp. 638–639	**12.** pp. 645–646
3. p. 639	**13.** pp. 646–647
4. p. 641	**14.** pp. 647–648
5. p. 641	**15.** p. 648
6. pp. 641–642	**16.** pp. 648–649
7. pp. 642–643	**17.** p. 649
8. p. 643	**18.** p. 649
9. pp. 643–644	**19.** pp. 649–650
10. p. 644	**20.** pp. 650–651

CHAPTER 35

Income Inequality and Poverty

Chapter 35 examines another current problem in the economy of the United States: the unequal distribution of total income and the poverty of many families in the nation.

The things which you should learn from this chapter are found in the checklist below. In addition, the following ideas have an important bearing on the discussion of inequality and poverty. First, you will recall from Chapter 6 that one of the functions of government in the American economy is to modify the economic results which a **pure** market system would yield: it is the market system and the institutions of capitalism which bring about an unequal distribution of income, and government in the United States has worked to reduce—but not eliminate—this unequal distribution.

Second, the critics of the market system attack the system because it has unequally distributed income. But American capitalism has replied by repairing many of its faults. It is for this reason that people and groups advocating drastically different economic systems have met with little success in the United States or in other nations of the world.

Third, the single most effective method of reducing the importance of income inequality and the extent of poverty in the United States has been the maintenance of full employment and an expanding average standard of living. Other programs have aided in the achievement of this goal, but the best cure has been the high and increasing output of the American economy.

Fourth, very few people advocate an absolutely equal distribution of income; the question to be decided is not one of inequality or equality, but of how much or how little inequality there should be. The question can be looked at either ethically or economically, and the economist has nothing to offer on the ethical question but a personal value judgment. From the economic point of view it is the task of the economist to observe that less income inequality may result in a smaller domestic output and a lower employment rate. This is the fundamental "tradeoff" confronting the economy and it requires that the people of the United States make a choice. The pros and cons of the income-inequality issue represent no more than different opinions on the degree to which we should reduce our economic efficiency (total output and employment) in order to reduce income inequality.

Finally, while poverty is caused by many forces, it is essentially an economic problem. Any attack on poverty will have to be an economic attack. Over the years a variety of programs have been established to provide income support for people in the United States. At the end of the chapter you will learn about the major features of the programs. Despite these established programs, there is still dissatisfaction with the income maintenance system. The final topic of the chapter focuses on comprehensive and partial proposals for reform of public assistance.

■ CHECKLIST

When you have studied this chapter you should be able to:

☐ Present data from the textbook to support the conclusion that there is considerable income inequality in the United States.

☐ Report what has happened to the distribution of income in the United States in three time periods since 1929.

☐ State what is measured on each axis when a Lorenz curve is used to describe the degree of income inequality; and what area measures the extent of income inequality.

☐ Explain the two ways in which Census Bureau data on income inequality have been adjusted; and what the adjusted data reveal about the degree of and the trends in income equality in the United States.

☐ Describe the effects of taxes and of transfer payments on the extent of inequality in the distribution of income and poverty in the American economy.

☐ Enumerate seven causes of an unequal distribution of income.

☐ State the case **for** and the case **against** income equality.

☐ Explain the trade-off between equality and efficiency that is at the heart of the debate over how much income inequality is desirable.

☐ Define poverty using current government standards.
☐ Identify the groups in which poverty is concentrated.
☐ Describe the trends in the poverty rate since 1960.
☐ Explain the "black underclass" view of ghetto poverty and poverty programs.
☐ Give three reasons why poverty tends to be invisible.
☐ Contrast social insurance with public assistance (welfare); and list the three programs in the former and the four programs in the latter category.
☐ State three major criticisms of the welfare system.
☐ Explain how a negative income tax (NIT) might be employed to reform the welfare system and the two crucial elements in any NIT plan.
☐ List the three goals of any NIT plan and explain why it is impossible to devise a program in which these three goals do not conflict.
☐ State five reasons why the AFDC program was subject to calls for reform.
☐ Explain what **workfare** means and describe the Family Support Act of 1988.

■ **CHAPTER OUTLINE**

1. There is considerable income inequality in the American economy.
 a. The extent of the inequality can be seen by examining a personal-distribution-of-income table.
 b. Since 1929 the real incomes received by all income classes have increased; and between 1929 and 1947 the relative distribution of personal income changed to reduce income inequality. From 1947–1969 there was a slight increase in the equality of income distribution, but from 1969–1990, the distribution of income moved to less equality. Comparing 1947 to 1990, the distribution of income has been relatively constant.
 c. The Lorenz curve is a geometric device for portraying the extent of inequality in any group at any time, for comparing the extent of inequality among different groups, and for contrasting the extent of inequality at different times.

2. The data published annually by the Bureau of the Census may overstate the extent of income inequality in the United States.
 a. By broadening the concept of income to include in-kind transfers, education provided by government, and capital gains, and by subtracting Federal personal income and payroll taxes, Browning concluded that inequality in the distribution of income is less than assumed and has lessened with the passage of time.
 b. By looking at earnings over a lifetime rather than in a single year Paglin found that there is less income inequality than census data indicate and that income equality has lessened since World War II.

3. The tax system and the transfer payments of govern-

ment in the United States significantly reduce the extent of income inequality and of poverty in the American economy.

4. The impersonal market system does not necessarily result in a just or fair distribution of income; at least seven factors explain why income inequality exists:
 (1) the distribution of abilities and skills of people;
 (2) differences in education and training;
 (3) preferences of certain types of jobs and willingness to accept risk on the job;
 (4) discrimination in labor markets;
 (5) inequalities in the ownership of property and in the accumulation of wealth;
 (6) market power in either resource or product markets; and
 (7) other factors such as luck, personal connections, and misfortunes.

5. The important question which society must answer is not whether there will or will not be income inequality but what is the best amount of inequality.
 a. Those who argue for equality contend that it leads to the maximum satisfaction of consumer wants (utility) in the economy.
 b. But those who argue for inequality contend that equality would reduce the incentives to work, save, invest, and take risks; and that these incentives are needed if the economy is to be efficient: to produce as large an output (and income) as it is possible for it to produce from its available resources.
 c. In the United States there is a trade-off between economic equality and economic efficiency. A more nearly equal distribution of income results in less economic efficiency (a smaller domestic output) and greater economic efficiency leads to a more unequal distribution of income. The debate over the right amount of inequality depends, therefore, upon how much output society is willing to sacrifice to reduce income inequality.

6. Aside from inequality in the distribution of income, there is great concern today with the problem of poverty in the United States.
 a. Using the generally accepted definition of poverty, 13.5% of the people in the American economy live in poverty.
 b. The poor tend to be concentrated among certain groups, such as blacks, Hispanics, female-headed families, and children.
 c. The poverty rate decreased significantly between 1960 and 1968, remained relatively constant from 1969–1978, increased in the early 1980s, and has gradually declined since then. When alternative poverty rates are calculated that take into account the monetary value of noncash transfer, the estimated rate for 1990 was 9.8%.

d. Some observers contend that ghettos produce a "black underclass" and a culture of poverty that cannot be corrected by antipoverty programs, and thus the poor must help themselves out of poverty. Critics of this view counter that it is simplistic, blames the victim, and fails to focus on larger social and economic problems; they think the poverty problem can be partially addressed by better jobs, work experiences, and income-maintenance programs.

e. Poverty in the United States tends to be invisible because the pool of poor people changes, the poor are isolated in large cities, and the poor do not have a political voice.

7. The income-maintenance system of the United States is intended to reduce poverty and includes both social insurance and public assistance (welfare) programs.

a. OASDI ("social security") and Medicare are the principal social insurance programs and are financed by taxes levied on employers and employees.

b. The unemployment insurance programs maintained by the states and financed by taxes on employers are also a part of the social insurance program of the United States.

c. The public assistance programs include SSI, AFDC, food stamps, and Medicaid.

d. The social security (or welfare) system has been criticized in recent years. Its critics argue that it is costly to administer, is inequitable, impairs incentives to work, and creates family problems.

8. One comprehensive approach to income maintenance would employ a negative income tax (NIT) to subsidize families whose incomes are below a certain level.

a. In any NIT plan a family would be guaranteed a minimum income and the subsidy to a family would decrease as its earned income increases. But a comparison of three alternative plans reveals that the guaranteed income, the (benefit-loss) rate at which the subsidy declines as earned income increases, and the (break-even) income at which the subsidy is no longer paid may differ.

b. The comparison of the plans also indicates there is a conflict among the goals of taking families out of poverty, maintaining incentives to work, and keeping the costs of the plan at a reasonable level; and that a trade-off among the three goals is necessary because no one plan can achieve all three goals.

9. A more recent, but more piecemeal, approach to welfare reform is **workfare**. This reform plan has focused primarily on the AFDC program. Under this plan, welfare recipients would be provided with education, training, and work activities to help move them from public assistance to employment. This welfare-to-work plan was enacted in the Family Assistance Act of 1988.

■ IMPORTANT TERMS

Income inequality
Lorenz curve
In-kind transfer
Optimal distribution of income
Equality vs. efficiency trade-off
Poverty rate
Income-maintenance system
Social security programs
Public assistance (welfare) programs
Old age, survivors, and disability insurance (OASDI)
Medicare

Unemployment insurance (compensation)
Supplemental security income (SSI)
Aid to Families with Dependent Children (AFDC)
Food stamp program
Medicaid
Negative income tax (NIT)
Guaranteed income
Benefit-loss rate
Break-even income
Workfare plans
Family Support Act of 1988

■ FILL-IN QUESTIONS

1. It can fairly be said that the extent of income inequality in the United States is _____

a. The percentage of total personal income received by the highest quintile has since 1929 (increased, decreased) _____ and the percentage received by the lowest two quintiles has _____; and these changes can fairly be said to have been (slight, significant) _____

b. But since the close of World War II the distribution of personal income in the United States (has, has not) _____ changed significantly.

2. Income inequality can be portrayed graphically by drawing a _____ curve.

a. When such a curve is plotted, the cumulative percentage of (income, families) _____ is measured along the horizontal and the cumulative percentage of _____ is measured along the vertical axis.

b. The curve which would show a completely (perfectly) equal distribution of income is a diagonal line which would run from the (lower, upper) _____ left to the _____ right corner of the graph.

c. The extent or degree of income inequality is measured by the area which lies between the _____ and the _____

3. Two major criticisms of the census data on the distribution of income in the United States are that the income concept used in the census is too (narrow, broad) _____ and that the income-accounting period is too (short, long) _____. When the data are adjusted to take account of these two criticisms the distribution of income is (more, less) _____ unequal and over time the inequality has become (greater, smaller) _____

4. The tax system and the transfer programs in the American economy significantly (reduce, expand) _____ the degree of inequality in the distribution of income.

5. The important factors which explain (or cause) income inequality are differences in _____; in _____ and _____; in job _____ and risk; in labor market _____; in the ownership of _____; in market _____; and in luck, connections, misfortune, and discrimination.

6. Those who argue for the:
a. equal distribution of income contend that it results in the maximization of total (income, utility) _____ in the economy;
b. unequal distribution of income believe it results in a greater total (income, utility) _____

7. The fundamental trade-off is between economic _____ and economic _____ This means that:
a. less income inequality leads to a (greater, smaller) _____ total output; and
b. a larger total output requires (more, less) _____ income inequality.
c. The problem for a society that wants more equality is how to (minimize, maximize) _____ the adverse effects on economic efficiency. Recent studies suggest that the (gain, loss) _____ from the redistribution of income may be higher than originally thought.

8. Using the more or less official definition of poverty,
a. The poor includes any family of four with less than $_____ and any individual with less than $_____ a year to spend.

b. Approximately _____% of the population and about _____ million people are poor.

9. Poverty tends to be concentrated:
a. among the (young, elderly) _____
b. among (whites, blacks and Hispanics) _____
c. in families headed by _____

10. Alleviating ghetto poverty is difficult.
a. One view holds that city ghettos are spawning a _____ which traps people in a permanent cycle of poverty; the responsibility for solving this poverty problem largely rests with _____ and not with government programs or laws.
b. Critics of this view contend that it is _____ _____ and blames the _____ of poverty. They suggest that poverty in ghettos may be alleviated by providing residents with more and better _____, improved _____ and _____; and that a program of income _____ be instituted.

11. In the affluent economy of the United States much of the poverty in the country is (visible, invisible) _____ _____ because the poverty _____ changes from year to year, the poor are isolated in large _____, and the poor do not have a _____ voice.

12. The income-maintenance system in the United States consists of social _____ programs and public _____ programs.
a. In the first category of programs are
(1) _____ and medi-_____; and
(2) _____ compensation.
b. In the second category are
(1) (use initials) _____ and _____;
(2) the _____ program; and
(3) medi-_____

13. Critics of the income-maintenance system often refer to "the welfare mess" and point to its three *in*s: they contend that it is administratively *in*-_____, is *in-_____*, and impairs work

in-_____

14. The two critical elements of any negative income tax plan are a _____ income below which family incomes would not be allowed to fall and a _____rate which specifies the rate at which the subsidy would be reduced if earned income increases.

15. The three goals of any negative income tax plan:

a. are to get families out of _____,

provide _____ to work, and ensure

the _____ of the program are reasonable;

b. are (complementary, conflicting) _____

16. Recent reforms of the income supplement system have focused on _____ because among other reasons the program tends to encourage family _____, encourage or at least subsidize _____, and promote a _____ of poverty.

17. The criticisms of AFDC have resulted in a variety of _____ proposals, where people on welfare would receive help through education, training, and work to move from public assistance to _____.

In 1988, the _____ Act was passed to reform welfare in this manner.

■ **PROBLEMS AND PROJECTS**

1. The distribution of personal income among families in a hypothetical economy is shown in the table below.
   a. Complete the table by computing:
   (1) The percentage of all families in each income class and all lower classes; enter these figures in column 4.
   (2) The percentage of total income received by each income class and all lower classes; enter these figures in column 5.
   b. From the distribution of income data in columns 4 and 5 it can be seen that:
   (1) Consumer units with less than $15,000 a year income constitute the lowest _____% of all families and receive _____% of the total income.
   (2) Families with incomes of $50,000 a year or more constitute the highest _____% of all families and receive _____% of the total income.
   c. Use the figures you entered in columns 4 and 5 to draw a Lorenz curve on the graph on the next page. (Plot the seven points and the zero-zero point and connect them with a smooth curve.) Be sure to label the axes.
   (1) On the same graph draw a diagonal line which would indicate complete equality in the distribution of income.
   (2) Shade the area of the graph that shows the degree of income inequality.

(1) Personal income class	(2) Percentage of all families in this class	(3) Percentage of total income received by this class	(4) Percentage of all families in this and all lower classes	(5) Percentage of total income received by this and all lower classes
Under $10,000	18	4	_____	_____
$10,000–$14,999	12	6	_____	_____
$15,000–$24,999	14	12	_____	_____
$25,000–$34,999	17	14	_____	_____
$35,000–$49,000	19	15	_____	_____
$50,000–$74,999	11	20	_____	_____
$75,000 and over	9	29	_____	_____

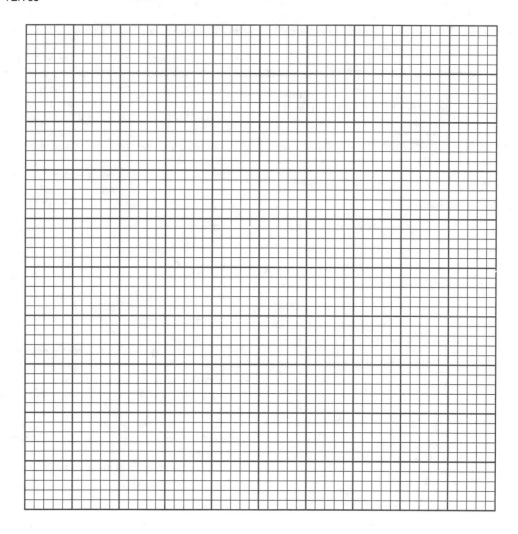

2. The table below contains different possible earned incomes for a family of a certain size.

Earned income	NIT subsidy	Total income
$ 0	$5,000	$5,000
5,000	_____	_____
10,000	_____	_____
15,000	_____	_____
20,000	_____	_____
25,000	_____	_____

a. Assume that $5,000 is the guaranteed income for a family of this size and that the benefit-loss rate is 20%. Enter the NIT subsidy and the total income at each of the five remaining earned-income levels. (*Hint*: 20% of $5,000 is $1,000.)

(1) This NIT program retains strong incentives to work because whenever the family earns an additional $5,000 its total income increases by $_____

(2) But this program is costly because the family receives a subsidy until its earned income, the break-even income, is $_____

b. To reduce the break-even income the benefit-loss rate is raised to 50%. Complete the table below.

Earned income	NIT subsidy	Total income
$ 0	$5,000	$5,000
2,500	_____	_____
5,000	_____	_____
7,500	_____	_____
$10,000	_____	_____

(1) This program is less costly than the previous one because the family only receives a subsidy until it earns the break-even income of $_____ ;

(2) but the incentives to work are less because whenever the family earns an additional $5,000 its total income increases by only $_____

c. Both of the previous two NIT programs guaranteed an income of only $5,000. Assume that that guaranteed income is raised to $7,500 and the benefit-loss rate is kept at 50%. Complete the table below.

Earned income	NIT subsidy	Total income
$ 0	$7,500	$7,500
3,000	———	———
6,000	———	———
9,000	———	———
12,000	———	———
15,000	———	———

(1) This program is more costly than the previous one because the break-even income has risen to

$_____

(2) The incentives to earn additional income are no better in this program than in the previous one. But to improve these incentives by reducing the benefit-loss rate to 40% would raise the break-even income to (divide the guaranteed income by the benefit-loss rate)

$_____

d. To summarize:

(1) given the guaranteed income, the lower the benefit-loss rate the (greater, less) _____ are the incentives to earn additional income and the

(greater, less) _____ is the break-even income and the cost of the NIT program;

(2) and given the benefit-loss rate, the greater the guaranteed income, the (greater, less) _____ is the break-even income and the cost of the program;

(3) but to reduce the break-even income and the cost of the program requires either a(n) (increase, decrease)

_____ in the benefit-loss rate or a(n)

_____ in the guaranteed income.

■ **SELF-TEST**

Circle the T if the statement is true; the F if it is false.

1. According to the authors of the text, there is considerable income inequality in the United States.　　**T　F**

2. Since 1929 the percentage of total personal income received by families in the highest income quintile has decreased.　　**T　F**

3. There was a significant increase in income inequality in the 1929–1947 period.　　**T　F**

4. The distribution of income has been relatively stable when you compare 1947 with 1990.　　**T　F**

5. In a Lorenz curve, the percentage of families in each income class is measured along the horizontal axis and the percentage of the total income received by those families is measured on the vertical axis.　　**T　F**

6. After the adjustments made by Edgar Browning in the Census Bureau data, the distribution of personal income in the United States is less unequal, and there is a trend over time toward less inequality.　　**T　F**

7. Adjustments for differences in the ages of receivers of income seem to make the distribution of personal income in the United States more unequal.　　**T　F**

8. The distribution of income in the United States *after* taxes and transfers are taken into account is less unequal than it is before they are taken into account.　　**T　F**

9. Differences in "job tastes" is one explanation for income differences in the United States.　　**T　F**

10. Those who favor equality in the distribution of income contend that equality will lead to stronger incentives to work, save, invest, and take risks and to a greater national output and income.　　**T　F**

11. In the tradeoff between equality and economic efficiency, an increase in efficiency requires a decrease in inequality.　　**T　F**

12. Using the semiofficial definition of poverty, about 13.5% of the population of the United States is poor.　　**T　F**

13. The incidence of poverty is extremely high among female-headed families.　　**T　F**

14. Including the value of noncash transfers in poverty rate calculations tends to decrease the estimate of the poverty rate.　　**T　F**

15. OASDI, Medicare, and unemployment compensation are public assistance (or welfare) programs.　　**T　F**

16. Those who have been critical of the American system of income maintenance contend that the welfare system impairs incentives to work.　　**T　F**

17. In a NIT program, the benefit-loss rate is the rate at which subsidy benefits decrease as the earned income of a family increases.　　**T　F**

18. The lower the benefit-loss rate the smaller are the incentives to earn additional income.　　**T　F**

19. Workfare plans are basically designed to provide public funds for transportation so that people on welfare can get to work.   **T   F**

20. In 1988 Congress passed the Family Support Act, which revised the welfare provisions of OASDHI.   **T   F**

Circle the letter that corresponds to the best answer.

1. According to the Census Bureau statistics, families making less than $10,000 a year account for about:
   (a) 6% of all families and receive about 1% of total personal income
   (b) 9% of all families and receive about 1% of total personal income
   (c) 12% of all families and receive about 2% of total personal income
   (d) 15% of all families and receive about 4% of total personal income

2. In 1990, the top 5% of families received about what percentage of total income before taxes?
   (a) 13%
   (b) 18%
   (c) 21%
   (d) 25%

3. Which of the following would be evidence of a decrease in income inequality in the United States?
   (a) a decrease in the percentage of total personal income received by the lowest quintile
   (b) an increase in the percentage of total personal income received by the highest quintile
   (c) an increase in the percentage of total personal income received by the four lowest quintiles
   (d) a decrease in the percentage of total personal income received by the four lowest quintiles

4. In the post-World War II period there has been;
   (a) a significant decrease in the percentage of total personal income received by the highest quintile
   (b) a significant increase in the percentage of total personal income received by the lowest quintile
   (c) a significant increase in the percentage of total personal income received by the middle three quintiles
   (d) no significant change in the percentage of total personal income received by any of the five quintiles

5. When a Lorenz curve has been drawn, the degree of income inequality in an economy is measured by:
   (a) the slope of the diagonal that runs from the southwest to the northeast corner of the diagram
   (b) the slope of the Lorenz curve
   (c) the area between the Lorenz curve and the axes of the graph
   (d) the area between the Lorenz curve and the southwest-northeast diagonal

Use the graph below to answer the next four questions (6, 7, 8, and 9). The graph shows four different Lorenz curves (1, 2, 3, and 4).

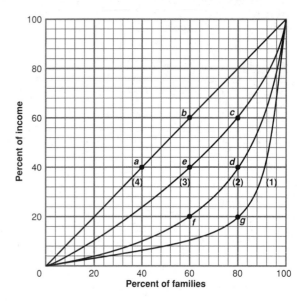

6. The greatest increase in income equality would occur with a shift in a Lorenz curve from:
   (a) 1 to 2
   (b) 1 to 4
   (c) 4 to 1
   (d) 3 to 1

7. What point indicates that 80% of the families receive only 40% of the income?
   (a) *c*
   (b) *d*
   (c) *e*
   (d) *g*

8. The movement from point *b* to point *f* in the graph would indicate that:
   (a) 60% of families now receive 40% of income instead of 60% of income
   (b) 60% of income goes to 20% of families instead of 60% of families
   (c) 20% of income goes to 20% of families instead of 60% of families
   (d) 60% of families now receive 20% of income instead of 60% of income

9. Which change would indicate that there has been an increase in income *inequality*? A movement from point:
   (a) *b* to *a*
   (b) *g* to *d*
   (c) *g* to *f*
   (d) *e* to *d*

10. Suppose that Laura earns $5000 in year 1 and $50,000 in year 2, while Kristin earns $50,000 in year 1 and only $5000 in year 2. Is there income inequality for the two individuals?
(a) both the annual and the two-year data indicate equality
(b) both the annual and the two-year data indicate inequality
(c) the annual data indicate inequality, but two-year data indicate equality
(d) the annual data indicate equality, but two-year data indicate inequality

11. The empirical data indicate that the tax system and the transfer programs of the government:
(a) significantly reduces the degree of inequality in the distribution of income
(b) produces only a slight reduction in the degree of inequality in the distribution of income
(c) significantly increases the degree of inequality in the distribution of income
(d) produces only a slight increase in the degree of inequality in the distribution of income

12. Which of the following is *not* one of the causes of the unequal distribution of income in the United States?
(a) the unequal distribution of property
(b) in-kind transfers
(c) the inability of the poor to invest in human capital
(d) luck and the unequal distribution of misfortune

13. Suppose that Ms. Anne obtains 5 units of utility from the last dollar of income received by her and that Mr. Charles obtains 8 units of utility from the last dollar of his income. Those who favor an equal distribution of income would:
(a) advocate redistributing income from Charles to Anne
(b) advocate redistributing income from Anne to Charles
(c) be content with this distribution of income between Anne and Charles
(d) argue that any redistribution of income between them would increase total utility

14. The case for income inequality is primarily made on the basis that income inequality:
(a) is reduced by the transfer payment programs for the poor
(b) is necessary to maintain incentives to work and produce output
(c) depends on luck and chance, which cannot be corrected by government action
(d) is created by education and training programs that distort the distribution of income

15. The debate over income redistribution focuses on the tradeoff between equality and:
(a) efficiency
(b) unemployment
(c) economic growth
(d) economic freedom

16. The leaky-bucket analogy is used to describe the:
(a) welfare reform mess
(b) trends in the poverty rate
(c) economic loss from income redistribution programs
(d) piecemeal approach toward income maintenance programs

17. Poverty does not have a precise definition, but the officially accepted poverty line for a family of four in 1990 was about:
(a) $ 6,652
(b) $ 7,300
(c) $ 9,100
(d) $13,359

18. In 1990, which group had the largest percentage in poverty?
(a) Hispanics
(b) families headed by women
(c) children under 18 years of age
(d) the elderly (65 years and older)

19. Which of the following would best characterize the trend in the poverty rate in the 1980s?
(a) it decreased steadily during the 1980s
(b) it increased steadily during the 1980s
(c) it increased during the early 1980s and then decreased
(d) it decreased during the early 1980s and then increased

20. The position that city ghettos create a culture of poverty that is not alleviated by social programs and that require the self-help of the poor is most closely associated with which view of ghetto poverty?
(a) workfare
(b) black underclass
(c) income maintenance
(d) "invisible poor"

21. An example of a social insurance program would be:
(a) Medicare
(b) Medicaid
(c) food stamps
(d) Aid to Families with Dependent Children

22. Which of the following is designed to provide a nationwide minimum income for the aged, the blind, and the disabled?
(a) SSI
(b) FFS

(c) AFDC
(d) OASDI

23. The income maintenance system has been criticized for a number of reasons. What is **not** one of the criticisms?
(a) the system is dependent on a costly and large bureaucracy for administration
(b) freedom of consumer choice is enhanced with the use of noncash transfer payments
(c) there are inequities in the program benefits for those with similar needs
(d) the programs is detrimental to incentives to work and may keep people on welfare

24. Negative income tax plans have been criticized because it is difficult to construct a plan that:
(a) provides reasonable income levels and incentives to work for the poor, but is not too costly
(b) is not subject to substantial administrative costs and bureaucratic red tape
(c) does not discriminate against those individuals with similar circumstances, but who have similar needs
(d) promotes family unity and does not create a "culture of poverty" among the participants in the program

25. Workfare proposals, as incorporated into the Family Support Act of 1988, would:
(a) provide a reasonable level of guaranteed income for low-income working families
(b) provide education and job training opportunities for welfare recipients to help and require them to become employed
(c) decrease the level of support for social security programs and transfer the funds to improve the Aid to Families with Dependent Children program
(d) substitute the payment of cash for the use of food stamps for those willing that are willing to go to work

■ **DISCUSSION QUESTIONS**

1. How much income inequality is there in the American economy? Cite figures to support your conclusion. What causes income inequality in American capitalism?

2. Has the distribution of income changed in the United States during the past 60 to 65 years? If it has, in what way, to what extent, and why has it changed? Has income distribution changed in the past 45 to 50 years?

3. What is measured along each of the two axes when a Lorenz curve is drawn?
(a) If the distribution of income were completely equal, what would the Lorenz curve look like?
(b) If one family received all of the income of the economy, what would the Lorenz curve look like?
(c) After the Lorenz curve for an economy has been drawn, how is the degree of income inequality in that economy measured?

4. How does the Bureau of the Census measure income in its published data on the distribution of income in the United States. What are the two major criticisms of these data?

5. How did:
(a) Edgar Browning and
(b) Morton Paglin adjust the census data on the distribution of income? What do their adjusted figures reveal about the distribution of income in the United States?

6. What effect do taxes and transfers have upon the distribution of income in the United States? How much of this change in the distribution of income is the result of the transfer payments made by government?

7. What are seven factors contributing to income inequality in the United States?

8. State the case for an equal distribution of income and the case for an unequal distribution. What would be traded for what in the fundamental "tradeoff"? Describe the leaky-bucket analogy.

9. What is the currently accepted and more or less official definition of poverty? How many people and what percentage of the American population are poor if we use this definition of poverty?

10. What characteristics—other than the small amounts of money they have to spend—do the greatest concentrations of the poor families of the nation **tend** to have?

11. What have been the trends in the poverty rate since 1960? In the 1980s?

12. What is the black underclass view of poverty? What do critics of this view think can be done to alleviate ghetto poverty?

13. Why does poverty in the United States tend to be invisible or hidden?

14. Explain the difference between social insurance and public assistance (or welfare). List and briefly describe the three social insurance and the four public assistance programs that constitute the income-maintenance system of the United States.

15. State at least three basic reasons why the income maintenance system has been criticized. Are there other criticisms of the system?

16. Explain how poverty and the unequal distribution of income would be reduced by a negative income tax. Be sure to include in your explanation definitions of guaranteed income, the benefit-loss rate, and break-even income.

17. What are the three goals or objectives of any NIT plan? Explain why there is a conflict among these objectives—why all three goals cannot be achieved simultaneously.

18. What were some of the problems with AFDC? How was this program changed by the Family Support Act of 1988?

■ **ANSWERS**

Chapter 35 Income Inequality and Poverty

FILL-IN QUESTIONS

1. considerable; *a.* decreased, increased, significant; *b.* has not

2. Lorenz; *a.* families, income; *b.* lower, upper; *c.* Lorenz curve, line of complete equality (either order)

3. narrow, short, less, smaller

4. reduce

5. ability, education, training, tastes, discrimination, property, power

6. *a.* utility; *b.* income

7. equality, efficiency (either order); *a.* smaller; *b.* more; *c.* minimize, loss

8. *a.* 13,359, 6,652; *b.* 13.5, 34

9. *a.* young; *b.* blacks and Hispanics; *c.* women

10. *a.* black underclass, the poor; *b.* simplistic, victims, jobs, education, training, maintenance

11. invisible, pool, cities, political

12. insurance, assistance; *a.* (1) OASDI, care, (2) unemployment; *b.* (1) SSI, AFDC (either order), (2) food-stamp, (3) caid

13. efficient, equitable, centives

14. guaranteed, benefit-loss

15. *a.* poverty, incentives, costs; *b.* conflicting

16. AFDC, dissolution, illegitimate births, culture

17. workfare, employment (work), Family Support (Welfare Reform)

PROBLEMS AND PROJECTS

1. *a.* (1) column 4: 18, 30, 44, 61, 80, 91, 100; (2) column 5: 4, 10, 22, 36, 51, 71, 100; *b.* (1) 30, 10; (2) 20, 49

2. *a.* NIT subsidy: 4,000, 3,000, 2,000, 1,000, 0; Total income: 9,000, 13,000, 17,000, 21,000, 25,000; (1) 4,000, (2) 25,000; *b.* NIT subsidy: 3,750, 2,500, 1,250, 0; Total income 6,250, 7,500, 8,750, 10,000; (1) 10,000 (2) 2,500; *c.* NIT subsidy; 6,000, 4,500, 3,000, 1,500, 0; Total income: 9,000, 10,500, 12,000, 13,500, 15,000; (1) 15,000, (2) 18,750; *d.* (1) greater, greater, (2) greater, (3) increase, decrease

SELF-TEST

1. T, p. 654	**11.** F, pp. 661–662
2. T, p. 655	**12.** T, p. 662
3. F, p. 655	**13.** T, p. 662
4. T, pp. 655–656	**14.** T, p. 663
5. T, p. 656	**15.** F, pp. 664–665
6. T, p. 657	**16.** T, p. 666
7. F, pp. 657–658	**17.** T, p. 667
8. T, p. 658	**18.** F, p. 667
9. T, p. 658	**19.** F, p. 668
10. F, p. 660	**20.** F, p. 668

1. *b*, p. 655	**14.** *b*, pp. 660–661
2. *b*, p. 656	**15.** *a*, p. 661
3. *c*, p. 656	**16.** *c*, p. 662
4. *d*, pp. 655–656	**17.** *d*, p. 662
5. *d*, p. 656	**18.** *b*, p. 662
6. *b*, pp. 656–657	**19.** *c*, p. 663
7. *b*, pp. 656–657	**20.** *b*, pp. 663–664
8. *d*, pp. 656–657	**21.** *a*, p. 664
9. *d*, pp. 656–657	**22.** *a*, p. 666
10. *c*, pp. 657–658	**23.** *b*, p. 666
11. *a*, p. 657	**24.** *a*, p. 668
12. *b*, pp. 658–659	**25.** *b*, p. 668
13. *b*, p. 660	

DISCUSSION QUESTIONS

1. p. 655	**10.** pp. 662–663
2. pp. 655–656	**11.** p. 663
3. p. 656	**12.** pp. 663–664
4. pp. 657–658	**13.** p. 664
5. pp. 657–658	**14.** pp. 664–665
6. p. 658	**15.** p. 666
7. pp. 658–659	**16.** pp. 667–668
8. pp. 660–661	**17.** p. 668
9. p. 662	**18.** pp. 668–669

Labor-Market Issues: Unionism, Discrimination, and Immigration

Chapter 36 completes the examination of government and current economic problems by looking at three major issues in labor markets—unionism, discrimination, and immigration. Most of the chapter focuses on unionism and labor-management relations. This topic is almost always in the news for one reason or another—strikes, new labor legislation, wage increases, employee "wage concessions," union demands, and collective bargaining. Discrimination was cited as a factor contributing to poverty in Chapter 35, but Chapter 36 now extends the discussion by analyzing discrimination in labor markets. Finally, you learn in Chapter 36 that labor is a resource that can move between nations and you learn how this movement can affect the market for labor in nations.

The labor union is an important institution in American capitalism. But labor unions did not always occupy the position in the economy that they now do. The first part of Chapter 36 is devoted to a historical review of their development in the Unites States and is separated into three periods. The important thing for you to see is that the growth and power of unions in each of these periods clearly depended upon the rights and recognition given to them by Federal law. At first the law repressed them, then it encouraged them, and finally it has sought to curb and control their greatly increased power.

Until 1955 the labor movement in the United States was divided into those unions affiliated with the AFL and those affiliated with the CIO. But in 1955 the labor movement was united when the AFL and CIO merged. Since then, however, unionism in the American economy has declined: the percentage of the labor force organized in unions has declined; and in more recent years the number of union members has decreased. The second section of Chapter 36 examines two possible hypotheses which separately or together might explain this decline in unionism in the U.S.

In Chapter 28 you learned how unions directly and indirectly seek to influence wage rates. The impact of the union upon its own membership, upon employers, and upon the rest of the economy is more than just a matter of wages, however. The third section of Chapter 36 examines the contents usually found in a contract between a union and an employer. The purpose of this examination is to give you some idea of the goals which unions seek and other issues over which employers and employees bargain and upon which they must reach an agreement. Another extremely important idea which you will find in the section is this: Labor-management relations mean more than the periodic signing of a contract; they also mean the day-to-day working relations between the union and the employer and the new problems and issues not specifically settled in the contract which must be resolved under the general provisions of that contract.

The fourth section of the chapter examines the economic effects or impact of unions on the economy. Unions affect the economy in four principle ways: they affect the wage rates of their members relative to the wage rates of nonunionized workers; the productivity of labor and, therefore, the efficiency with which the economy uses its resources; the inequality with which the earnings of labor are distributed among workers; and the rate of inflation in the economy. Just how unions affect these four economic variables is, to a large extent, uncertain and debatable. The authors of the text present you with both sides of the issues, however, and draw whatever conclusions can be obtained from the empirical evidence.

Discrimination has always been present in labor markets and is therefore one of the three major topics studied in the fifth section of this chapter. The section first looks at the four forms of economic discrimination—wage, employment, human-capital, and occupational—to give you an understanding of the dimension of the problem. The analysis then focuses on occupational segregation and presents the crowding model which is similar to the one presented earlier in the chapter to study the efficiency effects of unions. After a brief comment on the discrimination costs, the section ends by discussing the topic of comparable worth and some nondiscriminatory factors.

The third major topic discussed in the final section of the chapter is immigration. The migration of workers from a poor nation (such as Mexico) to a rich nation (such as the United States) creates economic effects on wage rates, output and employment, and business incomes in the two nations. The method employed to find the effects of this immigration is similar to the analysis of unions and discrimination you studied earlier in the chapter. The conclusions drawn about immigration using the supply and demand analysis are definite and you should be sure you understand them. The conclusions, however, are only approximations of reality. The real world is more complicated than a supply-and-demand model. Be sure you understand the four complications which are introduced toward the end of this section and how these complications modify the conclusions obtained by using supply and demand.

■ **CHECKLIST**

When you have studied this chapter you should be able to:

☐ Describe the attitudes and behavior of the courts and business toward labor unions during the repression phase.

☐ Identify the three fundamental ideas of Samuel Gompers.

☐ Explain how the Norris-LaGuardia Act and the Wagner Act contributed to the revival and rapid growth of the labor movement during the encouragement phase.

☐ Contrast the beliefs of John L. Lewis and the founders of the CIO with those of the leaders of the AFL during the 1930s.

☐ Identify the four headings into which the provisions of the Taft-Hartley Act can be put.

☐ Outline the provisions of the Landrum-Griffin Act.

☐ State the extent to which unionism in the United States has declined over the past 35 years; and present two hypotheses to explain this decline.

☐ Enumerate and explain the contents of the four basic areas of a collective-bargaining agreement.

☐ Describe the effects unions have on the wages of their members, on the wages of unorganized (nonunion) workers, and on the average level of real wages in the American economy; and state the size of the wage advantage of unionized workers.

☐ List the three ways in which unions might have a negative impact and the three ways in which they might have a positive impact on efficiency in the economy.

☐ Explain in detail how the unionization of a particular labor market leads to the misallocation of labor and a decline in the domestic output.

☐ Identify a way in which unions increase and the two ways in which they decrease, the inequality with which the earnings of labor are distributed.

☐ Contrast the causes of inflation in the demand-pull and cost-push models; discuss wage increases as an inflationary factor.

☐ List four kinds of discrimination.

☐ Use the crowding model to explain why women and blacks receive lower wages and why the labor resources of the economy are more efficiently allocated when occupational discrimination is eliminated.

☐ Estimate how much racial or other kinds of discrimination costs the United States each year.

☐ State the comparable worth doctrine and three objections to using it to set wages for women.

☐ List a few of the nondiscriminatory factors that have resulted in women receiving lower incomes than men.

☐ Recount briefly the history of immigration into the United States and the estimates of the number of legal and illegal immigrants entering the U.S. in recent years.

☐ Use a supply-and-demand model to explain the effects of the migration of workers from a poor to a rich nation on wage rates, output, and business incomes in the two nations.

☐ Explain how the four complicating factors modify the effects of migration on the two economies.

☐ Describe other economic and noneconomic complexities about immigration.

■ **CHAPTER OUTLINE**

1. The history of labor unions in the United States can be divided into three periods or phrases.

   a. During the *repression* phase, between 1790 and 1930, the growth of unions was severely limited by the judicial application of the criminal conspiracy doctrine and by the refusal of many firms to recognize and bargain with unions; but between 1886 and 1930 the AFL, following the union philosophy of Samuel Gompers, was able to organize many crafts and expand its membership.

   b. Between 1930 and 1947, the *encouragement* phase, labor union membership grew rapidly, encouraged by pro-labor legislation; and the CIO was formed to unionize industrial workers.

   c. In the *intervention* phase from 1947 onward, government regulation and control of labor-management relations increased with the passage of the Taft-Hartley and Landrum-Griffin acts.

2. The merger of the AFL and the CIO in 1955 reunited the American labor movement, but since then membership in unions as a percentage of the labor force has declined; and there are two complementary explanations of the relative decline in union membership.

   a. The structural-change explanation (or hypothesis) is that a number of changes in the structure of the economy and of the labor force have occurred and these changes have not been favorable to the expansion of union membership.

   b. The managerial-opposition hypothesis is that the opposition of management to unions has increased and become more aggressive in recent years, and the legal and illegal tactics employed by management against unions have decreased union membership.

3. Collective bargaining between labor and management results in collective-bargaining (or work) agreements between them.

a. This bargaining and the resulting agreements are more often than not the result of compromise; strikes and violence are actually quite rare.

b. The work agreements reached take many different forms; but the agreement between the employer and the union usually covers four basic areas: union status and managerial prerogatives, wages and hours, seniority and the control of job opportunities, and the grievance procedure.

4. Labor unions may increase wage rates, increase or decrease economic efficiency, make the distribution of income more or less unequal, and contribute to inflation.

a. While unions have increased the wages of their members relative to the wages of nonunion members, they have had little or no effect on the average level of real wages in the economy.

b. Whether unions result in more or less efficiency and an increase or a decrease in the productivity of labor in the economy is a question with two sides.

(1) The negative view is that they decrease efficiency by their featherbedding and work rules, by engaging in strikes, and by fostering a misallocation of labor resources.

(2) The positive view is that they increase efficiency by having a shock effect on the performance of management, by reducing worker turnover, and by the informal transfer of skills from the more- to the less-skilled workers fostered by the seniority system.

(3) The empirical evidence shows that unions have increased labor productivity in some industries and decreased it in other industries; but this evidence has not led to any general conclusion on the effect of unionization on the productivity of labor in the economy.

c. There is also no agreement on the effect of unions on the distribution of earnings among workers.

(1) Some economists argue that unions increase earnings and reduce employment in the labor markets which are unionized; but this increases the supply of labor and lowers earnings in the labor markets which are not unionized: the result is an increase in the inequality with which earnings are distributed.

(2) Other economists observe that unions try to obtain equal wage rates for all workers performing the same jobs both within a single firm and among different firms; and that the effect is to decrease the inequality with which earnings are distributed.

d. Whether unions generate cost-push inflation is a controversial issue.

(1) In the demand-pull model of inflation increases in wage rates are a result (or the effect) of an increase in aggregate demand and not the cause of inflation; but in the cost-push model of inflation union-imposed increases in wage rates greater than the increases in the productivity of labor lead to higher price levels in the economy.

(2) Most experts would agree that inflation in the past has been the result of increases in aggregate demand or of supply-side shocks and has not been the result of increases in wage rates.

5. The greater incidence of poverty among blacks, Hispanics, and women is in part the result of discrimination.

a. This discrimination is found in the wage, employment, human-capital, and occupational discrimination to which these groups are subject.

b. Women and blacks have been subjected to occupational discrimination which has crowded them into a small number of occupations in which the supply of workers is large relative to the demand for them and wage rates and incomes are, therefore, lower; and the crowding model illustrates these effects and the effects of the elimination of this discrimination.

c. The costs of this discrimination to the economy are estimated at 4% of the domestic output.

d. It is necessary to add to the examination of income inequality, poverty, and discrimination in the United States that

(1) the comparable worth doctrine has been suggested as a further method of reducing occupational discrimination against women; and while his suggestion has been subjected to several criticisms, it will be an important public-policy issue in the future; and

(2) the differences between the incomes of men and women and between those of whites and nonwhites are not all due to discrimination and are instead partly due to nondiscriminatory factors.

6. The immigration of workers into the United States is a controversial issue because this international movement of labor has economic effects on the American economy.

a. Largely unimpeded until World War I but then curtailed by law until liberalized after World War II, annual entry into the United States now consists of approximately 700,000 legal and 500,000 illegal immigrants.

b. In a simple model, the movement of workers from one economy into another economy lowers the average level of wage rates, expands the domestic output, and increases business incomes in the latter economy; has the opposite effects in the former economy; and increases output in the world.

c. These conclusions must, however, be modified to take into account the costs of migration, remittances and backflows, the levels of employment in the two economies, and the effects on tax revenues and government spending in the economy receiving the immigrants.

d. In addition to its economic effects, immigration raises several noneconomic issues in the United States.

■ IMPORTANT TERMS

Criminal-conspiracy
doctrine

Injunction

Discriminatory discharge

Blacklisting

Lockout

Yellow-dog contract

Company union

Business unionism

American Federation
of Labor

Norris-LaGuardia Act
of 1932

Wagner (National Labor
Relations) Act of 1935

National Labor Relations
Board

Congress of Industrial
Organizations

Taft-Hartley (Labor-
Management Relations)
Act of 1947

Jurisdictional strike

Sympathy strike

Secondary boycott

Featherbedding

Closed shop

Landrum-Griffin (Labor-
Management Reporting
and Disclosure) Act
of 1959

Structural-change
hypothesis

Managerial-opposition
hypothesis

Union shop

Open shop

Nonunion shop

Right-to-work law

Managerial prerogatives

Cost-of-living adjustment
(COLA)

Grievance procedure

Seniority

Fringe benefit

Collective voice

Exit mechanism

Voice mechanism

Wage discrimination

Employment
discrimination

Human-capital
discrimination

Occupational
discrimination

Crowding model
of occupational
discrimination

Comparable worth
doctrine

Legal immigrant

Illegal immigrant

Simpson-Rodino Act
of 1986

Remittances

Backflows

Two terms for review:

Craft unionism

Industrial unionism

■ FILL-IN QUESTIONS

1. About _____ million workers belong to labor unions in the United States. This is approximately what percentage of the civilian labor force? _____

2. During the repression phase of labor union history, union growth was slow because of the hostility of the _____ toward labor unions and the reluctance of American businesses to _____ and _____ with labor unions.

3. Unions were limited in their growth between 1790 and 1930 by courts which applied the _____ doctrine to labor unions and issued _____ to prevent strikes, picketing, and boycotts.

4. Employers used the following nonjudicial means of retarding the growth of labor unions in the repression phase: _____, _____, _____, _____, _____, _____, and _____.

5. The philosophy of the AFL under the leadership of Samuel Gompers was _____ _____, _____, and _____.

6. In the encouragement phase of labor union history, unions grew as a consequence of such favorable legislation as the _____ and _____ acts; and the (AFL, CIO) _____, based on the principle of (craft, industrial) _____ unionism, was formed to organize (skilled, both skilled and unskilled) _____ workers in a particular industry or group of related industries.

7. The National Labor Relations Act of 1935 guaranteed the "twin rights" of labor; the right to _____ and the right to _____; in addition it established the _____ Board and listed a number of unfair labor practices by (management, unions) _____

8. Three important events that occurred in the history of labor unions after 1946 were the passage of the _____ and _____ acts and the _____ of the AFL and the CIO.

9. Since the merger of the AFL and CIO in 1955 union membership as a percentage of the labor force has (increased, decreased, remained constant) _____

_____ and the number of unionized workers has

_____

10. The two complementary hypotheses which can be used to explain the changes in the size of the union membership are the _____ and the _____ hypotheses.

11. A typical work agreement between a union and an employer covers the following four basic areas:

a. _____

b. _____

c. _____

d. _____

12. Unionization of workers in the American economy has tended to (increase, decrease, have no effect on) _____ the wage rates of union members, to _____ the wage rates of nonunion workers, and to _____ the average level of real wage rates received by all workers.

13. Unions have a
a. negative effect on productivity and efficiency in the economy to the extent that they

(1) engage in _____ and impose _____ rules on their employers,

(2) engage in _____ against their employers, or

(3) impose (above-, below-) _____ equilibrium wage rates on employers that lead to the _____ of labor resources;
b. positive effect on productivity and efficiency in the economy to the extent that

(1) the wage increases they obtain have a _____ effect that induces employers to substitute (labor, capital) _____ for _____ and to hasten their search for technologies that (increase, decrease) _____ the costs of production,

(2) they (increase, decrease) _____ labor turnover, or

(3) the _____ system results in the (formal, informal) _____ training of (younger, older) _____ by _____ employees.

14. Unionization has the effect of:
a. increasing the inequality with which labor earnings are distributed when it displaces workers from (high, low) _____-wage employment in (unionized, nonunionized) _____ labor markets to _____-wage employment in _____ labor markets;
b. decreasing the inequality with which labor earnings are distributed if it results in a wage rate for a particular job that is (the same, different) _____ within the firm and is _____ among firms.

15. In the:
a. demand-pull model of inflation increases in wage rates are the (result, cause) _____ of inflation; and in the cost-push model of inflation increases in wage rates in excess of increases in the productivity of labor are the _____ of inflation;
b. American economy the major episodes of rapid inflation have been the result of expansions in aggregate (demand, supply) _____ or shocks on the _____ side.

16. The four principal kinds of _economic_ discrimination are:

a. _____

b. _____

c. _____

d. _____

17. The occupational discrimination that pushes women and blacks into a small number of occupations in which the supply of labor is large relative to the demand for it is explained by the _____ model.
a. Because supply is large relative to demand, wages and incomes in these occupations are (high, low) _____
b. The reduction or elimination of this occupational discrimination would result in a (more, less) _____ efficient allocation of the labor resources of the economy, and a(n) (expansion, contraction) _____ in the national income and output.

18. The number of legal immigrants to the U.S. under current legislation is about _____ a year, and the number of illegal immigrants in recent years is estimated to be about _____ a year.

19. The movement of workers from a poor nation to a rich nation tends:

    a. in the rich nation to (increase, decrease) _____

_____ the national output, to

_____ wage rates, and to

_____ business incomes;

    b. in the poor nation to _____ national

output, to _____ wage rates, and

to _____ business incomes; and

    c. in the world to _____ the real output of goods and services.

20. List the four complications that may modify the conclusions reached in question 19 above.

    a. _____

    b. _____

    c. _____

    d. _____

■ PROBLEMS AND PROJECTS

1. Below is a list of frequently employed terms, and following the terms is a series of identifying phrases. Match the term with the phrase by placing the appropriate letter after each of the phrases. *Note:* All the terms will not be needed.

    A. Injunction
    B. Blacklisting
    C. Lockout
    D. Yellow-dog contract
    E. Company union
    F. Business union
    G. Jurisdictional strike
    H. Sympathy strike
    I. Secondary boycott
    J. Featherbedding
    K. Closed shop
    L. Union shop
    M. Open shop
    N. Nonunion shop
    O. Checkoff
    P. Craft union
    Q. Industrial union

    1. A worker must be a member of the union before he or she is eligible for employment. _____

    2. A worker agrees when employed not to join a union. _____

    3. A union open to all workers employed by a given firm or in a given industry. _____

    4. A union organized and encouraged by an employer to prevent the formation of a union which might make "unreasonable" demands. _____

    5. The refusal of a labor union to buy or to work with the products produced by another union or group of nonunion workers. _____

    6. A dispute between two unions over whose members are to perform a certain job. _____

    7. A court order which forbids a person or group of persons to perform some act. _____

    8. The closing of the place of employment by the employer as a means of preventing the formation of a union. _____

    9. Concern of unions with better pay, hours, and working conditions rather than with plans for social and economic reform. _____

    10. Payment of workers for work not actually performed. _____

2. Below is a list of provisions found in four important pieces of labor legislation. Identify the act in which the provision is found by putting either **(N)** for the Norris-LaGuardia Act, **(W)** for the Wagner Act, **(T)** for the Taft-Hartley Act, or **(L)** for the Landrum-Griffin Act in the space following each provision.

    a. Specified that contracts between a union and an employer must contain a termination or reopening clause. _____

    b. Established a board to investigate unfair labor practices and to conduct elections among workers. _____

    c. Guaranteed to workers the right to organize unions to bargain collectively. _____

    d. Declared that yellow-dog contracts were unenforceable and limited the use of injunctions against unions. _____

    e. Regulated union elections and finances and guaranteed certain rights to union members in their dealings with the union and its officers. _____

    f. Outlawed the closed shop, jurisdictional and certain sympathy strikes, secondary boycotts, and featherbedding. _____

    g. Provided a procedure whereby strikes affecting the health and safety of the nation might be delayed. _____

h. Outlawed company unions, antiunion discrimination in hiring and discharging workers, and interfering with the rights of workers to form unions. _____

3. Suppose there are two identical labor markets in the economy. The supply of workers and the demand for workers in each of these markets are shown in the table below.

Quantity of labor demanded	Wage rate (MRP of labor)	Quantity of labor supplied
10	$100	70
20	90	60
30	80	50
40	70	40
50	60	30
60	50	20
70	40	10

a. In each of the two labor markets the equilibrium wage rate in a competitive labor market would be

$_____ and employment would be

_____ workers.

b. Now suppose that in the first of these labor markets workers form a union and the union imposes an above-equilibrium wage rate of $90 on employers.

(1) Employment in the unionized labor market will (rise,

fall) _____ to _____ workers; and

(2) the output produced by workers employed by the firms in the unionized labor market will (expand, con-

tract) _____ by $_____

c. If the workers displaced by the unionization of the first labor market all enter and find employment in the second labor market which remains nonunionized and competitive.

(1) the wage rate in the second labor market will (rise,

fall) _____ to _____

(2) the output produced by the workers employed by firms in the second labor market will (expand, contract)

_____ by $_____

d. While the total employment of labor in the two labor markets has remained constant, the total output produced by the employers in the two labor markets

has (expanded, contracted) _____ by

$_____

4. Suppose there are only three labor markets in the economy and each of these markets is perfectly competitive. The table at the top of the next column contains the demand (or marginal-revenue-product) schedule for labor in each of these three markets.

Wage rate (marginal revenue product of labor per hour)	Quantity of labor (millions per hour)
$11	4
10	5
9	6
8	7
7	8
6	9
5	10
4	11
3	12

a. Assume there are 24 million homogeneous workers in the economy and that one-half of these workers are male and one-half are female.

(1) If the 12 million female workers can be employed only in labor market Z, for all of them to find employ-

ment the hourly wage rate must be $_____

(2) If of the 12 million male workers, 6 million are employed in labor market X and 6 million are employed in labor market Y, the hourly wage rate in labor markets

X and Y will be $_____

b. Imagine now that the impediment to the employment of females in labor markets X and Y is removed; and that as a result (and because the demand and marginal revenue product of labor is the same in all three markets) 8 million workers find employment in each labor market.

(1) in labor market Z (in which only females had previously been employed):

(a) the hourly wage rate will rise to $_____

(b) the **decrease** in national output that results from the decrease in employment from 12 to 8 million workers is equal to the loss of the marginal revenue products of the workers no longer employed; and it totals

$_____

(2) In labor market X and in labor market Y (in each of which only males had previously been employed):

(a) the hourly wage rate will fall to $_____

(b) the **increase** in national output that results from the increase in employment from 6 to 8 million workers is equal to the marginal revenue products of the additional workers employed; and the gain in **each** of these mar-

kets is $ _____ million and the total gain

in the two markets is $_____

(c) the _net_ gain to society from the reallocation of fe-

male workers is $_____ million.

5. In the tables on the next page are the demands for labor and the levels of domestic output that can be produced at each level of employment in two countries.

Country A		
Wage rate	Quantity of labor demanded	Real output
$20	95	$1900
18	100	1990
16	105	2070
14	110	2140
12	115	2200
10	120	2250
8	125	2290

Country B		
Wage rate	Quantity of labor demanded	Real output
$20	10	$200
18	15	290
16	20	370
14	25	440
12	30	500
10	35	550
8	40	590

a. If there were full employment in both countries and if:

(1) the labor force in Country A were 110, the wage rate in Country A would be $_____

(2) the labor force in Country B were 40, the wage rate in Country B would be $_____

b. With these labor forces and wage rates:

(1) total wages paid in A would be $_____ and the incomes of businesses (capitalists) in A would be $_____. (*Hint:* Subtract the total wages paid from the real output.)

(2) total wages paid in B would be $_____ and business incomes in B would be $_____

c. Assume the difference between the wage rates in the two countries induces 5 workers to migrate from B to A. So long as both countries maintain full employment,

(1) the wage rate in A would (rise, fall) _____ to $_____;

(2) and the wage rate in B would _____ to $_____

d. The movement of workers from B to A would

(1) (increase, decrease) _____ the output of A by $_____;

(2) _____ the output of B by $_____

(3) _____ their combined (and the world's) output by $_____

e. This movement of workers from B to A also (in- creased, decreased) _____ business incomes in A by $_____ and _____ business incomes in B by $_____

■ **SELF-TEST**

Circle the T if the statement is true; the F if it is false.

1. An injunction is a court order which declares that com- binations of workers to raise wages are illegal. **T F**

2. Blacklisting was a device employed by early labor unions to cut off a firm's labor supply. **T F**

3. The CIO was based on the principle of industrial unionism while the AFL was operated on the craft union philosophy. **T F**

4. The Taft-Hartley Act lists a number of unfair labor practices on the part of management. **T F**

5. Under the provisions of the Labor-Management Re- lations Act of 1947 yellow-dog contracts and featherbed- ding are prohibited. **T F**

6. The merger of the AFL and CIO in 1945 was one of the main causes of a feeling that labor unions had become too powerful that led to the enactment of the Taft-Hartley Act in 1947. **T F**

7. Union membership has increased in every year since the end of World War II. **T F**

8. Strikes precede nearly 25% of the contracts negoti- ated by labor unions and management. **T F**

9. Collective bargaining between labor and manage- ment means no more than deciding upon the wage rates employees will receive during the life of the contract. **T F**

10. The four-points criteria employed by unions in arguing for higher wages can also be used by management to re- sist higher wages and to argue for decreased wages. **T F**

11. Seniority means that the worker with the longest con- tinuous employment by a firm is the last to be laid off and the first to be recalled from a layoff. **T F**

12. The wages of union members exceed the wages of nonunion members on the average by more than 40%. **T F**

13. Strikes in the American economy result in fairly little lost work time and reductions in total output. **T F**

14. The imposition of an above-equilibrium wage rate in a particular labor market tends to reduce the employment of labor in that market. **T F**

15. The loss of output in the American economy that is the result of increases in wage rates imposed by unions on employers is relatively large. **T F**

16. Reduced labor turnover tends to decrease the productivity of labor. **T F**

17. The seniority system, its advocates argue, expands the informal training of less-skilled, younger workers and improves the productivity of a firm's work force. **T F**

18. It is generally agreed that unions decrease the productivity of labor in the American economy. **T F**

19. An authoritative study concludes that unionization, on balance, increases income inequality by about 3%. **T F**

20. In the demand-pull model of inflation increased wage rates are the result of increases in aggregate demand that increase the demand for labor in the economy. **T F**

21. The cost of discrimination against blacks in the United States is equal to approximately 4% of the national output. **T F**

22. The difference between the average earnings of full-time female and male workers is only partly the result of occupational discrimination. **T F**

23. The annual number of *illegal* immigrants entering the United States in recent years may be as large as 500,000. **T F**

24. The movement of workers from low- to high-average-income nations tends to increase the world's real output of goods and services. **T F**

25. Remittances to their families in Mexico from Mexican workers who have migrated to the United States expands the gain in the national output of the United States and expands the loss of national output in Mexico. **T F**

Circle the letter that corresponds to the best answer.

1. About what percentage of all civilian workers are members of unions?
 (a) 5%
 (b) 16%
 (c) 24%
 (d) 27%

2. Which of the following would *not* be used by a firm to prevent the organization of a genuine union among its employees?
 (a) lockout
 (b) featherbedding
 (c) company union
 (d) yellow-dog contract

3. Which one of the following was an essential part of Samuel Gompers' union philosophy?
 (a) industrial unionism

 (b) support of the Democratic Party at the polls
 (c) establishment of producer cooperatives operated by labor and management
 (d) business unionism

4. The Norris-LaGuardia Act outlawed:
 (a) yellow-dog contracts
 (b) the closed shop
 (c) company unions
 (d) blacklisting

5. The Wagner Act outlawed:
 (a) company unions
 (b) the closed shop
 (c) featherbedding
 (d) injunctions against unions

6. The Taft-Hartley Act outlawed:
 (a) the nonunion shop
 (b) the open shop
 (c) the union shop
 (d) the closed shop

7. Which one of the following is *not* a provision of the Landrum-Griffin Act?
 (a) allows a worker to sue a union if the union denies the member certain rights
 (b) unions are prohibited from making political contributions in elections for Federal offices
 (c) requires regularly scheduled union elections and the use of secret ballots
 (d) guarantees union members the right to attend union meetings, to vote and to participate in the meeting, and to nominate union officers

8. Which one of the following is *not* presently an unfair practice?
 (a) the refusal of either unions or companies to bargain in good faith
 (b) the coercion of employees by unions to join and by companies not to join unions
 (c) the practices of company and business unionism
 (d) both jurisdictional strikes and secondary boycotts

9. The decline in union membership in the United States in recent years can be explained by the:
 (a) managerial-growth hypothesis
 (b) structural-change hypothesis
 (c) relative-income hypothesis
 (d) complementary-expansion hypothesis

10. If workers at the time they are hired have a choice of joining the union and paying dues or of not joining the union and paying no dues, there exists:
 (a) a union shop
 (b) an open shop
 (c) a nonunion shop
 (d) a closed shop

11. Unionization has tended to:
(a) increase the wages of union workers and decrease the wages of nonunion workers
(b) increase the wages of nonunion workers and decrease the wages of union workers
(c) increase the wages of both union and nonunion workers
(d) increase the average level of real wages in the economy

12. Which of the following tends to decrease (to have a negative effect on) productivity and efficiency in the economy?
(a) reduced labor turnover
(b) featherbedding and union-imposed work rules
(c) the seniority system
(d) the shock effect of higher union-imposed wage rates

13. The higher wages imposed on employers in a unionized labor market tend to result in:
(a) lower wage rates in nonunionized labor markets and a decline in national output
(b) lower wage rates in nonunionized labor markets and an expansion in national output
(c) higher wage rates in nonunionized labor markets and a decline in national output
(d) higher wage rates in nonunionized labor markets and an expansion in national output

14. The reallocation of labor from employment where its MRP is $50,000 to employment where its MRP is $40,000 will:
(a) increase the output of the economy by $10,000
(b) increase the output of the economy by $90,000
(c) decrease the output of the economy by $10,000
(d) decrease the output of the economy by $90,000

15. Which of the following tends to increase (have a positive effect on) productivity and efficiency in the economy?
(a) reduced labor turnover
(b) featherbedding and union-imposed work rules
(c) strikes
(d) the unionization of a particular labor market

16. A wage increase imposed by unions on employers has a shock effect if it induces employers to:
(a) accelerate the substitution of capital for labor
(b) hasten their search for productivity-increasing technologies
(c) speed their employment of productive techniques that reduce their costs
(d) do any or all of the above

17. Unions tend to reduce labor turnover by providing workers with all but one of the following. Which one?
(a) an exit mechanism
(b) a voice mechanism
(c) a collective voice
(d) a wage advantage

18. The effect of union-imposed wage increases in the unionized labor markets of the economy is to:
(a) decrease inequality in the distribution of labor earnings
(b) leave unchanged the distribution of labor earnings
(c) increase inequality in the distribution of labor earnings
(d) destabilize the distribution of earnings between unionized and nonunionized workers

19. In the cost-push model of inflation, increases in nominal-wage rates that exceed increases in the productivity of labor:
(a) increase aggregate supply and the price level in the economy
(b) increase aggregate supply and decrease the price level in the economy
(c) decrease aggregate supply and the price level in the economy
(d) decrease aggregate supply and increase the price level in the economy

20. Most of the sustained and rapid inflation in the United States has **not** been the result of:
(a) increases in aggregate demand
(b) supply-side shocks
(c) increases in the money supply
(d) increases in money-wage rates

21. The average weekly earnings of full-time female workers is about what percentage of the average annual earnings of full-time male employees?
(a) 70%
(b) 75%
(c) 90%
(d) 95%

22. Which of the following is **not** one of the four dimensions of *economic* discrimination?
(a) wage discrimination
(b) racial and sexual discrimination
(c) occupational discrimination
(d) human-capital discrimination

23. The crowding of women and minorities into certain occupations:
(a) is the result of occupational discrimination
(b) results in the misallocation of resources
(c) explains the lower wage rates in the crowded occupations
(d) all of the above

24. If there is full employment in both nations, the effect of the migration of workers from a poor to a rich nation is to increase:
(a) the average wage rate in the rich nation
(b) the output in the rich nation
(c) business incomes in the poor nation
(d) the total wages received by nonmigrant workers in the poor nation

25. Which of the following would increase the gains realized in the world from the migration of workers?

(a) the explicit and implict costs of migration

(b) the remittances of workers to their native countries

(c) the migration of unemployed workers to nations in which they find employment

(d) the migration of employed workers to nations in which the taxes they pay are less than the welfare benefits they receive

■ **DISCUSSION QUESTIONS**

1. What are the three phases in the history of labor unions in the United States? What was the law with respect to unions, what was the extent of unionization, and what were the principal events in each of these periods?

2. How were the courts able to retard the growth of unions between 1790 and 1930? How did employers attempt to limit union growth?

3. Explain the union philosophy of Samuel Gompers.

4. What were the chief provisions of the Norris-La-Guardia Act and the Wagner Act?

5. Explain how the principles of the CIO differed from those on which the AFL was based.

6. Contrast the philosophy and policy embodied in the Wagner Act with that found in the Taft-Hartley Act.

7. What are the four main sections of the Taft-Hartley Act? What specific practices are outlawed by the act and what specific things are required of unions, union officers, and bargaining agreements?

8. Explain the major provisions of the Landrum-Griffin Act.

9. What evidence is there that the labor movement in the United States has declined? What are two possible causes of this decline?

10. What are the four basic areas usually covered in the collective-bargaining agreement between management and labor?

11. What are the four arguments employed by labor (management) in demanding (resisting) higher wages? Why are these arguments "two-edged"?

12. How large is the union wage advantage in the United States? How has the unionization of many labor markets affected the average level of real wages in the American economy?

13. By what basic means do unions have a positive and a negative effect on economic efficiency in the economy? What appears to have been the overall effect of unions on economic efficiency in the American economy?

14. What effect does the unionization of a particular labor market have upon:

(a) the wage rate in that market,

(b) the wage rates in other labor markets, and

(c) the total output of the economy?

15. Explain how unions:

(a) reduce labor turnover and

(b) improve the skills of younger workers.

16. How and in what ways do unions affect

(a) the distribution of earnings among workers and

(b) the price level (the rate of inflation)?

17. What is meant by economic discrimination and what are the four major types of such discrimination? How does this discrimination affect the earnings of blacks (and other minorities) and women relative to the earnings of white men in the United States?

18. If labor markets were competitive, what would be the effect of reducing or eliminating occupational discrimination in these labor markets upon the wage rates received by men and women and upon the national output?

19. What:

(a) are the comparable worth doctrine and the objections to it; and

(b) are the factors other than discrimination that lead to differences in the earnings of men and women in the United States?

20. Construct a supply-and-demand model to explain the effects of the migration of labor from a poor to a rich nation on the average wage rate, output, and business income in the two nations. What is the effect of this migration on the real output of the world?

21. What four complications make it necessary to modify the conclusions you reached in question 20? Explain how each of these complications alters your conclusions.

22. How do the types of workers who immigrate and economic conditions in the economy to which they migrate change the benefits from immigrants to the nation into which workers migrate?

■ **ANSWERS**

Chapter 36 Labor-Market Issues: Unionism, Discrimination, and Immigration

FILL-IN QUESTIONS

1. 17, 16

2. courts, recognize, bargain

3. criminal conspiracy, injunctions

4. discriminatory discharge, blacklisting, lockout, strikebreakers, yellow-dog contracts, paternalism, company unions

5. business unionism, political neutrality, craft unionism

6. Norris-LaGuardia, Wagner, CIO, industrial, both skilled and unskilled

7. organize, bargain collectively, National Labor Relations, management

8. Taft-Hartley, Landrum-Griffin, merger

9. decreased, decreased

10. structural-change, managerial-opposition (any order)

11. *a.* the degree of recognition and status accorded the union and the prerogatives of management; *b.* wages and hours; *c.* seniority and job opportunities; *d.* a procedure for settling grievances (any order)

12. increase, decrease, have no effect on

13. *a.* (1) featherbedding, work, (2) strikes, (3) above-, misallocation; *b.* (1) shock, capital, labor, decrease, (2) decrease, (3) seniority, informal, younger, older

14. *a.* high, unionized, low, nonunionized; *b.* the same, the same

15. *a.* result, cause; *b.* demand, supply

16. *a.* wage discrimination; *b.* employment discrimination; *c.* human-capital discrimination; *d.* occupational discrimination

17. crowding; *a.* low; *b.* more, expansion

18. 700,000, 500,000

19. *a.* increase, decrease, increase; *b.* decrease, increase, decrease; *c.* increase

20. *a.* including the costs of migration; *b.* remittances and backflows; *c.* the amounts of unemployment in the two nations; *d.* the fiscal aspects in the country receiving the immigrants

PROBLEMS AND PROJECTS

1. 1. K; 2. D; 3. Q; 4. E; 5. I; 6. G; 7. A; 8. C; 9. F; 10. J

2. *a.* T; *b.* W; *c.* W; *d.* N; *e.* L; *f.* T; *g.* T; *h.* W

3. *a.* 70, 40; *b.* (1) fall, 20, (2) contract, 150; *c.* (1) fall, 50 (2) expand, 110; *d.* contracted, 40

4. *a* (1) 3, (2) 9; *b* (1) (*a*) 7, (*b*) 18, (2) (*a*) 7, (*b*) 15, 30 (*c*) 12

5. *a.* (1) 14, (2) 8; *b.* (1) 1540, 600, (2) 320, 270; *c.* (1) fall, 12, (2) rise, 10; *d.* (1) increase, 60, (2) decrease, 40, (3) increase, 20; *e.* increased, 220, decreased, 70

SELF-TEST

1. F, p. 673	**14.** T, p. 682
2. F, p. 674	**15.** F, p. 682
3. T, p. 676	**16.** F, p. 683
4. F, p. 675	**17.** T, p. 683
5. F, p. 676	**18.** F, p. 683
6. F, p. 677	**19.** F, p. 684
7. F, p. 677	**20.** T, p. 684
8. F, p. 678	**21.** T, p. 688
9. F, p. 678	**22.** T, p. 688
10. T, p. 679	**23.** T, p. 689
11. T, p. 679	**24.** T, p. 690
12. F, p. 680	**25.** F, p. 691
13. T, p. 682	

1. *b*, p. 672	**14.** *c*, p. 682
2. *b*, p. 674	**15.** *a*, p. 683
3. *d*, p. 674	**16.** *d*, p. 683
4. *a*, p. 675	**17.** *a*, p. 683
5. *a*, p. 675	**18.** *c*, p. 684
6. *d*, pp. 676–677	**19.** *d*, pp. 684–685
7. *b*, p. 677	**20.** *d*, p. 685
8. *c*, p. 676	**21.** *a*, p. 685
9. *b*, p. 677	**22.** *b*, p. 686
10. *b*, p. 679	**23.** *d*, p. 687
11. *a*, p. 680	**24.** *b*, p. 690
12. *b*, p. 681	**25.** *c*, p. 691
13. *a*, pp. 681–682	

DISCUSSION QUESTIONS

1. pp. 672–673	**12.** p. 680
2. pp. 673–674	**13.** pp. 681–683
3. pp. 674–675	**14.** pp. 678–681
4. p. 675	**15.** p. 683
5. p. 676	**16.** pp. 684–685
6. pp. 676–677	**17.** pp. 685–686
7. p. 677	**18.** pp. 687–688
8. p. 677	**19.** p. 688
9. pp. 677–678	**20.** pp. 689–690
10. pp. 678–679	**21.** pp. 691–692
11. p. 679	**22.** pp. 690–691

CHAPTER 37

International Trade: Comparative Advantage and Protectionism

This is the first of two chapters dealing with international trade and finance. International trade is a subject with which most people have little firsthand experience. For this reason many of the terms, concepts, and ideas encountered in these chapters will be unfamiliar and may not be readily grasped. However, most of this material is fairly simple if you will take some pains to examine it. The ideas and concepts employed are new, but they are not especially complex or difficult.

At the beginning it is essential to recognize that international trade is important to the United States. Exports from and imports into the American economy were $593 and $622 billion in 1991. The United States **absolutely** is the greatest exporting and importing nation in the world. In **relative** terms, other nations have exports and imports which are larger percentages of their GDPs. They may export and import more than 35 percent of GDP, while the United States exports and imports only about 10% to 11% of GDP. It is equally important for you to understand from the beginning that international trade differs from the trade that goes on within nations. Different nations use different monies, not just one money; resources are less mobile internationally than they are **intra**nationally; and nations place more political restrictions on international trade than they do on intranational trade.

But while foreign trade differs from domestic trade, nations trade for the same basic reason that people within a nation trade: to take advantage of the benefits of specialization. Nations specialize in and export those goods and services in the production of which they have a comparative advantage. A comparative advantage means that the opportunity cost of producing a particular good or service is lower in that nation than in another nation. These nations will avoid the production of and import the goods and services in the production of which other nations have a comparative advantage. In this way all nations are able to obtain products which are produced as inexpensively as possible. Put another way, when nations specialize in those products in which they have a comparative advantage, the world as a whole can obtain more goods and services from its resources; and each of the nations of the world can enjoy a standard of living higher than it would have if it did not specialize and export and import.

But regardless of the advantages of specialization and trade among nations, people in the United States and throughout the world have for well over 200 years debated whether free trade or protection was the better policy for their nation. Economists took part in this debate and, with few exceptions, argued for free trade and against protection. Those who favor free trade contend that free trade benefits both the nation and the world as a whole. "Free traders" argue that tariffs, import quotas, and other barriers to international trade prevent or reduce specialization and decrease both a nation's and the world's production and standard of living.

But nations have and continue to erect barriers to trade with other nations. The questions upon which the latter part of this chapter focuses attention are (1) what motivates nations to impose tariffs and to limit the quantities of goods imported from abroad; (2) what effects do protection have upon a nation's own prosperity and upon the prosperity of the world; and (3) what kinds of arguments do those who favor protection employ to support their position—on what grounds do they base their contention that their nation will benefit from the erection of barriers which reduce imports from foreign nations.

The chapter's final major section is a brief review of American policy toward trade barriers since 1934. That year began a series of gradual but substantial tariff-rate reductions which have continued almost up to the present year under the General Agreement on Tariffs and Trade (GATT). There has also been economic integration among nations in an area that reduces trade restrictions. The European Economic Community, or Common Market, the United States–Canadian Free-Trade Agreement and more recently, the proposal for a North American free-trade zone are examples of economic integration. Despite this progress in decreasing the barriers to trade with other nations, protectionism is not dead. Advocates of protection are alive—though not quite well—and the causes and costs of this rebirth of protectionism in the United States conclude the chapter.

Whether free trade or protection will be the policy of the United States in the years to come may well depend upon whether you understand that free trade helps everyone and that protection is costly for a nation and for the world economy.

■ **CHECKLIST**

When you have studied this chapter you should be able to:

☐ Explain the importance of international trade to the American economy in terms of volume, dependence, trade patterns, and output effects.

☐ Identify three features of international trade which distinguish it from the trade that takes place within a nation.

☐ State the two economic circumstances which make it desirable for nations to specialize and trade.

☐ Explain the basic principle of comparative advantage based on an individual example.

☐ Compute the costs of producing two commodities when you are given the necessary data in a two-nation example.

☐ Determine which nation has the comparative advantage in the production of each commodity using the cost data you computed for the two-nation example.

☐ Calculate the range in which the terms of trade will occur in the two-nation example.

☐ Explain how nations benefit from trade and specialization based on the two-nation example.

☐ Restate the case for free trade.

☐ Identify the four principal types of artificial barriers to international trade and the motive for erecting these barriers.

☐ Explain the economic effects of a protective tariff on resource allocation, the price of the commodity, the total production of the commodity, and the outputs of foreign and domestic producers of the commodity.

☐ Analyze the economic effects of an import quota and compare them with the economic effects of a tariff.

☐ Enumerate six arguments used to support the case for protection and find the weakness in each of these arguments.

☐ List the major provisions of the Reciprocal Trade Agreements Act of 1934 and of the General Agreement on Tariffs and Trade (GATT) of 1947; and explain why the former was a sharp change in the trade policy of the United States.

☐ Describe the recent focus of GATT negotiations.

☐ Identify the four major goals of the European Economic Community (the Common Market).

☐ Explain the features and the economic significance of the United States–Canadian Free-Trade Agreement of 1988.

☐ Discuss the proposal for a North American free-trade zone.

☐ Identify the causes of the rebirth of protectionism in the United States, give examples of it, and discuss its cost.

■ **CHAPTER OUTLINE**

1. Trade among nations is large enough and unique enough to warrant special attention.

   a. While the relative importance of international trade to the United States is less than it is to other nations:

   (1) this country's imports and exports are about 10% to 11% of its GDP (about $622 billion imports and $593 billion exports in 1991), and the United States is the largest trading nation in the world;

   (2) the American economy depends on this trade for important raw materials and markets for its finished goods;

   (3) the United States imports more from the rest of the world as a whole, Japan, and the OPEC nations than it exports to them, most American trade is with other developed nations, and Canada is the largest trading partner; and

   (4) changes in the net exports (exports minus imports) have a multiplier effect on American output, employment, and prices.

   b. International trade has three characteristics that distinguish it from domestic trade: resources are less mobile, the nations use different currencies (or money), and the trade is subjected to more political restrictions.

2. Specialization and trade among nations is advantageous because the world's resources are not evenly distributed and the efficient production of different commodities necessitates different methods and combinations of resources.

3. Two simple hypothetical examples explain comparative advantage and the gains from trade.

   a. In an individual example, suppose that an accountant wants to have his house painted, but the accountant can either do it himself (he is a skilled painter) or hire a professional painter to do the job.

   (1) The law of comparative advantage suggests that the accountant will specialize in that work where the opportunity cost is lower relative to the work where the opportunity cost is higher.

   (2) The same principle applies to the professional painter in deciding whether to prepare his own tax return, or specialize in painting and hire an accountant to prepare the tax return for him.

   (3) Given the hypothetical labor time and wage data in the textbook example, both the accountant and the painter reduce their opportunity costs when they specialize in their respective jobs and exchange money for other services they desire.

   b. In an international trade example, suppose the world is composed of only two nations, each of which is capable of producing two different commodities and in which the production possibilities curves are different straight lines (whose opportunity cost ratios are constant but different).

(1) With different opportunity cost ratios, each nation will have a comparative (cost) advantage in the production of one of the two commodities; and if the world is to use its resources economically each nation must specialize in the commodity in the production of which it has a comparative advantage.

(2) The ratio at which one product is traded for another—the terms of trade—lies between the opportunity cost ratios of the two nations.

d. Each nation gains from this trade because specialization permits a greater total output from the same resources and a better allocation of the world's resources.

e. If opportunity cost ratios in the two nations are not constant, specialization may not be complete.

f. The basic argument for free trade among nations is that it leads to a better allocation of resources and a higher standard of living in the world; but it also increases competition and deters monopoly in these nations.

4. Nations, however, retard international trade by erecting artificial barriers; and tariffs, import quotas, a variety of nontariff barriers, and voluntary export restrictions are the principal barriers to trade.

a. Special interest groups within nations benefit from protection and persuade their nations to erect trade barriers; but the costs to consumers of this protection exceed the benefits to the economy.

b. The imposition of a tariff on a good imported from abroad has both direct and indirect effects on an economy.

(1) The tariff increases the domestic price of the good, reduces its domestic consumption, expands its domestic production, decreases foreign production, and transfers income from domestic consumers to government.

(2) It also reduces the income of foreign producers and the ability of foreign nations to purchase goods and services in the nation imposing the tariff, causes the contraction of relatively efficient industries in that nation, decreases world trade, and lowers the real output of goods and services.

c. The imposition of a quota on an imported product has the same direct and indirect effects as that of a tariff on that product, with the exception that a tariff generates revenue for government use whereas an import quota transfers that revenue to foreign producers.

5. The arguments for protectionism are many but they often are of questionable validity.

a. The military self-sufficiency argument can be challenged because it is difficult to determine which industry is "vital" to national defense and must be protected; it

would be more efficient economically to provide a direct subsidy to military producers rather than impose a tariff.

b. Trade barriers do not necessarily increase domestic employment because:

(1) imports may eliminate some jobs, but create others; therefore, imports may only change the composition of employment, not the overall level of employment;

(2) the exports of one nation become the imports of another; tariffs barriers can be viewed as "beggar thy neighbor" policies;

(3) there is likely to be retaliation from other nations from the imposition of trade barriers that will reduce domestic output and employment; and,

(4) they create a less efficient allocation of resources by shielding protected domestic industries from the rigors of competition.

c. Using tariff barriers to permit diversification for stability in economy is not necessary for advanced economies such as the United States and there may be economic costs to diversification in less developed nations.

d. It is alleged that infant-industries need protection until they are sufficiently large to compete. But the argument may not apply to developed economies; it is difficult to select which industries will prosper; protectionism tends to persist long after it is needed; and direct subsidies may be more economically efficient. A variant of this argument for advanced nations is "strategic trade policy" to justify barriers that protect the investment in high risk, growth industries for a nation, but these policies often lead to retaliation and smaller policies from other trading nations.

e. Sometimes protection is sought against the "dumping" of excess foreign goods on American markets. Dumping is a legitimate concern and is restricted under United States trade law, but to use dumping as an excuse for widespread tariff protection is unjustified and the number of documented cases is few. If foreign companies are more efficient (low cost) producers, what may appear to be dumping may actually be comparative advantage at work.

f. Protection is sometimes sought because of the cheap foreign labor argument; it should be realized that nations gain from trade based on comparative advantage and without trade living standards will be lower.

g. In summary, most of the protectionist arguments are fallacious or based on half-truths. The only points that have some validity, under certain conditions, are the infant-industry and military-sufficiency arguments, but both are subject to abuse. The historical evidence suggests that free trade promotes and protectionism deters prosperity and economic growth in the world.

6. International trade policies have changed over the years.

a. Until 1934, the United States steadily increased tariff rates to protect private-interest groups. Since the passage of the Reciprocal Trade Agreement Act of 1934, tariff rates have been substantially reduced.

b. Many nations, including the United States, signed the General Agreement on Tariffs and Trade (GATT) in an attempt to eliminate trade barriers. The Uruguay "round" of negotiations, begun in 1986, is the current forum for multination trade negotiations and they involve reducing agricultural subsidies worldwide, removal of trade barriers in services, ending restrictions on foreign investments, and establishing worldwide recognition for patents, copyrights, and trademarks. GATT negotiations temporarily collapsed in 1990 mainly over issues related to agricultural subsidies for domestic production and exports.

c. Economic integration, or the combining of markets of two or more nations into free trade zones, is another method for trade liberalization. There are three examples of economic integration:

(1) The European Common Market sought the economic integration of thirteen Western European nations to create mass markets and increase economic growth; a number of specific goals were set for 1992; but the success of the integration creates problems for non-member nations such as the United States because of potential tariff barriers.

(2) The United States–Canadian Free-Trade Agreement of 1989 eliminated many trade restrictions between the two nations and should be a benefit to both countries given the volume of trade between them.

(3) A proposed North American free-trade zone would add Mexico to the free-trade zone created by the United States and Canada in 1989. The three nations would constitute a sizable trading bloc to counter the development of the European Common Market. Proponents cite the usual advantages of free trade, while critics worry about job losses from the United States to Mexico and the potential for abuse of the agreement by trading partners.

d. In recent years pressures for protection from goods produced abroad have reemerged in the United States.

(1) There are several interrelated causes of these pressures including a backlash from past tariff reductions, more firms are affected by foreign competition, other nations are now more competitive with the United States, and American imports have exceeded exports in recent years.

(2) There are examples of restrictions placed on imports into the United States, and although tariffs overall are low, some very high tariffs and restrictions have been placed on a select list of goods.

(3) The costs to consumers in the United States of protection are high; protection is similar to a regressive tax because it redistributes income from the lowest to the highest income groups; the gains that trade barriers create for protected industries produce a much greater loss for the overall economy.

■ IMPORTANT TERMS

Labor- (land-, capital-) intensive commodity

Cost ratio

Comparative advantage

Specialization

Terms of trade

Trading possibilities line

Tariff

Revenue tariff

Protective tariff

Import quota

Nontariff barriers (NTBs)

Voluntary export restrictions (VERs)

Smoot-Hawley Tariff Act of 1930

Dumping

Reciprocal Trade Agreements Act of 1934

Most-favored-nation clause

General Agreement on Tariffs and Trade (GATT)

Export subsidies

Economic integration

European Common Market (European Economic Community)

United States–Canadian Free-Trade Agreement

North American free-trade zone

■ FILL-IN QUESTIONS

1. Trade is important to the United States in many ways.
   a. The imports of the United States amount to about

   _____% of the economy's GDP and exports

   amount to about _____%. In absolute volume of imports and exports the United States is the world's

   _____ trading nation.

   b. The United States is _____ on world trade and the bulk of its trade is with (less developed,

   developed) _____ nations. The largest trading partner of the United States is (Japan, Can-

   ada) _____

   c. Changes in net exports have _____ effects on the level of national income, employment, and prices.

2. Special attention is devoted to international trade be-

cause resources are (more, less) _____ mobile between nations than within a nation; because

each nation employs a different _____; and because international trade is subject to a (greater,

smaller) _____ number of political interferences and controls than domestic trade.

3. Nations tend to trade among themselves because the distribution of economic resources among them is (even,

uneven) _____ and because the efficient production of various goods and services necessitates (the same,

different) _____
technologies or combinations of resources.

4. The nations of the world tend to specialize in those goods in the production of which they have a

_____, to export those goods, and to import those goods in the production of which they do not

have a _____

5. If the cost ratio in country X is 4 Panama hats equal 1 pound of bananas, while in country Y, 3 Panama hats equal 1 pound of bananas:

   a. In country X hats are relatively (expensive, inex-

pensive) _____ and bananas

relatively _____

   b. In country Y hats are relatively _____

and bananas relatively _____
   c. X has a comparative advantage and should spe-

cialize in the production of _____ and Y has a comparative advantage and should specialize in

the production of _____
   d. When X and Y specialize and trade, the terms of

trade will be somewhere between _____ and

_____

hats for each pound of bananas; and will depend upon

_____

   e. When the actual terms of trade turn out to be 3½ hats for 1 pound of bananas, the cost of obtaining:

(1) 1 Panama hat has been decreased from _____

to _____ pounds of bananas in Y.
(2) 1 pound of bananas has been decreased from

_____ to _____ Panama hats in X.
   f. This international specialization will not be complete if the cost of producing either good (increases, de-

creases, remains constant) _____ as a nation produces more of it.

6. The basic argument for free trade is that it results in

a better _____ of resources and a higher _____ of living.

7. The barriers to international trade include _____,

_____ quotas, the non _____ bar-

riers, and _____ restrictions.

8. Nations erect barriers to international trade to benefit

the economic positions of _____
groups even though these barriers (increase, decrease)

_____ economic efficiency and trade among nations, and the benefits to a nation are (greater,

less) _____ than the costs to it.

9. When the United States imposes a tariff on a good which is imported from abroad:
   a. the price of that good in the United States will (in-

crease, decrease) _____
   b. the total purchases of the good in the United States

will _____
   c. the output of:

(1) American producers of the good will _____

_____

(2) foreign producers will _____
   d. the ability of foreigners to buy goods and services

in the United States will _____ and, as a result, output and employment in American industries

that sell goods and services abroad will _____

10. When comparing the effects of a tariff with the effects of a quota to restrict the U.S. imports of a product, the

basic difference is that with a (tariff, quota) _____ the U.S. government will receive revenue, but with a

_____ foreign producers will receive the revenue that would have gone to the U.S. government.

11. List the six arguments which protectionists employ to justify trade barriers.

   a. _____

   b. _____

   c. _____

   d. _____

   e. _____

   f. _____

12. The only two protectionism arguments containing any reasonable justification for protection are the

_____ argument and the _____ argument.

13. Until 1930 the trend of tariff rates in the United States

was (upward, downward) _____; but

since the passage of the _____ Act in 1934

the trend has been _____. This act em-

powered the President to lower _____

rates by up to _____% in return for a reduction in foreign restrictions on American goods and in-

corporated _____ clauses in American trade agreements.

14. The three main principles set down in the General Agreement on Tariffs and Trade are:

    a. _____

    b. _____

    c. _____

15. The Uruguay _____ negotiations is focused on proposals to eliminate trade barriers and domestic subsidies in _____; to remove barriers to trade in _____; to end restrictions on foreign economic _____; and to establish and enforce _____, _____, and _____ rights on an international basis; but the negotiations temporarily broke down in 1990 primarily over issues related to subsidies in _____.

16. The specific aims of the European Common Market were the abolition of _____ _____ among member nations, the establishment of common tariffs on goods imported from _____ nations, the free movement of _____ and _____ among member nations, and common policies with respect to other matters.

17. A recent example of economic integration in the Western hemisphere was the _____ of 1989. Under terms of the agreement all trade restrictions will be eliminated over a ____-year period. It has been estimated that the agreement will produce annual gains to each nation of $____ to $____ billion when fully implemented.

18. A recent proposal for a free-trade zone in North America would include three nations: _____, _____, and _____. Supporters contend that it would increase total output from scarce resources in each nation because of specialization according to _____, but U.S. critics complain about the potential loss of _____

19. What are four interrelated factors which have resulted in the recent resurgence of pressures for the protection of American industries?

    a. _____

    b. _____

    c. _____

    d. _____

20. The costs of protecting American producers from foreign competition are equal to the rise in the _____ American consumers have to pay for the protected goods.

    a. These costs are (greater, less) _____ than the benefits to American producers.

    b. The costs of protection were borne mostly by those consumers in the (highest, lowest) _____ income group.

■ **PROBLEMS AND PROJECTS**

1. Shown on the next page are the production possibilities curves for two nations: the United States and Chile. Suppose these two nations do not currently engage in international trade or specialization, and suppose that points **A** and **a** show the combinations of wheat and copper they now produce and consume.

    a. The straightness of the two curves indicates that the cost ratios in the two nations are (changing, constant) _____

    b. Examination of the two curves reveals that the cost ratio in:

    (1) The United States is _____ million tons of wheat for _____ thousand pounds of copper.

    (2) Chile is _____ million tons of wheat for _____ thousand pounds of copper.

    c. If these two nations were to specialize and trade wheat for copper,

    (1) The United States would specialize in the production of wheat because _____

    (2) Chile would specialize in the production of copper because _____

    d. The terms of trade, if specialization and trade occur, will be greater than 2 and less than 4 million tons of wheat for 1 thousand pounds of copper because ____ _____

    e. Assume the terms of trade turn out to be 3 million tons of wheat for 1 thousand pounds of copper. Draw in the trading possibilities curve for the United States and Chile.

f. With these trading possibilities curves, suppose the United States decides to consume 5 million tons of wheat and 1 thousand pounds of copper while Chile decides to consume 3 million tons of wheat and 1 thousand pounds of copper. The gains from trade to:

(1) The United States are _____ million tons of wheat and _____ thousand pounds of copper.

(2) Chile are _____ million tons of wheat and _____ thousand pounds of copper.

2. The following table shows the quantities of woolen gloves demanded (**D**) in the United States at several different prices (**P**). Also shown in the table are the quantities of woolen gloves that would be supplied by American producers (**S_a**) and the quantities that would be supplied by foreign producers (**S_f**) at the nine different prices.

P	D	S_a	S_f	S_t	S'_f	S'_t
$2.60	450	275	475	_____	_____	_____
2.40	500	250	450	_____	_____	_____
2.20	550	225	425	_____	_____	_____
2.00	600	200	400	_____	_____	_____
1.80	650	175	375	_____	_____	_____
1.60	700	150	350	_____	_____	_____
1.40	750	125	325	_____	_____	_____
1.20	800	0	300	_____	_____	_____
1.00	850	0	0	_____	_____	_____

a. Compute and enter in the table the total quantities that would be supplied (**S_t**) by American and foreign producers at each of the prices.

b. If the market for woolen gloves in the United States is a competitive one the equilibrium price for woolen gloves is $_____ and the equilibrium quantity is _____

c. Suppose now that the United States government imposes an 80 cent ($0.80) per pair of gloves tariff on all gloves imported into the United States from abroad. Compute and enter into the table the quantities that would be supplied (**S'_f**) by foreign producers at the nine different prices. (**Hint**: If foreign producers were willing to supply 300 pairs at a price of $1.20 when there was no tariff they are now willing to supply 300 pairs at $2.00, the $0.80 per pair tariff plus the $1.20 they will receive for themselves. The quantities supplied at each of the other prices may be found in a similar fashion.)

d. Compute and enter into the table the total quantities that would be supplied (**S'_t**) by American and foreign producers at each of the nine prices.

e. As a result of the imposition of the tariff the equilibrium price has risen to $_____ and the equilibrium quantity has fallen to _____

f. The number of pairs sold by:

(1) American producers has (increased, decreased) _____ by _____

(2) foreign producers has (increased, decreased) _____ by _____

g. The total revenues (after the payment of the tariff) of:

(1) American producers—who **do not** pay the tariff—have (increased, decreased) _____ by $_____

(2) foreign producers—who **do** pay the tariff—have (increased, decreased) _____ by $_____

h. The total amount spent by American buyers of woolen gloves has _____ by $_____

i. The total number of dollars earned by foreigners has _____ by $_____; and, as a result, the total foreign demand for goods and services produced in the United States will _____ by $_____

j. The tariff revenue of the United States government has _____ by $_____

k. If an import quota was imposed that had the same effect as the tariff on price and output, the amount of the tariff revenue, $_____, would now be received as revenue by _____ producers.

■ **SELF-TEST**

Circle the T if the statement is true; the F if it is false.

1. Since 1975 the dollar volume of U.S. imports has increased and the dollar volume of its exports has decreased. **T F**

2. The American economy's share of world trade has decreased since 1947. **T F**

3. The United States exports and imports goods and services with a dollar value greater than any other nation in the world. **T F**

4. The United States is completely dependent on trade for certain commodities which cannot be obtained in domestic markets. **T F**

5. Canada is the most important trading partner for the United States in terms of the volume of exports and imports. **T F**

Use the following production possibilities to answer the next five questions (6, 7, 8, 9, and 10).

NEPAL PRODUCTION POSSIBILITIES TABLE

	Production alternatives					
Product	A	B	C	D	E	F
Yak fat	0	4	8	12	16	20
Camel hides	40	32	24	16	8	0

KASHMIR PRODUCTION POSSIBILITIES TABLE

	Production alternatives					
Product	A	B	C	D	E	F
Yak fat	0	3	6	9	12	15
Camel hides	60	48	36	24	12	0

6. In Kashmir the cost of 1 camel hide is 3 units of yak fat. **T F**

7. Nepal has a comparative advantage in producing camel hides. **T F**

8. The best terms of trade for Nepal and Kashmir are 5 camel hides for 1 yak fat. **T F**

9. With specialization and trade, the trading possibilities curves of both nations would move to the right of their production possibilities curves. **T F**

10. Assume that prior to specialization and trade, Nepal and Kashmir produced combination B. If these two nations now specialized by comparative advantage, the total gains from specialization and trade would be 60 camel hides. **T F**

11. Increasing production costs tend to prevent specialization among trading nations from being complete. **T F**

12. Trade among nations tends to bring about a more efficient use of the world's resources and a greater world output of goods and services. **T F**

13. Free trade among nations tends to increase monopoly and lessen competition in these nations. **T F**

14. A tariff on coffee in the United States is an example of a protective tariff. **T F**

15. The imposition of a tariff on a good imported from abroad will raise the price of the good and lower the quantity of it bought and sold. **T F**

16. The major difference between a tariff and a quota on an imported product is that a quota produces revenue for the government. **T F**

17. To advocate tariffs which would protect domestic producers of goods and materials essential to national defense is to substitute a political-military objective for the economic objectives of efficiently allocating resources. **T F**

18. An increase in a nation's imports will, other things remaining constant, expand aggregate demand, real output, and employment in that nation. **T F**

19. The Smoot-Hawley Tariff Act of 1930 reduced tariffs in the United States to the lowest level ever in an attempt to pull the nation out of the Great Depression. **T F**

20. One crop economies may be able to make themselves more stable and diversified by imposing tariffs on goods imported from abroad; but these tariffs are apt also to lower the standard of living in these economies. **T F**

21. Protection against the "dumping" of foreign goods at low prices on the American market is one good reason for widespread, permanent tariffs. **T F**

22. The only argument for tariffs that has, in the appropriate circumstances, any economic justification is the increase-domestic-employment argument. **T F**

23. If the United States concludes a tariff agreement which lowers the tariff rates on goods imported from another nation and that trade agreement contains a most-favored-nation clause, the lower tariff rates are then applied to those goods when they are imported from (most) other nations in the world. **T F**

24. Export subsidies are government payments to reduce the price of a product to buyers from other nations. **T F**

25. The members of the European Economic Community have experienced freer trade since they formed the Common Market in 1958. **T F**

26. The economic integration of nations creates larger markets for firms within the nations that integrate and makes it possible for these firms and their customers to benefit from the economies of large-scale (mass) production. **T F**

27. The formation of the European Economic Community (Common Market) has made it more difficult for American firms to compete with firms located within the Community for customers there. **T F**

28. The United States–Canadian Free-Trade Agreement of 1988 is an example of the gains to be obtained from voluntary export restrictions. **T F**

29. The proposed North American free-trade zone also includes Central American nations. **T F**

30. The cost of protecting American firms and employees from foreign competition is the rise in the prices of products produced in the United States, and this cost almost always exceeds its benefits. **T F**

Circle the letter that corresponds to the best answer.

1. In 1991 the imports of the United States amounted to approximately what percentage of the United States' GDP?
   (a) 5%
   (b) 7%
   (c) 9%
   (d) 11%

2. Which nation is our most important trading partner in terms of the quantity of trade volume?
   (a) Japan
   (b) Canada
   (c) Germany
   (d) United Kingdom

3. Which of the following is **not** true?
   (a) the greater part of the export-import trade in merchandise is with the less developed nations

   (b) the U.S. imports more merchandise from the OPEC nations than it exports to them
   (c) the U.S. imports more merchandise from Japan than it exports to it
   (d) the merchandise imports of the U.S. exceed its exports of merchandise

4. In recent years the total exports and imports of goods and services of the U.S have been about:
   (a) $200 billion and $300 billion
   (b) $300 billion and $400 billion
   (c) $400 billion and $500 billion
   (d) $600 billion and $600 billion

5. International trade is a special and separate area of economic study because:
   (a) international trade involves the movement of goods over greater distances than trade within a nation
   (b) resources are more mobile internationally than domestically
   (c) countries engaged in international trade use different monies
   (d) international trade is based on comparative advantage

6. Nations would not need to engage in trade if:
   (a) all products were produced from the same combinations of resources
   (b) world resources were evenly distributed among nations
   (c) world resources were perfectly mobile
   (d) all of the above

*Use the tables preceding true-false question **6** to answer the following four questions (**7, 8, 9** and **10**).*

7. The data in the table show that production in:
   (a) both Nepal and Kashmir are subject to increasing opportunity costs
   (b) both Nepal and Kashmir are subject to constant opportunity costs
   (c) Nepal is subject to increasing opportunity costs and Kashmir to constant opportunity costs
   (d) Kashmir to increasing opportunity costs and Nepal to constant opportunity costs

8. If Nepal and Kashmir engage in trade, the terms of trade will be:
   (a) between 2 and 4 camel hides for 1 unit of yak fat
   (b) between $\frac{1}{3}$ and $\frac{1}{2}$ units of yak fat for 1 camel hide
   (c) between 3 and 4 units of yak fat for 1 camel hide
   (d) between 2 and 4 units of yak fat for 1 camel hide

9. Assume that prior to specialization and trade Nepal and Kashmir both choose production possibility "C." Now if each specializes according to its comparative advantage, the resulting gains from specialization and trade will be:

   (a) 6 units of yak fat
   (b) 8 units of yak fat
   (c) 6 units of yak fat and 8 camel hides
   (d) 8 units of yak fat and 6 camel hides

10. Each nation produced only one product in accordance with its comparative advantage and the terms of trade were set at 3 camel hides for 1 yak fat. In this case, the Nepal could obtain a maximum combination of 8 yak fat and:

   (a) 12 camel hides
   (b) 24 camel hides
   (c) 36 camel hides
   (d) 48 camel hides

11. Which one of the following is characteristic of tariffs?

   (a) they prevent the importation of goods from abroad
   (b) they specify the maximum amounts of specific commodities which may be imported during a given period of time
   (c) they often protect domestic producers from foreign competition
   (d) they enable nations to reduce their exports and increase their imports during periods of depression

12. The motive for the erection by a nation of barriers to the importation of goods and services from abroad is to:

   (a) improve economic efficiency in that nation
   (b) protect and benefit special interest groups in that nation
   (c) reduce the prices of the goods and services produced in that nation
   (d) expand the export of goods and services to foreign nations

13. When a tariff is imposed on a good imported from abroad:

   (a) the demand for the good increases
   (b) the demand for the good decreases
   (c) the supply of the good increases
   (d) the supply of the good decreases

Answer the next five questions (14, 15, 16, 17, and 18) on the basis of the following diagram, where S_d and D_d are the domestic supply and demand for a product and P_w is the world price of that product.

14. In a closed economy (without international trade), the equilibrium price would be:

   (a) $0P_d$ but in an open economy, the equilibrium price will be $0P_t$
   (b) $0P_d$ but in an open economy, the equilibrium price will be $0P_w$
   (c) $0P_w$ but in an open economy, the equilibrium price will be $0P_d$

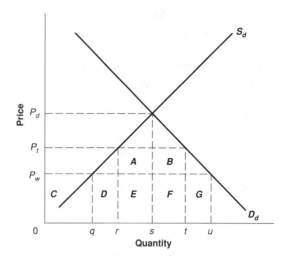

   (d) $0P_w$ but in an open economy, the equilibrium price will be $0P_t$

15. If there is free trade in this economy and no tariffs, the total revenue going to the foreign producers is represented by:

   (a) area *C*
   (b) areas *A* and *B* combined
   (c) areas *A, B, E,* and *F* combined
   (d) areas *D, E, F,* and *G* combined

16. If a per unit tariff was imposed in the amount of P_wP_t, then domestic producers would supply:

   (a) $0q$ units and foreign producers would supply *qu* units
   (b) $0s$ units and foreign producers would supply *su* units
   (c) $0r$ units and foreign producers would supply *rt* units
   (d) $0t$ units and foreign producers would supply *tu* units

17. Given a per unit tariff in the amount of P_wP_t, the amount of the tariff revenue paid by consumers of this product is represented by:

   (a) area *A*
   (b) area *B*
   (c) areas *A* and *B* combined
   (d) areas *D, E, F,* and *G* combined

18. Assume an import quota of *rt* units is imposed on the foreign nation producing this product. The amount of **total** revenue going to foreign producers is represented by areas:

   (a) *A + B*
   (b) *E + F*
   (c) *A + B + E + F*
   (d) *D + E + F + G*

19. Tariffs lead to:

   (a) the contraction of relatively efficient industries

(b) an overallocation of resources to relatively efficient industries

(c) an increase in the foreign demand for domestically produced goods

(d) an underallocation of resources to relatively inefficient industries

20. "The nation needs to protect itself from foreign countries that sell their products in our domestic markets at less than the cost of production." This quotation would be most closely associated with which protectionist argument?

(a) diversification for stability

(b) increase domestic employment

(c) protection against dumping

(d) cheap foreign labor

21. Which one of the following arguments for protection is the least fallacious and most pertinent in the United States today?

(a) the military self-sufficiency argument

(b) the increase-domestic-employment argument

(c) the cheap foreign labor argument

(d) the infant-industry argument

22. Which of the following is the likely result of the United States employing tariffs to protect its high wages and standard of living from cheap foreign labor?

(a) an increase in U.S. exports

(b) a rise in the American real GDP

(c) a decrease in the average productivity of American workers

(d) a decrease in the quantity of labor employed by industries producing the goods on which tariffs have been levied

23. Which of the following is a likely result of imposing tariffs to increase domestic employment?

(a) a short-run increase in domestic employment

(b) retaliatory increases in the tariff rates of foreign nations

(c) a long-run decline in exports

(d) all of the above

24. The infant-industry argument for tariffs:

(a) is especially pertinent for the European Economic Community

(b) generally results in tariffs that are removed after the infant industry has matured

(c) makes it rather easy to determine which infant industries will become mature industries with comparative advantages in producing their goods

(d) might better be replaced by an argument for outright subsidies for infant industries

25. Which one of the following specifically empowered the President of the United States to reduce its tariff rates up to 50% if other nations would reduce their tariffs on American goods?

(a) the Underwood Act of 1913

(b) the Hawley-Smoot Act of 1930

(c) the Trade Agreements Act of 1934

(d) the General Agreement on Tariffs and Trade of 1947

26. Which of the following is **not** characteristic of the General Agreement on Tariffs and Trade? Nations signing the agreement were committed to:

(a) the elimination of import quotas

(b) the reciprocal reduction of tariffs by negotiation

(c) the nondiscriminatory treatment of all trading nations

(d) the establishment of a world customs union

27. One important topic for discussion during the Uruguay round of GATT was:

(a) removing voluntary export restraints in manufacturing

(b) eliminating trade barriers and subsidies in agriculture

(c) abolishing the need for patent, copyright, and trademark protection

(d) increasing tariff barriers on services but reducing tariff barriers on foreign economic investments

28. The European Common Market:

(a) is designed to eliminate tariffs and import quotas among its members

(b) aims to allow the eventual free movement of capital and labor within the member nations

(c) imposes common tariffs on goods imported into the member nations from outside the Common Market area

(d) does all of the above

29. An example of economic integration would be the:

(a) Smoot-Hawley Tariff Act

(b) United States–Canadian Free-Trade Agreement

(c) Reciprocal Trade Agreements Act

(d) General Agreements on Tariffs and Trade

30. Pressures for the protection of American industries have increased in recent years because of:

(a) previous decreases in the barriers to trade

(b) persistent trade deficits in the United States

(c) increased competition from imported products

(d) all of the above

■ **DISCUSSION QUESTIONS**

1. In relative and absolute terms, how large is the volume of the international trade of the United States? What has happened to these figures over the past thirty or so years?

2. What are the principal exports and imports of the American economy? What commodities used in the economy come almost entirely from abroad and what American industries sell large percentages of their outputs abroad?

3. Which nations are the principal "trading partners" of the United States? How much of this trade is with the developed and how much of it is with the less developed nations of the world?

4. Are the American economy's exports of merchandise to greater or less than its imports of merchandise from:
(a) Japan,
(b) the OPEC nations, and
(c) the rest of the world?

5. In what ways is international trade different from the trade which takes place within a nation?

6. Why do nations specialize in certain products and export their surplus production of these goods at the same time that they are importing other goods? Why do they not use the resources employed to produce the surpluses which they export to produce the goods which they import?

7. What two facts—one dealing with the distribution of the world's resources and the other related to the technology of producing different products—are the basis for the trade among nations?

8. Explain:
(a) the theory or principle of comparative advantage;
(b) what is meant by and what determines the terms of trade; and
(c) the gains from trade.

9. What is the "case for free trade"?

10. What motivates nations to erect barriers to the importation of goods from abroad and what types of barriers do they erect?

11. Suppose the United States were to increase the tariff on automobiles imported from Germany (and other foreign countries). What would be the effect of this tariff-rate increase on:
(a) the price of automobiles in the United States;
(b) the total number of cars sold in the United States during a year;
(c) the number of cars produced by and employment in the German automobile industry;
(d) production by and employment in the American automobile industry;
(e) German income obtained by selling cars in the United States;
(f) the German demand for goods produced in the U.S.;
(g) the production of and employment in those American industries which now export goods to Germany;
(h) the standards of living in the U.S. and in Germany;
(i) the allocation of resources in the American economy; and
(j) the allocation of the world's resources?

12. Compare and contrast the economic effects of a tariff with the economic effects of an import quota on a product. Give an example of a recent import quota and explain how it affected foreign producers.

13. Critically evaluate the military self-sufficiency and infant-industry arguments (including strategic trade policy) as a basis for protectionism.

14. Is there a "strong case" for protectionism that can be made on the basis of one of the following reasons: increasing domestic employment, diversifying for stability, defending against the "dumping" of products, or shielding domestic workers from competition from "cheap" foreign labor? Summarize the case for and the case against protectionism.

15. What was the tariff policy of the United States between 1920 and 1930? What has been the policy since 1934? Explain the basic provisions of the Reciprocal Trade Agreements Act.

16. How has the United States cooperated with other nations since 1945 to reduce trade barriers? What were the three cardinal principles contained in the General Agreements on Tariffs and Trade? What were the basic objectives and what were the results of the "Uruguay Round" of GATT negotiations?

17. What were the four main goals of the European Economic Community? How does the achievement of these goals bring about an increased standard of living within the Community? What problems and what benefits does the success of the EC create for the United States?

18. What was the United States–Canadian Free-Trade Agreement and what is its economic significance?

19. What recent actions have been taken to create a free-trade zone? What are the pros and cons of this proposal?

20. Why have the pressures for the protection of American firms and workers increased in the last few years? What:
(a) are several examples of this increased protection; and
(b) are the costs to the American economy of protection?

■ **ANSWERS**

Chapter 37 International Trade: Comparative Advantage and Protectionism

FILL-IN QUESTIONS

1. *a.* 11, 10, largest; *b.* dependent, developed, Canada; *c.* multiple

2. less, money (currency), greater

3. uneven, different

4. comparative advantage, comparative advantage

5. *a.* inexpensive, expensive; *b.* expensive, inexpensive; *c.* hats, bananas; *d.* 3, 4, world demand and supply for hats and bananas; *e.* (1) ⅓, ²⁄₇, (2) 4, 3½; *f.* increases

6. allocation, standard

7. tariffs, import, tariff, voluntary export

8. special interest, decrease, less

9. *a.* increase; *b.* decrease; *c.* (1) increase, (2) decrease; *d.* decrease, decrease

10. tariff, quota

11. *a.* military self-sufficiency; *b.* infant industry; *c.* increase domestic employment; *d.* diversification for stability; *e.* protection against dumping; *f.* cheap foreign labor

12. military self-sufficiency, infant-industry

13. upward, Reciprocal Trade Agreements, downward, tariff, 50, most-favored-nation

14. *a.* equal, nondiscriminatory treatment of all trading nations; *b.* reduction of tariffs by negotiation; *c.* elimination of import quotas

15. Round, agriculture, services, investments, patents, copyrights, trademarks, agriculture

16. tariffs and import quotas, nonmember, capital, labor

17. United States–Canadian Free-Trade Agreement, 10, 1, 3

18. United States, Canada, Mexico; comparative advantage, jobs (or employment)

19. *a.* the freer trade that resulted from past reductions in trade barriers; *b.* the increased competition from abroad that resulted from a more open economy; *c.* the increased competitiveness of foreign products that resulted from lower labor costs and prices abroad; *d.* persistent trade deficits

20. prices; *a.* greater; *b.* lowest

PROBLEMS AND PROJECTS

1. *a.* constant; *b.* (1) 8, 2, (2) 4, 2; *c.* (1) it has a comparative advantage in producing wheat (its cost of producing wheat is less than Chile's), (2) it has a comparative advantage in producing copper (its cost of producing copper is less than the United States), *d.* one of the two nations would be unwilling to trade if the terms of trade are outside this range; *f.* (1) 1, 0, (2) 1, 0

2. *a.* 750, 700, 650, 600, 550, 500, 450, 300, 0; *b.* $2.00, 600; *c.* 375, 350, 325, 300, 0, 0, 0, 0, 0; *d.* 650, 600, 550, 500, 175, 150, 125, 0, 0; *e.* $2.20, 550; *f.* (1) increased, 25, (2) decreased, 75; *g.* (1) increased, $95, (2) decreased, $345; *h.* increased, $10; *i.* decreased, $345, decrease, $345; *j.* increased, $260; *k.* $260, foreign

SELF-TEST

1. F, p. 698	**16.** F, p. 708
2. T, p. 698	**17.** T, p. 708
3. T, p. 698	**18.** F, p. 709
4. T, p. 698	**19.** F, p. 709
5. T, p. 699	**20.** T, p. 709
6. F, pp. 701–703	**21.** F, p. 710
7. F, pp. 701–703	**22.** F, p. 711
8. F, p[. 702–703	**23.** T, p. 712
9. T, p. 703	**24.** T, p. 713
10. F, pp. 703–704	**25.** T, pp. 713–714
11. T, p. 704–705	**26.** T, p. 713
12. T, p. 705	**27.** T, p. 714
13. F, p. 705	**28.** F, p. 714
14. F, p. 706	**29.** F, p. 714
15. T, pp. 706–707	**30.** T, p. 717

1. *d,* p. 698	**16.** *c,* pp. 707–708
2. *b,* p. 699	**17.** *c,* p. 707
3. *a,* p. 698	**18.** *c,* p. 708
4. *d,* p. 698	**19.** *a,* p. 707
5. *c,* p. 699	**20.** *c,* p. 710
6. *d,* pp. 699–700	**21.** *a,* p. 711
7. *b,* p. 701	**22.** *c,* p. 711
8. *a,* pp. 702–703	**23.** *d,* pp. 708–709
9. *a,* pp. 703–704	**24.** *d,* p. 710
10. *c,* pp. 703–704	**25.** *c,* p. 712
11. *c,* p. 706	**26.** *d,* p. 712
12. *b,* p. 706	**27.** *b,* pp. 712–713
13. *d,* p. 706	**28.** *d,* p. 713
14. *b,* pp. 706–707	**29.** *b,* p. 714
15. *d,* p. 707	**30.** *d,* pp. 715–716

DISCUSSION QUESTIONS

1. p. 698	**11.** pp. 706–707
2. pp. 698–699	**12.** pp. 706–708
3. pp. 698–699	**13.** pp. 708; 710
4. pp. 698–699	**14.** pp. 708–711
5. p. 699	**15.** p. 712
6. pp. 699–700	**16.** pp. 712–713
7. p. 700	**17.** pp. 713–714
8. pp. 700–704	**18.** p. 714
9. p. 705	**19.** pp. 714–715
10. p. 706	**20.** pp. 715–717

Exchange Rates, the Balance of Payments, and Trade Deficits

In the last chapter you learned **why** nations engage in international trade and **why** they erect barriers to trade with other nations. In Chapter 38 you will learn **how** nations using different monies (or currencies) are able to trade with each other.

The means nations employ to overcome the difficulties that result from the use of different monies is fairly simple. When the residents of a nation (its consumers, business firms, or governments) wish to buy goods or services or real or financial assets from, make loans or gifts to, or pay interest and dividends to the residents of other nations they **buy** some of the money used in that nation. They pay for the foreign money with some of their own money. In other words, they **exchange** their own money for foreign money.

When the residents of a nation sell goods or services or real or financial assets to, receive loans or gifts from, or are paid dividends or interest by the residents of foreign nations and obtain foreign money they **sell** this foreign money—often called foreign exchange—in return for some of their own money. That is, they **exchange** foreign money for their own money.

The markets in which one money is sold and is paid for with another money are called foreign exchange markets. The price that is paid (in one money) for a unit of another money is called the foreign exchange rate (or the rate of exchange). And like most prices, the foreign exchange rate for any foreign currency is determined by the demand for and the supply of that foreign currency.

As you know from Chapter 37, nations buy and sell large quantities of goods and services across national boundaries. But the residents of these nations also buy and sell such financial assets as stocks and bonds and such real assets as land and capital goods in other nations; and the governments and individuals in one nation make gifts (remittances) in other nations. At the end of a year, nations summarize their foreign transactions with the rest of the world. This summary is called the nation's international balance of payments: a record of how it obtained foreign money during the year and what it did with this foreign money.

Of course, all foreign money obtained was used for some purpose—it did not evaporate—and consequently the balance of payments **always** balances. The international balance of payments is an extremely important and useful device for understanding the amounts and kinds of international transactions in which the residents of a nation engage. But it also enables us to understand the meaning of a balance of payments imbalance (a deficit or a surplus), the causes of these imbalances, and how to deal with them.

Probably the most difficult section of this chapter is concerned with balances of payments deficits and surpluses. A balance of payments deficit (surplus) is found when the receipts of foreign money are less (greater) than the payments of foreign money and the nation must reduce (expand) its official reserves to make the balance of payments balance. You should pay particular attention to the way in which a system of **flexible** exchange rates and the way in which a system of **fixed** exchange rates will correct balance of payments deficits and surpluses; and the advantages and disadvantages of these two alternative methods of eliminating imbalances.

As examples of these two types of exchange rate systems you will find in the third section of the chapter an examination of the gold standard, of the Bretton Woods system, and of the managed floating exchange rate system. In the first two systems exchange rates are fixed; and in the third system exchange rates are fixed in the short run (to obtain the advantages of fixed exchange rates) and flexible in the long run (to enable nations to correct balance of payments deficits and surpluses).

The final section of the chapter examines trade deficits of the United States of the 1980s and early 1990s. The problem is that during the early 1980s the United States imported goods and services with a dollar-and-cents value greater than the value of the goods and services it exported; and it incurred very large current-account deficits in those years. It was able to do this only by increasing its debts to (by borrowing from) the rest of the world; and by 1985 it owed more to foreigners than they owed to people in the United States. The primary (though not the only) cause of the trade deficit was the high international value of (exchange rate for) the American dollar during the mid-1980s. The high exchange rate for the dollar meant that the exchange rates for foreign currencies were low. The low exchange rates for other currencies and the high exchange rate for the dollar expanded American imports, contracted American exports, and produced the foreign-trade problem in the United States.

The relatively high exchange rate for the dollar in the mid-1980s was the result of real interest rates which were higher in the United States than in the rest of the world. Real interest rates were higher in the American economy than in the rest of the world because the large budget deficits of the Federal government forced it to borrow in the American money market; and these high real interest rates in the United States increased the attractiveness to foreigners of financial investment (buying bonds or lending) in the U.S., increased the foreign demand for dollars in the foreign exchange markets, and drove the price of the dollar upward in these markets. Although the value of the dollar fell over the 1985–1987 period, the trade deficit persisted for several reasons, and only in mid-1988 did the deficit begin to fall. Even today, however, the trade deficit remains large.

The undesirable effects of the trade deficit have led to a search for policy options. Two are worthy of note while five others are more limited remedies. First, it is thought by many economists that a reduction in the budget deficit of the Federal government would help reduce real interest rates in the United States relative to other nations, increase foreign investment in the United States and the demand for dollars, and cause the value of the dollar to fall. Putting the nation's "fiscal house" in order would help reduce the value of the dollar and move exports and imports to balance in a way that would be more acceptable to the major trading partners of the United States. Second, it is thought that if nations with large trade surpluses with the United States, such as Japan and Germany, would take actions to increase their rate of economic growth, this condition would help increase exports from the United States to those nations.

One last word for you. This chapter is filled with new terms. Some of these are just special words used in international economies to mean things with which you are already familiar. Be very sure you learn what all of the new terms mean. It will simplify your comprehension of this chapter and enable you to understand more readily the foreign trade "crisis" of the United States examined at the end of the chapter.

■ **CHECKLIST**

When you have studied this chapter you should be able to:

☐ Explain how American exports create a demand for dollars and generate a supply of foreign exchange; and how American imports create a demand for foreign exchange and generate a supply of dollars.

☐ Define each of the five balances found in a nation's international balance of payments; and distinguish between a deficit and a surplus in each of these five balances.

☐ Explain the relationship between the current and capital account balances; and between the balance of payments and changes in the official reserves of a nation.

☐ Using a supply and demand graph, illustrate how a foreign exchange market works to establish the price and quantity of a currency.

☐ Identify the five principal determinants of the demand for and supply of a particular foreign money.

☐ Explain how a change in each of these determinants would affect the rate of exchange for that foreign money.

☐ Provide an explanation of how flexible (floating) exchange rates function to eliminate payments deficits and surpluses; and enumerate the three disadvantages of this method of correcting imbalances.

☐ Enumerate the four means by which a nation may fix (or "peg") foreign exchange rates.

☐ Explain how a nation with a payments deficit might employ its international reserves to prevent a rise in foreign exchange rates.

☐ Describe how a nation with a payments deficit might use trade policies, fiscal and monetary policies, and exchange controls to eliminate the deficit.

☐ List the three conditions which a nation had to fulfill if it was to be on the gold standard.

☐ Explain how gold flows operated to reduce payments deficits and surpluses; and identify its basic advantages and its disadvantages.

☐ Explain how the Bretton Woods system stabilized exchange rates and attempted to provide for orderly changes in exchange rates to eliminate payments imbalances.

☐ Define the international monetary reserves of nations in the Bretton Woods system.

☐ Explain why the United States had to incur balance of payments deficits to expand these reserves, and describe the dilemma this created for the United States.

☐ Describe how the United States severed the link between gold and the international value of the dollar in 1971 that led to the floating of the dollar and brought to an end the old Bretton Woods system.

☐ Explain what is meant by a system of managed floating exchange rates.

☐ Enumerate its two alleged virtues and three alleged shortcomings of a system of managed floating exchange rates.

☐ Contrast the adjustments necessary to correct payments deficits and surpluses when exchange rates are flexible and when they are fixed.

☐ Describe and explain the causes of the large trade deficits of the 1980s and early 1990s.

☐ Analyze the effects of the trade deficit on output and employment and prices in the United States and on the indebtedness of Americans to foreigners.

☐ State what two major policies are proposed for reducing the foreign-trade deficit of the United States.
☐ Discuss five other "remedies" for large trade deficits.

■ **CHAPTER OUTLINE**

1. Trade between two nations differs from domestic trade because the nations use different monies; but this problem is resolved by the existence of foreign-exchange markets in which the money used by one nation can be purchased and paid for with the money of the other nation.

a. American exports create a demand for dollars and generate a supply of foreign money in the foreign-exchange markets; increase the money supply in the United States and decrease foreign money supplies; and earn monies that can be used to pay for American imports.

b. American imports create a supply of dollars and generate a demand for foreign money in foreign-exchange markets; decrease the money supply in the United States and increase foreign money supplies; and use monies obtained by exporting.

2. The international balance of payments for a nation is an annual record of all its transactions with the other nations in the world; and it records all the payments received from and made to the rest of the world.

a. The current-account section of a nation's international balance of payments records its trade in currently produced goods and services; and within this section:
(1) the trade balance of the nation is equal to its exports of goods (merchandise) less its imports of goods (merchandise), and the nation has a trade surplus (deficit) if the exports are greater (less) than the imports;
(2) the balance on goods and services is equal to its exports of goods and services less its imports of goods and services; and
(3) the balance on the current account is equal to its balance on goods and services plus its net investment income (dividends and interest) from other nations and its net private and public transfers to other nations, and this balance may be either a surplus or a deficit.

b. The capital-account section of a nation's international balance of payments records its sales of real and financial assets (which earn it foreign money) and its purchases of real and financial assets (which use up foreign money), and the nation has a capital-account surplus (deficit) if its sales are greater (less) than its purchases of real and financial assets.

c. The current and capital accounts in a nation's international balance of payments are interrelated: a nation with a current-account deficit can finance the deficit by borrowing or selling assets abroad (with a capital-account surplus) and a nation with a current-account

surplus can lend or buy assets abroad (incur a capital-account deficit).

d. The official reserves of a nation are the foreign currencies (monies) owned by its central bank: these reserves a nation uses to finance a net deficit on its current and capital accounts, and these reserves increase when a nation has a net surplus on its current and capital accounts; and in this way the nation's total outpayments and inpayments are made to equal each other (to balance).

e. A nation is said to have a balance-of-payments surplus (deficit) when the current and capital account balance is positive (negative) and its official reserves increase (decrease).

f. The merchandise or trade deficit of a nation implies its producers are losing their competitiveness in foreign markets, but is beneficial to consumers in that nation who receive more goods (imports) from abroad than they must pay for (export); and a balance-of-payments deficit is undesirable to the extent that the nation's official reserves are limited and require the nation to take painful macroeconomic adjustments to correct it.

3. The kinds of adjustments a nation with a balance-of-payments deficit or surplus must make to correct the imbalance depends upon whether exchange rates are flexible (floating) or fixed.

a. If foreign exchange rates float freely the demand for and the supply of foreign exchange determine foreign exchange rates; and the exchange rate for any foreign money is the rate at which the quantity of that money demanded is equal to the quantity of it supplied.
(1) A change in the demand for or supply of a foreign money will cause the exchange rate for that money to rise or fall; and when there is a rise (fall) in the price paid in dollars for a foreign money it is said that the dollar has depreciated (appreciated) and that the foreign money has appreciated (depreciated).

A HELPFUL HINT

The application of the terms *depreciate* and *appreciate* to foreign exchange confuses many students. Here are some hints that will help reduce the confusion.
   First:
● depreciate means decrease; and appreciate means increase.
   Second: what decreases when Country A's currency depreciates and increases when its currency appreciates is
● the quantity of Country B's currency that can be purchased for *one unit* of Country A's currency.
   Third: when the exchange rate for B's currency:
● *rises* the quantity of B's currency that can be purchased for one unit of A's currency *decreases* (just as a rise in the price of cigars decreases the number of cigars that can be bought for a dollar) and A's currency has *depreciated;*
● *falls* the quantity of B's currency that can be purchased for one unit of A's currency *increases* (just as a fall in the price of cigars increases the number of cigars that can be bought for a dollar) and A's currency has *appreciated.*

(2) Changes in the demand for or supply of a foreign currency are largely the result of changes in tastes, relative income changes, relative price changes, changes in relative real interest rates, and speculation.

(3) When a nation has a payments deficit (surplus), foreign exchange rates will rise (fall); this will make foreign goods and services more (less) expensive, decrease (increase) imports, make a nation's goods and services less (more) expensive for foreigners to buy, increase (decrease) its exports; and these adjustments in foreign exchange rates and in imports and exports correct the nation's payments deficit (surplus).

(4) But flexible exchange rates increase the uncertainties faced by exporters, importers, and investors (and reduce international trade); change the terms of trade; and destabilize economies (by creating inflation or unemployment).

b. When nations fix (or "peg") foreign exchange rates, the governments of these nations must intervene in the foreign exchange markets to prevent shortages and surpluses of foreign monies.

(1) One way for a nation to stabilize foreign exchange rates is for its government to sell (buy) a foreign money in exchange for its own money (or gold) when there is a shortage (surplus) of the foreign money.

(2) A nation with a payments deficit might also discourage imports by imposing tariffs, import quotas, and special taxes; and encourage exports by subsidizing them.

(3) To eliminate a payments deficit a nation might require exporters who earn foreign exchange to sell it to the government; and the government would then ration the available foreign exchange among importers and make the value of imports equal to the value of exports.

(4) Another way for a nation to stabilize foreign exchange rates is to employ fiscal and monetary policies to reduce its national income and price level and to raise interest rates relative to those in other nations; and, thereby, reduce the demand for and increase the supply of the different foreign monies.

4. The nations of the world in their recent history have employed three different exchange rate systems.

a. Between 1879 and 1934 (with the exception of the World War I years) the operation of the gold standard kept foreign exchange rates relatively stable.

(1) A nation was on the gold standard when it:

(a) defined its monetary unit in terms of a certain quantity of gold;

(b) maintained a fixed relationship between its stock of gold and its money supply; and

(c) allowed gold to be exported and imported without restrictions.

(2) Foreign exchange rates between nations on the gold standard would fluctuate only within a narrow range (determined by the cost of packing, insuring, and

shipping gold from country to country); and if a foreign exchange rate rose (fell) to the upper (lower) limit of the range gold would flow out of (into) a nation.

(3) But if a nation has a balance-of-payments deficit (surplus) and gold flowed out of (into) the country, its money supply would decrease (increase); this would raise (lower) interest rates and reduce (expand) aggregate demand, national output, employment, and prices in that country; and the balance-of-payments deficit (surplus) would be eliminated.

(4) The gold standard resulted in nearly stable foreign-exchange rates (which by reducing uncertainty stimulated international trade), and automatically corrected balance-of-payments deficits and surpluses; but it required that nations accept such unpleasant adjustments as recession and inflation to eliminate their balance-of-payments deficits and surpluses.

(5) During the worldwide Great Depression of the 1930s nations felt that remaining on the gold standard threatened their recoveries from the Depression, and the devaluations of their currencies (to expand exports and reduce imports) led to the breakdown and abandonment of the gold standard.

b. From the end of World War II until 1971 the Bretton Woods system, committed to the adjustable-peg system of exchange rates and managed by the International Monetary Fund (IMF), kept foreign-exchange rates relatively stable.

(1) The adjustable-peg system required the United States to sell gold to other member nations at a fixed price and the other members of the IMF to define their monetary units in terms of either gold or dollars (which established fixed exchange rates among the currencies of all member nations); and for the other member nations to keep the exchange rates for their currencies from rising by selling foreign currencies, selling gold, or borrowing on a short-term basis from the IMF.

(2) The system also provided for orderly changes in exchange rates to correct a fundamental imbalance (persistent and sizable balance-of-payments deficits) by allowing a nation to devalue its currency (increase its defined gold or dollar equivalent).

(3) The other nations of the world used gold and dollars as their international monetary reserves in the Bretton Woods system: for these reserves to grow the United States had to continue to have balance-of-payments deficits, but to continue the convertibility of dollars into gold it had to reduce the deficits; and, faced with this dilemma, the United States in 1971 suspended the convertibility of the dollar, brought an end to the Bretton Woods system of fixed exchange rates, and allowed the exchange rates for the dollar and the other currencies to float.

c. Exchange rates today are managed by individual nations to avoid short-term fluctuations and allowed to float in the long term to correct balance-of-payments deficits and surpluses; and this new system of managed floating exchange rates is favored by some and criticized by others.

(1) Its proponents contend that this system has not led to any decrease in world trade and it has enabled the world to adjust to severe economic shocks.

(2) Its critics argue that it has resulted in volatile exchange rates and has not reduced balance-of-payments deficits and surpluses; and that it is a "nonsystem" that a nation may employ to achieve its own domestic economic goals.

5. During the 1980s and into the 1990s, the United States has been running large trade deficits because its exports grew slowly but its imports grew rapidly. There are now large merchandise and current-account deficits.

a. These deficits have had three major causes.

(1) The international value of the dollar rose from 1980–1985 because of large Federal-budget deficits, a tighter monetary policy during the early 1980s, and lower rates of inflation in the United States and higher real interest rates than in the rest of the world. The value of the dollar declined from 1985–1987 because of intervention by five industrial nations to supply dollars to the foreign exchange market and the increasing demand for foreign currency to purchase imports. The dollar's fall helped increase American exports, but imports continued to rise until mid-1988 in part because foreign producers kept price increases low by accepting low per unit profits.

(2) The more rapid recover of the American economy from the 1980–1982 recession increased its imports by large amounts; and the less rapid recovery of the rest of the world increased. American exports by only small amounts.

(3) American exports to the less developed nations fell and its imports from them rose because they used restrictive monetary and fiscal policies and devalued their currencies to cope with their international debts to the developed nations.

b. The trade deficits of the United States lowered real output and employment, restrained inflation, lessened the prices of imported goods in the United States, and increased the indebtedness of Americans to foreigners; had the opposite effects on its industrialized trading partners.

c. To deal with the trade deficit several policies have been considered:

(1) It is argued that a decline in the Federal-budget deficits will lower the real rate of interest in the United States compared to other nations; G-7 nations would like the United States to "put its fiscal house in order" rather than just relying on "managed" depreciation of the dollar to ease the trade imbalance.

(2) The adoption of expansionary monetary and fiscal policies by the major trading partners of the United

States would tend to increase economic growth in those nations and thereby increase exports from the United States to those nations.

(3) Other "remedies"—easy money, protective tariffs, recession, increasing competitiveness, and direct foreign investment—are possible but some have limitations and drawbacks.

■ **IMPORTANT TERMS**

Financing exports
and imports

Foreign exchange market

Export transaction

Import transaction

Rate of exchange (foreign
exchange rate)

International balance
of payments

Current account

Trade balance

Trade surplus

Trade deficit

Balance on goods
and services

Balance on current
account

Net investment income

Net transfers

Capital account

Capital inflow

Capital outflow

Balance on the capital
account

Current account deficit

Current account surplus

Capital account deficit

Capital account surplus

Official reserves

Balance of payments
deficit

Balance of payments
surplus

Flexible (floating)
exchange rate

Fixed exchange rate

Exchange rate (currency)
depreciation

Exchange rate (currency)
appreciation

Purchasing power parity

Exchange control

Gold standard

Gold flow

Gold export point

Gold import point

Devaluation

Bretton Woods system

Adjustable pegs

International Monetary
Fund

International monetary
reserves

Managed floating
exchange rate

G-7 nations

■ **FILL-IN QUESTIONS**

1. The rate of exchange for the French franc is the number of (francs, dollars) _____ which an American must pay to obtain one (franc, dollar) _____

2. When the rate of exchange for the Saudi Arabian riyal is 30 American cents, the rate of exchange for the American dollar is _____ riyals.

3. American:

a. exports create a (demand for, supply of) _____ foreign money, generate a _____ dollars, (increase, decrease) _____ the money supply in the United States, and _____ money supplies abroad;

b. imports create a _____ foreign money, generate a _____ dollars, and _____ the money supply in the United States, and _____ money supplies abroad.

4. In addition to the demand for foreign currency by American firms that wish to import goods from foreign countries, Americans also demand foreign money to purchase _____ and _____ services abroad and to pay _____ and _____ on foreign investments in the United States.

5. The balance of payments of a nation records all payments its residents make to and receive from residents in

_____

a. Any transaction that **earns** foreign exchange for that nation is a (debit, credit) _____ and is shown with a $(+, -)$ _____ sign.

b. A transaction that **uses up** foreign exchange is a _____ and is shown with a _____ sign.

6. When a nation has a:

a. balance of trade deficit its exports are (greater, less) _____ than its imports of _____;

b. balance-on-goods-and-services surplus its exports are _____ than its imports of goods and services;

c. current-account deficit its balance on goods and services plus its net _____ income and net _____ is (positive, negative) _____

7. The capital account records the capital inflows and capital outflows of a nation.

a. The capital inflows are the expenditures made (in that nation, abroad) _____ by residents of (that nation, other nations) _____; and the capital outflows are the expenditures made _____ by residents of _____ for _____ and _____ assets.

b. A nation has a capital-account surplus when its capital-account inflows are (greater, less) _____ than its outflows.

8. A nation:

a. may finance a current-account deficit by (buying, selling) _____ assets or by (borrowing, lending) _____ abroad; and

b. may use a capital-account surplus to (buy, sell) _____ assets or to (borrow, lend) _____ abroad.

9. The official reserves of a nation are the quantities of (foreign monies, its own money) _____ owned by its _____ bank. If that nation has

a. a deficit on the current and capital accounts its official reserves (increase, decrease) _____;

b. a surplus on the current and capital accounts its official reserves _____;

c. either a current and capital account deficit or surplus, the sum of the current and capital balances and the increases or decreases in its official reserves total

_____

10. A country has a balance-of-payments deficit if the sum of its current and capital accounts balance is (positive, negative) _____ and its official reserves (increase, decrease) _____; and a payments surplus when the sum of its current and capital accounts balance is _____ and its official reserves _____

11. If foreign exchange rates float freely and a nation has a balance of payments **deficit:**

a. that nation's money in the foreign exchange markets will (appreciate, depreciate) _____ and foreign monies will _____

b. as a result of these changes in foreign exchange rates, the nation's imports will (increase, decrease) _____, its exports will _____, and the size of its deficit will _____

12. What effect (depreciation or appreciation) would each of the following have upon the French franc in the foreign exchange market (**ceteris paribus**)?

a. The increased preference in the United States for domestic wines over wines produced in France: _____

b. A rise in the national income of the United States:

_____

c. An increase in the price level in France: _____

_____

d. A rise in real interest rates in the United States:

_____

e. The belief of speculators in France that the dollar

will appreciate in the foreign exchange market: _____

13. There are three disadvantages of freely floating foreign exchange rates: The risks and uncertainties associated with flexible rates tend to (expand, diminish)

_____ trade between nations; when a nation's currency depreciates, its terms of trade with other

nations are (worsened, bettered) _____;
and fluctuating exports and imports can destabilize an

economy and result in _____ or in

_____ in that economy.

14. To fix or "peg" the rate of exchange for the German mark when:
a. the exchange rate for the mark is rising, the United

States would (buy, sell) _____ marks in exchange for dollars;
b. the exchange rate for the mark is falling, the United

States would _____ marks in exchange for dollars.

15. Under a fixed exchange rate system, a nation with a balance of payments deficit:
a. might attempt to eliminate the deficit by (taxing, sub-

sidizing) _____ imports or by _____
exports;
b. might employ exchange controls and ration foreign exchange among those who wish to (export, import)

_____ goods and services and re-

quire all those who _____ goods and services to sell the foreign exchange they earn to the

_____

16. If the United States has a payments deficit with Japan and the exchange rate for the Japanese yen is rising, then under a fixed exchange rate system the United States might employ (expansionary, contractionary)

_____ fiscal and monetary policies to reduce the demand for the yen; but this would bring about

(inflation, recession) _____ in the United States.

17. A nation is on the gold standard when it defines its

money in terms of _____, maintains a

fixed relationship between its _____

supply and gold _____, and allows gold to

be freely _____

from and _____
into the nation.

18. When the nations of the world were on the gold standard
a. exchange rates were relatively (stable, unstable)

_____,
b. but when a nation had a payments deficit:
(1) gold flowed (into, out of) _____ the nation;
(2) its money supply and price level (increased, de-

creased) _____ and its interest rates

_____;

(3) its payments deficit (rose, fell) _____

and it experienced (inflation, recession) _____

_____

19. The Bretton Woods system was established to bring

about (flexible, fixed) _____ exchange rates;

and, to accomplish this, if employed the _____
system of exchange rates. Under the Bretton Woods system;
a. a member nation defined its monetary unit in terms

of _____ or _____;
b. each member nation stabilized the exchange rate for its currency and prevented it from rising by (buying,

selling) _____ foreign currency which it

obtained from its _____

fund, by (buying, selling) _____ gold,

or by (borrowing from, lending to) _____
the International Monetary Fund;
c. a nation with a deeply rooted payments deficit could

(devalue, revalue) _____ its currency;
d. international monetary reserves included both

_____ and _____;
e. it was hoped that exchange rates in the short run

would be (stable, flexible) _____ enough to promote international trade and in the long run would

be _____ enough to correct balance of payments imbalances.

20. The role of the dollar as a component of international monetary reserves produced a dilemma:
a. For these reserves to grow the United States had to incur balance of payments (surpluses, deficits)

_____

b. This resulted in an increase in the foreign holding

CHAPTER 38

of American dollars and in a decrease in the American

reserves (stock) of _____

c. The ability of the United States to convert dollars into gold and the willingness of foreigners to hold dollars (because they were "as good as gold") therefore

(increased, decreased) _____

d. For the dollar to remain an acceptable international monetary reserve the U.S. payments deficits had to be

(eliminated, continued) _____; but for international monetary reserves to grow the U.S.

payments deficits had to be _____

21. The United States completed the destruction of the Bretton Woods system in 1971 when it suspended the

convertibility of dollars into _____ and allowed the value of the dollar to be determined by

_____.

Since then the international monetary system has moved from exchange rates which (for all practical purposes)

were (fixed, floating) _____ to exchange

rates which are _____

22. The system of exchange rates which has developed

since 1971 has been labeled a system of _____ exchange rates. This means that individual nations will:

a. in the short term buy and sell foreign exchange to

keep exchange rates _____

b. in the long term allow exchange rates to rise or fall

to correct payments _____

23. The advantages of the current system of exchange

rates are that it did not reduce the _____ of trade over the years and it has survived much economic

_____, but its disadvantages are the

_____ of the system, and the lack of clear rules

and guidelines for nations that make it a "_____"

24. The major problem with foreign trade in the United States concerns the American merchandise and current-

account (surpluses, deficits) _____ which were brought about by the sharp increases in its (exports,

imports) _____ and the small increases in

its _____

25. The three causes of the trade deficits during the 1980s were

a. the (strong, weak) _____ dollar,

b. the (slow, rapid) _____ growth of the American economy, and

c. the (expanded, reduced) _____ exports of the United States to less developed nations.

26. Changes in the international value of the dollar contributed to the trade deficit problem.

a. From 1980–1985, the rise in the value of the dollar

made American goods (more, less) _____ expensive and foreign goods _____ expensive,

(increased, decreased) _____ American exports,

and _____ American imports and

b. was the result of relatively (high, low) _____ real interest rates in the United States caused by large

Federal-budget (surpluses, deficits) _____,

a (light, easy) _____ monetary policy, and

relatively (high, low) _____ rates of inflation in the United States.

c. From 1985–1987, the value of the dollar (rose, fell)

_____ but imports continued to rise because foreign producers accepted lower per unit

_____ and in 1987 _____ nations agreed to halt the decline of the dollar.

d. Finally, from 1988–1991 the deficit began to (increase, decrease) _____

27. American:

a. imports increased sharply in the mid-1980s because its national income (rose, fell) _____ rapidly after the 1980–1982 recession.

b. exports to many less developed nations declined because their foreign debt problem forced them to

apply (expansionary, restrictive) _____ monetary and fiscal policies to their economies and to

(revalue, devalue) _____ their currencies in

order to expand their (exports, imports) _____

and reduce their _____

28. The effects of the large American foreign-trade deficits have been to (expand, contract) _____ real domestic output and employment in the United States,

to (speed, slow) _____ its rate of inflation, to

(raise, lower) _____ the prices of goods it imported, and to (increase, decrease) _____ American indebtedness to foreigners. It has also changed the United States from a net (creditor, debtor) _____ to a net _____ nation.

29. Two policies to correct the trade deficit include a(n) (expansion, contraction) _____ in the budget deficit of the Federal government to help lower real interest rates in the United States relative to other nations, and a(n) _____ in the economies of major trading partners, such as Japan and Germany, to help increase demand for exports for the United States.

30. Other "remedies" for large trade deficits include: _____ money, protective _____, forced _____, increased _____ of American products, and direct foreign _____

■ **PROBLEMS AND PROJECTS**

1. Assume an American exporter sells $3 million worth of wheat to an importer in Colombia. If the rate of exchange for the Colombian peso is $0.02 (two cents), the wheat has a total value of 150 million pesos.

a. There are two ways the importer in Colombia may pay for the wheat. It might write a check for 150 million pesos drawn on its bank in Botogá and send it to the American exporter.

(1) The American exporter would then sell the check to its bank in New Orleans and its demand deposit there would increase by $_____ million.

(2) This New Orleans bank now sells the check for 150 million pesos to a correspondent bank (an American commercial bank that keeps an account in the Botogá bank).

(a) The New Orleans bank's account in the correspondent bank increases by _____ million (dollars, pesos) _____; and

(b) the correspondent bank's account in the Botogá bank increases by _____ million (pesos, dollars) _____

b. The second way for the importer to pay for the wheat is to buy from its bank in Botogá a draft on an American bank for $3 million, pay for this draft by writing a check for 150 million pesos drawn on the Botogá bank, and send the draft to the American exporter.

(1) The American exporter would then deposit the draft in its account in the New Orleans bank and its demand deposit account there would increase by $_____ million.

(2) The New Orleans bank collects the amount of the

draft from the American bank on which it is drawn through the Federal Reserve Banks.

(a) Its account at the Fed increases by $_____ million; and

(b) the account of the bank on which the draft was drawn decreases by $_____ million.

c. Regardless of the way employed by the Colombian importer to pay for the wheat:

(1) The export of the wheat created a (demand for, supply of) _____ dollars and a _____ pesos

(2) The number of dollars owned by the American exporter has (increased, decreased) _____ and the number of pesos owned by the Colombian importer has _____

2. The table below contains hypothetical international balance of payments data for the United States. All figures are in billions.

Current account	
(1) U.S. merchandise exports	$+150
(2) U.S. merchandise imports	−200
(3) Balance of trade	_____
(4) U.S. exports of services	+75
(5) U.S. imports of services	−60
(6) Balance on goods and services	_____
(7) Net investment income	+12
(8) Net transfers	−7
(9) Balance on current account	_____
Capital account	
(10) Capital inflows to the U.S.	+80
(11) Capital outflows from the U.S.	−55
(12) Balance on capial account	_____
(13) Current and capital account balance	_____
(14) Official reserves	_____
	$____0

a. Compute with the appropriate sign (+ or −) and enter in the table the six missing items.

b. The United States had a payments (deficit, surplus) _____ of $_____

3. In the table below are the supply and demand schedules for the British pound.

Quantity of pounds supplied	Price	Quantity of pounds demanded
400	$5.00	100
360	4.50	200
300	4.00	300
286	3.50	400
267	3.00	500
240	2.50	620
200	2.00	788

a. If the exchange rates are flexible:

(1) What will be the rate of exchange for the pound?

$_____

(2) What will be the rate of exchange for the dollar?

£_____

(3) How many pounds will be purchased in the market?

_____

(4) How many dollars will be purchased in the market?

_____

b. If the government of the United States wished to fix or "peg" the price of the pound at $5.00 it would have to (buy, sell) _____ (how many) _____ pounds for $_____

c. And if the British government wishes to fix the price of the dollar at £⅖ it would have to (buy, sell) _____ (how many) _____ pounds for $_____

■ **SELF-TEST**

Circle the T if the statement is true; the F if it is false.

1. The importation of goods and services by Americans from abroad creates a supply of dollars in the foreign exchange market. **T F**

2. American exports expand foreign money supplies and reduce the supply of money in the United States. **T F**

3. The international balance of payments of the United States records all the payments its residents receive from and make to the residents of foreign nations. **T F**

4. Exports are a debit item and are shown with a plus sign (+) and imports are a credit item and are shown with a minus sign (−) in the international balance of payments of a nation. **T F**

5. The United States had a balance of trade deficit in 1990. **T F**

6. The balance on goods and services of the United States in 1990 was positive (a surplus). **T F**

7. In 1990 the United States had positive net investment income and negative net transfers from the rest of the world. **T F**

8. In 1990 there was a net capital outflow from the United States and the United States had a capital-account deficit. **T F**

9. The United States would have a balance of payments surplus if the balance on its current and capital accounts were positive. **T F**

10. Any nation with a balance of payments deficit must reduce its official reserves. **T F**

11. The sum of a nation's current-account balance, its capital-account balance, and the change in its official reserves in any years is always equal to zero. **T F**

12. A large trade deficit in Brazil is harmful to consumers in Brazil. **T F**

13. If a nation has a balance of payments deficit and exchange rates are flexible, the price of that nation's money in the foreign exchange markets will fall and this will reduce its imports and increase its exports. **T F**

14. The purchasing power parity theory basically explains why there is an inverse relationship between the price of dollars and the quantity demanded. **T F**

15. The expectations of speculators in the United States that the exchange rate for the Japanese yen will fall in the future will increase the supply of yen in the foreign exchange market and decrease the exchange rate for the yen. **T F**

16. Were the United States' terms of trade with Nigeria to worsen, Nigeria would obtain a greater quantity of American goods and services for every barrel of oil it exported to the United States. **T F**

17. If a nation wishes to fix (or "peg") the foreign exchange rate for the Swiss franc, it must buy Swiss francs with its own currency when the rate of exchange for the Swiss franc rises. **T F**

18. If exchange rates are stable or fixed and a nation has a payments surplus, prices and money incomes in that nation will tend to rise. **T F**

19. A nation using exchange controls to eliminate a balance of payments surplus might depreciate its currency. **T F**

20. If country A defined its money as worth 100 grains of gold and country B defined its money as worth 20 grains of gold, then, ignoring packing, insuring, and shipping charges, 5 units of country A's money would be worth 1 unit of country B's money. **T F**

21. When nations were on the gold standard, foreign exchange rates fluctuated only within limits determined by the cost of moving gold from one nation to another. **T F**

22. If a nation maintains an exchange stabilization fund it would purchase its own money with gold or foreign monies when the value of its money falls in foreign exchange markets. **T F**

23. In the Bretton Woods system a nation could not devalue its currency by more than 10% without the permission of the International Fund. **T F**

24. In the Bretton Woods system a nation with persistent balance of payments surpluses had an undervalued currency and should have increased the pegged value of its currency. **T F**

25. Because the world's stock of gold did not grow very rapidly it became necessary for the United States to have payments deficits if international monetary reserves were to increase. **T F**

26. One of the basic shortcomings of the Bretton Woods system was its inabiity to bring about the changes in exchange rates needed to correct persistent payments deficits and surpluses. **T F**

27. Another basic shortcoming of the Bretton Woods system was its failure to maintain stable foreign exchange rates. **T F**

28. The United States shattered the Bretton Woods system in August 1971 by raising tariff rates on nearly all the goods it imported by an average of 40%. **T F**

29. Using the managed floating system of exchange rates, a nation with a persistent balance of payments surplus should allow the value of its currency in foreign exchange markets to decrease. **T F**

30. Two criticisms of the current managed floating exchange rate system are its potential for volatility and its lack of clear policy rules or guidelines for nations to manage exchange rates. **T F**

31. The foreign-trade deficits experienced by the American economy in the 1980s were caused by sharp increases in American exports and slight increases in American imports. **T F**

32. The principal reason for the strong dollar in the early 1980s was the high real interest rates in the United States. **T F**

33. High real interest rates in the United States would tend to increase the attractiveness of financial investment in the United States to foreigners and the foreign demand for American dollars. **T F**

34. The rapid growth of the American economy after 1982 lessened foreign-trade deficits because exports were directly related to national income. **T F**

35. The strong international value of the dollar in the mid-1980s imposed special hardships on American firms dependent on export markets and those that competed with imported goods. **T F**

36. The negative net exports of the United States have increased the indebtedness of Americans to foreigners. **T F**

37. In 1985 the status of the United States was changed from net-debtor to net-creditor nation. **T F**

38. The major trading partners in the United States contend that it must work to reduce the Federal budget deficit if it is to achieve a better balance of international trade. **T F**

39. Improved economic growth in the major economies of the major trading partners of the United States would tend to worsen the trade deficit. **T F**

40. Under the right circumstances, an easy money policy can help reduce a trade deficit. **T F**

Circle the letter that corresponds to the best answer.

1. If an American could buy £25,000 for $100,000, the rate of exchange for the pound would be:
- **(a)** $40
- **(b)** $25
- **(c)** $4
- **(d)** $.25

2. American residents demand foreign currencies in order:
- **(a)** to pay for goods and services imported from foreign countries
- **(b)** to receive interest payments and dividends on their investments outside the United States
- **(c)** to make real and financial investments in foreign nations
- **(d)** to do all of the above

3. A nation's balance of trade is equal to its:
- **(a)** exports less its imports of merchandise (goods)
- **(b)** exports less its imports of goods and services
- **(c)** exports less its imports of goods and services plus its net investment income and net transfers
- **(d)** exports less its imports of goods, services, and capital

4. A nation's balance on the current account is equal to its:
- **(a)** exports less its imports of merchandise (goods)
- **(b)** exports less its imports of goods and services
- **(c)** exports less its imports of goods and services plus its net investment income and net transfers
- **(d)** exports less its imports of goods, services, and capital

5. The net investment income of the United States in its international balance of payments is:
- **(a)** the interest income it receives from foreign residents

(b) the dividends it receives from foreign residents
(c) the interest payments and dividends it receives from foreign residents
(d) the interest payments, dividends, and transfers it receives from foreign residents

6. Capital flows into the United States include the purchase by foreign residents of:
   (a) a factory building owned by Americans
   (b) shares of stock owned by Americans
   (c) bonds owned by Americans
   (d) all of the above

7. An American current account deficit may be financed by:
   (a) borrowing abroad
   (b) selling real assets to foreigners
   (c) selling financial assets to foreigners
   (d) doing any of the above

8. The official reserves of the United States are:
   (a) the stock of gold owned by the Federal government
   (b) the foreign currencies owned by the Federal Reserve Banks
   (c) the money supply of the United States
   (d) all of the above

9. A nation may be able to correct or eliminate a persistent (long-term) balance of payments deficit by:
   (a) lowering the barriers on imported goods
   (b) reducing the international value of its currency
   (c) expanding its national income
   (d) reducing its official reserves

10. If exchange rates float freely the exchange rate for any currency is determined by:
    (a) the demand for it
    (b) the supply of it
    (c) the demand for and the supply of it
    (d) the official reserves that "back" it

11. If a nation had a balance of payments surplus and exchange rates floated freely:
    (a) the foreign exchange rate for its currency would rise, its exports would increase, and its imports would decrease
    (b) the foreign exchange rate for its currency would rise, its exports would decrease, and its imports would increase
    (c) the foreign exchange rate for its currency would fall, its exports would increase, and its imports would decrease
    (d) the foreign exchange rate for its currency would fall, its exports would decrease, and its imports would increase

12. Assuming exchange rates are flexible, which of the following should increase the dollar price of the Swedish krona?

    (a) a rate of inflation greater in Sweden than in the United States
    (b) real interest-rate increases greater in Sweden than in the United States
    (c) national-income increases greater in Sweden than in the United States
    (d) the increased preference of Swedes for American over Swedish automobiles

13. Which of the following would be one of the results associated with the use of freely floating foreign exchange rates to correct a nation's balance of payments surplus?
    (a) the nation's terms of trade with other nations would be worsened
    (b) importers in the nation who had made contracts for the future delivery of goods would find that they had to pay a higher price than expected for the goods
    (c) if the nation were at full employment the decrease in exports and the increase in imports would be inflationary
    (d) exporters in the nation would find their sales abroad had decreased

14. When exchange rates are fixed and a nation at full employment has a balance of payments surplus, the result in that nation will be:
    (a) a declining price level
    (b) falling money income
    (c) inflation
    (d) rising real income

15. The use of exchange controls to eliminate a nation's balance of payments deficit results in:
    (a) decreasing the nation's imports
    (b) decreasing the nation's exports
    (c) decreasing the nation's price level
    (d) decreasing the nation's income

16. A nation with a balance of payments surplus might attempt to eliminate this surplus by employing:
    (a) import quotas
    (b) higher tariffs
    (c) subsidies on items which the nation exports
    (d) none of the above

17. Which one of the following conditions did a nation *not* have to fulfill if it was to be one under the gold standard?
    (a) use only gold as a medium of exchange
    (b) maintain a fixed relationship between its gold stock and its money supply
    (c) allow gold to be freely exported from and imported into the nation
    (d) define its monetary unit in terms of a fixed quantity of gold

18. If the nations of the world were on the gold standard and one nation has a balance of payments surplus:
    (a) foreign exchange rates in that nation would rise toward the gold import point

(b) gold would tend to be imported into that country

(c) the level of prices in that country would tend to fall

(d) employment and output in that country would tend to fall

19. Under the gold standard a nation with a balance of payments deficit would experience all but one of the following. Which one?

(a) gold would flow out of the nation

(b) the nation's money supply would contract

(c) interest rates in the nation would fall

(d) real national output, employment, and prices in the nation would decline

20. Which of the following was the principal disadvantage of the gold standard?

(a) unstable foreign exchange rates

(b) persistent payments imbalances

(c) the uncertainties and decreased trade that resulted from the depreciation of gold

(d) the domestic macroeconomic adjustments experienced by a nation with a payments deficit or surplus

21. All but one of the following were elements in the adjustable-peg system of foreign exchange rates. Which one?

(a) each nation defined its monetary unit in terms of gold or dollars

(b) nations bought and sold their own currencies to stabilize exchange rates

(c) nations were allowed to devalue their currencies freely within a range when faced with persistent payments deficits

(d) the gold deposits of all member nations were held by the IMF

22. Which one of the following was *not* characteristic of the International Monetary Fund in the Bretton Woods system?

(a) made short-term loans to member nations with balance of payments deficits

(b) tried to maintain relatively stable exchange rates

(c) required member nations to maintain exchange stabilization funds

(d) extended long-term loans to less developed nations for the purpose of increasing their productive capacities

23. The objective of the adjustable-peg system was exchange rates which were:

(a) adjustable in the short run and fixed in the long run

(b) adjustable in both the short and long run

(c) fixed in both the short and long run

(d) fixed in the short run; adjustable in the long run

24. Which of the following is the best definition of international monetary reserves in the Bretton Woods system?

(a) gold

(b) dollars

(c) gold and dollars

(d) gold, dollars, and British pounds

25. The dilemma created by the U.S. payments deficits was that:

(a) to maintain the status of the dollar as an acceptable international monetary reserve the deficit had to be reduced and to increase these reserves the deficits had to be continued

(b) to maintain the status of the dollar the deficit had to be continued and to increase reserves the deficit had to be eliminated

(c) to maintain the status of the dollar the deficit had to be increased and to expand reserves the deficit had to be reduced

(d) to maintain the status of the dollar the deficit had to be reduced and to expand reserves the deficit had to be reduced

26. "Floating" the dollar means:

(a) the value of the dollar is determined by the demand for and the supply of the dollar

(b) the dollar price of gold has been increased

(c) the price of the dollar has been allowed to crawl upward at the rate of one-fourth of 1% a month

(d) the IMF decreased the value of the dollar by 10%

27. A system of managed floating exchange rates:

(a) allows nations to stabilize exchange rates in the short term

(b) requires nations to stabilize exchange rates in the long term

(c) entails stable exchange rates in both the short and long term

(d) none of the above

28. Floating exchange rates:

(a) tend to correct balance of payments imbalances

(b) reduce the uncertainties and risks associated with international trade

(c) increase the world's need for international monetary reserves

(d) tend to expand the volume of world trade

29. The foreign-trade problem facing the United States is:

(a) its merchandise and current-account surpluses

(b) its merchandise deficit and current-account surplus

(c) its merchandise and current-account deficit

(d) its merchandise surplus and current-account deficit

30. Which of the following is *not* one of the causes of the growth of American trade deficits during the 1980s?

(a) the strong dollar

(b) the rapid growth of the American economy

(c) the reduced imports of heavily indebted less developed nations from the United States

(d) the high rate of inflation experienced by the American economy relative to rates in other nations

31. High real interest rates in the United States during the mid-1980s were the result of all but one of the following. Which one?

(a) the budget deficits of the Federal government

(b) the low demand of foreign investors for the dollar

(c) the tight money policy of the Federal Reserve Banks

(d) the relatively low rate of inflation in the United States

32. The external debt problems of less developed nations forced many of them to apply:

(a) restrictive monetary and fiscal policies and to devalue their currencies

(b) restrictive monetary and fiscal policies and to revalue their currencies

(c) expansionary monetary and fiscal policies and to devalue their currencies

(d) expansionary monetary and fiscal policies and to revalue their currencies

33. The effect of the trade deficit in the United States during the early and mid-1980s was to:

(a) increase the rate of inflation

(b) increase output and employment

(c) decrease aggregate demand

(d) decrease the international value of the dollar

34. One policy solution for large trade deficits is a reduction in the Federal budget deficit because this change would tend to:

(a) increase real interest rates and increase the demand for dollars in the United States

(b) decrease real interest rates and increase the demand for dollars in the United States

(c) decrease real interest rates and decrease the demand for dollars in the United States

(d) increase real interest rates and decrease the demand for dollars in the United States

35. It is suggested that the large trade deficits of the United States can best be reduced with:

(a) an easy money policy in the United States

(b) an expansionary fiscal policy in the United States

(c) economic policies that increase the rate of growth in the G-7 nations

(d) an appreciation in the value of the currencies of less developed nations

■ DISCUSSION QUESTIONS

1. What is foreign exchange and the foreign exchange rate? Who are the demanders and suppliers of a particular foreign exchange, say, the French franc? Why is a buyer (demander) in the foreign exchange markets always a seller (supplier) also?

2. What is meant when it is said that "a nation's exports pay for its imports"? Do nations pay for all their imports with exports?

3. What is an international balance of payments? What are the principal sections in a nation's international balance of payments and what are the principal "balances" to be found in it?

4. How can a nation finance a current account deficit and what can it do with a current account surplus? How does a nation finance a balance of payments deficit and what does it do with a balance of payments surplus?

5. Is it good or bad for a nation to have a balance of payments deficit or surplus?

6. What types of events cause the exchange rate for a foreign currency to appreciate or to depreciate? How will each of these events affect the exchange rate for a foreign money and for a nation's own money?

7. How can freely floating foreign exchange rates eliminate balance of payments deficits and surpluses? What are the problems associated with this method of correcting payments imbalances?

8. How may a nation employ its international monetary reserves to fix or "peg" foreign exchange rates? Be precise. How does a nation obtain or acquire these monetary reserves?

9. What kinds of trade controls may nations with payments deficits employ to eliminate their deficits?

10. How can foreign exchange controls to be used to restore international equilibrium? Why do such exchange controls necessarily involve the rationing of foreign exchange? What effect do these controls have upon prices, output, and employment in nations that use them?

11. If foreign exchange rates are fixed, what kind of domestic macroeconomic adjustments are required to eliminate a payments deficit? To eliminate a payments surplus?

12. When was a nation on the gold standard? How did the international gold standard correct payments imbalances? What were the disadvantages of this method of eliminating payments deficits and surpluses?

13. Why does the operation of the international gold standard ensure relatively stable foreign exchange rates, that is, rates which fluctuate only within very narrow limits? What are limits and what are the advantages of stable exchange rates?

14. What is the "critical difference" between the adjustments necessary to correct payments deficits and surpluses under the gold standard and those necessary when exchange rates are flexible? How did this difference lead to the demise of the gold standard during the 1930s?

15. Explain:
(a) why the International Monetary Fund was established and what the objectives of the adjustable-peg (or Bretton Woods) system were
(b) what the adjustable-peg system was and the basic means it employed to stabilize exchange rates in the short run; and
(c) when and how the system was to adjust exchange rates in the long run.

16. What did nations use as international monetary reserves under the Bretton Woods system? Why was the dollar used by nations as an international money and how could they acquire additional dollars?

17. Explain the dilemma created by the need for expanding international monetary reserves and for maintaining the status of the dollar.

18. Why and how did the United States shatter the Bretton Woods system in 1971? If the international value of the dollar is no longer determined by the amount of gold for which it can be exchanged, what does determine its value?

19. Explain what is meant by a managed floating system of foreign exchange rates. When are exchange rates managed and when are they allowed to float?

20. Explain the arguments of the proponents and the critics of the managed floating system.

21. What was the foreign-trade problem of the United States during the 1980s and early 1990s? What were
(a) its causes; and
(b) its effects on the American economy?

22. What two major policies are suggested for reducing the large trade deficits in the United States? How would such policies affect national output and employment? What other five remedies have also been discussed?

■ **ANSWERS**

Chapter 38 Exchange Rates, the Balance of Payments, and Trade Deficits

FILL-IN QUESTIONS

1. francs, dollar

2. $3\frac{1}{3}$

3. *a.* supply of, demand for, increase, decrease; *b.* demand for, supply of, decrease, increase

4. transportation, insurance (either order), interest, dividends (either order)

5. the other nations of the world: *a.* credit, $+$; *b.* debit, $-$

6. *a.* less, merchandise; *b.* greater; *c.* investment, transfers, negative

7. *a.* in that nation, other nations, in other nations, that nation, real, financial (either order); *b.* greater

8. *a.* selling, borrowing; *b.* buy, lend

9. foreign monies, central; *a.* decrease; *b.* increase; *c.* zero

10. negative, decrease, positive, increase

11. *a.* depreciate, appreciate; *b.* decrease, increase, decrease

12. *a.* depreciate; *b.* appreciate; *c.* depreciate; *d.* depreciate; *e.* depreciate

13. diminish, worsened, recession, inflation (either order)

14. *a.* sell; *b.* buy

15. *a.* taxing, subsidizing; *b.* import, export, government

16. contractionary, recession

17. gold, money, stock, exported, imported

18. *a.* stable; *b.* (1) out of, (2) decreased, rose, (3) fell, recession

19. fixed, adjustable-peg; *a.* gold, dollars (either order); *b.* buying, exchange-stabilization, selling, borrowing from; *c.* devalue; *d.* gold, dollars (either order); *e.* stable, flexible

20. *a.* deficits; *b.* gold; *c.* decreased; *d.* eliminated, continued

21. gold, market forces (demand and supply), fixed, floating

22. managed floating; *a.* stable; *b.* imbalances

23. growth, turbulence, volatility, nonsystem

24. deficits, imports, exports

25. *a.* strong; *b.* rapid; *c.* reduced

26. *a.* more, less, decreased, increased; *b.* high, deficits, tight, low; *c.* fell, profits, G-7; *d.* decrease

27. *a.* rose; *b.* restrictive, devalue, exports, imports

28. contract, slow, lower, increase, creditor, debtor

29. contraction, expansion

30. easy, tariffs, recession, competitiveness, investment

PROBLEMS AND PROJECTS

1. *a.* (1) 3, (2) (a) 3, dollars, (b) 150, pesos; *b.* (1) 3, (2) (a) 3, (b) 3; *c.* (1) demand for, supply of, (2) increased, decreased

2. *a.* −50, −35, −30, +25, −5, +5; *b.* deficit, 5

3. *a.* (1) 4.00, (2) ¼, (3) 300, (4) 1200; *b.* buy, 300, 1500; *c.* sell, 380, 950

SELF-TEST

1. T, pp. 721–722
2. F, pp. 721–722
3. T, pp. 722–723
4. F, p. 723
5. T, p. 723
6. F, p. 723
7. T, p. 723
8. F, p. 723
9. T, pp. 723–725
10. T, pp. 723–725
11. T, pp. 723–725
12. F, p. 725
13. T, pp. 728–729
14. F, p. 728
15. T, p. 728
16. T, p. 730
17. F, p. 730
18. T, p. 731
19. F, p. 731
20. F, p. 732

21. T, p. 732
22. T, pp. 732–733
23. T, pp. 734–735
24. T, pp. 734–735
25. T, pp. 735–736
26. T, pp. 735–736
27. F, pp. 735–736
28. F, p. 736
29. F, p. 736
30. T, pp. 736–737
31. F, pp. 737–738
32. T, pp. 737–738
33. T, pp. 737–738
34. F, p. 738
35. T, pp. 739–740
36. T, pp. 740–741
37. F, p. 740
38. T, pp. 741–742
39. F, p. 742
40. T, p. 742

1. *c*, pp. 721–722
2. *d*, pp. 721–722
3. *a*, p. 723
4. *c*, pp. 723–724
5. *c*, pp. 723–724
6. *d*, p. 724
7. *d*, p. 724
8. *b*, p. 725
9. *b*, p. 725
10. *c*, pp. 726–727
11. *b*, pp. 728–729
12. *b*, p. 728
13. *d*, pp. 728–729
14. *c*, pp. 731–732
15. *a*, p. 731
16. *d*, p. 731
17. *a*, p. 732
18. *b*, p. 733

19. *c*, p. 733
20. *d*, p. 733
21. *d*, pp. 734–735
22. *d*, pp. 734–735
23. *d*, p. 735
24. *c*, p. 735
25. *a*, pp. 735–736
26. *a*, p. 736
27. *a*, p. 736
28. *a*, p. 736
29. *c*, p. 737
30. *d*, pp. 737–738
31. *b*, pp. 737–738
32. *a*, p. 739
33. *c*, p. 739
34. *c*, p. 741
35. *c*, p. 742

DISCUSSION QUESTIONS

1. pp. 721–722
2. p. 722
3. pp. 722–724
4. pp. 723–724
5. p. 725
6. pp. 726–728
7. pp. 728–729
8. pp. 730–731
9. pp. 730–731
10. p. 731
11. p. 731

12. pp. 732–733
13. pp. 732–733
14. pp. 733–734
15. pp. 734–735
16. pp. 734–735
17. pp. 734–735
18. pp. 735–736
19. p. 736
20. p. 737
21. pp. 737–739
22. pp. 741–742

CHAPTER 39

Growth and the Less Developed Countries

This chapter looks at the problem of raising the standard of living faced by the less developed countries of the world. Economic growth both in these less developed countries and in the developed or the industrially advanced countries requires that the country's resources and technological knowledge be expanded. Application of this principle in the less developed countries, however, faces a set of obstacles quite different from those that limit economic growth in the United States. The emphasis in this chapter is on the obstacles to economic growth in the poor and less developed countries of the world. You should concentrate your attention on these obstacles. You will then understand why increasing the quantity and quality of resources and improving technology is especially difficult in the world's less developed countries.

These obstacles do not mean that increases in the living standards of the less developed countries are impossible. What they do mean is that the less developed countries must do things to encourage growth that did not need to be done in the United States, or in the other industrial countries. Governments of the less developed countries will have to take an active role in promoting growth and limit public sector problems for economic development. Large population increases are going to have to be reduced. Dramatic changes in social practices and institutions will be required. If these actions are not taken it will not be possible to reduce the obstacles to growth.

No matter how successful the less developed countries are in reducing these obstacles they probably will still not be able to grow very rapidly without the help of the developed countries. There are at least two reasons why the developed countries will offer the less developed ones some assistance. The citizens of the more advanced countries feel some moral obligation to aid the less fortunate peoples of the world; and they may feel it is in their own self-interest to aid the poor of the world.

The debts of less developed countries rose significantly in the past two decades. In fact, in 1990 the external debt of less developed countries that was owed to foreign governments and financial institutions was equal to about 45% of the combined gross domestic products of the less developed countries. The causes of this debt problem were

due in part to the events of the 1970s and early 1980s. During this period, less developed countries paid more for imported oil, incurred high borrowing costs because of higher interest rates, and faced lower net export earnings because of the appreciation of the dollar. To reduce the debt burdens, these nations were forced to enact restrictive domestic programs that often had adverse effects on net export earnings and economic growth. There are two proposed solutions to the persistent debt crisis, but as you will learn, each proposal has some adverse secondary effects.

Less developed countries have grown during the past thirty years, but the rate at which they grew was about the same as that at which the developed countries grew. Because the per capita income in the less developed countries were initially so much smaller, equal rates of growth increase the gap between the two groups over this period of time. For this and other reasons, less developed countries have become increasingly dissatisfied with their relationships with the advanced industrial nations. They have argued for the establishment of a New International Economic Order to address the problem. Here you should look at these relationships from the viewpoint of the less developed countries that are not oil exporters. To understand the proposals they have made, you must understand why they feel their relationships with the developed countries mostly benefit the developed and largely hurt the less developed countries.

■ CHECKLIST

When you have studied this chapter you should be able to:

☐ Distinguish between industrially advanced, oil-exporting, and less developed countries and describe the economic characteristics of the three groups.
☐ Explain the widening gap between the standards of living in less developed countries and the industrially advanced countries and calculate differences when given a simple example.

☐ Enumerate the human implications of the poverty in the less developed countries.

☐ Identify the four factors which make economic growth possible.

☐ Describe natural resource problems in less developed countries.

☐ Identify the three specific problems related to human resources that plague the less developed countries.

☐ Explain the difficulties for economic growth that are created by population growth in less developed countries.

☐ Describe the conditions of unemployment and underemployment in less developed countries.

☐ State reasons for low labor productivity in less developed countries.

☐ Present three reasons for the emphasis on capital formation in the less developed countries.

☐ Identify two obstacles to domestic capital formation through saving.

☐ List two obstacles to domestic capital formation through investment.

☐ Explain why transferring the technologies used in the industrially advanced countries to the less developed ones may not be a realistic method of improving the technology of the latter nations.

☐ Identify three potential sociocultural factors that can inhibit economic growth.

☐ Describe the institutional obstacles to growth.

☐ Explain why poverty in the poor nations is a vicious circle.

☐ List five reasons why governments in the less developed countries will have to play a crucial role if the vicious circle of poverty is to be broken.

☐ Describe the problems with the public sector in fostering economic development.

☐ Identify the three ways in which the industrially advanced countries may help the less developed countries to grow economically.

☐ Explain the importance of a reduction in international trade barriers to economic growth in less developed countries.

☐ Describe the two sources of and the general results from foreign aid for less developed countries.

☐ Discuss the importance of private capital flows for economic development in less developed countries.

☐ Describe the debt problem in less developed countries and identify four potential causes.

☐ Explain the economic consequences of the debt problem in less developed countries.

☐ Evaluate the proposed solutions to the debt problem in less developed countries.

☐ List and describe six proposals made by less developed countries that would result in a New International Economic Order.

■ CHAPTER OUTLINE

1. There is considerable inequality in income among nations.

a. Nations can be classified into three major groups.

(1) *Industrially advanced countries* (IACs) are characterized by high per capita incomes, large stocks of capital goods, advanced technology for production, and a highly educated work force. These nations include the United States, Canada, Japan, Australia, New Zealand, and most of the nations in Western Europe.

(2) *Oil-exporting countries* such as Saudi Arabia and Kuwait have high per capita incomes, but are not highly industrialized.

(3) Most of the remaining 97 nations are considered *less developed countries* (LDCs). LDCs are poor, not industrialized, are heavily dependent on agriculture, have high population growth, and have low rates of literacy. These countries comprise about three-fourths of the world's population. Of this group, there are 56 middle-income LDCs with average annual per capita income of $2,040 and 41 low-income LDCs with per capita income averaging $330.

b. The newly industrialized countries such as Hong Kong, South Korea, Taiwan, and Singapore have experienced high rates of economic growth over the past thirty years, while many other LDCs have experienced a decrease in GNP per capita; if the growth rates were the same for high and low income countries, the gap in per capita income would widen because the income base is higher.

c. The human implications of extreme poverty are important. Compared with the developed countries, LDCs have not only lower per capita incomes but also lower life expectancies, higher infant mortality, lower literacy rates, less food per person, and fewer nonhuman sources of energy.

2. Economic growth requires that the quantity and quality of economic resources be increased, that economic resources be used efficiently, and that technological knowledge be expanded. There are many obstacles to such factors in LDCs.

a. Many (but not all) LDCs possess inadequate natural resources and the farm products which LDCs typically export are subject to significant price variation.

b. Many LDCs are overpopulated, there is substantial unemployment and underemployment of labor, and labor productivity is low.

c. LDCs are short of capital goods and these countries find it difficult to accumulate capital because of low savings potential, the flight of capital to IACs, and the absence of investors or incentives to invest.

d. Technological knowledge is primitive in LDCs; although they might adopt the technologies of the advanced nations, those technologies are not always appropriate to the resource endowments of the LDCs and they must therefore develop their own technologies.

e. In addition, it is difficult for LDCs to alter the social, cultural, and institutional environment in the process of promoting economic growth.

3. In summary, LDCs save little and, therefore, invest little in real and human capital because they are poor; and because they do not invest, their outputs per capita remain low and they remain poor. Even if the vicious circle were to be broken, a rapid increase in population would leave the standard of living unchanged.

4. There are differing views about the role that government plays in fostering economic growth in LDCs.

a. The positive view holds that in the initial stages of economic development government action is needed to help overcome such obstacles as the lack of law and order, entrepreneurship, and infrastructure. Government policies may also assist capital formation, and in resolving social and institutional problems.

b. There are also problems and disadvantages with government involvement in promoting growth from such factors as bureaucratic impediments, corruption, maladministration, and the importance of political objectives over economic goals. Central planning does not work because it restricts competition and individual incentives, which are important ingredients in the growth process.

5. Industrially advanced nations of the world can help the poor countries develop in a number of ways.

a. They can lower the trade barriers which prevent the LDCs from selling their products in the developed countries.

b. Loans and grants from governments and from international organizations such as the World Bank also enable the LDCs to accumulate capital.

c. The flow of private capital from industrially advanced countries helps the LDCs increase their productive capacities and per capita outputs.

6. The large external debts of LDCs are a continuing problem.

a. The debt that LDCs owe to foreign governments and foreign financial institutions increased significantly over the last two decades, and is roughly equal to 45% of the total amount of the gross domestic products of LDCs, but for some countries it is much larger.

b. The causes of the debt crisis rest with world events during the 1970s and early 1980s.

(1) Higher prices for imported oil during the 1970s and early 1980s forced LDCs to borrow to cover current account deficits.

(2) The United States and other industrially advanced nations imposed tight monetary policies in the early 1980s to restrain inflation but this policy raised interest rates and costs for LDC borrowing and brought on

recession to industrially advanced countries, which reduced imports from LDCs.

(3) The appreciation in the international value of the dollar during the 1981–1985 period forced LDCs to pay more for imported manufactured goods from the United States and to receive less in return for exports to the United States.

(4) And, severe debt problems in Mexico in 1982 signaled problems with LDC loans in the financial community and resulted in reduced loans from private sources; increasing Federal budget deficits in the United States during most of the 1980s absorbed more private capital that might otherwise be lent to LDCs.

c. In recent years, the International Monetary Fund worked with countries on an individual basis to resolve debt problems. In return for debt rescheduling, LDCs often must impose austerity measures and use net export earning to pay for debt retirement, but these conditions have reduced economic development funds, retarded economic growth, and lowered capital income.

d. For the future, the two basic solutions to the LDC debt problem focus on continuation of country-by-country negotiations, which may require too many years to solve the problem, and debt forgiveness by industrially advanced countries, which might have an adverse effect on private lending.

7. Because they have not grown so rapidly as they had hoped and are dissatisfied with their relationship with industrially advanced nations, the LDCs have urged the creation of a ***New International Economic Order*** which would involve six controversial features: changing the rules of the game in world economic institutions, preferential tariff treatment, less exploitation by and dependence on foreign corporations, improved terms of trade for LDC products, debt relief, and increased foreign aid from governments in industrially advanced countries.

■ IMPORTANT TERMS

Less developed countries (LDCs)	**Capital-saving technological advance**
Industrially advanced countries (IACs)	**Capital-using technological advance**
Unemployment	**The will to develop**
Underemployment	**World Bank**
Investment in human capital	**Neocolonialism**
Brain drain	**New International Economic Order (NIEO)**
Domestic capital formation	**Preferential tariff treatment**
Capital flight	**Stabilization fund**
Infrastructure	**Terms of trade**
Nonfinancial (in-kind) investment	

■ **FILL-IN QUESTIONS**

1. There is income inequality among countries.
   a. Industrially advanced countries (IACs) have (high, low) _____ per capita incomes while there are less developed countries (LDCs) that have _____ per capita incomes. Oil exporting countries have _____ per capita income but are not highly industrialized.

   b. Among the _____ LDCs, there is a group of 56 countries which are classified as (middle, low) _____-income LDCs with per capita GNP of $_____ and 41 countries which are classified as _____-income LDCs with per capita GNP of $_____. In 1989, GNP of the United States was $_____ trillion, but the combined GNP of the _____ LDCs that year was $_____ trillion.

2. Singapore, Hong Kong, South Korea, and Taiwan are considered _____ countries and had rates of economic growth in real GNP from 1960–1989 of _____ to _____%; many LDCs have experienced _____ real per capita GNP in the 1980s.

3. IACs have a (higher, lower) _____ starting base for per capita income than LDCs, so the same percentage growth rate for both IACs and LDCs means an increase in the _____ income gap.

4. Low per capita income in LDCs means that life _____, adult _____, daily _____ supply, and _____ consumption are (higher, lower) _____ and infant mortality is _____

5. The process for economic growth is the same for IACs and LDCs. It involves more _____ use of existing resources and also increasing supplies of _____
_____, _____,
_____, and improving its
_____

6. The distribution of natural resources among LDCs is (even, uneven) _____; many LDCs lack vital natural resources. Although _____ nations have been able to use oil resources for economic growth, much of the natural resources in LDCs are owned or controlled by companies in _____; exports of products from LDCs are subject to _____ fluctuations.

7. In terms of human resources:
   a. Many LDCs are _____ and have population growth rates of about _____% compared to _____% for IACs; given the growth rate for LDCs, "rule of 70" would suggest that the population of LDCs will double in about _____ years. Rapid population growth can cause per capita GDP to (increase, decrease) _____

   b. There is both _____ and _____ among workers in LDCs.

   c. Labor _____ is also very low in most LDCs in part because these countries have not been able to invest in _____; and the so-called _____ contributes to the decline in skill level and productivity as the best-trained workers leave LDCs to work in IACs.

8. Capital accumulation is critical to the development of LDCs. If there were more capital goods, this would improve _____ and help boost per capita GDP; an increase in capital goods is necessary because the _____ of arable land is limited; the process of capital formation is "cumulative," investment increases the (population, output, natural resources) _____ of the economy and this in turn makes it possible for the economy to save more and invest more in capital goods.

9. The formation of domestic capital requires that a nation save and invest.
   a. The former is difficult in LDCs because of a low _____ and the latter is difficult because of a lack of _____ and of _____ to invest; there is also the problem of _____ where savings are transferred to IACs.
   b. Many LDCs do not have much public capital goods, or _____, that are necessary for productive _____ investment.
   c. Nonfinancial (or in-kind) investment involves the transfer of surplus labor from (agriculture, industry) _____ to the improvement of agricultural facilities or the _____

10. The technologies used in the advanced industrial countries might be borrowed by and used in the less developed countries; but

 a. the technologies used in the advanced countries are based upon a labor force that is (skilled, unskilled)

_____, labor that is relatively (abundant,

scarce) _____, and capital that is rela-

tively _____, and their technologies

tend to be (labor, capital)-_____ using; while

 b. the technologies required in the underdeveloped countries must be based on a labor force that is

_____, labor that is relatively

_____, and capital that is rela-

tively _____, and their technologies

need to be _____-using.

 c. If technological advances make it possible to replace a worn-out plow, costing $10 when new, with a new $5 plow, the technological advance is capital (sav-

ing, using) _____

11. The "will to develop" in less developed countries involves a willingness to change the _____

and _____ arrangements of the country.

12. In most less developed countries, there is a vicious cycle of poverty. Saving is small because the

_____ per capita is small. Because sav-

ing is small, _____ in real and human

capital is also small. And for this reason the _____

of labor and _____ per capita remain small.

13. List five reasons why the role of government in fostering economic development will need to be large in the less developed countries, especially during the early stages of development:

 a. _____

 b. _____

 c. _____

 d. _____

 e. _____

14. There can also be _____ with government's role in the economy of LDCs because government

_____ can impede social and economic change, central planners give too much emphasis to

_____ objectives rather than economic objectives, and there can be _____-administration

and _____ in government. Central planning

models also restrict _____ and individ-

ual _____ which are factors in economic development.

15. The three major ways in which the United States can assist economic development in the LDCs are _____

_____,

_____,

and _____

16. The LDC debt crisis arose from the large (internal,

external) _____ debts that were accumulated over the past two decades. In 1990, these debts were

about $_____ billion and equal to about

_____% of the total of the gross domestic products of LDCs.

17. The causes of the LDC debt problem were due to world events during the 1970s and early 1980s.

 a. Oil prices (increased, decreased) _____

during the 1970s and this event _____ the borrowing needs of LDCs to pay for imported oil.

 b. In the early 1980s, the United States had a (tight,

easy) _____ monetary policy that (in-

creased, decreased) _____ real interest

rates and _____ the cost to LDCs of servicing debts; the recession of the early 1980s in the

United States also _____ the exports of farm products from LDCs to the United States.

 c. Over the 1981–1984 period, the international value

of the dollar (appreciated, depreciated) _____

which meant that LDCs had to pay (more, less) _____

for imports and receive _____ in return for exports.

 d. The debt crisis in _____ in 1982 shook

confidence in LDCs and reduced private _____ by banks and financial institutions; the increasing Fed-

eral budget _____ during the early 1980s also absorbed more private capital.

18. The economic consequences of the LDC debt crisis were that creditor nations and the International Monetary

Fund _____ debts to reduce the annual

burden of interest and principal repayments; in return, LDCs had to implement domestic _____ programs that tended to reduce the _____ of living and transferred _____ earnings to debt repayment and away from investments. Some experts also worried that the LDCs' debts are a threat to the _____ systems of the _____.

19. One solution to the lingering LDC debt crisis is to negotiate (separately with, with the group of) _____ indebted countries, but the problem is that it will take too many _____ and thwart _____ in those LDCs; another solution is to _____ the debts but this action might have an adverse effect on private lending and encourage further _____.

20. In pressing for the establishment of a New International Economic Order the LDCs have argued (among other things) that:

   a. because LDCs had no part in their formation and because they are "stacked" against them, there should be a change in the _____ by which international trade, finance, and investment are conducted;

   b. the IACs, to deprive LDCs of their export markets, have erected barriers to _____ and the LDCs should be accorded preferential _____

   c. the dealings of the LDCs with corporations in the advanced nations have led to the greater part of the benefits from the _____ of their natural resources going to others and to the increased _____ of LDCs on world markets;

   d. there has been, as a result of the higher prices charged for manufactured goods by corporations in the IACs, a shift against them in the _____ of _____ and that these might be improved by the establishment of _____ funds and by _____.

   e. except for the oil-exporting countries, the size of their _____ abroad has increased and these should either be _____ or _____

   f. the foreign aid which they have received has been _____ and should be increased to _____% of the GDP of the IACs, have no _____ attached to it, and should be provided on a long-term and _____ basis.

■ **PROBLEMS AND PROJECTS**

1. Suppose that the real per capita income in the average industrially advanced country is $8000 per year and in the average less developed country is $500 per year.

   a. The gap between their standards of living is $_____ per year.

   b. If GDP per capita were to grow at a rate of 5% during a year in both the industrially advanced and the less developed countries:

   (1) the standard of living in the industrially advanced countries would rise to $_____ a year;

   (2) the standard of living in the less developed countries would rise to $_____ a year; and

   (3) the gap between their standards of living would (narrow, widen) _____ to $_____ a year.

2. While economic conditions are not identical in all less developed countries, there are certain conditions common to or typical of most of them. In the spaces after each of the following characteristics, indicate briefly the nature of this characteristic in most less developed countries.

   a. Standard of living (per capita income). _____

   _____

   b. Average life expectancy. _____

   c. Extent of unemployment. _____

   d. Literacy. _____

   e. Technology. _____

   f. Percentage of the population engaged in agriculture. _____

   g. Size of the population relative to the land and capital available. _____

   h. The birth and death rates. _____

   i. Quality of the labor force. _____

   j. Amount of capital equipment relative to the labor force. _____

   k. Level of saving. _____

   l. Incentive to invest. _____

   m. Amount of basic social capital. _____

   n. Extent of industrialization. _____

   o. Size and quality of the entrepreneurial class and the supervisory class. _____

   _____

p. Per capita public expenditures for education and per capita energy consumption. _____

q. Per capita consumption of food. _____

r. Disease and malnutrition. _____

3. Suppose that it takes a minimum of 5 units of food to keep a person alive for a year, that the population can double itself every 10 years, and that the food supply can increase every 10 years by an amount equal to what it was in the beginning (year 0).

a. Assume that both the population and the food supply grow at these rates. Complete the following table by computing the size of the population and the food supply in years 10 through 60.

Year	Food supply	Population
0	200	20
10	_____	_____
20	_____	_____
30	_____	_____
40	_____	_____
50	_____	_____
60	_____	_____

b. What happens to the relationship between the food supply and the population in the 30th year?

_____

c. What would actually prevent the population from growing at this rate following the 30th year?

_____

d. Assuming that the actual population growth in the years following the 30th does not outrun the food supply, what would be the size of the population in:

(1) Year 40: _____

(2) Year 50: _____

(3) Year 60: _____

e. Explain why the standard of living failed to increase in the years following the 30th even though the food supply increased by 75% between years 30 and 60.

_____

■ **SELF-TEST**

Circle the T if the statement is true; the F if it is false.

1. About three-fourths of the world's population lives in 97 less developed countries.   **T F**

2. The United States has about 5% of the world's pop-

ulation and produces approximately one-fourth of the world's output.   **T F**

3. Per capita GNP in 1989 was about $6000 in India and about $21,000 in the United States.   **T F**

4. The difference between the per capita incomes in the less developed countries and the per capital incomes in the developed countries has decreased over the past years.   **T F**

5. Economic growth in both industrially advanced and less developed countries requires using economic resources more efficiently and increasing the supplies of some of these resources.   **T F**

6. It is impossible to achieve a high standard of living with a small supply of natural resources.   **T F**

7. Countries with large populations are less developed.   **T F**

8. The chief factor preventing the elimination of unemployment in the less developed countries is the small number of job openings available in the cities.   **T F**

9. Saving in LDCs is a smaller percentage of domestic output than in IACs, and this is the chief reason total saving in LDCs is small.   **T F**

10. Before private investment can be increased in less developed countries it is necessary to reduce the amount of investment in infrastructure.   **T F**

11. Technological advances in LDCs will be made rapidly because they do not require pushing forward the frontiers of technological knowledge and the technologies used in IACs can be easily transferred to the less developed ones.   **T F**

12. When technological advances are capital-saving it is possible for an economy to increase its productivity without any *net* investment in capital goods.   **T F**

13. Emancipation from custom and tradition is often the fundamental prerequisite of economic development.**T F**

14. The policies of the governments of less developed countries have often tended to reduce the incentives of foreigners to invest in the less developed countries. **T F**

15. Governments always play a positive role in the economic development of LDCs.   **T F**

16. LDCs will not need foreign aid if the developed countries will reduce tariffs and import quotas on the goods which the less developed countries export.   **T F**

17. An increase in the output and employment of the United States works to the advantage of the less developed countries because it provides the less developed countries with larger markets for their exports.   **T F**

18. Foreign aid from the United States to the less developed countries has consistently exceeded 1% of its GDP. **T   F**

19. Many in LDCs believe that the public and private aid extended by the IACs to the LDCs is designed to increase profits in the former and to exploit the latter countries. **T   F**

20. In 1992 the total external debts of LDCs was equal to about 26% of the total of the gross domestic products of LDCs. **T   F**

21. During the early 1980s, an appreciation of the dollar, and a decrease in private lending contributed to the LDC debt crisis. **T   F**

22. The simplest solution to the lingering LDC debt problem and the one with fewest repercussions would be to have the creditors in IACs forgive the debts of LDCs. **T   F**

23. Were a fund to be established to stabilize the price of a commodity such as copper, the fund would be used to purchase the commodity when its price fell. **T   F**

24. Preferential tariff treatment for LDCs means that the IACs would set their tariffs on commodities imported from LDCs below those established for the same commodities imported from IACs. **T   F**

25. One of the proposals associated with the establishment of a New International Economic Order is that the aid from IACs to LDCs be automatic, have no "strings" attached to it. **T   F**

Circle the letter that corresponds to the best answer.

1. Which of the following would be considered a LDC?
  (a) China
  (b) Kuwait
  (c) Taiwan
  (d) New Zealand

2. If per capita income is $600 a year in a LDC and per capita income is $12,000 in an IAC, then a 2% growth rate increases the absolute income gap by:
  (a) $120
  (b) $228
  (c) $240
  (d) $252

3. When the average annual rate of growth in per capita GDP in a LDC is 1%, approximately how many years will it take for the standard of living to double?
  (a) 27 years
  (b) 35 years
  (c) 57 years
  (d) 70 years

4. Which of the following is high in the less developed countries?
  (a) life expectancy
  (b) infant mortality
  (c) literacy
  (d) per capita energy consumption

5. Which of the following is an obstacle to economic growth in most less developed countries?
  (a) the supply of national resources
  (b) the size and quality of the labor force
  (c) the supply of capital equipment
  (d) all of the above

6. An increase in the total output of consumer goods in a less developed country may not increase the average standard of living because:
  (a) of capital flight
  (b) it may lead to an increase in the population
  (c) of disguised unemployment
  (d) the quality of the labor force is so poor

7. Which of the following best describes the unemployment found in the less developed countries?
  (a) the result of cyclical fluctuations in aggregate demand
  (b) the agricultural workers who have migrated from rural to urban areas and failed to find employment in the cities
  (c) the workers in excess of the optimum population
  (d) workers whose productivity is subject to diminishing returns

8. Which of the following is *not* a reason for placing special emphasis on capital accumulation in less developed countries?
  (a) the inflexible supply of arable land
  (b) the low productivity of workers
  (c) the low marginal contribution of capital equipment
  (d) the possibility that capital accumulation will be "cumulative"

9. Which of the following is *not* a factor limiting saving in less developed countries?
  (a) the output of the economy is too low to permit a large volume of saving
  (b) those who do save do not make their saving available to their own economies
  (c) the highly unequal distribution of income
  (d) the low marginal contribution of capital equipment to production

10. When citizens of LDCs transfer savings or invest savings in IACs, it is referred to as:
  (a) brain drain
  (b) capital flight
  (c) savings potential
  (d) in-kind investment

11. Which of the following is *not* an obstacle to capital formation (investment) in less developed countries?
(a) the absence of strong incentives to invest
(b) the lack of basic social capital
(c) the absence of a large entrepreneurial class
(d) the lack of capital-saving changes in technology

12. Which of the following is an example of infrastructure?
(a) a steel plant
(b) an electric power plant
(c) a farm
(d) a deposit in a financial institution

13. Which of the following seems to be the most acute institutional problem that needs to be resolved in many less developed countries?
(a) adoption of birth control
(b) development of strong labor unions
(c) increase in the nation's public capital
(d) land reform

14. Assume the total real output of a LDC increases from $100 billion to $115.5 billion while its population expands from 200 million to 210 million people. Real income per capita has, as a result, increased by:
(a) $50
(b) $100
(c) $150
(d) $200

15. The role of government in the early stages of economic development will probably be a major one for several reasons. Which one of the following is *not* one of these reasons?
(a) only government can provide a larger amount of the needed infrastructure
(b) the absence of private entrepreneurs to accumulate capital and take risks
(c) the necessity of creating *new* money to finance capital accumulation
(d) the slowness and uncertainty of the market system in fostering development

16. In recent years, many LDCs have come to recognize that:
(a) competition and economic incentives for individuals are necessary for economic development
(b) there are few disadvantages from government involvement in the development process
(c) private capital is not required for economic development
(d) the World Bank serves as an institutional barrier to economic growth

17. An event that occurred during the 1970s or early 1980s that contributed to the LDC debt crisis was:
(a) a sharp decline in price of oil charged by OPEC countries
(b) a depreciation in the international value of the dollar

(c) a tight monetary policy and recession in the United States
(d) a rise in net export earnings of the LDCs

18. To raise funds to pay interest and principal on external debt, LDCs had to adopt domestic economic policies that tended to:
(a) decrease imports, increase exports, and lower the standard of living
(b) increase imports, decrease exports, and lower the standard of living
(c) decrease imports, decrease exports, and lower the standard of living
(d) increase imports, decrease exports, and raise the standard of living

19. The terms of trade for a nation exporting tin worsen whenever:
(a) the price of tin rises
(b) the price of tin falls
(c) the price of tin rises and the prices of imported goods decline
(d) the price of tin falls and the prices of imported goods rise

20. Which one of the following is *not* one of the proposals included in the New International Economic Order for which LDCs have argued?
(a) a change in the rules by which international financial institutions are governed
(b) the elimination of OPEC
(c) the renegotiation and cancellation of the debts of LDCs to the IACs
(d) abandonment of the neo-colonial policies of the IACs

■ **DISCUSSION QUESTIONS**

1. What is the degree of income inequality among nations of the world? Classify nations into three groups and describe this inequality. What further division can be made among poor nations?

2. How do the overall level of economic growth per capita and the rates of economic growth compare among rich nations and poor countries? Why does the income gap widen?

3. What are the "human implications" of poverty found in LDCs? (Use the socioeconomic indicators found in Table 39-2 of the text to contrast the quality of life in IACs and LDCs).

4. Describe the basic avenues of economic growth. Do these avenues differ for IACs and LDCs?

5. How would you describe the natural resource situation for LDCs? In what ways do price fluctuations affect

LDC exports? Is a weak natural resource base an obstacle to economic growth?

6. Describe the implications of the high rate of growth in population and its effects on the standard of living. Can the standard of living be raised by merely increasing the output of consumer goods in LDCs? What is the meaning of the cliché, "the rich get richer and the poor get children," and how does it apply to LDCs?

7. What obstacles do the human resources of LDCs place in the path of economic development? What is the distinction between unemployment and underemployment and how do the concepts apply to LDCs? What are the reasons for the low level of labor productivity in LDCs? How does "brain drain" affect LDCs?

8. What reasons exist for placing special emphasis on capital accumulation as a means of promoting economic growth in LDCs?

9. Why is domestic capital accumulation difficult in LDCs? Answer both in terms of the saving side and the investment side of capital accumulation. Is there "capital flight" from LDCs?

10. In addition to the obstacles which limit domestic investment, what other obstacles tend to limit the flow of foreign capital into LDCs? What role does infrastructure play in capital formation?

11. How might the LDCs improve their technology without engaging in slow and expensive research? Why might this be an inappropriate method of improving the technology used in the LDCs?

12. What is meant by the "will to develop"? How is it related to social and institutional change in LDCs?

13. Explain the "vicious circle" of poverty found in the LDCs. How does population growth make an escape from this vicious circle difficult?

14. Why is the role of government expected to be a positive one in the early phases of development in LDCs? What have been the problems with the involvement of government in economic development?

15. How can the United States help LDCs? What types of aid can be offered? How is it possible for the United States to assist LDCs without spending a penny on "foreign aid"? Is this type of aid sufficient to ensure rapid and substantial development in LDCs?

16. Discuss the World Bank in terms of its purposes, characteristics, sources of funds, promotion of private capital flows, and success. What are its affiliates and their purposes?

17. Describe the dimensions of the lingering LDC debt crisis. What were the causes of the crisis? Explain the eco-nomic consequences for LDCs and IACs of the debt crisis. Are there any solutions?

18. Explain the principal proposals which constitute the program of the LDCs for the establishment of a New International Economic Order. Explain the arguments made by the LDCs to support each of these proposals.

■ **ANSWERS**

Chapter 39 Growth and the Less Developed Countries

FILL-IN QUESTIONS

1. *a.* high, low, high; *b.* 97, middle, 2040, low, 330, 5.2, 97, 3.1

2. new industrialized, 6, 7, declining

3. higher, absolute

4. expectancies, literacy, calorie, energy, lower, higher

5. efficient, natural resources, human resources, capital goods, technology

6. uneven, OPEC, IACs, price

7. *a.* overpopulated, 2, .7, 35, decrease; *b.* unemployment, underemployment; *c.* productivity, human capital, brain drain

8. *a.* labor productivity, supply, output

9. *a.* saving potential, investors, incentives, capital flight; *b.* infrastructure, private; *c.* agriculture, infrastructure

10. *a.* skilled, scarce, abundant, capital; *b.* unskilled, abundant, scarce, labor; *c.* saving

11. institutions, social

12. income, investment, productivity, output (income)

13. *a.* the existence of widespread banditry and intertribal warfare in the poorest less developed nations; *b.* the absence of a sizable and vigorous entrepreneurial class; *c.* the great need for public goods and services; *d.* government action may be the only means of promoting saving and investment; *e.* government can more effectively deal with the social-institutional obstacles to growth

14. public sector problems, bureaucracy, political, mal, corruption, competition, incentives

15. by expanding trade with the underdeveloped nations (lowering the barriers to trade), private flows of capital, foreign aid (public loans and grants)

16. external, 1530, 26

17. *a.* increased, increased; *b.* tight, increased, increased, decreased; *c.* appreciated, more, less; *d.* Mexico, lending, deficits

18. rescheduled, austerity, standard, net export, banking and financial, IACs

19. separately with, decades (years), economic growth, forgive, defaults

20. *a.* rules; *b.* trade, tariff treatments; *c.* exploitation, dependence; *d.* terms, trade, stabilization, indexing; *e.* debts, canceled, rescheduled; *f.* insufficient, 0.7, strings, automatic

PROBLEMS AND PROJECTS

1. *a.* 7500; *b.* (1) 8400, (2) 525, (3) widen, 7875

2. *a.* low; *b.* short; *c.* widespread; *d.* low; *e.* primitive; *f.* large; *g.* large; *h.* high; *i.* poor; *j.* small; *k.* low; *l.* absent; *m.* small; *n.* small; *o.* small and poor; *p.* small; *q.* low; *r.* common

3. *a.* food supply; 400, 600, 800, 1000, 1200, 1400; population; 40, 80, 160, 320, 640, 1280; *b.* the food supply is just able to support the population; *c.* the inability of the food supply to support a population growing at this rate; *d.* (1) 200, (2) 240, (3) 280; *e.* the population increased as rapidly as the food supply

SELF-TEST

1. T, p. 746
2. T, p. 746
3. F, p. 747
4. F, p. 746
5. T, p. 747
6. F, p. 748
7. F, p. 749
8. T, pp. 749–750
9. F, p. 751
10. F, pp. 751–752
11. F, pp. 752–753
12. T, p. 752
13. T, p. 753
14. T, pp. 751–753
15. F, p. 756
16. F, pp. 756–757
17. T, p. 757
18. F, p. 757
19. T, p. 761
20. T, p. 758
21. T, p. 759
22. F, p. 760
23. T, p. 761
24. T, p. 760
25. T, p. 761

1. *a*, p. 746
2. *b*, p. 746
3. *d*, p. 748
4. *b*, p. 747
5. *d*, p. 747
6. *b*, pp. 748–749
7. *b*, pp. 749–750
8. *c*, pp. 750–752
9. *d*, p. 751
10. *b*, p. 751
11. *d*, pp. 751–754
12. *b*, pp. 751–752
13. *d*, pp. 753–754
14. *a*, p. 746
15. *c*, p. 755
16. *a*, p. 756
17. *c*, p. 759
18. *a*, pp. 759–760
19. *d*, p. 761
20. *b*, pp. 760–761

DISCUSSION QUESTIONS

1. pp. 745–746
2. p. 746
3. p. 747
4. p. 747
5. p. 748
6. pp. 748–749
7. pp. 749–750
8. pp. 750–751
9. p. 751
10. pp. 751–752
11. pp. 752–753
12. p. 753
13. p. 754
14. pp. 754–756
15. pp. 756–758
16. p. 757
17. pp. 758–760
18. pp. 760–761

CHAPTER 40

The Soviet Economy in Transition

In the years following the Russian Revolution of 1917, many people in the United States were convinced that the economic system of the Soviet Union was unworkable and that it would break down sooner or later—proof that Marx and Lenin were unrealistic dreamers—and that the reconversion of the Soviet economy to a market system would follow. Now, some seventy-five years after the revolution, the economy of the former Soviet Union is being transformed into a market economy. Chapter 40 provides insights into this profound turn of events by examining the reasons why the Soviet economic system failed, and by discussing reforms and obstacles in the path to a market economy for the former Soviet Union.

The first two sections of the chapter explain the basic ideas behind Marxian ideology and discuss the two institutional features that were most characteristic of the economy of the former Soviet Union. For over seven decades, the Soviet economy operated under a system of state ownership of property resources and direct control. Central planning was used to set prices, to restrict consumption, and to direct investment to heavy industry and to the military. Although central planning served as a powerful form of economic decision-making, it had serious problems and flaws as a coordinating mechanism because it resulted in production bottlenecks, missed production targets, and reduced the economic freedom and decision-making for producers, workers, and consumers.

As you will learn in the third and fourth sections of the chapter, the slowing of economic growth in the Soviet economy in 1970s and 1980s set the stage for the failure of communism and for the final attempts to reform the faltering economic system of the former Soviet Union. What contributed to the deterioration of Soviet economy were many factors, among them being the economic burden of supporting a large military, inefficiencies in the agricultural sector that hurt other sectors of the economy, and the reliance of more inputs rather than increasing the productivity and efficiency of available inputs to fuel economic growth. By 1986, then-Soviet President Mikhail Gorbachev proposed a series of economic changes designed to restructure the economy (**perestroika**) and to give peo-ple more freedom in the conduct of economic and business affairs (**glasnost**). Although the Gorbachev reforms attempted to correct the deficiencies of central control and modernize the economy, the proposal did not eliminate central planning.

The fifth and sixth parts of Chapter 40 explain the elements of and obstacles to a more sweeping transformation of the economy of the former Soviet Union into a market economy. The transition will require the privatization of property resources, the promotion of competition, a reduced and altered role for government, major price reforms, and currency conversion. These transition policies will also result in high rates of inflation. A host of obstacles—technical problems, negative attitudes among bureaucrats and workers, the maintainence of order and national unity, and achieving simultaneous progress in all major reforms—must also be overcome in the movement to a market economy. The challenge is daunting, but it will be facilitated by several positive aspects of the economy of the former Soviet Union.

The final section discusses the actions that can be taken by the major capitalist nations to help transform the centrally planned economy into one based on markets and prices. The most obvious assistance is foreign aid, but as you will learn, it is not without much criticism. Private investment is the most important avenue for long-term change, yet the amount of investment and its effectiveness will depend on the progress in economic restructuring. The economy of the former Soviet Union will also benefit from the steps it takes to join international organizations that promote world trade and economic development.

The transformation of the economy of the former Soviet Union into a market economy is one of the most important economic events of this decade. Whether the sweeping economic reforms will work, or what the final outcomes will be, is still unknown and uncertain. Nevertheless, this examination of the sweeping change of an economic system from one based on central planning to one based on markets and prices should deepen your understanding of the principles of economics. This dramatic development is a fitting topic for the conclusion to your study of economics.

■ CHECKLIST

☐ Outline the key elements of Marxian ideology.
☐ Identify two outstanding institutions of the economy of the former Soviet Union.
☐ Make seven generalizations about the functioning of central economic planning in the former Soviet Union.
☐ Compare the coordination mechanism in a market economy with that in a centrally planned economy.
☐ Describe the deteriorating economic performance of the Soviet economy after the 1960s.
☐ Identify six factors that contributed to the collapse of the Soviet economic system.
☐ Discuss the six interrelated elements of the Gorbachev reforms.
☐ List six factors that are important in the transition to a market economy for the economy of the former Soviet Union.
☐ Explain the effects of privatization and competition in the transition.
☐ Describe the changed role for government in the transition.
☐ Use a supply and demand graph to discuss the difficulties posed by price reforms in the transition.
☐ Explain the importance of opening the economy to international trade and finance in the transition.
☐ Identify three reasons to expect high rates of inflation in the transition.
☐ List four major obstacles to the transformation of the economy of the former Soviet Union.
☐ Identify four positive factors in the former Soviet Union that will help in the change to a market economy.
☐ List three actions by the capitalist industrial nations of the world to assist the former Soviet Union to build a market economy.
☐ Evaluate the importance of foreign aid and private investment in the transformation of the economy of the former Soviet Union.
☐ Identify the key international organizations and actions that would help with the transition to a market economy for the former Soviet Union.

■ CHAPTER OUTLINE

1. The Soviet economy was based on ideology and institutions.
  a. The Soviet government was viewed as a dictatorship of the proletariat (or working class), and the economy was based on *Marxian* ideology.
  (1) The Marxian concept of a *labor theory of value* held that only labor creates value in production, and that profits are a *surplus value* expropriated from workers by capitalists, who because of the institution of private property, were able to control the means of production (capital goods).

(2) The communist system of the former Soviet Union sought to end this exploitation of workers by eliminating private property and by creating a classless society.
  b. The two major institutional features of the Soviet economy were state ownership of property resources and central economic planning.

2. Central planning was used throughout much of the history of the Soviet Union.
  a. Historically, the operation of central planning in the Soviet Union exhibited seven features:
  (1) the attachment of great importance to military strength and to industrialization;
  (2) the overcommitment of available resources and the missing of planning targets;
  (3) a stress on increasing the quantity of resources rather than using given resources more productively;
  (4) the use of directives to allocate inputs for production rather than markets and prices;
  (5) price fixing and price controls by government;
  (6) an emphasis on the self-sufficiency of the nation; and
  (7) passive use of monetary and fiscal policies.
  b. The basic problem encountered in a centrally planned economy such as that of the former Soviet Union is the difficulty of coordinating the many interdependent segments of the economy and the avoidance of the chain reaction that would result from a bottleneck in any one of the segments.

3. The failure of communism in the Soviet Union resulted in large part from the poor economic growth performance of the economy in the years since the 1960s. Technology lagged by Western standards and manufacturing goods were of poor quality. Consumers were also aware that they had received few material benefits from years of sacrifice for the rapid industrialization and the sizable public expenditures to support a large military.
  a. Six interrelated factors contributed to the collapse of the economy of the former Soviet Union.
  (1) The large financial burden for military expenditures diverted resources from the production of consumer and capital goods.
  (2) Inefficiencies in agriculture acted as a drag on economic growth and hurt productivity in other sectors of the economy.
  (3) Economic growth was achieved throughout much of the Soviet history by increasing the quantity of economic resources (especially labor) rather than by using the more difficult route of increasing the productivity of existing resources; however, growing labor shortages limited growth by the historical route and the lack of incentives and technology needs made the second route more difficult.
  (4) The increased complexity of production processes in a modern industrial society compounded the difficulties of central planning.

(5) There were inadequate measures of economic performance to determine the degree of success or failure of enterprises or to give clear signals to the economy. (6) Economic incentives were ineffective for encouraging initiative and work or for coordination of productive activities.

4. In 1986, President Mikhail Gorbachev offered a series of proposals for economic reform (***perestroika***) and also call for more openness (***glasnost***) in discussions about economic affairs, both designed to improve the economic performance of the centrally planned system. The Gorbachev reforms called for: the modernization of industry; the decentralization of decision-making; the encouragement of some private production of products; the increased use of economic incentives to motivate workers and fire incompetent managers; the institution of price reforms and a more rational price system; and a greater involvement in the world economy. The reforms did not work in large part because they only modified the major deficiencies of the centrally planned system.

5. There are six components to the transition from a command economy to a market economy for the former Soviet Union.
   a. Private property rights must be established and government property must be transferred to private ownership. Several options are possible to achieve the privatization objective: selling enterprises directly, employee stock ownership, or conversion of large government enterprises into corporations or publicly owned businesses.
   b. Competition must be promoted by splitting up or restructing large state-owned enterprises to reduce the potential for monopoly power by having only one privatized business in an industry.
   c. The government must reduce its extensive involvement in the economy to the more limited and traditional role of providing a legal system, maintaining competition, redistributing income, reallocating resources to necessary public goods, addressing the problems of spillovers, and stabilizing the economy.
   d. The government will need to eliminate price fixing and price controls so that prices for goods and services are free to change and reflect relative scarcities.
   e. Action must be taken to open the economy to international trade and finance by making the ruble a convertible currency. Eventually, this action will promote more competition and efficiency in production.
   f. The transition reforms will be accompanied by inflation because of the decontrol of prices, and because of a ***ruble overhang***, which is the excess currency created by the lack of opportunities for consumer spending. Also contributing to the inflation problem are the large, recent deficits of government and the printing of new currency to finance these deficits.

6. Obstacles to transforming the Soviet economy will make the transition difficult.
   a. The drastic reforms in the economy create many technical problems that must be solved.
   b. There may be public resistance to the reforms because they threaten job status and require workers and managers to change old methods and procedures of work.
   c. The demands for autonomy in new republics of the former Soviet Union may lead to disorder, reduce economic efficiency, and restrict trade between republics.
   d. The reforms must be pursued simultaneously; a failure to achieve one reform will affect the success of all the reforms.
   e. Four positive factors, however, may contribute to the success of the reforms:
   (1) the large endowment of natural resources;
   (2) the shift of resources and expenditures from military to civilian uses;
   (3) the experience and skills developed in the underground or second economy; and
   (4) the political reform and democratization that frees people to express ideas and to be more productive.

7. The major capitalist economies of the world will facilitate the transition of the economy of the former Soviet Union to a market economy.
   a. Foreign aid is being provided by capitalist nations. Critics contend, however, that foreign aid is wasteful under present circumstances, delays military cuts which would be more effective, is too little to be of much help to the average citizen, and would be better spent addressing problems in home countries.
   b. Private investment will be very important, but there are many obstacles for private businesses that desire to invest because of unclear ownership and control of enterprises, inadequacies in the private distribution system and in the public infrastructure, and the inconvertibility of the ruble.
   c. Membership in international organizations, such as the International Monetary Fund, the World Bank, and the General Agreement on Tariffs and Trade, will help integrate the former Soviet Union into the world's market economy.

8. The prospects are still uncertain for the current reform of the Soviet economy and its transition to a market economy.

■ **IMPORTANT TERMS**

Labor theory of value	**Gorbachev reforms**
Surplus value	***Perestroika***
State ownership	***Glasnost***
Central economic planning	**Ruble overhang**

■ FILL-IN QUESTIONS

1. The ideology of the economy of the former Soviet Union was that:

a. the value of any commodity is determined by the amount of _____ required to produce it;

b. in capitalist economies, capital is (privately, publicly) _____ owned, and capitalists exploit workers by paying them a wage that is equal to the _____ wage and obtain _____ value at the expense of workers; and

c. in a communist economy, capital and other property resources will be _____, society will be _____-less, and it will be governed by the Communist Party as a dictatorship of the _____.

2. The two major institutions of the former Soviet Union are the ownership of property resources by the _____ and _____ economic planning.

3. Economic planning in the former Soviet Union functioned in several ways.

a. The Soviet five-year plans sought to achieve rapid _____ and _____ strength, but these policies created an (over, under) _____-commitment of resources and resulted in an _____-production of goods for consumers.

b. Early economic growth was achieved by _____ resources and reallocating surplus labor from _____ to industry.

c. The government allocated inputs among industries by planning _____ and the government fixed _____ for goods and services and inputs.

d. The Soviet Union considered itself to be a (capitalist, socialist) _____ nation surrounded by _____ nations, and central plans were designed to achieve economic _____-sufficiency.

e. Monetary and fiscal policies in the Soviet Union were (active, passive) _____. Prices were _____ by government and ambitious planning targets essentially eliminated the _____ of workers. The _____ issued credit or working capital to state enterprises and accepted deposits, but it did not manipulate the supply of _____

4. Decision-making in a market economy is (centralized, decentralized) _____, but in the Soviet economy it was _____. The market system tends to produce a reasonably (efficient, inefficient) _____ allocation of resources, but central planning in the Soviet economy was _____ and resulted in production bottlenecks and failures to meet many production targets.

5. There are a number of reasons for the collapse of communism and the failure of the Soviet economy.

a. There was a large _____ burden on the economy that diverted resources from the production of investment and _____ goods.

b. Agriculture was (efficient, inefficient) _____ and (helped, hurt) _____ economic growth and productivity in other sectors of the economy.

c. Traditionally, economic growth was achieved by increasing the (quality, quantity) _____ of economic resources rather than by increasing the _____, or productivity, of existing resources, but shortages of labor and capital have limited economic growth in the traditional path, and improving the productivity of existing resources was difficult because of lagging _____ progress.

d. Central planning became (more, less) _____ complex and difficult as the Soviet economy grew and changed over time.

e. Measures of economic performance were (adequate, inadequate) _____ for determining the success or failure of economic activities.

f. Economic incentives were (effective, ineffective) _____ for encouraging work or for giving signals for efficient allocation of resources in the economy.

6. In 1986, reform of the Soviet economy was proposed by Mikhail _____. His economic program for reform and restructuring was referred to as _____; it was accompanied by _____, which means that there was to be more openness in the discussion of economic issues among participants in the economy.

7. List the six elements of the 1986 reforms.

a. _____

b. _____

c. _____

d. _____

e. _____

f. _____

8. The transition to a market economy for the former Soviet Union will require success in achieving more sweeping changes than the _____ reforms. One of the most important changes is the establishment of _____ rights and the transfer of government property to _____ ownership. This objective may be achieved by the _____ of state enterprises, by employee _____ ownership, and in the case of large state enterprise, conversion into _____ or into businesses owned by the _____

9. The economy must also promote _____ by splitting up the large state-owned enterprises so that there is more than one business producing a good or service and to reduce the potential for _____ power.

10. In the transition, the role of government will need to be _____ and refocused on the traditional functions of providing a _____ system, maintaining _____, redistributing _____, reallocating resources to essential _____ goods, addressing the problems of _____ costs and benefits, and macroeconomic _____ of the economy.

11. In the past, prices of goods and services were kept at low levels through price _____, but the movement to a market economy will require them to be lifted and the economy will experience _____

12. The former Soviet Union will need to join the international economy by making the ruble a _____ or exchangeable currency on international markets, and by opening the economy to more international _____ with other nations.

13. The move to a market economy will be accompanied by inflation because of the _____ of prices, a ruble _____, and government financing of large budget deficits by printing more _____

14. The obstacles to the transformation of the economy of the Soviet Union into a market economy will include _____ economic problems, the need to change public _____ among bureaucrats and workers, the political problems of maintaining national _____, and the need to make _____

rather than piecemeal progress on all the economic reforms.

15. List four positive factors that may contribute to the success of the transition of the former Soviet Union to a market economy.

a. _____
b. _____
c. _____
d. _____

16. The major capitalist economies of the world can assist with conversion of the Soviet economy to a market economy by providing foreign _____, by increasing private _____, and by allowing the former Soviet Union to become a _____ of such institutions as the International _____ Fund, the World _____, and the General Agreement on _____

17. The outlook for the effective transformation of the economy of the former Soviet Union from a system of central planning to one based on markets and prices is (certain, uncertain) _____ and will require time to work.

■ **PROBLEMS AND PROJECTS**

1. In the table below are several of the major institutions and characteristics of either the American economy or the economy of the former Soviet Union. In the appropriate space, name the corresponding institution or characteristic of the other economy.

American institution or characteristic	Soviet institution or characteristic
a. _____	labor theory of value
b. _____	surplus value
c. Private ownership of economic resources	_____
d. a market economy	_____
e. _____	state industrial enterprises
f. privately owned farms	_____
g. entrepreneurial freedom	_____
h. consumer sovereignty	_____
i. _____	price controls
j. _____	turnover tax
k. democracy	_____
l. underground economy	_____

2. Answer the next set of questions based on the table below. In the table are the columns for the price, quantity demanded (Q_d) by consumers, and a fixed quantity supplied by government (Q_{s1}) for a product in the former Soviet Union. The column for Q_{s2} shows the supply curve for the product **after** privatization in the industry producing the product.

Price (in rubles)	Q_d	Q_{s1}	Q_{s2}
90	25	25	55
80	30	25	50
70	35	25	45
60	40	25	40
50	45	25	35
40	50	25	30
30	55	25	25

a. When only the government supplies the product as shown in the Q_{s1} schedule, the equilibrium price will be

_____ rubles and the equilibrium quantity will be

_____ units.

b. If the government tries to make the product more accessible to lower-income consumers by setting the price at 30 rubles, then the quantity demanded will be

_____ units and the quantity supplied will be

_____ units, producing a shortage of _____ units.

c. If the government decontrolled prices but did not privatize industry, then prices will rise to _____ rubles and the government will still produce _____ units.

d. With privatization, there will be a new quantity supplied schedule (Q_{s2}). The equilibrium price will be

_____ rubles and the equilibrium quantity will be

_____ units. The equilibrium price has risen by

_____ rubles and the equilibrium quantity by

_____ units.

■ **SELF-TEST**

1. The labor theory of value is the Marxian idea that the exchange value of a product is determined by the supply and demand of labor resources. **T F**

2. Surplus value in Marxian ideology is the value or price of a commodity at equilibrium in a competitive market. **T F**

3. The economy of the former Soviet Union was characterized by both state ownership of resources and decentralized economic decision-making. **T F**

4. The Soviet government set the economic objectives of the economy, directed the resources of the economy toward the achievement of those objectives, and used the market system as one means of achieving those objectives. **T F**

5. Historically, the Soviet Union placed strong emphasis on rapid industrialization and economic self-sufficiency. **T F**

6. Economic resources tended to be undercommitted in the economy of the former Soviet Union. **T F**

7. The former Soviet Union actively used monetary and fiscal policies to manipulate aggregate levels of employment, output, and prices. **T F**

8. During 1990 and 1991, the real domestic output of the former Soviet Union increased. **T F**

9. Greater productivity and technological progress in the civilian sector were often sacrificed or limited by the demands to support a large military in the former Soviet Union. **T F**

10. Agriculture was one of the most productive sectors of the economy of the former Soviet Union. **T F**

11. Soviet economic growth slowed in the years after the 1970s because of a surplus of labor and extensive unemployment. **T F**

12. The problems of central planning became easier and less complex as the economy of the former Soviet Union grew over time, but the economy was undermined by calls for democratic reform. **T F**

13. *Glasnost* refers to the economic restructuring proposed in 1986 by Mikhail Gorbachev. **T F**

14. The Gorbachev reforms called for the development of a limited private enterprise sector and more use of economic incentives. **T F**

15. The current transition to a market economy in the former Soviet Union will require the breakup of large industries and actions to promote competition. **T F**

16. Price decontrol will be a minor problem in the conversion of the economy of the former Soviet Union to capitalism because the prices established by the Soviet government over the years are very similar to the economic value that would be established in a competitive market. **T F**

17. Government is more likely to expand rather than contract its role in the transition to a market economy in the former Soviet Union. **T F**

18. The financing of recent budget deficits in the former Soviet Union by printing and distributing more currency is an important source of inflation. **T F**

19. Old work habits and bureaucratic resistence will be obstacles in the movement to capitalize in the former Soviet Union. **T F**

20. The "simultaneity" problem refers to the need to achieve a simultaneous decrease in inflation and unemployment in the former Soviet Union. **T F**

21. Maintaining political and economic unity will be difficult in the former Soviet Union because of the specialization of production and the existence of state monopolies in different republics. **T F**

22. A positive factor contributing to the economic transformation of the former Soviet Union to a market economy will be the size and variety of the natural resource base. **T F**

23. The "second economy" refers to the state-run monopolies that control most of the production in the former Soviet Union and which need to be converted to private enterprises. **T F**

24. A critic of foreign aid to the former Soviet Union would argue that the aid is wasteful and ineffective until the transition to capitalism has been achieved. **T F**

25. Private investment from capitalist nations will be an important source of real capital and business skills in management, marketing and entrepreneurship for the former Soviet Union. **T F**

Circle the letter that corresponds to the best answer.

1. Which of the following was an element in the ideology of the Soviet Union?
(a) dictatorship over the business class
(b) the creation of surplus value by government
(c) the labor theory of value
(d) the private ownership of property

2. Marxian (or communist) ideology in the Soviet Union was highly critical of capitalist societies because in those societies:
(a) capitalists own the machinery and equipment necessary for production
(b) capitalists pay workers a wage that is less than the value of their production
(c) capitalists expropriate the surplus value of workers
(d) all of the above are true

3. The institution that was most characteristic of the Soviet Union was:
(a) private ownership of property
(b) authoritarian central planning
(c) a system of markets and prices
(d) consumer sovereignty

4. Industrialization and rapid economic growth in the Soviet Union were initially achieved by:
(a) the mobilization of economic resources

(b) the overcommitment of economic resources
(c) price controls and price fixing
(d) active use of fiscal policy by the government

5. The Soviet Union viewed itself historically as a single socialist nation surrounded by hostile capitalist nations, and as a consequence central planning stressed the need for:
(a) consumer sovereignty
(b) economic self-sufficiency
(c) allocation by directive
(d) manipulation of the money supply by the **Gosbank**

6. In the system of central planning in the Soviet Union, the outputs of some industries became the inputs for other industries, but a failure of one industry to meet its target would cause:
(a) inflation in wholesale and retail prices
(b) the decay of the infrastructure
(c) a chain reaction of production problems and bottlenecks
(d) widespread unemployment and underemployment among workers

Use the table below to answer the next question (7).

Years	Growth in real domestic output (percent)			
	A	**B**	**C**	**D**
1950s	3	4	5	6
1960s	4	3	3	5
1970s	5	6	1	3
1980s (mid)	6	2	1	2

7. The column that best portrays the record of Soviet economic growth from the 1950s through the mid-1980s is:
(a) A
(b) B
(c) C
(d) D

8. In 1990 and 1991, real domestic economic growth in the Soviet Union:
(a) increased slightly
(b) decreased significantly
(c) remained the same in both years
(d) increased in 1990, but decreased significantly in 1991

9. Which of the following is evidence of economic failure of communism in the Soviet Union?
(a) lagging technology compared to Western standards
(b) the inability to supply consumer goods that people wanted
(c) the poor quality of consumer goods
(d) all of the above

10. What was the size of expenditures for the military as a percentage of domestic output in the Soviet Union versus the United States?

(a) 15–20% in Soviet Union versus 15–20% in the United States

(b) 5–10% in the Soviet Union versus 10–15% in the United States

(c) 15–20% in the Soviet Union versus 6% in the United States

(d) 10% in the Soviet Union versus 6% in the United States

11. Which of the following was a cause of low productivity in agriculture in the Soviet Union?

(a) inability to make productive use of the abundance of good farmland in the country

(b) the failure to construct an effective incentive system for agriculture

(c) an increase in the length of the growing season

(d) the overuse of certain chemical fertilizers on crops

12. Which factor contributed to the slowing of Soviet economic growth in the 1980s?

(a) labor shortages

(b) unemployment

(c) idle plant capacity

(d) decreased consumption

13. What was the major success indicator for Soviet enterprises?

(a) profits

(b) the level of prices

(c) production targets

(d) the turnover tax

14. The restructuring of the Soviet economy under Mikhail Gorbachev is referred to as:

(a) *Gosbank*

(b) *glasnost*

(c) *perestroika*

(d) the "second economy"

15. The modernization proposal of Gorbachev's economic program basically involved:

(a) increased production of consumers goods and decreased production of investment goods

(b) reallocation of investment to research and development and to high-tech industries

(c) the building of new housing facilities to address the pressing problems of overcrowding and the deterioration in dwellings

(d) increasing the productivity of agriculture by improving the quality of equipment available to agricultural workers

16. Which of the following is *not* one of the components of the most recent and sweeping reform effort in the former Soviet Union?

(a) privatization

(b) promotion of competition

(c) an increased role for government

(d) more participation in the world economy

17. The effect of price controls on most consumer goods in the Soviet Union was that:

(a) shortages developed because quantity demanded was greater than the quantity supplied by the competitive market at the controlled price set by government

(b) prices rose because the quantity demanded by consumers was greater than the quantity supplied by government

(c) prices fell because the quantity supplied by the competitive market was greater than the quantity demanded by consumers

(d) shortages developed because the quantity demanded by consumers was greater than the quantity supplied by the government at the price set by government

18. Which set of factors contributed to the recent inflationary pressure in the former Soviet Union?

(a) the breakup of state monopolies, the extension of credit to enterprises by the *Gosbank*, the increase in the turnover tax

(b) central planning, production targets, and production bottlenecks

(c) the printing of new currency to finance government, the ruble overhang, and the decontrol of prices

(d) increased military spending, investment in new technology, and making the ruble a convertible currency

19. Which of the following would *not* be considered an important obstacle to the transformation of the former Soviet Union into a market economy?

(a) the need to make simultaneous progress on each component of the reform

(b) the need to change public attitudes and values

(c) the potential for national disintegration

(d) competition from the "second economy"

20. An important avenue that has been suggested for industrialized capitalist nations to assist in the development of a market economy in the former Soviet Union is for those nations to:

(a) eliminate the ruble overhang

(b) increase private investment

(c) forgive past debts

(d) reduce foreign aid

■ **DISCUSSION QUESTIONS**

1. What are the essential features of Marxian ideology on which the command economy of the Soviet Union was based?

2. What were the two principal economic institutions of the Soviet Union? How do these institutions compare with those of the United States?

3. Describe how Soviet planning functioned historically. What are some generalizations you can make about resource use, directives, prices, self-sufficiency, and macroeconomic policies?

4. Why does central planning result in a "coordination" problem? Compare the operation of central planning with the use of markets and prices for economic decision-making.

5. What economic evidence can you present on the failure of communism in the Soviet Union in the 1980s and early 1990s?

6. Discuss the six factors that contributed to the collapse of the Soviet economy. In particular, explain the difference between achieving economic growth by increasing the quantity of resources and increasing economic growth by increasing the productivity and efficiency with which existing resources are used.

7. What were the six elements of Gorbachev's economic reform program? How do these reforms compare with past economic reforms?

8. What problems are posed by privatization for the former Soviet Union as it moves to a market economy?

9. Discuss what must be done in the former Soviet Union to promote competition. To what extent are "state monopolies" a problem?

10. What is the traditional role for government in a market economy? Describe the anticipated changes in the role of government in the former Soviet Union as it adopts capitalism.

11. Why was there a need for price reform in the former Soviet Union in the transition to a market economy? What has been the *general* effect of this change? Use a supply and demand graph to explain the effect of the price decontrol on a specific product.

12. What is the major problem confronting the former Soviet Union as it seeks to join the world economy?

13. Present three reasons why there is inflation in the former Soviet Union as it transforms its economy into a market economy.

14. What are the major obstacles to the development of capitalism in the former Soviet Union? Describe the technical problems, the attitudinal problems, and the political problems. Why must the economic reforms be achieved simultaneously?

15. Cite and discuss the positive factors that will aid in the transition to capitalism for the former Soviet Union.

16. What are the contributions of foreign aid and private investment in helping the former Soviet Union? What are the criticisms of these efforts?

17. How will membership in international organizations help the former Soviet Union? What are the key international organizations or institutions in which membership has been or will be sought?

18. Evaluate the prospects for the transformation of the economy of the former Soviet Union.

■ **ANSWERS**

Chapter 40 The Soviet Economy in Transition

FILL-IN QUESTIONS

1. *a.* labor; *b.* privately, subsistence, surplus; *c.* publicly owned, class, proletariat

2. state, central

3. *a.* industrialization, military, over, under; *b.* mobilizing, agriculture; *c.* targets, prices; *d.* socialist, capitalist, self; *e.* passive, controlled, unemployment, *Gosbank*, money

4. decentralized, centralized, efficient, inefficient

5. *a.* military, consumer; *b.* inefficient, hurt; *c.* quantity, quality, technological; *d.* more; *e.* inadequate; *f.* ineffective

6. Gorbachev, *perestroika, glasnost*

7. *a.* modernization of industry; *b.* greater decentralization of decision-making; *c.* creation of a limited private enterprise sector; *d.* improved worker discipline and incentive; *e.* a more rational price system; *f.* increased role in the international economy

8. Gorbachev, property, private, sale, stock, corporations, government

9. competition, monopoly

10. limited, legal, competition, income, public, spillover, stabilization

11. controls, inflation

12. convertible, trade

13. decontrol, overhang, currency (or money)

14. technical, attitudes, unity, simultaneous

15. *a.* large and varied natural resources base; *b.* peace dividend (less military spending); *c.* the experiences from the "second economy"; *d.* democratization

16. aid, investment, member, Monetary, Bank, Tariffs and Trade

17. uncertain

PROBLEMS AND PROJECTS

1. *a.* supply and demand; *b.* profit; *c.* state ownership of resources; *d.* command or centrally planned economy; *e.* corporations; *f.* agricultural cooperatives or collective farms; *g.* central economic planning (or production targets); *h.* central economic planning; *i.* free markets and flexible prices; *j.* excise tax; *k.* dictatorship by the party; *l.* the "second economy"

2. *a.* 90, 25; *b.* 55, 25, 30; *c.* 90, 25; *d.* 60, 40, 30, 15

SELF-TEST

1. F, p. 766	**14.** T, p. 772
2. F, p. 766	**15.** T, p. 773
3. F, p. 767	**16.** F, p. 774
4. F, pp. 767–768	**17.** F, pp. 773–774
5. T, p. 767	**18.** T, p. 775
6. F, p. 767	**19.** T, p. 776
7. F, p. 768	**20.** F, p. 777
8. F, p. 769	**21.** T, pp. 776–777
9. T, p. 770	**22.** T, p. 777
10. F, p. 770	**23.** F, p. 777
11. F, p. 770	**24.** T, p. 779
12. F, p. 770	**25.** T, p. 780
13. F, p. 772	

1. *c*, pp. 766–777	**11.** *b*, p. 770
2. *d*, p. 766	**12.** *a*, p. 770
3. *b*, p. 767	**13.** *c*, p. 771
4. *a*, pp. 767–768	**14.** *c*, p. 772
5. *b*, p. 768	**15.** *b*, p. 772
6. *c*, p. 768	**16.** *c*, p. 773
7. *d*, p. 769	**17.** *d*, p. 774
8. *b*, p. 769	**18.** *c*, p. 775
9. *d*, p. 769	**19.** *d*, pp. 776–777
10. *c*, p. 770	**20.** *b*, pp. 779–780

DISCUSSION QUESTIONS

1. pp. 766–767	**10.** pp. 773–774
2. p. 767	**11.** pp. 774–775
3. pp. 767–768	**12.** pp. 775–776
4. pp. 768–769	**13.** pp. 775–776
5. pp. 769–770	**14.** pp. 776–777
6. pp. 770–771	**15.** p. 777
7. p. 772	**16.** pp. 778–779
8. p. 773	**17.** p. 780
9. p. 773	**18.** p. 780

Glossary

Ability-to-pay principle The belief that those who have greater income (or wealth) should be taxed absolutely and relatively more than those who have less.

Abstraction Elimination of irrelevant and noneconomic facts to obtain an economic principle.

Acreage-allotment program The program which determines the total number of acres that are to be used to produce various agricultural products and allocates these acres among individual farmers who are required to limit their plantings to the number of acres allotted to them if they wish to obtain the Support price for their crops.

Actual budget The amount spent by the Federal government (to purchase goods and services and for transfer payments) less the amount of tax revenue collected by it in any (fiscal) year; and which can *not* reliably be used to determine whether it is pursuing an expansionary or contractionary fiscal policy. Compare (*see*) the Full-employment budget.

Actual deficit The size of the Federal government's Budget deficit (*see*) or surplus actually measured or recorded in any given year.

Actual investment The amount which business Firms do invest; equal to Planned investment plus Unplanned investment.

Actual reserves The amount of funds which a Member bank has on deposit at the Federal Reserve Bank of its district (plus its vault cash).

Adaptive expectations theory The idea that people determine their expectations about future events (for example, inflation) on the basis of past and present events (rates of inflation) and only change their expectations as events unfold.

Adjustable pegs The device used in the Bretton Woods system (*see*) to change Exchange rates in an orderly way to eliminate persistent Payments deficits and surpluses: each nation defined its monetary unit in terms of (pegged it to) gold or the dollar, kept the Rate of exchange for its money stable in the short run, and changed (adjusted) it in the long run when faced with international disequilibrium.

Adverse selection problem A problem which arises when information known to one party to a contract is not known to the other party, causing the latter to incur major costs. Example: Individuals who have the poorest health are more likely to buy health insurance.

AFDC (*See* Aid to families with dependent children.)

Aggregate demand A schedule or curve which shows the total quantity of goods and services that will be demanded (purchased) at different price levels.

Aggregate demand-aggregate supply model The macroeconomic model which uses Aggregate demand and Aggregate supply (*see* both) to determine and explain the Price level and the real Domestic output.

Aggregate expenditures The total amount spent for final goods and services in the economy.

Aggregate expenditures–domestic output approach Determination of the Equilibrium gross domestic product (*see*) by finding the real GDP at which Aggregate expenditures are equal to the Domestic output.

Aggregate expenditures schedule A schedule or curve which shows the total amount spent for final goods and services at different levels of real GDP.

Aggregate supply A schedule or curve which shows the total quantity of goods and services that will be supplied (produced) at different price levels.

Aggregation Combining individual units or data into one unit or number. For example, all prices of individual goods and services are combined into a Price level, or all units of output are aggregated into Real gross domestic product.

Agricultural Adjustment Act The Federal act of 1933 which established the Parity concept (*see*) as the cornerstone of American agricultural policy and provided Price supports for farm products, restriction of agricultural production, and the disposal of surplus output.

Aid to families with dependent children (AFDC) A state-administered and partly federally funded program in the United States which provides aid to families in which dependent children do not have the support of a parent because of his or her death, disability, or desertion.

Alcoa case The case decided by the Federal courts in 1945 in which the courts ruled that the possession of monopoly power, no matter how reasonably that power had been used, was a violation of the antitrust laws; and which overturned the Rule of reason (*see*) applied in the U.S. Steel case (*see*).

Allocative efficiency The apportionment of resources among firms and industries to obtain the production of the products most wanted by society (consumers); the output of each product at which its Marginal cost and Price are equal.

Allocative factor The ability of an economy to reallocate resources to achieve the Economic growth which the Supply factors (*see*) make possible.

American Federation of Labor (AFL) The organization of affiliated Craft unions formed in 1886.

Annually balanced budget The equality of government expenditures and tax collections during a year.

Anticipated inflation Inflation (*see*) at a rate which was equal to the rate expected in that period of time.

Applied economics (*See* Policy economics.)

Appreciation of the dollar An increase in the value of the dollar relative to the currency of another nation; a dollar now buys a larger amount of the foreign currency. For example, if the dollar price of a British pound changes from $3 to $2, the dollar has appreciated.

Asset Anything of monetary value owned by a firm or individual.

Asset demand for money The amount of money people want to hold as a Store of value (the amount of their financial assets they wish to have in the form of Money); and which varies inversely with the Rate of interest.

Authoritarian capitalism As economic system (method of organization) in which property resources are privately owned and government extensively directs and controls the economy.

Average fixed costs The total Fixed cost (*see*) of a Firm divided by its output (the quantity of product produced).

Average product The total output produced per unit of a resource employed (total product divided by the quantity of a resource employed).

Average propensity to consume Fraction of Disposable income which households spend for consumer goods and services; consumption divided by Disposable income.

Average propensity to save Fraction of Disposable income which households save; Saving divided by Disposable income.

Average revenue Total revenue from the sale of a product divided by the quantity of the product sold (demanded); equal to the price at which the product is sold so long as all units of the product are sold at the same price.

Average tax rate Total tax paid divided by total (taxable) income; the tax rate on total (taxable) income.

Average (total) cost The Total cost of a Firm divided by its output (the quantity of product produced); equal to Average fixed cost (*see*) plus Average variable cost (*see*).

Average variable cost The total Variable cost (*see*) of a Firm divided by its output (the quantity of product produced).

Backflows The return of workers to the countries from which they originally migrated.

Balanced budget multiplier The effect of equal increases (decreases) in government spending for goods and services and in taxes is to increase (decrease) the Equilibrium gross domestic product by the amount of the equal increases (decreases).

Balance of payments deficit The sum of the Balance on current account (*see*) and the Balance on the capital account (*see*) is negative.

Balance of payments surplus The sum of the Balance on current account (*see*) and the Balance on the capital account (*see*) is positive.

Balance on current account The exports of goods (merchandise) and services of a nation less its imports of goods (merchandise) and services plus its Net investment income and Net transfers.

Balance on goods and services The exports of goods (merchandise) and services of a nation less its imports of goods (merchandise) and services.

Balance on the capital account The Capital inflows (*see*) of a nation less its Capital outflows (*see*).

Balance sheet A statement of the Assets (*see*), Liabilities (*see*), and Net worth (*see*) of a firm or individual at some given time.

Balanced-budget amendment Proposed constitutional amendment which would require Congress to balance the Federal budget annually.

Bank deposits The deposits which banks have at the Federal Reserve Banks (*see*).

Bankers' bank A bank which accepts the deposits of and makes loans to Depository institutions; a Federal Reserve Bank.

Bank reserves Bank reserves held at the Federal Reserve Banks (*see*) plus bank Vault cash (*see*).

Barrier to entry Anything that artificially prevents the entry of Firms into an industry.

Barter The exchange of one good or service for another good or service.

Base year The year with which prices in other years are compared when a Price index (*see*) is constructed.

Benefit-cost analysis Deciding whether to employ resources and the quantity of resources to employ for a project or program (for the production of a good or service) by comparing the marginal benefits with the marginal costs.

Benefit-loss rate The percentage by which subsidy benefits in a Negative income tax plan (*see*) are reduced as earned income rises.

Benefits-received principle The belief that those who receive the benefits of goods and services provided by government should pay the taxes required to finance them.

Big business A business Firm which either produces a large percentage of the total output of an industry, is large (in terms of number of employees or stockholders, sales, assets, or profits) compared with other Firms in the economy, or both.

Bilateral monopoly A market in which there is a single seller (Monopoly) and a single buyer (Monopsony).

Blacklisting The passing from one employer to another of the names of workers who favor the formation of labor unions and who ought not to be hired.

Board of Governors The seven-member group that supervises and controls the money and banking system of the United States; formally, the Board of Governors of the Federal Reserve System; the Federal Reserve Board.

Brain drain The emigration of highly educated, highly skilled workers from a country.

Break-even income The level of Disposable income at which Households plan to consume (spend) all of their income (for consumer goods and services) and to save none of it; also denotes that level of earned income at which subsidy payments become zero in an income maintenance program.

Break-even point Any output which a (competitive) Firm might produce at which its Total cost and Total revenue would be equal; an output at which it has neither an Economic profit nor a loss.

Bretton Woods system The international monetary system developed after World War II in which Adjustable pegs (*see*) were employed, the International Monetary Fund (*see*) helped to stabilize Foreign exchange rates, and gold and the dollar (*see*) were used as International monetary reserves (*see*).

Budget deficit The amount by which the expenditures of the Federal government exceed its revenues in any year.

Budget line A line which shows the different combinations to two products a consumer can purchase with a given money income.

Budget restraint The limit the size of the consumer's income (and the prices that must be paid for the goods and services) imposes on the ability of an individual consumer to obtain goods and services.

Built-in stability The effect of Nondiscretionary fiscal policy (*see*) on the economy; when Net taxes vary directly with the Gross domestic product, the fall (rise) in Net taxes during a recession (inflation) helps to eliminate unemployment (inflationary pressures).

Business cycle Recurrent ups and downs over a period of years in the level of economic activity.

Business unionism The belief that the labor union should concern itself with such practical and short-run objectives as higher wages, shorter hours, and improved working conditions and should not concern itself with long-run and idealistic changes in the capitalistic system.

Capital Human-made resources used to produce goods and services; goods which do not directly satisfy human wants; capital goods.

Capital account The section in a nation's International balance of payments (*see*) in which are recorded the Capital inflows (*see*) and the Capital outflows (*see*) of that nation.

Capital account deficit A negative Balance on the capital account (*see*).

Capital account surplus A positive Balance on the capital account (*see*).

Capital flight The transfer of savings from less developed to industrially advanced countries to avoid government expropriation, taxation, and high rates of inflation or to realize better investment opportunities.

Capital gain The gain realized when securities or properties are sold for a price greater than the price paid for them.

Capital goods (*See* Capital.)

Capital inflow The expenditures made by the residents of foreign nations to purchase real and financial capital from the residents of a nation.

Capital-intensive commodity A product which requires a relatively large amount of Capital to produce.

Capital outflow The expenditures made by the residents of a nation to purchase real and financial capital from the residents of foreign nations.

Capital-saving technological advance An improvement in technology that permits a greater quantity of a product to be produced with a given amount of Capital (or the same amount of the product to be produced with a smaller amount of Capital).

Capital-using technological advance An improvement in technology that requires the use of a greater amount of Capital to produce a given quantity of a product.

Cartel A formal written or oral agreement among Firms to set the price of the product and the outputs of the individual firms or to divide the market for the product geographically.

Causation A cause-and-effect relationship; one or several events bring about or result in another event.

CEA (*See* Council of Economic Advisers.)

Cease-and-desist order An order from a court or government agency (commission or board) to a corporation or individual to stop engaging in a specified practice.

Ceiling price (*See* Price ceiling.)

Celler-Kefauver Act The Federal act of 1950 which amended the Clayton Act (*see*) by prohibiting the acquisition of the assets of one firm by another firm when the effect would be to lessen competition.

Central bank A bank whose chief function is the control of the nation's money supply.

Central economic planning Government determination of the objectives of the economy and the direction of its resources to the attainment of these objectives.

Ceteris paribus assumption (*See* "Other things being equal" assumption.)

Change in amount consumed (Increase or decrease in consumption spending that results from an increase or decrease in Disposable income, the Consumption schedule (curve) remaining unchanged; movement from one row (point) to another on the same Consumption schedule (curve).

Change in amount saved Increase or decrease in Saving that results from an increase or decrease in Disposable income, the Saving schedule (curve) remaining unchanged; movement from one row (point) to another on the same Saving schedule (curve).

Change in the consumption schedule An increase or decrease in consumption at each level of Disposable income caused by changes in the Nonincome determinants of consumption and saving (*see*); an upward or downward movement of the Consumption schedule.

Change in the saving schedule An increase or decrease in Saving at each level of Disposable income caused by changes in the Nonincome determinants of consumption and saving (*see*); an upward or downward movement of the Saving schedule.

Checkable deposit Any deposit in a commercial bank or Thrift institution against which a check may be written; includes Demand deposits and now, ATS, and share draft accounts.

Checking account A Checkable deposit (*see*) in a Commercial bank or Thrift institution.

Circuit velocity of money (*See* Velocity of money.)

Circular flow of income The flow of resources from Households to Firms and of products from Firms to Households accompanied in an economy using money by flows of money from Households to Firms and from Firms to Households.

Classical range The vertical segment of the Aggregate supply curve along which the economy is at Full employment.

Classical theory The Classical theory of employment (*see*).

Classical theory of employment The Macroeconomic generalizations accepted by most economists before the 1930s which led to the conclusion that a capitalistic economy would employ its resources fully.

Clayton Act The Federal antitrust act of 1914 which strengthened the Sherman Act (*see*) by making it illegal for business firms to engage in certain specified practices.

Clean Air Act of 1990 Legislation embodying a variety of specific measures to deal with air pollution, urban smog, motor vehicle emissions, ozone depletion, and acid rain.

Closed economy An economy which neither exports nor imports goods and services.

Close-down case The circumstance in which a Firm would experience a loss greater than its total Fixed cost if it were to produce any output greater than zero; alternatively, a situation in which a firm would cease to operate when the price at which it can sell its product is less than its Average variable cost.

Closed shop A place of employment at which only workers who are already members of a labor union may be hired.

Coase theorem The idea that Externality problems may be resolved through private negotiations of the affected parties.

Coincidence of wants The item (good or service) which one trader wishes to obtain is the same item which another trader desires to give up and the item which the second trader wishes to acquire is the same item the first trader desires to surrender.

COLA (*See* Cost-of-living adjustment.)

Collection of checks The process by which funds are transferred from the checking accounts of the writers of checks to the checking accounts of the recipients of the checks; also called the "clearing" of checks.

Collective voice The function a union performs for its members as a group when it communicates their problems and grievances to management and presses management for a satisfactory resolution to them.

Collusion A situation in which Firms act together and in agreement (collude) to set the price of the product and the output each firm will produce or to determine the geographic area in which each firm will sell.

Collusive oligopoly Occurs when the few firms composing an oligopolistic industry reach an explicit or unspoken agreement to fix prices, divide a market, or otherwise restrict competition; may take the form of a Cartel (*see*), Gentlemen's agreement (*see*), or Price leadership (*see*).

Command economy An economic system (method of organization) in which property resources are publicly owned and Central economic planning (*see*) is used to direct and coordinate economic activities.

Commercial bank Firm which has a charter from either a state government or the Federal government to engage in the business of banking.

Commercial banking system All Commercial banks and Thrift institutions as a group.

Communism (*See* Command economy.)

Company union An organization of employees which is dominated by the employer (the company) and does not engage in genuine collective bargaining with the employer.

Comparable worth doctrine The belief that women should receive the same salaries (wages) as men when the levels of skill, effort, and responsibility in their different jobs are the same.

Comparative advantage A lower relative or Comparative cost (*see*) than another producer.

Comparative cost The amount the production of one product must be reduced to increase the production of another product; Opportunity cost (*see*).

Compensation to employees Wages and salaries paid by employers to workers plus Wage and salary supplements (*see*).

Competing goods (*See* Substitute goods.)

Competition The presence in a market of a large number of independent buyers and sellers and the freedom of buyers and sellers to enter and leave the market.

Competitive industry's short-run supply curve The horizontal summation of the short-run supply curves of the Firms in a purely competitive industry (*See* Pure competition); a curve which shows the total quantities that will be offered for sale at various prices by the Firms in an industry in the Short run (*see*).

Competitive labor market A market in which a large number of (noncolluding) firms demand a particular type of labor from a large number of nonunionized workers.

Complementary goods Goods or services for which there is an inverse relationship between the price of one and the demand for the other; when the price of one falls (rises) the demand for the other increases (decreases).

Complex multiplier The Multiplier (*see*) when changes in the Gross domestic product change Net taxes and Imports, as well as Saving.

Concentration ratio The percentage of the total sales of an industry made by the four (or some other number) largest sellers (Firms) in the industry.

Conglomerate combination A group of Plants (*see*) owned by a single Firm and engaged at one or more stages in the production of different products (of products which do not compete with each other).

Conglomerate merger The merger of a Firm in one Industry with a Firm in another Industry (with a Firm that is neither supplier, customer, nor competitor).

Congress of Industrial Organizations (CIO) The organization of affiliated Industrial unions formed in 1936.

Constant-cost industry An industry in which the expansion of the Industry by the entry of new Firms has no effect on the prices the Firms in the industry pay for resources and no effect, therefore, on their cost schedules (curves).

Consumer goods Goods and services which satisfy human wants directly.

Consumer sovereignty Determination by consumers of the types and quantities of goods and services that are produced from the scarce resources of the economy.

Consumption of fixed capital Estimate of the amount of Capital worn out or used up (consumed) in producing the Gross domestic product; depreciation.

Consumption schedule Schedule which shows the amounts Households plan to spend for Consumer goods at different levels of Disposable income.

Contractionary fiscal policy A decrease in Aggregate demand brought about by a decrease in Government expenditures for goods and services, an increase in Net taxes, or some combination of the two.

Corporate income tax A tax levied on the net income (profit) of Corporations.

Corporation A legal entity ("person") chartered by a state or the Federal government, and distinct and separate from the individuals who own it.

Correlation Systematic and dependable association between two sets of data (two kinds of events).

Cost-of-living adjustment An increase in the incomes (wages) of workers which is automatically received by them when there is inflation in the economy and guaranteed by a clause in their labor contracts with their employer.

Cost-plus pricing A procedure used by (oligopolistic) Firms to determine the price they will charge for a product and in which a percentage markup is added to the estimated average cost of producing the product.

Cost-push inflation Inflation that results from a decrease in Aggregate supply (from higher wage rates and raw material prices) and which is accompanied by decreases in real output and employment (by increases in the Unemployment rate).

Cost ratio The ratio of the decrease in the production of the product to the increase in the production of another product when resources are shifted from the production of the first to the production of the second product; the amount the production of one product decreases when the production of a second product increases by one unit.

Council of Economic Advisers A group of three persons which advises and assists the President of the United States on economic matters (including the preparation of the economic report of the President to Congress).

Craft union A labor union which limits its membership to workers with a particular skill (craft).

Credit An accounting notation that the value of an asset (such as the foreign money owned by the residents of a nation) has increased.

Credit union An association of persons who have a common tie (such as being employees of the same Firm or members of the same Labor union) which sells shares to (accepts deposits from) its members and makes loans to them.

Criminal-conspiracy doctrine The (now outdated) legal doctrine that combinations of workers (Labor unions) to raise wages were criminal conspiracies and, therefore, illegal.

Cross elasticity of demand The ratio of the percentage change in Quantity demanded of one good to the percentage change in the price of some other good. A negative coefficient indicates the two products are Substitute goods; a positive coefficient indicates Complementary goods.

Crowding model of occupational discrimination A model of labor markets that assumes Occupational discrimination (*see*) against women and blacks has kept them out of many occupations and forced them into a limited number of other occupations in which the large Supply of labor (relative to the Demand) results in lower wages and incomes.

Crowding-out effect The rise in interest rates and the resulting decrease in planned investment spending in the economy caused by increased borrowing in the money market by the Federal government.

Currency Coins and Paper money.

Currency appreciation (*See* Exchange rate appreciation.)

Currency depreciation (*See* Exchange rate depreciation.)

Current account The section in a nation's International balance of payments (*see*) in which are recorded its exports and imports of goods (merchandise) and services, its net investment income, and its net transfers.

Current account deficit A negative Balance on current account (*see*).

Current account surplus A positive Balance on current account (*see*).

Customary economy (*See* Traditional economy.)

Cyclical deficit A Federal Budget deficit which is caused by a recession and the consequent decline in tax revenues.

Cyclical unemployment Unemployment caused by insufficient Aggregate expenditures.

Cyclically balanced budget The equality of Government expenditures and Net tax collections over the course of a Business cycle; deficits incurred during periods of recession are offset by surpluses obtained during periods of prosperity (inflation).

Debit An accounting notation that the value of an asset (such as the foreign money owned by the residents of a nation) has decreased.

Declining economy An economy in which Net private domestic investment (*see*) is less than zero (Gross private domestic investment is less than Depreciation).

Declining industry An industry in which Economic profits are negative (losses are incurred) and which will, therefore, decrease its output as Firms leave the industry.

Decrease in demand A decrease in the Quantity demanded of a good or service at every price; a shift of the Demand curve to the left.

Decrease in supply A decrease in the Quantity supplied of a good or service at every price; a shift of the Supply curve to the left.

Deduction Reasoning from assumptions to conclusions; a method of reasoning that tests a hypothesis (an assumption) by comparing the conclusions to which it leads with economic facts.

Deflating Finding the Real gross domestic product (*see*) by decreasing the dollar value of the Gross domestic product produced in a year in which prices were higher than in the Base year (*see*).

Deflation A fall in the general (average) level of prices in the economy.

Demand A Demand schedule or a Demand curve (*see* both).

Demand curve A curve which shows the amounts of a good or service buyers wish to purchase at various prices during some period of time.

Demand deposit A deposit in a Commercial bank against which checks may be written; a Checking account or checking-account money.

Demand-deposit multiplier (*See* Monetary multiplier.)

Demand factor The increase in the level of Aggregate demand which brings about the Economic growth made possible by an increase in the productive potential of the economy.

Demand management The use of Fiscal policy (*see*) and Monetary policy (*see*) to increase or decrease Aggregate demand.

Demand-pull inflation Inflation which is the result of an increase in Aggregate demand.

Demand schedule A schedule which shows the amounts of a good or service buyers wish to purchase at various prices during some period of time.

Dependent variable A variable which changes as a consequence of a change in some other (independent) variable; the "effect" or outcome.

Depository institution A Firm that accepts the deposits of Money of the public (businesses and persons); Commercial banks, Savings and loan associations, Mutual savings banks, and Credit unions.

Depository Institutions Deregulation and Monetary Control Act Federal legislation of 1980 which, among other things, allowed Thrift institutions to accept Checkable deposits and to use the check-clearing facilities of the Federal Reserve and to borrow from the Federal Reserve Banks; subjected the Thrifts to the reserve requirements of the Fed; and provided for the gradual elimination of the maximum interest rates that could be paid by Depository institutions on Savings and Time deposits.

Depreciation (*See* Consumption of fixed capital.)

Depreciation of the dollar A decrease in the value of the dollar relative to another currency; a dollar now buys a smaller amount of the foreign currency. For example, if the dollar price of a British pound changes from $2 to $3, the dollar has depreciated.

Derived demand The demand for a good or service which is dependent on or related to the demand for some other good or service; the demand for a resource which depends on the demand for the products it can be used to produce.

Descriptive economics The gathering or collection of relevant economic facts (data).

Determinants of aggregate demand Factors such as consumption, investment, government, and net export spending which, if they change, will shift the aggregate demand curve.

Determinants of aggregate supply Factors such as input prices, productivity, and the legal-institutional environment which, if they change, will shift the aggregate supply curve.

Determinants of demand Factors other than its price which determine the quantities demanded of a good or service.

Determinants of supply Factors other than its price which determine the quantities supplied of a good or service.

Devaluation A decrease in the defined value of a currency.

DI (*See* Disposable income.)

DIDMCA (*See* Depository Institutions Deregulation and Monetary Control Act.)

Differentiated oligopoly An Oligopoly in which the firms produce a Differentiated product (*see*).

Differentiated product A product which differs physically or in some other way from the similar products produced by other Firms; a product which is similar to but not identical with and, therefore, not a perfect substitute for other products; a product such that buyers are not indifferent to the seller from whom they purchase it so long as the price charged by all sellers is the same.

Dilemma of regulation When a Regulatory agency (*see*) must establish the maximum legal price a monopolist may charge, it finds that if it sets the price at the Socially optimal price (*see*) this price is below Average cost (and either bankrupts the Firm or requires that it be subsidized) and if it sets the price at the Fair-return price (*see*) it has failed to eliminate fully the underallocation of resources that is the consequence of unregulated monopoly.

Directing function of prices (*See* Guiding function of prices.)

Directly related Two sets of economic data that change in the same direction; when one variable increases (decreases) the other increases (decreases).

Direct relationship The relationship between two variables which change in the same direction, for example, product price and quantity supplied.

Discount rate The interest rate which the Federal Reserve Banks charge on the loans they make to Depository institutions.

Discouraged workers Workers who have left the Labor force (*see*) because they have not been able to find employment.

Discretionary fiscal policy Deliberate changes in taxes (tax rates) and government spending (spending for goods and services and transfer payment programs) by Congress to achieve a full-employment noninflationary Gross domestic product and economic growth.

Discriminatory discharge The firing of workers who favor formation of labor unions.

Diseconomies of scale Forces which increase the

Average cost of producing a product as the Firm expands the size of its Plant (its output) in the Long run (*see*).

Disinflation A reduction in the rate of Inflation (*see*).

Disposable income Personal income (*see*) less personal taxes (*see*); income available for Personal consumption expenditures (*see*) and Personal saving (*see*).

Dissaving Spending for consumer goods and services in excess of Disposable income; the amount by which Personal consumption expenditures (*see*) exceed Disposable income.

Division of labor Dividing the work required to produce a product into a number of different tasks which are performed by different workers; Specialization (*see*) of workers.

Dollar votes The "votes" which consumers and entrepreneurs in effect cast for the production of the different kinds of consumer and capital goods, respectively, when they purchase them in the markets of the economy.

Domestic capital formation Adding to a nation's stock of Capital by saving part of its own domestic output.

Domestic economic goal Assumed to be full employment with little or no inflation.

Domestic output Gross (or net) domestic product; the total output of final goods and services produced in the economy.

Double counting Including the value of Intermediate goods (*see*) in the Gross domestic product; counting the same good or service more than once.

Double taxation Taxation of both corporate net income (profits) and the dividends paid from this net income when they become the Personal income of households.

Dumping The sale of products below cost in a foreign country.

Du Pont cellophane case The antitrust case brought against du Pont in which the U.S. Supreme Court ruled (in 1956) that while du Pont (and one licensee) had a monopoly in the narrowly defined market for cellophane it did not monopolize the more broadly defined market for flexible packaging materials, and was not guilty, therefore, of violating the Sherman Act.

Durable good A consumer good with an expected life (use) of one year or more.

Dynamic progress The development over time of more efficient (less costly) techniques of producing existing products and of improved products; technological progress.

Earnings The money income received by a worker; equal to the Wage (rate) multiplied by the quantity of labor supplied (the amount of time worked) by the worker.

Easy money policy Expanding the Money supply.

EC European Economic Community (*See* European Common Market.)

Economic analysis Deriving Economic principles (*see*) from relevant economic facts.

Economic concentration A description or measure of the degree to which an industry is monopolistic or competitive. (*See* Concentration ratio.)

Economic cost A payment that must be made to obtain and retain the services of a resource; the income a Firm must provide to a resource supplier to attract the resource away from an alternative use; equal to the quantity of other products that cannot be produced when resources are employed to produce a particular product.

Economic efficiency The relationship between the input of scarce resources and the resulting output of a good or service; production of an output with a given dollar-and-cents value with the smallest total expenditure for resources; obtaining the largest total production of a good or service with resources of a given dollar-and-cents value.

Economic growth (1) An increase in the Production possibilities schedule or curve that results from an increase in resource supplies or an improvement in Technology; (2) an increase either in real output (Gross domestic product) or in real output per capita.

Economic integration Cooperation among and the complete or partial unification of the economies of different nations; the elimination of the barriers to trade among these nations; the bringing together of the markets in each of the separate economies to form one large (a common) market.

Economic law (*See* Economic principle.)

Economic model A simplified picture of reality; an abstract generalization.

Economic perspective A viewpoint which envisions individuals and institutions making rational or purposeful decisions based on a consideration of the benefits and costs associated with their actions.

Economic policy Course of action that will correct or avoid a problem.

Economic principle Generalization of the economic behavior of individuals and institutions.

Economic profit The Total revenue of a firm less all its Economic costs; also called "pure profit" and "above normal profit."

Economic regulation (*See* Industrial regulation.)

Economic rent The price paid for the use of land and other natural resources, the supply of which is fixed (perfectly inelastic).

Economics Social science concerned with using scarce resources to obtain the maximum satisfaction of the unlimited material wants of society.

Economic theory Deriving economic principles (*see*) from relevant economic facts; an Economic principle (*see*).

Economies of scale The forces which reduce the Average cost of producing a product as the Firm expands the size of its Plant (its output) in the Long run (*see*); the economies of mass production.

Economizing problem Society's material wants are unlimited but the resources available to produce the goods and services that satisfy wants are limited (scarce); the inability of any economy to produce unlimited quantities of goods and services.

Efficiency loss of a tax The loss of net benefits to society because a tax reduces the production and consumption of a taxed good below the allocatively efficient level.

Efficiency wage A wage which minimizes wage costs per unit of output.

Efficient allocation of resources That allocation of the resources of an economy among the production of different products which leads to the maximum satisfaction of the wants of consumers.

Elastic demand The Elasticity coefficient (*see*) is greater than one; the percentage change in Quantity demanded is greater than the percentage change in price.

Elasticity coefficient The number obtained when the percentage change in Quantity demanded (or supplied) is divided by the percentage change in the price of the commodity.

Elasticity formula The price elasticity of demand (supply) is equal to

percentage change in quantity

$$\frac{\text{demanded (supplied)}}{\text{percentage change in price}}$$

which is equal to

$$\frac{\text{change in quantity demanded (supplied)}}{\text{original quantity demanded (supplied)}}$$

divided by $\dfrac{\text{change in price}}{\text{original price}}$

Elastic supply The Elasticity coefficient (*see*) is greater than one; the percentage change in Quantity supplied is greater than the percentage change in price.

Emission fees Special fees that might be levied against those who discharge pollutants into the environment.

Employment Act of 1946 Federal legislation which committed the Federal government to the maintenance of economic stability (Full employment, stable prices, and Economic growth); established the Council of Economic Advisers (*see*); and the Joint Economic Committee (*see*); and provided for the annual economic report of the President to Congress.

Employment discrimination The employment of whites before blacks (and other minority groups) are employed and the discharge of blacks (and other minority groups) before whites are discharged.

Employment rate   The percentage of the Labor force (*see*) employed at any time.

Entrepreneurial ability   The human resource which combines the other resources to produce a product, makes nonroutine decisions, innovates, and bears risks.

Equality vs. efficiency tradeoff   The decrease in Economic efficiency (*see*) that appears to accompany a decrease in Income inequality (*see*); the presumption that an increase in Income inequality is required to increase Economic efficiency.

Equalizing differences   The differences in the Wages received by workers in different jobs which compensate for nonmonetary differences in the jobs.

Equation of exchange $MV = PQ$; in which M is the Money supply (*see*), V is the Income velocity of money (*see*), P is the Price level, and Q is the physical volume of final goods and services produced.

Equilibrium domestic output   The real Domestic output at which the Aggregate demand curve intersects the Aggregate supply curve.

Equilibrium gross domestic product   The Gross domestic product at which the total quantity of final goods and services produced (the Domestic output) is equal to the total quantity of final goods and services purchased (Aggregate expenditures).

Equilibrium position   The point at which the Budget line (*see*) is tangent to an Indifference curve (*see*) in the indifference curve approach to the theory of consumer behavior.

Equilibrium price   The price in a competitive market at which the Quantity demanded (*see*) and the Quantity supplied (*see*) are equal; at which there is neither a shortage nor a surplus; and at which there is no tendency for price to rise or fall.

Equilibrium price level   The price level at which the Aggregate demand curve intersects the Aggregate supply curve.

Equilibrium quantity   The Quantity demanded (*see*) and Quantity supplied (*see*) at the Equilibrium price (*see*) in a competitive market.

Equilibrium real domestic output   The real domestic output which is determined by the equality (intersection) of Aggregate demand and Aggregate supply.

European Common Market   The association of twelve European nations initiated in 1958 to abolish gradually the Tariffs and Import quotas that exist among them, to establish common Tariffs for goods imported from outside the member nations, to allow the eventual free movement of labor and capital among them, and to create other common economic policies.

European Economic Community (EC)   (*See* European Common Market.)

Excess reserves   The amount by which a member bank's Actual reserves (*see*) exceeds its Required reserves (*see*); Actual reserves minus Required reserves.

Exchange control   (*See* Foreign exchange control.)

Exchange rate   The Rate of exchange (*see*),

Exchange rate appreciation   An increase in the value of a nation's money in foreign exchange markets; an increase in the Rates of exchange for foreign monies.

Exchange rate depreciation   A decrease in the value of a nation's money in foreign exchange markets; a decrease in the Rates of exchange for foreign monies.

Exchange rate determinant   Any factor other than the Rate of exchange (*see*) that determines the demand for and the supply of a currency in the Foreign exchange market (*see*).

Excise tax   A tax levied on the expenditure for a specific product or on the quantity of the product purchased.

Exclusion principle   The exclusion of those who do not pay for a product from the benefits of the product.

Exclusive unionism   The policies employed by a Labor union to restrict the supply of labor by excluding potential members in order to increase the Wages received by its members; the Policies typically employed by a Craft union (*see*).

Exhaustive expenditure   An expenditure by government that results directly in the employment of economic resources and in the absorption by government of the goods and services these resources produce; a Government purchase (*see*).

Exit mechanism   Leaving a job and searching for another one in order to improve the conditions under which a worker is employed.

Expanding economy   An economy in which Net private domestic investment (*see*) is greater than zero (Gross private domestic investment is greater than Depreciation).

Expanding industry   An industry in which Economic profits are obtained by the firms in the industry and which will, therefore, increase its output as new firms enter the industry.

Expansionary fiscal policy   An increase in Aggregate demand brought about by an increase in Government expenditures for goods and services, a decrease in Net taxes, or some combination of the two.

Expectations   What consumers, business Firms, and others believe will happen or what conditions will be in the future.

Expected rate of net profits   Annual profits which a firm anticipates it will obtain by purchasing Capital (by investing) expressed as a percentage of the price (cost) of the Capital.

Expenditures approach   The method which adds all the expenditures made for Final goods and services to measure the Gross domestic product.

Expenditures-output approach   (*See* Aggregate expenditures–domestic output approach.)

Explicit cost   The monetary payment a Firm must make to an outsider to obtain a resource.

Exports Goods and services produced in a given nation and sold to customers in other nations.

Export subsidies Government payments which reduce the price of a product to foreign buyers.

Export transactions A sale of a good or service which increases the amount of foreign money held by the citizens, firms, and governments of a nation.

External benefit (*See* Spillover benefit.)

External cost (*See* Spillover cost.)

External debt Public debt (*see*) owed to foreign citizens, firms, and institutions.

External economic goal (*See* International economic goal.)

Externality (*See* Spillover.)

Face value The dollar or cents value stamped on a coin.

Factors of production Economic resources: Land, Capital, Labor, and Entrepreneurial ability.

Fair-return price The price of a product which enables its producer to obtain a Normal profit (*see*) and which is equal to the Average cost of producing it.

Fallacy of composition Incorrectly reasoning that what is true for the individual (or part) is therefore necessarily true for the group (or whole).

Fallacy of limited decisions The false notion that there are a limited number of economic decisions to be made so that, if government makes more decisions, there will be fewer private decisions to render.

Farm Act of 1990 Farm legislation which reduces the amount of acreage covered by price supports and allows farmers to plant these uncovered acres in alternative crops.

Farm problem The relatively low income of many farmers (compared with incomes in the nonagricultural sectors of the economy) and the tendency for farm income to fluctuate sharply from year to year.

FDIC (*See* Federal Deposit Insurance Corporation.)

Featherbedding Payment by an employer to a worker for work not actually performed.

Federal Advisory Committee The group of twelve commercial bankers which advises the Board of Governors (*see*) on banking policy.

Federal Deposit Insurance Corporation (FDIC) The Federally chartered corporation which insures the deposit liabilities of Commercial banks and Thrift Institutions.

Federal funds rate The interest rate that lending depository institutions charge borrowing institutions for the use of excess reserves.

Federal Open Market Committee (*See* Open Market Committee.)

Federal Reserve Bank Any one of the twelve banks chartered by the United States government to control the Money supply and perform other functions. (*See* Central bank, Quasi-public bank, *and* Banker's bank.)

Federal Reserve Note Paper money issued by the Federal Reserve Banks.

Federal Trade Commission (FTC) The commission of five members established by the Federal Trade Commission Act of 1914 to investigate unfair competitive practices of business Firms, to hold hearings of the complaints of such practices, and to issue Cease-and-desist orders (*see*) when Firms were found to engage in such practices.

Federal Trade Commission Act The Federal act of 1914 which established the Federal Trade Commission (*see*).

Feedback effects The effects which a change in the money supply will have (because it affects the interest rate, planned investment, and the equilibrium GDP on the demand for money which is itself directly related to the GDP.

Female labor force participation rate The percentage of the female population of working age in the Labor force (*see*).

Fewness A relatively small number of sellers (or buyers) of a good or service.

Fiat money Anything that is Money because government has decreed it to be Money.

Final goods Goods which have been purchased for final use and not for resale or further processing or manufacturing (during the year).

Financial capital (*See* Money capital.)

Financing exports and imports The use of Foreign exchange markets by exporters and importers to receive and make payments for goods and services they sell and buy in foreign nations.

Firm An organization that employs resources to produce a good or service for profit and owns and operates one or more Plants (*see*).

(The) firm's short-run supply curve A curve which shows the quantities of a product a Firm in a purely competitive industry (*see* Pure competition) will offer to sell at various prices in the Short run (*see*); the portion of the Firm's short-run Marginal cost (*see*) curve which lies above its Average variable cost curve.

Fiscal federalism The system of transfers (grants) by which the Federal government shares its revenues with state and local governments.

Fiscal policy Changes in government spending and tax collections for the purpose of achieving a full-employment and noninflationary domestic output.

Five fundamental economic questions The five questions which every economy must answer: what to produce, how to produce, how to divide the total output, how to maintain Full employment, and how to assure economic flexibility.

Fixed cost Any cost which in total does not change when the Firm changes its output; the cost of Fixed resources (*see*).

Fixed exchange rate A Rate of exchange that is prevented from rising or falling.

Fixed resource Any resource employed by a Firm the quantity of which the firm cannot change.

Flexible exchange rate A rate of exchange that is determined by the demand for and supply of the foreign money and is free to rise or fall.

Floating exchange rate (*See* Flexible exchange rate.)

Food for peace program The program established under the provisions of Public Law 480 which permits less developed nations to buy surplus American agricultural products and pay for them with their own monies (instead of dollars).

Food stamp program A program in the United States which permits low-income persons to purchase for less than their retail value, or to obtain without cost, coupons that can be exchanged for food items at retail stores.

Foreign competition (*See* Import competition.)

Foreign exchange control The control a government may exercise over the quantity of foreign money demanded by its citizens and business firms and over the Rates of exchange in order to limit its outpayments to its inpayments (to eliminate a Payments deficit, *see*).

Foreign exchange market A market in which the money (currency) used by one nation is used to purchase (is exchanged for) the money used by another nation.

Foreign exchange rate (*See* Rate of exchange.)

Foreign purchases effect The inverse relationship between the Net exports (*see*) of an economy and its Price level (*see*) relative to foreign Price levels.

45-degree line A line along which the value of the GDP (measured horizontally) is equal to the value of Aggregate expenditures (measured vertically).

Fractional reserve A Reserve ratio (*see*) that is less than 100 percent of the deposit liabilities of a Commercial bank.

Freedom of choice Freedom of owners of property resources and money to employ or dispose of these resources as they see fit, of workers to enter any line of work for which they are qualified, and of consumers to spend their incomes in a manner which they deem to be appropriate (best for them).

Freedom of enterprise Freedom of business Firms to employ economic resources, to use these resources to produce products of the firm's own choosing, and to sell these products in markets of their choice.

Freely floating exchange rates Rates of exchange (*see*) which are not controlled and which may, therefore, rise and fall; and which are determined by the demand for and the supply of foreign monies.

Free-rider problem The inability of those who might provide the economy with an economically desirable and indivisible good or service to obtain payment from those who benefit from the good or service because the Exclusion principle (*see*) cannot be applied to it.

Free trade The absence of artificial (government imposed) barriers to trade among individuals and firms in different nations.

Frictional unemployment Unemployment caused by workers voluntarily changing jobs and by temporary lay-offs; unemployed workers between jobs.

Fringe benefits The rewards other than Wages that employees receive from their employers and which include pensions, medical and dental insurance, paid vacations, and sick leaves.

Full employment (1) Using all available resources to produce goods and services; (2) when the Unemployment rate is equal to the Full-employment unemployment rate and there is Frictional and Structural but no Cyclical unemployment (and the Real output of the economy is equal to its Potential real output).

Full-employment budget What government expenditures and revenues and its surplus or deficit would be if the economy were to operate at Full employment throughout the year.

Full-employment unemployment rate The Unemployment rate (*see*) at which there is no Cyclical unemployment (*see*) of the Labor force (*see*); and because some Frictional and Structural unemployment is unavoidable, equal to about 5 or 6 percent.

Full production The maximum amount of goods and services that can be produced from the employed resources of an economy; the absence of Underemployment (*see*).

Functional distribution of income The manner in which the economy's (the national) income is divided among those who perform different functions (provide the economy with different kinds of resources); the division of National income (*see*) into wages and salaries, proprietors' income, corporate profits, interest, and rent.

Functional finance Use of Fiscal policy to achieve a full-employment noninflationary Gross domestic product without regard to the effect on the Public debt (*see*).

Game theory A theory which compares the behavior of participants in games of strategy, such as poker and chess, with that of a small group of mutually interdependent firms (an Oligopoly).

GATT (*See* General Agreement on Tariffs and Trade.)

GDP (*See* Gross domestic product.)

GDP deflator The Price index (*see*) for all final goods and services used to adjust the money (or nominal) GDP to measure the real GDP.

GDP gap Potential Real gross domestic product less actual Real gross domestic product.

General Agreement on Tariffs and Trade The international agreement reached in 1947 by twenty-three nations (including the United States) in which each nation agreed to give equal and nondiscriminatory treatment to the other nations, to reduce tariff rates by multinational negotiations, and to eliminate Import quotas.

General equilibrium analysis A study of the Market system as a whole; of the interrelations among equilibrium prices, outputs, and employments in all the different markets of the economy.

Generalization Statistical or probability statement; statement of the nature of the relation between two or more sets of facts.

Gentleman's agreement An informal understanding on the price to be charged among the firms in an Oligopoly.

Glasnost A Soviet campaign of the mid-1980s for greater "openness" and democratization in political and economic activities.

Gold export point The rate of exchange for a foreign money above which—when nations participate in the International gold standard (*see*)—the foreign money will not be purchased and gold will be sent (exported) to the foreign country to make payments there.

Gold flow The movement of gold into or out of a nation.

Gold import point The Rate of exchange for a foreign money below which—when nations participate in the International gold standard (*see*)—a nation's own money will not be purchased and gold will be sent (imported) into that country by foreigners to make payments there.

Gorbachev's reforms A mid-1980s series of reforms designed to revitalize the Soviet economy. The reforms stressed the modernization of productive facilities, less centralized control, improved worker discipline and productivity, more emphasis on market prices, and an expansion of private economic activity.

Gosbank The state-owned and -operated bank in the former U.S.S.R.

Government purchases Disbursements of money by government for which government receives a currently produced good or service in return; the expenditures of all governments in the economy for Final goods (*see*) and services.

Government transfer payment The disbursement of money (or goods and services) by government for which government receives no currently produced good or service in return.

Gramm-Rudman-Hollings Act Legislation enacted in 1985 by the Federal government requiring annual reductions in Federal budget deficits and, as amended, a balanced budget by 1993; and mandating an automatic decrease in expenditures when Congress and the President cannot agree on how to meet the targeted reductions in the budget deficit.

Grievance procedure The methods used by a Labor union and the Firm to settle disputes that arise during the life of the collective bargaining agreement between them.

Gross domestic product (GDP) The total market value of all Final goods (*see*) and services produced annually within the boundaries of the United States, whether by American or foreign-supplied resources.

Gross national product (GNP) The total market value of all Final goods (*see*) and services produced annually by land, labor, and capital, and entrepreneurial tal-

ent supplied by American residents, whether these resources are located in the United States or abroad.

Gross private domestic investment Expenditures for newly produced Capital goods (*see*)—machinery, equipment, tools, and buildings—and for additions to inventories.

Guaranteed income The minimum income a family (or individual) would receive if a Negative income tax (*see*) were to be adopted.

Guiding function of prices The ability of price changes to bring about changes in the quantities of products and resources demanded and supplied (*See* Incentive function of price.)

Herfindahl index A measure of the concentration and competitiveness of an industry; calculated as the sum of the squared market shares of the individual firms.

Homogeneous oligopoly An Oligopoly in which the firms produce a Standardized product (*see*).

Horizontal axis The "left–right" or "west–east" axis on a graph or grid.

Horizontal combination A group of Plants (*see*) in the same stage of production which are owned by a single Firm (*see*).

Horizontal merger The merger of one or more Firms producing the same product into a single Firm.

Household An economic unit (of one or more persons) which provides the economy with resources and uses the money paid to it for these resources to purchase goods and services that satisfy material wants.

Human-capital discrimination The denial to blacks (and other minority groups) of the same quality and quantity of education and training received by whites.

Human-capital investment Any action taken to increase the productivity (by improving the skills and abilities) of workers; expenditures made to improve the education, health, or mobility of workers.

Hyperinflation A very rapid rise in the price level.

Illegal immigrant A person who unlawfully enters a country.

IMF (*See* International Monetary Fund.)

Immobility The inability or unwillingness of a worker or another resource to move from one geographic area or occupation to another or from a lower-paying to a higher-paying job.

Imperfect competition All markets except Pure competition (*see*); Monopoly, Monopsony, Monopolistic competition, Oligopoly, and Oligopsony (*see all*).

Implicit cost The monetary income a Firm sacrifices when it employs a resource it owns to produce a product rather than supplying the resource in the market; equal to what the resource could have earned in the best-paying alternative employment.

Import competition   Competition which domestic firms encounter from the products and services of foreign suppliers.

Import quota   A limit imposed by a nation on the quantity of a good that may be imported during some period of time.

Imports   Spending by individuals, Firms, and governments of an economy for goods and services produced in foreign nations.

Import transaction   The purchase of a good or service which decreases the amount of foreign money held by citizens, firms, and governments of a nation.

Incentive function of price   The inducement which an increase (a decrease) in the price of a commodity offers to sellers of the commodity to make more (less) of it available; and the inducement which an increase (decrease) in price offers to buyers to purchase smaller (larger) quantities; the Guiding function of prices (*see*).

Incentive pay plan   A compensation scheme which ties worker pay directly to performance. Such plans include piece rates, bonuses, commissions, and profit sharing.

Inclusive unionism   A union which attempts to include all workers employed in an industry as members.

Income approach   The method which adds all the incomes generated by the production of Final goods and services to measure the Gross domestic product.

Income effect   The effect which a change in the price of a product has on the Real income (purchasing power) of a consumer and the resulting effect on the quantity of that product the consumer would purchase after the consequences of the Substitution effect (*see*) have been taken into account (eliminated).

Income elasticity of demand   The ratio of the percentage change in the Quantity demanded of a good to the percentage change in income; it measures the responsiveness of consumer purchases to income changes.

Income inequality   The unequal distribution of an economy's total income among persons or families in the economy.

Income-maintenance system   The programs designed to eliminate poverty and to reduce inequality in the distribution of income.

Incomes policy   Government policy that affects the Nominal incomes of individuals (the wages workers receive) and the prices they pay for goods and services and thereby affects their Real incomes; (*see* Wage-price policy).

Income velocity of money   (*See* Velocity of money.)

Increase in demand   An increase in the Quantity demanded of a good or service at every price; a shift in the Demand curve to the right.

Increase in supply   An increase in the Quantity supplied of a good or service at every price; a shift in the Supply curve to the right.

Increasing-cost industry   An Industry in which the expansion of the Industry through the entry of new firms increases the prices the Firms in the Industry must pay for resources and, therefore, increases their cost schedules (moves their cost curves upward).

Increasing returns   An increase in the Marginal product (*see*) of a resource as successive units of the resource are employed.

Independent goods   Goods or services such that there is no relationship between the price of one and the demand for the other; when the price of one rises or falls the demand for the other remains constant.

Independent variable   The variable which causes a change in some other (dependent) variable.

Indifference curve   A curve which shows the different combinations of two products which give a consumer the same satisfaction or Utility (*see*).

Indifference map   A series of Indifference curves (*see*), each of which represents a different level of Utility; and which together show the preferences of the consumer.

Indirect business taxes   Such taxes as Sales, Excise, and business Property taxes (*see all*), license fees, and Tariffs (*see*) which Firms treat as costs of producing a product and pass on (in whole or in part) to buyers of the product by charging them higher prices.

Individual demand   The Demand schedule (*see*) or Demand curve (*see*) of a single buyer of a good or service.

Individual supply   The Supply schedule (*see*) or Supply curve (*see*) of a single seller of a good or service.

Induction   A method of reasoning that proceeds from facts to Generalization (*see*).

Industrially advanced countries (IACs)   Countries such as the United States, Canada, Japan, and the nations of western Europe which have developed Market economies based on large stocks of technologically advanced capital goods and skilled labor forces.

Industrial policy   Any policy in which government takes a direct and active role in shaping the structure and composition of industry to promote economic growth.

Industrial regulation   The older and more traditional type of regulation in which government is concerned with the prices charged and the services provided the public in specific industries; in contrast to Social regulation (*see*).

Industrial union   A Labor union which accepts as members all workers employed in a particular industry (or by a particular firm) and which contains largely unskilled or semiskilled workers.

Industry   The group of (one or more) Firms that produce identical or similar products.

Inelastic demand   The Elasticity coefficient (*see*) is less than one; the percentage change in price is greater than the percentage change in Quantity demanded.

Inelastic supply   The Elasticity coefficient (*see*) is less than one; the percentage change in price is greater than the percentage change in Quantity supplied.

Inferior good   A good or service of which consumers purchase less (more) at every price when their incomes increase (decrease).

Inflating Finding the Real gross domestic product (*see*) by increasing the dollar value of the Gross domestic product produced in a year in which prices are lower than they were in the Base year (*see*).

Inflation A rise in the general (average) level of prices in the economy.

Inflationary expectations The belief of workers, business Firms, and consumers that there will be substantial inflation in the future.

Inflationary gap The amount by which the Aggregate-expenditures schedule (curve) must decrease (shift downward) to decrease the nominal GDP to the full-employment noninflationary level.

Inflationary recession (*See* Stagflation.)

Infrastructure For the economy, the capital goods usually provided by the Public sector for the use of its citizens and Firms (e.g., highways, bridges, transit systems, wastewater treatment facilities, municipal water systems, and airports). For the Firm, the services and facilities which it must have to produce its products, which would be too costly for it to provide for itself, and which are provided by governments or other Firms (e.g., water, electricity, waste treatment, transportation, research, engineering, finance, and banking).

Injection An addition of spending to the income-expenditure stream: Investment, Government purchases, and Exports.

Injunction An order from a court of law that directs a person or organization not to perform a certain act because the act would do irreparable damage to some other person or persons; a restraining order.

In-kind investment Nonfinancial investment (*see*).

In-kind transfer The distribution by government of goods and services to individuals and for which the government receives no currently produced good or service in return; a Government transfer payment (*see*) made in goods or services rather than in money.

Innovation The introduction of a new product, the use of a new method of production, or the employment of a new form of business organization.

Inpayments The receipts of (its own or foreign) money which the individuals, Firms, and governments of one nation obtain from the sale of goods and services, investment income, Remittances, and Capital inflows from abroad.

Input-output analysis Using an Input-output table (*see*) to examine interdependence among different parts (sectors and industries) of the economy and to make economic forecasts and plans.

Input-output table A table which lists (along the left side) the producing sectors and (along the top) the consuming or using sectors of the economy and which shows quantitatively in each of its rows how the output of a producing sector was distributed among consuming sectors and quantitatively in each of its columns the producing

sectors from which a consuming sector obtained its inputs during some period of time (a year).

Insurable risk An event, the average occurrence of which can be estimated with considerable accuracy, which would result in a loss that can be avoided by purchasing insurance.

Interest The payment made for the use of money (of borrowed funds).

Interest income Income of those who supply the economy with Capital (*see*).

Interest rate The Rate of interest (*see*).

Interest-rate effect The tendency for increases (decreases) in the Price level to increase (decrease) the demand for money; raise (lower) interest rates; and, as a result, to reduce (expand) total spending in the economy.

Interindustry competition Competition or rivalry between the products produced by Firms in one Industry (*see*) and the products produced by Firms in another industry (or in other industries).

Interlocking directorate A situation in which one or more of the members of the board of directors of one Corporation are also on the board of directors of another Corporation; and which is illegal when it reduces competition among the Corporations.

Intermediate goods Goods which are purchased for resale or further processing or manufacturing during the year.

Intermediate range The upsloping segment of the Aggregate supply curve that lies between the Keynesian range and the Classical range (*see both*).

Internal economic goal (*See* Domestic economic goal.)

Internal economics The reduction in the cost of producing or marketing a product that results from an increase in output of the Firm [*see* Economies of (large) scale].

Internally held public debt Public debt (*see*) owed to (United States government securities owned by) American citizens, Firms, and institutions.

International balance of payments Summary statement of the transactions which took place between the individuals, Firms, and governments of one nation and those in all other nations during the year.

International balance of payments deficit (*See* Balance of payments deficit.)

International balance of payments surplus (*See* Balance of payments surplus.)

International Bank for Reconstruction and Development (*See* World Bank.)

International economic goal Assumed to be a current-account balance of zero.

International gold standard An international monetary system employed in the nineteenth and early twentieth centuries in which each nation defined its money in terms of a quantity of gold, maintained a fixed relationship between its gold stock and money supply, and allowed the free importation and exportation of gold.

International Monetary Fund   The international association of nations which was formed after World War II to make loans of foreign monies to nations with temporary Payments deficits (*see*) and to administer the Adjustable pegs (*see*).

International monetary reserves.   The foreign monies and such assets as gold a nation may use to settle a Payments deficit (*see*).

International value of the dollar   The price that must be paid in foreign currency (money) to obtain one American dollar.

Interstate Commerce Commission   The commission established in 1887 to regulate the rates and monitor the services of the railroads in the United States.

Interstate Commerce Commission Act   The Federal legislation of 1887 which established the Interstate Commerce Commission (*see*).

Intrinsic value   The market value of the metal in a coin.

Inverse relationship   The relationship between two variables which change in opposite directions, for example, product price and quantity demanded.

Investment   Spending for (the production and accumulation of) Capital goods (*see*) and additions to inventories.

Investment curve   A curve which shows the amounts firms plan to invest (along the vertical axis) at different income (Gross domestic product) levels (along the horizontal axis).

Investment-demand curve   A curve which shows Rates of interest (along the vertical axis) and the amount of Investment (along the horizontal axis) at each Rate of interest.

Investment-demand schedule   Schedule which shows Rates of interest and the amount of investment at each Rate of interest.

Investment in human capital   (*See* Human-capital investment.)

Investment schedule   A schedule which shows the amounts Firms plan to invest at different income (Gross domestic product) levels.

Invisible hand   The tendency of Firms and resource suppliers seeking to further their self-interests in competitive markets to further the best interest of society as a whole (the maximum satisfaction of wants).

JEC   (*See* Joint Economic Committee.)

Joint Economic Committee   Committee of Senators and members of Congress which investigates economic problems of national interest.

Jurisdictional strike   Withholding from an employer the labor services of its members by a Labor union that is engaged in a dispute with another Labor union over which is to perform a specific kind of work for the employer.

Keynesian economics   The macroeconomic generalizations which are today accepted by most (but not all) economists and which lead to the conclusion that a capitalistic economy does not always employ its resources fully and that Fiscal policy (*see*) and Monetary policy (*see*) can be used to promote Full employment (*see*).

Keynesianism   The philosophical, ideological, and analytical views of the prevailing majority of economists; and their employment theory and stabilization policies.

Keynesian range   The horizontal segment of the Aggregate-supply curve along which the price level is constant as real domestic output changes.

Kinked demand curve   The demand curve which a noncollusive oligopolist sees for its output and which is based on the assumption that rivals will follow a price decrease and will not follow a price increase.

Labor   The physical and mental talents (efforts) of people which can be used to produce goods and services.

Labor force   Persons sixteen years of age and older who are not in institutions and who are employed or are unemployed and seeking work.

Labor-intensive commodity   A product which requires a relatively large amount of Labor to produce.

Labor-Management Relations Act   (*See* Taft-Hartley Act.)

Labor-Management Reporting and Disclosure Act (*See* Landrum-Griffin Act.)

Labor productivity   Total output divided by the quantity of labor employed to produce the output; the Average product (*see*) of labor or output per worker per hour.

Labor theory of value   The Marxian notion that the economic value of any commodity is determined solely by the amount of labor required to produce it.

Labor union   A group of workers organized to advance the interests of the group (to increase wages, shorten the hours worked, improve working conditions, etc.).

Laffer curve   A curve which shows the relationship between tax rates and the tax revenues of government and on which there is a tax rate (between zero and 100 percent) at which tax revenues are a maximum.

Laissez faire capitalism   (*See* Pure capitalism.)

Land   Natural resources ("free gifts of nature") which can be used to produce goods and services.

Land-intensive commodity   A product which requires a relatively large amount of Land to produce.

Landrum-Griffin Act   The Federal act of 1959 which regulates the elections and finances of Labor unions and guarantees certain rights to their members.

Law of conservation of matter and energy The notion that matter can be changed to other matter or into energy but cannot disappear; all production inputs are ultimately transformed into an equal amount of finished product, energy, and waste (pollution).

Law of demand The inverse relationship between the price and the Quantity demanded (*see*) of a good or service during some period of time.

Law of diminishing marginal utility As a consumer increases the consumption of a good or service, the Marginal utility (*see*) obtained from each additional unit of the good or service decreases.

Law of diminishing returns When successive equal increments of a Variable resource (*see*) are added to the Fixed resources (*see*), beyond some level of employment, the Marginal product (*see*) of the Variable resource will decrease.

Law of increasing opportunity cost As the amount of a product produced is increased, the Opportunity cost (*see*)—Marginal cost (*see*)—of producing an additional unit of the product increases.

Law of supply The direct relationship between the price and the Quantity supplied (*see*) of a good or service during some period of time.

Leakage (1) a withdrawal of potential spending from the income-expenditures stream: Saving (*see*), tax payments, and Imports (*see*); (2) a withdrawal which reduces the lending potential of the Commercial banking system.

Leakages-injections approach Determination of the Equilibrium gross domestic product (*see*) by finding the Gross domestic product at which Leakages (*see*) are equal to Injections (*see*).

Least-cost combination rule (of resources) The quantity of each resource a Firm must employ if it is to produce any output at the lowest total cost; the combination on which the ratio of the Marginal product (*see*) of a resource to its Marginal resource cost (*see*) (to its price if the resource is employed in a competitive market) is the same for all resources employed.

Legal cartel theory of regulation The hypothesis that industries want to be regulated so that they may form legal Cartels (*see*) and that government officials (the government) provide the regulation in return for their political and financial support.

Legal immigrant A person who lawfully enters a country.

Legal reserves (deposit) The minimum amount which a Depository institution (*see*) must keep on deposit with the Federal Reserve Bank in its district, or in Vault cash (*see*).

Legal tender Anything that government has decreed must be accepted in payment of a debt.

Lending potential of an individual commercial bank The amount by which a single Commercial bank can safely increase the Money supply by making new loans to (or buying securities from) the public; equal to the Commercial bank's Excess reserves (*see*).

Lending potential of the banking system The amount by which the Commercial banking system (*see*) can increase the Money supply by making new loans to (or buying securities from) the public; equal to the Excess reserves (*see*) of the Commercial banking system multiplied by the Monetary multiplier (*see*).

Less developed countries (LDCs) Most countries of Africa, Asia, and Latin America which are characterized by a lack of capital goods, primitive production technologies, low literacy rates, high unemployment, rapid population growth, and labor forces heavily committed to agriculture.

Liability A debt with a monetary value; an amount owed by a Firm or an individual.

Limited liability Restriction of the maximum that may be lost to a predetermined amount; the maximum amount that may be lost by the owners (stockholders) of a Corporation is the amount they paid for their shares of stock.

Line-item veto A proposal to give the President the power to delete specific expenditure items from spending legislation passed by Congress.

Liquidity Money or things which can be quickly and easily converted into Money with little or no loss of purchasing power.

Loaded terminology Terms which arouse emotions and elicit approval or disapproval.

Loanable funds theory of interest The concept that the supply of and demand for loanable funds determines the equilibrium rate of interest.

Lockout The temporary closing of a place of employment and the halting of production by an employer in order to discourage the formation of a Labor union or to compel a Labor union to modify its demands.

Logrolling The trading of votes by legislators to secure favorable outcomes on decisions to provide public goods and services.

Long run A period of time long enough to enable producers of a product to change the quantities of all the resources they employ; in which all resources and costs are variable and no resources or costs are fixed.

Long-run aggregate supply curve The aggregate supply curve associated with a time period in which input prices (especially nominal wages) are fully responsive to changes in the price level.

Long-run competitive equilibrium The price at which Firms in Pure competition (*see*) neither obtain Economic profit nor suffer losses in the Long run and the total quantity demanded and supplied at that price are equal; a price equal to the minimum long-run average cost of producing the product.

Long-run farm problem The tendency for the incomes of many farmers to decline relative to incomes in the rest of the economy.

Long-run supply A schedule or curve which shows

the prices at which a Purely competitive industry will make various quantities of the product available in the Long run.

Lorenz curve A curve which shows the distribution of income in an economy; and when used for this purpose the cumulated percentage of families (income receivers) is measured along the horizontal axis and the cumulated percentage of income is measured along the vertical axis.

Loss-minimizing case The circumstances which result in a loss which is less than its Total fixed cost when a Firm produces the output at which total profit is a maximum (or total loss is a minimum): when the price at which the firm can sell its product is less than Average total but greater than Average variable cost.

M1 The narrowly defined Money supply; the Currency and Checkable deposits (*see*) not owned by the Federal government, Federal Reserve Banks, or Depository institutions.

M2 A more broadly defined Money supply; equal to M1 (*see*) plus Noncheckable savings deposits, small Time deposits (deposits of less than $100,000), Money market deposit accounts, and individual Money market mutual fund balances.

M3 A still more broadly defined Money supply; equal to M2 (*see*) plus large Time deposits (deposits of $100,000 or more).

Macroeconomics The part of economics concerned with the economy as a whole; with such major aggregates as the household, business, and governmental sectors and with totals for the economy.

Managed floating exchange rate An Exchange rate that is allowed to change (float) to eliminate persistent Payments deficit and surpluses and is controlled (managed) to reduce day-to-day fluctuations.

Managerial-opposition hypothesis The explanation that attributes the relative decline of unionism in the United States to the increased and more aggressive opposition of management to unions.

Managerial prerogatives The decisions, often enumerated in the contract between a Labor union and a business Firm, that the management of the Firm has the sole right to make.

Marginal cost The extra (additional) cost of producing one more unit of output; equal to the change in Total cost divided by the change in output (and in the short run to the change in Total variable cost divided by the change in output).

Marginal labor cost The amount by which the total cost of employing Labor increases when a Firm employs one additional unit of Labor (the quantity of other resources employed remaining constant); equal to the change in the total cost of Labor divided by the change in the quantity of Labor employed.

Marginal product The additional output produced when one additional unit of a resource is employed (the quantity of all other resources employed remaining constant); equal to the change in total product divided by the change in the quantity of a resource employed.

Marginal productivity theory of income distribution The contention that the distribution of income is equitable when each unit of each resource receives a money payment equal to its marginal contribution to the firm's revenue (its Marginal revenue product).

Marginal propensity to consume Fraction of any change in Disposable income which is spent for Consumer goods; equal to the change in consumption divided by the change in Disposable income.

Marginal propensity to save Fraction of any change in Disposable income which households save; equal to change in Saving (*see*) divided by the change in Disposable income.

Marginal rate of substitution The rate (at the margin) at which a consumer is prepared to substitute one good or service for another and remain equally satisfied (have the same total Utility); and equal to the slope of an Indifference curve (*see*).

Marginal resource cost The amount by which the total cost of employing a resource increases when a Firm employs one additional unit of the resource (the quantity of all other resources employed remaining constant); equal to the change in the Total cost of the resource divided by the change in the quantity of the resource employed.

Marginal revenue The change in the Total revenue of the Firm that results from the sale of one additional unit of its product; equal to the change in Total revenue divided by the change in the quantity of the product sold (demanded).

Marginal-revenue–marginal cost approach The method which finds the total output at which Economic profit (*see*) is a maximum (or losses a minimum) by comparing the Marginal revenue (*see*) and the Marginal cost (*see*) of each additional unit of output.

Marginal revenue product The change in the Total revenue of the Firm when it employs one additional unit of a resource (the quantity of all other resources employed remaining constant); equal to the change in Total revenue divided by the change in the quantity of the resource employed.

Marginal tax rate The fraction of additional (taxable) income that must be paid in taxes.

Marginal utility The extra Utility (*see*) a consumer obtains from the consumption of one additional unit of a good or service; equal to the change in total Utility divided by the change in the quantity consumed.

Market Any institution or mechanism that brings together the buyers (demanders) and sellers (suppliers) of a particular good or service.

Market demand (*See* Total demand.)

Market economy An economy in which only the private decisions of consumers, resource suppliers, and business Firms determine how resources are allocated; the Market system.

Market failure The failure of a market to bring about the allocation of resources that best satisfies the wants of society (that maximizes the satisfaction of wants). In particular, the over- or underallocation of resources to the production of a particular good or service (because of Spillovers or informational problems) and no allocation of resources to the production of Public goods (*see*).

Market for externality rights A market in which the Perfectly inelastic supply (*see*) of the right to pollute the environment and the demand for the right to pollute would determine the price which a polluter would have to pay for the right.

Market-oriented income stabilization The proposal to shift the goal of farm policy from the enhancement to the stabilization of farm prices and incomes; allow farm prices and incomes to move toward their free-market levels in the long run; and have government stabilize farm prices and incomes from year to year by purchasing farm products when their prices fell below and by selling surplus farm products when their prices rose above their long-run trend of prices.

Market period A period of time in which producers of a product are unable to change the quantity produced in response to a change in its price; in which there is Perfect inelasticity of supply (*see*); and in which all resources are Fixed resources (*see*).

Market policies Government policies designed to reduce the market power of labor unions and large business firms and to reduce or eliminate imbalances and bottlenecks in labor markets.

Market socialism An economic system (method of organization) in which property resources are publicly owned and markets and prices are used to direct and coordinate economic activities.

Market system All the product and resource markets of the economy and the relationships among them; a method which allows the prices determined in these markets to allocate the economy's scarce resources and to communicate and coordinate the decisions made by consumers, business firms, and resource suppliers.

Median-voter model The view that under majority rule the median (middle) voter will be in the dominant position to determine the outcome of an election.

Medicaid A Federal program in the United States which helps to finance the medical expenses of individuals covered by the Supplemental security income (*see*) and the Aid to families with dependent children (*see*) programs.

Medicare A Federal program which is financed by Payroll taxes (*see*) and provides for (1) compulsory hospital insurance for senior citizens and (2) low-cost voluntary insurance to help older Americans pay physicians' fees.

Medium of exchange Money (*see*); a convenient means of exchanging goods and services without engaging in Barter (*see*); what sellers generally accept and buyers generally use to pay for a good or service.

Microeconomics The part of economics concerned with such individual units within the economy as Industries, Firms, and Households; and with individual markets, particular prices, and specific goods and services.

Minimum wage The lowest Wage (rate) employers may legally pay for an hour of Labor.

Mixed capitalism An economy in which both government and private decisions determine how resources are allocated.

Monetarism An alternative to Keynesianism (*see*); the philosophical, ideological, and analytical view of a minority of American economists; and their employment theory and stabilization policy which stress the role of money.

Monetary multiplier The multiple of its Excess reserves (*see*) by which the Commercial banking system (*see*) can expand the Money supply and Demand deposits by making new loans (or buying securities); and equal to one divided by the Required reserve ratio (*see*).

Monetary policy Changing the Money supply (*see*) to assist the economy to achieve a full-employment, non-inflationary level of total output.

Monetary rule The rule suggested by Monetarism (*see*); the Money supply should be expanded each year at the same annual rate as the potential rate of growth of the Real gross domestic product; the supply of money should be increased steadily at from 3 to 5 percent.

Money Any item which is generally acceptable to sellers in exchange for goods and services.

Money capital Money available to purchase Capital goods (*see*).

Money income (*See* Nominal income.)

Money interest rate The Nominal interest rate (*see*).

Money market The market in which the demand for and the supply of money determine the Interest rate (or the level of interest rates) in the economy.

Money market deposit account (MMDA) Interest-earning accounts at banks and thrift institutions which pool the funds of depositors to buy various short-term securities.

Money market mutual funds (MMMF) Interest-bearing accounts offered by brokers which pool depositors' funds for the purchase of short-term securities; depositors may write checks in minimum amounts or more against their accounts.

Money supply Narrowly defined (*see*) $M1$, more broadly defined (*see*) $M2$ and $M3$.

Money wage The amount of money received by a worker per unit of time (hour, day, etc.); nominal wage.

Money wage rate (*See* Money wage.)

Monopolistic competition A market in which many Firms sell a Differentiated product (*see*), into which entry is relatively easy, in which the Firm has some control over the price at which the product it produces is sold, and in which there is considerable Nonprice competition (*see*).

Monopoly A market in which the number of sellers is so small that each seller is able to influence the total supply and the price of the good or service.

Monopsony A market in which there is only one buyer of the good, service, or resource.

Moral hazard problem The possibility that individuals or institutions will change their behavior in unanticipated ways as the result of a contract or agreement. Example: A bank whose deposits are insured against loss may make riskier loans and investments.

Most-favored-nation clause A clause in a trade agreement between the United States and another nation which provides that the other nation's Imports into the United States will be subjected to the lowest tariff levied then or later on any other nation's Imports into the United States.

MR = MC rule A Firm will maximize its Economic profit (or minimize its losses) by producing the output at which Marginal revenue (*see*) and Marginal cost (*see*) are equal—provided the price at which it can sell its products is equal to or greater than Average variable cost (*see*).

MRP = MRC rule To maximize Economic profit (or minimize losses) a Firm should employ the quantity of a resource at which its Marginal revenue product (*see*) is equal to its Marginal resource cost (*see*).

Multiplier The ratio of the change in the Equilibrium GDP to the change in Investment (*see*), or to the change in any other component of the Aggregate expenditures schedule or to the change in Net taxes; the number by which a change in any component in the Aggregate expenditures schedule or in Net taxes must be multiplied to find the resulting change in the Equilibrium GDP.

Multiplier effect The effect on Equilibrium gross domestic product of a change in the Aggregate expenditures schedule (caused by a change in the Consumption schedule, Investment, Net taxes, Government expenditures for goods and services, or Net exports).

Mutual interdependence Situation in which a change in price (or in some other policy) by one Firm will affect the sales and profits of another Firm (or other Firms) and any Firm which makes such a change can expect the other Firm(s) to react in an unpredictable (uncertain) way.

Mutually exclusive goals Goals which conflict and cannot be achieved simultaneously.

Mutual savings bank A Firm without stockholders which accepts deposits primarily from small individual savers and which lends primarily to individuals to finance the purchases of residences.

National bank A Commercial bank (*see*) chartered by the United States government.

National income Total income earned by resource suppliers for their contributions to the production of the Gross domestic product (*see*); equal to the Gross domestic product minus the Nonincome charges (*see*) plus net American income earned abroad (*see*).

National income accounting The techniques employed to measure (estimate) the overall production of the economy and other related totals for the nation as a whole.

National Labor Relations Act (*See* Wagner Act.)

National Labor Relations Board The board established by the Wagner (National Labor Relations) Act (*see*) of 1935 to investigate unfair labor practices, issue Cease-and-desist orders (*see*), and to conduct elections among employees to determine if they wish to be represented by a Labor union and which union they wish to represent them.

Natural monopoly An industry in which the Economies of scale (*see*) are so great that the product can be produced by one Firm at an average cost which is lower than it would be if it were produced by more than one Firm.

Natural rate hypothesis The idea that the economy is stable in the long run at the natural rate of unemployment; views the long-run Phillips Curve (*see*) as being vertical at the natural rate of unemployment.

Natural rate of unemployment (*See* Full-employment unemployment rate.)

NDP (*See* Net domestic product.)

Near-money Financial assets, the most important of which are Noncheckable savings accounts, Time deposits, and U.S. short-term securities and savings bonds, that are not a medium of exchange but can be readily converted into Money.

Negative income tax The proposal to subsidize families and individuals with money payments when their incomes fall below a Guaranteed income (*see*); the negative tax would decrease as earned income increases. (*See* Benefit-loss rate.)

Negative relationship (*See* Inverse relationship.)

Net American income earned abroad Receipts of resource income from the rest of the world minus payments of resource income to the rest of the world; the difference between GDP (*see*) and GNP (*see*).

Net capital movement The difference between the real and financial investments and loans made by individuals and Firms of one nation in the other nations of the world and the investments and loans made by individuals and Firms from other nations in a nation; Capital inflows less Capital outflows.

Net domestic product Gross domestic product (*see*) less that part of the output needed to replace the Capital goods worn out in producing the output (Consumption of fixed capital, *see*).

Net export effect The notion that the impact of a change in Monetary policy (Fiscal policy) will be strengthened (weakened) by the consequent change in Net exports (*see*). For example, a tight (easy) money policy will increase (decrease) domestic interest rates, thereby increasing (decreasing) the foreign demand for dollars. As a result, the dollar appreciates (depreciates) and causes American net exports to decrease (increase).

Net exports Exports (*see*) minus Imports (*see*).

Net investment income The interest and dividend income received by the residents of a nation from residents of other nations less the interest and dividend payments made by the residents of that nation to the residents of other nations.

Net private domestic investment Gross private domestic investment (*see*) less (Consumption of fixed capital, (*see*); the addition to the nation's stock of Capital during a year.

Net taxes The taxes collected by government less Government transfer payments (*see*).

Net transfers The personal and government transfer payments made to residents of foreign nations less the personal and government transfer payments received from residents of foreign nations.

Net worth The total Assets (*see*) less the total Liabilities (*see*) of a Firm or an individual; the claims of the owners of a firm against its total Assets.

New classical economics The theory that, although unanticipated price level changes may create macroeconomic instability in the short run, the economy is stable at the full-employment level of domestic output in the long run because of price and wage flexibility.

New International Economic Order A series of proposals made by the Less developed countries (LDCs) (*see*) for basic changes in their relationships with the advanced industrialized nations that would accelerate the growth of and redistribute world income to the LDCs.

New perspective view of advertising Envisions advertising as a low-cost source of consumer information which increases competition by making consumers more aware of substitute products.

NIEO New International Economic Order (*see*).

NIT (*See* Negative income tax.)

NLRB (*See* National Labor Relations Board.)

Nominal gross domestic output (GDP) The GDP (*see*) measured in terms of the price level at the time of measurement (unadjusted for changes on the price level).

Nominal income The number of dollars received by an individual or group during some period of time.

Nominal interest rate The rate of interest expressed in dollars of current value (not adjusted for inflation).

Nominal wage The Money wage (*see*).

Noncheckable savings account A Savings account (*see*) against which a check may not be written.

Noncollusive oligopoly An Oligopoly (*see*) in which the Firms do not act together and in agreement to determine the price of the product and the output each Firm will produce or to determine the geographic area in which each Firm will sell.

Noncompeting groups Groups of workers in the economy that do not compete with each other for employment because the skill and training of the workers in one group are substantially different from those of the workers in other groups.

Nondiscretionary fiscal policy The increases (decreases) in Net taxes (*see*) which occur without Congressional action when the gross domestic product rises (falls) and which tend to stabilize the economy.

Nondurable good A Consumer good (*see*) with an expected life (use) of less than one year.

Nonexhaustive expenditure An expenditure by government that does not result directly in the employment of economic resources or the production of goods and services; *see* Government transfer payment.

Nonfinancial investment An investment which does not require households to save a part of their money incomes; but which uses surplus (unproductive) labor to build Capital goods.

Nonincome charges Consumption of fixed capital (*see*) and Indirect business taxes (*see*).

Nonincome determinants of consumption and saving All influences on consumption spending and saving other than the level of Disposable income.

Noninterest determinants of investment All influences on the level of investment spending other than the rate of interest.

Noninvestment transaction An expenditure for stocks, bonds, or second-hand Capital goods.

Nonmarket transactions The production of goods and services not included in the measurement of the Gross domestic product because the goods and services are not bought and sold.

Nonprice competition The means other than decreasing the prices of their products which Firms employ to attempt to increase the sale of their products; and which includes Product differentiation (*see*), advertising, and sales promotion activities.

Nonproductive transaction The purchase and sale of any item that is not a currently produced good or service.

Nontariff barriers All barriers other than Tariffs (*see*) which nations erect to impede trade among nations: Import quotas (*see*), licensing requirements, unreasonable product-quality standards, unnecessary red tape in customs procedures, etc.

Nonunion shop A place of employment at which none of the employees are members of a Labor union (and at which the employer attempts to hire only workers who are not apt to join a union).

Normal good A good or service of which consumers will purchase more (less) at every price when their incomes increase (decrease).

Normal profit Payment that must be made by a Firm to obtain and retain Entrepreneurial ability (*see*); the minimum payment (income) Entrepreneurial ability must (expect to) receive to induce it to perform the entrepreneurial functions for a Firm; an Implicit cost (*see*).

Normative economics That part of economics which

pertains to value judgments about what the economy should be like; concerned with economic goals and policies.

Norris-LaGuardia Act The Federal act of 1932 which made it more difficult for employers to obtain Injunctions (*see*) against Labor unions in Federal courts and which declared that Yellow-dog contracts (*see*) were unenforceable.

NTBs (*See* Nontariff barriers.)

OASDHI (*See* Old age, survivors, and disability health insurance.)

Occupational discrimination The arbitrary restrictions which prevent blacks (and other minority groups) or women from entering the more desirable and higher-paying occupations.

Occupational licensure The laws of state or local governments which require a worker to obtain a license from a licensing board (by satisfying certain specified requirements) before engaging in a particular occupation.

Official reserves The foreign monies (currencies) owned by the central bank of a nation.

Okun's law The generalization that any one percentage point rise in the Unemployment rate above the Full-employment unemployment rate will increase the GDP gap by 2.5 percent of the Potential output (GDP) of the economy.

Old age, survivors, and disability health insurance The social program in the United States which is financed by Federal Payroll taxes (*see*) on employers and employees and which is designed to replace the Earnings lost when workers retire, die, or become unable to work.

Oligopoly A market in which a few Firms sell either a Standardized or Differentiated product, into which entry is difficult, in which the Firm's control over the price at which it sells its product is limited by Mutual interdependence (*see*) (except when there is collusion among firms), and in which there is typically a great deal of Nonprice competition (*see*).

Oligopsony A market in which there are a few buyers.

OPEC An acronym for the Organization of Petroleum Exporting Countries (*see*).

Open economy An economy which both exports and imports goods and services.

Open Market Committee The twelve-member group that determines the purchase-and-sale policies of the Federal Reserve Banks in the market for United States government securities.

Open-market operations The buying and selling of United States government securities by the Federal Reserve Banks.

Open shop A place of employment at which the employer may hire either Labor union members or workers who are not (and need not become) members of the union.

Opportunity cost The amount of other products that must be forgone or sacrificed to produce a unit of a product.

Optimal amount of externality reduction That reduction of pollution or other negative externality where society's marginal benefit and marginal cost of reducing the externality are equal.

Organization of Petroleum Exporting Countries The cartel formed in 1970 by thirteen oil-producing countries to control the price at which they sell crude oil to foreign importers and the quantity of oil exported by its members and which accounts for a large proportion of the world's export of oil.

"Other things being equal" assumption Assuming that factors other than those being considered are constant.

Outpayments The expenditures of (its own or foreign) money which the individuals, Firms, and governments of one nation make to purchase goods and services, for Remittances, as investment income, and Capital outflows abroad.

Output effect The impact which a change in the price of a resource has on the output a Firm finds it most profitable to produce and the resulting effect on the quantity of the resource (and the quantities of other resources) employed by the Firm after the consequences of the Substitution effect (*see*) have been taken into account (eliminated).

Paper money Pieces of paper used as a Medium of exchange (*see*); in the United States, Federal Reserve Notes (*see*).

Paradox of thrift The attempt of society to save more results in the same amount of, or less, Saving.

Paradox of voting A situation where voting by majority rule fails to provide a consistent ranking of society's preferences for public goods or services.

Parity concept The notion that year after year a given output of a farm product should enable a farmer to acquire a constant amount of nonagricultural goods and services.

Parity price The price at which a given amount of an agricultural product would have to be sold to enable a farmer to obtain year after year money income needed to purchase a constant total quantity of nonagricultural goods and services.

Parity ratio The ratio (index) of the price received by farmers from the sale of an agricultural commodity to the (index of the) prices paid by them; used as a rationale for Price supports (*see*).

Partial equilibrium analysis The study of equilibrium prices and equilibrium outputs or employments in a particular market which assumes prices, outputs, and employments in the other markets of the economy remain unchanged.

Partnership An unincorporated business Firm owned and operated by two or more persons.

Patent laws The Federal laws which grant to inventors and innovators the exclusive right to produce and sell a new product or machine for a period of seventeen years.

Payments deficit (*See* Balance of payments deficit.)

Payments surplus (*See* Balance of payments surplus.)

Payroll tax A tax levied on employers of Labor equal to a percentage of all or part of the wages and salaries paid by them; and on employees equal to a percentage of all or part of the wages and salaries received by them.

Perestroika The essential feature of Mikhail Gorbachev's reform program to "restructure" the Soviet economy; includes modernization, decentralization, some privatization, and improved worker incentives.

Perfect elasticity of demand A change in the Quantity demanded requires no change in the price of the commodity; buyers will purchase as much of a commodity as is available at a constant price.

Perfect elasticity of supply A change in the Quantity supplied requires no change in the price of the commodity; sellers will make available as much of the commodity as buyers will purchase at a constant price.

Perfect inelasticity of demand A change in price results in no change in the Quantity demanded of a commodity; the Quantity demanded is the same at all prices.

Perfect inelasticity of supply A change in price results in no change in the Quantity supplied of a commodity; the Quantity supplied is the same at all prices.

Per se violations Collusive actions, such as attempts to fix prices or divide a market, which are violations of the antitrust laws even though the actions are unsuccessful.

Personal consumption expenditures The expenditures of Households for Durable and Nondurable consumer goods and services.

Personal distribution of income The manner in which the economy's Personal or Disposable income is divided among different income classes or different households.

Personal income The income, part of which is earned and the remainder of which is unearned, available to resource suppliers and others before the payment of Personal taxes (*see*).

Personal income tax A tax levied on the taxable income of individuals (households and unincorporated firms).

Personal saving The Personal income of households less Personal taxes (*see*) and Personal consumption expenditures (*see*); Disposable income not spent for Consumer goods (*see*).

Phillips Curve A curve which shows the relationship between the Unemployment rate (*see*) (on the horizontal axis) and the annual rate of increase in the Price level (on the vertical axis).

Planned economy An economy in which only government determines how resources are allocated.

Planned investment The amount which business firms plan or intend to invest.

Plant A physical establishment (Land and Capital) which performs one or more of the functions in the production (fabrication and distribution) of goods and services.

P = MC rule A firm in Pure competition (*see*) will maximize its Economic profit (*see*) or minimize its losses by producing the output at which the price of the product is equal to Marginal cost (*see*), provided that price is equal to or greater than Average variable cost (*see*) in the short run and equal to or greater than Average (total) cost (*see*) in the long run.

Policy economics The formulation of courses of action to bring about desired results or to prevent undesired occurrences (to control economic events).

Political business cycle The tendency of Congress to destabilize the economy by reducing taxes and increasing government expenditures before elections and to raise taxes and lower expenditures after elections.

Positive economics The analysis of facts or data to establish scientific generalizations about economic behavior, compare Normative economics.

Positive relationship The relationship between two variables which change in the same direction, for example, product price and quantity supplied.

***Post hoc, ergo propter hoc* fallacy** Incorrectly reasoning that when one event precedes another the first event is the cause of the second.

Potential competition The possibility that new competitors will be induced to enter an industry if firms now in that industry are realizing large economic profits.

Potential output The real output (GDP) an economy is able to produce when it fully employs its available resources.

Poverty An existence in which the basic needs of an individual or family exceed the means to satisfy them.

Poverty rate The percentage of the population with incomes below the official poverty income levels established by the Federal government.

Preferential hiring A practice (often required by the provisions of a contract between a Labor union and an employer) which requires the employer to hire union members so long as they are available and to hire nonunion workers only when union members are not available.

Preferential tariff treatment Setting Tariffs lower for one nation (or group of nations) than for others.

Premature inflation Inflation (*see*) which occurs before the economy has reached Full employment (*see*).

Price The quantity of money (or of other goods and services) paid and received for a unit of a good or service.

Price ceiling A legally established maximum price for a good or service.

Price-decreasing effect The effect in a competitive market of a decrease in Demand or an increase in Supply upon the Equilibrium price (*see*).

Price discrimination The selling of a product (at a given time) to different buyers at different prices when the price differences are not justified by differences in the cost of producing the product for the different buyers; and a practice made illegal by the Clayton Act (*see*) when it reduces competition.

Price elasticity of demand The ratio of the percentage change in Quantity demanded of a commodity to the percentage change in its price; the responsiveness or sensitivity of the quantity of a commodity buyers demand to a change in the price of a commodity.

Price elasticity of supply The ratio of the percentage change in Quantity supplied of a commodity to the percentage change in its price; the responsiveness or sensitivity of the quantity of a commodity supplied to a change in the price of a commodity.

Price floor A legally determined price which is above the Equilibrium price.

Price guidepost The price charged by an industry for its product should increase by no more than the increase in the Unit labor cost (*see*) of producing the product.

Price increasing effect The effect in a competitive market of an increase in Demand or a decrease in Supply on the equilibrium price.

Price index An index number which shows how the average price of a "market basket" of goods changes through time. A price index is used to change nominal output (income) into real output (income).

Price leadership An informal method which the Firms in an Oligopoly (*see*) may employ to set the price of the product they produce; one firm (the leader) is the first to announce a change in price and the other firms (the followers) quickly announce identical (or similar) changes in price.

Price level The weighted average of the Prices paid for the final goods and services produced in the economy.

Price level surprises Unanticipated changes in the price level.

Price maker A seller (or buyer) of a commodity that is able to affect the price at which the commodity sells by changing the amount it sells (buys).

Price support The minimum price which government allows sellers to receive for a good or service; a price which is a legally established or maintained minimum price.

Price taker A seller (or buyer) of a commodity that is unable to affect the price at which a commodity sells by changing the amount it sells (or buys).

Price-wage flexibility Changes in the prices of products and in the Wages paid to workers; the ability of prices and Wages to rise or to fall.

Price war Successive and continued decreases in the prices charged by the firms in an oligopolistic industry by which each firm hopes to increase its sales and revenues and from which firms seldom benefit.

Prime interest rate The interest rate banks charge their most credit-worthy borrowers, for example, large corporations with impeccable financing credentials.

Principal-agent problem A conflict of interest which occurs when agents (workers) pursue their own objective to the detriment of the principal's (employer's) goals.

Private good A good or service to which the Exclusion principle (*see*) is applicable and which is provided by privately owned firms to those who are willing to pay for it.

Private property The right of private persons and Firms to obtain, own, control, employ, dispose of, and bequeath Land, Capital, and other Assets.

Private sector The Households and business firms of the economy.

Product differentiation Physical or other differences between the products produced by different Firms which result in individual buyers preferring (so long as the price charged by all sellers is the same) the product of one Firm to the Products of the other Firms.

Production possibilities curve A curve which shows the different combinations of two goods or services that can be produced in a Full-employment (*see*), Full-production (*see*) economy in which the available supplies of resources and technology are constant.

Production possibilities table A table which shows the different combinations of two goods or services that can be produced in a Full-employment (*see*), Full production (*see*) economy in which the available supplies of resources and technology are constant.

Productive efficiency The production of a good in the least costly way; occurs when production takes place at the output where Average total cost is at a minimum and where Marginal product per dollar's worth of each input is the same.

Productivity A measure of average output or real output per unit of input. For example, the productivity of labor may be determined by dividing hours of work into real output.

Productivity slowdown The recent decline in the rate at which Labor productivity (*see*) in the United States has increased.

Product market A market in which Households buy and Firms sell the products they have produced.

Profit (*See*) Economic profit and Normal profit; without an adjective preceding it, the income of those who supply the economy with Entrepreneurial ability (*see*) or Normal profit.

Profit-maximizing case The circumstances which result in an Economic profit (*see*) for a Firm when it produces the output at which Economic profit is a maximum; when the price at which the Firm can sell its product is greater than the Average (total) cost of producing it.

Profit-maximizing rule (combination of resources) The quantity of each resource a Firm must employ of its Economic profit (*see*) is to be a maximum or its losses a minimum; the combination in which the Marginal revenue product (*see*) of each resource is equal to its Marginal resource cost (*see*) (to its price if the resource is employed in a competitive market).

Progressive tax A tax such that the Average tax rate increases as the taxpayer's income increases and decreases as income decreases.

Property tax A tax on the value of property (Capital,

Land, stocks and bonds, and other Assets) owned by Firms and Households.

Proportional tax   A tax such that the Average tax rate remains constant as the taxpayer's income increases and decreases.

Proprietors' income   The net income of the owners of unincorporated Firms (proprietorships and partnerships).

Prosperous industry   (*See* Expanding industry.)

Protective tariff   A Tariff (*see*) designed to protect domestic producers of a good from the competition of foreign producers.

Public assistance programs   Programs which pay benefits to those who are unable to earn income (because of permanent handicaps or because they are dependent children) which are financed by general tax revenues, and which are viewed as public charity (rather than earned rights).

Public choice theory   Generalizations that describe how government (the Public sector) makes decisions for the use of economic resources.

Public debt   The total amount owned by the Federal government (to the owners of government securities) and equal to the sum of its past Budget deficits (less its budget surpluses).

Public finance   The branch of economics which analyzes government revenues and expenditures.

Public good   A good or service to which the Exclusion principle (*see*) is not applicable; and which is provided by government if it yields substantial benefits to society.

Public interest theory of regulation   The presumption that the purpose of the regulation of an Industry is to protect the public (consumers) from the abuse of the power possessed by Natural monopolies (*see*).

Public sector   The part of the economy that contains all its governments; government.

Public-sector failure   The failure of the Public sector (government) to resolve socioeconomic problems because it performs its functions in an economically inefficient fashion.

Public utility   A Firm which produces an essential good or service, has obtained from a government the right to be the sole supplier of the good or service in the area, and is regulated by that government to prevent the abuse of its monopoly power.

Purchasing power parity   The idea that exchange rates between nations equate the purchasing power of various currencies; exchange rates between any two nations adjust to reflect the price level differences between the countries.

Pure capitalism   An economic system (method of organization) in which property resources are privately owned and markets and prices are used to direct and coordinate economic activities.

Pure competition   (1) A market in which a very large number of Firms sells a Standardized product (*see*), into which entry is very easy, in which the individual seller has no control over the price at which the product sells, and in which there is no Nonprice competition (*see*); (2) A market in which there is a very large number of buyers.

Pure monopoly   A market in which one Firm sells a unique product (one for which there are no close substitutes), into which entry is blocked, in which the Firm has considerable control over the price at which the product sells, and in which Nonprice competition (*see*) may or may not be found.

Pure profit   (*See* Economic profit.)

Pure rate of interest   (*See The* rate of interest.)

Quantity-decreasing effect   The effect in a competitive market of a decrease in Demand or a decrease in Supply on the Equilibrium quantity (*see*).

Quantity demanded   The amount of a good or service buyers wish (or a buyer wishes) to purchase at a particular price during some period of time.

Quantity-increasing effect   The effect in a competitive market of an increase in Demand or an increase in Supply on the Equilibrium quantity (*see*).

Quantity supplied   The amount of a good or service sellers offer (or a seller offers) to sell at a particular price during some period of time.

Quasi-public bank   A bank which is privately owned but governmentally (publicly) controlled; each of the Federal Reserve Banks.

Quasi-public good   A good or service to which the Exclusion principle (*see*) could be applied, but which has such a large Spillover benefit (*see*) that government sponsors its production to prevent an underallocation of resources.

R&D   Research and development; activities undertaken to bring about Technological progress.

Ratchet effect   The tendency for the Price level to rise when Aggregate demand increases, but not fall when Aggregate demand declines.

Rate of exchange   The price paid in one's own money to acquire one unit of a foreign money; the rate at which the money of one nation is exchanged for the money of another nation.

Rate of interest   Price paid for the use of Money or for the use of Capital; interest rate.

Rational   An adjective that describes the behavior of any individual who consistently does those things that will enable him or her to achieve the declared objective of the individual; and that describes the behavior of a consumer who uses money income to buy the collection of goods and services that yields the maximum amount of Utility (*see*).

Rational expectations theory   The hypothesis that business firms and households expect monetary and fiscal policies to have certain effects on the economy and take, in pursuit of their own self-interests, actions which make these policies ineffective.

Rationing function of price The ability of a price in a competitive market to equalize Quantity demanded and Quantity supplied and to eliminate shortages and surpluses by rising or falling.

Reaganomics The policies of the Reagan administration based on Supply-side economics (*see*) and intended to reduce inflation and the Unemployment rate (Stagflation).

Real-balances effect The tendency for increases (decreases) in the price level to lower (raise) the real value (or purchasing power) of financial assets with fixed money values; and, as a result, to reduce (expand) total spending in the economy.

Real capital (*See* Capital.)

Real gross domestic product Gross domestic product (*see*) adjusted for changes in the price level; Gross domestic product in a year divided by the GDP deflator (*see*) for that year.

Real income The amount of goods and services an individual or group can purchase with his, her, or its Nominal income during some period of time. Nominal income adjusted for changes in the Price level.

Real interest rate The rate of interest expressed in dollars of constant value (adjusted for inflation); and equal to the Nominal interest rate (*see*) less the rate of inflation.

Real rate of interest The Real interest rate (*see*).

Real wage The amount of goods and services a worker can purchase with his or her Nominal wage (*see*); the purchasing power of the Nominal wage; the Nominal wage adjusted for changes in the Price level.

Real wage rate (*See* Real wage.)

Recessionary gap The amount by which the Aggregate expenditures schedule (curve) must increase (shift upward) to increase the real GDP to the full-employment noninflationary level.

Reciprocal Trade Agreements Act of 1934 The Federal act which gave the President the authority to negotiate agreements with foreign nations and lower American tariff rates by up to 50 percent if the foreign nations would reduce tariff rates on American goods and which incorporated Most-favored-nation clauses (*see*) in the agreements reached with these nations.

Refinancing the public debt Paying owners of maturing United States government securities with money obtained by selling new securities or with new securities.

Regressive tax A tax such that the Average tax rate decreases (increases) as the taxpayer's income increases (decreases).

Regulatory agency An agency (commission or board) established by the Federal or a state government to control for the benefit of the public the prices charged and the services offered (output produced) by a National monopoly (*see*).

Remittance A gift or grant; a payment for which no good or service is received in return; the funds sent by workers who have legally or illegally entered a foreign nation to their families in the nations from which they have migrated.

Rental income Income received by those who supply the economy with Land (*see*).

Rent-seeking behavior The pursuit through government of a transfer of income or wealth to a resource supplier, business, or consumer at someone else's or society's expense.

Required reserve ratio (*See* Legal reserves.)

Required reserves (*See* Legal reserves.)

Reserve ratio The specified minimum percentage of its deposit liabilities which a Member bank (*see*) must keep on deposit at the Federal Reserve Bank in its district, or in Vault cash (*see*).

Resolution Trust Corporation (RTC) A Federal institution created in 1989 to oversee the closing and sale of failed savings and loan institutions.

Resource market A market in which Households sell and Firms buy the services of resources.

Retiring the public debt Reducing the size of the Public debt by paying money to owners of maturing United States government securities.

Revaluation An increase in the defined value of a currency.

Revenue tariff A Tariff (*see*) designed to produce income for the (Federal) government.

Ricardian equivalence theorem The idea that an increase in the public debt will have little or no effect on real output and employers because taxpayers will save more in anticipation of future higher taxes to pay the higher interest expense on the debt.

Right-to-work law A law which has been enacted in twenty states that makes it illegal in those states to require a worker to join a Labor union in order to retain his or her job with an employer.

Roundabout production The construction and use of Capital (*see*) to aid in the production of Consumer goods (*see*).

Ruble overhang The large amount of forced savings held by Russian households due to the scarcity of consumer goods; these savings could fuel inflation when Russian prices are decontrolled.

Rule of reason The rule stated and applied in the U.S. Steel case (*see*) that only combinations and contracts that unreasonably restrain trade are subject to actions under the antitrust laws and that size and the possession of monopoly were not themselves illegal.

Rule of 70 A method by which the number of years it will take for the Price level to double can be calculated; divide 70 by the annual rate of inflation.

Sales tax A tax levied on expenditures for a broad group of products.

Saving Disposable income not spent for Consumer goods (*see*); not spending for consumption; equal to Disposal income minus Personal consumption expenditures (**see**).

Savings account A deposit in a Depository institution (**see**) which is interest-earning and which can normally be withdrawn by the depositor at any time.

Savings and loan association A Firm which accepts deposits primarily from small individual savers, and lends primarily to individuals to finance purchases of residences.

Saving schedule Schedule which shows the amounts Households plan to save (plan not to spend for Consumer goods, **see**) at different levels of Disposable income.

Savings institution A Thrift institution (**see**).

Say's law The (discredited) macroeconomic generalization that the production of goods and services (supply) creates an equal Aggregate demand for these goods and services.

Scarce resources The fixed (limited) quantities of Land, Capital, Labor, and Entrepreneurial ability (**see all**) which are never sufficient to satisfy the material wants of humans because their wants are unlimited.

Schumpeter-Galbraith view (of oligopoly) The belief shared by these two economists that large oligopolistic firms are necessary if there is to be a rapid rate of technological progress (because only this kind of firm has both the means and the incentive to introduce technological changes).

Seasonal variation An increase or decrease during a single year in the level of economic activity caused by a change in the season.

Secondary boycott The refusal of a Labor union to buy or to work with the products produced by another union or a group of nonunion workers.

"Second economy" The semilegal and illegal markets and activities which existed side by side with the legal and official markets and activities in the former U.S.S.R.

Secular trend The expansion or contraction in the level of economic activity over a long period of years.

Selective controls The techniques the Federal Reserve Banks employ to change the availability of certain specific types of credit.

Self-interest What each Firm, property owner, worker, and consumer believes is best for itself and seeks to obtain.

Seniority The length of time a worker has been employed by an employer relative to the lengths of time the employer's other workers have been employed; the principle which is used to determine which workers will be laid off when there is insufficient work for them all and who will be rehired when more work becomes available.

Separation of ownership and control Difference between the group that owns the Corporation (the stockholders) and the group that manages it (the directors and officers) and between the interests (goals) of the two groups.

Service That which is intangible (invisible) and for which a consumer, firm, or government is willing to exchange something of value.

Sherman Act The Federal antitrust act of 1890 which made monopoly, restraint of trade, and attempts, combinations, and conspiracies to monopolize or to restrain trade criminal offenses; and allowed the Federal government or injured parties to take legal action against those committing these offenses.

Shirking Attempts by workers to increase their utility or well-being by neglecting or evading work.

Shortage The amount by which the Quantity demanded of a product exceeds the Quantity supplied at a given (below-equilibrium) price.

Short run A period of time in which producers of a product are able to change the quantity of some but not all of the resources they employ; in which some resources—the Plant (**see**)—are Fixed resources (**see**) and some are Variable resources (**see**); in which some costs are Fixed costs (**see**) and some are Variable costs (**see**); a period of time too brief to allow a Firm to vary its plant capacity but long enough to permit it to change the level at which the plant capacity is used; a period of time not long enough to enable Firms to enter or to leave an Industry (**see**).

Short-run aggregate supply curve The aggregate supply curve relevant to a time period in which input prices (particularly nominal wages) remain constant when the price level changes.

Short-run competitive equilibrium The price at which the total quantity of a product supplied in the Short run (**see**) by a purely competitive industry and the total quantity of the product demanded are equal and which is equal to or greater than the Average variable cost (**see**) of producing the product.

Short-run farm problem The sharp year-to-year changes in the prices of agricultural products and in the incomes of farmers.

Simple multiplier The Multiplier (**see**) in an economy in which government collects no Net taxes (**see**), there are no Imports (**see**), and Investment (**see**) is independent of the level of income (Gross domestic product); equal to one divided by the Marginal propensity to save (**see**).

Simpson-Rodino Act of 1986 Immigration legislation which provides amnesty to qualified illegal aliens; includes penalties for employers who knowingly hire illegal aliens; and allows temporary migrants to harvest perishable crops.

Single-tax movement The attempt of a group which followed the teachings of Henry George to eliminate all taxes except one which would tax all Rental income (**see**) at a rate of 100 percent.

Slope of a line The ratio of the vertical change (the rise or fall) to the horizontal change (the run) in moving between two points on a line. The slope of an upward sloping line is positive, reflecting a direct relationship between two variables; the slope of a downward sloping line is negative, reflecting an inverse relationship between two variables.

Smoot-Hawley Tariff Act Passed in 1930, this legislation established some of the highest tariffs in United States history. Its objective was to reduce imports and stimulate the domestic economy.

Social accounting   (*See* National income accounting.)

Socially optimal price   The price of a product which results in the most efficient allocation of an economy's resources and which is equal to the Marginal cost (*see*) of the last unit of the product produced.

Social regulation   The type of regulation in which government is concerned with the conditions under which goods and services are produced, their physical characteristics, and the impact of their production on society; in contrast to Industrial regulation (*see*).

Social security programs   The programs which replace the earnings lost when people retire or are temporarily unemployed, which are financed by Payroll taxes (*see*), and which are viewed as earned rights (rather than charity).

Sole proprietorship   An unincorporated business firm owned and operated by a single person.

Special-interest effect   Effect on public decision making and the allocation of resources in the economy when government promotes the interests (goals) of small groups to the detriment of society as a whole.

Specialization   The use of the resources of an individual, a Firm, a region, or a nation to produce one or a few goods and services.

Spillover   A benefit or cost associated with the consumption or production of a good or service which is obtained by or inflicted without compensation on a party other than the buyer or seller of the good or service (*see* Spillover benefit and Spillover cost).

Spillover benefit   The benefit obtained neither by producers nor by consumers of a product but without compensation by a third party (society as a whole).

Spillover cost   The cost of producing a product borne neither by producers nor by consumers of the product but without compensation by a third party (society as a whole).

SSI   (*See* Supplemental security income.)

Stabilization fund   A stock of money and of a commodity that is used to prevent the price of the commodity from changing by buying (selling) the commodity when its price decreases (increases).

Stabilization policy dilemma   The use of monetary and fiscal policy to decrease the Unemployment rate increases the rate of inflation, and the use of monetary and fiscal policy to decrease the rate of inflation increases the Unemployment rate.

Stagflation   Inflation accompanied by stagnation in the rate of growth of output and a high unemployment rate in the economy; simultaneous increases in both the Price level and the Unemployment rate.

Standardized product   A product such that buyers are indifferent to the seller from whom they purchase it so long as the price charged by all sellers is the same; a product such that all units of the product are perfect substitutes for each other (are identical).

State bank   A Commercial bank chartered to engage in the business of banking by a state government.

State ownership   The ownership of property (Land and Capital) by government (the state); in the former U.S.S.R. by the central government (the nation).

Static economy   (1) An economy in which Net private domestic investment (*see*) is equal to zero—Gross private domestic investment (*see*) is equal to the Consumption of fixed capital (*see*); (2) an economy in which the supplies of resources, technology, and the tastes of consumers do not change and in which, therefore, the economic future is perfectly predictable and there is no uncertainty.

Store of value   Any Asset (*see*) or wealth set aside for future use.

Strategic trade policy   The use of trade barriers to reduce the risk of product development by domestic firms, particularly products involving advanced technology.

Strike   The withholding of their labor services by an organized group of workers (a Labor union).

Strikebreaker   A person employed by a Firm when its employees are engaged in a strike against the firm.

Structural-change hypothesis   The explanation that attributes the relative decline of unionism in the United States to changes in the structure of the economy and of the labor force.

Structural deficit   The difference between Federal tax revenues and expenditures when the economy is at full employment.

Structural unemployment   Unemployment caused by changes in the structure of demand for Consumer goods and in technology; workers who are unemployed either because their skills are not demanded by employers or because they lack sufficient skills to obtain employment.

Subsidy   A payment of funds (or goods and services) by a government, business firm, or household for which it receives no good or service in return. When made by a government, it is a Government transfer payment (*see*).

Substitute goods   Goods or services such that there is a direct relationship between the price of one and the Demand for the other; when the price of one falls (rises) the Demand for the other decreases (increases).

Substitution effect   (1) The effect which a change in the price of a Consumer good would have on the relative expensiveness of that good and the resulting effect on the quantity of the good a consumer would purchase if the consumer's Real income (*see*) remained constant; (2) the effect which a change in the price of a resource would have on the quantity of the resource employed by a firm if the firm did not change its output.

Superfund Law of 1980   Legislation which taxes manufacturers of toxic products and uses these revenues to finance the cleanup of toxic-waste sites; assigns liability for improperly dumped waste to the firms producing, transporting, and dumping that waste.

Superior good   (*See* Normal good.)

Supplemental security income   A program federally financed and administered which provides a uniform nationwide minimum income for the aged, blind, and disabled who do not qualify for benefits under the Old age, survivors, and disability health insurance (*see*) or Unemployment insurance (*see*) programs in the United States.

Supply A Supply schedule or a Supply curve (*see both*).

Supply curve A curve which shows the amounts of a good or service sellers (a seller) will offer to sell at various prices during some period of time.

Supply factor An increase in the available quantity of a resource, an improvement in its quality, or an expansion of technological knowledge which makes it possible for an economy to produce a greater output of goods and services.

Supply schedule A schedule which shows the amounts of a good or service sellers (or seller) will offer at various prices during some period of time.

Supply shock One of several events of the 1970s and early 1980s which increased production costs, decreased Aggregate supply, and generated Stagflation in the United States.

Supply-side economics The part of modern macroeconomics that emphasizes the role of costs and Aggregate supply in its explanation of Inflation, unemployed labor, and Economic growth.

Supply-side view The view of fiscal policy held by the advocates of Supply-side economics which emphasizes increasing Aggregate supply (*see*) as a means of reducing the Unemployment rate and Inflation and encouraging Economic Growth.

Support price (*See* Price support.)

Surplus The amount by which the Quantity supplied of a product exceeds the Quantity demanded at a given (above-equilibrium) price.

Surplus value A Marxian term; the amount by which the value of a worker's daily output exceeds his daily wage; the output of workers appropriated by capitalists as profit.

Sympathy strike Withholding from an employer the labor services of its members by a Labor union that does not have a disagreement with the employer but wishes to assist another Labor union that does have a disagreement with the employer.

Tacit collusion Any method used in a Collusive oligopoly (*see*) to set prices and output or the market area of each firm that does not involve outright (or overt) collusion (formal agreements or secret meetings); and of which Price leadership (*see*) is a frequent example.

Taft-Hartley Act The Federal act of 1947 which marked the shift from government sponsorship to government regulation of Labor unions.

Tangent The point at which a line touches, but does not intersect, a curve.

Target dilemma A problem which arises because

monetary authorities cannot simultaneously stabilize both the money supply and the level of interest rates.

Tariff A tax imposed (only by the Federal government in the United States) on an imported good.

Tax A nonvoluntary payment of money (or goods and services) to a government by a Household or Firm for which the Household or Firm receives no good or service directly in return and which is not a fine imposed by a court for an illegal act.

Tax incidence The income or purchasing power which different persons and groups lose as a result of the imposition of a tax after Tax shifting (*see*) has occurred.

Tax shifting The transfer to others of all or part of a tax by charging them a higher price or by paying them a lower price for a good or service.

Tax-transfer disincentives Decreases in the incentives to work, save, invest, innovate, and take risks that allegedly result from high Marginal tax rates and Transfer-payment programs.

Tax "wedge" Such taxes as Indirect business taxes (*see*) and Payroll taxes (*see*) which are treated as a cost by business firms and reflected in the prices of the products produced by them; equal to the price of the product less the cost of the resources required to produce it.

Technology The body of knowledge that can be used to produce goods and services from Economic resources.

Terms of trade The rate at which units of one product can be exchanged for units of another product; the Price (*see*) of a good or service; the amount of one good or service that must be given up to obtain one unit of another good or service.

Theory of human capital Generalization that Wage differentials (*see*) are the result of differences in the amount of Human-capital investment (*see*); and that the incomes of lower-paid workers are increased by increasing the amount of such investment.

The rate of interest The Rate of interest (*see*) which is paid solely for the use of Money over an extended period of time and which excludes the charges made for the riskiness of the loan and its administrative costs; and which is approximately equal to the rate of interest paid on the long-term and virtually riskless bonds of the United States government.

Thrift institution A Savings and loan association, Mutual savings bank, or Credit union (*see all*).

Tight money policy Contracting, or restricting the growth of, the nation's Money supply (*see*).

Till money (*See* Vault cash.)

Time deposit An interest-earning deposit in a Depository institution (*see*) which may be withdrawn by the depositor without a loss of interest on or after a specific date or at the end of a specific period of time.

Token money Coins which have a Face value (*see*) greater than their Intrinsic value (*see*).

Total cost The sum of Fixed cost (*see*) and Variable cost (*see*).

Total demand The Demand schedule (*see*) or the Demand curve (*see*) of all buyers of a good or service.

Total demand for money The sum of the Transactions demand for money (*see*) and Asset demand for money (*see*); the relationship between the total amount of money demanded, nominal GDP, and the Rate of Interest.

Total product The total output of a particular good or service produced by a firm (a group of firms or the entire economy).

Total revenue The total number of dollars received by a Firm (or Firms) from the sale of a product; equal to the total expenditures for the product produced by the Firm (or firms); equal to the quantity sold (demanded) multiplied by the price at which it is sold—by the Average revenue (*see*) from its sale.

Total-revenue test A test to determine whether Demand is Elastic (*see*), Inelastic (*see*), or of Unitary elasticity (*see*) between any two prices: Demand is elastic (inelastic, unit elastic) if the Total revenue (*see*) of sellers of the commodity increases (decreases, remains constant) when the price of the commodity falls; or Total revenue decreases (increases, remains constant) when its price rises.

Total-revenue–total-cost approach The method which finds the output at which Economic profit (*see*) is a maximum or losses a minimum by comparing the Total revenue and the Total costs of a Firm at different outputs.

Total spending The total amount buyers of goods and services spend or plan to spend.

Total supply The Supply schedule (*see*) or the Supply curve (*see*) of all sellers of a good or service.

Trade balance The export of merchandise (goods) of a nation less its imports of merchandise (goods).

Trade controls Tariffs (*see*), export subsidies, Import quotas (*see*), and other means a nation may employ to reduce Imports (*see*) and expand Exports (*see*).

Trade deficit The amount by which a nation's imports of merchandise (goods) exceed its exports of merchandise (goods).

Trade surplus The amount by which a nation's exports of merchandise (goods) exceed its imports of merchandise (goods).

Trading possibilities line A line which shows the different combinations of two products an economy is able to obtain (consume) when it specializes in the production of one product and trades (exports) this product to obtain the other product.

Traditional economy An economic system (method of organization) in which traditions and customs determine how the economy will use its scarce resources.

Traditional view of advertising The position that advertising is persuasive rather than informative; promotes industrial concentration; and is essentially inefficient and wasteful.

Transactions demand for money The amount of money people want to hold to use as a Medium of exchange (to make payments); and which varies directly with the nominal GDP.

Transfer payment A payment of money (or goods and services) by a government or a Firm to a Household or Firm for which the payer receives no good or service directly in return.

Truth in Lending Act Federal law enacted in 1968 that is designed to protect consumers who borrow; and that requires the lender to state in concise and uniform language the costs and terms of the credit (the finance charges and the annual percentage rate of interest).

Tying agreement A promise made by a buyer when allowed to purchase a product from a seller that it will make all of its purchases of certain other products from the same seller; and a practice forbidden by the Clayton Act (*see*).

Unanticipated inflation Inflation (*see*) at a rate which was greater than the rate expected in that period of time.

Underemployment Failure to produce the maximum amount of goods and services that can be produced from the resources employed; failure to achieve Full production (*see*).

Undistributed corporate profits The after-tax profits of corporations not distributed as dividends to stockholders; corporate or business saving.

Unemployment Failure to use all available Economic resources to produce goods and services; failure to the economy to employ fully its Labor force (*see*).

Unemployment compensation (*See* Unemployment insurance.)

Unemployment insurance The insurance program which in the United States is financed by state Payroll taxes (*see*) on employers and makes income available to workers who are unable to find jobs.

Unemployment rate The percentage of the Labor force (*see*) that is unemployed at any time.

Uninsurable risk An event, the occurrence of which is uncontrollable and unpredictable, which would result in a loss that cannot be avoided by purchasing insurance and must be assumed by an entrepreneur (*See* Entrepreneurial ability); sometimes called "uncertainty."

Union shop A place of employment at which the employer may hire either labor union members or workers who are not members of the union but who must become members within a specified period of time or lose their jobs.

Unitary elasticity The Elasticity coefficient (*see*) is equal to one; the percentage change in the quantity (demanded or supplied) is equal to the percentage change in price.

United States–Canadian Free-Trade Agreement An accord signed in 1988 to eliminate all trade barriers between the two nations over a ten-year period.

Unit labor cost Labor costs per unit of output; equal to the Nominal wage rate (*see*) divided by the Average product (*see*) of labor.

Unlimited liability Absence of any limit on the maximum amount that may be lost by an individual and that the individual may become legally required to pay; the amount that may be lost and that a sole proprietor or partner may be required to pay.

Unlimited wants The insatiable desire of consumers (people) for goods and services that will give them pleasure or satisfaction.

Unplanned investment Actual investment less Planned investment; increases or decreases in the inventories of business firms that result from production greater than sales.

Unprosperious industry (*See* Declining industry.)

U.S. Steel case The antitrust action brought by the Federal government against the U.S. Steel Corporation in which the courts ruled (in 1920) that only unreasonable restraints of trade were illegal and size and the possession of monopoly power were not violations of the antitrust laws.

Utility The want-satisfying power of a good or service; the satisfaction or pleasure a consumer obtains from the consumption of a good or service (or from the consumption of a collection of goods and services).

Utility-maximizing rule To obtain the greatest Utility (*see*) the consumer should allocate his Money income so that the last dollar spent on each good or service yields the same Marginal utility (*see*); so that the Marginal utility of each good or service divided by its price is the same for all goods and services.

Value added The value of the product sold by a Firm less the value of the goods (materials) purchased and used by the Firm to produce the product; and equal to the revenue which can be used for Wages, rent, interest, and profits.

Value-added tax A tax imposed on the difference between the value of the goods sold by a firm and the value of the goods purchased by the firm from other firms.

Value judgment Opinion of what is desirable or undesirable; belief regarding what ought or ought not to be (regarding what is right or just and wrong or unjust).

Value of money The quantity of goods and services for which a unit of money (a dollar) can be exchanged; the purchasing power of a unit of money; the reciprocal of the Price level.

Variable cost A cost which in total increases (decreases) when the firm increases (decreases) its output; the cost of Variable resources (*see*).

Variable resource Any resource employed by a firm the quantity of which can be increased or decreased (varied).

VAT Value-added tax (*see*).

Vault cash The Currency (*see*) a bank has in its safe (vault) and cash drawers.

Velocity of money The number of times per year the average dollar in the Money supply (*see*) is spent for Final goods (*see*).

VERs (*See* Voluntary export restrictions.)

Vertical axis The "up-down" or "north-south" axis on a graph or grid.

Vertical combination A group of Plants (*see*) engaged in different stages of the production of a final product and owned by a single Firm (*see*).

Vertical intercept The point at which a line meets the vertical axis of a graph.

Vertical merger The merger of one or more Firms engaged in different stages of the production of a final product into a single Firm.

Vicious circle of poverty A problem common to the less developed countries where their low per capita incomes are an obstacle to realizing the levels of saving and investment requisite to acceptable rates of economic growth.

Voice mechanism Communication by workers through their union to resolve grievances with an employer.

Voluntary export restrictions The limitations by firms of their exports to particular foreign nations to avoid the erection of other trade barriers by the foreign nations.

Wage The price paid for Labor (for the use or services of Labor, *see*) per unit of time (per hour, per day, etc.).

Wage and salary supplements Payments made by employers of Labor into social insurance and private pension, health, and welfare funds for workers; and a part of the employer's cost of obtaining Labor.

Wage differential The difference between the Wage (*see*) received by one worker or group of workers and that received by another worker or group of workers.

Wage discrimination The payments to blacks (or other minority groups) of a wage lower than that paid to whites for doing the same work.

Wage guidepost Wages (*see*) in all industries in the economy should increase at an annual rate equal to the rate of increase in the Average product (*see*) of Labor in the economy.

Wage-price controls A Wage-price policy (*see*) that legally fixes the maximum amounts by which Wages (*see*) and prices may be increased in any period of time.

Wage-price guideposts A Wage-price policy (*see*) that depends on the voluntary cooperation of Labor unions and business firms.

Wage-price inflationary spiral Increases in wage rates which bring about increases in prices which in turn result in further increases in wage rates and in prices.

Wage-price policy Government policy that attempts to alter the behavior of Labor unions and business firms in order to make their Wage and price decisions more nearly compatible with the goals of Full employment and a stable Price level.

Wage rate (*See* Wage.)

Wages The income of those who supply the economy with Labor (*see*).

Wagner Act The Federal act of 1935 which established the National Labor Relations Board (*see*), guaranteed the rights of Labor unions to organize and to bargain collectively with employers, and listed and prohibited a number of unfair labor practices by employers.

Wastes of monopolistic competition The waste of economic resources resulting from producing an output at which price is more than marginal cost and average cost is more than the minimum average cost.

Wealth effect (*See* Real balances effect.)

Welfare programs (*See* Public assistance programs.)

Wheeler-Lea Act The Federal act of 1938 which amended the Federal Trade Commission Act (*see*) by prohibiting and giving the commission power to investigate unfair and deceptive acts or practices on commerce (false and misleading and advertising and the misrepresentation of products).

(The) "will to develop" Wanting economic growth strongly enough to change from old to new ways of doing things.

Workfare plans Reforms of the welfare system, particularly AFDC, designed to provide education and training for recipients so that they may move from public assistance to gainful employment.

World Bank A bank which lends (and guarantees loans) to less developed nations to assist them to grow; formally, the International Bank for Reconstruction and Development.

X-inefficiency Failure to produce any given output at the lowest average (and total) cost possible.

Yellow-dog contract The (now illegal) contract in which an employee agrees when accepting employment with a Firm that he or she will not become a member of a Labor union while employed by the Firm.